Mathematics for GCSE

Thousands of practice questions and worked examples covering the new Grade 9-1 GCSE Maths courses.

Foundation Level

Contents

Number, Ratio and Algebra

Section 1 — Non-Calculator Arithmetic
1.1 Negative Numbers 1
1.2 Whole Number Arithmetic 3
1.3 Decimals 7
1.4 Adding and Subtracting Decimals 9
1.5 Multiplying and Dividing Decimals 11
1.6 Order of Operations 15
1.7 Non-Calculator Arithmetic Problems 17

Section 2 — Approximations
2.1 Rounding — Whole Numbers 18
2.2 Rounding — Decimal Places 19
2.3 Rounding — Significant Figures 21
2.4 Estimating Answers 23
2.5 Rounding Errors 25

Section 3 — Powers and Roots
3.1 Squares, Cubes and Roots 26
3.2 Indices 28
3.3 Laws of Indices 30
3.4 Standard Form 32

Section 4 — Multiples and Factors
4.1 Finding Multiples and Factors 34
4.2 Prime Numbers 36
4.3 LCM and HCF 38

Section 5 — Fractions
5.1 Equivalent Fractions 42
5.2 Mixed Numbers 44
5.3 Ordering Fractions 46
5.4 Adding and Subtracting Fractions 48
5.5 Multiplying and Dividing Fractions 51
5.6 Fractions and Decimals 56
5.7 Fractions Problems 60

Section 6 — Ratios
6.1 Ratios and Simplifying 63
6.2 Using Ratios 66
6.3 Dividing in a Given Ratio 70
6.4 Ratio Problems 72

Section 7 — Percentages
- 7.1 Percentages 73
- 7.2 Percentages, Fractions and Decimals 77
- 7.3 Percentage Increase and Decrease 80
- 7.4 Compound Growth and Decay 86
- 7.5 Percentages Problems 87

Section 8 — Algebraic Expressions
- 8.1 Collecting Like Terms 89
- 8.2 Expanding Brackets 91
- 8.3 Factorising 95

Section 9 — Equations and Inequalities
- 9.1 Solving Equations 98
- 9.2 Solving Harder Equations 102
- 9.3 Writing Your Own Equations 105
- 9.4 Solving Inequalities 107
- 9.5 Simultaneous Equations 111
- 9.6 Solving Quadratic Equations 113
- 9.7 Equations and Inequalities Problems 114

Section 10 — Formulas and Functions
- 10.1 Writing Formulas 116
- 10.2 Substituting into a Formula 118
- 10.3 Rearranging Formulas 121
- 10.4 Functions 124
- 10.5 Formulas and Functions Problems 125

Section 11 — Sequences
- 11.1 Sequences — Term-to-Term Rules 127
- 11.2 Sequences — Position-to-Term Rules 130
- 11.3 Finding a Position-to-Term Rule 132

Section 12 — Graphs and Equations
- 12.1 Coordinates 134
- 12.2 Horizontal and Vertical Graphs 136
- 12.3 Other Straight-Line Graphs 138
- 12.4 Gradients 140
- 12.5 Equations of Straight-Line Graphs 143
- 12.6 Quadratic Graphs 146
- 12.7 Harder Graphs 150
- 12.8 Graphs and Equations Problems 153

Section 13 — Real-Life Graphs
13.1 Interpreting Real-Life Graphs 155
13.2 Drawing Real-Life Graphs 159

Section 14 — Proportion
14.1 Direct Proportion 161
14.2 Inverse Proportion 165
14.3 Proportion Problems 167

Geometry and Measures

Section 15 — Angles and 2D Shapes
15.1 Basic Angle Properties 168
15.2 Triangles 170
15.3 Parallel and Intersecting Lines 172
15.4 Quadrilaterals 176
15.5 Interior and Exterior Angles 180
15.6 Symmetry 184
15.7 Angles and 2D Shapes Problems 187

Section 16 — Units, Measuring and Estimating
16.1 Reading Scales 189
16.2 Converting Metric Units — Length, Mass and Volume 192
16.3 Converting Units — Area and Volume 194
16.4 Metric and Imperial Units 197
16.5 Estimating in Real Life 199

Section 17 — Speed, Density, Pressure
17.1 Speed, Distance, Time Calculations 201
17.2 Density, Mass, Volume Calculations 203
17.3 Pressure, Force, Area Calculations 204
17.4 Distance-Time Graphs 205

Section 18 — Scale Drawings and Bearings
18.1 Scale Drawings 209
18.2 Bearings 213
18.3 Scale Drawings and Bearings Problems 216

Section 19 — Pythagoras and Trigonometry
19.1 Pythagoras' Theorem 217
19.2 Trigonometry — Sin, Cos and Tan 221
19.3 Pythagoras and Trigonometry Problems 224

Section 20 — Vectors
- 20.1 Column Vectors 225
- 20.2 Vectors Problems 228

Section 21 — Constructions
- 21.1 Circles 230
- 21.2 Lines, Angles and Triangles 232
- 21.3 Constructions 236
- 21.4 Loci 242

Section 22 — Area and Perimeter
- 22.1 Rectangles and Triangles 244
- 22.2 Other Quadrilaterals 248
- 22.3 Circumference of a Circle 252
- 22.4 Area of a Circle 255
- 22.5 Arcs and Sectors of Circles 258
- 22.6 Area and Perimeter Problems 258

Section 23 — 3D Shapes
- 23.1 Nets 261
- 23.2 Plans and Elevations 264
- 23.3 Isometric Drawings 267
- 23.4 Volume 270
- 23.5 Surface Area 275
- 23.6 3D Shapes Problems 280

Section 24 — Transformations
- 24.1 Reflection 283
- 24.2 Rotation 287
- 24.3 Translations 291
- 24.4 Enlargements 294
- 24.5 Combinations of Transformations 301
- 24.6 Congruence and Similarity 304

Statistics and Probability

Section 25 — Collecting Data
- 25.1 Using Different Types of Data 310
- 25.2 Data-Collection Sheets and Questionnaires 312
- 25.3 Sampling and Bias 316

Section 26 — Analysing Data
26.1 Using Lists and Tables 319
26.2 Averages and Range 320
26.3 Two-Way Tables 327
26.4 Bar Charts and Pictograms 328
26.5 Stem and Leaf Diagrams 330
26.6 Pie Charts 332
26.7 Time Series 336
26.8 Scatter Graphs 338

Section 27 — Probability
27.1 Probability — The Basics 342
27.2 Calculating Probabilities 344
27.3 Listing Outcomes 348
27.4 Probability from Experiments 351
27.5 The AND/OR Rules 355
27.6 Tree Diagrams 356
27.7 Sets and Venn Diagrams 358

Answers 360
Index 442

Throughout the book, the more challenging questions are marked like this: **1**

Editors:
Rob Harrison, Shaun Harrogate, Paul Jordin, Sarah Oxley, Andy Park, David Ryan, Ruth Wilbourne, Jonathan Wray

Contributors:
Jane Appleton, Katharine Brown, Pamela Chatley, Eva Cowlishaw, Alastair Duncombe, Stephen Green, Philip Hale, Phil Harvey, Judy Hornigold, Claire Jackson, Mark Moody, Charlotte O'Brien, Philip Potten, Rosemary Rogers, Manpreet Sambhi, Neil Saunders, Jan Walker, Kieran Wardell, Jeanette Whiteman

Proofreaders:
Peter Caunter, Janet Dickinson, Alastair Duncombe, Samantha Walker

Published by CGP

ISBN: 978 1 78294 438 6

Clipart from Corel®
Printed by Elanders Ltd, Newcastle upon Tyne.
Text, design, layout and original illustrations © Coordination Group Publications Ltd. (CGP) 2015
All rights reserved.

Photocopying more than one section of this book is not permitted, even if you have a CLA licence.
Extra copies are available from CGP with next day delivery • 0800 1712 712 • www.cgpbooks.co.uk

Section 1 — Non-Calculator Arithmetic

1.1 Negative Numbers

Adding and Subtracting Negative Numbers

Negative numbers are numbers which are **less than zero**.
You can count places on a **number line** to help with calculations involving negative numbers.

Example 1

Work out: a) $-1 + 4$ b) $-2 - 3 + 1$

Start at -1 and count 4 places to the right. $\Rightarrow$ a) $-1 + 4 = \underline{3}$
Start at -2, count 3 places to the left, and then 1 place to the right. $\Rightarrow$ b) $-2 - 3 + 1 = \underline{-4}$

Exercise 1

Answer **Questions 1-6** without using your calculator.

1. Work out the following.
   a) $-4 + 3$
   b) $-1 + 5$
   c) $-2 + 1$
   d) $2 - 6$
   e) $-5 + 9$
   f) $-5 - 3$
   g) $-9 - 2$
   h) $4 - 8$
   i) $-12 + 15$
   j) $6 - 17$
   k) $-13 + 18$
   l) $11 - 19$

2. Work out the following.
   a) $-3 + 2 - 1$
   b) $-2 + 8 - 5$
   c) $8 - 5 - 3$
   d) $6 - 2 + 1$
   e) $-1 - 7 - 4$
   f) $-5 + 8 - 12$
   g) $-9 + 13 + 11$
   h) $7 - 18 + 11$

The thermometer on the right shows temperature. Use it to answer **Questions 3-6**.

3. a) Find the temperature that is 3 °C lower than –1 °C.
   b) Find the temperature that is 8 °C higher than –5 °C.

4. Find the difference between the following temperatures.
   a) –6 °C and 3 °C
   b) –2 °C and –5 °C

5. At midday the temperature was 6 °C. By midnight, the temperature had decreased by 7 °C. What was the temperature at midnight?

6. At 5 am, the temperature was –6 °C. At 11 pm, the temperature was –1 °C. What was the difference in temperature between these two times?

Section 1 — Non-Calculator Arithmetic

Rules for Adding and Subtracting Negative Numbers

Adding a negative number is the same as subtracting a positive number. ⟶ '+' next to '–' means subtract

Subtracting a negative number is the same as adding a positive number. ⟶ '–' next to '–' means add

Example 2

Work out: a) $1 - (-4)$ b) $-5 + (-2)$

1. – next to – means add.

    a) $1 - (-4) = 1 + 4$
        $= \underline{5}$

2. + next to – means subtract.

    b) $-5 + (-2) = -5 - 2$
        $= \underline{-7}$

Exercise 2

Answer **Questions 1-4** without using your calculator.

1 Work out the following.
   a) $4 - (-2)$
   b) $-3 - (-5)$
   c) $-7 + (-2)$
   d) $-6 - (-2)$
   e) $-5 + (-5)$
   f) $-5 - (-5)$
   g) $9 + (-2)$
   h) $3 - (-7)$
   i) $-13 - (-3)$
   j) $8 + (-2)$
   k) $-6 + (-3)$
   l) $1 - (-12)$

2 Work out the following.
   a) $-1 + (-4) - 1$
   b) $3 + (-2) + (-5)$
   c) $6 - (-2) + (-3)$
   d) $7 + (-6) - (-8)$
   e) $-2 - (-9) - (-1)$
   f) $-8 + (-8) - (-12)$
   g) $9 - (-13) + (-2)$
   h) $-3 + (-11) + (-6)$

3 Find the difference between the following numbers by subtracting one from the other.
   a) 6 and –5
   b) –10 and –6
   c) –8 and 4
   d) –5 and –12

4 Copy the following calculations and fill in the blanks.
   a) $-3 + \square = -5$
   b) $5 - \square = 10$
   c) $\square + (-7) = 4$
   d) $\square - (-2) = -6$

Multiplying and Dividing Negative Numbers

When you multiply or divide two numbers which have the **same** sign, the answer is **positive**.
When you multiply or divide two numbers which have **opposite** signs, the answer is **negative**.

Example 3

Work out:

a) $24 \div (-6)$ The signs are opposite (one positive, one negative), so the answer is negative. ⟶ $24 \div -6 = \underline{-4}$

b) $-5 \times (-8)$ The signs are the same (both negative), so the answer is positive. ⟶ $-5 \times -8 = \underline{40}$

Section 1 — Non-Calculator Arithmetic

Exercise 3

Answer **Questions 1-3** without using your calculator.

1 Work out the following.

a) 3 × (−4) b) (−15) ÷ (−3) c) 12 ÷ (−4) d) 2 × (−8)
e) 5 ÷ (−5) f) (−15) ÷ 3 g) (−9) × 6 h) (−11) × (−8)
i) (−72) ÷ (−6) j) 56 ÷ (−8) k) (−7) × (−3) l) (−81) ÷ (−9)
m) (−24) ÷ 4 n) (−18) ÷ (−2) o) 6 × (−3) p) (−96) ÷ (−12)
q) (−12) × (−3) r) 7 × (−6) s) 45 ÷ (−9) t) (−12) × 2

2 Copy the following calculations and fill in the blanks.

a) −3 × ☐ = −6 b) −14 ÷ ☐ = −2 c) ☐ × 4 = −16 d) ☐ ÷ (−2) = −5
e) −8 × ☐ = −24 f) −18 ÷ ☐ = 3 g) ☐ × (−3) = 36 h) ☐ ÷ 11 = −7

3 Work out the following.

a) (−3) × 4 ÷ 2 b) 2 × 4 ÷ (−2) c) (−3) × 7 ÷ (−21) d) (−5) × (−6) ÷ 3
e) (−6) × 5 ÷ (−2) f) (−3) × (−5) × (−6) g) (−63) × (−2) ÷ (−9) h) (−12) × 3 × (−2)
i) (−60) × (−10) ÷ 12 j) [35 ÷ (−7)] × (−8) k) [55 ÷ (−11)] × (−9) l) [(−24) ÷ 8)] ÷ 3

1.2 Whole Number Arithmetic

Addition and Subtraction

When adding or subtracting large numbers, write one number above the other, then add or subtract one column at a time.

Example 1

Work out: a) 145 + 28   b) 364 − 128

1. Write one number above the other, making sure the columns line up.
2. Add or subtract one column at a time — you may have to 'carry' numbers when adding, or 'borrow' numbers when subtracting.

a)
```
  1 4 5        1 4 5        1 4 5
+   2 8      +   2 8      +   2 8
─────        ─────        ─────
      3         7 3       1 7 3     So 145 + 28 = 173.
      ₁           ₁
```

b)
```
   ⁵ ¹           ⁵ ¹           ⁵ ¹
  3 6̸ 4̸        3 6̸ 4̸        3 6̸ 4̸
− 1 2 8      − 1 2 8      − 1 2 8
─────        ─────        ─────
      6         3 6       2 3 6     So 364 − 128 = 236.
```

Exercise 1

Answer these questions without using your calculator.

1 Copy and work out the following.

a)
```
    2 3
+   5 6
─────
```

b)
```
    4 7
+   3 6
─────
```

c)
```
  1 2 2
+   9 7
─────
```

d)
```
  2 4 3
+ 1 7 8
─────
```

2 Copy and work out the following.

   a)   9 8   **b)**   7 3   **c)**   1 8 1   **d)**   2 3 3
       − 3 5   − 2 7   − 3 5   − 1 8 7

3 Work out the following.
   a) 25 + 68   **b)** 256 + 312   **c)** 342 + 679   **d)** 614 + 288
   e) 138 − 26   **f)** 262 − 54   **g)** 841 − 346   **h)** 307 − 128
   i) 2513 + 241   **j)** 1358 + 1296   **k)** 2942 − 324   **l)** 4003 − 1235

4 Work out the following.
   a) 41 + 112 + 213   **b)** 123 + 478 + 215   **c)** 341 + 162 − 145   **d)** 764 + 138 − 345
   e) 221 + 126 − 98   **f)** (498 − 137) + 556   **g)** (1841 − 346) + 141   **h)** (987 − 451) + 221

5 Lisa has 38 marbles, John has 52 marbles and Bina has 65 marbles. How many marbles do they have altogether?

6 An art club has £2146 in the bank. It spends £224 on art supplies. How much money does it have left?

7 The village of Great Missingham has a population of 1845. The neighbouring village of Fentley has a population of 1257. How many more people live in Great Missingham than Fentley?

Multiplication

There are different methods for multiplying large numbers.
Example 2 uses traditional **long multiplication**, while Example 3 uses a **grid method**.

Example 2

Work out 254 × 26.

1. Write one number above the other, making sure the columns line up.

2. Multiply each digit of 254 by 6, working from right to left. If the answer is 10 or more, carry the ten's digit. This is 254 × 6.

3. Now put a 0 in the right-hand column, and multiply each digit of 254 by 2, carrying digits where necessary. This is 254 × 20.

4. Add the two rows to find the final answer.

$$\begin{array}{r} 254 \\ \times\ 26 \\ \hline 1524 \\ 5080 \\ \hline 6604 \end{array}$$

So 254 × 26 = **6604**.

Section 1 — Non-Calculator Arithmetic

Example 3

Work out 254 × 26.

1. Split each number up into units, tens, hundreds etc.
2. Put these around the outside of a grid.
3. Multiply the numbers at the edge of each box. To multiply by 200, multiply by 2, then by 100. To multiply by 50, multiply by 5, then by 10.

	200	50	4
20	20 × 200 = 4000	20 × 50 = 1000	20 × 4 = 80
6	6 × 200 = 1200	6 × 50 = 300	6 × 4 = 24

4. Add the numbers from the boxes to find the final answer.

```
    4 0 0 0
    1 0 0 0
        8 0
    1 2 0 0
      3 0 0
  +     2 4
    6 6 0 4
      1
```

So 254 × 26 = **6604**.

Exercise 2

Answer **Questions 1-8** without using your calculator.

1 Work out the following.

a) 52 × 10
b) 11 × 17
c) 13 × 12
d) 16 × 24
e) 37 × 19
f) 43 × 15
g) 32 × 53
h) 87 × 24
i) 64 × 67
j) 71 × 49
k) 88 × 76
l) 93 × 98
m) 66 × 72
n) 79 × 86
o) 86 × 98
p) 83 × 81

2 Work out the following.

a) 100 × 26
b) 114 × 30
c) 125 × 71
d) 216 × 54
e) 245 × 31
f) 311 × 59
g) 409 × 63
h) 415 × 41
i) 367 × 62
j) 498 × 69
k) 511 × 55
l) 568 × 74

3 In November, Jilly tells her friend that there are 46 days until Christmas. How many hours is this?

4 Dom's monthly electricity bill is £33. How much does he spend on electricity each year?

5 Sheila earns £243 per week. How much does she earn in 52 weeks?

6 The weight of a storage container is 14 tonnes. A cargo ship can carry 230 of these containers. How many tonnes can the cargo ship carry?

7 A box of matches contains 85 matches. There are 160 boxes in a carton. How many matches are there in a carton?

8 Work out the following.

a) 1347 × 20
b) 2271 × 25
c) 3669 × 21
d) 5624 × 42
e) 3000 × 21
f) 1211 × 34
g) 2623 × 42
h) 4526 × 19

Division

There are different ways to divide numbers without using a calculator.
Example 4 shows '**short division**'. Example 5 shows '**long division**'.

Example 4

Work out 3144 ÷ 8.

Using short division:
1. 8 doesn't go into 3, so look at the first <u>two</u> digits.
2. 8 goes into 31 three times, with remainder 7.
3. 8 goes into 74 nine times, with remainder 2.
4. 8 goes into 24 three times exactly.

So 3144 ÷ 8 = **393**.

Example 5

Work out 7657 ÷ 34.

Using long division:
1. 34 goes into 76 twice. 34 × 2 = 68, so subtract 68 from 76 to find the remainder.
2. Bring the 5 down from above.
3. 34 goes into 85 twice. 34 × 2 = 68, so subtract 68 from 85 to find the remainder.
4. Bring the 7 down from above.
5. 34 goes into 177 five times. 34 × 5 = 170, so subtract 170 from 177 to find the remainder.

So 7657 ÷ 34 = **225 remainder 7**
$= \mathbf{225\frac{7}{34}}$

Exercise 3

Answer **Questions 1-10** without using your calculator.

1 Use short division to work out the following.
    a) 7)357   **b)** 7)238   **c)** 9)603   **d)** 8)3616
    e) 4)1312   **f)** 6)1350   **g)** 4)2240   **h)** 6)3732

2 Use short division to work out the following. In each case, give the remainder as a fraction.
   a) 361 ÷ 5   b) 5213 ÷ 3   c) 4198 ÷ 5   d) 4609 ÷ 9
   e) 300 ÷ 7   f) 671 ÷ 9   g) 2545 ÷ 6   h) 2674 ÷ 8

3 Use long division to work out the following.
   a) 23)644   b) 19)608   c) 18)738   d) 17)816
   e) 20)4120   f) 33)6633   g) 24)9624   h) 31)7936
   i) 22)6842   j) 34)9146   k) 28)8680   l) 26)9152

4 Use long division to work out the following. Give any remainders as fractions.
   a) 945 ÷ 45   b) 846 ÷ 32   c) 711 ÷ 21   d) 648 ÷ 18
   e) 608 ÷ 16   f) 1159 ÷ 19   g) 1218 ÷ 21   h) 1552 ÷ 33
   i) 7131 ÷ 18   j) 6718 ÷ 25   k) 8323 ÷ 31   l) 8539 ÷ 44

5 A postage stamp costs 41p. How many stamps could you buy for £5.00, and how much change would you receive?

6 672 people are to be divided into 24 equal groups. How many people will be in each group?

7 Eggs are packed into boxes that hold 6 eggs each. How many boxes are needed for 1350 eggs?

8 22 identical washing machines cost £7634 in total. How much does each washing machine cost?

9 a) Mike earns £22 464 per year. How much does he earn per week? (Assume 1 year = 52 weeks.)
   b) Andrea earns £24 636 per year. How much does she earn per month?

10 The local team played 14 games on their home ground. The same number of people went to each game and 17 584 people in total attended the games. How many people went to each game?

1.3 Decimals

Decimals are a way of showing parts of a whole number.

$$627.381$$

6 Hundreds, 2 Tens, 7 Units, Decimal Point, 3 Tenths, 8 Hundredths, 1 Thousandths

Example 1
What is the value of each of the digits in 0.692?

The 6 is in the tenths column.   Six tenths = $\frac{6}{10}$
The 9 is in the hundredths column.   Nine hundredths = $\frac{9}{100}$
The 2 is in the thousandths column.   Two thousandths = $\frac{2}{1000}$

Exercise 1

1 Write down the value of the 7 in 4.271.
2 Write down the value of the 3 in 6.382.
3 Write down the value of the 8 in 0.718.
4 Write down the value of the 1 in 9.0361.
5 Write down the value of the 2 in 2.37.
6 Write down the value of the 6 in 0.956.

Section 1 — Non-Calculator Arithmetic

7 Write down the following as decimal numbers.
   a) one tenth
   b) two hundredths
   c) five thousandths
   d) seven tenths
   e) $\frac{7}{100}$
   f) $\frac{1}{1000}$
   g) $\frac{9}{100}$
   h) $\frac{8}{10}$

Ordering Decimals

Use the **place value** of digits to put decimals in order of size — digits further to the left are 'worth more'.

Example 2
Put the decimals 8.09, 8.2, 8.092 and 8.9 in order of size, from smallest to largest.
1. Arrange the numbers in columns and fill in any gaps with 0's.
2. Compare the numbers one column at a time, from left to right.
3. Write the numbers in the correct order.

8.090
8.200
8.092
8.900

The correct order is
8.09, 8.092, 8.2, 8.9

Example 3
Put the decimals −1.02, −1.2, −0.12 and −2.1 in order, from lowest to highest.
1. Arrange the numbers in columns and fill in any gaps with 0's.
2. Compare the numbers one column at a time, from left to right.
3. With negative numbers, the larger the digit the lower the number is. For example, −2 is lower than −1.
4. Write the numbers in the correct order.

−1.02
−1.20
−0.12
−2.10

The correct order is
−2.1, −1.2, −1.02, −0.12

Exercise 2

1 Write down the larger number in each of the following pairs.
   a) 0.3, 0.31
   b) 0.21, 0.12
   c) 0.09, 0.009
   d) 0.427, 0.472
   e) 8.3, 8.03
   f) 0.006, 0.05
   g) 0.1, 0.01
   h) 0.11, 0.09
   i) 3.7, 3.07
   j) 7.19, 7.091
   k) 12.1, 12.099
   l) 18.07, 17.08

2 Put each of the following lists of decimals in order of size, from smallest to largest.
   a) 0.02, 0.2, 0.15
   b) 0.61, 0.51, 0.16
   c) 0.59, 0.591, 0.559
   d) 0.03, 0.035, 0.04
   e) 0.07, 0.007, 0.017, 0.7
   f) 1.4, 1.14, 0.41, 1.41
   g) 2.3, 2.03, 0.09, 0.75
   h) 0.78, 0.782, 0.708, 0.078
   i) 0.09, 0.101, 0.1, 0.11
   j) 1.6, 1.66, 0.61, 1.09
   k) 0.3, 0.31, 3.01, 3.1
   l) 4.05, 5.04, 5.4, 4.5

3 Put each of the following lists of decimals in order of size, from lowest to highest.
   a) 1.05, 1.5, –1.5, 1.55
   b) 0.6, 6.1, –0.6, –6
   c) –0.01, 0.1, –0.09, –0.1
   d) –0.5, –0.45, –0.55, –5
   e) –7, –7.1, –7.07, 0.007
   f) 0.9, –0.05, –0.09, –0.095

1.4 Adding and Subtracting Decimals

Adding and subtracting decimals is similar to using whole numbers — just make sure you line up the decimal points.

Example 1

Work out 4.53 + 1.6

1. Write one number above the other, lining up the decimal points.
2. Fill in any gaps with 0's.
3. Add the digits one column at a time.

```
   4.53        4.53        4.53
 + 1.60      + 1.60      + 1.60
 ─────       ─────       ─────
    .3        ₁.13       6₁.13
```

So 4.53 + 1.6 = **6.13**

Example 2

Work out 8.5 – 3.07

1. Write one number above the other, lining up the decimal points.
2. Fill in any gaps with 0's.
3. Subtract the digits one column at a time.

```
   8.⁴5̸¹0      8.⁴5̸¹0      8.⁴5̸¹0
 – 3.07      – 3.07      – 3.07
 ─────       ─────       ─────
    .3         .43       5.43
```

So 8.5 – 3.07 = **5.43**

Exercise 1

Answer these questions without using your calculator.

1 Copy and work out the following.

a)   5.1
   + 1.8

b)   6.3
   + 5.4

c) 11.7
   + 8.2

d)   2.5
   + 4.1

e)   0.4
   + 0.7

f)   8.9
   + 3.2

g)   5.7
   +12.6

h)   4.8
   + 5.3

2 Copy and work out the following.

a)   5.6
   – 0.3

b)   9.9
   – 4.2

c) 16.8
   – 7.5

d)   6.7
   – 5.1

e)   6.45
   – 3.23

f)   7.98
   – 6.12

g)   5.3
   – 2.8

h)   8.5
   – 1.9

Section 1 — Non-Calculator Arithmetic

3 Work out the following.
   a) 10.83 + 7.4
   b) 0.029 + 1.8
   c) 91.7 + 0.492
   d) 6.474 + 0.92
   e) 2.191 + 4.1
   f) 14.799 + 0.08
   g) 1.581 + 15.8
   h) 11.1 + 12.902
   i) 7.89 + 4.789
   j) 0.888 + 1.02
   k) 0.02 + 0.991
   l) 3.41 + 22.169

4 Work out the following.
   a) 24.63 – 7.5
   b) 6.78 – 5.6
   c) 9.915 – 3.7
   d) 73.46 – 8.5
   e) 67.5 – 4.31
   f) 16.3 – 5.16
   g) 9.241 – 2.8
   h) 0.946 – 0.07
   i) 3.52 – 0.126
   j) 9.1 – 7.02
   k) 11.2 – 1.89
   l) 1.1 – 0.839

5 Work out the following.
   a) 3.81 + 9.54
   b) 2.75 + 9.45
   c) 8.67 + 0.95
   d) 2.81 – 0.16
   e) 4.32 – 2.17
   f) 8.72 – 5.94
   g) 6.31 – 5.83
   h) 1.6 + 4.35
   i) 9.6 + 3.12
   j) 0.78 + 1.3
   k) 6.78 – 5.6
   l) 4.21 – 1.9
   m) 3.8 – 0.59
   n) 15.1 – 0.08
   o) 6.25 + 5.6
   p) 1.97 + 21.7

Example 3
Work out 4 – 0.91

1. Write any whole numbers as decimals by adding 0's, then line up the decimal points.
2. Subtract the digits one column at a time. As you can't borrow from 0, borrow from the 4 instead.

$$\begin{array}{r} 4.00 \\ -\ 0.91 \\ \hline . \end{array} \qquad \begin{array}{r} {}^3\!4.{}^9\!\!\not0\,{}^1\!0 \\ -\ 0.91 \\ \hline .\ 9 \end{array} \qquad \begin{array}{r} {}^3\!4.{}^9\!\!\not0\,{}^1\!0 \\ -\ 0.91 \\ \hline 3.09 \end{array}$$

So 4 – 0.91 = **3.09**

6 Work out the following.
   a) 6 – 5.1
   b) 23 – 18.51
   c) 12 – 5.028
   d) 13 – 6.453

7 Work out the following.
   a) 2 + 1.8
   b) 3.7 + 6
   c) 12.7 + 7.34
   d) 9.49 + 13
   e) 38 + 6.92
   f) 5 – 0.8
   g) 9 – 4.2
   h) 24 – 5.7

8 Work out the following.
   a) 6.474 + 0.92 + 1.1
   b) 2.39 + 8.8 + 0.26
   c) 12.24 + 3.7 + 1.2
   d) 13.56 + 1.5 + 7.06
   e) 2 + 4.123 + 1.86
   f) 16.8 + 4.17 + 2
   g) 2.64 + 13 + 1.012
   h) 1 + 0.07 + 0.012

9 Copy the following calculations and fill in the blanks.

a)
$$\begin{array}{r} \square\,.\,6\,\square \\ +\ 0\,.\,\square\,0 \\ \hline 8\,.\,2\,1 \end{array}$$

b)
$$\begin{array}{r} 5\,.\,\square\,8 \\ +\ \square\,.\,4\,\square \\ \hline 6\,.\,4\,0 \end{array}$$

c)
$$\begin{array}{r} 6\,.\,7\,5 \\ +\ \square\,.\,4\,\square \\ \hline 9\,.\,\square\,3 \end{array}$$

d)
$$\begin{array}{r} 5\,.\,\square\,3 \\ -\ 2\,.\,1\,\square \\ \hline \square\,.\,3\,1 \end{array}$$

Section 1 — Non-Calculator Arithmetic

Exercise 2

Answer **Questions 1-6** without using your calculator.

1. Malcolm travels 2.3 km to the shops, then a further 4.6 km to his aunt's house. How far does he travel in total?

2. Sunita buys a hat for £18.50 and a bag for £31. How much does she spend altogether?

3. A plank of wood is 4 m long. A 2.75 m long piece is cut from the plank. What length of wood is left?

4. Joan goes out for a meal. The bill for the meal comes to £66.50. She uses a voucher which entitles her to £15 off her meal. How much does she have left to pay?

5. Ashkan spends £71.42 at the supermarket. His receipt says that he has saved £11.79 on special offers. How much would he have spent if there had been no special offers?

6. On his first run, Ted sprints 100 m in 15.32 seconds. On his second run, he is 0.47 seconds quicker. How long did he take on his second run?

1.5 Multiplying and Dividing Decimals

Multiplying and Dividing by 10, 100, 1000

When multiplying by 10, 100 or 1000, each digit in the number moves to the **left**.

- × 10   each digit moves **one place** to the left
- × 100   each digit moves **two places** to the left
- × 1000   each digit moves **three places** to the left

Example 1

Work out:
a) 0.478×100 Move each digit two places to the left. ⇒ $0.478 \times 100 = \underline{\mathbf{47.8}}$
b) 1.35×1000 Move each digit three places to the left — fill in any gaps with 0's. ⇒ $1.35 \times 1000 = \underline{\mathbf{1350}}$

When dividing by 10, 100 or 1000, each digit in the number moves to the **right**.

- ÷ 10   each digit moves **one place** to the right
- ÷ 100   each digit moves **two places** to the right
- ÷ 1000   each digit moves **three places** to the right

Example 2

Work out:
a) $923.1 \div 100$ Move each digit two places to the right. ⇒ $923.1 \div 100 = \underline{\mathbf{9.231}}$
b) $51.4 \div 1000$ Move each digit three places to the right — fill in any gaps after the decimal point with 0's. ⇒ $51.4 \div 1000 = \underline{\mathbf{0.0514}}$

Section 1 — Non-Calculator Arithmetic

Exercise 1

Answer **Questions 1-2** without using your calculator.

1. Work out the following.
   a) 0.92 × 10
   b) 1.41 × 100
   c) 72.5 × 10
   d) 0.023 × 100
   e) 0.019 × 1000
   f) 14.6 × 100
   g) 6.07 × 1000
   h) 9.9 × 100
   i) 13.04 × 10
   j) 7.8 × 1000
   k) 0.006 × 100
   l) 0.23 × 1000

2. Work out the following.
   a) 25.9 ÷ 10
   b) 861.5 ÷ 100
   c) 381.7 ÷ 10
   d) 549.1 ÷ 1000
   e) 901.5 ÷ 100
   f) 6.3 ÷ 10
   g) 5.1 ÷ 1000
   h) 0.94 ÷ 100
   i) 0.08 ÷ 10
   j) 23.2 ÷ 1000
   k) 601.2 ÷ 100
   l) 17 ÷ 1000

Multiplying Decimals

When multiplying two decimals, ignore the decimal point and multiply them as whole numbers. Then add in the decimal point in the right place at the end.

Example 3

Work out 0.32 × 0.6

1. Ignore the decimal points and treat it as a whole number multiplication.
2. There are three digits in total after the decimal points in the question (two in 0.32 and one in 0.6).
3. The answer should also have three digits after the decimal point.

So 0.32 × 0.6 = **0.192**

Exercise 2

Answer **Questions 1-8** without using your calculator.

1. You are given that 132 × 238 = 31 416. Use this information to work out the following.
   a) 13.2 × 238
   b) 1.32 × 23.8
   c) 1.32 × 0.238
   d) 0.132 × 0.238

2. You are given that 401 × 119 = 47 719. Use this information to work out the following.
   a) 40.1 × 11.9
   b) 4.01 × 1.19
   c) 0.401 × 1.19
   d) 0.401 × 0.119

3. a) Work out 21 × 6.
   b) Use your answer to work out the following.
      (i) 2.1 × 6
      (ii) 2.1 × 0.6
      (iii) 0.21 × 0.06

4. a) Work out 11 × 23.
   b) Use your answer to work out the following.
      (i) 1.1 × 2.3
      (ii) 1.1 × 0.23
      (iii) 0.11 × 0.23

5 Work out the following.
   a) 6.7 × 8
   b) 3.2 × 6
   c) 8.8 × 3
   d) 5.6 × 8
   e) 0.65 × 9
   f) 9.7 × 2
   g) 2.7 × 4
   h) 9.3 × 5

6 Work out the following.
   a) 0.6 × 0.3
   b) 0.9 × 0.8
   c) 0.01 × 0.6
   d) 0.05 × 0.04
   e) 0.08 × 0.5
   f) 0.2 × 0.03
   g) 0.04 × 0.02
   h) 0.007 × 0.006

7 Work out the following.
   a) 2.1 × 0.6
   b) 3.5 × 0.4
   c) 8.1 × 0.5
   d) 2.2 × 0.3
   e) 3.6 × 0.3
   f) 0.51 × 0.3
   g) 1.6 × 0.04
   h) 8.2 × 0.008
   i) 0.61 × 0.6
   j) 0.33 × 0.02
   k) 5.2 × 0.09
   l) 4.7 × 0.002

8 Work out the following.
   a) 6.3 × 2.1
   b) 1.4 × 2.3
   c) 1.5 × 2.7
   d) 2.4 × 1.8
   e) 3.9 × 8.3
   f) 8.6 × 6.9
   g) 0.16 × 3.3
   h) 5.1 × 0.23
   i) 0.52 × 0.12
   j) 0.64 × 0.42
   k) 0.029 × 0.61
   l) 0.017 × 0.034

Example 4

Work out 1.36 × 200

1. 1.36 × 200 = 1.36 × 2 × 100, so break the multiplication down into two stages.
2. First calculate 1.36 × 2 by ignoring the decimal point and adding it in at the end.
3. Then multiply by 100 by moving each digit two places to the left.

$$\begin{array}{r} 136 \\ \times\ \ 2 \\ \hline 272 \end{array}$$

136 × 2 = 272, so 1.36 × 2 = 2.72
So 1.36 × 200 = 2.72 × 100
= **272**

Exercise 3

Answer **Questions 1-2** without using your calculator.

1 a) Work out 6.412 × 4.
   b) Use your answer to work out the following.
      (i) 6.412 × 40
      (ii) 6.412 × 400
      (iii) 6.412 × 4000

2 Work out the following.
   a) 3.1 × 40
   b) 0.7 × 600
   c) 12.1 × 30
   d) 11.06 × 80
   e) 0.061 × 2000
   f) 1.007 × 400
   g) 101.8 × 60
   h) 0.903 × 5000
   i) 4.112 × 90
   j) 0.003 × 8000
   k) 12.225 × 70
   l) 30.303 × 20

Dividing Decimals

When dividing decimals, you need to make sure you put the decimal point in the correct place.

When the number you're **dividing by** is a decimal, convert the calculation into a division by a whole number by multiplying both numbers by a power of 10.

Example 5

Work out $5.16 \div 8$

1. Position the decimal point in the answer directly above the one inside the division.
2. Divide as you would with whole numbers.
3. You may need to add zeros to the decimal inside the division sign.

So $5.16 \div 8 = \underline{\mathbf{0.645}}$

Example 6

Work out $8.16 \div 0.2$

1. Multiply both numbers by 10, so you are dividing by a whole number.
2. Divide as usual.

So $8.16 \div 0.2 = \underline{\mathbf{40.8}}$

Exercise 4

Answer **Questions 1-12** without using your calculator.

1 Copy and work out the following.
   a) $2\overline{)5.4}$
   b) $3\overline{)9.6}$
   c) $6\overline{)9.24}$
   d) $5\overline{)2.65}$
   e) $7\overline{)7.21}$
   f) $9\overline{)4.05}$
   g) $7\overline{)98.7}$
   h) $4\overline{)0.924}$

2 Work out the following.
   a) $8.52 \div 4$
   b) $0.0612 \div 6$
   c) $112.8 \div 4$
   d) $1.02 \div 3$
   e) $2.14 \div 4$
   f) $8.62 \div 5$
   g) $17.1 \div 6$
   h) $0.081 \div 9$
   i) $0.84 \div 5$
   j) $49.35 \div 7$
   k) $1.25 \div 4$
   l) $89.1 \div 2$
   m) $5.62 \div 8$
   n) $0.052 \div 5$
   o) $12.06 \div 8$
   p) $3.061 \div 5$

3 Consider the calculation $6.4 \div 0.4$.
   a) Multiply both numbers by 10 to form an equivalent calculation which involves dividing by a whole number.
   b) Use your answer to work out $6.4 \div 0.4$.

4 Consider the calculation $0.384 \div 0.12$.
   a) Multiply both numbers by 100 to form an equivalent calculation which involves dividing by a whole number.
   b) Use your answer to work out $0.384 \div 0.12$.

5 Consider the calculation 3.8 ÷ 0.008.
   a) Write down an equivalent calculation which involves dividing by a whole number.
   b) Use your answer to work out 3.8 ÷ 0.008.

6 Work out the following.
   a) 6.4 ÷ 0.2
   b) 1.56 ÷ 0.2
   c) 0.624 ÷ 0.3
   d) 8.8 ÷ 0.2
   e) 3.54 ÷ 0.4
   f) 3.774 ÷ 0.4
   g) 5.75 ÷ 0.5
   h) 0.275 ÷ 0.5

7 Work out the following.
   a) 22.56 ÷ 0.03
   b) 16.42 ÷ 0.02
   c) 0.028 ÷ 0.07
   d) 0.257 ÷ 0.05
   e) 1.08 ÷ 0.08
   f) 7.665 ÷ 0.03
   g) 0.252 ÷ 0.05
   h) 0.039 ÷ 0.06

8 Work out the following.
   a) 0.81 ÷ 0.009
   b) 4.68 ÷ 0.006
   c) 7.5 ÷ 0.005
   d) 50.4 ÷ 0.007

9 Work out the following.
   a) 0.9 ÷ 0.03
   b) 0.71 ÷ 0.002
   c) 63 ÷ 0.09
   d) 108 ÷ 0.4
   e) 1.76 ÷ 0.008
   f) 4.151 ÷ 0.7
   g) 15.33 ÷ 0.07
   h) 8.006 ÷ 0.2
   i) 20.16 ÷ 0.007
   j) 0.008 ÷ 0.4
   k) 0.01 ÷ 0.8
   l) 1.44 ÷ 1.2

Example 7
Work out 96.6 ÷ 300.
1. Break it down into stages — start by working out 96.6 ÷ 3.
2. Then divide your answer by 100.

$$\begin{array}{r}3\,2.2\\3\overline{)9\,6.6}\end{array}$$

32.2 ÷ 100 = **0.322**

10 Consider the calculation 7.3 ÷ 50.
   a) Work out 7.3 ÷ 5.
   b) Use your answer to work out 7.3 ÷ 50.

11 Consider the calculation 2.41 ÷ 400.
   a) Work out 2.41 ÷ 4.
   b) Use your answer to work out 2.41 ÷ 400.

12 Work out the following.
   a) 6.08 ÷ 40
   b) 5.74 ÷ 700
   c) 3.552 ÷ 80
   d) 13.722 ÷ 3000
   e) 25.47 ÷ 900
   f) 33.708 ÷ 6000
   g) 14.016 ÷ 120
   h) 28.6 ÷ 13 000

1.6 Order of Operations

Operations in mathematics are things like addition, subtraction, multiplication and division. The order in which each of these is carried out within a calculation is very important.

BODMAS tells you the correct order to carry out these operations.

Brackets, **O**ther, **D**ivision, **M**ultiplication, **A**ddition, **S**ubtraction

If there are two or more consecutive divisions and/or multiplications, they should be done in **order**, from **left to right**. The same goes for addition and subtraction.

Example 1
Work out:
a) 20 − 3 × 4   Multiply first, then subtract. ⟹ 20 − 3 × 4 = 20 − 12 = **8**
b) 30 ÷ (15 − 12)   Work out what's in the brackets first, then divide. ⟹ 30 ÷ (15 − 12) = 30 ÷ 3 = **10**

Exercise 1

Answer **Questions 1-5** without using your calculator.

1. Work out the following.
   a) $5 + 1 \times 3$
   b) $11 - 2 \times 5$
   c) $5 + 6 \times 2$
   d) $18 - 10 \div 5$
   e) $24 \div 4 + 2$
   f) $35 \div 5 + 2$
   g) $4 + 9 \times 2$
   h) $36 - 12 \div 4$

2. Work out the following.
   a) $2 \times (4 + 10)$
   b) $(7 - 2) \times 3$
   c) $4 + (48 \div 8)$
   d) $5 + (3 \times 7)$
   e) $56 \div (2 \times 4)$
   f) $(3 + 2) \times (9 - 4)$
   g) $(9 + 15) \div 4$
   h) $20 \div (5 - 3)$
   i) $6 \times (4 + 3)$
   j) $11 - (2 + 3)$
   k) $(8 - 7) \times (6 + 5)$
   l) $(8 \times 4) - 11$

3. Work out the following.
   a) $2 \times (8 + 4) - 7$
   b) $5 \times 6 - 8 \div 2$
   c) $18 \div (9 - 12 \div 4)$
   d) $100 \div (8 + 3 \times 4)$
   e) $7 + (10 - 9 \div 3)$
   f) $20 - (5 \times 3 + 2)$
   g) $48 \div 3 - 7 \times 2$
   h) $36 - (7 + 4 \times 4)$

4. Copy each of the following and insert brackets to make the calculation correct.
   a) $9 \times 7 - 5 = 18$
   b) $18 - 6 \div 3 = 4$
   c) $21 \div 4 + 3 = 3$
   d) $5 + 2 \times 6 - 2 = 28$
   e) $13 - 5 \times 13 - 1 = 96$
   f) $6 + 8 - 7 \times 5 = 35$

5. Copy each of the following and: **(i)** fill in the blanks with either $+$, $-$, $\times$ or $\div$,
   (ii) add any brackets necessary to complete the calculation.
   a) $6 + 7 \,\square\, 2 = 20$
   b) $16 \,\square\, 6 \div 3 = 14$
   c) $11 \,\square\, 3 + 5 = 38$
   d) $5 + 16 \,\square\, 2 = 13$
   e) $3 \,\square\, 6 \,\square\, 9 = 9$
   f) $18 \,\square\, 4 \,\square\, 6 = 8$
   g) $8 \,\square\, 2 \,\square\, 6 = 10$
   h) $35 \,\square\, 7 \,\square\, 2 = 56$
   i) $3 \,\square\, 7 \,\square\, 4 = 40$
   j) $13 \,\square\, 4 \,\square\, 1 = 10$
   k) $14 \,\square\, 6 \,\square\, 8 = 1$
   l) $45 \,\square\, 6 \,\square\, 3 = 5$

Example 2

Work out $\dfrac{2 \times 4 + 12}{9 - 5}$.

1. You need to divide the top line by the bottom line.
2. Work out what's on the top and the bottom separately — imagine brackets around the two parts.

$\dfrac{2 \times 4 + 12}{9 - 5} = (2 \times 4 + 12) \div (9 - 5)$
$= (8 + 12) \div (9 - 5)$
$= 20 \div 4 = \underline{\mathbf{5}}$

Exercise 2

Answer **Question 1** without using your calculator.

1. Work out the following.
   a) $\dfrac{4 + 5}{3}$
   b) $\dfrac{7 \times 4}{2 + 5}$
   c) $\dfrac{4 - 1 + 5}{2 \times 2}$
   d) $\dfrac{12 - 5 \times 2}{4 - 2}$
   e) $\dfrac{16}{4 \times (5 - 3)}$
   f) $\dfrac{8 + 2}{15 \div 3}$
   g) $\dfrac{4 \times (7 + 5)}{6 + 3 \times 2}$
   h) $\dfrac{6 + (11 - 8)}{7 - 5}$
   i) $\dfrac{12 \div (9 - 5)}{25 \div 5}$
   j) $\dfrac{8 \times 2 \div 4}{5 - 6 + 7}$
   k) $\dfrac{3 \times 3}{21 \div (12 - 5)}$
   l) $\dfrac{36 \div (11 - 2)}{8 - 8 \div 2}$

1.7 Non-Calculator Arithmetic Problems

Exercise 1

Answer **Questions 1-20** without using your calculator.

1. Work out the following.
   a) $-5 + 8$
   b) $3 \times (-7)$
   c) $-9 + (-4)$
   d) $-48 \div 3$
   e) $6 - (-2)$
   f) $-8 \times (-5)$
   g) $54 \div (-9)$
   h) $-11 - 3$

2. In New York, the evening temperature was -4 °C. During the night, the temperature dropped by 7 °C. What was the lowest temperature that night?

3. The melting point of nitrogen is -210 °C. The melting point of magnesium is 650 °C. What is the difference in melting points of the two elements?

4. Six supermarket shelves each contain 75 tins of soup. How many tins are there in total?

5. Tickets for the school play cost £6 each. £570 worth of tickets were sold altogether. How many tickets were sold?

6. Laura receives £14 pocket money each week. How much money does she get in 52 weeks?

7. 462 pupils are going on a school trip. A coach can seat 54 children. How many coaches will be needed for the trip?

Carry out the calculations in **Questions 8-10**.

8. a) $-8.7 + 3.94$
   b) $7.6 + (-3.82)$
   c) $16 - (-8.74)$
   d) $-6 + 0.9 - (-12.53)$

9. a) 3.4×0.01
   b) $3.48 \div 0.1$
   c) -9.5×1.14
   d) $86.2 \div (-0.04)$

10. a) $-0.051 \div 0.5$
    b) -0.09×8.2
    c) $-0.048 \div (-0.12)$
    d) $-0.072 \times (-0.5)$

11. Asha bought 2 CDs. One cost £11.95 and the other cost £6.59. She paid with a £20 note. How much change did she receive?

12. 1 litre is equal to 1.76 pints. How many pints are there in 5 litres?

13. A car uses 9 litres of petrol to travel 80 km. Petrol costs £1.35 per litre. How much does it cost to travel 400 km?

14. A school jumble sale raises £412.86. The money is to be split equally between three charities. How much will each charity receive?

15. A box of chocolates costs £4.65. A bunch of flowers costs £12.95. Mr O'Brien buys his wife six boxes of chocolates and 3 bunches of flowers. How much does he spend altogether?

16. It costs £35.55 to buy nine identical books. How much would it cost to buy seven of these books?

17. You are given that $221 \times 168 = 37\,128$. Work out the following.
    a) 2.21×1.68
    b) 0.221×1.68
    c) 221×0.168
    d) 22.1×16.8

18. A shop sells apples for £1.18 per kg. How much would it cost to buy 2.5 kg of apples?

19. A 2.72 m ribbon is cut into pieces of length 0.08 m. How many pieces will there be?

20. Work out the following.
    a) $3 - 8 \times 2$
    b) $2 - 18 \div 3$
    c) $6 + 4 \times (-2)$
    d) $0.5 \times 3 - 1.2$
    e) $3.4 \div 1.7 - 2$
    f) $0.48 \div (5 + 1)$
    g) $(5 - 13) \times 1.2$
    h) $12.8 \div [3 - (-1)]$

Section 2 — Approximations

2.1 Rounding — Whole Numbers

Numbers are sometimes **approximated** (or **rounded**) to make them easier to work with.

For example, a number like 5468.9 could be rounded:
- to the nearest **whole number** (= 5469)
- to the nearest **ten** (= 5470)
- to the nearest **hundred** (= 5500)
- to the nearest **thousand** (= 5000)

Example 1

a) Round 18.6 to the nearest whole number.
Look at the digit in the <u>tenths</u> column.
It's <u>greater than 5</u>, so round <u>up</u>.

a) 18.⑥ — rounds up to **19**

b) Round 34.2 to the nearest ten.
Look at the digit in the <u>units</u> column.
It's <u>less than 5</u>, so round <u>down</u>.

b) 3④.2 — rounds down to **30**

c) Round 150 to the nearest hundred.
Look at the digit in the <u>tens</u> column.
It's <u>equal to 5</u>, so round <u>up</u>.

c) 1⑤0 — rounds up to **200**

Exercise 1

1 Write down all the numbers from the box that round to 14 to the nearest whole number.

| 14.1 | 13.3 | 14.02 | 15.499 | 14.5 | 15.01 |
| 13.7 | 14.09 | 14.9 | 13.4999 | 14.4999 | 13.901 |

2 Round the following to the nearest whole number.
a) 9.7   b) 8.4   c) 12.2   d) 7.5   e) 39.8
f) 7.8   g) 45.5   h) 1.1   i) 117.4   j) 662.5

3 Round the following to the nearest whole number.
a) 11.79   b) 7.41   c) 25.12   d) 45.58   e) 11.04

4 Round the following to the nearest ten.
a) 27   b) 32   c) 78   d) 68   e) 48.5
f) 55   g) 54   h) 485   i) 658   j) 187 523

5 Round the following to the nearest hundred.
a) 158   b) 596   c) 650   d) 449   e) 486
f) 5685   g) 6321   h) 4714   i) 2369   j) 12 345

6 Round the following to the nearest thousand.
a) 2536   b) 8516   c) 7218   d) 9500   e) 8596
f) 1658   g) 4328   h) 12   i) 3258   j) 56 985

7 Round the numbers on these calculator displays to the nearest: **(i)** whole number **(ii)** ten

a) 18.2   b) 16.479   c) 20150001   d) 14999999

Exercise 2

1 378 people visited a museum. Round this number to the nearest 10.

2 Flora picked 417 blackberries. How many is this to the nearest 10?

3 Matilda says Italy has an area of 301 225 km². Round this figure to the nearest thousand.

4 Seven thousand four hundred and fifty-two people attended a football match.
   a) Write this number in digits.
   b) Round this number to the nearest:
      (i) ten   **(ii)** hundred   **(iii)** thousand

5 At its closest, Jupiter is about 390 682 810 miles from Earth. Write this distance to the nearest million miles.

6 The number of sweets in a jar is 670, to the nearest 10.
   a) What is the maximum possible number of sweets in the jar?
   b) What is the minimum possible number of sweets in the jar?

7 Bryony keeps 1600 chickens, rounded to the nearest hundred. What is the maximum number of chickens Bryony could have?

2.2 Rounding — Decimal Places

You can also round to different numbers of decimal places (d.p.).

For example, a number like 8.9471 could be rounded:
- to **one** decimal place (= 8.9)
- to **two** decimal places (= 8.95)
- to **three** decimal places (= 8.947)

Example 1

a) Round 4.7625 to one decimal place.
   Look at the digit in the <u>second</u> decimal place.
   It's greater than 5, so round up.

   a) 4.7⑥25 — rounds <u>up</u> to **4.8**

b) Round 4.7625 to two decimal places.
   Look at the digit in the <u>third</u> decimal place.
   It's less than 5, so round down.

   b) 4.76②5 — rounds <u>down</u> to **4.76**

c) Round 4.7625 to three decimal places.
   Look at the digit in the <u>fourth</u> decimal place.
   It's equal to 5, so round up.

   c) 4.762⑤ — rounds <u>up</u> to **4.763**

Section 2 — Approximations

Exercise 1

1 Write down all the numbers from the box that round to 0.4 to one decimal place.

| 0.41 | 0.45 | 0.347 | 0.47204 | 0.335 | 0.405 |
| 0.35 | 0.4295 | 0.5216 | 0.4124 | 0.4671 | 0.307 |

2 Round the following numbers to one decimal place.
a) 0.23
b) 0.678
c) 2.6893
d) 7.147
e) 13.5561
f) 1.3493
g) 72.355
h) 8.3812
i) 0.0324
j) 5.6023
k) 1.85223
l) 4.69999

Exercise 2

1 Write down all the numbers from the box that round to 0.35 to two decimal places.

| 0.362 | 0.357 | 0.345 | 0.359 | 0.3493 | 0.3509 |
| 0.355 | 0.3405 | 0.339 | 0.3498 | 0.3545 | 0.3573 |

2 Round the following numbers to two decimal places.
a) 4.567
b) 0.0424
c) 6.2571
d) 0.35273
e) 3.103695
f) 23.74902
g) 0.34457
h) 0.666666
i) 0.07953
j) 10.30436
k) 1.165725
l) 0.087462

3 Round the following numbers to three decimal places.
a) 0.96734
b) 0.25471
c) 2.43658
d) 6.532561
e) 0.03056
f) 3.638205
g) 5.68414
h) 3.26861
i) 0.008723
j) 13.68543
k) 5.855486
l) 4.57034

4 Round these numbers to the number of decimal places (d.p.) specified.
a) 0.13475 — to 2 d.p.
b) 0.68361 — to 1 d.p.
c) 5.73174 — to 3 d.p.
d) 0.000635 — to 3 d.p.
e) 21.3532 — to 2 d.p.
f) 0.25623 — to 1 d.p.
g) 0.39641 — to 2 d.p.
h) 3.3041 — to 2 d.p.
i) 0.00563 — to 2 d.p.
j) 3.25953 — to 3 d.p.
k) 11.399627 — to 3 d.p.
l) 29.5425 — to 2 d.p.
m) 5.9998 — to 2 d.p.
n) 0.0045789 — to 4 d.p.

5 The mass of the field vole on the right is 0.0384 kg. Round this mass to two decimal places.

6 The length of a snake is 1.245 metres. Round this length to one decimal place.

7 The average distance that a group of students live from a school is 2.4575 km. Round this figure to three decimal places.

8 A number, when rounded to two decimal places, equals 0.40. Write down the smallest possible value of the number.

Not shown actual size.

Section 2 — Approximations

2.3 Rounding — Significant Figures

You can also round to different numbers of **significant figures** (s.f.).

For example, 217 304 could be rounded:
- to **one** significant figure (= 200 000)
- to **two** significant figures (= 220 000)
- to **three** significant figures (= 217 000)

Example 1

a) Round 52 691 to one significant figure.
Look at the <u>second</u> digit.
It's less than 5, so round down.

a) 5②691 — rounds <u>down</u> to **50 000**

b) Round 6.578 to two significant figures.
Look at the <u>third</u> digit.
It's more than 5, so round up.

b) 6.5⑦8 — rounds <u>up</u> to **6.6**

c) Round 958 542 to three significant figures.
Look at the <u>fourth</u> digit.
It's equal to 5, so round up.

c) 958 ⑤42 — rounds <u>up</u> to **959 000**

Exercise 1

1 Round the following numbers to one significant figure.
- a) 476
- b) 31
- c) 7036
- d) 867
- e) 3729
- f) 79 975
- g) 146 825
- h) 993

2 Round the following numbers to two significant figures.
- a) 741
- b) 6551
- c) 7067
- d) 2649
- e) 11.806
- f) 674.81
- g) 136 164
- h) 974.008

3 Round the following numbers to three significant figures.
- a) 4762
- b) 46.874
- c) 5067
- d) 594.5
- e) 35 722
- f) 693 704
- g) 80.569
- h) 925 478

4 Round the following numbers to the number of significant figures (s.f.) indicated.
- a) 45.89 — to 1 s.f.
- b) 5689.6 — to 3 s.f.
- c) 6.792 — to 1 s.f.
- d) 360.8 — to 2 s.f.
- e) 6527 — to 2 s.f.
- f) 756 557 — to 3 s.f.
- g) 146.745 — to 1 s.f.
- h) 376.25 — to 2 s.f.
- i) 79 477 — to 2 s.f.
- j) 624 595 — to 1 s.f.
- k) 579 — to 1 s.f.
- l) 4 567 296 — to 3 s.f.

5 The speed of sound is approximately 1236 km/h. Round this speed to two significant figures.

6 The diameter of Saturn is 120 536 km.
Round this diameter to three significant figures.

7 The average length of a dragon's tail is 258 cm.
Round this length to two significant figures.

8 The table on the right shows the areas of five European countries.
Round each area to two significant figures.

Country	Area (km²)
Austria	83 871
Greece	131 960
Italy	301 263
Luxembourg	2586
Sweden	449 960

Section 2 — Approximations

Rounding Decimals to Significant Figures

Zeros at the start of a decimal do **not** count as significant figures.
The first significant figure is the first **non-zero** digit.

For example, 0.00152839 could be rounded:
- to **one** significant figure (= 0.002)
- to **two** significant figures (= 0.0015)
- to **three** significant figures (= 0.00153)

Example 2

a) Round 0.06826 to one significant figure.
Look at the <u>second</u> significant figure.
It's more than 5, so round up.

a) 0.06⑧26 — rounds <u>up</u> to **0.07**

b) Round 0.006325 to two significant figures.
Look at the <u>third</u> significant figure.
It's less than 5, so round down.

b) 0.0063②5 — rounds <u>down</u> to **0.0063**

c) Round 0.00097151 to three significant figures.
Look at the <u>fourth</u> significant figure.
It's equal to 5, so round up.

c) 0.000971⑤1 — rounds <u>up</u> to **0.000972**

Exercise 2

1 Round the following numbers to one significant figure.
  a) 0.0672
  b) 0.349
  c) 0.000555
  d) 0.0197
  e) 0.47892
  f) 0.000798
  g) 0.11583
  h) 0.00825

2 Round each of the following numbers to two significant figures.
  a) 0.003753
  b) 0.02644
  c) 0.0001792
  d) 0.08735
  e) 3570.4
  f) 0.5635
  g) 0.0007049
  h) 167 489

3 Round each of the following numbers to three significant figures.
  a) 0.5787
  b) 0.08521
  c) 0.10653
  d) 0.00041769
  e) 146.83
  f) 34.726
  g) 0.0084521
  h) 0.437501

4 Round the following numbers to the number of significant figures (s.f.) indicated.
  a) 0.004567 — to 1 s.f.
  b) 0.1932 — to 2 s.f.
  c) 0.0043862 — to 3 s.f.
  d) 0.006204 — to 1 s.f.
  e) 0.009557 — to 2 s.f.
  f) 0.00060384 — to 3 s.f.
  g) 1567.9 — to 2 s.f.
  h) 2364.8 — to 1 s.f.
  i) 0.57863 — to 3 s.f.
  j) 0.02727 — to 1 s.f.
  k) 0.0348657 — to 4 s.f.
  l) 0.04962 — to 2 s.f.
  m) 0.35952 — to 3 s.f.
  n) 0.09625 — to 1 s.f.
  o) 0.069496 — to 2 s.f.

5 The table shows the masses (in kilograms) of some mammals.
Round each mass to two significant figures.

6 The density of the hydrogen gas in a balloon is 0.0899 kg/m^3.
Round this density to one significant figure.

Mammal	Mass (kg)
Common vole	0.0279
Gerbil	0.1472
Meerkat	0.7751
Red squirrel	0.1998
Shrew	0.00612

Section 2 — Approximations

2.4 Estimating Answers

An **approximate** answer to a calculation can be obtained by rounding all the numbers in the calculation to **one significant figure**. Even though the answer isn't exact, it can still be useful. An estimate higher than the exact answer is called an **overestimate**.
If it's lower than the exact answer, it's an **underestimate**.

Example 1
1. a) By rounding each number to one significant figure, estimate $43 + 31.7$
   Replace: 43 with 40 $\longrightarrow$ $43 + 31.7 \approx 40 + 30 =$ **70**
   31.7 with 30

   b) Say whether this is an underestimate or an overestimate.
   $40 < 43$, and $30 < 31.7$. So the estimated
   answer is lower than the exact answer. **Underestimate**

2. By rounding each number to one significant figure, estimate $\dfrac{78.43 \times 6.24}{19.76}$

   Replace: 78.43 with 80
   6.24 with 6 $\longrightarrow$ $\dfrac{78.43 \times 6.24}{19.76} \approx \dfrac{80 \times 6}{20} = \dfrac{480}{20} =$ **24**
   19.76 with 20

Exercise 1

1 By rounding each number to one significant figure, estimate the following.
   a) $437 + 175$
   b) $310 + 876$
   c) $784 - 279$
   d) $0.516 - 0.322$
   e) $184 + 722$
   f) $838 - 121$

2 By rounding each number to one significant figure:
   (i) estimate the calculation, and **(ii)** say whether this is an overestimate or an underestimate.
   a) 23×43
   b) 59×5.7
   c) 40.4×5.1
   d) 18×79
   e) 276×19
   f) 587×8.81

3 Sam has done the calculation 56.2×34.7 on his calculator.
   His calculator display is shown on the right. `17686.14`
   Beth says Sam must have pressed the wrong button at some point.
   a) By rounding each number in the calculation to one significant figure, estimate 56.2×34.7.
   b) Do you think Sam pressed the wrong button at some point? Explain your answer.

4 Use rounding to choose the correct answer (A, B or C) for each of the following calculations.
   a) 1.76×6.3 A: 1.328   B: 5.788   C: 11.088
   b) 582×2.1 A: 119.52   B: 1222.2   C: 4545.2
   c) $\dfrac{57.5 \times 3.78}{16.1}$ A: 1.65   B: 6.3   C: 13.5

5 By rounding each number to one significant figure, estimate the following.

a) $\frac{18}{4.8}$ b) $\frac{8.9}{3.1}$ c) $\frac{32}{5.1}$ d) $\frac{38}{9.7}$ e) $\frac{57}{18}$

f) $\frac{37.3}{5.2}$ g) $\frac{39.4}{3.86}$ h) $\frac{9.98}{2.14}$ i) $\frac{765.4}{18.2}$ j) $\frac{586.2}{186}$

6 By rounding each number to one significant figure, estimate the following.

a) $\frac{68.8 + 27.3}{23.7}$ b) $\frac{\sqrt{8.67}}{3.32}$ c) $\frac{5.6 \times 9.68}{5.14}$ d) $\frac{\sqrt{38.6} + 56.3}{1.678}$

7 The decimal points have been missed out from each of the answers to these calculations. Use rounding to find an approximate answer in each case, and then decide where the decimal point should be.

a) $18.5 \times 3.2 = 592$

b) $\frac{325.26}{5.2} = 6255$

c) $82.2 \times 1.8 = 14796$

d) $41 \times 4.85 = 19885$

e) $7.2 \times 69 = 4968$

f) $\frac{160.05}{3.75} = 4268$

g) $\frac{85.399}{11.5} = 7426$

h) $4.2 \times 5.1 = 2142$

i) $\frac{19.74}{2.4} = 8225$

j) $\frac{19.8 \times 27.4}{3.3} = 1644$

k) $\frac{52.668 \times \sqrt{104.04}}{3.78} = 14212$

l) $\frac{\sqrt{48.4} \times 8.1}{4.8} = 4125$

8 Pens cost 32 pence each. Estimate the cost of 18 pens. Give your answer in pounds.

9 It costs £4.70 to buy the toys needed for one 'Child's Party Bag'.
If 21 children attend a party, estimate how much it would cost to buy all the toys for the party bags.

10 Karen works 42 hours one week, and earns £6.85 per hour.
Estimate the amount of money she earns for the week.

11 A total of 6922 people enter a city-centre marathon.

  a) They each pay a fee of £10.50 to enter.
  Estimate the total amount of money paid to enter the marathon.

  b) The average amount of sponsorship money collected by each runner is £217.
  Estimate the total amount of sponsorship money collected by the runners.

12 A group of 28 children are going on a trip to watch a pantomime.
The total cost of the trip to the pantomime is £584.
Estimate the cost per child for the trip.

13 A smoothie factory operates for 62 hours per week.
It makes 324 litres of smoothie per hour.
Each litre of smoothie contains 18 strawberries.
Estimate the number of strawberries used each week.

Section 2 — Approximations

2.5 Rounding Errors

Error Intervals for Rounded Numbers

When a number has been rounded to a **given unit**, the actual number could be up to **half a unit** bigger or smaller than the rounded number.

Example 1

$m = 20$ rounded to 1 significant figure. Find the interval within which the actual value of m lies.

1. The first significant figure is in the tens column so the rounding unit is 10. Half the rounding unit is $10 \div 2 = 5$.

   Min value of $m = 20 - 5 = 15$
   Max value of $m = 20 + 5 = 25$

2. The actual value can be greater than or equal to the minimum value and less than the maximum value.

   The error interval is $\underline{15 \leq m < 25}$.

Exercise 1

1. Find the minimum and maximum values of the following rounded values.
   a) 80 rounded to the nearest whole number
   b) 400 rounded to 1 significant figure.

2. Write an inequality to show the interval in which the actual value lies for each of the following.
   a) $a = 60$ rounded to the nearest ten
   b) $b = 9$ rounded to the nearest whole number
   c) $c = 500$ rounded to the nearest hundred
   d) $d = 15\,000$ rounded to the nearest thousand

3. The following values have been rounded to the given number of significant figures. Write down an inequality for each to show the range of possible actual values.
   a) $e = 50$ to 1 s.f.
   b) $f = 0.3$ to 1 s.f.
   c) $g = 540$ to 2 s.f.
   d) $h = 14$ to 2 s.f.

4. The following values have been rounded to the given number of decimal places. Find the error interval for each value.
   a) $i = 7.6$ to 1 d.p.
   b) $j = 109.9$ to 1 d.p.
   c) $k = 2.55$ to 2 d.p.
   d) $l = 1.333$ to 3 d.p.

Error Intervals for Truncated Numbers

You **truncate** a number by chopping off decimal places — e.g. 77.88976 truncated to 1 d.p. is 77.8.

The **actual value** of a truncated number can be up to a whole unit bigger but no smaller.

Example 2

$x = 62.1$ truncated to 1 decimal place. Find the error interval for x.

The actual value can be up to 0.1 bigger but no smaller. $\underline{62.1 \leq x < 62.2}$

Exercise 2

1. Truncate the following values to the given number of decimal places.
   a) 1.354 to 1 d.p.
   b) 19.133 to 2 d.p.
   c) 55.78 to 1 d.p.
   d) 103.67183 to 3 d.p.

2. Find the error interval for the following truncated numbers.
   a) $x = 1.3$ truncated to 1 d.p.
   b) $y = 5.13$ truncated to 2 d.p.
   c) $z = 7.731$ truncated to 3 d.p.

Section 3 — Powers and Roots

3.1 Squares, Cubes and Roots

Squares and **cubes** show that a number is multiplied by itself.
For example, $4 \times 4 = 4^2$ is the **square** of 4. The square of a number is always **positive**.
And $4 \times 4 \times 4 = 4^3$ is the **cube** of 4.
The cube of a **positive** number is **positive**, but the cube of a **negative** number is **negative**.

Example 1

Find:
a) 4^2 $4^2 = 4 \times 4 =$ **16**
b) $(-4)^2$ $(-4)^2 = -4 \times -4 =$ **16**
c) 4^3 $4^3 = 4 \times 4 \times 4 =$ **64**
d) $(-4)^3$ $(-4)^3 = -4 \times -4 \times -4 =$ **−64**

Exercise 1

1 Copy and complete the table below without using a calculator.

x	1	2	3	4	5	6	7	8	9	10
x^2				16						

2 Evaluate the following. Use a calculator where necessary.
a) 11^2 b) 12^2 c) 15^2 d) 20^2 e) 30^2

3 Evaluate the following. Use a calculator where necessary.
a) $(-4)^2$ b) 0.1^2 c) $(-10)^2$ d) 0.3^2 e) 0.8^2
f) 0.6^2 g) $(-3)^2$ h) $(-0.2)^2$ i) $(-0.4)^2$ j) $(-15)^2$

4 Copy and complete the table below without using a calculator.

x	1	2	3	4	5
x^3				64	

5 Evaluate the following. Use a calculator where necessary.
a) 6^3 b) 10^3 c) 11^3 d) 20^3 e) 30^3

6 Evaluate the following. Use a calculator where necessary.
a) $(-3)^3$ b) $(-5)^3$ c) $(-10)^3$ d) 0.4^3 e) 0.5^3
f) $(-0.5)^3$ g) $(-6)^3$ h) $(-0.3)^3$ i) $(-0.8)^3$ j) $(-12)^3$

7 Evaluate the following. Use a calculator where necessary.
a) $(-2)^2$ b) $(-2)^3$ c) $(-0.1)^2$ d) $((-2)^2)^3$ e) $((-2)^3)^2$

Square Roots

Finding the **square root** of a number is the opposite of squaring it.
Every **positive** number has **two** square roots — one **positive** ($\sqrt{x}$) and one **negative** ($-\sqrt{x}$).

For example, the positive square root of 2 is $\sqrt{2}$.
And the negative square root of 2 is $-\sqrt{2}$.

Negative numbers **don't have** square roots.

$$\sqrt{x} \times \sqrt{x} = (\sqrt{x})^2 = x$$
$$(-\sqrt{x}) \times (-\sqrt{x}) = (-\sqrt{x})^2 = x$$

Example 2

Find both square roots of 16.

1. $4^2 = 16$, so the positive square root is 4. $\sqrt{16} = \underline{4}$
2. There's also the negative square root. Remember, $(-4) \times (-4) = 16$ too. $-\sqrt{16} = \underline{-4}$

Exercise 2

1 Copy and complete the table below without using a calculator.

x	1	4	9	16	25	36	100
$\sqrt{x}$		2					
$-\sqrt{x}$		−2					

2 Without using a calculator, find:
 a) $\sqrt{49}$ b) $-\sqrt{49}$ c) $\sqrt{81}$ d) $-\sqrt{81}$
 e) $\sqrt{121}$ f) $\sqrt{169}$ g) $-\sqrt{144}$ h) $\sqrt{400}$

3 Find both square roots of the following numbers. Use a calculator where necessary.
 a) 64 b) 121 c) 169 d) 10 000 e) 196

Cube Roots

Every number has exactly one **cube root**. The symbol $\sqrt[3]{}$ is used for cube roots.

$$\sqrt[3]{x} \times \sqrt[3]{x} \times \sqrt[3]{x} = (\sqrt[3]{x})^3 = x$$

Example 3

Find the cube root of: a) 64 b) −64

a) $4^3 = 64$, so the cube root of 64 is 4. a) $\sqrt[3]{64} = \underline{4}$
b) $(-4)^3 = -64$, so the cube root of −64 is −4. b) $\sqrt[3]{-64} = \underline{-4}$

Exercise 3

1 Copy and complete this table without using a calculator.

x	1	8	27	1000	−1	−8	−27	−1000
$\sqrt[3]{x}$				10				

2   Find the following cube roots. Use a calculator where necessary.
   a) $\sqrt[3]{64}$ b) $\sqrt[3]{125}$ c) $\sqrt[3]{1331}$ d) $\sqrt[3]{-64}$
   e) $\sqrt[3]{-125}$ f) $\sqrt[3]{512}$ g) $\sqrt[3]{216}$ h) $\sqrt[3]{-729}$

Exercise 4 — Mixed Exercise

In this exercise use a calculator where you need to.

1   Evaluate the following.
   a) 16^2 b) 12^3 c) $\sqrt[3]{729}$ d) $\sqrt{10000}$
   e) $\sqrt[3]{-343}$ f) 13^2 g) 15^3 h) $\sqrt[3]{-1000000}$

2   Work out the following.
   a) 2.7^3 b) 1.9^2 c) $\sqrt{10}$ d) $\sqrt[3]{80}$
   e) 0.1^2 f) 0.1^3 g) $\sqrt{0.000001}$ h) $\sqrt[3]{-0.000001}$

3   Work out which number in each pair is greater.
   a) 5^2 or $\sqrt{5}$ b) 0.5^2 or $\sqrt{0.5}$ c) $\sqrt{27}$ or $\sqrt[3]{125}$
   d) 5^2 or 5^3 e) 0.5^2 or 0.5^3 f) $\sqrt{200}$ or $\sqrt[3]{2000}$
   g) 100^2 or 10^3 h) $\sqrt{1000}$ or 3^3 i) 4^3 or $\sqrt[3]{250000}$

4   Use a calculator to work out the following.
   a) $\sqrt[4]{81}$ b) $\sqrt[4]{625}$ c) $\sqrt[5]{32}$ d) $\sqrt[5]{16807}$

3.2 Indices

Squares and cubes are two examples of **powers**.

Powers show something that is being multiplied by itself. Powers are usually written using 'index notation' — involving a **base** and an **index**.

base $\Rightarrow 2^3 \Leftarrow$ index

For example, $2 \times 2 \times 2 \times 2 = 2^4$ — this is four 2's multiplied together, and is read as "**2 to the power 4**".
And $5 \times 5 \times 5 \times 5 \times 5 \times 5 = 5^6$ — this is six 5's multiplied together, and is read as "**5 to the power 6**".

Example 1

a) Rewrite $3 \times 3 \times 3 \times 3 \times 3$ using index notation.
    $$3 \times 3 \times 3 \times 3 \times 3 = \underline{\mathbf{3^5}}$$

b) Rewrite 100 000 using powers of 10.
    $$100\,000 = 10 \times 10 \times 10 \times 10 \times 10 = \underline{\mathbf{10^5}}$$

c) Evaluate 5^4.
    $$5^4 = 5 \times 5 \times 5 \times 5 = \underline{\mathbf{625}}$$

Exercise 1

1   Write the following using index notation.
   a) 3×3 b) $2 \times 2 \times 2$ c) $7 \times 7 \times 7 \times 7 \times 7$
   d) $9 \times 9 \times 9 \times 9 \times 9 \times 9$ e) $12 \times 12 \times 12 \times 12$ f) $17 \times 17 \times 17$

2   Use a calculator to evaluate these powers.
   a) 2^4 b) 2^5 c) 3^4 d) 4^6
   e) 6^4 f) 17^3 g) 5^5 h) 3^5

3 a) Use a calculator to evaluate these powers of 10.
    (i) 10^2 **(ii)** 10^3 **(iii)** 10^4 **(iv)** 10^5
    (v) 10^6 **(vi)** 10^7 **(vii)** 10^8 **(viii)** 10^9

  b) Copy and complete the following sentences. (Here, n is a positive whole number.)
    (i) "10^{15} can be written as a '1' followed by _____ zeros."
    (ii) "10^n can be written as a '1' followed by _____ zeros."

4 Rewrite the following as powers of 10.
  a) 100   **b)** 1000   **c)** 10 000   **d)** 100 000
  e) 1 million   **f)** 10 million   **g)** 1 000 000 000   **h)** 1 000 000 000 000

5 Evaluate the following using a calculator.
(Remember to work out powers **before** carrying out any addition or subtraction.)
  a) $3^2 + 2^3$ **b)** $2^3 + 3^3$ **c)** $3^4 - 4^2$ **d)** $5^2 + 6^2$ **e)** $10^3 - 6^2$
  f) $2^6 + 10^3$ **g)** $3^5 - 5^3$ **h)** $10^4 - 7^3$ **i)** $3^4 - 9^2$ **j)** $2^7 + 10^5$

6 Evaluate the following using a calculator.
  a) $3^2 - 2^3$ **b)** $5^2 - 6^2$ **c)** $2^6 - 10^2$ **d)** 3×2^8 **e)** 8×5^4
  f) $8 + 2^5$ **g)** $150 - 3^4$ **h)** $2^7 + 10^6$ **i)** $3^4 \times 2^5$ **j)** $7^5 + 8^4$
  k) $8^7 \div 4^6$ **l)** $10^4 \times 10^3$ **m)** $2^4 \times 2^2$ **n)** $9^3 + 4^2$ **o)** $3^4 \div 5^4$

7 Evaluate the following using a calculator.
  a) $(5 - 2)^3$ **b)** $(5 - 6)^2$ **c)** $(2^2)^2$ **d)** $(3^2)^2$ **e)** $(8 - 5)^4$
  f) $(7 + 3)^5$ **g)** $6^4 - 7^2$ **h)** $2 + 10^5$ **i)** $3^5 \times 2^3$ **j)** $(150 - 50)^6$

Example 2
a) Rewrite $a \times a \times a \times a \times a \times a$ using index notation.
There are 6 a's multiplied together. $a \times a \times a \times a \times a \times a = \underline{\boldsymbol{a^6}}$

b) Rewrite $b \times b \times b \times b \times c \times c$ using index notation.
There are 4 b's multiplied together, and 2 c's. $b \times b \times b \times b \times c \times c = b^4 \times c^2$
                                                                                                       $= \underline{\boldsymbol{b^4 c^2}}$

Exercise 2

1 Rewrite the following using index notation.
  a) $h \times h \times h \times h$ **b)** $t \times t \times t \times t \times t$ **c)** $s \times s \times s \times s \times s \times s \times s$
  d) $k \times k \times k \times k \times k \times k$ **e)** $y \times y \times y \times y$ **f)** $m \times m \times m \times m \times m$

2 Rewrite the following using index notation.
  a) $a \times a \times b \times b \times b$ **b)** $k \times k \times k \times k \times f \times f \times f$ **c)** $m \times m \times m \times m \times n \times n$
  d) $s \times s \times s \times s \times t$ **e)** $w \times w \times w \times v \times v \times v$ **f)** $p \times p \times q \times q \times q \times q \times q$

3 Evaluate these powers using a calculator, given that $x = 2$ and $y = 5$.
  a) $x^2 y^2$ **b)** $x^3 y^2$ **c)** $x^2 y^3$
  d) $x^5 y^2$ **e)** $x^4 y^3$ **f)** $x^4 y^4$

3.3 Laws of Indices

Use the **laws of indices** ('indices' = plural of 'index') to multiply and divide powers with the **same base**.

1) To **multiply** two powers with the same base, **add** the indices: $a^m \times a^n = a^{m+n}$
2) To **divide** two powers with the same base, **subtract** the indices: $a^m \div a^n = a^{m-n}$
3) To **raise** one power to another power, **multiply** the indices: $(a^m)^n = a^{m \times n}$
4) To raise a **fraction** to a power, apply the power to the **numerator** and **denominator**: $\left(\frac{a}{b}\right)^n = \frac{a^n}{b^n}$
5) To raise a number or fraction to a **negative** power, apply the **positive** power to the **reciprocal**: $a^{-n} = \frac{1}{a^n}$

There are two other important index facts you need to know.

1) Anything to the **power 1** is itself: $a^1 = a$
2) Anything to the **power 0** is 1: $a^0 = 1$

Example 1

Simplify the following, leaving the answers in index form.

a) $3^8 \times 3^5$
This is multiplication, so add the indices.
$3^8 \times 3^5 = 3^{8+5} = \underline{\mathbf{3^{13}}}$

b) $\frac{10^8}{10^5}$
This is division ($\frac{10^8}{10^5} = 10^8 \div 10^5$), so subtract the indices.
$10^8 \div 10^5 = 10^{8-5} = \underline{\mathbf{10^3}}$

c) $(2^7)^2$
For one power raised to another power, multiply the indices.
$(2^7)^2 = 2^{7 \times 2} = \underline{\mathbf{2^{14}}}$

d) $\left(\frac{7}{5}\right)^6$
Apply the power to the top and bottom of the fraction.
$\left(\frac{7}{5}\right)^6 = \underline{\mathbf{\frac{7^6}{5^6}}}$

e) 12^{-5}
Find the reciprocal of 12, then raise it to the power of 5.
$12^{-5} = \left(\frac{1}{12}\right)^5 = \frac{1^5}{12^5} = \underline{\mathbf{\frac{1}{12^5}}}$

f) $a^7 \times a^3$
The laws of indices work in exactly the same way with variables.
$a^7 \times a^3 = a^{7+3} = \underline{\mathbf{a^{10}}}$

Exercise 1

1 Simplify these without using a calculator. Leave your answers in index form.
a) $3^2 \times 3^6$
b) $10^7 \times 10^3$
c) $4^7 \times 4^4$
d) 7×7^6
e) $2^3 \times 2^{10}$

2 Simplify these without using a calculator. Leave your answers in index form.
a) $6^7 \div 6^4$
b) $8^6 \div 8^3$
c) $5^7 \div 5^2$
d) $6^8 \div 6^6$
e) $2^{18} \div 2^{11}$

3 Simplify these without using a calculator. Leave your answers in index form.
a) $(4^3)^3$
b) $(11^2)^5$
c) $(100^3)^{23}$
d) $(14^7)^4$
e) $(9^{11})^8$

4 Evaluate the following without using a calculator. Give fractions in their simplest form.
a) 8^{-2}
b) 2^{-3}
c) 5^{-2}
d) 3^{-3}
e) 2^{-4}
f) $\left(\frac{1}{2}\right)^3$
g) $\left(\frac{4}{3}\right)^2$
h) $\left(\frac{2}{6}\right)^3$
i) $\left(\frac{1}{9}\right)^{-2}$
j) $\left(\frac{4}{5}\right)^{-2}$

Section 3 — Powers and Roots

5 Simplify these without using a calculator. Leave your answers in index form.
   a) $4^5 \times 4^{11}$
   b) $12^7 \div 12^3$
   c) $8^2 \times 8^9$
   d) $(6^8)^4$
   e) $(3^{12})^4$
   f) $7^{11} \div 7^6$
   g) $4^{15} \div 4^7$
   h) $(11^2)^9$
   i) $8^8 \times 8^{-4}$
   j) $15^{12} \div 15^{-14}$
   k) $29^{-5} \times 29^{-2}$
   l) $72^{-13} \div 72^7$
   m) $(45^2)^{-9}$
   n) $18^{-8} \times 18^4$
   o) $\dfrac{20^{222}}{20^{210}}$

6 For each of the following, find the number that should replace the square.
   a) $3^3 \times 3^6 = 3^\blacksquare$
   b) $8^\blacksquare \times 8^{10} = 8^{12}$
   c) $(6^{10})^4 = 6^\blacksquare$
   d) $(15^6)^\blacksquare = 15^{24}$
   e) $(9^\blacksquare)^{10} = 9^{30}$
   f) $5^\blacksquare \div 5^6 = 5^7$
   g) $6^5 \times 6^\blacksquare = 6^{12}$
   h) $10^\blacksquare \div 10^2 = 10^4$
   i) $12^{-4} \times 12^\blacksquare = 12^7$
   j) $13^{-6} \div 13^\blacksquare = 13$
   k) $(2^\blacksquare)^{-5} = 2^{40}$
   l) $2^{-24} \div 2^\blacksquare = 2^{17}$

7 Simplify the following.
   a) $a^6 \times a^4$
   b) $e^{12} \div e^3$
   c) $(c^5)^4$
   d) $b^8 \div b^5$
   e) $(m^6)^8$
   f) $y^8 \div y^2$
   g) $h^{17} \times h^2$
   h) $g^7 \times g^5$
   i) $(k^3)^6$
   j) $\dfrac{b^8}{b^5}$
   k) $d^{-7} \times d^2$
   l) $j^{-13} \div j^7$
   m) $(n^7)^{-3}$
   n) $p^{-8} \times p^{-6}$
   o) $\dfrac{x^{60}}{x^{-8}}$

8 For each of the following, find the number that should replace the square.
   a) $s^9 \times s^\blacksquare = s^{14}$
   b) $t^5 \div t^\blacksquare = t^3$
   c) $r^7 \times r^\blacksquare = r^{13}$
   d) $(p^7)^\blacksquare = p^{49}$
   e) $k^\blacksquare \div k^5 = k^3$
   f) $a^\blacksquare \times a^7 = a^{15}$
   g) $m^5 \times m^\blacksquare = m^8$
   h) $(q^5)^\blacksquare = q^{25}$
   i) $l^\blacksquare \times l^{-8} = l^3$
   j) $b^\blacksquare \div b^7 = b^{-10}$
   k) $c^{-15} \times c^\blacksquare = c^8$
   l) $(y^{-4})^\blacksquare = y^{16}$

Example 2

Simplify each expression without using a calculator. Leave your answers in index form.
a) $2^6 \times 2^8 \div 2^2$
   The index of the result will be $6 + 8 - 2$.
   $2^6 \times 2^8 \div 2^2 = 2^{6+8-2} = \underline{\mathbf{2^{12}}}$

b) $\dfrac{2^3 \times 2^5}{2^8 \div 2^6}$
   1. Work out the top and bottom lines of the fraction separately.
   2. Then you can do the final division.

   $\dfrac{2^3 \times 2^5}{2^8 \div 2^6} = \dfrac{2^{3+5}}{2^{8-6}} = \dfrac{2^8}{2^2}$
   $= 2^{8-2}$
   $= \underline{\mathbf{2^6}}$

Exercise 2

In **Questions 1-3**, simplify each expression without using a calculator.
Leave your answers in index form.

1 a) $3^2 \times 3^5 \times 3^7$
   b) $5^4 \times 5 \times 5^8$
   c) $(8^6)^2 \times 8^5$
   d) $(9^4 \times 9^3)^5$
   e) $7^3 \times 7^5 \div 7^6$
   f) $8^3 \times 8^7 \div 8^9$
   g) $(12^8 \div 12^4)^3$
   h) $(4^3)^6 \div 4^4$

2 a) $\dfrac{3^4 \times 3^5}{3^6}$
   b) $\dfrac{8^5 \times 8^4}{8^2 \times 8^3}$
   c) $\dfrac{2^5 \times 2^5}{2^3}$
   d) $\dfrac{4^4 \times 4^6}{4^8 \times 4}$
   e) $\dfrac{7 \times 7^8}{7^2 \times 7^3}$
   f) $\dfrac{5^5 \times 5^5}{5^8 \div 5^3}$
   g) $\dfrac{10^8 \div 10^3}{10^4 \div 10^4}$
   h) $\dfrac{8^{25} \div 8^2}{8^6 \times 8^{10}}$

3 a) $\left(\dfrac{6^3 \times 6^9}{6^7}\right)^3$ b) $\dfrac{2^3 \times 2^4}{(2^2)^2}$ c) $\dfrac{(8^5)^7 \div 8^{12}}{8^6 \times 8^{10}}$ d) $\dfrac{(5^{10} \div 5^8)^4}{5^4 \div 5^2}$

4 Which of the expressions in the box below are equal to 1?

$$\dfrac{4^4 \div 4^3}{4} \qquad \dfrac{7^{16}}{7^8 \times 7^2} \qquad \dfrac{3^8 - 3^7}{3} \qquad \dfrac{5^5 \times 5^9}{(5^2)^7} \qquad \dfrac{(9^2)^2 - 9^0}{9^3}$$

5 Simplify these without using a calculator. Leave your answers in index form.

a) $\left(\dfrac{2^{-5} \times 2^7}{2^3}\right)^5$ b) $\left(\dfrac{7^3}{7}\right)^3 \times 7^{-2}$ c) $\dfrac{9^{-3} \times 9^{15}}{(9^{-3})^{-2}}$ d) $\left(\dfrac{3^{-8} \times 3^{12}}{3^2}\right)^{-6}$

Simplify each of the expressions in **Questions 6-8**.

6 a) $a^6 \times a^5 \div a^4$ b) $z^8 \div z^2 \times z$ c) $(m^4)^3 \times m^3$ d) $(p^5 \div p^3)^6$

7 a) $\dfrac{r \times r^4}{r^2}$ b) $\dfrac{s^{18} \div s^4}{s^3 \times s^6}$ c) $\dfrac{y^8 \div y^3}{y^4 \div y^4}$ d) $\dfrac{(t^6 \div t^3)^4}{t^9 \div t^4}$

8 a) $\dfrac{b \times b^4}{b^{-8}}$ b) $\dfrac{(x^6)^{-4}}{x^9 \div x^3}$ c) $\dfrac{(c^{-4})^3}{c^{-8} \div c^4}$ d) $\left(\dfrac{n^{-18}}{n^3 \times n^6}\right)^{-2}$

3.4 Standard Form

In **standard form** (or standard index form), numbers are written like this:

A can be any number between 1 and 10 (but not 10 itself) ⇒ **A × 10ⁿ** ← **n** can be any integer.

Example 1
Write these numbers in standard form.
a) 360 000
   360 000 = 3.6 × 100 000 = **3.6 × 10⁵**
b) 0.000036
   0.000036 = 3.6 × 0.00001 = **3.6 × 10⁻⁵**

Exercise 1
Write the following numbers in standard form.

1 a) 250 b) 1100 c) 330 d) 48 000 e) 5 900 000
   f) 2 750 000 g) 8560 h) 7340 i) 808 080 j) 7450

2 a) 0.0025 b) 0.0067 c) 0.0303 d) 0.00048 e) 0.000056
   f) 0.375 g) 0.000078 h) 0.07070 i) 0.00000021 j) 0.0005002

Example 2
Write the following standard form numbers as ordinary numbers.
a) 3.5 × 10³
   3.5 × 10³ = 3.5 × 1000
            = **3500**
b) 4.67 × 10⁻⁵
   4.67 × 10⁻⁵ = 4.67 ÷ 10⁵
              = 4.67 ÷ 100 000 = **0.0000467**

Section 3 — Powers and Roots

Exercise 2

1 Write the following out as ordinary numbers.
   a) 3×10^6
   b) 4×10^2
   c) 9.4×10^4
   d) 8.8×10^5
   e) 4.09×10^3
   f) 1.989×10^8
   g) 6.69×10^1
   h) 7.20×10^0
   i) 3.56×10^{-6}
   j) 4.23×10^{-2}
   k) 9.45×10^{-4}
   l) 8.88×10^{-5}
   m) 1.9×10^{-8}
   n) 6.69×10^{-1}
   o) 7.05×10^{-6}

Calculations in Standard Form

To **multiply/divide** in standard form, multiply/divide the numbers and powers of 10 **separately**.
To **add** or **subtract** in standard form, the powers of 10 have to be the **same**.

Example 3

Find the following without using a calculator. Give your answers in standard form.

a) $(2 \times 10^6) \times (3.5 \times 10^5)$
   1. Rearrange to put the numbers and powers of 10 together. $2 \times 3.5 \times 10^6 \times 10^5$
   2. Multiply the numbers and add the indices of the powers of 10. $= 7 \times 10^{6+5}$
   3. Check your answer is in standard form. $= \underline{7 \times 10^{11}}$

b) $(3.7 \times 10^3) + (8.2 \times 10^3)$
   1. The powers of 10 match so add the numbers. $(3.7 + 8.2) \times 10^3$
   2. This isn't in standard form (because 11.9 is bigger than 10) so convert it, $11.9 = 1.19 \times 10$. $= 11.9 \times 10^3$
   $= 1.19 \times 10 \times 10^3 = \underline{1.19 \times 10^4}$

Exercise 3

1 Convert the following numbers to standard form.
   a) 0.034×10^4
   b) 0.00567×10^9
   c) 0.0505×10^3
   d) 907×10^5
   e) 95.32×10^2
   f) 0.034×10^{-4}
   g) 0.0505×10^{-3}
   h) 567×10^{-5}

Do **Questions 2-6** without using a calculator. Give your answers in standard form.

2 a) $(3 \times 10^7) \times (2 \times 10^4)$
   b) $(4 \times 10^9) \times (2 \times 10^{-4})$
   c) $(6 \times 10^5) \times (1.4 \times 10^2)$
   d) $(3.4 \times 10^{-4}) \times (2 \times 10^2)$
   e) $(3.4 \times 10^{-5}) \times (5 \times 10^5)$
   f) $(2.1 \times 10^4) \times (7 \times 10^6)$

3 a) $(9 \times 10^6) \div (3 \times 10^4)$
   b) $(8 \times 10^7) \div (2 \times 10^4)$
   c) $(8.4 \times 10^4) \div (7 \times 10^8)$
   d) $(3.6 \times 10^7) \div (1.2 \times 10^4)$
   e) $(1.8 \times 10^{-4}) \div (0.9 \times 10^8)$
   f) $(8.1 \times 10^{-1}) \div (9 \times 10^{-3})$

4 a) $(5 \times 10^3) + (3 \times 10^3)$
   b) $(6.4 \times 10^2) + (3.2 \times 10^2)$
   c) $(1.8 \times 10^5) + (3.2 \times 10^5)$
   d) $(9.9 \times 10^8) + (5.5 \times 10^8)$
   e) $(3.2 \times 10^{-2}) + (4.9 \times 10^{-2})$
   f) $(6.9 \times 10^{-4}) + (3.8 \times 10^{-4})$

5 a) $(5.2 \times 10^4) - (3.3 \times 10^4)$
   b) $(7.2 \times 10^{-3}) - (1.5 \times 10^{-3})$
   c) $(5.6 \times 10^7) - (3.4 \times 10^7)$
   d) $(4.5 \times 10^{-2}) - (3.3 \times 10^{-2})$
   e) $(1.8 \times 10^4) - (1.2 \times 10^4)$
   f) $(6.4 \times 10^2) - (6.3 \times 10^2)$

6 A country has a population of 5.76×10^7 people. There are 1.8×10^4 branches of the supermarket Spendalot in the country. How many people are there per Spendalot store?

Section 4 — Multiples and Factors

4.1 Finding Multiples and Factors

Multiples

A **multiple** of a number is one that is in its times table.
So the multiples of 2 are: 2, 4, 6, 8, 10, 12, 14... and the multiples of 5 are: 5, 10, 15, 20, 25, 30, 35...
10 is in both lists, so 10 is a **common multiple** of 2 and 5. Both 2 and 5 divide into 10 exactly.

Example 1

a) List the multiples of 5 between 23 and 43.
Starting at 20, the times table of 5 is: 20, 25, 30, 35, 40, 45...
— so the multiples between 23 and 43 are: **25, 30, 35, 40**

b) Which of the numbers in the box on the right are: | 24 7 28 35 39 |
(i) multiples of 3?
3 divides into 24 and 39 exactly — so 24 and 39 are multiples of 3.
But 3 doesn't divide exactly into 7, 28 or 35 — these aren't multiples of 3. (i) **24 and 39**

(ii) multiples of 5?
The only number in the box that 5 divides into exactly is 35. (ii) **35**

(iii) common multiples of 4 and 7?
The multiples of 4 are 24 and 28, while the multiples of 7 (iii) **28**
are 7, 28 and 35. So the only common multiple is 28.

Exercise 1

1 List the first five multiples of: **a)** 4   **b)** 10   **c)** 3   **d)** 6   **e)** 7

2 Write down the numbers from the box that are:
   a) multiples of 3
   b) multiples of 4 | 2   5   8   9   11   12 |
   c) multiples of 5 | 14 15 16 18 20   21 |

3 **a)** List the multiples of 8 between 10 and 20.
   b) List the multiples of 9 between 20 and 50.
   c) List the multiples of 6 between 25 and 35.

4 Write down the numbers from the box that are: | 5   10 15 20 25 30 35 |
   a) multiples of 10 | 40 45 50 55 60 65 70 |
   b) multiples of 15 | 75 80 85 90 95 100 105|
   c) common multiples of 10 and 15

5 **a)** List the multiples of 3 between 19 and 35.
   b) List the multiples of 4 between 19 and 35.
   c) List the common multiples of 3 and 4 between 19 and 35.

6 List all the common multiples of 5 and 6 between 1 and 40.

7 List all the common multiples of 8 and 10 between 1 and 100.

Section 4 — Multiples and Factors

Factors

A number's **factors** divide into it exactly.
For example, the factors of 12 are 1, 2, 3, 4, 6 and 12 — all these numbers divide into 12 exactly.
5 is a factor of both 15 and 20, so 5 is a **common factor** of 15 and 20.

Example 2

Write down all the factors of: a) 18   b) 16

1. Check if 1, 2, 3, 4... divide into the number. Write down each number that divides in exactly, and also its 'factor partner' in a multiplication.
2. Stop checking when you reach a number already in an earlier multiplication, or when a factor is repeated in a multiplication.
3. List all the numbers in your multiplications.

a) $18 = 1 \times 18$ $18 = 2 \times 9$ $18 = 3 \times 6$
4 and 5 don't divide exactly into 18.
So the factors of 18 are **1, 2, 3, 6, 9, 18**.

b) $16 = 1 \times 16$ $16 = 2 \times 8$ $16 = 4 \times 4$
3 doesn't divide exactly into 16.
So the factors of 16 are **1, 2, 4, 8, 16**.

Exercise 2

1 List the numbers from the box on the right that are factors of:

| 1 | 3 | 4 | 7 | 8 | 20 |

a) 8   b) 15   c) 21
d) 40   e) 28   f) 25

2 List the numbers from the box on the right that are factors of:

| 2 | 3 | 5 | 6 | 12 | 15 |

a) 6   b) 24   c) 30
d) 36   e) 20   f) 45

3 List all the factors of the following numbers.

a) 10   b) 4   c) 13   d) 20   e) 25
f) 24   g) 35   h) 32   i) 40   j) 50
k) 9   l) 15   m) 36   n) 49   o) 48

4 a) Which number is a factor of all other numbers?
b) Which two numbers are factors of all even numbers?
c) Which two numbers must be factors of all numbers whose last digit is 5?
d) Which four numbers must be factors of all numbers whose last digit is 0?

Example 3

Find the common factors of 6 and 20.

1. Find the factors of 6 and 20.

$6 = 1 \times 6$ $6 = 2 \times 3$
So the factors of 6 are: 1, 2, 3, 6

$20 = 1 \times 20$ $20 = 2 \times 10$ $20 = 4 \times 5$
So the factors of 20 are: 1, 2, 4, 5, 10, 20

2. The common factors are the numbers that appear in both lists.

So the common factors of 6 and 20 are **1 and 2**.

Section 4 — Multiples and Factors

5   a) List all the factors of 15.
    b) List all the factors of 21.
    c) List the common factors of 15 and 21.

6   List the common factors of the following pairs of numbers.
    a) 15, 20   b) 12, 15   c) 30, 45   d) 50, 90   e) 25, 50

7   List the common factors of the following sets of numbers.
    a) 15, 20, 25   b) 12, 18, 20   c) 30, 45, 50   d) 15, 16, 17

4.2 Prime Numbers

A **prime number** is a number that has no factors except itself and 1.
In other words, the only numbers that divide exactly into a prime number are itself and 1.

But remember... 1 is **not** a prime number.

Example 1

Which of the numbers in the box on the right are prime? | 16 17 18 19 20 |

1. Look for factors of each of the numbers.
2. If you can find factors other than 1 and the number itself, then the number isn't prime.
3. If there are no factors other than 1 and the number itself, then the number is prime.

$16 = 2 \times 8$, and so 16 isn't prime
$18 = 3 \times 6$, and so 18 isn't prime
$20 = 4 \times 5$, and so 20 isn't prime
17 has no factors other than 1 and 17.
19 has no factors other than 1 and 19.
So the prime numbers are **17 and 19**

Exercise 1

1 Look at the following list of numbers: 11, 13, 15, 17, 19
    a) Which number in the list is <u>not</u> prime?
    b) Find two factors greater than 1 that can be multiplied together to give this number.

2 a) Which three numbers in the box on the right are <u>not</u> prime? | 31 33 35 37 39 |
    b) Find two factors greater than 1 that multiply together to give each of your answers to **a)**.

3 Write down the prime numbers in this list: 5, 15, 22, 34, 47, 51, 59

4 a) Write down all the prime numbers less than 10.
    b) Find all the prime numbers between 20 and 30.

5 a) For each of the following, find a factor greater than 1 but less than the number itself:
        (i) 4   (ii) 14   (iii) 34   (iv) 74
    b) Explain why any number with last digit 4 <u>cannot</u> be prime.

6 Without doing any calculations, explain how you can tell that none of the numbers in this list are prime. | 20 30 40 50 70 90 110 130 |

Section 4 — Multiples and Factors

Writing a Number as a Product of Primes

Whole numbers which are **not** prime can be broken down into **prime factors**. The **product** of these prime factors is the original number. (Remember, 'product' means the result of multiplying things.)

Example 2

Write 12 as the product of prime factors.

Make a factor tree.
1. First find <u>any</u> two factors whose product is 12 (here, 12 = 2 × 6). Circle any of these factors that are prime.
2. Repeat step 1 for any factors you didn't circle (here, 6 = 2 × 3).
3. Stop when all the factor tree's branches end in a circle. The product of all the circled primes is the number you started with.

12 = 2 × 2 × 3, or **12 = $2^2 \times 3$**

Exercise 2

In the following questions, write any repeated prime factors as powers.

1 a) Copy and complete the following factor trees.
   (i) 14 — 2, ?
   (ii) 33 — ?, 3
   (iii) 10 — ?, ?
   (iv) 25 — ?, ?

b) Use your factor trees to write the following as products of prime factors.
   (i) 14   (ii) 33   (iii) 10   (iv) 25

2 Write the following numbers as the product of two prime factors.
   a) 15   b) 21   c) 22   d) 35   e) 39

3 a) Copy and complete the following factor trees.
   (i) 30
   (ii) 44
   (iii) 24
   (iv) 72

b) Use your factor trees to write the following as the product of prime factors.
   (i) 30   (ii) 44   (iii) 24   (iv) 72

4 Use factor trees to write the following numbers as the product of prime factors.
   a) 42   b) 66   c) 70   d) 190   e) 210

5 Use factor trees to write the following numbers as the product of prime factors.
   a) 18   b) 50   c) 36   d) 150   e) 32

6 a) Copy and complete the three factor trees below.

(i) [factor tree for 64]

(ii) [factor tree for 64]

(iii) [factor tree for 64]

b) Use each of your factor trees to write 64 as the product of prime factors. What do you notice?

7 Write the following as the product of prime factors.
- **a)** 8
- **b)** 6
- **c)** 28
- **d)** 27
- **e)** 16
- **f)** 60
- **g)** 40
- **h)** 98
- **i)** 24
- **j)** 128
- **k)** 168
- **l)** 225
- **m)** 325
- **n)** 1000
- **o)** 46

8 Square numbers have all their prime factors raised to even powers.
For example, $36 = 2^2 \times 3^2$ and $64 = 2^6$.
- **a)** Write 75 as a product of prime factors.
- **b)** What is the smallest number you could multiply 75 by to form a square number? Explain your answer.

4.3 LCM and HCF

Least Common Multiple (LCM)

The **least common multiple** (**LCM**) of a set of numbers is the smallest of their common multiples. It's the lowest number that they all divide into exactly.

Example 1

Find the least common multiple (LCM) of 4, 6 and 8.

1. Find the multiples of 4, 6 and 8.

   Multiples of 4 are: 4, 8, 12, 16, 20, 24, 28...
   Multiples of 6 are: 6, 12, 18, 24, 30, 36...
   Multiples of 8 are: 8, 16, 24, 32, 40, 48...

2. The LCM is the smallest number that appears in all three lists.

   So the LCM of 4, 6 and 8 is **24**.

Exercise 1

1 Find the LCM of each of the following pairs of numbers.
- **a)** 3 and 4
- **b)** 3 and 5
- **c)** 6 and 8
- **d)** 2 and 10
- **e)** 6 and 7
- **f)** 4 and 9
- **g)** 10 and 15
- **h)** 15 and 20

2 Find the LCM of each of the sets of numbers below.
   a) 3, 6, 8
   b) 2, 5, 6
   c) 3, 5, 6
   d) 4, 9, 12
   e) 5, 7, 10
   f) 5, 6, 9

Example 2

Jane and Alec are running around a small circular track.
It takes Jane 10 seconds to run one lap and Alec 12 seconds.

If they both start from the same point on the track at exactly the same time, how long will it be before they next cross the start line together?

Jane crosses the start line after the following numbers of seconds: 10, 20, 30, 40, 50, ⓞ60, 70...
Alec crosses the start line after the following numbers of seconds: 12, 24, 36, 48, ⓞ60, 72...

So they will next cross the start line together after **60 seconds**.

Exercise 2

1 Laurence and Naima are cycling around a circular course. They leave the start-line at the same time and need to do 10 laps. It takes Laurence 8 minutes to do one lap and Naima 12 minutes.
   a) After how many minutes does Laurence pass the start-line? Write down all possible answers.
   b) After how many minutes does Naima pass the start-line? Write down all possible answers.
   c) When will they first pass the start-line together?

2 Mike visits Oscar every 4 days, while Narinda visits Oscar every 5 days. If they both visited today, how many days will it be before they visit on the same day again?

3 Jill divides a pile of sweets into 5 equal piles. Kay then divides the same sweets into 7 equal piles. What is the smallest number of sweets there could be?

Example 3

Given that $18 = 2 \times 3^2$ and $42 = 2 \times 3 \times 7$, find the LCM of 18 and 42.

1. List the prime factors that appear for **either** number.
   3 appears twice for 18 so list it twice — 2, 3, 3, 7

2. Multiply the listed numbers together to find the least common multiple.
   LCM = $2 \times 3 \times 3 \times 7 =$ **126**

4 Use the prime factorisations below to find the LCM of each pair of numbers.
   a) $30 = 2 \times 3 \times 5$ and $110 = 2 \times 5 \times 11$
   b) $20 = 2^2 \times 5$ and $21 = 3 \times 7$
   c) $6 = 2 \times 3$ and $16 = 2^4$
   d) $18 = 2 \times 3^2$ and $15 = 3 \times 5$
   e) $104 = 2^3 \times 13$ and $96 = 2^5 \times 3$
   f) 11 and 13
   g) 17 and $68 = 2^2 \times 17$
   h) $132 = 2^2 \times 3 \times 11$ and $84 = 2^2 \times 3 \times 7$

5 At a wholesaler, oranges can only be bought in bags of 13. Apples can only be bought in bags of 23. John wants to buy an equal number of apples and oranges. What is the smallest number of apples that John can buy?

Section 4 — Multiples and Factors

6 Gary divides his DVDs into equal groups of 12. He then rearranges them into equal groups of 9. Use prime factors to find the smallest number of DVDs he could have.

Highest Common Factor (HCF)

The **highest common factor** (**HCF**) of a set of numbers is the largest of their common factors. It's the biggest number that divides into all of them exactly.

Example 4

Find the highest common factor of: a) 12 and 15 b) 4 and 8

1. Find the factors of both numbers. The common factors are the numbers in both lists.

   a) The factors of 12 are: ①, 2, ③, 4, 6, 12
      The factors of 15 are: ①, ③, 5, 15
      So the highest common factor of 12 and 15 is **3**.

2. The HCF is the biggest number that appears in both lists.

   b) The factors of 4 are: ①, ②, ④
      The factors of 8 are: ①, ②, ④, 8
      So the highest common factor of 4 and 8 is **4**.

Exercise 3

1 a) Find the common factors of 12 and 20.
     b) Hence find the highest common factor (HCF) of 12 and 20.

2 a) List the common factors of 20 and 30.
     b) Use your list to find the HCF of 20 and 30.

3 Find the HCF of the following pairs of numbers.
   a) 8 and 12   b) 24 and 32   c) 18 and 24   d) 36 and 60
   e) 14 and 15   f) 12 and 36   g) 35 and 42   h) 56 and 63

4 Write down the following:
   a) the HCF of 5 and 6
   b) the HCF of 11 and 12
   c) the HCF of 21 and 22

5 Find the HCF of the following sets of numbers.
   a) 6, 8, 16   b) 12, 15, 18   c) 24, 30, 36
   d) 18, 36, 72   e) 36, 48, 60   f) 25, 50, 75

Example 5

Given that $60 = 2^2 \times 3 \times 5$ and $110 = 2 \times 5 \times 11$, find the highest common factor of 60 and 110.

1. List the prime factors that appear in **both** numbers.   2, 5
2. Multiply the listed numbers together to find the highest common factor.
   HCF = $2 \times 5 =$ **10**

Section 4 — Multiples and Factors

6 Use the prime factorisations below to find the HCF of each pair of numbers.
   a) $18 = 2 \times 3^2$ and $38 = 2 \times 19$
   b) $42 = 2 \times 3 \times 7$ and $70 = 2 \times 5 \times 7$
   c) $14 = 2 \times 7$ and $4 = 2^2$
   d) $18 = 2 \times 3^2$ and $30 = 2 \times 3 \times 5$
   e) $30 = 2 \times 3 \times 5$ and $84 = 2^2 \times 3 \times 7$
   f) $104 = 2^3 \times 13$ and $39 = 3 \times 13$
   g) 17 and $68 = 2^2 \times 17$
   h) $132 = 2^2 \times 3 \times 11$ and $96 = 2^5 \times 3$
   i) $81 = 3^4$ and $99 = 3^2 \times 11$
   j) $126 = 2 \times 3^2 \times 7$ and $108 = 2^2 \times 3^3$

Exercise 4 — Mixed Exercise

1 a) Find the highest common factor of the following pairs of numbers.
   (i) 5 and 9   (ii) 9 and 12   (iii) 10 and 15   (iv) 12 and 20
   b) Find the least common multiple of the following pairs of numbers.
   (i) 5 and 9   (ii) 9 and 12   (iii) 10 and 15   (iv) 12 and 20

2 Anna has 36 identical sweets, and wants to arrange them all into equal piles.
   a) First she makes piles of 2 sweets. How many piles could she make?
   b) Could she make piles of 5 sweets using all the sweets? Explain your answer.
   c) In total, how many different ways are there for Anna to divide the 36 sweets into equal piles? List all the different possibilities.

3 A baker has 12 identical cakes. In how many different ways can he divide them up into equal packets (without cutting them up)? List the possibilities.

4 In how many different ways can 100 identical chairs be arranged in rows of equal length? List all the ways the chairs can be arranged.

5 A zoo has between 95 and 155 animals. The number of animals divides exactly by 20 and exactly by 30.
   a) Write down all the multiples of 20 between 95 and 155.
   b) Write down all the multiples of 30 between 95 and 155.
   c) How many animals are there?

6 A garden centre has between 95 and 205 potted plants. They can be arranged exactly in rows of 25 and exactly in rows of 30. How many plants are there?

7 There are between 240 and 300 decorated plates hanging on a wall, and the number of plates divides exactly by both 40 and 70. How many plates are there?

8 Use prime factors to find **(i)** the HCF and **(ii)** the LCM of each of the following pairs of numbers.
   a) $36 = 2^2 \times 3^2$ and $8 = 2^3$
   b) $12 = 2^2 \times 3$ and $75 = 3 \times 5^2$
   c) $54 = 2 \times 3^3$ and $96 = 2^5 \times 3$
   d) $108 = 2^2 \times 3^3$ and $124 = 2^2 \times 31$
   e) $200 = 2^3 \times 5^2$ and $240 = 2^4 \times 3 \times 5$
   f) $84 = 2^2 \times 3 \times 7$ and $196 = 2^2 \times 7^2$
   g) $140 = 2^2 \times 5 \times 7$ and $308 = 2^2 \times 7 \times 11$
   h) $150 = 2 \times 3 \times 5^2$ and $180 = 2^2 \times 3^2 \times 5$

9 a) Copy and complete the factor trees to write 78 and 92 as products of their prime factors.
   b) Use the prime factors of 78 and 92 to find their LCM and HCF.

Section 5 — Fractions

5.1 Equivalent Fractions

The fraction $\frac{a}{b}$ means 'a out of b' or 'a divided by b'. The top number in a fraction (a) is called the **numerator**. The bottom number (b) is called the **denominator**.

Equivalent fractions are fractions that are equal in value.

To find an equivalent fraction, multiply or divide the numerator and denominator by the **same thing**.

Example 1

Find the value that needs to replace the square: $\frac{1}{5} = \frac{\square}{20}$

1. Find what you need to multiply by to get from one denominator to the other.
2. Multiply the numerator by the same number.

$$\frac{1}{5} \xrightarrow{\times 4} \frac{\square}{20}$$

$$\frac{1}{5} \xrightarrow{\times 4} \frac{4}{20}$$

Example 2

Find the value of b if $\frac{12}{30} = \frac{4}{b}$

1. Find what you need to divide by to get from one numerator to the other.
2. Divide the denominator by the same number.

$$\frac{12}{30} \xrightarrow{\div 3} \frac{4}{b}$$

$$\frac{12}{30} \xrightarrow{\div 3} \frac{4}{10} \quad \text{So } \underline{\mathbf{b = 10}}$$

Exercise 1

1 a) How many sections of each square do you need to shade to show a fraction equivalent to $\frac{1}{2}$?
  b) Use your answers to replace the stars and make fractions equivalent to $\frac{1}{2}$.

$$\frac{1}{2} = \frac{\star}{4} = \frac{\star}{6} = \frac{\star}{8}$$

2 Replace the stars and make fractions equivalent to $\frac{1}{3}$. Use the circles to help.

$$\frac{1}{3} = \frac{\star}{6} = \frac{\star}{9} = \frac{\star}{12}$$

3 Find the values of the letters in the following fractions.
a) $\frac{1}{5} = \frac{a}{10}$
b) $\frac{1}{4} = \frac{b}{12}$
c) $\frac{3}{4} = \frac{c}{16}$
d) $\frac{1}{20} = \frac{d}{60}$
e) $\frac{1}{5} = \frac{5}{e}$
f) $\frac{1}{6} = \frac{3}{f}$
g) $\frac{7}{12} = \frac{35}{g}$
h) $\frac{9}{10} = \frac{81}{h}$

4 Find the values of the letters in the following fractions.
a) $\frac{1}{a} = \frac{5}{15}$
b) $\frac{3}{b} = \frac{12}{20}$
c) $\frac{c}{3} = \frac{10}{15}$
d) $\frac{d}{14} = \frac{9}{42}$
e) $\frac{e}{9} = \frac{15}{27}$
f) $\frac{f}{51} = \frac{9}{17}$
g) $\frac{11}{g} = \frac{55}{80}$
h) $\frac{1}{h} = \frac{11}{121}$

Simplifying Fractions

Simplifying a fraction by **cancelling down** means writing an equivalent fraction using the smallest possible numbers. This is also known as 'expressing a fraction in its **lowest terms**'.

Example 3
Express $\frac{24}{30}$ as a fraction in its lowest terms.

1. Divide the numerator and denominator by any common factor. Here, 3 is a common factor of 24 and 30.
2. Repeat this until the numerator and denominator have no more common factors. Here, 2 is a common factor of 8 and 10.
3. 4 and 5 have no common factors, so this is in its lowest terms.
4. Dividing 24 and 30 by their highest common factor (= 6) will get the answer in a single step.

$\frac{24}{30} = \frac{8}{10}$ (÷3)

$\frac{8}{10} = \frac{4}{5}$ (÷2)

Exercise 2

Answer **Questions 1-4** without using a calculator.

1 a) Find a common factor of 2 and 10 that's greater than 1.
b) Use your answer to simplify $\frac{2}{10}$.
c) Is your answer to **b)** in its lowest terms? Explain your answer.

2 a) Which of the following is a common factor of 45 and 75? [9 25 2 5]
b) (i) Simplify $\frac{45}{75}$ by dividing the numerator and denominator by your answer to **a)**.
(ii) Is this fraction in its lowest terms?
If not, find another common factor of the numerator and denominator and simplify the fraction again. Repeat this process until the fraction is in its lowest terms.

3 Write the following fractions in their lowest terms.
a) $\frac{3}{9}$
b) $\frac{5}{20}$
c) $\frac{8}{16}$
d) $\frac{4}{32}$
e) $\frac{9}{45}$
f) $\frac{15}{36}$
g) $\frac{15}{20}$
h) $\frac{12}{15}$
i) $\frac{21}{35}$
j) $\frac{24}{64}$
k) $\frac{30}{40}$
l) $\frac{25}{100}$

4 Simplify these fractions. Then state which fraction is not equivalent to the other two.
a) $\frac{6}{18}, \frac{5}{20}, \frac{9}{27}$
b) $\frac{6}{8}, \frac{9}{15}, \frac{15}{25}$
c) $\frac{4}{18}, \frac{6}{33}, \frac{10}{45}$
d) $\frac{18}{24}, \frac{60}{80}, \frac{24}{40}$

5   Simplify each of these fractions. Use a calculator where necessary.
    a) $\frac{91}{130}$ b) $\frac{175}{230}$ c) $\frac{204}{348}$ d) $\frac{1029}{3486}$

Example 4
Express 20 as a fraction of 100 in its simplest form.
Write the first number over the second number and simplify.

$$\frac{20}{100} = \frac{1}{5} \quad (\div 20)$$

6   Without using a calculator, express the following in their simplest terms.
    a) 4 as a fraction of 24   b) 11 as a fraction of 88   c) 20 as a fraction of 54
    d) 12 as a fraction of 66   e) 35 as a fraction of 150   f) 108 as a fraction of 256
    g) 0.6 as a fraction of 0.8   h) 0.9 as a fraction of 7.2   i) 1.8 as a fraction of 3.8

5.2 Mixed Numbers

A **mixed number** is a whole number combined with a fraction. $\Rightarrow 2\frac{1}{2}$

A fraction where the numerator is bigger than the denominator is a **top-heavy** or **improper** fraction. $\Rightarrow \frac{5}{2}$

Example 1
Write the mixed number $4\frac{3}{5}$ as an improper fraction.
1. Find the fraction which is equivalent to 4 and which has 5 as the denominator. Remember, $4 = \frac{4}{1}$.

   $\frac{4}{1} = \frac{20}{5}$ (× 5)

2. Combine the two fractions into one improper fraction.

   So $4\frac{3}{5} = \frac{20}{5} + \frac{3}{5} = \frac{23}{5}$

Exercise 1
Answer **Questions 1-6** without using the fractions button on your calculator.

1   Use the diagrams to form improper fractions equivalent to the whole numbers.
    a) $2 = \frac{★}{3}$ b) $3 = \frac{★}{4}$
    Clue: *How many thirds are there in 2?*   Clue: *How many quarters are there in 3?*

2   Find the values of the letters to write the following whole numbers as improper fractions.
    a) $2 = \frac{a}{6}$ b) $5 = \frac{b}{5}$ c) $6 = \frac{30}{c}$ d) $13 = \frac{65}{d}$

3   a) Find the value of a if $4 = \frac{a}{3}$.
    b) Use your answer to write the mixed number $4\frac{1}{3}$ as an improper fraction.

4   a) Find the value of b if $3 = \frac{b}{5}$.
    b) Use your answer to write the mixed number $3\frac{2}{5}$ as an improper fraction.

Section 5 — Fractions

5 Find the values of the letters to write the following mixed numbers as improper fractions.
   a) $1\frac{1}{3} = \frac{a}{3}$
   b) $1\frac{2}{7} = \frac{b}{7}$
   c) $2\frac{1}{2} = \frac{c}{2}$
   d) $3\frac{4}{7} = \frac{d}{7}$

6 Write the following mixed numbers as improper fractions.
   a) $1\frac{4}{5}$
   b) $1\frac{5}{12}$
   c) $2\frac{9}{10}$
   d) $5\frac{3}{10}$
   e) $4\frac{3}{4}$
   f) $9\frac{5}{6}$
   g) $12\frac{2}{5}$
   h) $15\frac{5}{7}$
   i) $6\frac{5}{6}$
   j) $3\frac{1}{9}$
   k) $10\frac{3}{10}$
   l) $7\frac{2}{3}$

Example 2
Write the improper fraction $\frac{13}{5}$ as a mixed number in its simplest terms.
1. Split the numerator into:
   (i) a multiple of the denominator,
   plus (ii) a 'remainder' (since $13 \div 5 = 2$, with remainder 3).
2. Separate the fraction to write it as a mixed number. The first part will always simplify to a whole number.

$\frac{13}{5} = \frac{10 + 3}{5}$
$= \frac{10}{5} + \frac{3}{5}$
$= 2 + \frac{3}{5} = 2\frac{3}{5}$

Exercise 2
Answer **Questions 1-7** without using your calculator.

1 Write the whole number that is equivalent to these improper fractions.
   a) $\frac{14}{2}$
   b) $\frac{22}{11}$
   c) $\frac{45}{5}$
   d) $\frac{72}{12}$

2 a) Write down the value of a if $\frac{11}{7} = \frac{7 + a}{7}$.
   b) Use your answer to write $\frac{11}{7}$ as a mixed number in its simplest terms.

3 a) Write down the value of c if $\frac{17}{3} = \frac{c + 2}{3}$.
   b) Use your answer to write $\frac{17}{3}$ as a mixed number in its simplest terms.

4 Write the following improper fractions as mixed numbers.
   a) $\frac{5}{3}$
   b) $\frac{9}{5}$
   c) $\frac{17}{10}$
   d) $\frac{12}{7}$
   e) $\frac{13}{11}$
   f) $\frac{9}{4}$
   g) $\frac{13}{6}$
   h) $\frac{16}{5}$
   i) $\frac{20}{9}$
   j) $\frac{11}{3}$

5 a) Simplify the improper fraction $\frac{26}{4}$ so that it is in its lowest terms.
   b) Use your answer to write $\frac{26}{4}$ as a mixed number.

6 Write the following improper fractions as mixed numbers in their lowest terms.
   a) $\frac{18}{12}$
   b) $\frac{10}{4}$
   c) $\frac{50}{15}$
   d) $\frac{18}{4}$
   e) $\frac{24}{18}$
   f) $\frac{35}{25}$
   g) $\frac{18}{8}$
   h) $\frac{51}{12}$
   i) $\frac{34}{6}$
   j) $\frac{98}{8}$

7 Find the number in each list that is not equivalent to the other two.
   a) $\frac{5}{2}, \frac{6}{4}, 1\frac{1}{2}$
   b) $2\frac{1}{3}, 3\frac{1}{2}, \frac{7}{3}$
   c) $\frac{19}{4}, 4\frac{3}{4}, \frac{15}{4}$
   d) $2\frac{2}{3}, \frac{11}{3}, \frac{16}{6}$

5.3 Ordering Fractions

Finding a Common Denominator

Putting two (or more) fractions over a **common denominator** means rewriting them so they have the same denominator (the number on the bottom of the fraction).

The common denominator will be a **multiple** of both fractions' denominators.

Example 1

Rewrite the following pairs of fractions so they have a common denominator.

a) $\frac{1}{2}$ and $\frac{1}{8}$

You can use 8 as the common denominator, since 8 is a multiple of 2 and 8. So find a fraction equivalent to $\frac{1}{2}$ with 8 as the denominator.

$\frac{1}{2} = \frac{4}{8}$ (× 4)

So these fractions are equivalent to $\frac{4}{8}$ and $\frac{1}{8}$.

b) $\frac{5}{6}$ and $\frac{3}{8}$

24 is a multiple of both 6 and 8, so use this as the common denominator. Rewrite the two fractions so that they have 24 as the denominator.

$\frac{5}{6} = \frac{20}{24}$ (× 4) $\frac{3}{8} = \frac{9}{24}$ (× 3)

These fractions are equivalent to $\frac{20}{24}$ and $\frac{9}{24}$.

Exercise 1

Answer **Questions 1-4** without using a calculator.

1 Rewrite the following pairs of fractions so they have a common denominator.
a) $\frac{1}{3}, \frac{1}{6}$ b) $\frac{1}{5}, \frac{3}{10}$ c) $\frac{1}{4}, \frac{5}{16}$ d) $\frac{2}{5}, \frac{7}{20}$
e) $\frac{3}{8}, \frac{1}{4}$ f) $\frac{1}{12}, \frac{2}{3}$ g) $\frac{5}{18}, \frac{2}{9}$ h) $\frac{2}{7}, \frac{5}{28}$

2 Rewrite the following pairs of fractions so they have a common denominator.
a) $\frac{1}{2}, \frac{1}{5}$ b) $\frac{1}{3}, \frac{1}{4}$ c) $\frac{1}{7}, \frac{1}{10}$ d) $\frac{1}{3}, \frac{1}{7}$
e) $\frac{1}{8}, \frac{2}{5}$ f) $\frac{1}{4}, \frac{1}{12}$ g) $\frac{1}{6}, \frac{1}{4}$ h) $\frac{1}{8}, \frac{1}{6}$

3 Rewrite the following pairs of fractions so they have a common denominator.
a) $\frac{2}{9}, \frac{1}{3}$ b) $\frac{2}{3}, \frac{3}{4}$ c) $\frac{5}{6}, \frac{1}{7}$ d) $\frac{2}{9}, \frac{1}{2}$
e) $\frac{3}{8}, \frac{4}{5}$ f) $\frac{5}{6}, \frac{7}{12}$ g) $\frac{7}{8}, \frac{3}{10}$ h) $\frac{2}{5}, \frac{4}{9}$

4 Rewrite the following groups of fractions so they have a common denominator.
a) $\frac{3}{4}, \frac{5}{8}, \frac{7}{12}$ b) $\frac{1}{5}, \frac{7}{10}, \frac{9}{20}$ c) $\frac{1}{7}, \frac{4}{21}, \frac{5}{14}$ d) $\frac{1}{2}, \frac{3}{8}, \frac{2}{3}$
e) $\frac{2}{5}, \frac{5}{12}, \frac{11}{30}$ f) $\frac{1}{8}, \frac{7}{20}, \frac{3}{5}$ g) $\frac{2}{3}, \frac{5}{7}, \frac{5}{6}$ h) $\frac{5}{18}, \frac{7}{24}, \frac{11}{30}$

Ordering Fractions

If fractions have a common denominator, then you can use their **numerators** to put them in order.

Example 2

Put the fractions $\frac{1}{2}, \frac{3}{8}$, and $\frac{3}{4}$ in order, from smallest to largest.

1. Put the fractions over a common denominator first.
   Use 8 as the common denominator, since 8 is a multiple of 2, 4 and 8. So rewrite $\frac{1}{2}$ and $\frac{3}{4}$ as fractions with a denominator of 8.

   $\frac{1}{2} = \frac{4}{8}$ (×4) $\frac{3}{4} = \frac{6}{8}$ (×2)

   So the fractions are equivalent to $\frac{4}{8}, \frac{3}{8}$ and $\frac{6}{8}$.

2. Use the numerators to put the fractions in order. In order, these are: $\frac{3}{8}, \frac{4}{8}, \frac{6}{8}$.

3. Write the ordered fractions in their original form. So in order, the original fractions are $\frac{3}{8}, \frac{1}{2}, \frac{3}{4}$.

Exercise 2

Answer **Questions 1-9** without using a calculator.

1 a) Rewrite the fractions $\frac{5}{6}$ and $\frac{2}{3}$ so they have a common denominator.
   b) Which of the fractions $\frac{5}{6}$ and $\frac{2}{3}$ is larger?

2 a) Rewrite the fractions $\frac{2}{5}$ and $\frac{3}{8}$ so they have a common denominator.
   b) Which of the fractions $\frac{2}{5}$ and $\frac{3}{8}$ is larger?

3 Write down the larger fraction in each pair below.
   a) $\frac{1}{4}, \frac{5}{8}$ b) $\frac{3}{5}, \frac{7}{10}$ c) $\frac{4}{7}, \frac{9}{14}$ d) $\frac{11}{18}, \frac{2}{3}$
   e) $\frac{5}{6}, \frac{3}{4}$ f) $\frac{2}{3}, \frac{3}{5}$ g) $\frac{2}{3}, \frac{3}{4}$ h) $\frac{7}{10}, \frac{3}{4}$

4 a) Rewrite the fractions $\frac{1}{3}, \frac{4}{15}$ and $\frac{2}{9}$ so they have a common denominator.
   b) Use your answer to write the fractions $\frac{1}{3}, \frac{4}{15}$ and $\frac{2}{9}$ in order, from smallest to largest.

In **Questions 5-7**, put each of the sets of fractions in order, from smallest to largest.

5 a) $\frac{1}{2}, \frac{5}{8}, \frac{7}{16}$ b) $\frac{2}{5}, \frac{3}{10}, \frac{7}{20}$ c) $\frac{3}{4}, \frac{7}{12}, \frac{5}{8}$ d) $\frac{5}{6}, \frac{11}{12}, \frac{19}{24}$

6 a) $\frac{4}{9}, \frac{5}{12}, \frac{2}{3}$ b) $\frac{9}{10}, \frac{11}{12}, \frac{4}{5}$ c) $\frac{1}{4}, \frac{3}{11}, \frac{5}{22}$ d) $\frac{7}{9}, \frac{4}{5}, \frac{13}{15}$

7 a) $\frac{7}{8}, \frac{5}{6}, \frac{13}{16}$ b) $\frac{4}{15}, \frac{7}{27}, \frac{13}{45}$ c) $\frac{5}{16}, \frac{7}{20}, \frac{9}{25}$ d) $\frac{11}{36}, \frac{4}{15}, \frac{9}{24}$

8 Annette scores $\frac{5}{6}$ on a test. Ben scores $\frac{7}{8}$. Who does better?

9 Charlene runs $\frac{3}{4}$ of a mile, while Dave runs $\frac{7}{10}$ of a mile. Who runs further?

Section 5 — Fractions

5.4 Adding and Subtracting Fractions

Add or subtract fractions with a **common denominator** by adding or subtracting the **numerators**.
If fractions have **different denominators**, then rewrite them with a common denominator first.

Example 1

Work out $\frac{2}{5} + \frac{2}{3}$.

1. Rewrite the fractions with a common denominator of 15.

   $\frac{2}{5} = \frac{6}{15}$ (×3) $\frac{2}{3} = \frac{10}{15}$ (×5)

2. Rewrite the addition using your new fractions. Then add or subtract the numerators.

   So $\frac{2}{5} + \frac{2}{3} = \frac{6}{15} + \frac{10}{15}$

   $= \frac{6 + 10}{15}$

3. Give your answer in its simplest terms.

   $= \frac{16}{15}$ or $1\frac{1}{15}$

Exercise 1

Answer **Questions 1-7** without using your calculator.

1. Work out the following. Give your answers in their simplest form.
   a) $\frac{1}{3} + \frac{1}{3}$
   b) $\frac{4}{5} - \frac{2}{5}$
   c) $\frac{5}{11} - \frac{3}{11}$
   d) $\frac{1}{10} + \frac{3}{10}$
   e) $\frac{1}{12} + \frac{5}{12}$
   f) $\frac{8}{9} - \frac{2}{9}$
   g) $\frac{3}{20} + \frac{7}{20}$
   h) $\frac{11}{16} - \frac{5}{16}$

2. Work out the following. Give your answers as mixed numbers in their simplest form.
   a) $\frac{5}{8} + \frac{7}{8}$
   b) $\frac{3}{4} + \frac{3}{4}$
   c) $\frac{7}{10} + \frac{9}{10}$
   d) $\frac{11}{20} + \frac{13}{20}$
   e) $\frac{5}{11} + \frac{8}{11} + \frac{7}{11}$
   f) $\frac{5}{7} + \frac{4}{7} + \frac{6}{7}$
   g) $\frac{8}{15} + \frac{13}{15} - \frac{2}{15}$
   h) $\frac{17}{20} + \frac{19}{20} - \frac{7}{20}$

3. a) Rewrite the fractions $\frac{1}{2}$ and $\frac{1}{4}$ with a common denominator.
   b) Work out $\frac{1}{2} + \frac{1}{4}$.

4. Work out the following. Give your answers in their simplest form.
   a) $\frac{3}{5} + \frac{1}{10}$
   b) $\frac{1}{4} + \frac{3}{8}$
   c) $\frac{1}{6} + \frac{1}{2}$
   d) $\frac{3}{14} + \frac{2}{7}$
   e) $\frac{4}{9} - \frac{1}{3}$
   f) $\frac{3}{4} - \frac{3}{8}$
   g) $\frac{7}{10} - \frac{2}{5}$
   h) $\frac{5}{18} - \frac{2}{9}$

5. a) Rewrite the fractions $\frac{9}{10}$ and $\frac{5}{6}$ with a common denominator.
   b) Work out $\frac{9}{10} - \frac{5}{6}$. Give your answer in its simplest form.

6 Work out the following. Give your answers in their simplest form.

a) $\frac{1}{5} + \frac{1}{3}$
b) $\frac{9}{10} - \frac{5}{6}$
c) $\frac{1}{2} + \frac{3}{5}$
d) $\frac{2}{3} - \frac{1}{4}$
e) $\frac{2}{3} + \frac{4}{5}$
f) $\frac{5}{6} + \frac{9}{10}$
g) $\frac{6}{7} - \frac{3}{4}$
h) $\frac{6}{11} + \frac{7}{9}$
i) $\frac{23}{24} - \frac{7}{10}$
j) $\frac{8}{9} + \frac{12}{21}$
k) $\frac{3}{5} - \frac{3}{7}$
l) $\frac{15}{16} + \frac{3}{5}$

7 Work out the following. Give your answers in their simplest form.

a) $\frac{1}{9} + \frac{5}{9} + \frac{11}{18}$
b) $\frac{3}{4} + \frac{1}{8} - \frac{7}{16}$
c) $\frac{6}{7} + \frac{1}{14} - \frac{1}{2}$
d) $\frac{1}{4} + \frac{2}{3} + \frac{5}{6}$

Example 2

A maths exam has 24 questions. $\frac{1}{2}$ of the questions are on number topics, $\frac{1}{3}$ of the questions are on algebra, and the rest are on geometry.
What fraction of the questions are geometry questions?

1. The fractions of number questions, algebra questions and geometry questions must add up to 1.

   Fraction of geometry questions $= 1 - \frac{1}{2} - \frac{1}{3}$

2. Put the fractions over a common denominator. (Remember, anything divided by itself is 1, so you can write $1 = \frac{6}{6}$.)

   $1 = \frac{6}{6}$ $\frac{1}{2} = \frac{3}{6}$ $\frac{1}{3} = \frac{2}{6}$

3. Subtract to find the fraction of geometry questions.

   Fraction of geometry questions $= \frac{6}{6} - \frac{3}{6} - \frac{2}{6} = \frac{6 - 3 - 2}{6}$
   $= \frac{1}{6}$

Exercise 2

1 $\frac{4}{9}$ of the pupils in one class are boys. What fraction of the class are girls?

2 Jake, Frank and Olga are sharing a cake. Jake eats $\frac{2}{7}$ of the cake, Frank eats $\frac{3}{7}$ and Olga eats the rest. What fraction of the cake does Olga eat?

3 $\frac{1}{5}$ of the flowers in a garden are roses. $\frac{3}{10}$ of the flowers are tulips.
What fraction of the flowers are neither roses nor tulips?

4 A bag contains a mixture of sweets. $\frac{2}{5}$ of the sweets are chocolates, $\frac{1}{4}$ are toffees and the rest are mints. What fraction of the sweets are mints?

5 In a school survey, $\frac{1}{2}$ of the pupils said they walk to school. $\frac{1}{5}$ said they catch the bus.
The rest arrive by car. What fraction come to school by car?

Adding and Subtracting Mixed Numbers

To add or subtract mixed numbers, first change them into **improper fractions** with a **common denominator**.

Example 3

Work out $1\frac{1}{3} + 2\frac{5}{6}$.

1. Write the mixed numbers as improper fractions.

   $1 = \frac{3}{3}$, so $1\frac{1}{3} = \frac{3}{3} + \frac{1}{3} = \frac{4}{3}$

   $2 = \frac{12}{6}$, so $2\frac{5}{6} = \frac{12}{6} + \frac{5}{6} = \frac{17}{6}$

2. Rewrite the improper fractions with a common denominator of 6.

   $\frac{4}{3} = \frac{8}{6}$ (×2)

3. Add the numerators.

   So $1\frac{1}{3} + 2\frac{5}{6} = \frac{8}{6} + \frac{17}{6} = \frac{25}{6}$

4. Give your answer as a mixed number in its simplest form.

   $= \frac{24}{6} + \frac{1}{6} = \mathbf{4\frac{1}{6}}$

Exercise 3

Answer **Questions 1-8** without using your calculator.

1 a) Write the mixed number $1\frac{4}{5}$ as an improper fraction.

b) Use your answer to work out $1\frac{4}{5} + \frac{3}{5}$.

2 Work out the following. Give your answers in their simplest form.

a) $1\frac{2}{3} + \frac{1}{3}$ b) $2\frac{3}{8} + \frac{7}{8}$ c) $3\frac{1}{5} + \frac{2}{5}$

d) $1\frac{5}{6} + 1\frac{1}{6}$ e) $1\frac{3}{7} - \frac{4}{7}$ f) $2\frac{5}{9} - \frac{8}{9}$

3 a) Write the following as improper fractions: (i) $2\frac{1}{5}$ (ii) $1\frac{3}{5}$

b) Use your answers to work out $2\frac{1}{5} - 1\frac{3}{5}$.

4 Work out the following. Give your answers in their simplest form.

a) $2\frac{1}{5} + 1\frac{3}{5}$ b) $4\frac{5}{12} - 2\frac{11}{12}$ c) $5\frac{7}{11} + \frac{5}{11}$

d) $3\frac{2}{5} - \frac{4}{5}$ e) $4\frac{1}{3} + \frac{2}{3}$ f) $6\frac{3}{8} - \frac{7}{8}$

5 a) Write the following as improper fractions: (i) $2\frac{3}{4}$ (ii) $1\frac{1}{2}$

b) Rewrite your answers to part **a)** with a common denominator.

c) Work out $2\frac{3}{4} + 1\frac{1}{2}$.

Section 5 — Fractions

6 Work out the following. Give your answers in their simplest form.
a) $3\frac{3}{10} + \frac{2}{5}$
b) $2\frac{5}{9} + \frac{1}{3}$
c) $3\frac{1}{2} + 1\frac{3}{4}$
d) $2\frac{5}{8} + 3\frac{3}{4}$
e) $2\frac{3}{8} - \frac{3}{4}$
f) $4\frac{5}{12} - 2\frac{5}{6}$
g) $4\frac{3}{14} - 1\frac{6}{7}$
h) $7\frac{5}{9} - 1\frac{11}{18}$

7 a) Write the following as improper fractions: (i) $1\frac{1}{6}$ (ii) $3\frac{1}{8}$
b) Rewrite your answers to part a) with a common denominator.
c) Work out $1\frac{1}{6} + 3\frac{1}{8}$.

8 Work out the following. Give your answers in their simplest form.
a) $1\frac{3}{5} + \frac{3}{4}$
b) $2\frac{5}{8} + \frac{2}{3}$
c) $3\frac{1}{5} + 2\frac{3}{7}$
d) $1\frac{1}{6} + 4\frac{7}{15}$
e) $3\frac{3}{4} - \frac{5}{7}$
f) $5\frac{2}{5} - 3\frac{7}{9}$
g) $2\frac{1}{4} - 1\frac{6}{7}$
h) $2\frac{5}{11} + 3\frac{2}{3}$
i) $5\frac{7}{12} + 3\frac{2}{5}$
j) $4\frac{3}{8} - 1\frac{2}{9}$
k) $1\frac{4}{7} + 3\frac{5}{9}$
l) $5\frac{3}{20} - 1\frac{7}{12}$

5.5 Multiplying and Dividing Fractions

Multiplying by Unit Fractions

A **unit fraction** has 1 as its numerator — for example, these are all unit fractions: $\frac{1}{2}, \frac{1}{3}, \frac{1}{5}, \frac{1}{10}$
Multiplying by a **unit fraction** is the same as **dividing** by a **whole number**.
For example, multiplying by $\frac{1}{2}$ is the same as dividing by 2.

Example 1
Work out:
a) $12 \times \frac{1}{3}$ — Multiplying by $\frac{1}{3}$ is the same as dividing by 3.
Remember, $\frac{12}{3}$ means the same as $12 \div 3$.
$12 \times \frac{1}{3} = \frac{12}{3} = \underline{\mathbf{4}}$

b) $10 \times \frac{1}{4}$ — Multiplying by $\frac{1}{4}$ is the same as dividing by 4.
Remember, $\frac{10}{4}$ means the same as $10 \div 4$.
$10 \times \frac{1}{4} = \frac{10}{4} = \underline{\mathbf{2\frac{1}{2}}}$

Exercise 1

Answer **Questions 1-2** without using your calculator.

1 Work out the following.
a) $8 \times \frac{1}{4}$
b) $10 \times \frac{1}{5}$
c) $15 \times \frac{1}{5}$
d) $45 \times \frac{1}{3}$
e) $27 \times \frac{1}{9}$
f) $40 \times \frac{1}{8}$
g) $16 \times \frac{1}{4}$
h) $35 \times \frac{1}{5}$
i) $39 \times \frac{1}{3}$
j) $42 \times \frac{1}{7}$
k) $48 \times \frac{1}{6}$
l) $80 \times \frac{1}{10}$

Section 5 — Fractions 51

2 Work out the following. Write your answers as mixed numbers.

a) $18 \times \frac{1}{4}$
b) $15 \times \frac{1}{6}$
c) $17 \times \frac{1}{2}$
d) $25 \times \frac{1}{10}$
e) $16 \times \frac{1}{5}$
f) $21 \times \frac{1}{4}$
g) $39 \times \frac{1}{4}$
h) $29 \times \frac{1}{5}$
i) $10 \times \frac{1}{3}$
j) $-20 \times \frac{1}{9}$
k) $25 \times -\frac{1}{6}$
l) $40 \times -\frac{1}{3}$

Multiplying Whole Numbers by Fractions

To multiply a whole number by any fraction:
- **multiply** by the **numerator**
- **divide** by the **denominator**

You can do these two steps in any order.

Example 2

Work out:

a) $15 \times \frac{2}{5}$ You need to multiply 15 by 2, and then divide by 5. (Or you can divide by 5, and then multiply by 2 — you'll get the same answer.)

$$15 \times \frac{2}{5} = \frac{15 \times 2}{5} = \frac{30}{5} = \underline{\mathbf{6}}$$

b) $5 \times \frac{3}{4}$ You need to multiply 5 by 3, and then divide by 4. (Or you can divide by 4, and then multiply by 3.)

$$5 \times \frac{3}{4} = \frac{5 \times 3}{4} = \frac{15}{4} = \underline{\mathbf{3\frac{3}{4}}}$$

Exercise 2

Answer **Questions 1-3** without using your calculator.

1 Work out the following. Write your answers as simply as possible.

a) $12 \times \frac{2}{3}$
b) $28 \times \frac{3}{4}$
c) $15 \times \frac{4}{5}$
d) $48 \times \frac{3}{8}$
e) $60 \times \frac{5}{12}$
f) $32 \times \frac{7}{16}$
g) $35 \times \frac{3}{7}$
h) $40 \times \frac{9}{10}$
i) $18 \times \frac{2}{9}$
j) $-24 \times \frac{5}{6}$
k) $100 \times -\frac{7}{25}$
l) $-96 \times -\frac{7}{12}$

2 Work out the following. Write your answers as mixed numbers.

a) $15 \times \frac{3}{4}$
b) $22 \times \frac{2}{5}$
c) $42 \times \frac{3}{10}$
d) $38 \times \frac{3}{5}$
e) $48 \times \frac{2}{7}$
f) $27 \times \frac{5}{6}$
g) $32 \times \frac{2}{3}$
h) $34 \times \frac{4}{5}$
i) $80 \times \frac{2}{9}$
j) $45 \times \frac{5}{12}$
k) $72 \times -\frac{3}{11}$
l) $62 \times -\frac{5}{8}$

Example 3

Find $\frac{3}{5}$ of 20.

You can replace 'of' with a multiplication sign. $\frac{3}{5}$ of $20 = \frac{3}{5} \times 20 = \frac{3 \times 20}{5} = \frac{60}{5} = \underline{\mathbf{12}}$

Section 5 — Fractions

3 Find the following.

    a) $\frac{3}{4}$ of 36   **b)** $\frac{2}{3}$ of 33   **c)** $\frac{3}{8}$ of 64   **d)** $\frac{5}{12}$ of 72

    e) $\frac{5}{6}$ of 18   **f)** $\frac{3}{5}$ of 15   **g)** $\frac{5}{6}$ of 33   **h)** $\frac{7}{12}$ of 45

4 Find the following.

    a) $\frac{3}{2}$ of 18   **b)** $\frac{5}{3}$ of 21   **c)** $\frac{11}{9}$ of 72   **d)** $\frac{20}{7}$ of 63

Multiplying Fractions and Mixed Numbers

To multiply two or more fractions, multiply the numerators and denominators **separately**.
To multiply **mixed numbers**, change them to improper fractions first.

Example 4
Work out:

a) $\frac{2}{3} \times \frac{4}{5}$ The numerator of the result will be 2 × 4. $\frac{2}{3} \times \frac{4}{5} = \frac{2 \times 4}{3 \times 5} = \frac{8}{15}$
The denominator of the result will be 3 × 5.

b) $\frac{3}{4} \times \frac{2}{9}$ The numerator of the result will be 3 × 2. $\frac{3}{4} \times \frac{2}{9} = \frac{3 \times 2}{4 \times 9} = \frac{6}{36} = \frac{1}{6}$
The denominator of the result will be 4 × 9.
Simplify your answer as much as possible.

Exercise 3

Answer **Questions 1-6** without using your calculator.

1 Work out the following.

    a) $\frac{1}{6} \times \frac{1}{3}$ **b)** $\frac{2}{5} \times \frac{1}{3}$ **c)** $\frac{3}{4} \times \frac{1}{7}$ **d)** $\frac{1}{5} \times \frac{3}{5}$

    e) $\frac{5}{6} \times \frac{1}{4}$ **f)** $\frac{4}{5} \times \frac{2}{7}$ **g)** $-\frac{2}{7} \times \frac{5}{7}$ **h)** $-\frac{3}{8} \times -\frac{7}{10}$

2 Work out the following. Give your answers in their lowest terms.

    a) $\frac{1}{4} \times \frac{2}{3}$ **b)** $\frac{3}{5} \times \frac{1}{6}$ **c)** $\frac{5}{6} \times \frac{2}{15}$ **d)** $\frac{5}{12} \times \frac{3}{4}$

    e) $\frac{4}{7} \times \frac{3}{8}$ **f)** $\frac{2}{5} \times \frac{15}{16}$ **g)** $-\frac{6}{7} \times -\frac{7}{8}$ **h)** $\frac{7}{10} \times -\frac{5}{14}$

Example 5
Work out $4\frac{1}{2} \times 3\frac{3}{5}$.

1. Write the mixed numbers as improper fractions.

$4\frac{1}{2} = \frac{8}{2} + \frac{1}{2} = \frac{9}{2}$

$3\frac{3}{5} = \frac{15}{5} + \frac{3}{5} = \frac{18}{5}$

2. Multiply the two fractions.

So $4\frac{1}{2} \times 3\frac{3}{5} = \frac{9}{2} \times \frac{18}{5} = \frac{9 \times 18}{2 \times 5} = \frac{162}{10}$

3. Simplify your answer and write it as a mixed number.

$\frac{162}{10} = \frac{81}{5} = \frac{80}{5} + \frac{1}{5} = \mathbf{16\frac{1}{5}}$

Section 5 — Fractions   **53**

3   **a)** Write the mixed number $1\frac{3}{7}$ as an improper fraction.
     b) Use your answer to work out $1\frac{3}{7} \times \frac{2}{3}$.

4   Work out the following.
     a) $1\frac{1}{2} \times \frac{1}{3}$ **b)** $2\frac{1}{5} \times \frac{3}{4}$ **c)** $1\frac{5}{6} \times \frac{2}{3}$ **d)** $3\frac{3}{4} \times \frac{2}{5}$
     e) $2\frac{1}{7} \times \frac{2}{9}$ **f)** $1\frac{11}{12} \times \frac{1}{4}$ **g)** $4\frac{3}{5} \times \frac{4}{5}$ **h)** $2\frac{4}{9} \times \frac{3}{8}$

5   **a)** Write the mixed number $3\frac{2}{5}$ as an improper fraction.
     b) Write the mixed number $1\frac{1}{2}$ as an improper fraction.
     c) Use your answer to work out $3\frac{2}{5} \times 1\frac{1}{2}$.

6   Work out the following.
     a) $1\frac{1}{5} \times 1\frac{1}{4}$ **b)** $2\frac{2}{5} \times 1\frac{2}{3}$ **c)** $1\frac{1}{9} \times 2\frac{2}{3}$ **d)** $1\frac{3}{5} \times 1\frac{3}{4}$
     e) $2\frac{3}{7} \times 3\frac{1}{6}$ **f)** $3\frac{4}{9} \times 1\frac{7}{8}$ **g)** $2\frac{6}{7} \times 2\frac{1}{9}$ **h)** $4\frac{3}{10} \times 3\frac{5}{6}$

Dividing by Fractions

Swapping the numerator and the denominator of a fraction gives you the **reciprocal** of that fraction.
Dividing by a fraction is the same as **multiplying by its reciprocal**.

Example 6
Find the reciprocal of:

    a) $\frac{3}{5}$ Swap the numerator and denominator.   The reciprocal of $\frac{3}{5}$ is $\frac{5}{3}$.

    b) 6   Remember, $6 = \frac{6}{1}$.   The reciprocal of 6 is $\frac{1}{6}$.

Exercise 4

1   Find the reciprocal of each of the following.
     a) $\frac{1}{3}$ **b)** $\frac{1}{7}$ **c)** $\frac{4}{5}$ **d)** $\frac{5}{8}$
     e) $\frac{12}{27}$ **f)** $\frac{9}{10}$ **g)** $\frac{6}{19}$ **h)** $\frac{84}{107}$

2   Find the reciprocal of each of the following.
     a) 5   **b)** 12   **c)** 9   **d)** 27

3   **a)** Write the mixed number $1\frac{1}{4}$ as an improper fraction.
     b) Use your answer to find the reciprocal of $1\frac{1}{4}$.

4 By first writing them as improper fractions, find the reciprocal of each of the following.
   a) $1\frac{3}{5}$ b) $2\frac{1}{7}$ c) $1\frac{4}{9}$ d) $2\frac{3}{4}$
   e) $1\frac{11}{12}$ f) $3\frac{1}{4}$ g) $5\frac{2}{3}$ h) $4\frac{2}{7}$

Example 7
Work out:
a) $\frac{1}{2} \div \frac{2}{3}$ Multiply $\frac{1}{2}$ by the reciprocal of $\frac{2}{3}$. $\frac{1}{2} \div \frac{2}{3} = \frac{1}{2} \times \frac{3}{2} = \frac{1 \times 3}{2 \times 2} = \frac{3}{4}$

b) $\frac{4}{7} \div 2$ Multiply $\frac{4}{7}$ by the reciprocal of 2. Simplify your answer if possible. $\frac{4}{7} \div 2 = \frac{4}{7} \times \frac{1}{2} = \frac{4 \times 1}{7 \times 2} = \frac{4}{14} = \frac{2}{7}$

Exercise 5

Answer **Questions 1-7** without using your calculator.

1 Work out the following.
   a) $\frac{1}{5} \div \frac{2}{3}$ b) $\frac{1}{6} \div \frac{2}{5}$ c) $\frac{1}{4} \div \frac{3}{7}$ d) $\frac{2}{3} \div \frac{5}{7}$
   e) $\frac{5}{12} \div \frac{4}{5}$ f) $\frac{2}{7} \div \frac{5}{6}$ g) $-\frac{3}{8} \div \frac{2}{5}$ h) $-\frac{7}{10} \div \frac{5}{7}$

2 Work out the following. Give your answers in their simplest form.
   a) $\frac{1}{6} \div \frac{3}{8}$ b) $\frac{1}{4} \div \frac{1}{2}$ c) $\frac{2}{5} \div \frac{7}{10}$ d) $\frac{4}{7} \div \frac{8}{21}$
   e) $\frac{3}{8} \div \frac{9}{11}$ f) $\frac{3}{5} \div \frac{9}{20}$ g) $\frac{3}{4} \div -\frac{9}{16}$ h) $-\frac{5}{7} \div -\frac{11}{14}$

3 Work out the following.
   a) $1 \div \frac{1}{2}$ b) $2 \div \frac{2}{3}$ c) $3 \div \frac{3}{5}$ d) $4 \div \frac{7}{8}$
   e) $\frac{2}{3} \div 4$ f) $\frac{2}{5} \div 3$ g) $\frac{1}{4} \div 4$ h) $\frac{3}{7} \div 6$

4 a) Write the mixed number $1\frac{3}{4}$ as an improper fraction.
   b) Find the reciprocal of $1\frac{3}{4}$.
   c) Use your answer to work out $\frac{2}{5} \div 1\frac{3}{4}$.

5 By first writing any mixed numbers as improper fractions, work out the following.
   a) $1\frac{1}{2} \div 4$ b) $3\frac{1}{3} \div 6$ c) $2\frac{3}{7} \div 3$ d) $4\frac{4}{9} \div 6$
   e) $5 \div 1\frac{3}{5}$ f) $2 \div 1\frac{7}{8}$ g) $6 \div 2\frac{1}{3}$ h) $4 \div 4\frac{1}{5}$

6 a) Write the mixed numbers $2\frac{1}{3}$ and $1\frac{4}{5}$ as improper fractions.
   b) Find the reciprocal of $1\frac{4}{5}$.
   c) Hence work out $2\frac{1}{3} \div 1\frac{4}{5}$. Give your answer as a mixed number in its simplest form.

Section 5 — Fractions

7 By first writing any mixed numbers as improper fractions, work out the following.
a) $1\frac{1}{3} \div \frac{2}{5}$
b) $2\frac{1}{2} \div \frac{1}{3}$
c) $1\frac{1}{6} \div \frac{1}{4}$
d) $3\frac{1}{5} \div \frac{2}{3}$
e) $\frac{2}{3} \div 3\frac{2}{5}$
f) $\frac{3}{4} \div 2\frac{1}{3}$
g) $\frac{4}{7} \div 3\frac{1}{2}$
h) $\frac{4}{9} \div 1\frac{3}{5}$
i) $1\frac{1}{4} \div 1\frac{1}{5}$
j) $2\frac{2}{3} \div 1\frac{1}{4}$
k) $4\frac{5}{6} \div 2\frac{1}{3}$
l) $3\frac{2}{3} \div -2\frac{1}{10}$
m) $4\frac{3}{4} \div 1\frac{1}{6}$
n) $6\frac{2}{5} \div -2\frac{3}{10}$
o) $-5\frac{1}{7} \div -1\frac{4}{5}$
p) $-3\frac{3}{10} \div 2\frac{1}{7}$

5.6 Fractions and Decimals

All fractions can be written as either a **terminating** or **recurring** decimal. In a terminating decimal the digits stop. A recurring decimal has a repeating pattern in its digits which goes on forever.
A recurring decimal is shown using a dot above the first and last repeated digits.
For example, $0.111... = 0.\dot{1}$, $0.151515... = 0.\dot{1}\dot{5}$, $0.12341234... = 0.\dot{1}23\dot{4}$.

Converting Fractions to Decimals Using a Calculator

Use a calculator to convert a fraction to a decimal by **dividing** the numerator by the denominator.

Example 1

Use a calculator to convert the following fractions to decimals:

a) $\frac{5}{16}$ Divide the numerator by the denominator. $\frac{5}{16} = 5 \div 16 = \underline{\mathbf{0.3125}}$

b) $1\frac{2}{5}$ Either: Think of this as $1 + (2 \div 5) = 1 + 0.4$. $1\frac{2}{5} = 1 + (2 \div 5) = 1 + 0.4 = \underline{\mathbf{1.4}}$
Or: Convert this to the improper fraction $\frac{7}{5}$,
and use your calculator to find $7 \div 5 = 1.4$.

Exercise 1

1 Use a calculator to help decide whether these decimals are terminating or recurring.
a) $\frac{3}{8}$
b) $\frac{2}{5}$
c) $\frac{5}{6}$
d) $\frac{5}{8}$
e) $\frac{2}{11}$
f) $\frac{11}{20}$
g) $\frac{5}{9}$
h) $\frac{13}{16}$
i) $\frac{15}{32}$
j) $\frac{6}{11}$
k) $\frac{23}{40}$
l) $\frac{1}{15}$

2 Use a calculator to convert the following fractions to decimals.
a) $\frac{3}{4}$
b) $\frac{4}{5}$
c) $\frac{5}{8}$
d) $\frac{7}{20}$
e) $\frac{7}{16}$
f) $\frac{5}{32}$
g) $\frac{7}{40}$
h) $\frac{23}{50}$
i) $\frac{176}{200}$
j) $\frac{53}{64}$
k) $\frac{329}{500}$
l) $\frac{97}{128}$

3 Use a calculator to convert the following mixed numbers to decimals.
  a) $1\frac{3}{5}$
  b) $2\frac{1}{8}$
  c) $6\frac{7}{20}$
  d) $2\frac{37}{100}$
  e) $4\frac{719}{1000}$
  f) $5\frac{19}{25}$
  g) $7\frac{11}{32}$
  h) $8\frac{7}{16}$

Example 2
Use a calculator to convert the following fractions to decimals:

  a) $\frac{1}{6}$ This is a 'recurring decimal' — one that repeats forever. The calculator tells you the answer is 0.1666... Show the repeating digit with a dot.
  $\frac{1}{6} = 1 \div 6 = 0.1666... = \mathbf{0.1\dot{6}}$

  b) $\frac{41}{333}$ The calculator tells you the answer is 0.123123123... Show the repeating pattern by putting dots over the first and last digits of the repeated group.
  $\frac{41}{333} = 41 \div 333$
  $= 0.123123123... = \mathbf{0.\dot{1}2\dot{3}}$

4 Use a calculator to convert the following fractions to decimals.
  a) $\frac{1}{3}$
  b) $\frac{2}{11}$
  c) $\frac{5}{6}$
  d) $\frac{4}{9}$

5 By first writing these fractions as decimals, put each of the following lists in order, from smallest to largest.
  a) $\frac{3}{10}, \frac{1}{4}, \frac{7}{16}$
  b) $\frac{7}{8}, \frac{17}{20}, \frac{5}{6}$
  c) $\frac{4}{10}, \frac{3}{8}, \frac{9}{25}$

6 Use a calculator to convert the following fractions to decimals.
  a) $\frac{67}{111}$
  b) $\frac{1111}{9000}$
  c) $\frac{4}{15}$
  d) $\frac{1234}{9999}$

Converting Fractions to Decimals Without Using a Calculator

There are a couple of ways to convert fractions to decimals if you don't have a calculator.

1) You can use the following to convert fractions with denominators of **10**, **100** or **1000**.

$$\frac{1}{10} = 0.1, \quad \frac{1}{100} = 0.01, \quad \frac{1}{1000} = 0.001$$

For fractions with **other denominators**, you can first convert them to an equivalent fraction whose denominator is 10, 100 or 1000.

2) Or you can divide the numerator by the denominator using **pen and paper** (instead of a calculator).

Example 3
Write the following fractions as decimals.

  a) $\frac{7}{10}$ Write the fraction as a multiple of $\frac{1}{10}, \frac{1}{100}$ or $\frac{1}{1000}$. Then rewrite as a decimal.
  $\frac{7}{10} = 7 \times \frac{1}{10} = 7 \times 0.1 = \mathbf{0.7}$

  b) $\frac{9}{100}$
  $\frac{9}{100} = 9 \times \frac{1}{100} = 9 \times 0.01 = \mathbf{0.09}$

Section 5 — Fractions

Exercise 2

Answer **Questions 1-10** without using your calculator.

Write the fractions in **Questions 1-4** as decimals.

1. a) $\frac{9}{10}$ b) $\frac{2}{10}$ c) $\frac{3}{10}$ d) $\frac{8}{10}$

2. a) $\frac{91}{100}$ b) $\frac{42}{100}$ c) $\frac{99}{100}$ d) $\frac{8}{100}$

3. a) $\frac{7}{1000}$ b) $\frac{201}{1000}$ c) $\frac{41}{1000}$ d) $\frac{27}{1000}$

4. a) $\frac{52}{100}$ b) $\frac{6}{10}$ c) $\frac{635}{1000}$ d) $\frac{34}{100}$
   e) $\frac{86}{1000}$ f) $\frac{46}{100}$ g) $\frac{9}{10}$ h) $\frac{492}{1000}$

Example 4

Write these fractions as decimals.

a) $\frac{4}{5}$
1. Multiply top and bottom to find an equivalent fraction with a denominator of 10.
2. Then rewrite as a decimal.

$\frac{4}{5} = \frac{8}{10}$ (× 2)

$\frac{8}{10} = 8 \times \frac{1}{10} = 8 \times 0.1 = \underline{\mathbf{0.8}}$

b) $\frac{123}{300}$
1. Divide top and bottom to find an equivalent fraction with a denominator of 10.
2. Then rewrite as a decimal.

$\frac{123}{300} = \frac{41}{100}$ (÷ 3)

$\frac{41}{100} = 41 \times \frac{1}{100} = 41 \times 0.01 = \underline{\mathbf{0.41}}$

5. a) Find the value of a if $\frac{13}{20} = \frac{a}{100}$.
   b) Use your answer to write the fraction $\frac{13}{20}$ as a decimal.

6. a) Find a fraction which is equivalent to $\frac{8}{25}$ and which has a denominator of 100.
   b) Use your answer to write $\frac{8}{25}$ as a decimal.

Write the fractions in **Questions 7-10** as decimals.

7. a) $\frac{1}{5}$ b) $\frac{9}{30}$ c) $\frac{45}{50}$ d) $\frac{3}{5}$

8. a) $\frac{17}{50}$ b) $\frac{22}{25}$ c) $\frac{43}{50}$ d) $\frac{96}{300}$

9. a) $\frac{1}{500}$ b) $\frac{33}{250}$ c) $\frac{103}{200}$ d) $\frac{306}{3000}$

10. a) $\frac{2}{5}$ b) $\frac{12}{25}$ c) $\frac{333}{500}$ d) $\frac{24}{50}$
    e) $\frac{180}{2000}$ f) $\frac{43}{50}$ g) $\frac{7}{20}$ h) $\frac{123}{200}$

Example 5

Write $\frac{1}{8}$ as a decimal.

You need to work out $1 \div 8$.
1. 8 doesn't go into 1.
2. 8 goes into 10 once, with remainder 2.
3. 8 goes into 20 twice, with remainder 4.
4. 8 goes into 40 exactly 5 times.
   Remember, the decimal point in the answer goes directly above the decimal point in 1.000.

$$8)\overline{1.^10}$$
$$8)\overline{1.^10^20}$$
$$8)\overline{1.^10^20^40}$$
$$8)\overline{1.^10^20^40}$$

So $\frac{1}{8} = \textbf{0.125}$

Exercise 3

Answer **Questions 1-2** without using your calculator.

1 a) Write $\frac{3}{8}$ as a decimal by finding $3 \div 8$. b) Write $\frac{5}{16}$ as a decimal by finding $5 \div 16$.

2 Write the following fractions as decimals by dividing the numerator by the denominator.
   a) $\frac{1}{4}$ b) $\frac{3}{4}$ c) $\frac{1}{20}$ d) $\frac{1}{40}$
   e) $\frac{1}{16}$ f) $\frac{7}{8}$ g) $\frac{7}{40}$ h) $\frac{13}{80}$

Converting Terminating Decimals to Fractions

You can quickly convert a **terminating decimal** to a fraction with a denominator of 10, 100, 1000 or another power of 10.

Example 6

Write the following decimals as fractions.

a) 0.24 The final digit is in the 'hundredths' column — so write as a fraction with denominator 100. Then simplify your answer.

$0.24 = \frac{24}{100} = \frac{6}{25}$

b) 0.025 The final digit is in the 'thousandths' column — so write this as a fraction with denominator 1000.

$0.025 = \frac{25}{1000} = \frac{1}{40}$

Exercise 4

Convert the decimals in **Questions 1-4** to fractions without using your calculator.
Give your answers in their simplest form.

1 a) 0.7   b) 0.9   c) 0.1   d) 0.4
2 a) 0.93   b) 0.07   c) 0.23   d) 0.47
3 a) 0.004   b) 0.801   c) 0.983   d) 0.098
4 a) 0.6   b) 0.12   c) 0.236   d) 0.35
   e) 0.05   f) 0.084   g) 0.24   h) 0.175
   i) 0.014   j) 0.08   k) 0.125   l) 0.375

Converting Fractions to Recurring Decimals

Example 7

Write $\frac{3}{11}$ as a decimal without using a calculator.

1. Work out 3 ÷ 11 using a written method.

2. The digits in your answer have started to repeat — first 2, then 7, then 2, then 7, and so on. The remainders are repeating as well — 3, 8, 3, 8.

3. You've found the repeating pattern of the recurring decimal — so mark the first and last digits of the repeating group.

① $11 \overline{)3.^30}$ 0.

② $11 \overline{)3.^30^80}$ 0. 2

③ $11 \overline{)3.^30^80^30}$ 0. 2 7

④ $11 \overline{)3.^30^80^30^80}$ 0. 2 7 2

⑤ $11 \overline{)3.^30^80^30^80^30}$ 0. 2 7 2 7

So $\frac{3}{11} = 0.\dot{2}\dot{7}$

Exercise 5

Answer **Questions 1-4** without using your calculator.

1 Write $\frac{6}{11}$ as a recurring decimal by finding 6 ÷ 11.

Write the fractions in **Questions 2-3** as recurring decimals.

2 a) $\frac{1}{3}$ b) $\frac{1}{9}$ c) $\frac{1}{12}$ d) $\frac{4}{9}$
   e) $\frac{1}{6}$ f) $\frac{1}{11}$ g) $\frac{2}{3}$ h) $\frac{4}{11}$
   i) $\frac{7}{15}$ j) $\frac{5}{6}$ k) $\frac{4}{15}$ l) $\frac{7}{9}$

3 a) $\frac{11}{30}$ b) $\frac{28}{45}$ c) $\frac{47}{90}$ d) $\frac{27}{110}$

4 a) Write the following fractions as recurring decimals.
     (i) $\frac{1}{7}$ (ii) $\frac{2}{7}$ (iii) $\frac{3}{7}$ (iv) $\frac{4}{7}$ (v) $\frac{5}{7}$
   b) What do you notice about the repeating pattern?
   c) Use your answers to parts **a)** and **b)** to write down the decimal which is equivalent to $\frac{6}{7}$.

5.7 Fractions Problems

Exercise 1

Unless told otherwise, answer the questions in this Exercise without using your calculator.

1 Which of the fractions on the right are equivalent to $\frac{2}{3}$? $\frac{18}{27}$ $\frac{21}{31}$ $\frac{40}{60}$ $\frac{4}{9}$ $\frac{12}{18}$

2 Which of the fractions on the right are equivalent to $1\frac{1}{4}$? $\frac{11}{4}$ $\frac{10}{8}$ $\frac{18}{16}$ $\frac{17}{12}$ $\frac{25}{20}$

Section 5 — Fractions

3 Use a calculator to write the following fractions as decimals.
   a) $\frac{7}{20}$ b) $\frac{21}{250}$ c) $\frac{3}{40}$ d) $\frac{7}{8}$

4 Use equivalent fractions to write $\frac{3}{4}, \frac{2}{3}, \frac{5}{6}$ and $\frac{11}{16}$ in order, from smallest to largest.

5 a) Convert the fractions $\frac{39}{100}, \frac{7}{20}, \frac{8}{25}$ and $\frac{3}{10}$ into decimals.
   b) Put the fractions in order, from smallest to largest.

6 Copy the scale on the right, making sure it's divided into 24 parts. Then mark the positions of the following fractions on the scale.
   a) $\frac{1}{3}$ b) $\frac{5}{8}$ c) $\frac{5}{12}$ d) $\frac{5}{6}$

Evaluate the expressions in **Questions 7-10**.

7 a) $\frac{5}{7} + \frac{2}{3}$ b) $\frac{3}{8} - \frac{2}{9}$ c) $\frac{6}{10} + \frac{3}{6}$ d) $\frac{2}{5} - \frac{1}{8}$

8 a) $\frac{7}{12} \times \frac{6}{11}$ b) $\frac{3}{5} \div \frac{7}{15}$ c) $\frac{4}{7} \times \frac{6}{8}$ d) $\frac{5}{9} \div \frac{15}{24}$

9 a) $2\frac{1}{8} + 3\frac{2}{5}$ b) $2\frac{3}{10} - 1\frac{7}{8}$ c) $3\frac{2}{5} + 4\frac{1}{4}$ d) $4\frac{5}{8} - 2\frac{1}{2}$

10 a) $1\frac{1}{6} \times 2\frac{1}{3}$ b) $3\frac{3}{4} \div 1\frac{1}{2}$ c) $3\frac{1}{2} \times 6\frac{7}{8}$ d) $5\frac{1}{2} \div 1\frac{1}{4}$

11 A plank of wood is 20 inches long. Three pieces of length $7\frac{3}{4}$ inches, $5\frac{5}{16}$ inches and $2\frac{1}{8}$ inches are cut from the plank. What length of wood is left over?

12 Work out the following (remembering the rules of BODMAS).
   a) $\frac{1}{4} \times \frac{2}{3} + \frac{5}{12}$ b) $\frac{7}{30} + \frac{2}{3} \times \frac{4}{5}$ c) $\frac{2}{3} \div \frac{5}{6} - \frac{1}{5}$ d) $\frac{15}{16} - \frac{3}{8} \div \frac{1}{3}$
   e) $1\frac{1}{2} + \frac{2}{5} \times \frac{3}{4}$ f) $1\frac{1}{2} \times \frac{2}{5} + \frac{3}{4}$ g) $1\frac{1}{6} - 3\frac{3}{4} \div \frac{3}{8}$ h) $3\frac{3}{4} \div 1\frac{1}{6} - \frac{3}{8}$

13 a) Find the reciprocal of each of these fractions. Give your answers in their simplest form.
      (i) $\frac{2}{5}$ (ii) $\frac{1}{3}$ (iii) $\frac{4}{5}$
   b) Multiply each fraction by its reciprocal. What do you notice?

14 This question involves the fractions $\frac{2}{7}, \frac{4}{5}, \frac{1}{3}$ and $\frac{1}{6}$.
   a) Put these fractions in order, starting with the smallest.
   b) Find the reciprocal of each of the fractions.
   c) Put the reciprocals in order, starting with the largest. What do you notice?

15 Using a calculator, find which of these fractions are equivalent to recurring decimals, and which are equivalent to terminating decimals.
   a) $\frac{7}{8}$ b) $\frac{1}{3}$ c) $\frac{3}{11}$ d) $\frac{4}{21}$ e) $\frac{7}{32}$

16 Which of the fractions $\frac{4}{5}, \frac{5}{6}, \frac{9}{16}, \frac{17}{40}$ and $\frac{2}{9}$ are equivalent to recurring decimals?

17 The length of a rectangle is $3\frac{3}{5}$ cm and the width is $1\frac{5}{8}$ cm.
   a) Find the rectangle's perimeter.
   b) Find the rectangle's area.

18 Amy, Ben and Carl are sharing a bar of chocolate. They each eat $\frac{1}{5}$ of the bar.
   a) What fraction of the bar of chocolate is left?

   Dave joins the group and the four of them share the rest of the bar equally.
   b) What fraction of the whole bar does Dave eat?

19 Pat's cat eats $\frac{2}{3}$ of a tin of cat food every morning and every evening.
   How many tins of cat food will Pat need to buy to feed the cat for a week?

20 It takes Ella $1\frac{1}{4}$ minutes to answer each question on her maths homework.
   How many questions can she answer in 20 minutes?

21 A bag contains a mixture of different coloured counters. $\frac{1}{3}$ of the counters are red, $\frac{2}{5}$ are blue, and the rest are yellow.
   a) What fraction of the counters are yellow?
   b) If there are 60 counters altogether, work out how many of each colour are in the bag.

22 Which of the fractions on the right is closest to $\frac{3}{4}$? $\frac{11}{15} \quad \frac{7}{10} \quad \frac{4}{5} \quad \frac{5}{6}$

23 What numbers need to go in the boxes to make the following true?
   a) $\frac{1}{3}$ of 60 = $\frac{1}{2}$ of ☐
   b) $\frac{2}{5}$ of 100 = ☐ of 50
   c) $\frac{3}{4}$ of ☐ = $\frac{2}{3}$ of 90

24 In ancient Egypt, fractions were written using sums of unit fractions.
   For example, instead of writing $\frac{3}{5}$, ancient Egyptians would write $\frac{1}{2} + \frac{1}{10}$.
   Find the fractions that ancient Egyptians would have written in the following ways:
   a) $\frac{1}{2} + \frac{1}{5}$
   b) $\frac{1}{3} + \frac{1}{12}$
   c) $\frac{1}{2} + \frac{1}{3} + \frac{1}{7}$

25 The large square on the right is split into 4 equal squares.
   One of these squares is split evenly into 4 small squares, then
   one of these small squares is split evenly into 4 smaller squares.
   a) What fraction of the large square is shaded?
   b) Make an unshaded copy of the diagram on the right,
      then shade in $\frac{11}{64}$ of the large square.

26 Dani and Graham split a bag of sweets equally between them.
   $\frac{2}{5}$ of the sweets Dani got were blue and $\frac{4}{7}$ of the sweets Graham got were blue.
   What fraction of all the sweets were blue? Give your answer in its simplest form.

Section 6 — Ratios

6.1 Ratios and Simplifying

Ratios are used to compare quantities.
For example, here the ratio of circles to squares is 6:4.

You can simplify ratios by dividing the numbers by common factors, just like you do with fractions.

Example 1
There are 15 fiction books and 10 non-fiction books on a shelf.
a) Write down the ratio of fiction books to non-fiction books.
   It's fiction to non-fiction, so the '15' comes first. ⟹ The ratio is **15:10**
b) Write this ratio in its simplest form.
   1. Look for a number that divides into both 15 and 10.   5 divides into both 15 and 10.
   2. Divide both sides of the ratio by this number, and rewrite the ratio. $15 \div 5 = 3$ and $10 \div 5 = 2$
   3. When no other numbers divide into both sides of the ratio, the ratio is in its simplest form.   So the ratio can be written **3:2**, and this is the ratio's simplest form.

Exercise 1

1 Write down the ratio of stars to triangles.

2 Write down the ratio of triangles to stars.

3 Write down the ratio of people to pigeons.

4 There are 17 boys and 14 girls in a class. Write down the ratio of boys to girls.

5 On a farm there are 15 pigs and 23 cows. Write down the ratio of cows to pigs.

For questions **6** and **7**, write down the given ratio. Then simplify your answer.

6 Shaded squares to white squares.

7 Shaded circles to white circles.

8 Write down each of the following ratios in its simplest form.
a) 2:8   b) 5:15   c) 40:10   d) 4:6   e) 24:6
f) 20:8   g) 7:28   h) 15:9   i) 16:12   j) 25:3
k) 40:60   l) 21:35   m) 55:5   n) 16:40   o) 18:27
p) 48:36   q) 18:72   r) 80:32   s) 150:350   t) 121:33

9 Write down each of the following ratios in its simplest form.
a) 6:2:4   b) 15:12:3   c) 14:10:2   d) 24:12:20   e) 6:3:15
f) 30:10:25   g) 16:24:80   h) 21:49:42   i) 12:32:16   j) 27:30:54

10 A floor is made up of 24 black tiles and 8 white tiles. Find the ratio of black tiles to white tiles in its simplest form.

11 At a party there are 36 girls and 27 boys. What is the ratio of girls to boys? Give your answer in its simplest form.

12 A school has 595 pupils and 170 computers. Write down the ratio of computers to pupils in its simplest form.

13 There are 18 boys in a class of 33 pupils. Find the ratio of boys to girls, giving your answer in its simplest form.

14 Isabel and Sophia share a bag of 42 sweets. Isabel has 16 sweets and Sophia has the rest. Find the ratio of Sophia's sweets to Isabel's sweets, giving your answer in its simplest form.

Example 2

Write the ratio 1 m : 40 cm in its simplest form.

1. Rewrite the ratio so that the units are the same on both sides.
   Then remove the units altogether.

2. Simplify as normal.

1 m : 40 cm is the same as 100 cm : 40 cm.
This is the same as 100 : 40.

$$\div 20 \searrow \underset{5 : 2}{100 : 40} \swarrow \div 20$$

So the simplest form is **5 : 2**

Exercise 2

1 Write these ratios in their simplest form.
  a) 10p : £1
  b) 20 mm : 4 cm
  c) 10 g : 1 kg
  d) 2 weeks : 7 days
  e) 40p : £1
  f) 30 cm : 2 m
  g) 18 mins : 1 hour
  h) 6 days : 3 weeks

2 Give the following ratios in their simplest form.
  a) 1 m : 150 mm
  b) 12 weeks : 1 year
  c) 8 cm : 1.1 m
  d) 9 g : 0.3 kg
  e) 2.5 hours : 20 mins
  f) £1.25 : 75p
  g) 65 m : 1.3 km
  h) 1.2 kg : 480 g

3 A jug of orange squash is made using 50 ml of orange concentrate and 1 litre of water. Find the ratio of concentrate to water in its simplest form.

4 A model of a house has a height of 15 cm. The actual house is 6 m tall. Write the ratio of the model's height to the actual height in its simplest form.

5 Emma's mass is 54 kg. Her award-winning pumpkin has a mass of 6000 g. Find the ratio of the pumpkin's mass to Emma's mass. Give your answer in its simplest form.

6 Alexsy runs in two cross-country races. He runs the first in 45 minutes and the second in 3½ hours. Find the ratio of his first race time to his second race time in its simplest form.

7 A small bag of crisps costs 44p and a king-size bag costs £1.21. Find the ratio of the cost of the small bag to the cost of the king-size bag in its simplest form.

8 The icing for some cupcakes is made by mixing 1.6 kg of icing sugar with 640 g of butter. Find the ratio of butter to icing sugar. Give your answer in its simplest form.

Writing Ratios in the Form 1 : n

Another way to simplify ratios is to write them in the form 1 : n, where n is a number.
In making the left-hand side equal to 1, you might end up with a fraction or a decimal on the right.

Example 3
Write the ratio 16 : 24 in the form 1 : n.
1. To get '1' on the left-hand side, divide both sides by 16.
2. Now the ratio is in the form 1 : n, where n = 1.5.

$$\div 16 \left(\begin{array}{c} 16 : 24 \\ \mathbf{1 : 1.5} \end{array} \right) \div 16$$

Example 4
Nigel makes his favourite smoothie by mixing half a litre of blueberry juice with
100 millilitres of plain yoghurt. How much yoghurt does he use for every millilitre of juice?

1. Write down the ratio of juice to yoghurt.   0.5 l : 100 ml

2. Rewrite the ratio so that it's all in millilitres.   0.5 l : 100 ml is the same
   Then get rid of the units altogether.   as 500 ml : 100 ml, or just 500 : 100

3. Simplify the ratio.
   And remember to give the units in your answer.

$$\div 500 \left(\begin{array}{c} 500 : 100 \\ 1 : 0.2 \end{array} \right) \div 500$$

So he uses 0.2 ml for every 1 ml of juice.

Exercise 3

1 Write down the following ratios in the form 1 : n.
 a) 2 : 6   b) 7 : 35   c) 6 : 24   d) 30 : 120
 e) 2 : 7   f) 4 : 26   g) 8 : 26   h) 2 : 1
 i) 10 : 3   j) 6 : 21   k) 8 : 5   l) 5 : 9

2 Write down each of these ratios in the form 1 : n.
 a) 10 mm : 5 cm   b) 12p : £6   c) 30 mins : 2 hours   d) 500 g : 20 kg
 e) 90 m : 7.2 km   f) 14 cm : 5.6 m   g) 50p : £6.25   h) 4.5 m : 900 mm

3 In a pond there are 7 frogs and 56 fish. Find the ratio of frogs to fish in the form 1 : n.

4 On a garage forecourt there are 15 red cars and 45 silver cars. Find the ratio of red cars to silver cars in the form 1 : n.

5 A recipe uses 125 ml of chocolate syrup and 2½ litres of milk. Write the ratio of chocolate syrup to milk in the form 1 : n.

6 Two towns 4.8 km apart are shown on a map 12 cm apart. Find the ratio of the map distance to the true distance in the form 1 : n.

7 A shade of purple paint is made using 4 parts of red paint to 5 parts of blue paint. How much blue paint is needed for every 1 part of red paint?

8 When Ellie went on holiday to Denmark she changed £50 into 425 Danish krone. Write down a ratio showing the exchange rate in the form £1 : n krone.

9 An animal sanctuary has 120 animals, 40 of which are donkeys. Write the ratio of donkeys to other animals in the form 1 : n.

Section 6 — Ratios

6.2 Using Ratios

If you know the **ratio** of one quantity to another and you know **how big** one of them is, you can use the ratio to find the size of the other.

Example 1

The ratio of men to women in an office is 3:4.
If there are 9 men in the office, how many women are there?

1. Write down what you know and what you need to find out.
2. Work out what you have to multiply the left-hand side by to get from 3 to 9.
3. Multiply the right-hand side by the same number.

$$3:4 = 9:?$$

$$\times 3 \begin{pmatrix} 3:4 \\ 9:12 \end{pmatrix} \times 3$$

So there are **12 women**.

Example 2

A cereal contains raisins, nuts and oats in the ratio 2:3:5. If a box of the cereal contains 200 g of raisins and 300 g of nuts, find how many grams of oats it contains.

1. Write the ratio of one of the quantities you know to the one you want to find. ⟹ The ratio of nuts to oats is 3:5
2. Find the number both sides of the ratio have to be multiplied by.
And remember to give the mass in grams.

$$3:5 = 300:?$$

$$\times 100 \begin{pmatrix} 3:5 \\ 300:500 \end{pmatrix} \times 100$$

So it contains **500 g oats**

Exercise 1

1. For a class of pupils, the ratio of blue eyes to brown eyes is 2:3. If 8 pupils have blue eyes, how many pupils have brown eyes?

2. Ben feeds his horses carrots. For every 12 carrots they eat, Ben eats 1. If the horses eat 24 carrots, how many does Ben eat?

3. The ages of a father and son are in the ratio 8:3. If the father is 48, how old is the son?

4. The ratio of red to yellow sweets in a bag is 3:4. If the bag contains 12 yellow sweets, how many red sweets are there?

5. In a wood there are oak trees and beech trees in the ratio 2:9. If there are 42 oak trees, how many beech trees are there?

6. In a supermarket the ratio of apples to bananas is 5:3. If there are 450 bananas, how many apples are there?

For questions **7–18**, remember to give the correct units in your answer.

7. A recipe uses sugar and butter in the ratio 2:1. How much butter would be needed with 100 g of sugar?

8. A photo of width 10 cm is enlarged so that the ratio of the two pictures' widths is 2:7.
How wide is the enlarged picture?

9. Meera and Sabrina share a holiday job. They split the money they make in the ratio 7:6. If Sabrina gets £48, how much does Meera get?

10. Tim has a cardboard cut-out of his favourite footballer. The height of the cut-out and the footballer's actual height are in the ratio 5:6. If the cut-out is 165 cm high, find the footballer's actual height in metres.

Section 6 — Ratios

11 A fruit punch is made by mixing pineapple juice, orange juice, and lemonade in the ratio 1:3:6. If 500 ml of pineapple juice is used, how much orange juice is needed?

12 Jem is unusually fussy about pizza toppings. She always orders olives, slices of courgette and slices of goat's cheese in the ratio 8:3:4. How many slices of courgette and goat's cheese would she order with 24 olives?

13 Mai, Lizzy and Dave have heights in the ratio 31:33:37. Mai is 155 cm tall. How tall are Lizzy and Dave?

14 Max, Molly and Maisie are at a bus stop. The number of minutes they have waited can be represented by the ratio 3:7:2. Molly has been waiting for 1 hour and 10 minutes. Calculate how long Max and Maisie have been waiting for.

15 The ratio of children to adults in a swimming pool must be 5:1 or less. If there are 32 children, how many adults must there be?

16 A TV-show producer is selecting a studio audience. He wants the ratio of under 30s to those aged 30 or over to be at least 8:1. If 100 under 30s are selected, find the maximum number of people aged 30 or over.

17 Harry is cooking for friends. His recipe says to use 1 aubergine for every 3 people. How many aubergines should he buy if there are 10 people eating?

18 Olga allows herself no more than 5 minutes of reality TV for every minute of news programmes she watches. If she watches 45 minutes of reality TV, what's the least amount of news she should watch?

Using Ratios to Find Fractions

You can use a ratio to express a quantity as a fraction of a total amount.
Or you can start with a fraction and use it to write a ratio between two quantities.

Example 3

A box of doughnuts contains jam doughnuts and chocolate doughnuts in the ratio 3:5. What fraction of the doughnuts are chocolate flavoured?

1. Add the numbers to find the total number of parts. $3 + 5 = 8$ parts altogether.

2. Divide the number of parts that are chocolate by the total number of parts.   5 of the parts are chocolate.
Fraction that are chocolate is $\frac{5}{8}$.

Exercise 2

1 A tiled floor has blue and white tiles in the ratio 1:3. What fraction of the tiles are blue?

2 A necklace has yellow beads and red beads in the ratio 3:2. What fraction of the beads are yellow?

3 The ratio of girls to boys in a class is 4:3. What fraction of the class are girls?

4 A recipe uses white flour and brown flour in the ratio 2:1. What fraction of the flour is brown?

5 A zoo has Gentoo penguins and King penguins in the ratio 9:4. What fraction of the penguins are King penguins?

6 The ratio of women to men in a tennis club is 13:7. What fraction of the players are men?

7 In a football tournament the numbers of home wins, away wins and draws were in the ratio 7:2:5. What fraction of the games were home wins?

8 A bag contains blue, green and red balls in the ratio 1:2:4. Decide whether each of these statements is true or false. There are:
   a) 2 times as many green balls as blue balls.
   b) $\frac{1}{2}$ as many red balls as green balls.
   c) 8 times as many red balls as blue balls.
   d) $\frac{1}{4}$ as many blue balls as red balls.
   e) $\frac{1}{2}$ as many blue balls as green balls.

9 In Amy's sock drawer there are spotty, stripy and plain socks in the ratio 5:1:4. What fraction of Amy's socks are stripy?

10 At a music festival there are men, women and children in the ratio 13:17:5. What fraction of the people are children?

11 James has peaches, pears and pomegranates in the ratio of 5:3:2.
   a) What fraction of the fruit are peaches?
   b) What fraction of the fruit are pears?

12 At a birthday party there are purple, red and blue balloons in the ratio 3:8:11.
   a) What fraction of the balloons are blue?
   b) What fraction of the balloons are purple?
   c) What fraction of the balloons aren't red?

Example 4

All of Hannah's DVDs are either horror films or comedies.
If $\frac{2}{7}$ of her DVDs are horror films, find the ratio of comedies to horror films.

1. Use the fraction to find the number of parts corresponding to each type of film.
2. Write this in ratio form, making sure you put the numbers the right way round.

$\frac{2}{7}$ = 2 parts out of 7 are horror

So 7 – 2 = 5 parts are comedies

Ratio of comedies to horror is **5:2**

Exercise 3

1 Aiden has a bag of red and green jelly babies. $\frac{1}{3}$ of the jelly babies are red. Write down the ratio of red to green jelly babies.

2 $\frac{1}{8}$ of the items made in a factory have defects. What is the ratio of items with defects to items without defects?

3 Jack has watched $\frac{3}{10}$ of the episodes in a DVD box set. Write down the ratio of episodes he's watched to episodes he hasn't watched.

4 $\frac{5}{12}$ of the children at a school eat school dinners and the rest bring a packed lunch. What is the ratio of children who bring a packed lunch to those who eat school dinners?

5 $\frac{3}{19}$ of the members of a chess club are left handed. Write down the ratio of right-handed club members to left-handed club members.

6 $\frac{1}{8}$ of the balls in a bag are red, $\frac{5}{8}$ are blue and the rest are green. What is the ratio of red to blue to green balls in the bag?

7 A cycling challenge has three routes — A, B and C. $\frac{3}{5}$ of the competitors choose route A, $\frac{1}{5}$ choose route B and the rest choose route C. What is the ratio of competitors choosing route A to those choosing route C?

8 On a street there are detached and terraced houses. There are 5 times as many terraced houses as detached houses. What is the ratio of detached to terrace houses?

9 In a fruit salad there are $\frac{1}{4}$ as many strawberries as blueberries and there are $\frac{2}{3}$ as many raspberries as blueberries.
   a) What is the ratio of strawberries to blueberries?
   b) What is the ratio of blueberries to raspberries?

10 A rugby team won half of their matches by more than 10 points, won a quarter of their matches by less than 10 points, and lost the rest.
Write the ratio of games they won to games they lost.

11 During one day at a pizza restaurant, $\frac{3}{8}$ of the pizzas ordered were pepperoni, $\frac{1}{2}$ were cheese and tomato and the rest were spicy chicken.
Write down the ratio of pepperoni to cheese and tomato to spicy chicken.

Part : Whole Ratios

Example 5

A shop only sells green and brown garden sheds.
The ratio of green sheds sold to the total number of sheds sold is 5 : 7.
What is the ratio of green sheds sold to brown sheds sold?
5 out of every 7 sheds sold are green, so 2 in every 7 are brown. $7 - 5 = 2$
For every 5 green sheds sold, 2 brown sheds are sold.   green : brown = **5 : 2**

Exercise 4

1 A reptile house only contains snakes and lizards.
   The ratio of snakes to the total number of reptiles is 3 : 8.
   a) What fraction of the reptiles are snakes?   b) What fraction of the reptiles are lizards?
   c) What is the ratio of lizards to the total number of reptiles?
   d) What is the ratio of snakes to lizards?

2 A biscuit tin only contains digestives and bourbons.
   The ratio of digestives to the total number of biscuits is 4 : 7.
   a) What fraction of the biscuits are bourbons?
   b) What is the ratio of bourbons to the total number of biscuits in the tin?
   c) What is the ratio of digestives to bourbons?

3 When Dan makes a cup of tea, the ratio of water to milk is 15 : 2.
   What is the ratio of water to the total amount of liquid in the cup?

4 A rock album is sold as a digital download and on a CD.
   The ratio of digital downloads to CDs sold is 53 : 46.
   What is the ratio of CDs sold to the total number of albums sold?

5 A bouquet of flowers contains only roses, tulips and daisies in the ratio 3 : 5 : 9.
   a) What fraction of the total number of flowers are daisies?
   b) What is the ratio of roses to the total number of flowers?
   c) What is the ratio of tulips to daises to the total number of flowers?

6 A bag of marbles contains only blue and green marbles.
   There are $\frac{1}{4}$ as many green marbles as blue marbles.
   What is the ratio of blue marbles to the total number of marbles?

6.3 Dividing in a Given Ratio

Ratios can be used to divide an amount into two or more shares.
The numbers in the ratio show how many parts of the whole each share gets.

Example 1

Divide £54 in the ratio $4:5$.

1. Add the numbers to find the total number of parts. $4 + 5 = 9$ parts altogether
2. Work out the amount for one part.
   9 parts = £54
   So 1 part = £54 ÷ 9 = £6
3. Then multiply the amount for one part by the number of parts for each share.
   (Check the shares add up to the original amount: £20 + £34 = £54)
   £6 × 4 = £24
   £6 × 5 = £30
   So the shares are **£24** and **£30**.

Example 2

A drink is made using apple juice, blackcurrant juice and lemonade in the ratio $3:2:5$. How much lemonade is needed to make 5 litres of the drink?

1. Add the numbers to find the total number of parts. $3 + 2 + 5 = 10$ parts altogether
2. Work out the amount for one part.
   10 parts = 5 litres
   So 1 part = 0.5 litres
3. Then multiply the amount for one part by the 'lemonade number' in the ratio.
   0.5 litres × 5
   = **2.5 litres of lemonade**

Exercise 1

1. Divide £48 in the following ratios.
   a) $2:1$ b) $1:3$ c) $5:1$ d) $7:5$

2. Share 90 kg in these ratios.
   a) $4:1$ b) $7:2$ c) $8:7$ d) $12:18$

3. Share 56 m in these ratios.
   a) $1:7$ b) $4:4$ c) $10:4$ d) $22:6$

4. Divide 1000 ml in these ratios.
   a) $1:9$ b) $25:25$ c) $3:17$ d) $57:43$

5. Divide 72 cm in the following ratios.
   a) $2:3:1$ b) $2:2:5$ c) $5:3:4$ d) $7:6:5$

6. Share £150 in these ratios.
   a) $1:4:5$ b) $15:5:30$ c) $6:7:2$ d) $13:11:6$

7 Find the smallest share when each amount below is divided in the given ratio.
   a) £22 in the ratio 5:6
   b) 450 g in the ratio 22:28
   c) 45 kg in the ratio 2:3:4
   d) 1800 ml in the ratio 5:6:7

8 Find the largest share when each amount below is divided in the given ratio.
   a) £30 in the ratio 1:3
   b) 36 g in the ratio 3:2
   c) 150 kg in the ratio 10:7:3
   d) 24 000 ml in the ratio 5:7:20

Exercise 2

1. Kat and Lindsay share 30 cupcakes in the ratio 3:2. How many do they each get?

2. Share 32 sandwiches in the ratio 3:5.

3. There are 112 people in an office. The ratio of men to women is 9:5. How many men and how many women are there?

4. Lauren is 16 and Cara is 14. Their grandad gives them £1200 to share in the ratio of their ages. How much money do they each get?

5. Orange paint is made by mixing yellow and red paint in the ratio 4:3. How much of each colour is needed to make 42 litres of orange paint?

6. There are 28 passengers on a bus. The ratio of passengers talking on their phones to those not talking on their phones is 5:2. How many passengers are on their phones?

7. In a school of 600 pupils, the ratio of right-handed pupils to left-handed pupils is 7:1. How many right-handed pupils are there?

8. Elsa and Daniel put money into their business in the ratio 2:3. If they share the profits in the same ratio, how much of a £5700 profit would Daniel get?

Exercise 3

1. Nicky, Jacinta and Charlie share a bag of 36 sweets in the ratio 2:4:3. How many sweets does each of them get?

2. Three friends win £6000 between them. They decide to share the money in the ratio 3:5:4. Calculate the amounts they receive.

3. Gemma, Alisha and Omar have a combined height of 490 cm. If their heights are in the ratio 31:32:35, how tall are they?

4. A fruit salad is made from raspberries, strawberries and redcurrants in the ratio 2:3:1. How much of each fruit is needed to make 450 g of fruit salad?

5. A quiz team share their prize money in the ratio 2:4:6. What is the least amount any team member wins if the prize is £150?

6. A box of 48 chocolates contains dark, milk and white chocolates in the ratio 2:7:3. Jeff doesn't like dark chocolates. How many of the chocolates can he happily eat?

7. Claire owns 20 handbags, which are black brown and purple in the ratio 5:3:2. She is choosing a bag and doesn't want it to be brown. How many bags does she have to choose from?

8. The four angles in a quadrilateral are in the ratio 2:4:1:3. Calculate the sizes of all four angles.

9. The length and width of a rectangle are in the ratio 5:1. If the perimeter of the rectangle is 72 cm, calculate the length and the width of the rectangle.

6.4 Ratio Problems

Exercise 1

1 A builder mixes 10 bags of cement with 25 bags of sand. Write down the ratio of cement to sand:
   a) in its simplest form
   b) in the form $1:n$
   c) in the form $n:1$

2 During one day, a shop has 63 customers. 18 of them are men.
   a) Write down the ratio of male to female customers. Give your answer in its simplest form.
   b) What fraction of the customers are men?

3 A field of sheep contains white sheep and black sheep in the ratio $8:1$.
   a) What fraction of the sheep are white?
   b) If there are 7 black sheep in the field, how many white sheep are there?

4 Evie is making wedding invitation cards in three different colours — blue, green and purple. She uses the different colours in the ratio $2:7:3$. Evie has made 12 green cards so far and has 72 more green cards to make. Work out how many purple cards she will need to make.

5 In a car park there are 6 times as many red cars as yellow cars.
   a) What is the ratio of red cars to yellow cars?
   b) 42 of the cars in the car park are either red or yellow. How many red cars are there?

6 One morning at a cafe the ratio of customers who bought coffee to the total number of customers was $2:5$.
   a) What fraction of the cafe's customers didn't buy coffee?
   b) If there were 72 customers who didn't buy coffee, how many customers did the cafe have that morning?

7 Natasha and Arun share a holiday job. They share the hours in the ratio $4:5$. If Natasha works for 12 hours, and they're each paid £6 an hour, how much does Arun earn?

8 A plank of wood is cut up into 3 pieces A, B and C with their lengths in the ratio $2:6:1$. The original piece of wood was 90 cm long.
   a) How long is piece A?
   b) How much longer is piece B than C?

9 A map has a scale of $1:200\,000$. The real distance between two towns is 60 km. How many centimetres apart are the towns on the map?

10 Jordan has 30 books. 18 of them are fiction books and 12 of them are non-fiction books. Jade's collection of non-fiction books is shown below.

If Jade has the same ratio of fiction to non-fiction books as Jordan, how many books does she have altogether?

11 Jonathan makes orange squash by mixing orange concentrate and water in the ratio $1:10$. Caroline mixes the concentrate and water in the ratio $2:15$. Whose squash is stronger?

12 In a bakery, the ratio of fruit scones to cheese scones is $3:4$.
   a) Given that there are 24 cheese scones, how many fruit scones are there?
   b) If 6 fruit scones were sold, what would be the new ratio of fruit scones to cheese scones? Give your answer in its simplest form.

13 One week, the ratio of flats sold to houses sold in a town was $3:7$. 12 more houses were sold than flats. How many flats were sold?

Section 7 — Percentages

7.1 Percentages

Writing One Number as a Percentage of Another

'Per cent' means '**out of 100**'. Writing an amount as a **percentage** means writing it as a number out of 100.

Example 1

Out of 100 cars in a car park, 38 are red. What percentage of the cars are red?

1. Write the amount as a fraction. ⟶ $\frac{38}{100}$
2. The amount is already written 'out of 100'.
3. Write the amount as a percentage.   So **38%** of the cars are red.

Example 2

Express 15 as a percentage of 50.

1. Write the amount as a fraction.
2. Write an equivalent fraction which is 'out of 100' by multiplying the top and bottom by the same number.
3. Write the amount as a percentage.

$$\frac{15}{50} \xrightarrow{\times 2} \frac{30}{100}$$

So 15 is **30%** of 50.

Exercise 1

Answer **Questions 1-11** without using your calculator.

1 Each grid below is made up of 100 small squares.
Find the percentage of each grid that is shaded.

a)   b)   c)   d)

2 Write each of the following amounts as a percentage.
   a) 13 out of 100   b) 27 out of 100   c) 76 out of 100   d) 243 out of 100

3 A football team scored 100 goals in one season. 13 of these goals were penalties.
What percentage of the goals scored were penalties?

4 a) Find the fraction equivalent to $\frac{23}{50}$ which has 100 as the denominator.
   b) Use your answer to express '23 out of 50' as a percentage.

5 A chess club has 25 members. 12 of these members are female.
   a) Write the number of female members as a fraction of the total number of members.
   b) Find the fraction equivalent to your answer to part **a)** which has 100 as the denominator.
   c) Hence express the number of female members of the club as a percentage.

6 There are 300 coloured counters in a bag. 45 of these counters are green.
   a) Write the number of green counters as a fraction of the total number of counters.
   b) Find the fraction equivalent to your answer to part **a)** which has 100 as the denominator.
   c) Hence express the amount of green counters as a percentage.

7 Write each of the following amounts as a percentage.
   a) 11 out of 25   **b)** 33 out of 50   **c)** 3 out of 20   **d)** 21 out of 10
   e) 12 out of 200   **f)** 99 out of 300   **g)** 600 out of 400   **h)** 890 out of 1000

Example 3

Express 45 as a percentage of 180.
1. Write the amount as a fraction.
2. It may take more than one step to write the fraction out of 100.
3. Write the amount as a percentage.

$$\frac{45}{180} = \frac{5}{20} = \frac{25}{100}$$ (÷9, ×5)

So 45 is **25%** of 180.

8 Write each of the following amounts as a percentage.
   a) 8 out of 32   **b)** 36 out of 60   **c)** 24 out of 40   **d)** 30 out of 150
   e) 72 out of 45   **f)** 56 out of 80   **g)** 63 out of 75   **h)** 120 out of 160
   i) 48 out of 120 **j)** 34 out of 170   **k)** 42 out of 35   **l)** 54 out of 180

9 Out of 24 pupils in a class, 18 walk to school.
   a) What percentage of the class walk to school?
   b) What percentage of the class do not walk to school?

10 There are 55 chocolates in a tin. 33 of the chocolates are milk chocolate. The rest are dark chocolate. What percentage are dark chocolate?

11 39 out of 65 people in a book club have blonde hair. What percentage do not have blonde hair?

Example 4

Express 333 as a percentage of 360.
1. Write the amount as a fraction.
2. It's not easy to rewrite this as a fraction out of 100. So instead, divide the top number by the bottom number, using a calculator if necessary.
3. Multiply by 100% to write as a percentage.

$\frac{333}{360}$

$333 \div 360 = 0.925$

$0.925 \times 100\% = 92.5$

So 333 is **92.5%** of 360.

Section 7 — Percentages

Exercise 2

You may use a calculator to answer these questions.

1. Write each of the following amounts as a percentage.
   a) 15 out of 24
   b) 221 out of 260
   c) 61 out of 500
   d) 896 out of 800
   e) 77 out of 275
   f) 101 out of 250
   g) 323 out of 850
   h) 1512 out of 375

2. A school has 875 pupils. 525 are boys. What is this as a percentage?

3. Express £252 as a percentage of £560.

4. 171 out of 180 raffle tickets were sold for a summer fete. What percentage of the tickets were sold?

5. Write each of the following amounts as a percentage.
   a) 116.6 out of 212
   b) 41.6 out of 128
   c) 588.5 out of 428
   d) 16.8 out of 210
   e) 47.25 out of 126
   f) 315.15 out of 382
   g) 85.86 out of 265
   h) 1809.92 out of 512

6. a) Express 31.36 as a percentage of 32.
   b) Express £117.30 as a percentage of £782.

7. The jackpot for a lottery was £10 250. John won £1896.25. What percentage of the total jackpot did he win?

8. Curtis receives £5.60 pocket money per week from his parents, and £2.40 pocket money per week from his grandparents. What percentage of his total pocket money comes from his grandparents?

Finding a Percentage without a Calculator

You can find some percentages without a calculator using the following rules.
- **50%** = $\frac{1}{2}$, so find 50% of something by **dividing by 2** (which is the same as multiplying by $\frac{1}{2}$).
- **25%** = $\frac{1}{4}$, so find 25% of something by **dividing by 4** (which is the same as multiplying by $\frac{1}{4}$).
- **10%** = $\frac{1}{10}$, so find 10% of something by **dividing by 10** (which is the same as multiplying by $\frac{1}{10}$).

Example 5
Find 75% of 44.
1. First find 25% by dividing by 4.   25% of 44 = 44 ÷ 4 = 11
2. 75% = 3 × 25%, so multiply by 3.   So 75% of 44 = 3 × 11 = **33**

Example 6
Find 35% of 70.
1. First find 10% of 70 by dividing by 10.   10% of 70 = 70 ÷ 10 = 7
2. 30% = 3 × 10%, so multiply 7 by 3 to find 30%.   30% of 70 = 3 × 7 = 21
3. 5% = 10% ÷ 2, so divide 7 by 2 to find 5%.   5% of 70 = 7 ÷ 2 = 3.5
4. 35% = 30% + 5%, so add the two amounts to find 35%.   So 35% of 70 = 21 + 3.5 = **24.5**

Exercise 3

Answer **Questions 1-7** without using your calculator.

1. Find each of the following.
   - a) 50% of 24
   - b) 50% of 82
   - c) 50% of 15
   - d) 25% of 36
   - e) 25% of 80
   - f) 25% of 120
   - g) 10% of 90
   - h) 10% of 270

2. a) Find 25% of 48.
   b) Use your answer to find 75% of 48.

3. a) Find 10% of 120.
   b) Use your answer to find the following.
      - (i) 5% of 120
      - (ii) 20% of 120
      - (iii) 25% of 120
      - (iv) 40% of 120

4. Find each of the following.
   - a) 75% of 12
   - b) 125% of 20
   - c) 5% of 140
   - d) 5% of 260
   - e) 30% of 90
   - f) 40% of 150
   - g) 70% of 110
   - h) 110% of 70
   - i) 15% of 220
   - j) 35% of 340
   - k) 45% of 500
   - l) 65% of 120

5. What is 85% of £70?

6. A wooden plank is 9 m long. 55% of the plank is cut off. What length of wood has been cut off?

7. Shima has £1400 in her savings account. She gives 95% of her savings to charity. How much does she give to charity?

Finding a Percentage with a Calculator

To find a percentage of an amount, first **divide** the percentage by 100% to change the percentage into a decimal. Then **multiply** the amount by the decimal.

Example 7

Find 67% of 138.

1. Divide by 100% to turn 67% into a decimal. $67\% \div 100\% = 0.67$
2. Multiply 138 by the decimal. $0.67 \times 138 = \underline{\mathbf{92.46}}$

Exercise 4

You may use a calculator to answer these questions.

1. Find each of the following.
   - a) 17% of 200
   - b) 9% of 11
   - c) 3% of 210
   - d) 41% of 180
   - e) 68% of 320
   - f) 21% of 370
   - g) 158% of 615
   - h) 73% of 801
   - i) 59% of 713
   - j) 282% of 823
   - k) 91% of 769
   - l) 96% of 911

2. What is 12% of 68 kg?

3. Jeff is on a journey of 385 km. So far, he has completed 31% of his journey. How far has he travelled?

4 125 people work in an office. 12% of the office workers are men. How many workers is this?

5 The cost of an adult's ticket for a theme park is £42. A child's ticket is 68% of the price of an adult's ticket. How much does a child's ticket cost?

6 Which is larger, 22% of £57 or 46% of £28? By how much?

7 A jug can hold 2.4 litres of water. It is 34% full. How much more water will fit in the jug?

7.2 Percentages, Fractions and Decimals

You can switch between percentages, fractions and decimals in the following ways.

Fraction —Divide→ Decimal —× 100%→ Percentage

Fraction ←Use Place Value (tenths, hundredths etc.)— Decimal ←÷ 100%— Percentage

Example 1

Write 24% as: a) a decimal b) a fraction in its simplest terms.

1. Divide by 100% to write as a decimal.

   a) $24\% \div 100\% = \mathbf{0.24}$

2. The final digit of 0.24 (the '4') is in the hundredths column, so write 0.24 as 24 hundredths, and then simplify.

   b) $0.24 = \frac{24}{100} = \frac{6}{25}$ (÷ 4)

Example 2

Write $\frac{3}{8}$ as: a) a decimal b) a percentage.

1. Calculate 3 ÷ 8 to write as a decimal.

   a) $8\overline{)3.^30^60^40}$ gives 0.375 So $\frac{3}{8} = \mathbf{0.375}$

2. Multiply the decimal by 100% to write as a percentage.

   b) $0.375 \times 100\% = \mathbf{37.5\%}$

Exercise 1

1 Each grid below is made up of 100 small squares. Find the proportion of each grid that is shaded as **(i)** a percentage, **(ii)** a decimal, and **(iii)** a fraction in its simplest terms.

a)   b)   c)   d)

Section 7 — Percentages 77

2 **a)** Find the fraction equivalent to $\frac{3}{20}$ which has 100 as the denominator.
   b) Write $\frac{3}{20}$ as **(i)** a percentage, and **(ii)** a decimal.

3 **a)** By calculating 5 ÷ 11, write $\frac{5}{11}$ as a recurring decimal.
   b) Hence write $\frac{5}{11}$ as a percentage.

4 Write each of the following percentages as **(i)** a decimal, and **(ii)** a fraction in its simplest terms.
   a) 75%   **b)** 30%   **c)** 40%   **d)** 65%
   e) 125%   **f)** 95%   **g)** 24%   **h)** 32%
   i) 48%   **j)** 12%   **k)** 2%   **l)** 6%
   m) 5%   **n)** 13%   **o)** 96%   **p)** 74%

5 Write each of the following fractions as **(i)** a decimal, and **(ii)** a percentage.
   a) $\frac{79}{100}$ **b)** $\frac{43}{100}$ **c)** $\frac{3}{10}$ **d)** $\frac{7}{10}$
   e) $\frac{3}{2}$ **f)** $\frac{1}{5}$ **g)** $\frac{2}{5}$ **h)** $\frac{7}{5}$
   i) $\frac{3}{4}$ **j)** $\frac{7}{8}$ **k)** $\frac{1}{3}$ **l)** $\frac{1}{9}$
   m) $\frac{2}{15}$ **n)** $\frac{7}{11}$ **o)** $\frac{1}{6}$ **p)** $\frac{4}{25}$

6 Write each of the following decimals as **(i)** a percentage, and **(ii)** a fraction in its simplest terms.
   a) 0.35   **b)** 0.86   **c)** 0.7   **d)** 0.52
   e) 0.6   **f)** 0.48   **g)** 0.05   **h)** 0.72
   i) 0.36   **j)** 0.4   **k)** 0.01   **l)** 0.68
   m) 0.14   **n)** 1.2   **o)** 0.125   **p)** 0.325

7 Raj answers 86% of the questions in a test correctly. Write this as a decimal.

8 8% of the members of a drama group have green eyes. Write this as a decimal.

9 $\frac{3}{5}$ of the pupils in a class are right-handed. What percentage of the class are right-handed?

10 Raphael eats 36% of a cake. Write this percentage as a fraction in its lowest terms.

11 The probability of it raining tomorrow is $\frac{17}{25}$. Write this probability as a percentage.

Example 3

Put $\frac{1}{3}$, 33% and 0.3 in order, from smallest to largest.

Write the amounts in the same form.
(Here, I've chosen to write them all as decimals.)
1. Calculate 1 ÷ 3 to write $\frac{1}{3}$ as a decimal.

$$\begin{array}{r} 0.33 \\ 3\overline{)1.^10^10} \end{array}$$ So $\frac{1}{3} = 0.33... = 0.\dot{3}$

2. Calculate 33% ÷ 100% to write 33% as a decimal.   33% ÷ 100% = 0.33

3. Put the decimals in order, from smallest to largest.   0.3, 0.33, 0.$\dot{3}$

4. Rewrite in their original forms.   0.3, 33%, $\frac{1}{3}$

Section 7 — Percentages

Exercise 2

Answer **Questions 1-8** without using your calculator.

1. **a)** Write 24% as a decimal.
   b) Write $\frac{1}{5}$ as a decimal.
   c) Hence put 24%, $\frac{1}{5}$ and 0.25 in order, from smallest to largest.

2. For each of the following pairs, write down which is larger.
   a) 0.35, 32%
   b) 0.58, 68%
   c) 0.4, 4%
   d) 0.09, 90%
   e) 0.2, $\frac{21}{100}$
   f) 0.6, $\frac{7}{10}$
   g) 0.7, $\frac{3}{4}$
   h) 0.55, $\frac{3}{5}$

3. For each of the following lists, write down which amount is not equal to the others.
   a) 0.25, 40%, $\frac{1}{4}$
   b) 0.5, 20%, $\frac{1}{2}$
   c) 0.125, 1.25%, $\frac{1}{8}$
   d) 0.44, 44%, $\frac{4}{9}$
   e) 0.8, 8%, $\frac{4}{5}$
   f) 0.615, 40%, $\frac{6}{15}$
   g) 0.22, 22%, $\frac{22}{50}$
   h) 1.5, 150%, $\frac{7}{4}$

4. Put the numbers in each of the following lists in order, from smallest to largest.
   a) 0.42, 25%, $\frac{2}{5}$
   b) 0.505, 45%, $\frac{1}{2}$
   c) 0.15, 0.2%, $\frac{1}{5}$
   d) 0.37, 38%, $\frac{3}{8}$
   e) 0.2, 22%, $\frac{2}{9}$
   f) 0.07, 0.7%, $\frac{7}{10}$
   g) 0.111, 11%, $\frac{1}{9}$
   h) 0.13, 12.5%, $\frac{3}{20}$
   i) 0.25, 23%, $\frac{9}{40}$
   j) 0.02, 0.5%, $\frac{1}{20}$
   k) 0.006, 0.06%, $\frac{3}{50}$
   l) 1.23, 127%, $\frac{6}{5}$

5. Two shops are having a sale. Shop A is offering $\frac{1}{8}$ off all items, while Shop B is offering 15% off all items. Which shop is reducing its prices by the greater percentage?

6. Margaret is buying a car. She needs to pay $\frac{2}{5}$ of the total cost as a deposit. Her parents give her 35% of the cost of the car to help her buy it. Is this enough to pay the deposit?

7. In a game, the winner is the person who transfers more of their 60 counters from one box to another. Oliver transfers 65% of his counters. Jen transfers $\frac{11}{20}$ of her counters. Who has won?

8. In a season, Team X won 14 out of the 20 matches they played. Team Y won 60% of their matches. Which team had the higher proportion of wins?

Example 4

$\frac{1}{4}$ of pupils in a school bring a packed lunch, 65% have school dinners, and the rest go home for lunch. What percentage of pupils go home for lunch?

1. Write $\frac{1}{4}$ as a percentage by writing it as a fraction out of 100. (Or you could divide the top number by the bottom number and multiply by 100%.)
2. Find the percentage that don't go home for lunch by adding the percentages for 'packed lunches' and 'school dinners'.
3. Subtract this from 100% to find the percentage who <u>do</u> go home for lunch.

$\frac{1}{4} = \frac{25}{100}$ (× 25) So $\frac{1}{4} = 25\%$

25% + 65% = 90%
100% − 90% = **10%**

Exercise 3

Answer **Questions 1-9** without using your calculator.

1. In a school survey of food preferences, 50% of pupils said they prefer pizza, $\frac{1}{5}$ said they prefer shepherd's pie and the rest said they prefer roast chicken.
   a) Write the percentage of pupils that prefer shepherd's pie.
   b) Use your answer to find the percentage that prefer roast chicken.

2. In a car park, $\frac{2}{5}$ of the cars are red, 0.12 are white, 15% are blue, and the rest are black.
   a) Write the proportion of red cars as a percentage.
   b) Write the proportion of white cars as a percentage.
   c) Use your answers to find the percentage of cars in the car park that are black.

3. A bag contains coloured counters. 0.37 of the counters are green, 12% are pink and the rest are yellow. What percentage of the counters are yellow?

4. Ainslie is keeping a record of the birds in his garden. Of the birds he has seen this month, $\frac{3}{8}$ were sparrows, 41.5% were blackbirds, and the rest were robins. What percentage were robins?

5. $\frac{3}{4}$ of the people at a concert arrived by train, 0.05 walked, and the rest came by car. What percentage came by car?

6. $\frac{3}{5}$ of the chocolates in a tin are milk chocolate, 20% are white chocolate, and the rest are dark chocolate. What percentage are dark chocolate?

7. Beverley eats 0.3 of a pie, Victoria eats $\frac{1}{10}$, Patrick eats 20%, and Gus eats the rest. What percentage of the pie does Gus eat?

8. $\frac{1}{4}$ of Hattie's jackets are leather, $\frac{1}{5}$ are denim, 30% are suede, and the rest are corduroy. Find the percentage of Hattie's jackets that are corduroy.

9. In a choir, the ratio of men to women is 4 : 7. 25% of the men prefer classical songs, and 80% of the women prefer classical songs. What percentage of the choir prefer classical songs?

7.3 Percentage Increase and Decrease

Finding the New Amount without a Calculator

To **increase** an amount by a percentage — (i) **calculate** the percentage,
(ii) **add** it to the original amount.
To **decrease** an amount by a percentage, **subtract** the percentage from the original amount.

Example 1

Increase 450 by 15% without using your calculator.

1. Find 10% and 5% of 450.   10% of 450 = 450 ÷ 10 = 45
   5% of 450 = 45 ÷ 2 = 22.5
2. Add these to find 15% of 450.   So 15% of 450 = 45 + 22.5 = 67.5
3. Add this to the original amount.   450 + 67.5 = **517.5**

Section 7 — Percentages

Exercise 1

Answer **Questions 1-6** without using your calculator.

1. a) Find 50% of 360.
   b) Increase 360 by 50%.

2. a) Find 30% of 120.
   b) Increase 120 by 30%.

3. a) Find 10% of 160.
   b) Decrease 160 by 10%.

4. a) Find 20% of 84.
   b) Decrease 84 by 20%.

5. Increase each of the following amounts by the percentage given.
   a) 90 by 10%   b) 30 by 50%   c) 60 by 25%   d) 80 by 75%
   e) 270 by 20%   f) 110 by 60%   g) 150 by 40%   h) 25 by 30%
   i) 11 by 80%   j) 480 by 15%   k) 140 by 45%   l) 100 by 85%

6. Decrease each of the following amounts by the percentage given.
   a) 60 by 50%   b) 55 by 10%   c) 24 by 25%   d) 48 by 75%
   e) 25 by 30%   f) 75 by 20%   g) 120 by 60%   h) 125 by 40%
   i) 11 by 70%   j) 150 by 55%   k) 140 by 35%   l) 520 by 15%

Finding the New Amount with a Calculator

1) Find the **multiplier** — convert the percentage to a **decimal**, then add it to 1 for a percentage increase, or subtract it from 1 for a percentage decrease.
2) **Multiply** the amount in the question by the multiplier.

Example 2

Decrease 326 by 12%.

1. Convert the percentage to a decimal.   12% = 0.12
2. It's a percentage decrease, so subtract from 1 to find the multiplier.   Multiplier = 1 − 0.12 = 0.88
3. Multiply 326 by the multiplier.   326 × 0.88 = **286.88**

Exercise 2

1. Increase each of the following amounts by the percentage given.
   a) 490 by 11%   b) 101 by 16%   c) 55 by 37%   d) 89 by 61%
   e) 139 by 28%   f) 426 by 34%   g) 854 by 89%   h) 761 by 77%
   i) 2523 by 67%   j) 1036 by 23%   k) 36 500 by 32%   l) 450 000 by 93%

2. Decrease each of the following amounts by the percentage given.
   a) 77 by 8%   b) 36 by 21%   c) 82 by 13%   d) 101 by 43%
   e) 189 by 38%   f) 313 by 62%   g) 645 by 69%   h) 843 by 91%
   i) 4679 by 11%   j) 8612 by 39%   k) 75 250 by 4%   l) 116 000 by 18%

Percentage Increase and Decrease Problems

Example 3

Fabian deposits £150 into an account which pays 5% simple interest per year.
Without using a calculator, work out how much will be in the account after one year.

1. Find 5% of £150.   10% of 150 = 15
   So 5% of 150 = 15 ÷ 2 = 7.5

2. Add this to £150.   £150 + £7.50 = **£157.50**

Exercise 3

Answer **Questions 1-6** without using your calculator.

1. Leroy deposits £230 into an account which pays 5% simple interest per year. How much will be in the account after one year?

2. Damelza's salary of £24 500 is increased by 15%. What is her new salary?

3. A farmer has 380 acres of land. He sells 35% of his land. How much does he have left?

4. A kettle originally costing £42 is reduced by 75% in a sale. What is the sale price of the kettle?

5. 20% VAT is added to the basic price of a TV to give the selling price. The basic price of the TV is £485. What is the selling price?

6. A population decreases by 15% from 2400. What is the new population?

You may use a calculator to answer **Questions 7-13**.

7. Kimberley deposits £895 into an account which pays 3% simple interest per year. How much will be in the account after one year?

8. A computer costing £365 is reduced by 7% in a sale. What is the sale price of the computer?

9. A household spends £643 on electricity per year. The electricity company increases its prices by 11%. How much would the same amount of electricity now cost the family?

10. A couple go out for a meal in a restaurant. The bill is £63, but the restaurant adds a 13% service charge. How much are the couple being asked to pay in total?

11. David's height increased by 20% between the ages of 6 and 10. He was 50 inches tall when he was 6. How tall was he when he was 10?

12. A dining room suite costs £975. One week, it is reduced by 11% in a sale. The following week, it is reduced by a further 8% of the new price.
    a) How much does it cost after the first reduction?
    b) How much does it cost after the second reduction?

13. Alison earns £31 000 per year. One year, she gets a pay rise of 3%. The following year, she gets a pay cut of 2%. How much does she now earn?

Example 4

Shop A sells a type of oven for £300 and then increases its prices by 5%.
Shop B sells the same type of oven for £290 and increases its prices by 10%.
Without using a calculator, work out which shop now sells the oven more cheaply.

1. Calculate the new price in Shop A.
2. Calculate the new price in Shop B.
3. Compare the new prices to see which is cheaper.

Shop A:
10% of 300 = 30
So 5% of 300 = 15
£300 + £15 = £315

Shop B:
10% of 290 = 29
£290 + £29 = £319

So **Shop A** is cheaper.

Exercise 4

Answer **Questions 1-4** without using your calculator.

1. Roberto's weekly wage of £400 is **decreased** by 5%.
   Mary's weekly wage of £350 is **increased** by 10%.
   a) How much does Roberto now earn?
   b) How much does Mary now earn?
   c) Who now earns more? By how much?

2. A car priced at £11 000 decreases in value at a rate of 10% per year.
   A van priced at £12 400 decreases in value at a rate of 15% per year.
   a) Find the cost of the car after one year.
   b) Find the cost of the van after one year.
   c) Which costs more after one year? By how much?

3. At the start of a journey, Natalie's car had 8 gallons of fuel, and Jason's car had 12 gallons of fuel.
   During the journey, Natalie used 25% of her fuel, and Jason used 40% of his fuel.
   Who had more fuel left at the end of the journey? By how much?

4. Gerry puts £5500 into an account which pays 10% simple interest per year.
   Raj puts £6000 into an account which pays 5% simple interest per year.
   Who has more money in their account after one year? By how much?

You may use a calculator to answer **Questions 5-7**.

5. House A is valued at £245 000. Over the next year, it increases in value by 2%.
   House B is valued at £225 000. Over the next year, it increases in value by 9%.
   Which house is worth more at the end of the year? By how much?

6. Last year, Elsie's gas bill was £480 and her electricity bill was £612.
   This year, her gas bill has increased by 2% and her electricity bill has decreased by 4%.
   Which is now the more expensive bill? By how much?

7. The population of Barton is 152 243, and increases by 11% each year.
   The population of Meristock is 210 059, and decreases by 8% each year.
   Which town has the larger population after one year? By how much?
   Give your answer to the nearest whole number.

Section 7 — Percentages

Finding a Percentage Increase or Decrease

To find a percentage increase:
(i) calculate the **difference** between the new amount and the original amount,
(ii) find this as a percentage of the **original** amount.

Example 5

In a sale, the cost of a CD is reduced from £15 to £9. Find the percentage decrease.

1. Find the difference between the new cost and the original cost.

    $15 - 9 = 6$

2. Write the difference as a fraction of the original cost...

    $\dfrac{6}{15} = \dfrac{2}{5} = \dfrac{40}{100} = 40\%$ (÷3, ×20)

3. ...then write the fraction out of 100 to find the percentage decrease.

    So it is a **40%** decrease.

Exercise 5

Answer **Questions 1-7** without using your calculator.

1 Find the percentage increase when:
   a) a price of £10 is increased to £12.
   b) a price of £20 is increased to £22.
   c) a price of £140 is increased to £161.

2 Find the percentage decrease when:
   a) a price of £10 is decreased to £8.
   b) a price of £25 is decreased to £22.
   c) a price of £150 is decreased to £138.

3 The number of people working for a company increases from 45 to 72.
   a) Find the difference in the number of people working for the company.
   b) Write your answer to part **a)** as a fraction of the original amount.
   c) Find the percentage increase in the number of people working for the company.

4 Percy is on a healthy eating plan. His weight drops from 80 kg to 68 kg.
   a) Find the amount of weight Percy has lost.
   b) Find the percentage decrease in Percy's weight.

5 In an experiment, the mass of a chemical drops from 75 g to 69 g. Find the percentage decrease.

6 The price of a local newspaper increases from 80p to £1. Find the percentage increase.

7 In a sale, the price of a toaster is reduced from £50 to £30. Find the percentage reduction.

Example 6

A house price increases from £145 000 to £187 050. Find the percentage increase.

1. Calculate the difference.

    $187\,050 - 145\,000 = 42\,050$

2. Write as a fraction of the original amount, then divide the top number by the bottom number.

    $\dfrac{42\,050}{145\,000} = 42\,050 \div 145\,000 = 0.29$

3. Multiply by 100% to write as a percentage.

    $0.29 \times 100\% = 29\%$

    So it is a **29%** increase.

Section 7 — Percentages

You may use a calculator to answer **Questions 8-12**.

8 The price of a holiday increases from £320 to £364.80. Find the percentage increase.

9 A shop owner buys a pair of trainers for £52 and sells them for £70.20.
What is her percentage profit?

10 The height of a sunflower increases from 1.3 m to 2.08 m over the course of summer.
What is the percentage increase in its height?

11 During a season, the average attendance for a local sports team's matches was 11 350.
The following season, the average attendance was 11 123. Find the percentage decrease.

12 A car is bought for £12 950. Three years later, it is sold for £8806.
After another three years, it is sold again for £4403.
  a) Find the percentage decrease in the car's price over the first three years.
  b) Find the percentage decrease in the car's price over the next three years.
  c) Find the percentage decrease in the car's price over the whole six years.

Finding the Original Value

If you know the new amount after a percentage increase or decrease,
you can find the original value using the following steps:
  (i) write the new amount as a **percentage of the original value**,
  (ii) **divide to find 1%** of the original value,
  (iii) **multiply by 100** to find the original value.

Example 7

The value of a painting increases by 12% to £1680.
What was the painting worth before it increased in value?

1. A 12% increase means the new amount is 112% of the original value.
2. Divide by 112 to find 1% of the original value.
3. Multiply by 100 to get the original value.

112% = £1680
1% = £15
100% = **£1500**

Exercise 6

1 A fridge costs £200 after a 50% reduction. Calculate the original price of the fridge.

2 Andy buys a top hat that has been reduced in a sale by 35%.
If the sale price is £13.00, find the original price.

3 The owner of a furniture shop increased the price of a bookcase by 26%.
If the bookcase is now priced at £819, what was the price before the increase?

4 An estate agent reduced the price of a house by 4%.
If the house is now for sale at £192 000, what was its original price?

5 In the past year, the number of frogs living in a pond has increased by 10% to 528,
and the number of newts living there has increased by 15% to 621.
How many frogs and how many newts lived in the pond a year ago?

7.4 Compound Growth and Decay

Compound growth and decay are types of percentage change. The amount added on or taken away each time is a percentage of the **new** amount, **not** the **original** amount.

Compound interest is a type of compound **growth**. The interest is **added on** to the money in the account each time it's calculated, and the next amount of interest is calculated from the **new total**.

Depreciation is where the value of something decreases over time. It's a type of compound **decay**.

Example 1

Mr Zupnik invests £600 in a bank account at 5% per annum compound interest. How much money will he have in the bank after two years?

1. Find the multiplier for the percentage increase.   5% = 0.05
2. 'Per annum' means 'per year'. Multiply to find the amount after one year.   Multiplier = 1 + 0.05 = 1.05
   £600 × 1.05 = £630
3. Multiply again to find the amount after two years.   £630 × 1.05 = **£661.50**

Exercise 1

1 A bank pays 3% per annum compound interest.
Calculate how much interest these accounts will earn. Give your answer to the nearest penny.
   a) £250 invested for 1 year.   **b)** £45 invested for 3 years.   **c)** £1500 invested for 2 years.

2 Josephine invests £3500 in a bank account that pays annual compound interest of 4.5%.
How much money (to the nearest penny) will she have in the bank after: **a)** 2 years?   **b)** 3 years?

3 Alan buys a television for £320. Its value depreciates at a rate of 15% per year.
What is its value after: **a)** 2 years?   **b)** 3 years?

4 A car is bought for £12 000. The value of the car depreciates at a rate of 6% per year for the first two years, and then at a rate of 17% per year for the following three years.
What is the value of the car five years after it was bought? Give your answer to the nearest penny.

Example 2

A motorbike is valued at £2500. If its value depreciates at a rate of 6% per month, after how many months will its value be less than £2000?

1. Find the multiplier for the percentage decrease.   6% = 0.06
   Multiplier = 1 − 0.06 = 0.94
2. Find the value of the car at the end of each month, until you reach a value below £2000.
   Value after 1 month = £2500 × 0.94 = £2350
   Value after 2 months = £2350 × 0.94 = £2209
   Value after 3 months = £2209 × 0.94 = £2076.46
   Value after 4 months = £2076.46 × 0.94 = £1951.87

   So it takes **4 months** for the value to fall below £2000.

Section 7 — Percentages

5   Mr Quasar is visiting Las Vegas and has taken $1000 to gamble in the casino. He is unlucky and loses money at a rate of 15% a day. After how many days will Mr Quasar have less than $650?

6   There are 500 harmful bacteria in a colony. When the population of harmful bacteria reaches 1000 it becomes unsafe and must be destroyed. The growth in the number of bacteria is at a rate of 18% per hour. How many full hours does it take for the population of harmful bacteria to be over 1000?

The Formula

The **formula** for compound growth and decay is: $P_n = P_0 \times (\text{multiplier})^n$

P_n = amount after n hours/days/years, P_0 = initial amount,   n = number of hours/days/years

Example 3

Calculate the total compound interest paid on £500 over 6 years if it's paid at a rate of 4% per year.

1. Use the formula for compound growth: $P_n = P_0 \times (\text{multiplier})^n$

2. Plug in the numbers... $P_0 = £500$, multiplier $= 1.04$, $n = 6$
   $P_n = £500 \times (1.04)^6 = £632.6595...$

3. Subtract the initial figure from the final value to find the interest paid.   Interest $= P_n - P_0 = £632.6595... - £500$
   $= £132.6595... = \mathbf{£132.66}$

Exercise 2

1   Calculate the amount of money (to the nearest penny) you would have if you invested:
    a) £1000 at an annual rate of 4% for 8 years.   b) £600 at an annual rate of 5.2% for 7 years.

2   Calculate the value (to the nearest £100) of a house after six years if it was bought for £650 000 and house prices are falling at a rate of 2% per annum.

3   A colony of ants has set up home in Mr Murphy's shed. At 9 am on Monday there were 250 ants. If the colony of ants grows at a rate of 6% per day, how many ants will there be at 9 am on Saturday?

4   Mr Butterworth is on a diet and is losing weight at a rate of 2% of his total body weight every week. If he weighs 110 kg when he starts his diet, what will his body weight be at the end of 8 weeks?

7.5   Percentages Problems

Exercise 1

Answer **Questions 1-6** without using your calculator.

1   Sandra gets paid £1385 per month. In December she gets a Christmas bonus of £138.50. What percentage of her monthly wage is this bonus?

2   A coat normally costs £160. In a sale, the coat's price was reduced by 35%.
    a) What is 35% of £160?
    b) What is the new price of the coat?

3   Each grid below is made up of 25 small squares. Find the proportion of each grid that is shaded as **(i)** a fraction in its simplest terms, **(ii)** a percentage, and **(iii)** a decimal.

   a)   b)   c)   d)

4   A pot of yoghurt normally contains 450 g. A special offer pot contains 35% extra free. How many grams of yoghurt does the special offer pot contain?

5   A newborn baby weighs 3.2 kg. His weight increases by 5% over the next fortnight. What does he weigh at the end of the fortnight?

6   House A is valued at £420 000 and House B is valued at £340 000. After 5 years the value of House A has **decreased** by 15% and the value of House B has **increased** by 5%. What is the difference in value of the two houses after 5 years?

You may use a calculator to answer **Questions 7-17**.

7   Write $\frac{2}{33}$, 0.061 and 6% in order, from smallest to largest.

8   Kelly and Nasir both had maths tests last week. Kelly scored $\frac{47}{68}$ and Nasir scored $\frac{35}{52}$. Who got the higher percentage score?

9   Two shops had a sale on a suit that had previously cost £92. Shop A had 70% off the original price, while Shop B had $\frac{7}{8}$ off. Which shop had the lower price, and by how much?

10 Last summer, 385 000 people visited a holiday resort. $\frac{1}{8}$ were German, 0.11 were French and the rest were British.
   a) What percentage were British?
   b) How many British people visited the resort?

11 The insurance for a car normally costs £356. With a no-claims discount, the cost is reduced by 27%. What is the reduced cost of the insurance?

12 Tony deposits £3250 into a savings account that earns 8.5% simple interest per year. How much will he have at the end of the year?

13 Dave loves a bargain and buys a feather boa which has been reduced in price by 70%. If the sale price is £2.85, what was the original price of the boa?

14 The population of an island is 12 500. Each year, the population increases by 8%.
   a) What is the population of the island after 5 years?
   b) What is the population of the island after 7 years?

15 Philip runs a clothes shop. He buys 5 pairs of lime-green trousers costing £14 each. They prove not to be very popular, so he is only able to sell them at a cut price. He sells 2 pairs at £10 each and 3 pairs at £6 each. Calculate Philip's percentage loss on the trousers.

16 Claire the Evil Genius buys a laser for £68 000. It will depreciate at 20% per annum for the first two years and at 15% per annum for the next three years. What is the value of the laser after 5 years?

17 30% of the animals in a wildlife park are lemurs. 40% of the lemurs are ring-tailed lemurs. What percentage of the animals in the wildlife park are ring-tailed lemurs?

Section 7 — Percentages

Section 8 — Algebraic Expressions

8.1 Collecting Like Terms

An **algebraic expression** involves letters that represent numbers.

For example, these are all algebraic expressions: a $6b$ xyz $a + b$ $x^2 + y^2 + z^2$

(Remember — a is the same as **1a**, and **6b** is the same as **6 × b**.)

Expressions do **not** contain an equals sign (=).

Expressions can sometimes be simplified by **collecting like terms**.
'**Like terms**' contain exactly the same combination of letters.

Example 1

Simplify these expressions by collecting like terms: a) $5p - 2p + 4p$ b) $4a + 3b - a - 7b$

a) This expression contains three 'like terms' — each only contains the letter p.
They combine to give a total of $7p$.

a) $5p - 2p + 4p = \underline{\mathbf{7p}}$

b) First write the like terms next to each other.

'$4a$' and '$-a$' are like terms — they just contain a.
Together these give $4a - a = 3a$.

And '$3b$' and '$-7b$' are like terms — they just contain b.
Together these give $3b - 7b = -4b$.

Remember, the + or – sign in front of a term actually belongs to that term.

b) $4a + 3b - a - 7b$
$= 4a - a + 3b - 7b$
$= \underline{\mathbf{3a - 4b}}$

Exercise 1

1. Simplify these expressions by collecting like terms.
   a) $b + b + b + b$
   b) $a + a + a$
   c) $2x + 3x + x$
   d) $p + 7p + 2p + 4p$
   e) $4s + s + 2s + 7s$
   f) $11n + 8n + n$

2. Simplify these expressions by collecting like terms.
   a) $3y + 5y - 2y$
   b) $8z + 7z - 3z$
   c) $7p - 2p + 3p - 4p$
   d) $10m - 7m + 2m$
   e) $8y - y - 3y$
   f) $3x + 5x - 8x$
   g) $q - 3q - 2q$
   h) $5m - 2m + 8m - 6m$
   i) $2y - y - 3y - 5y + 6y$

3. Simplify these expressions by collecting like terms.
   a) $c + c + c + d + d$
   b) $a + b + a - a + b$
   c) $x + y + x + y + x - y$
   d) $3m + m + 2n$
   e) $5x + 2y + 3x$
   f) $3a + 5b + 8a + 2b$
   g) $6p + q + p + 3q$
   h) $5a - 2a + 5b + 2b$
   i) $4b + 8c - b - 5c$

Example 2

Simplify the expression $x + 4y + 4 - 2x - y - 3$ by collecting like terms.

1. Terms involving no letters at all are like terms.
2. Collect them together in the same way as terms containing letters.

$x + 4y + 4 - 2x - y - 3$
$= x - 2x + 4y - y + 4 - 3$
$= \underline{-x + 3y + 1}$

4 Simplify these expressions by collecting like terms.
   a) $2c + 4 + c + 7$
   b) $3x + 6 - 6x - 4$
   c) $5y + 12 - 9y - 7$
   d) $-m + 5 - 8m + 16$
   e) $-4x - 2 + 7x + 12$
   f) $13a + 8 + 8a + 2$

5 Simplify these expressions by collecting like terms.
   a) $x + 7 + 4x + y + 5$
   b) $a + 2b + b - 8 - 5a$
   c) $5x + 2y + 6 + 4y + 2x - 9$
   d) $13m + 7 + 2n - 8m - 3$
   e) $5x + 2y + 3x - 2y - 3$
   f) $13a - 5b + 8a + 12b + 7$

6 Simplify these expressions.
   a) $16p + 4q + 4 - 2p + 3q - 8$
   b) $5a - 7b + 5b - 2 + 2a + 11$
   c) $14b + 8c - b + 3 - 5c - 5b + 4$
   d) $-3x + 9y + 2z - 2x - 5 + 4y - 8x$
   e) $-5m + 3 - 6n - 4 + 3n - 6m - 2n$
   f) $8p + 6q + 14 - 6r - 4p - 14r - 2q - 23$

Example 3

Simplify the expression $x + x^2 + yx + 7 + 4x + 2xy - 3$ by collecting like terms.

There are four sets of like terms:
(i) terms involving just x
(ii) terms involving x^2
(iii) terms involving xy (or yx, which means the same)
(iv) terms involving just numbers

Collect the different sets together separately.

$x + x^2 + xy + 7 + 4x + 2xy - 3$
$= (x + 4x) + x^2 + (xy + 2xy) + (7 - 3)$
$= \underline{5x + x^2 + 3xy + 4}$

7 Simplify the following expressions by collecting like terms.
   a) $x^2 + 3x + 2 + 2x + 3$
   b) $x^2 + 4x + 1 + 3x - 3$
   c) $x^2 + 4x + x^2 + 2x + 4$
   d) $x^2 + 2x^2 + 4x - 3x$
   e) $p^2 - 5p + 2p^2 + 3p$
   f) $3p^2 + 6q + p^2 - 4q + 3p^2$
   g) $8 + 6p^2 - 5 + pq + p^2$
   h) $4p + 5q - pq + p^2 - 7q$
   i) $6b^2 + 7b + 9 - 4b^2 + 5b - 2$

8 Simplify the following expressions by collecting like terms.
   a) $ab + cd - xy + 3ab - 2cd + 3yx + 2x^2$
   b) $pq + 3pq + p^2 - 2qp + q^2$
   c) $3ab - 2b + ab + b^2 + 5b$
   d) $4abc - 3bc + 2ab + b^2 + 5b + 2abc$

9 By collecting number terms and root terms, simplify the following.
   a) $7 + 3\sqrt{3} + 6 - 2\sqrt{3}$
   b) $-2 - 13\sqrt{7} - 7 + 3\sqrt{7}$
   c) $11 - 7\sqrt{5} - 11 - 8\sqrt{5}$
   d) $2 - 5\sqrt{10} - 6 - 6\sqrt{10}$
   e) $9 - 13\sqrt{2} - 10 + 6\sqrt{2}$
   f) $2 - 3\sqrt{6} + 3 - 5\sqrt{6}$

Section 8 — Algebraic Expressions

8.2 Expanding Brackets

You can **expand** (or remove) brackets by multiplying everything **inside** the brackets by the letter or number **in front**.

$$a(b + c) = ab + ac$$
$$a(b - c) = ab - ac$$

Remember, **powers** work with **letters** in exactly the same way as they work with numbers.

$$a^2 = a \times a$$
$$a^3 = a \times a \times a$$

$$a^m \times a^n = a^{m+n}$$

Example 1

Expand the brackets in these expressions: a) $3(a + 2)$ b) $8(n - 3)$

a) Multiply both a and 2 by 3.
b) Multiply both n and 3 by 8.

a) $3(a + 2) = (3 \times a) + (3 \times 2) = \underline{\mathbf{3a + 6}}$
b) $8(n - 3) = (8 \times n) - (8 \times 3) = \underline{\mathbf{8n - 24}}$

Exercise 1

1 Expand the brackets in these expressions.

a) $2(a + 5)$ b) $4(b + 3)$ c) $5(d + 7)$ d) $3(p + 4)$
e) $4(x + 8)$ f) $6(5 - r)$ g) $2(7 + y)$ h) $8(h - 2)$
i) $9(q - 3)$ j) $2(t + 6)$ k) $4(b - 4)$ l) $3(k + 6)$
m) $3(5 + p)$ n) $7(6 + g)$ o) $5(3 - y)$ p) $8(a - b)$

Example 2

Expand the brackets in these expressions: a) $m(n + 7)$ b) $a(a - 4)$

a) Multiply both n and 7 by m.
b) Multiply both a and 4 by a.

a) $m(n + 7) = (m \times n) + (m \times 7) = \underline{\mathbf{mn + 7m}}$
b) $a(a - 4) = (a \times a) - (a \times 4) = \underline{\mathbf{a^2 - 4a}}$

2 Expand the brackets in these expressions.

a) $x(y + 5)$ b) $p(q + 2)$ c) $a(b + 4)$ d) $m(p + 8)$
e) $q(p - 4)$ f) $s(5 - t)$ g) $y(5 + x)$ h) $n(n - 7)$
i) $x(x - 2)$ j) $p(8 - q)$ k) $x(8 - x)$ l) $a(b - 12)$

Example 3

Simplify these expressions: a) $b \times b \times b \times b$ b) $4a \times 5b$ c) $3a \times 6a$

1. If the same letter is multiplied by itself, write it as a power.
2. Multiply numbers and letters separately.

a) $b \times b \times b \times b = \underline{\mathbf{b^4}}$
b) $4a \times 5b = 4 \times 5 \times a \times b = \underline{\mathbf{20ab}}$
c) $3a \times 6a = 3 \times 6 \times a \times a = \underline{\mathbf{18a^2}}$

Section 8 — Algebraic Expressions

Exercise 2

1 Simplify the following expressions.
  a) $a \times a \times a$
  b) $2a \times 3a$
  c) $8p \times 2q$
  d) $3a \times 7a$
  e) $5x \times 3y$
  f) $m \times m \times m \times m$
  g) $12a \times 4b$
  h) $6p \times 8p$

2 Simplify the following expressions.
  a) $a \times ab$
  b) $4a^2 \times 5a$
  c) $2p \times 7q^2$
  d) $4ab \times 2ab$

Example 4

Expand the brackets in the following expressions.
  a) $4(5a + 3)$
  b) $3(4 - 7n)$

a) Multiply both 5a and 3 by 4.

a) $4(5a + 3) = (4 \times 5a) + (4 \times 3)$
$= \underline{\mathbf{20a + 12}}$

b) Multiply both 4 and 7n by 3.

b) $3(4 - 7n) = (3 \times 4) - (3 \times 7n)$
$= \underline{\mathbf{12 - 21n}}$

Exercise 3

1 Expand the brackets in the following expressions.
  a) $3(2p + 4)$
  b) $5(4t - 8)$
  c) $7(3h + 9)$
  d) $2(5d + 4)$
  e) $8(7k - 5)$
  f) $4(7 + 4p)$
  g) $4(5 + 7b)$
  h) $3(4 - 2z)$
  i) $2(8 - 6m)$
  j) $9(2 + 8v)$
  k) $6(n - 6m)$
  l) $9(u + 8v)$

2 Expand the brackets in the following expressions.
  a) $3(2n - 6m)$
  b) $5(4u + 8v)$
  c) $7(5n - 6m)$
  d) $3(u + 8v)$
  e) $4(4x - 7y)$
  f) $3(2p - 11q)$
  g) $8(2s - 12t)$
  h) $6(4x + 5y)$

Example 5

Expand the brackets in the following expressions: a) $-(q + 4)$ b) $-3(4 - 2a)$

a) You can think of $-(q + 4)$ as $-1 \times (q + 4)$.
See how a minus sign outside the brackets reverses the sign of everything inside the brackets.

a) $-(q + 4) = (-1 \times q) + (-1 \times 4)$
$= (-q) + (-4)$
$= \underline{\mathbf{-q - 4}}$

b) Again, the sign of everything inside the brackets changes.
Remember: $-(-6a) = 6a$.

b) $-3(4 - 2a) = (-3 \times 4) - (-3 \times 2a)$
$= (-12) - (-6a)$
$= \underline{\mathbf{-12 + 6a}}$

3 Expand the brackets in the following expressions.
  a) $-(q + 2)$
  b) $-(x + 7)$
  c) $-(h + 3)$
  d) $-(g + 3)$
  e) $-4(n + 2)$
  f) $-2(7 + r)$
  g) $-8(3 + 5a)$
  h) $-5(4 + z)$
  i) $-6(a + 4)$
  j) $-7(b + 2)$
  k) $-2(11 + c)$
  l) $-5(12 + d)$

4 Expand the brackets in the following expressions.
   a) $-(p-3)$
   b) $-(q-5)$
   c) $-(r-6)$
   d) $-(s-2)$
   e) $-4(u-7)$
   f) $-2(12-v)$
   g) $-8(7-w)$
   h) $-5(5-x)$

5 Expand the brackets in the following expressions.
   a) $-(m+3)$
   b) $-(n-11)$
   c) $-(p+4)$
   d) $-(q-7)$
   e) $-4(r-9)$
   f) $-2(13+s)$
   g) $-8(2-t)$
   h) $-5(6+u)$
   i) $-v(v+4)$
   j) $-v(v-5)$
   k) $-x(12-x)$
   l) $-y(4+y)$

6 Expand the brackets in the following expressions.
   a) $-6(5g-3)$
   b) $-7(4v+8)$
   c) $-2(5+4m)$
   d) $-5(10-8v)$
   e) $-5(2+3n)$
   f) $-4z(8-2z)$
   g) $-2(6b-3)$
   h) $-4y(2y+6)$

Example 6

Simplify the following expressions.
   a) $2(a+5) + 3(a+2)$
   b) $3(x+2) - 5(2x+1)$

a) Multiply out both sets of brackets. Then collect like terms.

   a) $2(a+5) + 3(a+2) = (2a+10) + (3a+6)$
   $= 2a + 10 + 3a + 6$
   $= \mathbf{5a + 16}$

b) Multiply out the individual brackets. The minus sign before the second set of brackets reverses the sign of each term inside those brackets.

   b) $3(x+2) - 5(2x+1) = (3x+6) - (10x+5)$
   $= 3x + 6 - 10x - 5$
   $= \mathbf{-7x + 1}$

Exercise 4

1 Simplify the following expressions.
   a) $2(z+3) + 4(z+2)$
   b) $3(c+1) + 5(c+7)$
   c) $4(u+6) + 8(u+5)$
   d) $2(c+2) + 3(c+5)$
   e) $3(v+5) + 6(v+7)$
   f) $3(w+4) + 5(w+2)$
   g) $5(b-6) + 7(b+4)$
   h) $7(t-3) + 2(t+12)$
   i) $8(m-2) + 9(m+5)$

2 Simplify the following expressions.
   a) $5(p-3) - (p+6)$
   b) $2(c-6) - (c+5)$
   c) $5(q-3) - (q+1)$
   d) $2(j-5) - (j-3)$
   e) $5(y-4) - (y-2)$
   f) $5(3c-6) - (c-3)$

3 Simplify the following expressions.
   a) $5(2q+5) - 2(q-2)$
   b) $2(3c-8) - 8(c+4)$
   c) $4(5q-1) - 2(q+2)$
   d) $3(a-6) - 4(a-1)$
   e) $5(4z-3) - 3(z-5)$
   f) $5(q-2) - 3(q-4)$

4 Simplify the following expressions.
   a) $2(z+2) + 3(z+6)$
   b) $8(c+4) - (c+2)$
   c) $4(u+4) + 3(u+5)$
   d) $4p(3p+5) - 3(p+1)$
   e) $6(4m+5) + 7m(2m+3)$
   f) $4(3k+1) - k(7k+9)$
   g) $9b(2b+5) + 4b(6b+6)$
   h) $4(t+1) - 7t(8t-11)$
   i) $7h(3h+2) - 10h(4h-1)$

Example 7

Expand the brackets in the following expressions.   a) $(q + 4)(p + 3)$ b) $3(x - 2)^2$

a) Multiply each term in the left bracket by each term in the right bracket. Write the letters in each term of the answer in alphabetical order.

b) Write out $(x - 2)^2$ as $(x - 2)(x - 2)$.
Multiply each term in the left bracket by each term in the right bracket.
Collect like terms, then multiply the whole lot by 3.

a) $(q + 4)(p + 3) = pq + 3q + 4p + 12$

b) $3(x - 2)^2 = 3 \times (x - 2)(x - 2)$
$= 3 \times (x^2 - 2x - 2x + 4)$
$= 3 \times (x^2 - 4x + 4)$
$= \mathbf{3x^2 - 12x + 12}$

Exercise 5

1 Expand the brackets in the following expressions.
a) $(a + 2)(b + 3)$
b) $(j + 4)(k - 5)$
c) $(x - 4)(y - 1)$
d) $(x + 6)(y + 2)$
e) $(2 + x)(8 + y)$
f) $(9 - a)(b - 3)$
g) $(t - 5)(s + 3)$
h) $(y + 12)(z - 3)$

2 Expand the brackets in the following expressions.
a) $2(a + 1)(p + 6)$
b) $5(x + 3)(y - 7)$
c) $3(j - 2)(k + 4)$
d) $8(g + 5)(h + 9)$
e) $2(w - 6)(z - 8)$
f) $6(x - 5)(y - 2)$
g) $9(x + 4)(3 - y)$
h) $7(a - 7)(b - 8)$

3 Expand the brackets in the following expressions.
a) $(x + 8)(x + 3)$
b) $(b + 2)(b - 4)$
c) $(a - 1)(a + 2)$
d) $(d + 7)(d + 6)$
e) $(c + 5)(3 - c)$
f) $(y - 8)(6 - y)$
g) $(z - 12)(z + 9)$
h) $2(x + 2)(x + 1)$

4 Expand the brackets in the following expressions.
a) $(x + 1)^2$
b) $(x + 4)^2$
c) $(x + 5)^2$
d) $(x - 2)^2$
e) $(x - 3)^2$
f) $(x - 7)^2$
g) $4(x + 3)^2$
h) $2(x - 6)^2$

Identities

You can show that two expressions are the **same** by using the **identity** symbol '≡'.
E.g. $x + 1 \equiv 1 + x$ — it's always true, for any value of x.

Example 8

Show that $(x + 6)(x - 3) \equiv x(x + 3) - 18$

1. Expand and simplify both sides of the identity separately.
2. Both sides give the same expression.

$(x + 6)(x - 3) = x^2 - 3x + 6x - 18 = x^2 + 3x - 18$
$x(x + 3) - 18 = x^2 + 3x - 18$
So $(x + 6)(x - 3) \equiv x(x + 3) - 18$

Exercise 6

1 For each of the following, state whether or not you could you replace the box with the symbol '≡'.
a) $4x \square 10$
b) $x^2 + 2x + 1 \square 0$
c) $-x^2 + 3 \square 3 - x^2$
d) $2(x + 1) \square x - 1$
e) $3(x + 2) - x \square 2(x + 3)$
f) $3(2 - 3x) + 2 \square 8x$

2 Show that: a) $(x + 4)^2 - 4 \equiv (x + 6)(x + 2)$ b) $5(x + 2) + (x^2 - 4) \equiv (x + 4)(x + 1) + 2$

Section 8 — Algebraic Expressions

8.3 Factorising

Factorising is the opposite of expanding brackets.
You look for a **common factor** of all the terms in an expression, and 'take it outside' the brackets.
If there is more than one common factor, the **highest common factor** goes outside the brackets.

For a lot of these questions, you'll need to remember how to **divide** two powers: $a^m \div a^n = \dfrac{a^m}{a^n} = a^{m-n}$

Example 1

Factorise these expressions: a) $6p + 8$ b) $12x - 18y$

a) 2 is a common factor of $6p$ and 8.
So 2 goes outside the brackets.

Divide each term by the common factor, and write
the results inside the brackets: $6p \div 2 = 3p$ and $8 \div 2 = 4$

a) $6p + 8 = 2(\ \ +\ \ )$
$= 2(3p +\ \ )$
$= \underline{\mathbf{2(3p + 4)}}$

b) 6 is the highest common factor of $12x$ and $18y$.
So 6 goes outside the brackets.

Divide each term by the common factor, and write the
results inside the brackets: $12x \div 6 = 2x$ and $18y \div 6 = 3y$

b) $12x - 18y = 6(\ \ -\ \ )$
$= 6(2x -\ \ )$
$= \underline{\mathbf{6(2x - 3y)}}$

Exercise 1

1 Factorise the following expressions.
a) $2a + 10$ b) $3b + 12$ c) $5c + 15$ d) $4 + 12x$
e) $15 + 3y$ f) $28 + 7v$ g) $10d + 35$ h) $8x + 12$

2 Factorise the following expressions.
a) $5a + 15b$ b) $9c + 12d$ c) $3x + 12y$ d) $21u + 7v$
e) $8c + 12f$ f) $25d + 35e$ g) $12x + 16y$ h) $3x + 9y$

3 Factorise the following expressions.
a) $4a^2 + 12b$ b) $3c + 15d^2$ c) $5c^2 + 25f$ d) $6x + 12y^2$

Example 2

Factorise $3x^2 + 2x$.

1. x is a common factor of $3x^2$ and $2x$.
   So x goes outside the brackets.

2. Divide each term by the common factor, and write the
   results inside the brackets: $3x^2 \div x = 3x$ and $2x \div x = 2$

$3x^2 + 2x = x(\ \ +\ \ )$
$= x(3x +\ \ )$
$= \underline{\mathbf{x(3x + 2)}}$

4 Simplify the following.
a) $x^2 \div x$ b) $2y^2 \div y$ c) $8p^2 \div p$ d) $35n^2 \div 7n$
e) $10d^2 \div 2d$ f) $24m^2 \div 3m$ g) $12a^2 \div 2a$ h) $22b^2 \div 11b$

5 Factorise the following expressions.
a) $3a^2 + 7a$ b) $4b^2 + 19b$ c) $2x^2 + 9x$ d) $7y + 15y^2$
e) $10d^2 + 27d$ f) $4y^2 + 13y$ g) $11y + 3y^2$ h) $22w + 5w^2$
i) $4x^2 - 9x$ j) $21q^2 - 16q$ k) $15y - 7y^2$ l) $27z^2 + 11z$

Section 8 — Algebraic Expressions   **95**

Example 3

Factorise these expressions: a) $6p + 9p^2$ b) $15x^2 - 10xy$

a) 3 and p are common factors of $6p$ and $9p^2$.
So $3p$ goes outside the brackets.
Divide each term by the common factor, and write the results inside the brackets: $6p \div 3p = 2$ and $9p^2 \div 3p = 3p$

b) 5 and x are common factors of $15x^2$ and $10xy$.
So $5x$ goes outside the brackets.
Divide each term by the common factor, and write the results inside the brackets: $15x^2 \div 5x = 3x$ and $10xy \div 5x = 2y$

a) $6p + 9p^2 = 3p(\quad + \quad)$
$= 3p(2 + \quad)$
$= \mathbf{3p(2 + 3p)}$

b) $15x^2 - 10xy = 5x(\quad - \quad)$
$= 5x(3x - \quad)$
$= \mathbf{5x(3x - 2y)}$

Exercise 2

1   Factorise these expressions.
   a) $5a^2 + 10a$
   b) $4b + 8b^2$
   c) $3c^2 - 9c$
   d) $9d - 18d^2$
   e) $6f^2 + 2f$
   f) $7p^2 + 21p$
   g) $2y + 18y^2$
   h) $3h - 15h^2$

2   Factorise these expressions.
   a) $10c^2 - 5cd$
   b) $20x^2 - 10xy$
   c) $9x^2 + 6xy$
   d) $12x^2 + 8xy$
   e) $2ab - 6b^2$
   f) $6a^2 + 3a$
   g) $4xy - 8x^2$
   h) $2ab + 12b^2$

3   Factorise these expressions.
   a) $10p^2 + 15pq$
   b) $12xy + 8y^2$
   c) $15ab - 20a^2$
   d) $12q^2 - 18pq$
   e) $6a^2 + 9ab$
   f) $12pq - 8p^2$
   g) $8a^2 + 6ab^2$
   h) $24x^2y - 16x$

Factorising Quadratics

A **quadratic expression** is one of the form $\mathbf{ax^2 + bx + c}$ where a, b and c are constants ($a \neq 0$).
You can **factorise** some quadratics using the method shown in the example below.

Example 4

Factorise: a) $x^2 + 7x + 10$ b) $x^2 + 2x - 15$

1. Find two numbers that add up to 7 and multiply to give 10:
2. You can check this by expanding the brackets.

You need two numbers that add up to 2 and multiply to give −15, so one must be positive and the other must be negative.

a) $5 + 2 = 7$ and $5 \times 2 = 10$
Then $x^2 + 7x + 10 = \mathbf{(x + 5)(x + 2)}$
$(x + 5)(x + 2) = x^2 + 2x + 5x + 10$

b) $5 + -3 = 2$ and $5 \times -3 = -15$
Then $x^2 + 2x - 15 = \mathbf{(x + 5)(x - 3)}$

Exercise 3

1   Factorise each of the following expressions.
   a) $x^2 + 5x + 6$
   b) $x^2 + 7x + 12$
   c) $x^2 + 8x + 7$
   d) $x^2 + 8x + 12$
   e) $x^2 + 5x + 4$
   f) $x^2 + 6x + 9$
   g) $x^2 + 6x + 8$
   h) $y^2 + 8y + 15$
   i) $z^2 + 9z + 14$
   j) $p^2 + 6p + 5$
   k) $s^2 + 10s + 24$
   l) $v^2 + 11v + 24$

Section 8 — Algebraic Expressions

2 Factorise each of the following expressions.
a) $x^2 + 2x - 3$
b) $x^2 - 6x + 8$
c) $x^2 - 7x + 10$
d) $x^2 - 5x + 4$
e) $x^2 + 3x - 10$
f) $x^2 + 2x - 8$
g) $k^2 + k - 6$
h) $m^2 - 2m - 8$
i) $n^2 + 4n - 21$
j) $q^2 - 8q + 15$
k) $r^2 + 6r - 27$
l) $u^2 - 15u + 54$

3 By first taking a common factor out of all the terms, fully factorise each of the following.
a) $3x^2 + 15x + 18$
b) $2x^2 + 18x + 36$
c) $5x^2 - 30x + 40$
d) $2x^2 + 24x + 70$
e) $6x^2 - 24x + 18$
f) $3x^2 - 27x + 60$
g) $5x^2 + 10x - 75$
h) $4x^2 - 4x - 24$

Difference of Two Squares

Some quadratic expressions have no middle term, e.g. $x^2 - 49$.
These quadratics have factors that are the same, except that one has a **positive** term and one has a **negative** term. For example, $x^2 - 49$ factorises to $(x + 7)(x - 7)$.

More generally: $a^2 - b^2 = (a + b)(a - b)$ This is known as the **difference of two squares**.

Example 5
Factorise $x^2 - 16$

$16 = 4^2$
Difference of two squares says: $x^2 - a^2 = (x + a)(x - a)$.
$x^2 - 16 = x^2 - 4^2$ So, $x^2 - 16 = \underline{\mathbf{(x + 4)(x - 4)}}$

Exercise 4

1 Factorise each of the following expressions.
a) $x^2 - 25$
b) $x^2 - 9$
c) $x^2 - 36$
d) $x^2 - 81$

2 A quadratic expression is of the form $16x^2 - 9$.
a) Find $\sqrt{16x^2}$
b) Write the expression $16x^2 - 9$ in the form $a^2 - b^2$.
c) Hence factorise $16x^2 - 9$.

3 Factorise each of the following expressions.
a) $4x^2 - 49$
b) $x^2 - 64$
c) $36x^2 - 4$
d) $9x^2 - 100$
e) $b^2 - 121$
f) $16z^2 - 1$
g) $25x^2 - 16$
h) $t^2 - 144$

4 Factorise each of the following expressions.
a) $x^2 - 7$
b) $x^2 - 3$
c) $x^2 - 11$
d) $5x^2 - 10$

Exercise 5 — Mixed Exercise

1 Factorise these expressions.
a) $2x + 4y$
b) $2x + x^2$
c) $2x + 4x^2$
d) $8x + 24$
e) $7m^2n + 4m^2p$
f) $4y - 6y^2$
g) $20y + 12xy$
h) $9pr + 6pq$

2 Factorise these expressions.
a) $28a - 35b$
b) $15ab - 10a^2$
c) $60x + 144y$
d) $28rst + 40r^2s$
e) $4abc^2 - 6a^2bc$
f) $5pq + 10qr$
g) $20m^2n - 24m$
h) $23pq - 92p$
i) $10pq^2 - 15p^2q$
j) $8cd^2 - 6c^2d$
k) $14m^2n - 35mn^2$
l) $16pq^2 - 6qp^2$

3 Factorise each of the following expressions.
a) $x^2 - 4x - 5$
b) $t^2 - 8t + 16$
c) $x^2 - 49$
d) $y^2 - y - 20$
e) $x^2 - x - 12$
f) $y^2 + 10y + 21$
g) $x^2 + 5x - 6$
h) $x^2 - 4x - 45$
i) $16a^2 - 25$
j) $100x^2 - 64$
k) $z^2 - 1$
l) $36x^2 - 169$

Section 8 — Algebraic Expressions

Section 9 — Equations and Inequalities

9.1 Solving Equations

Solving an equation means finding the value of an unknown letter that makes both sides **equal**.
For example, the solution to $2x + 3 = 11$ is $x = 4$ — because if $x = 4$, **both** sides equal 11.

Example 1

Solve the equation $x + 8 = 15$.
1. You need to get x on its own on one side of the equation, so you need to subtract 8 from the left-hand side.
2. But you must always do the same to both sides of an equation. So subtract 8 from the right-hand side too.
3. Check your answer by putting it in the original equation. $x + 8 = 7 + 8 = 15$, which is the same as the right-hand side.

$x + 8 = 15$
$x + 8 - 8 = 15 - 8$
$x = 15 - 8$
$\underline{x = 7}$

Exercise 1

1 Get x alone on one side of the equation to solve these equations.
a) $x + 9 = 12$
b) $x + 5 = 16$
c) $x - 2 = 14$
d) $x - 7 = 19$
e) $x - 3 = 12$
f) $x + 8 = 14$
g) $x - 5 = -3$
h) $x - 12 = -1$
i) $6 = x + 10$
j) $18 = x - 8$
k) $-2 = 7 + x$
l) $40 = x - 12$
m) $24 = x - 11$
n) $32 = x - 17$
o) $x - 22 = 27$
p) $x + 31 = 30$

Example 2

Solve the equation $15 - x = 7$.
1. Add x to both sides of the equation — this means you don't have a minus sign in front of x.
2. Now you can solve the equation as before.
3. Don't forget to check your answer.

$15 - x = 7$
$15 = x + 7$
$\underline{x = 8}$

2 Solve these equations. Start by adding x to both sides.
a) $12 - x = 9$
b) $4 - x = 2$
c) $15 - x = 14$
d) $14 - x = 19$
e) $2 - x = 7$
f) $4 - x = 12$
g) $8 - x = 14$
h) $5 - x = 7$

3 Solve the following equations.
a) $x + 7 = 12$
b) $x + 8 = 26$
c) $5 - x = 21$
d) $28 = 20 - x$
e) $16 = x + 10$
f) $18 - x = 9$
g) $28 = 7 + x$
h) $12 - x = 23$
i) $x - 9 = 12$
j) $x - 8 = 14$
k) $35 = 31 - x$
l) $32 - x = 17$

4 Solve the following equations.
a) $x + 2.5 = 2$
b) $x - 7.3 = 1.6$
c) $5.6 + x = 2.1$
d) $5.2 = 2.8 - x$
e) $1.6 = x + 2.3$
f) $6.2 - x = 9.8$
g) $3.47 = 7.18 + x$
h) $6.03 - x = 0.58$

Example 3

Solve the equation $5x = 15$.

1. Get x on its own by dividing both sides of the equation by 5.
2. Remember: $5x \div 5 = x$

$5x = 15$
$5x \div 5 = 15 \div 5$
$\underline{x = 3}$

Exercise 2

1 Get x alone on one side of the equation to solve these equations.
   a) $7x = 35$ b) $8x = 24$ c) $9x = 54$ d) $10x = 110$
   e) $11x = 143$ f) $12x = 18$ g) $16x = 56$ h) $14x = 91$
   i) $4x = 6$ j) $9x = 1.8$ k) $2x = 1.5$ l) $5x = 22.5$

2 Solve the following equations.
   a) $3.5x = 49$ b) $4.5x = 81$ c) $7.5x = 75$ d) $10.5x = 126$
   e) $12.5x = 250$ f) $22.5x = 180$ g) $37.5x = 600$ h) $62.5x = 1125$

3 Solve the following equations.
   a) $6x = -18$ b) $5x = -20$ c) $7x = -14$ d) $15x = -150$
   e) $2.5x = -25$ f) $1.5x = -1.8$ g) $3.5x = -7$ h) $6.5x = -1.3$

Example 4

Solve the equation $-6x = 9$.

1. This time, divide both sides by -6.
2. Remember: $-6x \div (-6) = x$

$-6x = 9$
$-6x \div (-6) = 9 \div (-6)$
$\underline{x = -1.5}$

4 Solve these equations by dividing both sides by a negative number.
   a) $-5x = 50$ b) $-8x = 24$ c) $-3x = 27$ d) $-7x = 35$
   e) $-4x = -16$ f) $-7x = -56$ g) $-9x = 108$ h) $-13x = 195$

5 Solve the following equations.
   a) $-3x = -12$ b) $40x = -32$ c) $-4.5x = -2.7$ d) $50x = -3.4$
   e) $60x = -36$ f) $-6.4x = -0.48$ g) $75x = -45$ h) $-80x = -56$

Example 5

Solve the equation $\frac{x}{5} = 3$.

1. Multiply both sides by 5.
2. Remember: $\frac{x}{5} \times 5 = x$

$\frac{x}{5} = 3$
$\frac{x}{5} \times 5 = 3 \times 5$
$\underline{x = 15}$

Exercise 3

1 Solve the following equations.

a) $\frac{x}{3} = 2$ b) $\frac{x}{10} = 4$ c) $\frac{x}{4} = 11$ d) $\frac{x}{6} = -3$

e) $\frac{x}{5} = 1.5$ f) $\frac{x}{3} = 0.4$ g) $\frac{x}{11} = -0.5$ h) $\frac{x}{2} = -3.2$

2 Solve these equations by multiplying both sides by a negative number.

a) $-\frac{x}{4} = 3$ b) $-\frac{x}{5} = 6$ c) $-\frac{x}{10} = 1.1$ d) $-\frac{x}{3} = 0.5$

e) $-\frac{x}{2.1} = 2.5$ f) $-\frac{x}{3.3} = 1.4$ g) $-\frac{x}{0.2} = 3.2$ h) $-\frac{x}{2.5} = 6.3$

Example 6

Solve the equation $\frac{3x}{4} = 6$.

1. Multiply both sides by 4.
2. Then divide both sides by 3.

$\frac{3x}{4} = 6$

$3x = 6 \times 4 = 24$

$x = 24 \div 3 = 8$

$x = 8$

3 Solve the following equations.

a) $\frac{4x}{3} = 12$ b) $\frac{2x}{5} = 6$ c) $\frac{6x}{7} = 12$ d) $\frac{5x}{6} = 3$

e) $\frac{7x}{5} = 1.4$ f) $\frac{2x}{1.5} = -0.2$ g) $\frac{3x}{0.1} = -0.6$ h) $\frac{11x}{2.2} = 6.3$

Two-Step Equations

"Two-step equations" need to be solved in two stages — and you need to do them in the **right order**.

Example 7

Solve the equation $2x + 3 = 11$.

1. $2x + 3$ means "take your value of x and then: (i) multiply it by 2, (ii) add 3".
   To get x on its own, "undo" these steps, but in the opposite order.
2. First, subtract 3.
3. Then divide by 2.
4. Check your answer: $(2 \times 4) + 3 = 8 + 3 = 11$

$2x + 3 = 11$

$2x = 11 - 3 = 8$

$x = 8 \div 2 = 4$

$x = 4$

Exercise 4

1 Solve the following two-step equations.
  a) $8x + 10 = 66$
  b) $10x + 15 = 115$
  c) $12x + 9 = 105$
  d) $15x + 12 = 72$
  e) $20x + 86 = 6$
  f) $25x + 140 = 15$
  g) $27x + 99 = 18$
  h) $35x + 80 = 10$

2 Solve the following equations.
  a) $16x - 6 = 10$
  b) $15x - 8 = 22$
  c) $14x - 17 = 25$
  d) $28x - 14 = 42$
  e) $1.5x - 3 = -24$
  f) $1.8x - 8 = -62$
  g) $2.6x - 7 = -59$
  h) $4.8x - 9 = -57$

3 Solve the following equations.
  a) $6x - 12 = 48$
  b) $8x + 15 = 71$
  c) $10x - 7 = 73$
  d) $12x + 8 = 44$
  e) $18x - 6 = -60$
  f) $20x - 12 = -132$
  g) $4x + 12 = -8$
  h) $2x + 9 = -2$

4 The expression $\frac{x}{2} - 1$ means: (i) divide x by 2, (ii) subtract 1.
"Undo" these two steps in the opposite order to solve the equation: $\frac{x}{2} - 1 = 3$

5 Solve the following equations
  a) $\frac{x}{2} + 1 = 7$
  b) $\frac{x}{3} - 2 = 2$
  c) $\frac{x}{6} + 4 = 16$
  d) $\frac{x}{10} - 3 = -1$
  e) $\frac{x}{4} - 5 = -9$
  f) $\frac{x}{2} - 1 = 3.5$
  g) $\frac{x}{5} + 3 = -5$
  h) $\frac{x}{7} - 8 = -11$

6 a) Write down the equation you get if you add $5x$ to both sides of the equation $20 - 5x = 10$.
  b) Solve your equation to find x.

7 Solve the following equations.
  a) $12 - 4x = 8$
  b) $47 - 9x = 11$
  c) $8 - 7x = 22$
  d) $17 - 10x = 107$

Example 8

Solve the equation $8(x + 2) = 36$.

There are two ways to do this — you'll get the same result both ways.

<u>Either</u>:
1. $8(x + 2)$ means: "add 2 to x, then multiply by 8". $8(x + 2) = 36$
2. So to find x, first divide by 8. $x + 2 = 36 \div 8 = 4.5$
3. And then subtract 2. $x = 4.5 - 2 = 2.5$
     $x = 2.5$

<u>Or</u>:
1. Multiply out the brackets. $8x + 16 = 36$
2. Subtract 16. $8x = 36 - 16 = 20$
3. And then divide by 8. $x = 20 \div 8 = 2.5$
     $x = 2.5$

Exercise 5

1 Solve the following equations.
   a) $7(x + 4) = 63$
   b) $8(x + 4) = 88$
   c) $11(x + 3) = 132$
   d) $14(x + 5) = 98$
   e) $16(x - 3) = -80$
   f) $13(x - 4) = -91$
   g) $14(x - 2) = -98$
   h) $18(x - 3) = -180$
   i) $2.5(x + 4) = 30$
   j) $1.5(x + 2) = 12$
   k) $3.5(x + 6) = 63$
   l) $4.5(x + 3) = 72$
   m) $7.5(x - 4) = 60$
   n) $4.2(x - 5) = 63$
   o) $12.5(x - 4) = 75$
   p) $6.5(x - 6) = 78$
   q) $98 = 7(2 - x)$
   r) $165 = 15(4 - x)$
   s) $315 = 21(6 - x)$
   t) $171 = 4.5(8 - x)$

9.2 Solving Harder Equations

Sometimes equations have an 'unknown' on both sides.

Example 1

Solve the equation $5x + 6 = 2x + 18$.

1. First subtract $2x$ from both sides.
   This leaves x on only one side of the equation.
2. Now you can solve the equation as before.
   Subtract 6 from both sides...
   ...and then divide by 3.
3. Remember to check your answer:
   $(5 \times 4) + 6 = 26$ and $(2 \times 4) + 18 = 26$.

$5x + 6 = 2x + 18$
$3x + 6 = 18$
$3x = 12$
$x = 12 \div 3$
$\underline{x = 4}$

Exercise 1

1 Solve these equations. Start by subtracting a multiple of x from both sides.
   a) $6x - 4 = 2x + 16$
   b) $17x - 2 = 7x + 8$
   c) $9x - 26 = 5x - 14$
   d) $10x - 5 = 3x + 9$
   e) $14x - 7 = 6x + 41$
   f) $15x - 12 = 6x + 15$
   g) $8x - 4 = 2x + 44$
   h) $15x - 8 = 4x + 47$
   i) $21x - 5 = 5x + 11$

2 Solve the following equations. Start by adding a multiple of x to both sides.
   a) $13x - 35 = 45 - 3x$
   b) $20x - 18 = 54 - 16x$
   c) $17x - 9 = 57 - 5x$
   d) $14x - 9 = 31 - 6x$
   e) $6x - 12 = 51 - 3x$
   f) $5x - 13 = 87 - 5x$
   g) $82 - 8x = 10 - 6x$
   h) $7x - 8 = 70 - 6x$
   i) $4x - 15 = 147 - 14x$

3 Solve the following equations.
   a) $4x - 3 = 0.5 - 3x$
   b) $10x - 18 = 10.2 + 4x$
   c) $4x + 9 = 6 - x$
   d) $6x - 2 = -18 - 2x$
   e) $11x - 1 = 5.3 + 2x$
   f) $2x - 2 = -11.6 - 2x$
   g) $56 - 7x = -48 + 6x$
   h) $4x - 8.6 = 48.1 - 5x$
   i) $-x + 1 = 28 + 2x$

Example 2

Solve the equation $4(x + 2) = 2(x + 6)$.
1. Multiply out the brackets.
2. Now you can solve the equation as before.
3. Remember to check your answer:
   $4 \times (2 + 2) = 16$ and $2 \times (2 + 6) = 16$.

$4(x + 2) = 2(x + 6)$
$4x + 8 = 2x + 12$
$2x + 8 = 12$
$2x = 4$
$\underline{x = 2}$

Exercise 2

1 Solve the following equations by first multiplying out the brackets.
a) $3(x + 2) = x + 14$
b) $9(x - 1) = x + 15$
c) $6(x + 2) = 3x + 48$
d) $5(x + 3) = 2x + 57$
e) $7(x - 2) = 2x + 36$
f) $10(x + 2) = 5x + 90$
g) $8(x - 8) = 2(x - 2)$
h) $6(x - 3) = 3(x + 8)$
i) $20(x - 2) = 5(x + 1)$

2 Solve the following equations.
a) $5(x - 5) = 2(x - 14)$
b) $4(x - 3) = 2(x - 8)$
c) $6(x - 2) = 3(x + 6)$
d) $6(x - 1.5) = 2(x - 3.5)$
e) $7(x - 2.5) = 14(x - 3)$
f) $9(x - 3.3) = -6(x + 1.7)$
g) $-4(x - 3) = 8(0.7 - x)$
h) $6(x - 1) = 4(6.2 - 2x)$
i) $8(x + 3) = 9(12.3 - x)$

3 Solve the following equations.
a) $4(2x + 1) = 2x + 34$
b) $11(3x - 5) = 5x - 195$
c) $5(4x - 1) = 2x + 7$
d) $5(6x - 2) = 2(2x - 31)$
e) $7(3x + 2) = 5(9x - 0.08)$
f) $7(2x + \frac{1}{7}) = 14(3x - 0.5)$
g) $10(x - 2) = -2(\frac{4}{3} + 7x)$
h) $4(3x - 3) = -2(\frac{76}{9} + 5x)$

Example 3

Solve the equation $\frac{x}{3} = 7 - 2x$.

1. Multiply both sides by 3.
2. Then solve in the normal way.
3. Remember to check your answer.

$\frac{x}{3} = 7 - 2x$
$x = 3(7 - 2x)$
$x = 21 - 6x$
$7x = 21$
$\underline{x = 3}$

Exercise 3

1 Solve the following equations. Start by multiplying both sides by a number.
a) $\frac{x}{4} = 1 - x$
b) $\frac{x}{3} = 8 - x$
c) $\frac{x}{5} = 11 - 2x$
d) $\frac{x}{2} = 5 - x$
e) $\frac{x}{6} = 1 - 2x$
f) $\frac{x}{3} = x + 4$
g) $\frac{x}{4} = 10 - x$
h) $\frac{x}{5} = x + 4$
i) $\frac{x}{5} = -22 - 2x$

2 Solve the following equations.

a) $\frac{x}{3} = 2(x-5)$
b) $\frac{x}{2} = 4(x-7)$
c) $\frac{x}{5} = 2(x+9)$
d) $\frac{x}{2} = 2(x+5)$
e) $\frac{x}{4} = -2(x+18)$
f) $\frac{x}{4} = 3(x-55)$

Example 4
Solve the equation $\frac{x-2}{2} = \frac{6-x}{6}$.

1. Cross-multiply — multiply the top of each fraction by the bottom of the other.
   (This is the same as first multiplying both sides by 2 and then multiplying both sides by 6.)
2. Then solve in the normal way.
3. Remember to check your answer.

$6(x-2) = 2(6-x)$
$6x - 12 = 12 - 2x$
$8x = 24$
x = 3

Exercise 4

1 Solve the following equations.

a) $\frac{x+4}{2} = \frac{x+10}{3}$
b) $\frac{x+2}{2} = \frac{x+4}{6}$
c) $\frac{x+3}{4} = \frac{x+9}{7}$
d) $\frac{x-2}{3} = \frac{x+4}{5}$
e) $\frac{x-3}{4} = \frac{x+2}{8}$
f) $\frac{x-6}{5} = \frac{x+3}{8}$

2 Solve the following equations.

a) $\frac{x-17}{4} = \frac{8-x}{5}$
b) $\frac{x-2}{4} = \frac{15-2x}{3}$
c) $\frac{x-4}{6} = \frac{12-3x}{2}$
d) $\frac{x-6}{2} = \frac{8-2x}{4}$
e) $\frac{x-9}{2} = \frac{2-3x}{4}$
f) $\frac{x-12}{6} = \frac{4-2x}{3}$

Exercise 5 — Mixed Exercise
Solve the following.

1
a) $24x - 3 = -21$
b) $32x - 8 = -16$
c) $35x - 14 = -42$
d) $45x - 7 = -52$
e) $7 - 6x = 43$
f) $14 - 8x = 46$
g) $8 - 3x = 47$
h) $10 - 2.5x = 27.5$
i) $5.5x + 0.8 = 7.2$

2
a) $12(x-3) = 4x + 92$
b) $15(x-4) = 6x + 21$
c) $9(x-4) = 4(x+6)$
d) $7(x-2) = 3(2-x)$
e) $9(x-1) = 3(-8-x)$
f) $12(x-2) = 4(3-x)$

3
a) $\frac{x}{2} = 5$
b) $\frac{x}{3} = 18$
c) $\frac{x}{12} = 3.7$
d) $\frac{x}{7} = 1.8$

4
a) $\frac{3x}{7} = x + 4$
b) $\frac{2x}{3} = 4 - 5x$
c) $\frac{x}{4} = 2(4.5 - x)$
d) $\frac{5x}{2} = 2(6.75 - x)$

5
a) $\frac{x+5}{3} = \frac{x+9}{2}$
b) $\frac{x+7}{3} = \frac{x+13}{6}$
c) $\frac{7x+3}{2} = \frac{x+19}{4}$

9.3 Writing Your Own Equations

Sometimes you'll need to write your own equation based on a description of a situation. Always read the question very carefully. And always **simplify** your equations as much as possible.

Example 1

I think of a number, double it, and add 3. The result equals 17.
What is the number I thought of?

1. You don't know what the number is yet. Call the number x.

2. Doubling x gives $2x$. Then: $2x + 3 = 17$.
   Then adding 3 gives $2x + 3$.
   The result is 17.

   So: $2x = 14$
   $x = 14 \div 2$
   $\underline{x = 7}$

3. Solve the equation in the normal way.
   Then check your answer.

Exercise 1

1 Which number did I think of in each situation below?
"*I think of a number, and then...*"

a) ...I add 5 to it. The result equals 12.
b) ...I add 8 to it. The result equals 23.
c) ...I subtract 12 from it. The result equals 7.
d) ...I subtract 14 from it. The result equals 15.
e) ...I multiply it by 2. The result equals 22.
f) ...I multiply it by 6. The result equals 54.
g) ...I divide it by 3. The result equals 12.
h) ...I divide it by 7. The result equals 16.

2 Which number did I think of in each situation below?
"*I think of a number, and then...*"

a) ...I double it, and then add 3. The result equals 19.
b) ...I multiply it by 3, and then add 7. The result equals 43.
c) ...I multiply it by 2, and then subtract 5. The result equals 15.
d) ...I multiply it by 4, and then subtract 10. The result equals 44.

Example 2

Use the triangle to write an equation involving x.
Solve your equation to find x.

1. The angles in a triangle always add up to 180°. $x + 2x + 60° = 180°$

2. Simplify your equation. $3x + 60° = 180°$

3. Solve the equation in the normal way. $3x = 180° - 60° = 120°$
   Then check your answer. $x = 120° \div 3$
   $\underline{x = 40°}$

Section 9 — Equations and Inequalities

Exercise 2

1 For each triangle below:
   (i) Write an equation involving x. (All the angles are measured in degrees.)
   (ii) Solve your equation to find x.

a) Triangle with angles $3x$, $5x$, $20°$

b) Triangle with angles $110°$, $3x$, $4x$

c) Triangle with angles $23x$, $7x$, $30x$

d) Triangle with angles $2x + 40°$, $3x$, $5x$

e) Triangle with angles $3x - 10°$, $10x$, $6x$

f) Triangle with angles $3x - 5°$, $5x$, $5x - 10°$

Example 3

The perimeter of this rectangle is 78 cm.
Write an equation involving x to show this.
Then solve your equation to find x.

Rectangle: $(x + 12)$ cm by $(x + 3)$ cm

1. Find the perimeter by adding together the lengths of all the sides. This must equal 78.

   Perimeter $= (x + 12) + (x + 3) + (x + 12) + (x + 3)$
   $= 4x + 30$
   So $4x + 30 = 78$.

2. Solve the equation in the normal way. Then check your answer.

   $4x = 78 - 30 = 48$
   $x = 48 \div 4$
   $\underline{x = 12}$

2 For each shape below:
   (i) Write an equation involving x.
   (ii) Solve your equation to find x.

a) Rectangle: $4x$ cm by $(x + 8)$ cm, Perimeter = 146 cm

b) Rectangle: $(x + 10)$ cm by $(x + 3)$ cm, Perimeter = 196 cm

3 The length of each side of this regular hexagon is $(x + 4)$ cm, and the total perimeter is 180 cm.
   a) Write an equation involving x.
   b) Solve your equation to find the value of x.

4 A regular octagon has a perimeter of 320 cm. Each side measures $(2x + 4)$ cm. Find the value of x.

Example 4

One day a furniture store sells 3 times as many leather sofas
as it does fabric sofas. On this day it sells a total of 28 sofas.
How many leather sofas were sold?
1. Call the number of fabric sofas sold x. Then the number of leather sofas sold is $3x$.
2. 28 sofas are sold in total, so use this to write an equation. $x + 3x = 4x$, $4x = 28$
3. Solve the equation to find x.   So $x = 7$, and $3x = 21$
4. Multiply by 3 to find the number of leather sofas sold.   **21** leather sofas were sold.

5   A bride and groom each invite an equal number of guests to their wedding.
All of the groom's guests are able to come, but 8 of the bride's guests can't come.
If a total of 60 guests **can** attend, how many guests did the groom invite?

6   One day a bed shop sells a total of 54 beds. 10 fewer king-size beds were sold than single beds,
and 16 more double beds were sold than single beds. How many single beds were sold?

7   Rufina makes and sells 20 fruit scones and 10 cheese scones. The ingredients cost £y in total.
She sells each fruit scone for £x and each cheese scone for 10p more than a fruit scone.
    a) Write an expression in terms of x and y for the profit, in £, that she makes.
    b) If she spent £6 on ingredients and made a profit of £10,
what was the selling price of a fruit scone?

9.4 Solving Inequalities

Write **inequalities** using these symbols: $>$ greater than $\geq$ greater than or equal to
    $<$ less than $\leq$ less than or equal to

Solving inequalities is very similar to solving equations. Your answer will also be an inequality.

Example 1

Show the following inequalities on a number line: a) $x > 1$ b) $x \leq 1$

The empty circle shows 1 is **not** included —
$x = 1$ does **not** make the inequality true.

The solid circle shows 1 **is** included —
$x = 1$ **does** make the inequality true.

Exercise 1

1   Insert $>$ or $<$ in each of the boxes to complete the following inequalities.
    a) 6 ☐ 1   **b)** 2 ☐ 8   **c)** –1 ☐ –3   **d)** –7 ☐ 1

2   Describe in words what is meant by the following inequalities.
    a) $x \geq 1$ **b)** $x < 7$ **c)** $x > -4$ **d)** $x \leq 9$
    e) $x < 8$ **f)** $x \leq -5$ **g)** $x \geq 3$ **h)** $x > -4$

3 Write each of the following as an inequality.
   a) x is greater than 4
   b) x is less than or equal to 12
   c) x is greater than or equal to 8
   d) x is less than 3

4 Show the following inequalities on a number line.
   a) $x \geq 12$
   b) $x < 22$
   c) $x > -6$
   d) $x \leq -3$
   e) $x < 18$
   f) $x > -25$
   g) $x \leq 34$
   h) $x < 45$
   i) $x \geq 57$
   j) $x < 65$
   k) $x \geq -7$
   l) $x \leq -4$

Example 2

Solve the inequalities: a) $x + 4 < 8$ b) $x - 7 \geq 2$
Show your solutions on a number line.

1. You need to get x on its own on one side. But you must always do the same to both sides of an inequality.

   a) $x + 4 < 8$
   $x + 4 - 4 < 8 - 4$
   $\underline{x < 4}$

2. If the question uses < or >, so will your answer.
   If the question uses ≤ or ≥, so will your answer.

   b) $x - 7 \geq 2$
   $x - 7 + 7 \geq 2 + 7$
   $\underline{x \geq 9}$

Exercise 2

1 Solve the following inequalities. Show each of your solutions on a number line.
   a) $x + 9 > 14$
   b) $x + 3 \leq 12$
   c) $x - 2 \geq 14$
   d) $x - 7 < 19$
   e) $x - 13 \geq 17$
   f) $x + 5 > 2$
   g) $x - 5 < -3$
   h) $x + 1 \leq -1$

2 Solve the following inequalities.
   a) $x - 9 > 8$
   b) $x + 7 < 17$
   c) $x + 4 \geq 5$
   d) $x - 2 \leq 11$
   e) $x + 16 \geq 20$
   f) $x - 4 > 9$
   g) $x + 12 < -18$
   h) $x - 8 \leq -3$

Example 3

Solve the inequality $2 > x - 5$. Show your solution on a number line.

1. This time x is on the right-hand side of the inequality. But as before, just do the same to both sides (so here, add 5).

   $2 > x - 5$
   $2 + 5 > x - 5 + 5$

2. So $7 > x$ (that is, '7 is greater than x').

   $7 > x$

3. To move x to the left-hand side, you have to swap the direction that the inequality points (showing that 'x is less than 7').

   $\underline{x < 7}$

Section 9 — Equations and Inequalities

3 This question is about the inequality $6 > x$.
   a) Describe in words what is meant by this inequality.
   b) Rewrite the inequality by completing the following: $x \square 6$
   c) Show the solution to this inequality on a number line.

4 Rewrite each of these inequalities with x on the left-hand side.
   a) $12 \geq x$ **b)** $4 < x$ **c)** $15 \leq x$ **d)** $14 > x$

5 Solve the following inequalities. Show each of your solutions on a number line.
   a) $18 < x + 2$ **b)** $12 \leq x - 4$ **c)** $1 > x - 17$ **d)** $31 \geq x + 30$

Example 4

Solve the following inequalities: a) $4x < 12$ b) $\frac{x}{3} \geq 5$

1. Do the same to both sides of an inequality.
2. Multiplying or dividing by a positive number doesn't change the direction of the inequality sign.

a) $4x < 12$
$4x \div 4 < 12 \div 4$
$\underline{x < 3}$

b) $\frac{x}{3} \geq 5$
$\frac{x}{3} \times 3 \geq 5 \times 3$
$\underline{x \geq 15}$

6 Solve the following inequalities by dividing both sides by a positive number.
   a) $3x \geq 9$ **b)** $5x < 25$ **c)** $2x > 8$ **d)** $7x \leq 21$
   e) $4x < -16$ **f)** $9x > -72$ **g)** $11x \leq 33$ **h)** $2x < 45$
   i) $6x \geq 57$ **j)** $2x < 15$ **k)** $4x \geq -32$ **l)** $2x \leq -1.5$

7 Solve the following inequalities by multiplying both sides by a positive number.
   a) $\frac{x}{2} \geq 3$ **b)** $\frac{x}{5} < 2$ **c)** $\frac{x}{3} < 8$ **d)** $\frac{x}{7} \leq 5$
   e) $\frac{x}{8} < -1$ **f)** $\frac{x}{6} \leq 0.5$ **g)** $\frac{x}{1.1} \geq 10$ **h)** $\frac{x}{0.2} < -3.2$
   i) $\frac{x}{5.5} < 1.2$ **j)** $\frac{x}{4} \geq -0.3$ **k)** $\frac{x}{0.1} \leq 1.8$ **l)** $\frac{x}{0.3} < -2.3$

Example 5

Solve the following inequalities: a) $2x + 4 > 10$ b) $\frac{x+4}{2} \leq 3$

1. Solve these in the same way that you'd solve two-step equations.
2. In a), first subtract 4, then divide by 2. In b), first multiply by 2, then subtract 4.

a) $2x + 4 > 10$
$2x > 6$
$\underline{x > 3}$

b) $\frac{x+4}{2} \leq 3$
$x + 4 \leq 6$
$\underline{x \leq 2}$

Solve each of the inequalities in **Questions 8-10**.

8   **a)** $4x + 11 < 23$ **b)** $5x + 3 \leq 43$ **c)** $3x - 7 \geq -1$ **d)** $7x - 12 > 65$
   e) $2x + 16 \geq -8$ **f)** $9x - 14 > -5$ **g)** $8x - 4.2 < 12.6$ **h)** $4x + 2.6 \leq 28.6$

9 a) $\frac{x+2}{3} < 1$ b) $\frac{x+4}{5} \geq 2$ c) $\frac{x-8}{2} > 7$ d) $\frac{x-8}{4} \leq 0.5$

10 a) $\frac{x}{4} - 2.5 \geq 1$ b) $\frac{x}{2} + 5.5 > 7$ c) $\frac{x}{8} - 3.1 < -1$ d) $\frac{x}{3.2} + 1.3 \leq 5$

Compound Inequalities

A compound inequality is like "two inequalities in one".
For example, $3 < x \leq 9$ means that **both** the following are true: $3 < x$ **and** $x \leq 9$.
So $3 < x \leq 9$ means: x is between 3 and 9 (including 9, but not including 3).

Example 6
Show the inequality $2 \leq x < 4$ on a number line.

1. Write down the two separate inequalities. $2 \leq x < 4$ means $2 \leq x$ and $x < 4$.
2. Find the number x is greater than... $2 \leq x$ is the same as $x \geq 2$
   ...and the number x is less than.   So $x \geq 2$ and $x < 4$.
3. Draw the number line. Here, x is between 2 and 4 (including 2, but not including 4).

Example 7
Solve the inequality $-1 < 2x + 2 < 4$. Show your solution on a number line.

1. Write down the two separate inequalities.
   $-1 < 2x + 2$ and $2x + 2 < 4$
   Or: $2x + 2 > -1$ and $2x + 2 < 4$

2. Solve the inequalities separately.
   ① $2x + 2 > -1$
      $2x > -3$
      $x > -1.5$
   ② $2x + 2 < 4$
      $2x < 2$
      $x < 1$

3. Draw the number line.   So $\underline{x > -1.5 \text{ and } x < 1}$.
   Or you can write: $\underline{-1.5 < x < 1}$.

Exercise 3

1 Show the following inequalities on a number line.
   a) $1 < x \leq 6$ b) $12 \leq x \leq 15$ c) $-1 \leq x < 8$
   d) $25 \leq x \leq 30$ e) $4 \leq x < 9$ f) $35 < x < 40$
   g) $0 < x < 7$ h) $36 < x \leq 42$ i) $-2.4 \leq x < 1.6$

2 Solve the following inequalities. Show each of your solutions on a number line.
   a) $7 < x + 3 \leq 15$ b) $2 \leq x - 4 \leq 12$ c) $-1 \leq x + 5 \leq 4$
   d) $21 \leq x - 16 \leq 44$ e) $5.1 \leq x + 2.5 < 9.7$ f) $-5.6 < x - 6.8 < 12.9$

Section 9 — Equations and Inequalities

3 Solve the following inequalities.
   a) $16 < 4x < 28$
   b) $32 < 2x \leq 42$
   c) $-24 < 8x \leq 40$
   d) $27 < 4.5x \leq 72$
   e) $-22.5 \leq 7.5x < 30$
   f) $62.72 < 11.2x \leq 94.08$

4 Solve the following inequalities.
   a) $17 < 6x + 5 < 29$
   b) $8 < 3x - 4 \leq 26$
   c) $-42 < 7x + 7 \leq 91$
   d) $9 < 1.5x + 3 \leq 9.9$
   e) $-18.8 \leq 10x + 14.2 < -6.8$
   f) $61.7 < 12x - 6.3 \leq 101.7$

Exercise 4 — Mixed Exercise
Solve the following inequalities.

1 a) $x + 7 > 22$
   b) $x - 6 \leq 14$
   c) $x + 11 \geq 17$
   d) $x - 7 < 21$
   e) $x + 5.6 \leq 14.6$
   f) $x - 6.23 \geq 9.75$
   g) $x + 7.01 < 33.25$
   h) $x + 11.08 > 21.82$

2 a) $4x \geq 84$
   b) $3x < 28.5$
   c) $9x \geq -56$
   d) $6x \leq -5.4$
   e) $\frac{x}{2} \leq 6$
   f) $\frac{x}{3} > 25$
   g) $\frac{x}{5} \geq -4$
   h) $\frac{x}{4} < -16$

3 a) $5x + 12 < 37$
   b) $11x + 7 \leq -15$
   c) $21x - 33 \geq -12$
   d) $4x - 5 > 2$
   e) $4x + 11 < 11$
   f) $12x - 3 \leq -8$
   g) $17x + 8 \geq -9$
   h) $4.6x - 5.6 > 2.3$

4 a) $\frac{x+5}{5} < 5$
   b) $\frac{x - 5.6}{3} \geq 6$
   c) $\frac{x}{3} - 4 \leq 6.2$
   d) $\frac{x}{4} + 3.7 > 8.4$

5 a) $-2 < 2x + 3 < 5$
   b) $-30 < 7x + 12 \leq 61$
   c) $-9 < 13x - 9 \leq 17$
   d) $-12 < 5x + 3 \leq 58$

9.5 Simultaneous Equations

Simultaneous equations have two unknowns, and you will be given two equations. The solution will be the values of the unknowns that make both equations true.

Example 1

Solve the simultaneous equations:
(1) $x + y = 11$
(2) $x - 3y = 7$

1. Subtract equation (2) from equation (1) to eliminate x.
$$x + y = 11$$
$$- \ x - 3y = 7$$
$$4y = 4$$
2. Solve the equation for y.
$$y = 1$$
3. Put $y = 1$ into one of the original equations and solve for x.
$$x + 1 = 11$$
$$x = 10$$
4. Use the other equation to check the answer.
Check: $x - 3y = 10 - 3(1) = 7$
$x = 10, y = 1$

Exercise 1

Solve each of the following pairs of simultaneous equations.

1 a) $x + 3y = 10$; $x + y = 6$
   b) $4x + 3y = 31$; $x + 3y = 10$
   c) $x + 3y = 13$; $x - y = 5$
   d) $2x - y = 7$; $4x + y = 23$
   e) $x + 2y = 6$; $x + y = 2$
   f) $3x - 2y = 16$; $2x + 2y = 14$
   g) $x - y = 8$; $x + 2y = -7$
   h) $2x + 4y = 16$; $3x + 4y = 24$

Example 2

Solve the simultaneous equations: (1) $5x - 4y = 13$
(2) $2x + 6y = -10$

1. Multiply equation (1) by 3 and equation (2) by 2 to get $+12y$ in one and $-12y$ in the other.
2. Add the resulting equations to eliminate y.
3. Solve the equation for x.
4. Put $x = 1$ into one of the original equations and solve for y.
5. Use the other equation to check the answer.

$3 \times$ (1): $15x - 12y = 39$
$2 \times$ (2): $4x + 12y = -20$
$19x = 19$
$x = 1$

$5 - 4y = 13$
$-4y = 8$
$y = -2$

Check: $2x + 6y = 2(1) + 6(-2) = -10$

$x = 1, \; y = -2$

2. a) $3x + 2y = 16$; $2x + y = 9$
   b) $4x + 3y = 16$; $5x - y = 1$
   c) $4x - y = 22$; $3x + 4y = 26$
   d) $5x - 3y = 12$; $2x - y = 5$
   e) $2x + 3y = 10$; $x - y = 5$
   f) $4x - 2y = 8$; $x - 3y = -3$
   g) $4x + 2y = 16$; $8x + y = 14$
   h) $2x - y = 6$; $-4x - 7y = 6$
   i) $8y - 2d = -2$; $5y + 4d = 25$
   j) $3e - 5r = 4$; $9e + 2r = 29$
   k) $4p + 3m = 6$; $7p - 9m = 39$
   l) $2c + 4v = 30$; $3c + 2v = 37$

3. a) $2c + 3d = 9$; $3c + 2d = 11$
   b) $4x + 3y = 10$; $3x + 4y = 11$
   c) $3x - 2y = 8$; $5x - 3y = 14$
   d) $4p + 3q = 17$; $3p - 4q = 19$
   e) $4u + 7v = 15$; $5u - 2v = 8$
   f) $5k + 3l = 4$; $3k + 2l = 3$
   g) $2e + 5f = 16$; $3e - 2f = 5$
   h) $2m - 3n = 7$; $5m + 4n = 6$

Example 3

Sue buys 4 dining chairs and 1 table for £142. Ken buys 6 of the same chairs and 2 of the same tables for £254. What is the price of one chair? What is the price of one table?

1. Choose some variables. Let the cost of one chair be £c and the cost of one table be £t.
2. Write the question as two simultaneous equations.

   (1) $4c + t = 142$
   (2) $6c + 2t = 254$

3. Multiply equation (1) by 2 so that when you subtract equation (2) the $2t$ cancels out.

   $2 \times$ (1): $8c + 2t = 284$
   (2): $-\;\; 6c + 2t = 254$
   $2c = 30$

4. Solve the resulting equation for c.
   $c = 15$

5. Put $c = 15$ into one of the original equations and solve for t.

   $4(15) + t = 142$
   $60 + t = 142$
   $t = 82$

6. Use the other equation to check the answer. Check: $6c + 2t = 6(15) + 2(82) = 254$

7. Write the answer in terms of the original question.

   The chairs cost £15 each.
   The tables cost £82 each.

4 The sum of two numbers, x and y, is 58, and the difference between them is 22. Given that x is greater than y, use simultaneous equations to find both numbers.

5 A grandfather with 7 grandchildren bought 6 sherbet dips and 1 Supa-Choc bar for £1.70 last week. He bought 3 sherbet dips and 4 Supa-Choc bars for £2.60 the week before. Calculate the price of each item.

9.6 Solving Quadratic Equations

Quadratic equations are equations of the form **ax^2 + bx + c = 0**, where a, b and c are constants (a ≠ 0).

Example 1
Solve the equation $x^2 - 16 = 0$.
1. There's no x term, so just rearrange the equation to get x^2 on its own. $x^2 = 16$
2. Square root both sides. $x = \pm 4$
3. Write down the positive and negative values for x.   **$x = 4$** or **$x = -4$**

Exercise 1
1 Solve the following equations giving exact solutions.
a) $x^2 - 4 = 0$ b) $x^2 - 1 = 0$ c) $x^2 - 25 = 0$ d) $x^2 - 64 = 0$
e) $x^2 - 121 = 0$ f) $x^2 - 100 = 0$ g) $x^2 - 2 = 0$ h) $x^2 - 7 = 0$

You'll often need to use **factorisation** to solve quadratic equations. If you can factorise an equation to give **($x - m$)($x - n$) = 0**, then either $x - m = 0$ or $x - n = 0$, so **$x = m$ or $x = n$**.

Example 2
Solve the equation $x^2 - 7x = 0$.
1. Factorise the left-hand side. $x(x - 7) = 0$
2. Set each factor equal to zero. $x = 0$ or $x - 7 = 0$
3. Solve to find the two possible values for x.   **$x = 0$** or **$x = 7$**

Exercise 2
1 Find the possible values of x for each of the following.
a) $x(x + 8) = 0$ b) $x(x - 5) = 0$ c) $x(x + 6) = 0$ d) $x(3 - x) = 0$

2 Solve the following equations.
a) $x^2 + 6x = 0$ b) $x^2 + x = 0$ c) $x^2 - 6x = 0$ d) $x^2 - 24x = 0$
e) $x^2 - 3x = 0$ f) $x^2 + 5x = 0$ g) $x - x^2 = 0$ h) $12x - x^2 = 0$

Example 3
Solve the equation $x^2 - 3x + 2 = 0$.
1. Factorise the left-hand side. $(x - 1)(x - 2) = 0$
2. Put each factor equal to zero. $x - 1 = 0$ or $x - 2 = 0$
3. Solve to find the two possible values for x.   **$x = 1$** or **$x = 2$**

Exercise 3

1 Find the possible values of x for each of the following.
   a) $(x - 5)(x - 1) = 0$
   b) $(x + 2)(x + 6) = 0$
   c) $(x - 9)(x + 7) = 0$

2 a) Factorise the following expressions.
   (i) $x^2 + 7x + 10$ (ii) $x^2 + 9x + 20$ (iii) $x^2 + 13x + 36$ (iv) $x^2 + 2x - 24$

   b) Use your answers to part (a) to solve the following equations.
   (i) $x^2 + 7x + 10 = 0$ (ii) $x^2 + 9x + 20 = 0$ (iii) $x^2 + 13x + 36 = 0$ (iv) $x^2 + 2x - 24 = 0$

3 Solve the following equations by factorising.
   a) $x^2 + 2x + 1 = 0$
   b) $x^2 + 3x + 2 = 0$
   c) $x^2 - 7x + 12 = 0$
   d) $x^2 + 4x + 4 = 0$
   e) $x^2 - 4x + 4 = 0$
   f) $x^2 + 2x - 15 = 0$
   g) $x^2 - 10x + 24 = 0$
   h) $x^2 - 5x + 6 = 0$
   i) $x^2 - 4x - 21 = 0$

9.7 Equations and Inequalities Problems

Exercise 1

1 Solve the following equations.
   a) $\frac{x + 8}{3} = 4$
   b) $\frac{x - 5}{6} = 5$
   c) $\frac{x - 2.5}{7} = 3$
   d) $\frac{x + 6}{5} = 4.2$
   e) $9 + 5x = 54$
   f) $12 - 6x = 84$
   g) $30 + 7x = 9$
   h) $13 - 3.5x = 34$
   i) $\frac{x + 3}{5} = -12$
   j) $\frac{x - 3}{7} = -5$
   k) $24 - 8x = -16$
   l) $17 - 12x = 149$

2 Solve the following equations.
   a) $72 = 4.5(8 + 2x)$
   b) $7(x - 3) = 3(x - 6)$
   c) $6(x - 2) = 4(x - 3)$
   d) $12(x + 3) = 6(x + 15)$
   e) $108 = 6(2 - x)$
   f) $9x - 144 = 42 + 15x$
   g) $5x - 9 = 54 - 8x$
   h) $12(x - 3) = 4(6 + 2x)$
   i) $12(4x - 3) = 4(2x + 1)$

3 Solve the following equations.
   a) $\frac{x - 2}{5} = \frac{9 - x}{3}$
   b) $\frac{x - 5}{6} = \frac{12 - 3x}{4}$
   c) $\frac{x - 7}{8} = \frac{15 - 4x}{6}$
   d) $\frac{x}{7} = 10 - 3x$
   e) $\frac{3x}{8} = 16 + 3x$
   f) $\frac{2x}{5} = 18 - 2x$

4 An electrician charges £x for each hour worked plus a £35 call-out charge. He does a job lasting 4 hours for which his total bill is £170. How much does the electrician charge per hour?

5 Jane bought 7 cereal bars costing x pence each. She also bought 4 cans of drink for 45p each. The total cost was £4.25. How much does each cereal bar cost?

6 a) Use the triangle to write an equation involving x.

(Triangle with angles $3x + 10°$, $x + 10°$, $x + 10°$)

b) Use your equation to find the sizes of the triangle's angles.

7 Find the sizes of this triangle's angles.

(Triangle with angles $2x + 30°$, $3x - 10°$, $4x - 11°$)

Section 9 — Equations and Inequalities

8 The perimeter of this rectangle is 158 cm. What is the value of x?

$\frac{x}{2}$ cm
$(2x + 4)$ cm

9 The perimeter of this rectangle is 191 m. Find the value of x.

$\left(\frac{1}{2}x - 4\right)$ m
$3(x - 3)$ m

Exercise 2

1 Solve the following inequalities. Show each of your solutions on a number line.
a) $x - 8 > 17$
b) $x - 11 \leq -3$
c) $x + 24 \geq 6$
d) $x + 7 > -3$
e) $x + 2.7 \geq 6.2$
f) $x + 6.9 < -3.1$
g) $x - 6.2 \leq 81.6$
h) $x - 3.25 < -7.48$
i) $\frac{x}{7} \geq 4$
j) $7x < 84$
k) $\frac{x}{9} < 7$
l) $6.5x \leq 45.5$
m) $5x \geq 35$
n) $\frac{x}{40} < 20$
o) $2.5x > 20$
p) $\frac{x}{2.5} \leq 6$

2 Solve the following inequalities.
a) $3x + 6 \leq 39$
b) $8x - 7 \geq 33$
c) $9x - 6 < 111$
d) $18x + 24 > 132$
e) $0.4x + 2.3 > 12.3$
f) $7 \leq 33 - x$
g) $3x - 5 < -11$
h) $0.24x + 3.7 \geq 1.5$

3 Solve the following inequalities. Show each of your solutions on a number line.
a) $70 < 13x + 5 \leq 96$
b) $49 < 15x + 4 < 79$
c) $-5 \leq 12x + 7 < 43$
d) $-37 \leq 7x + 12 \leq -2$
e) $15 < 12x + 3 < 27$
f) $-17 < 6x + 7 \leq 49$

4 Solve the following simultaneous equations.
a) $4x + 3y = 1$
   $6x - 6y = -30$
b) $3p - 2q = 19$
   $-2p + 4q = -10$
c) $2r + 4s = 24$
   $6r - 5s = 21$
d) $2m + 3n = -16$
   $5m - 4n = 6$

5 Solve the following equations.
a) $x^2 - 36 = 0$
b) $x^2 - 81 = 0$
c) $x^2 - 3 = 0$
d) $x^2 - 5 = 0$
e) $2x^2 - 18 = 0$
f) $4x^2 - 64 = 0$

6 Solve the following equations.
a) $x^2 - 4x - 5 = 0$
b) $x^2 - 14x + 24 = 0$
c) $x^2 - 7x + 6 = 0$
d) $x^2 - 10x + 21 = 0$
e) $x^2 + 9x + 18 = 0$
f) $x^2 + 9x - 22 = 0$

7 The area of this rectangle is 10 cm². Find x.

$(x + 3)$ cm
x cm

8 The area of this rectangle is 45 cm². Find x.

$(x + 2)$ cm
$(x - 2)$ cm

9 The quadratic expression $x^2 + 10x + 25$ represents the area of a square with side length $(x + a)$ cm.
a) Factorise the expression $x^2 + 10x + 25$ to find the value of a.
b) Given that the area of the square is 81 cm², find the value of x.

Section 10 — Formulas and Functions

10.1 Writing Formulas

A **formula** is like a set of instructions for working something out.
For example, $s = 4t + 3$ is a formula for s — it tells you how to find s, assuming you know the value of t.

The part after the equals sign is an **algebraic expression** — here, the algebraic expression involves t.

Example 1

Write an expression for the number of marbles I have in each case below.

a) I have a bag containing m marbles. I then lose 8 marbles.
   1. "I have a bag containing m marbles." $\quad m$
   2. "I then lose 8 marbles" — so you need to subtract 8. $\quad \mathbf{m - 8}$

b) My brother has 12 marbles, which is m marbles more than I own.
   1. "My brother has 12 marbles..." $\quad 12$
   2. "...which is m marbles more than I own."
      This means I have m marbles less than my brother. $\quad \mathbf{12 - m}$

Exercise 1

1 Write an algebraic expression for each of the quantities asked for below.

   a) I have c carrots. Su has 6 carrots more than me. How many carrots does Su have?
   b) Harry has s sugar cubes. Zurab takes 3 of them. How many sugar cubes does Harry now have?
   c) Daisy has p plants. Iris has 8 fewer plants. How many plants does Iris have?
   d) Elmer has r rabbits. Sam gives him 20 more rabbits. How many rabbits does Elmer have now?

2 Write an algebraic expression for each of the quantities asked for below.

   a) Genevieve has d daffodils, which is 8 more than Mariella has.
      How many daffodils does Mariella have?
   b) Jessica has 6 shirts, which is s more than Becky. How many shirts does Becky have?
   c) George spends m minutes on his maths homework, which is half as long as Chris.
      How many minutes does Chris spend on his homework?
   d) Emily has c chairs, which is 3 times more than Sara. How many chairs does Sara have?

Example 2

I have m marbles. I lose half of those marbles, but then someone gives me 6 of their marbles. Write an expression for how many marbles I have now.

1. "I have m marbles." $\quad m$
2. "I lose half of those marbles" — so divide m by 2. $\quad \dfrac{m}{2}$
3. "...someone gives me 6 of their marbles" — so add 6. $\quad \dfrac{m}{2} + 6$

3 Claudia owns f films. Barry owns twice as many films as Claudia.
   a) How many films does Barry own?
   b) How many films do Claudia and Barry own in total?
   c) How many films would they own in total if they each gave away 3 of their films?

4 I have b flower bulbs. To find the number of flowers that should grow from them, multiply the number of bulbs by 3 and then add 5. How many flowers can I expect?

5 Alf has £18. He then works in a shop for h hours. For each hour he works, he is paid £8. How much money (in pounds) does Alf have now?

6 To hire a go-kart, you have to pay: (i) 25p for each lap of the track you do (the variable charge)
     plus (ii) a fixed fee of £7
   I do n laps of the track.
   a) Write an expression for the cost (in pounds) of the variable charge.
   b) Write an expression for the total cost (in pounds) I will have to pay.

Example 3

Write a formula to show how much it costs to hire a boat for h hours if the total cost in pounds (C) is made up of: (i) a charge of £5 for each hour
           plus (ii) a fixed cost of £25

1. You need an expression showing the total cost. Cost (in pounds) for 1 hour = 5
2. Multiply the number of hours (h) by 5. ⟹ Cost (in pounds) for h hours = $h \times 5 = 5h$
   Then you need to add the fixed cost of £25. ⟹ Fixed cost (in pounds) = 25
3. A formula for C must start with "$C = ...$". So $\underline{C = 5h + 25}$

Exercise 2

1 It costs £3 per hour to park a car. Write a formula for the cost in pounds (C) to park for h hours.

2 It takes 2 minutes to drive 1 km. Write a formula for the time taken in minutes (T) to drive k km.

3 Tom gets paid w pounds for each hour he works in his local shop.
   Write a formula for the total amount he gets paid in pounds (P) if he works for 8 hours.

4 Katie always eats 2 more apples for her pudding than Laura does.
   Write a formula for the number of apples (n) that Katie eats if Laura eats a apples.

5 Sue runs r km, but Ellie runs 5 km less. Write a formula for the distance in km (d) that Ellie runs.

6 Write a formula for the cost in pounds (C) of hiring a minibus
   for n hours if it costs £5.50 for each hour plus a fixed charge of £F.

7 Write a formula for the cost in pounds (C) of having t trees
   cut down if it costs p pounds per tree plus a fixed amount of £25.

8 To hire a boat costs a £10 fixed fee plus 22 pence per mile for each mile covered.
   Write a formula for finding the cost in pounds (C) of hiring a boat and covering m miles.

9 To hire a bouncy castle costs a £125 fixed fee plus 80 pence per minute it is used.
   Write a formula for the cost in pounds (C) of hiring a bouncy castle for h hours.

10.2 Substituting into a Formula

Substituting numbers into a formula means replacing any letters with numbers.

Example 1

The area (A) of a rectangle is given by the formula $A = bh$.
Find the value of A when $b = 5$ and $h = 6$.

1. Write down the formula.
2. Replace each letter with its value, and carry out the calculation.

$A = bh = b \times h$
$= 5 \times 6$
$= \underline{\mathbf{30}}$

Exercise 1

1 Find the value of y in each of the following given that $x = 7$.
   a) $y = x + 4$ **b)** $y = x - 3$ **c)** $y = 12 - x$ **d)** $y = 6x$

2 Find the value of y in each of the following given that $m = -3$.
   a) $y = m - 8$ **b)** $y = m + 2$ **c)** $y = -4 + m$ **d)** $y = \frac{12}{m}$

3 If $x = 4$ and $y = 3$, then find the value of z in each of the following.
   a) $z = x + 2$ **b)** $z = y - 1$ **c)** $z = x + y$ **d)** $z = y - x$
   e) $z = 2x$ **f)** $z = 3y$ **g)** $z = 3y - 2$ **h)** $z = 6x - y$

4 The area (A, in cm²) of this rectangle is given by the formula $A = 6w$.
Find A for the values of w below.
   a) $w = 7$ **b)** $w = 8$ **c)** $w = 14$
   d) $w = 23$ **e)** $w = 37$ **f)** $w = 41$

5 The temperature in degrees Fahrenheit (f) is given by the formula $f = 1.8c + 32$, where c is the temperature in degrees Celsius.
Convert the following temperatures to degrees Fahrenheit.
   a) 15 °C   **b)** 6 °C   **c)** 24 °C   **d)** 100 °C

6 The formula for working out the speed (s, in metres per second) of a moving object is $s = \frac{d}{t}$, where d is the distance travelled (in metres) and t is the time taken (in seconds).
Find the speed (in metres per second) of each of the following.
(Give your answers to 3 significant figures.)
   a) a runner who travels 800 metres in 110 seconds
   b) a cheetah that travels 400 metres in 14 seconds
   c) a car that travels 1000 metres in 60 seconds
   d) a plane that travels 640 000 metres in 3600 seconds
   e) a satellite that travels 40 000 000 metres in 5000 seconds

Section 10 — Formulas and Functions

Example 2

The sum of the first n square numbers is $1^2 + 2^2 + 3^2 + 4^2 + \ldots + n^2$.

This sum (S) is given by the formula $S = \frac{n}{6}(2n^2 + 3n + 1)$.

Use the formula to find S when $n = 10$.

1. Write down the formula.

2. Replace n with 10.

3. Remember BODMAS:
   Evaluate the brackets first.
   Inside the brackets: (i) Find 10^2 first.
   (ii) Then do the multiplications.
   (iii) Then do the additions.

   Now evaluate the rest.

$S = \frac{n}{6}(2n^2 + 3n + 1)$

$= \frac{10}{6}(2 \times 10^2 + 3 \times 10 + 1)$

$= \frac{10}{6}(2 \times 100 + 3 \times 10 + 1)$

$= \frac{10}{6}(200 + 30 + 1) = \frac{10}{6} \times 231$

$S = \frac{10}{6} \times 231 = \underline{\mathbf{385}}$

7 If $m = 4$ and $n = 3$, then find the value of p in each of the following.
 a) $p = mn$
 b) $p = m^2$
 c) $p = m - n^2$
 d) $p = \frac{3m}{n}$
 e) $p = m(m - n)$
 f) $p = n^2 + n$
 g) $p = \frac{n}{m}$
 h) $p = mn^2$

8 Use the formula $S = \frac{1}{2}n(n + 1)$ to find S when:
 a) $n = 10$
 b) $n = 100$
 c) $n = 1000$
 d) $n = 5000$

Example 3

Use the formula $f = 1.8c + 32$ to find the temperature in degrees Fahrenheit (f) equivalent to the following temperatures in degrees Celsius (c).
 a) $c = -17$ b) $c = 37.4$

1. Write down the formula.
2. Replace each letter with its value, and do the calculation.

a) $f = 1.8c + 32$
   $= 1.8 \times (-17) + 32$
   $= -30.6 + 32 = \underline{\mathbf{1.4}}$

b) $f = 1.8c + 32$
   $= 1.8 \times 37.4 + 32$
   $= 67.32 + 32 = \underline{\mathbf{99.32}}$

9 If $a = -4$ and $b = -3$, then find the value of c in each of the following.
 a) $c = a - 4$
 b) $c = b + a$
 c) $c = 4b$
 d) $c = 6b - a$
 e) $c = b^3$
 f) $c = -\frac{4b}{3a}$
 g) $c = 5a - b^2$
 h) $c = 6a^2 - 2ab + 2b^2$

10 If $p = -4.8$ and $q = 3.2$, then find the value of r in each of the following.
 a) $r = p + 6.7$
 b) $r = q - p$
 c) $r = -4q$
 d) $r = 8.4q - p$
 e) $r = -q^3$
 f) $r = \frac{2.1q}{3.5p}$
 g) $r = -3.2p + q^2$
 h) $r = 4.1p^2 - 2.8pq$

11 Find the value of x in each of the following given that $r = \frac{3}{4}$ and $s = -\frac{1}{3}$.
  a) $x = 4r$
  b) $x = -2s$
  c) $x = \frac{s}{r}$
  d) $x = rs$
  e) $x = r + s$
  f) $x = r - s$
  g) $x = 4r + s$
  h) $x = 3s + 2r$

12 Use the formula $c = \frac{5}{9}(f - 32)$ to convert the following temperatures in degrees Fahrenheit (f) to degrees Celsius (c).
  a) 212 °F
  b) 64.4 °F
  c) −40 °F
  d) 98.6 °F

13 The area (A, in cm²) of this circle is given by the formula $A = \pi r^2$.
Find A for the values of r below. Give your answers to 1 decimal place.
  a) $r = 5$ cm
  b) $r = 3.5$ cm
  c) $r = 11.1$ cm
  d) $r = 6.4$ cm

14 The number of seconds (T) taken for a pendulum to swing forwards and then backwards once is given by the formula $T = 2\pi\sqrt{\frac{l}{10}}$, where l is the length of the pendulum in metres.

Taking π to be 3.142, calculate (to 1 decimal place) how long it will take a pendulum to swing backwards and forwards once if:
  a) $l = 1$ metre
  b) $l = 0.5$ metres
  c) $l = 0.25$ metres
  d) $l = 16$ metres

15 Use the formula $A = \frac{1}{2}bh$ to find the area (A, in m²) of a triangle with base b and height h, if:
  a) $b = 4$ m, $h = 6$ m
  b) $b = 2$ m, $h = 3$ m
  c) $b = 4$ m, $h = 6$ m
  d) $b = 0.4$ m, $h = 1.8$ m

16 Find the volumes (V, in cm³) of the cylinders below, using the formula on the left.
Give your answers to 3 significant figures.

  $V = \pi r^2 h$

  a) 3 cm, 8 cm
  b) 11 cm, 5 cm

17 Find the volumes (V, in cm³) of the cones below, using the formula on the left.
Give your answers to 3 significant figures.

  $V = \frac{\pi r^2 h}{3}$

  a) 2 cm, 6 cm
  b) 8.2 cm, 4.3 cm

Section 10 — Formulas and Functions

Example 4

Use the formula $v = u + at$ to find v if $u = 2.6$, $a = -18.3$ and $t = 4.9$.

1. You have three values to substitute this time — u, a and t.
2. Replace each letter with its value...
3. ...and carry out the calculation.

$v = u + at$
$= 2.6 + (-18.3 \times 4.9)$
$= 2.6 + (-89.67)$
$= \underline{\mathbf{-87.07}}$

18 Use the formula $v = u + at$ to find v if:
- a) $u = 3$, $a = 7$ and $t = 5$
- b) $u = 12$, $a = 17$ and $t = 15$
- c) $u = 2.3$, $a = 4.1$ and $t = 3.4$
- d) $u = 5.25$, $a = 9.81$ and $t = 4.39$
- e) $u = 3$, $a = -10$ and $t = 5.6$
- f) $u = -34$, $a = -1.37$ and $t = 63.25$

19 Use the formula $s = ut + \frac{1}{2}at^2$ to find s if:
- a) $u = 7$, $a = 2$ and $t = 4$
- b) $u = 24$, $a = 11$ and $t = 13$
- c) $u = 3.6$, $a = 5.3$ and $t = 14.2$
- d) $u = 9.8$, $a = 48.2$ and $t = 15.4$
- e) $u = -11$, $a = -9.81$ and $t = 12.2$
- f) $u = 66.6$, $a = -1.64$ and $t = 14.2$

10.3 Rearranging Formulas

Making a letter the **subject** of a formula means rearranging the formula so that that letter is on its own. It's a bit like solving an equation — you always have to do the same thing on **both sides**.

Example 1

Make b the subject of the formula $A = bh$.

1. Write down the original formula.
2. Divide both sides by h.
   Then b is on its own, since $bh \div h = b$.
3. In your final answer, always write the letter that's on its own on the left-hand side of the formula. All the other letters should be on the right-hand side.

$A = bh$

$\frac{A}{h} = b$

$\underline{b = \frac{A}{h}}$

Exercise 1

1 Make x the subject of the following formulas. All your answers should begin "$x =$".
- a) $y = x + 2$
- b) $b = x - 5$
- c) $z = 7 + x$
- d) $m = x + 2.3$
- e) $p = x - 8.4$
- f) $z = 12 + x$

2 Make x the subject of the following formulas.
- a) $z = x + r$
- b) $3y = x + 4r$
- c) $16r = 23t + x$

3 Make x the subject of the following formulas.
   a) $z = 4x$
   b) $p = 17x$
   c) $r = 4.2x$
   d) $s = 3.7x$
   e) $s = 6x$
   f) $s = 3.5x$

4 Make x the subject of the following formulas.
   a) $y = \frac{x}{8}$
   b) $z = \frac{x}{17}$
   c) $t = \frac{x}{8.6}$
   d) $m = \frac{x}{4}$
   e) $n = \frac{x}{6.1}$
   f) $p = \frac{x}{17.4}$

5 Make x the subject of the following formulas.
   a) $abc = 2x$
   b) $t = xy$
   c) $uv + y = 4.2x$
   d) $v = 7.3wx$
   e) $vwy = 6x$
   f) $2z + 4 = 2.2xy$

Example 2

Make x the subject of the formula $y = -2x$.

1. Write down the original formula. $y = -2x$
2. Divide both sides by -2.
   Then x is on its own, since $\frac{-2x}{-2} = x$. $\frac{y}{-2} = x$
3. Write your final answer with x on the left-hand side.
   Remember, $\frac{y}{-2} = -\frac{y}{2}$. $x = -\frac{y}{2}$

Example 3

Make x the subject of the formula $c = \frac{5}{6}x$.

1. Write down the original formula. $c = \frac{5}{6}x$
2. Multiply both sides by 6.
   Remember, $\frac{5}{6} \times 6 = 5$. $6c = 5x$
3. Divide both sides by 5. Remember, $\frac{6c}{5} = \frac{6}{5}c$. $\frac{6}{5}c = x$
4. Write your final answer with x on the left-hand side.
   You could also write this as $x = \frac{6c}{5}$. $x = \frac{6}{5}c$

6 Make x the subject of the following formulas.
   a) $p = -3x$
   b) $q = -\frac{x}{5}$
   c) $n = -6x$
   d) $m = -\frac{x}{9}$
   e) $r = -2.1x$
   f) $s = -\frac{x}{2.5}$

7 Make y the subject of the following formulas.
   a) $a = \frac{4}{5}y$
   b) $b = \frac{3}{4}y$
   c) $c = \frac{2}{3}y$
   d) $d = \frac{7}{11}y$
   e) $e = \frac{10}{3}y$
   f) $f = \frac{20}{7}y$

Section 10 — Formulas and Functions

8 Make s the subject of the following formulas.

a) $y = s - 4$
b) $t = \frac{s}{11}$
c) $d = \frac{3}{4}s$
d) $m = \frac{4}{5}s$
e) $r = -16s$
f) $p = -14.2s$
g) $a = \frac{5}{4}s$
h) $b = -\frac{6}{7}s$
i) $c = -11.6s$

9 The volume (V) of a cylinder is given by the formula $V = \pi r^2 h$, where r is the radius of the cylinder and h is its height.

a) Make h the subject of the formula.
b) Find the height of each of these cylinders.

(i) 3 cm, $V = 18\pi$ cm³
(ii) 5 cm, $V = 60\pi$ cm³

Two-Step Rearrangements

Example 4

Make x the subject of the formula $y = 4 + bx$.

1. $4 + bx$ means "take your value of x and then: (i) multiply by b (ii) add 4"
   To get x on its own, undo these steps, but in the opposite order.
2. First, subtract 4 from both sides.
3. Then divide both sides by b.
4. Write x on the left-hand side of the formula.

$y = 4 + bx$
$y - 4 = bx$
$\frac{y - 4}{b} = x$
$x = \frac{y - 4}{b}$

Exercise 2

1 Make x the subject of the following formulas.

a) $y = 5x + 3$
b) $z = 8x - 2$
c) $p = 15x + 18$
d) $m = 6x + 3$
e) $n = 5x + 4$
f) $r = 2x - 8$

2 Make y the subject of the following formulas.

a) $z = \frac{y + 4}{3}$
b) $x = \frac{7 + y}{4}$
c) $s = \frac{y - 2}{9}$
d) $t = \frac{y - 5.3}{9.7}$
e) $v = \frac{y + 11}{-3}$
f) $w = \frac{-65 + y}{5}$

3 Make x the subject of the following formulas.

a) $u = 4(x - 2)$
b) $v = 8(x + 4)$
c) $w = 3(x - 4)$
d) $p = -6(x - 8)$
e) $q = -5(x + 1)$
f) $r = -0.2(x + 5)$

4 Make y the subject of the following formulas.

a) $p + 3 = 4y - 2$
b) $q + 7 = 9y + 11$
c) $r - 5 = 21y - 9$
d) $s - 8 = 8y + 7$
e) $t + 6 = 3y - 2$
f) $u - 11 = 13y - 14$

5 a) Rearrange the formula $v = u + at$ to make a the subject.
　　b) Find a if $u = 3$, $v = 38$ and $t = 5$.
　　c) Find a if $u = 2.3$, $v = 16.24$ and $t = 3.4$.
　　d) Find a if $u = 5.25$, $v = 48.32$ and $t = 4.39$.

6 The temperature in degrees Fahrenheit (f) is given by the formula $f = \frac{9}{5}c + 32$, where c is the temperature in degrees Celsius.
　　a) Rearrange the formula to make c the subject.
　　b) Find c if:　　(i) $f = 50$　　(ii) $f = 80$　　(iii) $f = -30$　　(iv) $f = 32$

7 The surface area (A) of the shape on the right is given approximately by the formula $A = 21.5d^2$.
　　a) Rearrange the formula to make d the subject.
　　b) Find d if:
　　　　(i) $A = 344$ cm²　　(ii) $A = 134.375$ cm²

8 The perimeter (P) of the shape on the right is given by the formula $P = 2(2x + y)$.
　　a) Rearrange the formula to make x the subject.
　　b) Find x if:
　　　　(i) $P = 14$ and $y = 3$　　(ii) $P = 32$ and $y = 4$

9 Make x the subject of these formulas:
　　a) $\frac{x + y}{x} = 6$　　b) $\frac{3 + xy + x}{x + 1} = y$　　c) $y = xy + x$

10.4 Functions

A **function** takes a number, applies some **operations** to it, then outputs a new number. Function machines can be used forwards or backwards to find an output or input.

Example 1

This function machine represents the function 'multiply by 3 then add 4'.

$x \longrightarrow \boxed{\times 3} \longrightarrow \boxed{+ 4} \longrightarrow y$

a) Find the value of y when $x = 3$.
　Put 3 into the machine:　$3 \xrightarrow{\times 3} 9 \xrightarrow{+4} 13$　　So $\underline{y = 13}$.

b) Find the value of x when $y = 37$.
　Put 37 into the end of the machine and work backwards by doing the opposite operations in reverse order.
　　$37 \xrightarrow{-4} 33 \xrightarrow{\div 3} 11$　　So $\underline{x = 11}$.

Section 10 — Formulas and Functions

Exercise 1

1 The function machine below represents the function 'divide by 5 then add 7'.

$$x \longrightarrow \boxed{\div 5} \longrightarrow \boxed{+7} \longrightarrow y$$

Find the value of y for the following values of x.
- **a)** $x = 20$
- **b)** $x = 35$
- **c)** $x = 45$
- **d)** $x = -10$

2 The function machine below represents the function 'subtract 3 then multiply by 6'.

$$x \longrightarrow \boxed{-3} \longrightarrow \boxed{\times 6} \longrightarrow y$$

- **a)** What is the value of y when $x = 11$?
- **b)** Given that $y = 72$, find the value of x.

3 The equation $y = 7x - 2$ is represented by the function machine below.

$$x \longrightarrow \boxed{\times 7} \longrightarrow \boxed{-2} \longrightarrow y$$

- **a)** Given that $x = -1$, find the value of y.
- **b)** When $y = 19$, find the value of x.

4 Jared wants to write the equation $y = 4x + 1$ as a function machine.

- **a)** Copy and complete this function machine to show Jared's equation.

$$x \longrightarrow \boxed{} \longrightarrow \boxed{} \longrightarrow y$$

- **b)** Use the function machine to find the value of x when $y = 17$.

5 For each of the function machines below, write down the equation they represent.

- **a)** $x \longrightarrow \boxed{\times 6} \longrightarrow \boxed{-3} \longrightarrow y$
- **b)** $x \longrightarrow \boxed{+2} \longrightarrow \boxed{\div 4} \longrightarrow y$
- **c)** $x \longrightarrow \boxed{+5} \longrightarrow \boxed{\times 2} \longrightarrow y$
- **d)** $x \longrightarrow \boxed{\div 7} \longrightarrow \boxed{+3} \longrightarrow y$

10.5 Formulas and Functions Problems

Example 1

An isosceles triangle with one angle of size x has two angles of size y.

a) Write a formula for y in terms of x.
1. The angles in a triangle add up to 180°, so first subtract x from 180°.
2. Then divide by 2 to find the size of y.

$$y = \frac{180° - x}{2}$$

b) Find y when $x = 30°$.
Substitute $x = 30°$ into the formula.

$$y = \frac{180° - x}{2} = \frac{180° - 30°}{2} = \frac{150°}{2} = \underline{75°}$$

c) Rearrange the formula to make x the subject.
1. Multiply both sides by 2.
2. Add x to both sides.
3. Subtract $2y$ from both sides.

$$y = \frac{180° - x}{2}$$
$$2y = 180° - x$$
$$2y + x = 180°$$
$$\underline{x = 180° - 2y}$$

Exercise 1

1 Chloe gets 45 fewer free minutes on her mobile phone each month than Wassim.
  a) If Wassim gets w free minutes, write a formula for the number of free minutes (c) Chloe gets.
  b) Find c when $w = 125$.

2 The number of matchsticks (m) needed to make h hexagons as shown is given by the formula $m = 5h + 1$.
  a) Rearrange this formula to make h the subject.
  b) Use your formula to find h when $m = 36$.

3 The formula for calculating the cost (C, in £) of gas is $C = 0.06n + 7.5$, where n is the units used.
  a) Find the cost if 275 units of gas were used.
  b) Rearrange this formula to make n the subject.
  c) Use your formula to find how many units of gas were used if the gas bill is £40.50.

4 To book a swimming pool for a party, there is a fixed charge of £30 plus a fee of £1.25 for each person who attends.
  a) Write a formula to calculate the hire cost (C, in £) for n people.
  b) Calculate the hire cost when $n = 32$.
  c) Rearrange your formula to make n the subject.
  d) If the total cost of hiring the pool was £80, how many people attended the party?

5 A joint of beef needs to be cooked for 35 minutes for each kilogram it weighs, plus an extra 25 minutes.
  a) Write a formula for the cooking time needed (T, in minutes) for a joint weighing w kilograms.
  b) Use your formula to find the cooking time needed for a joint weighing 5.2 kg.
  c) Rearrange your formula to make w the subject.
  d) Use your formula to find the weight of a joint that must be cooked for 3 hours and 48 minutes.

6 Debi is decorating her bathroom walls with black tiles and white tiles.
She uses 3 white tiles for every black tile, plus an extra 50 white tiles.
  a) Copy and complete the function machine below to represent the number of white tiles used, w, given the number of black tiles used, b.

  $b \longrightarrow \boxed{} \longrightarrow \boxed{} \longrightarrow w$

  b) If Debi uses 200 black tiles, how many white tiles does she use?
  c) Copy and complete the function machine to show the total number of tiles used, t, given the number of black tiles used, b.

  $b \longrightarrow \boxed{} \longrightarrow \boxed{} \longrightarrow t$

  d) If Debi uses 530 tiles in total, how many black tiles does she use?

Section 11 — Sequences

11.1 Sequences — Term-to-Term Rules

A **sequence** is a list of numbers or shapes which follows a particular **rule**.
Each number or shape in the sequence is called a **term**.
Sequences where you add or subtract the same number each time are called **arithmetic** sequences.
Sequences where you multiply or divide by the same number each time are called **geometric** sequences.

Example 1

The first term of a sequence is 3. The rule for finding the next term in the sequence is 'add 4 to the previous term'. Write down the first 5 terms of the sequence.

1. The first term is 3, so write this down.
2. Add 4 each time to find the terms.

3, 7, 11, 15, 19
+4 +4 +4 +4

Example 2

Consider the sequence 2, 6, 18, 54...

a) Explain the rule for finding the next term in the sequence.
b) Write down the next three terms in the sequence.

1. This time the rule for finding the next term involves multiplication.

   2 ×3→ 6 ×3→ 18 ×3→ 54...

2. Multiply each term by 3 to get the next term.

a) Multiply the previous term by 3.
b) 54, **162, 486, 1458**.
   ×3 ×3 ×3

Exercise 1

1. The first term of a sequence is 5. The rule for finding the next term in the sequence is 'add 4 to the previous term'. Write down the first 5 terms of the sequence.

2. The first term of a sequence is 2. The rule for finding the next term in the sequence is 'multiply the previous term by 2'. Write down the first 5 terms of the sequence.

3. Write down the first 5 terms of the sequence with:
   a) first term = 100; further terms generated by the rule 'subtract 6 from the previous term'.
   b) first term = 40; further terms generated by the rule 'divide the previous term by 2'.
   c) first term = 11; further terms generated by the rule 'multiply the previous term by –2'.

4. The first four terms of a sequence are 3, 6, 9, 12.
   a) Write down what you add to each term in the sequence to find the next term.
   b) Write down the next three terms in the sequence.

5. The first four terms of a sequence are 3, 6, 12, 24.
   a) Write down what you multiply each term in the sequence by to find the next term.
   b) Write down the next three terms in the sequence.

For **Questions 6-7**: (i) explain the rule for finding the next term in the sequence.
(ii) find the next three terms in the sequence.

6 a) 3, 5, 7, 9...   b) 1, 2, 4, 8...   c) 4, 12, 36, 108...   d) 4, 7, 10, 13...
   e) 5, 3, 1, –1...   f) 1, 1.5, 2, 2.5...   g) 0.01, 0.1, 1, 10...   h) 192, 96, 48, 24...

7 a) 0, –4, –8, –12...   b) –1, –3, –9, –27...   c) 16, 8, 4, 2...   d) 1, –2, 4, –8...

8 The first four terms of a sequence are 4, 10, 16, 22.
   a) Explain the rule for finding the next term in this sequence.
   b) Use your rule to find: (i) the 5th term   (ii) the 6th term   (iii) the 8th term

9 The first four terms of a sequence are 1, 3, 9, 27.
   a) Explain the rule for finding the next term in this sequence.
   b) Use your rule to find: (i) the 5th term   (ii) the 7th term   (iii) the 9th term

10 Copy the following sequences and fill in the blanks.
   a) 7, 13, 19 , 25, ☐, 37   b) 9, 5, ☐, –3, –7, –11   c) ☐, –3, –9, –27, ☐, –243
   d) –72, ☐, –18, –9, ☐, –2.25   e) ☐, 0.8, 3.2, 12.8, ☐, 204.8   f) –63, –55, ☐, ☐, ☐, –23

Example 3

Find the next three terms in the sequence 4, 5, 7, 10...

1. Try finding the difference between neighbouring terms.
2. Here, the difference is **increasing by 1** each time.
3. Use this to find the next three terms in the sequence.
   Start with 10. Then add 4. Then add 5. Then add 6.

4 5 7 10
 +1 +2 +3

10 14 19 25
  +4 +5 +6

Exercise 2

1 Consider the sequence 7, 8, 10, 13, 17...
   a) Find the difference between each term and the next for the first 5 terms.
   b) Find the next three terms in the sequence.

2 For each sequence below, find: (i) the difference between neighbouring terms for the first 5 terms,
                                   (ii) the next three terms in the sequence.
   a) 4, 5, 7, 10, 14...   b) 5, 7, 11, 17, 25...   c) 20, 18, 15, 11, 6...

3 Consider the sequence 1, 2, 0, 3, –1...
   a) Find the difference between each term and the next for the first 5 terms.
   b) Find the next three terms in the sequence.

4 The sequence 1, 1, 2, 3, 5... is known as the Fibonacci sequence. Each term in the sequence is found by adding together the previous two terms. Find the next three terms in the sequence.

5 The first 5 terms of a sequence are 1, 1, 2, 6, 24.
   a) For the first 5 terms, find the number you multiply by each time to get the next term.
   b) Find the next two terms in the sequence.

Example 4

The matchstick shapes below form the first three patterns in a sequence.

a) Draw the fourth and fifth patterns in the sequence.
b) How many matchsticks are needed to make the sixth pattern in the sequence?

1. You have to add an extra square to the previous pattern.
2. Adding an extra square means you have to add 3 matchsticks to the previous pattern.
3. There are 16 + 3 = 19 matchsticks in the sixth pattern.

a) *(fourth and fifth patterns shown)*
b) **19 matchsticks**.

Exercise 3

1 The first three patterns of several sequences are shown below.
For each of the sequences: **(i)** explain the rule for making the next pattern,
(ii) draw the fourth and fifth patterns in the sequence,
(iii) find the number of matches needed to make the sixth pattern.

a)
b)
c)

2 Below is a sequence of triangles made up of different numbers of circles.
The numbers of circles in each triangle form a sequence called the 'triangle numbers'.
For example, the first three triangle numbers are 1, 3 and 6.

a) Draw the next three triangles in the sequence, and write down the corresponding triangle numbers.
b) Explain the rule for generating the next triangle number in the sequence.
c) Find the 7th triangle number.

3 For each of the sequences below:
  (i) Draw the next three patterns in the sequence.
  (ii) Explain the rule for generating the number of circles in the next pattern.
  (iii) Work out how many circles there are in the 7th pattern.
  (iv) Work out how many circles there are in the 10th pattern.

a)
b)
c)

Section 11 — Sequences

11.2 Sequences — Position-to-Term Rules

You can also work out a term by using its **position** (n) in the sequence.
For example, the 1st term has $n = 1$, the 2nd term has $n = 2$, the 10th term has $n = 10$, and so on.

Example 1

The nth term of a sequence is $2n - 1$. Find the first four terms of the sequence.

1. To find the 1st, 2nd, 3rd and 4th terms of the sequence, substitute the values $n = 1$, $n = 2$, $n = 3$ and $n = 4$ into the formula.

    $(2 \times 1) - 1 = 1$
    $(2 \times 2) - 1 = 3$
    $(2 \times 3) - 1 = 5$
    $(2 \times 4) - 1 = 7$

2. Write the terms in order to form the sequence.   So the first four terms are **1, 3, 5, 7**.

Exercise 1

1 The nth term of a sequence is $2n + 3$.
   Find the value of the nth term when:
   a) $n = 1$ b) $n = 2$ c) $n = 3$ d) $n = 4$.

2 The nth term of a sequence is $20 - 2n$.
   Find the value of:
   a) the 1st term   b) the 2nd term   c) the 3rd term   d) the 4th term

3 The nth term of a sequence is $7n - 11$. Write down the first four terms of the sequence.

4 Find the first four terms of a sequence if the nth term is given by:
   a) $n + 5$ b) $3n + 2$ c) $4n - 2$ d) $5n - 1$
   e) $10 - n$ f) $3 - 4n$ g) $10n - 8$ h) $-7 - 3n$

5 Find the first four terms of a sequence if the nth term is given by:
   a) $n^2 + 1$ b) $2n^2 + 1$ c) $3n^2 - 1$ d) $n(n - 1)$

6 The nth term of a sequence is $2n + 20$. Find the value of:
   a) the 5th term   b) the 10th term   c) the 20th term   d) the 100th term

7 The nth term of a sequence is $100 - 3n$. Find the value of:
   a) the 3rd term   b) the 10th term   c) the 30th term   d) the 40th term

8 Each of the following gives the nth term for a different sequence.
   For each sequence, find: **(i)** the 5th term   **(ii)** the 10th term   **(iii)** the 100th term
   a) $n + 11$ b) $2n + 3$ c) $6n - 1$ d) $4n + 12$
   e) $100 - n$ f) $30 - 3n$ g) $100n - 8$ h) $-20 + 2n$

9 Each of the following gives the nth term for a different sequence.
   For each sequence, find: **(i)** the 2nd term   **(ii)** the 5th term   **(iii)** the 20th term
   a) $2n^2$ b) $2n^2 + 3$ c) $4n^2 - 5$ d) $n(n + 1)$

Section 11 — Sequences

Example 2

The nth term of a sequence is $4n + 5$. Which term has the value 41?

1. Make the nth term equal to 41. $\quad\quad 4n + 5 = 41$
2. Solve the equation to find n. $\quad\quad 4n = 36$
$\quad\quad\quad\quad\quad\quad\quad\quad\quad\quad\quad\quad\quad\quad n = 9$

So the **9th term** is 41.

Exercise 2

1 a) Find the value of n when $2n + 6 = 20$.
   b) The nth term of a sequence is $2n + 6$. Write down which term has the value 20.

2 a) Find the value of n when $6n - 3 = 15$.
   b) The nth term of a sequence is $6n - 3$. Write down which term has the value 15.

3 a) The nth term of a sequence is $7n + 4$. Which term of the sequence has the value 53?
   b) The nth term of a sequence is $5n - 8$. Which term of the sequence has the value 37?
   c) The nth term of a sequence is $4n + 3$. Which term of the sequence has the value 27?
   d) The nth term of a sequence is $2n - 5$. Which term of the sequence has the value 11?

4 The nth term of a sequence is $17 - 2n$.
   a) Which term of the sequence has the value 3?
   b) Which term of the sequence has the value 9?

5 The nth term of a sequence is $50 - 6n$. Find which terms have the following values.
   a) 2   b) 8   c) 14   d) 26

6 The nth term of a sequence is $n^2 - 1$.
   a) Which term of the sequence has the value 8?
   b) Which term of the sequence has the value 99?

7 The nth term of a sequence is $n^2 + 1$. Find which terms have the following values.
   a) 5   b) 26   c) 50   d) 82

8 The formulas for the number of matches in the nth pattern of the following 'matchstick sequences' are shown below. For each of the sequences:
   (i) find the number of matches needed to make the 6th pattern,
   (ii) find the number of matches needed to make the 100th pattern.

   a) Number of matches in nth pattern = $2n + 1$

   b) Number of matches in nth pattern = $4n - 1$

9 The formula for the number of circles in the nth triangle in this sequence is $\frac{n(n + 1)}{2}$.
   a) Find the number of circles needed to make the 6th triangle.
   b) Find the number of circles needed to make the 10th triangle.

11.3 Finding a Position-to-Term Rule

You need to be able to write a formula for the nth term of a sequence.

Example 1

Find the nth term of the sequence 5, 7, 9, 11...

1. Find the difference between each term and the next.

    5, 7, 9, 11 (+2, +2, +2)

2. Here, the terms increase by 2 each time, so the formula for the nth term must include '$2n$'.
    The complete formula for the nth term will be '$2n + a$', where a is a number you need to find using the first term of the sequence.

    nth term is $2n + a$

3. Substitute $n = 1$ into $2n + a$, and put it equal to 5. Then solve your equation to find a.

    $(2 \times 1) + a = 5$
    $a = 5 - 2 = 3$
    So the nth term is **$2n + 3$**.

4. Check your formula by using it to find another term. (Check: 2nd term is $2 \times 2 + 3 = 7$ ✔)

Example 2

Find the nth term of the sequence 45, 42, 39, 36...

1. Find the difference between each term and the next.

    45, 42, 39, 36 (−3, −3, −3)

2. Here, the terms decrease by 3 each time, so the nth term is $-3n + a$.

    nth term is $-3n + a$

3. Use the first term of the sequence to find a.
    Substitute $n = 1$ into $-3n + a$ and put it equal to 45.
    Solve the equation to find a.

    $(-3 \times 1) + a = 45$
    $a = 45 + 3 = 48$

4. Write down and check your formula.

    So the nth term is **$-3n + 48$**, or **$48 - 3n$**.
    (Check: 2nd term is $-3 \times 2 + 48 = 42$ ✔)

Exercise 1

1 The first 4 terms of a sequence are: 9, 13, 17, 21
   a) Find the difference between each term and the next.
   b) Copy and complete this formula for the nth term of the sequence: ☐$n + a$
   c) Use the first term of the sequence to find the value of a.
   d) Write down and check your formula for the nth term of the sequence.

2 Find the formula for the nth term of each of the following sequences.
   a) 7, 13, 19, 25...
   b) 3, 10, 17, 24...
   c) 4, 8, 12, 16...
   d) 6, 16, 26, 36...
   e) 5, 10, 15, 20...
   f) 7, 27, 47, 67...
   g) 41, 81, 121, 161...
   h) 3, 11, 19, 27...

3 Find the formula for the nth term of each of the following sequences.
   a) −1, 1, 3, 5...
   b) −2, 1, 4, 7...
   c) −9, −5, −1, 3...
   d) −45, −26, −7, 12...

4 Find the formula for the *n*th term of each of the following sequences.
   a) 10, 8, 6, 4...
   b) 5, 4, 3, 2...
   c) 15, 10, 5, 0...
   d) 40, 37, 34, 31...
   e) 70, 60, 50, 40...
   f) 78, 69, 60, 51...
   g) 60, 55, 50, 45...
   h) 100, 92, 84, 76...

5 Find the formula for the *n*th term of each of the following sequences.
   a) 4, −1, −6, −11...
   b) 6, 3, 0, −3...
   c) −10, −25, −40, −55...
   d) −39, −51, −63, −75...

6 Find the number of matchsticks in the *n*th pattern of the following sequences.
   a)
   b)

7 a) Find the *n*th term of sequence A, which starts 4, 7, 10, 13...
   b) Find the *n*th term of sequence B, which starts 5, 8, 11, 14...
   c) (i) How does each term in sequence B compare with the corresponding term in sequence A?
      (ii) What do you notice about the formulas giving the *n*th term for these two sequences?

8 a) Find the *n*th term of the sequence 6, 11, 16, 21...
   b) Use your answer to part **a)** to write down the *n*th term of the sequence 7, 12, 17, 22...

9 a) Find the *n*th term of the sequence 13, 9, 5, 1...
   b) Use your answer to part **a)** to write down the *n*th term of the sequence 11, 7, 3, −1...

Example 3

A sequence has *n*th term $3n + 2$. Is 37 a term in the sequence?

1. Make an equation by setting the formula for the *n*th term equal to 37. Then solve your equation to find *n*.
$$3n + 2 = 37$$
$$3n = 35$$
$$n = 11.666...$$

2. Since *n* is not a whole number, 37 is not a term in the sequence.

So 37 **is not** a term in the sequence.

Exercise 2

1 A sequence has *n*th term $2n + 1$. Show that 54 is **not** a term in this sequence.

2 Show that 80 is a term in the sequence with *n*th term equal to $3n − 1$.

3 A sequence has *n*th term $21 − 2n$. Show that −1 is a term in this sequence, and write down the corresponding value of *n* to show its position.

4 a) Find the *n*th term of the sequence whose first four terms are 4, 9, 14, 19...
   b) Is 34 a term in this sequence? If so, write down its position.

5 a) Find the *n*th term of the sequence whose first four terms are 12, 18, 24, 30...
   b) Is 34 a term in this sequence?

6 A sequence has *n*th term equal to $17 + 3n$. Determine whether each of the following is a term in this sequence.
   a) 52   b) 98   c) 105   d) 248   e) 996

7 A sequence starts −5, −1, 3, 7... Determine whether each of the following is a term in this sequence. For those that are, state the corresponding value of *n*.
   a) 43   b) 71   c) 138   d) 384   e) 879

Section 11 — Sequences **133**

Section 12 — Graphs and Equations

12.1 Coordinates

Coordinates describe the **position** of a point. They are written in pairs inside brackets, with the x-coordinate (left or right) first and the y-coordinate (up or down) second.

Example 1
Write down the coordinates of the vertices of the triangle ABC shown below.

1. Follow the grid line down from each point and read off the x-coordinate.
2. Follow the grid line across from each point and read off the y-coordinate.
3. Write the coordinates in brackets with the x-coordinate first.

The coordinates are **$A(2, 2)$, $B(4, 8)$, $C(8, 4)$**.

Example 2
Draw the shape $WXYZ$ with vertices $W(-4, 5)$, $X(3, 2)$, $Y(4, -3)$ and $Z(-5, -2)$.

1. Here, some of the coordinates are negative, so your axes need to go below zero.
2. Read across the horizontal axis for the x-coordinates.
3. Read up and down the vertical axis for the y-coordinates.
4. Plot the points and connect them to draw the shape.

Exercise 1

1 Use the grid on the right to answer this question.
   a) Write down the coordinates of the following points.
      (i) A (ii) M (iii) Q (iv) U (v) Y
   b) Write down the sentence given by the letters with the following coordinates.
      (3, 4) - (2, 0) (4, 2) (4, 2) (2, 3) (3, 0) (3, 1) (3, 2) (0, 0) (4, 3) (4, 0)
      (2, 0) (4, 2) (2, 2) (4, 0) (3, 3)
      (0, 1) (3, 1) (2, 3) (3, 3) (4, 3)

Section 12 — Graphs and Equations

2 On separate copies of the grid on the right, draw the shapes whose vertices are given by the following sets of coordinates.
   a) A(2, 1), B(2, 4), C(5, 4), D(5, 1)
   b) E(1, 1), F(6, 3), G(3, 5)
   c) H(1, 3), I(3, 5), J(6, 3), K(3, 1)
   d) L(2, 6), M(5, 5), N(5, 3), O(2, 1)

3 Use the grid on the left for this question.
   a) The following sets of coordinates spell out the names of shapes. Write down the name of each shape.
      (i)   (2, −4) (−4, −4) (−5, −6) (−4, 5) (−2, −4) (−5, 3)
      (ii) (2, 5) (−4, 1) (−2, −4) (2, 5) (4, 1) (−5, 3)
      (iii) (2, 5) (−5, −6) (−2, 5) (3, −2) (−4, 1) (4, 5)
   b) Write down the sets of coordinates which spell out the names of the following shapes.
      (i) kite   (ii) sphere   (iii) triangle

4 Draw a coordinate grid ranging from −5 to 5 on the x-axis and y-axis. Plot the following points on your grid. Join the points you have plotted.
   A(0, 5)   B(1, 1)   C(5, 1)   D(2, −1)   E(3, −4)
   F(0, −2)   G(−3, −4) H(−2, −1) I(−5, 1)   J(−1, 1)

Midpoint of a Line Segment

The midpoint of a line segment is **halfway** between the end points. The midpoint's x- and y-coordinates equal the **average** of the end points' **x-coordinates** and the **average** of the end points' **y-coordinates**.

Example 3

Find the midpoint of the line segment AB.

1. Write down the coordinates of the end points A and B.   A(−3, 4) and B(5, 2)

2. Find the average of the x-coordinates by adding them together and dividing by 2. $\left(\frac{-3+5}{2}, \frac{4+2}{2}\right) = (1, 3)$

3. Find the average of the y-coordinates in the same way.   The midpoint has coordinates **(1, 3)**.

Section 12 — Graphs and Equations   135

Exercise 2

1 A line segment XY is shown on the grid on the right.
  a) Write down the coordinates of the points X and Y.
  b) Use the coordinates of X and Y to calculate the coordinates of M, the midpoint of XY.
  c) Plot the point M on a copy of the diagram. Use a ruler to check that the distances XM and MY are equal.

2 The points P and Q have coordinates P(1, 0) and Q(3, 5).
  a) Find the coordinates of M, the midpoint of PQ.
  b) Check your answer: **(i)** Plot P and Q on a square grid. Join the points to form the line segment PQ.
  (ii) Plot the point M. Check that M is the midpoint of PQ.

3 Find the coordinates of the midpoint of the line segment AB, where A and B have coordinates:
  a) A(1, 1), B(3, 5)   **b)** A(0, 1), B(6, 3)   **c)** A(0, 0), B(4, 4)   **d)** A(2, 7), B(6, 7)

4 Find the coordinates of the midpoint of the line segment AB, where A and B have coordinates:
  a) A(−1, 2), B(1, 2)   **b)** A(−2, 3), B(−4, 5)
  c) A(−1, −6), B(5, 8)   **d)** A(3, −2), B(−1, 4)
  e) A(−1, −9), B(−3, −4)   **f)** A(2, 5), B(−7, −8)
  g) A(0, −4), B(−5, 1)   **h)** A(−2, 0), B(1, −8)

5 Use the diagram on the right to find the midpoints of the following line segments.
  a) AF   **b)** AC   **c)** DF
  d) BE   **e)** BF   **f)** CE

12.2 Horizontal and Vertical Graphs

All **horizontal** lines on a graph have the equation $y = a$ (where a is a number), since every point on the same horizontal line has the same y-coordinate (a).

All **vertical** lines on a graph have the equation $x = b$ (where b is a number), since every point on the same vertical line has the same x-coordinate (b).

Example 1

Write down the equations of the lines marked A and B.

1. Every point on the line marked A has y-coordinate −3. $\Rightarrow$ A is the line $\underline{y = -3}$

2. Every point on the line marked B has x-coordinate 2. $\Rightarrow$ B is the line $\underline{x = 2}$

136   Section 12 — Graphs and Equations

Example 2

Plot the graphs of the equations: a) $x = -1$ b) $y = 3$

1. The line with equation $x = -1$ is a vertical line through -1 on the x-axis.

2. The line with equation $y = 3$ is a horizontal line through 3 on the y-axis.

Exercise 1

1 Write down the equations of each of the lines labelled A to E on this diagram.

2 Draw a set of coordinate axes and plot the graphs with the following equations.
  a) $y = 3$
  b) $y = -6$
  c) $y = -1$
  d) $x = 2$
  e) $x = 4$
  f) $x = -4$

3 a) What is the y-coordinate of every point on the x-axis?
  b) Write down the equation of the x-axis.

4 Write down the equation of the y-axis.

5 Draw a set of coordinate axes.
  a) Plot the line which is parallel to the x-axis, and which passes through the point $(2, -2)$.
  b) What is the equation of this line?

6 Draw a set of coordinate axes.
  a) Plot the line which is parallel to the y-axis, and which passes through the point $(1, -3)$.
  b) What is the equation of this line?

7 Write down the equation of the line which is parallel to the x-axis, and which passes through the point $(4, 8)$.

8 Write down the equation of the line which is parallel to the y-axis, and which passes through the point $(-2, -6)$.

9 Write down the equation of the line which is parallel to the line $x = 4$, and which passes through the point $(1, 2)$.

10 Write down the equation of the line which is parallel to the line $y = -5$, and which passes through the point $(0, 6)$.

11 Draw a set of coordinate axes.
  a) Plot the points $P(3, -1)$ and $Q(-1, -1)$.
  b) What is the equation of the line that contains points P and Q?

12 Find the equation of the line containing points $M(2, 0)$ and $N(2, -3)$.

13 Draw a set of coordinate axes.
  a) Plot the lines with the equations $x = -2$ and $y = 4$.
  b) Write down the coordinates of the point where the two lines intersect (cross).

14 Write down the coordinates of the points where the following pairs of lines intersect.
  a) $x = 2$ and $y = 4$
  b) $x = -3$ and $y = 7$
  c) $x = 8$ and $y = -11$
  d) $x = -5$ and $y = -13$

Section 12 — Graphs and Equations

12.3 Other Straight-Line Graphs

The equation of a straight line which **isn't** horizontal or vertical contains **both** x and y.

Example 1

a) Complete the table to show the value of $y = 2x + 1$ for values of x from 0 to 5.

b) Draw the graph of $y = 2x + 1$ for values of x from 0 to 5.

x	0	1	2	3	4	5
y						
Coordinates						

a)

x	0	1	2	3	4	5
y	$2 \times 0 + 1$ = 1	$2 \times 1 + 1$ = 3	$2 \times 2 + 1$ = 5	$2 \times 3 + 1$ = 7	$2 \times 4 + 1$ = 9	$2 \times 5 + 1$ = 11
Coordinates	(0, 1)	(1, 3)	(2, 5)	(3, 7)	(4, 9)	(5, 11)

1. Use the equation $y = 2x + 1$ to find the y-value corresponding to each value of x.
2. Use the numbers from the first and second rows to fill in the third row.
3. Plot the coordinates from your table on a grid, and join them up to draw the graph.

Exercise 1

1 a) Copy and complete the table below to show the value of $y = x + 2$ for values of x from 0 to 5.

x	0	1	2	3	4	5
y	2	3				
Coordinates	(0, 2)					

b) Copy the grid on the right and plot the coordinates from your table.

c) Join up the points to draw the graph of $y = x + 2$ for values of x from 0 to 5.

2 a) Copy and complete the table below to show the value of $y = x - 4$ for values of x from 0 to 5.

x	0	1	2	3	4	5
y	–4					
Coordinates						

b) Copy the grid on the right and plot the coordinates from your table.

c) Join up the points to draw the graph of $y = x - 4$ for values of x from 0 to 5.

Section 12 — Graphs and Equations

3 a) Copy and complete the table on the right to show the value of $y = 8 - x$ for values of x from 0 to 4.

x	0	1	2	3	4
y					
Coordinates					

  b) Draw a set of axes with x-values from -5 to 5 and y-values from 0 to 13. Plot the coordinates from your table.

  c) Join up the points to draw the graph of $y = 8 - x$ for values of x from 0 to 4. Use a ruler to extend your line to show the graph of $y = 8 - x$ for values of x from -5 to 5.

4 For each of the following equations:
  (i) complete a table like the one on the right to show the value of y for values of x from -1 to 2,
  (ii) draw a graph of the equation for values of x from -5 to 5.

x	-1	0	1	2
y				
Coordinates				

  a) $y = x + 3$
  b) $y = x + 5$
  c) $y = x - 1$
  d) $y = x - 3$
  e) $y = 3x$
  f) $y = 4x$
  g) $y = \frac{x}{2}$
  h) $y = 3x - 1$
  i) $y = 2x + 5$
  j) $y = 4x - 3$
  k) $y = 3 - x$
  l) $y = 4 - x$
  m) $y = 6 - 2x$
  n) $y = 8 - 3x$
  o) $y = 1 - 2x$
  p) $y = 5 - \frac{x}{2}$

5 Draw a graph of the following equations for the given range of x-values.
  a) $y = x$ for x from -4 to 4
  b) $y = x - 2$ for x from 0 to 6
  c) $y = x + 7$ for x from -7 to 0
  d) $y = 3x - 5$ for x from 0 to 4
  e) $y = 7 - 5x$ for x from 0 to 2
  f) $y = -2x + 8$ for x from 0 to 5

Solving Simultaneous Equations Graphically

You can solve **simultaneous equations** by plotting the graphs of both equations and finding the point where they **intersect**.

Example 2
a) Plot the graphs $y = 8 - x$ and $y = 2x + 2$.
b) Use your graphs to solve the simultaneous equations $y = 8 - x$ and $y = 2x + 2$.

1. Both equations are straight lines. Make a table of values for each equation and plot their graphs.

  a) $y = 8 - x$

x	0	4	8
y	8	4	0

  $y = 2x + 2$

x	-1	0	1
y	0	2	4

2. Find the x- and y-values of the point where the graphs intersect.

  b) The graphs cross at (2, 6), so the solution is $\underline{x = 2 \text{ and } y = 6}$.

Section 12 — Graphs and Equations

Exercise 2

1. The diagram on the right shows the graphs $y = x + 3$ and $y = -x + 7$.

   Use the diagram to find the solution to the simultaneous equations $y = x + 3$ and $y = -x + 7$.

Draw the graphs in **Questions 2–4** for $-8 \leq x \leq 8$ and $-8 \leq y \leq 8$.

2. **a)** Draw the graph of $y = 5 - x$.
   b) On the same axes, draw the graph of $y = x - 3$.
   c) Use your graphs to solve the simultaneous equations $y = 5 - x$ and $y = x - 3$.

3. Solve the following simultaneous equations by drawing graphs.
   a) $y = 7 - x$ and $y = x - 3$
   b) $y = 8 - x$ and $y = x$
   c) $y = 9 - x$ and $y = 2x$
   d) $y = 3x$ and $y = 2x + 2$
   e) $y = 2 - 2x$ and $y = x + 5$
   f) $y = 2x - 1$ and $y = x + 1$
   g) $y = 6 - x$ and $y = 2x - 3$
   h) $y = -7 - 2x$ and $y = x + 2$
   i) $y = 2x + 3$ and $y = 4x + 2$

4. **a)** Draw the graphs of $y = x + 3$ and $y = x - 2$.
   b) Explain how this shows that the simultaneous equations $y = x + 3$ and $y = x - 2$ have no solutions.

12.4 Gradients

The **gradient** of a straight line is a measure of **how steep** it is.
To find the gradient of a line divide the 'vertical distance' between two points on the line by the 'horizontal distance' between those points.

$$\text{Gradient} = \frac{\text{Vertical distance}}{\text{Horizontal distance}} = \frac{y_2 - y_1}{x_2 - x_1}$$

A line sloping upwards from left to right has a **positive gradient**.
A line sloping downwards from left to right has a **negative gradient**.

Gradients can be given in different ways — e.g. if the gradient is $\frac{1}{4}$, it has a ratio of **1 : 4**, a percentage of **25%** and you can say that the slope is "**1 in 4**".

Example 1

Find the gradient of the line segment AB.
Each square on the grid measures 1 unit.

1. The vertical distance between A and B is 3 squares.
   The horizontal distance between A and B is 4 squares.

   $$\frac{\text{Vertical distance}}{\text{Horizontal distance}} = \frac{3}{4}$$

2. The line slopes downwards from left to right, so the gradient is negative.

   $$\text{Gradient of } AB = -\frac{3}{4}$$

Section 12 — Graphs and Equations

Exercise 1

1. The grid spacing in this question is 1 unit.
   a) Write down the vertical distance between the points X and Y.
   b) Write down the horizontal distance between X and Y.
   c) State whether the gradient is positive or negative.
   d) Calculate the gradient of the line segment XY.

2. Find the gradient of each of the following line segments. The grid spacing is 1 unit.
   a)   b)   c)   d)
   e)   f)   g)   h)

3. Express the following gradients:
   (i) as a ratio   (ii) as a percentage   (iii) in the form "y in x" where y and x are integers.
   a) $\frac{1}{2}$ b) $\frac{3}{4}$ c) $\frac{3}{5}$ d) 2   e) $\frac{5}{4}$

Example 2
Find the gradient of the line containing points P(–3, 1) and Q(4, 5).

1. Call the coordinates of P (x_1, y_1), and the coordinates of Q (x_2, y_2).
2. Use the formula for the gradient.
3. The line slopes upwards from left to right. So you should get a positive answer.

Gradient $= \dfrac{y_2 - y_1}{x_2 - x_1}$
$= \dfrac{5 - 1}{4 - (-3)}$
$= \dfrac{4}{7}$

4. Points $P(x_1, y_1)$ and $Q(x_2, y_2)$ are plotted on this graph.
   a) Without doing any calculations, state whether the gradient of the line containing P and Q is positive or negative.
   b) Calculate the vertical distance $y_2 - y_1$ between P and Q.
   c) Calculate the horizontal distance $x_2 - x_1$ between P and Q.
   d) Find the gradient of the line containing P and Q.

Section 12 — Graphs and Equations

5 Use the points shown to find the gradient of each of the following lines.

a) A(1, 5), B(6, 3)

b) C(−4, 6), D(6, 1)

c) E(−5, 0), F(4, 6)

6 For each line shown below:
  (i) Use the axes to find the coordinates of each of the marked points.
  (ii) Find the gradient of each of the lines.

a) points G and H

b) points I and J

c) Line 1 through K and M; Line 2 through L and N

7 a) Plot the points U(−1, 2) and V(2, 5) on a square grid.
  b) Find the gradient of the line containing points U and V.

8 Use the gradient formula to find the gradient of the line containing the points Y(2, 0) and Z(−4, −3).

9 Find the gradients of the lines containing the following points.
  a) A(0, 4), B(2, 10)
  b) C(1, 3), D(5, 11)
  c) E(−1, 3), F(5, 7)
  d) G(−3, −2), H(1, −5)
  e) I(5, −2), J(−1, 1)
  f) K(−4, −3), L(−8, −6)

10 Find the gradients of the lines containing each of the following pairs of points.
  Give each answer as: (i) a ratio in its simplest form (ii) a percentage
  a) (0, 0) and (5, 1)
  b) (3, 3) and (8, 8)
  c) (3, 0) and (6, 6)
  d) (9, 7) and (−1, 1)
  e) (2, 9) and (−2, 3)
  f) (2, 5) and (12, 13)

11 Find the missing coordinates, marked by letters, in each of the following.
  a) A line with a gradient of 1 that goes through points (3, 5) and (7, a).
  b) A line with a gradient of 2 that goes through points (1, 1) and (b, 5).
  c) A line with a gradient of $\frac{1}{2}$ that goes through points (0, 0) and (8, c).

12.5 Equations of Straight-Line Graphs

The equation of a straight line is often written in the form $y = mx + c$, where m and c are numbers — for example, $y = 3x + 5$ ($m = 3$ and $c = 5$), or $y = -7x + 1$ ($m = -7$ and $c = 1$).

When written in this form:
- m is the **gradient** of the line,
- c tells you the **y-intercept** — the point where the line crosses the y-axis.

Example 1

Find the gradient and coordinates of the y-intercept of the line $y = 3x + 1$.

1. Comparing $y = 3x + 1$ to $y = mx + c$ gives $m = 3$ and $c = 1$.   gradient is **3**

2. Since $c = 1$, the line crosses the y-axis when $y = 1$. So the y-intercept has coordinates (0, 1). y-intercept is at **(0, 1)**

Exercise 1

For each of the lines in **Questions 1 and 2**, write down:

    (i) the gradient   **(ii)** the coordinates of the y-intercept

1   a) $y = 3x + 2$ b) $y = 2x - 4$ c) $y = 5x - 11$

     d) $y = -3x + 7$ e) $y = 4x$ f) $y = \frac{1}{2}x - 1$

2   a) $y = -x - \frac{1}{2}$ b) $y = 3 - x$ c) $y = 3$

3   Match the graphs to the correct equation from the box.

$$y = x + 2 \qquad y = \frac{7}{3}x - 1 \qquad y = -x + 6 \qquad y = 3x \qquad y = -\frac{1}{3}x + 4 \qquad y = \frac{1}{3}x + 2$$

Section 12 — Graphs and Equations

4 Sketch the graphs of the following equations, marking the coordinates of the x- and y-intercepts.
a) $y = 3x + 6$
b) $y = x - 2$
c) $y = 2x - 4$
d) $y = -x + 5$
e) $y = -3x + 9$
f) $y = -2x + 6$

Parallel Lines

Lines that are **parallel** have the **same gradient**.

Example 2

Which of the following lines is parallel to the line $2x + y = 5$?
    a) $y = 3 - 2x$ b) $x + y = 5$ c) $y - 2x = 6$

1. Rearrange the equation into the form $y = mx + c$ to find its gradient.

$2x + y = 5$
$y = 5 - 2x$
$y = -2x + 5$ So the gradient (m) = -2.

2. Rearrange the other equations in the same way. Any that have $m = -2$ will be parallel to $2x + y = 5$.

a) $y = 3 - 2x$
   $y = -2x + 3$
   $m = -2$

b) $x + y = 5$
   $y = -x + 5$
   $m = -1$

c) $y - 2x = 6$
   $y = 2x + 6$
   $m = 2$

So **line a)** is parallel to $2x + y = 5$.

Example 3

Find the equation of line L, which passes through the point (5, 8) and is parallel to $y = 3x + 2$.

1. Find the gradient of the line $y = 3x + 2$.

   Equation of a straight line: $y = mx + c$
   The gradient of $y = 3x + 2$ is 3.

2. The lines are parallel, so line L will have the same gradient.

   So the equation of line L must be $y = 3x + c$.

3. Substitute the values for x and y at point (5, 8) into the equation. Solve to find c and hence the equation of line L.

   At (5, 8), $x = 5$ and $y = 8$:
   $8 = 3(5) + c$
   $8 = 15 + c$
   $c = -7$ So the equation of line L is **$y = 3x - 7$**.

Exercise 2

1 Match the letters to show which of the following lines are parallel.

| A: $y = 3x + 1$ | B: $y = -x$ | C: $y = -2x - 9$ |
| D: $y = -x - 9$ | E: $y = 3x - 2$ | F: $y = -2x + 2$ |

2 Write down the equations of three lines that are parallel to: **a)** $y = 5x - 1$ **b)** $x + y = 7$

3 Which of the following are equations of lines parallel to: **(i)** $y = 2x - 1$? **(ii)** $2x - 3y = 0$?
  a) $y - 2x = 4$
  b) $2y = 2x + 5$
  c) $2x - y = 2$
  d) $2x + y + 7 = 0$
  e) $2x + 6 = 3y$
  f) $3y + 2x = 2$
  g) $y = 1 + 2x$
  h) $3y = 3 + 2x$
  i) $6x - 9y = -2$

4 Which of the lines listed below are parallel to the line shown in the diagram?
  a) $y + 3x = 2$
  b) $3y = 7 - x$
  c) $y = 4 - 3x$
  d) $x - 3y = 8$
  e) $y = 3 - \frac{1}{3}x$
  f) $6y = -2x$

5 For each of the following, find the equation of the line which is parallel to the given line and passes through the given point. Give your answers in the form $y = mx + c$.
  a) $y = 3x + 2$, (0, 5)
  b) $y = 5x - 3$, (1, –4)
  c) $y = 2x + 1$, (1, 6)
  d) $y = 5x - 7$, (1, 8)
  e) $y = 2x$, (–1, 5)
  f) $y = \frac{1}{2}x + 3$, (6, –7)
  g) $y = 4x - 9$, (7, 13)
  h) $y = 8x - 1$, (–3, –5)
  i) $y = x + 17$, (5, –7)
  j) $2y = 6x + 3$, (–3, 4)
  k) $y = 7 - 9x$, (1, –11)
  l) $x + y = 4$, (8, 8)

Equation of a Line through Two Points

Example 4
Find the equation of the straight line that passes through the points $A(-3, -4)$ and $B(-1, 2)$.

1. Write down the equation for a straight line. $y = mx + c$, m = gradient and c = y-intercept.

2. Find the gradient (m) of the line.   gradient $= \dfrac{y_2 - y_1}{x_2 - x_1} = \dfrac{2 - (-4)}{-1 - (-3)} = \dfrac{6}{2} = 3$
   So the equation of the line must be $y = 3x + c$.

3. Substitute the value for the gradient and the x and y values for one of the points into $y = mx + c$, then solve to find c.
   At point B, $x = -1$ and $y = 2$.
   $2 = 3 \times (-1) + c$
   $2 = -3 + c$
   $c = 5$ so the equation of the line is **$y = 3x + 5$**.

Exercise 3

1 Find the equations of the following lines based on the information given.
  a) gradient = 8, passes through (0, 2)
  b) gradient = –1, passes through (0, 7)
  c) gradient = 11, passes through (0, –5)
  d) gradient = –6, passes through (0, –1)
  e) gradient = 3, passes through (4, 10)
  f) gradient = 6, passes through (–1, 2)

2 Find the equations of the lines passing through the following points.
  a) (3, 7) and (5, 11)
  b) (1, 4) and (3, 14)
  c) (2, 0) and (5, 6)
  d) (3, 1) and (7, 13)
  e) (2, –5) and (5, 1)
  f) (–3, –6) and (4, 1)
  g) (–2, 1) and (1, 7)
  h) (–1, –1) and (2, 8)

Section 12 — Graphs and Equations

12.6 Quadratic Graphs

Drawing Quadratic Graphs

Quadratic functions always involve an **x^2 term** (but no higher powers of x, such as x^3, x^4...).

The graph of a quadratic function is always a curve called a **parabola**.
A parabola can be **u-shaped** or **n-shaped**.

Example 1

a) Complete the table to find the value of $y = x^2 - 3$ for values of x from -3 to 3.

x	-3	-2	-1	0	1	2	3
x^2							
$x^2 - 3$							

b) Draw the graph of $y = x^2 - 3$ for values of x from -3 to 3.

1. Fill in the table one row at a time.
2. Now plot each x-value from the first row against the corresponding y-value ($= x^2 - 3$) from the third row, and join the points with a smooth curve.

x	-3	-2	-1	0	1	2	3
x^2	9	4	1	0	1	4	9
$x^2 - 3$	6	1	-2	-3	-2	1	6

Exercise 1

1 a) Copy and complete the table below to find the value of $y = x^2 + 2$ for values of x from -3 to 3.

x	-3	-2	-1	0	1	2	3
x^2	9		1			4	
$x^2 + 2$	11		3			6	

b) Copy the grid on the right and plot the points from your table.
c) Join up the points to draw the graph of $y = x^2 + 2$.

2 a) Copy and complete the table to show the value of $y = x^2 - 1$ for values of x from -3 to 3.

b) Draw a set of axes with x-values from -3 to 3 and y-values from -1 to 8.
Draw the graph of $y = x^2 - 1$ on your axes.

x	-3	-2	-1	0	1	2	3
x^2		4					9
$x^2 - 1$		3					8

3 For each of the following equations:
(i) Complete a table like the one below to show the value of y for values of x from -3 to 3.
(ii) Draw a graph of the equation on suitable axes.

a) $y = x^2$ b) $y = x^2 + 3$ c) $y = x^2 - 2$
d) $y = x^2 + 4$ e) $y = 5 - x^2$ f) $y = 10 - x^2$

x	-3	-2	-1	0	1	2	3
x^2							
y							

146 *Section 12 — Graphs and Equations*

Example 2

a) Complete the table to find the value of $y = x^2 - x$ for values of x from -3 to 3.

b) Draw the graph of $y = x^2 - x$ for values of x from -3 to 3.

x	-3	-2	-1	0	1	2	3
x^2		4			1		
$-x$		2			-1		
$x^2 - x$		6			0		

1. Fill in the table one row at a time. Find the entry for the '$x^2 - x$' row by adding the entries in the 'x^2' and '$-x$' rows.
2. Now plot each x-value from the first row against the corresponding y-value ($= x^2 - x$) from the fourth row. Join the points with a smooth curve.

x	-3	-2	-1	0	1	2	3
x^2	9	4	1	0	1	4	9
$-x$	3	2	1	0	-1	-2	-3
$x^2 - x$	12	6	2	0	0	2	6

Exercise 2

1 a) Copy and complete the table below to find the value of $y = x^2 + x$ for values of x from -3 to 3.

x	-3	-2	-1	0	1	2	3
x^2	9					4	
x	-3					2	
$x^2 + x$	6					6	

b) Copy the grid on the right and plot the points from your table.
c) Join up the points to draw the graph of $y = x^2 + x$ for values of x from -3 to 3.

2 a) Copy and complete the table to show the value of $y = x^2 - 2x$ for values of x from -3 to 3.

x	-3	-2	-1	0	1	2	3
x^2		4					9
$-2x$		4					-6
$x^2 - 2x$		8					3

b) Draw a set of axes with x-values from -3 to 3 and y-values from -1 to 15. Draw the graph of $y = x^2 - 2x$ on your axes.

3 For each of the following quadratic equations:
   (i) Complete a table to show the value of y for values of x from -3 to 3.
   (ii) Draw a graph of the equation on suitable axes.

a) $y = x^2 + 3x$
b) $y = x^2 + 2x$
c) $y = x^2 - 4x$
d) $y = x^2 + 5x$
e) $y = x^2 - 3x$
f) $y = x^2 + 4x$

Example 3
Draw the graph of $y = x^2 + 3x - 2$ for values of x from -3 to 3.

1. Make a table — include separate rows for x^2, $3x$ and -2. The last row should add the three entries above.

x	-3	-2	-1	0	1	2	3
x^2	9	4	1	0	1	4	9
$3x$	-9	-6	-3	0	3	6	9
-2	-2	-2	-2	-2	-2	-2	-2
$x^2 + 3x - 2$	-2	-4	-4	-2	2	8	16

2. Now plot each x-value from the first row against the corresponding y-value ($= x^2 + 3x - 2$) from the final row. Join the points with a smooth curve.

4 For each of the following quadratic equations:
  (i) Complete a table to show the value of y for values of x from -3 to 3.
  (ii) Draw a graph of the equation on suitable axes.
  a) $y = x^2 + 2x + 5$
  b) $y = x^2 + x - 3$
  c) $y = x^2 - 3x - 2$
  d) $y = x^2 - 2x - 3$
  e) $y = x^2 - 3x - 1$
  f) $y = -x^2 - x - 1$

Using Graphs to Solve Quadratic Equations

Example 4
This graph shows the curve $y = x^2 - 2x - 1$.
Use the graph to estimate both solutions (or roots) to the equation $x^2 - 2x - 1 = 0$. Give your answers to 1 decimal place.

1. The left hand side of the equation $x^2 - 2x - 1 = 0$ is represented by the curve $y = x^2 - 2x - 1$ and the right-hand side is represented by the line $y = 0$ (the x-axis).

2. So, the estimated solutions are found where the curve crosses the x-axis. Read off the x-values.

$\underline{x = -0.4}$ and $\underline{x = 2.4}$

Exercise 3

1 Use these graphs to find the solutions to the following equations.
  a) $x^2 + 4x = 0$
  b) $x^2 - 2x - 3 = 0$
  c) $-x^2 + 4 = 0$

148 Section 12 — Graphs and Equations

2. **a)** Draw the graph of $y = x^2 - 5x + 3$ for values of x from 0 to 5.
   b) Use your graph to estimate the solutions to the equation $x^2 - 5x + 3 = 0$.
   Give your answers to 1 decimal place.

3. By drawing their graphs over the range of x values indicated, estimate the roots of these equations.
   Give your answers to 1 decimal place.
   a) $x^2 + 3x - 5 = 0$ for $-6 \leq x \leq 3$
   b) $x^2 - x - 3 = 0$ for $-3 \leq x \leq 4$
   c) $x^2 - 4x + 2 = 0$ for $-2 \leq x \leq 5$
   d) $x^2 - 7x + 9 = 0$ for $0 \leq x \leq 7$

4. The graph on the right shows the curve $y = x^2 - 1$.
   Use the graph to estimate the solutions to these equations.
   Where appropriate give your answers to 1 decimal place.
   a) $x^2 - 1 = 0$ **b)** $x^2 - 1 = 1$
   c) $x^2 - 1 = 2$ **d)** $x^2 - 1 = 3$
   e) $x^2 - 1 = 4$

Turning Points of Quadratics

The **turning point** of a quadratic graph is at the minimum y-value if the curve is u-shaped or the maximum y-value if the curve is n-shaped.

If the number in front of the x^2 term is **positive** then the curve is u-shaped, if it's **negative** then the curve is n-shaped.

Example 5

The graph on the right shows the equation $y = x^2 + x - 6$.
Find the turning point of the graph of $y = x^2 + x - 6$.

1. Find two points on the curve with the same y-value.
   $y = 0$ at $x = -3$ and $x = 2$
2. The x-coordinate of the turning point is halfway between these two x-values.
   x-coordinate $= (-3 + 2) \div 2 = -0.5$
3. Put the x-coordinate back into the equation to find the y-coordinate.
   y-coordinate $= (-0.5)^2 + (-0.5) - 6 = -6.25$
   So the turning point has coordinates **(−0.5, −6.25)**.

Exercise 4

1. For each of the following graphs, decide whether the turning point is a maximum or minimum.
   a) $y = x^2 + 2$ **b)** $y = 7 - x^2$ **c)** $y = x^2 + 2x$
   d) $y = x^2 - 8x + 32$ **e)** $y = 3x^2 - 10x + 7$ **f)** $y = -x^2 + 9x - 5$
   g) $y = -5x^2 + 16x - 5$ **h)** $y = 6x^2 + 11x + 9$ **i)** $y = -4x^2 + 6x + 7$

2 Find the coordinates of the turning points of these graphs.

a) $y = x^2 + 5x + 4$

b) $y = -x^2 - 3x + 4$

c) $y = x^2 - 5x + 2$

3 Find the turning points of these equations given the two points on the curve.
   a) $y = x^2 - 6x$ goes through points (–1, 7) and (7, 7).
   b) $y = x^2 - 2x + 3$ goes through points (0, 3) and (2, 3).
   c) $y = 8x - x^2$ goes through points (2, 12) and (6, 12).
   d) $y = x^2 + 4x + 6$ goes through points (–3, 3) and (–1, 3).
   e) $y = -x^2 - 2x + 8$ goes through points (–5, –7) and (3, –7).
   f) $y = 4x^2 - 8x - 9$ goes through points (–2, 23) and (4, 23).

Example 6

Find the turning point of the graph of $y = x^2 - 3x + 7$.

1. Draw a table of values and look for two x-values that give the same y-value.

x	–2	–1	0	1	2
y	17	11	7	5	5

   $x = 1$ and $x = 2$ both give $y = 5$

2. The x-coordinate of the turning point is halfway between these two x-values.

   x-coordinate = (1 + 2) ÷ 2 = 1.5

3. Put the x-coordinate back into the equation to find the y-coordinate.

   y-coordinate = $1.5^2 - (3 \times 1.5) + 7 = 4.75$
   So the turning point = **(1.5, 4.75)**.

4 By drawing tables for x values in the range $-3 \leq x \leq 3$, find the turning points of each of these curves.
   a) $y = x^2 - 2x$
   b) $y = x^2 + 3x + 11$
   c) $y = x^2 + 5x - 9$
   d) $y = -x^2 - x + 11$
   e) $y = 2x^2 + 8x - 3$
   f) $y = 3x^2 + 12x - 8$
   g) $y = -2x^2 - 2x + 9$
   h) $y = 4x^2 + 12x - 5$
   i) $y = -6x^2 + 18x - 3$

12.7 Harder Graphs

Cubic Graphs

Cubic functions have x^3 as the highest power of x.

Cubic graphs all have the same basic shape of a curve with a 'wiggle' in the middle.

The curve goes up from the bottom left if the number in front of the x^3 term is positive, and down from the top left if it's negative.

Example 1

Draw the graph of $y = x^3 + 1$.

1. Draw a table with rows for each term to help you work out the y-value for each value of x.

x	–3	–2	–1	0	1	2
x^3	–27	–8	–1	0	1	8
+1	1	1	1	1	1	1
$x^3 + 1$	–26	–7	0	1	2	9

2. Plot the coordinates and join the points with a smooth curve.

Exercise 1

1 Copy and complete each table and draw graphs for the following cubic equations.

a) $y = x^3$

x	–3	–2	–1	0	1	2	3
x^3		–8			1		

b) $y = x^3 + 5$

x	–3	–2	–1	0	1	2	3
x^3	–27					8	
$x^3 + 5$	–22					13	

c) $y = -x^3$

x	–3	–2	–1	0	1	2	3
$-x^3$			1			–8	

d) $y = 5 - x^3$

x	–3	–2	–1	0	1	2	3
5	5		5				5
$-x^3$		8					–27
$5 - x^3$		13					–22

e) $y = -4 - x^3$

x	–3	–2	–1	0	1	2	3
–4	–4	–4			–4		
$-x^3$		27			–1		
$-4 - x^3$		23			–5		

2 Draw the graph of $y = x^3 + 3$ for values of x between –3 and 3.

3 Draw the graph of $y = x^3 - 3x + 7$ for values of x between –4 and 4.

Section 12 — Graphs and Equations

Reciprocal Graphs

The equations of basic **reciprocal graphs** have the form: $y = \frac{A}{x}$ where A is a constant.

A reciprocal graph appears as **two curves** which are symmetrical about the lines $y = x$ and $y = -x$.

When A is **positive** the curves are in the top-right and bottom-left quadrants.

When A is **negative** the curves are in the top-left and bottom-right quadrants.

Example 2

Draw the graph of $y = \frac{1}{x}$ for values of x between -5 and 5.

1. Draw a table of values for the equation.

x	-5	-4	-2	-1	-0.5	-0.2
$\frac{1}{x}$	-0.2	-0.25	-0.5	-1	-2	-5

x	0.2	0.5	1	2	4	5
$\frac{1}{x}$	5	2	1	0.5	0.25	0.2

2. Plot the coordinates and join the points to make two smooth curves.

Exercise 2

1 Which of these equations would produce a basic reciprocal graph?

A: $y = \frac{x}{3}$ B: $y = \frac{9}{x}$ C: $y = \frac{6}{-x}$ D: $y = \frac{4}{x} + 1$

E: $xy = 5$ F: $y = \frac{9}{x} - 8$ G: $y = \frac{8}{2x}$ H: $y = \frac{2}{x} + x$

2 Copy and complete each table and draw graphs for the following reciprocal functions.

a) $y = \frac{2}{x}$

x	-5	-4	-2	-1	-0.5	-0.1	0.1	0.5	1	2	4	5
$\frac{2}{x}$		-0.5		-2						1		

b) $y = -\frac{1}{x}$

x	-5	-4	-2	-1	-0.5	-0.1	0.1	0.5	1	2	4	5
$-\frac{1}{x}$		0.25		1								

Section 12 — Graphs and Equations

12.8 Graphs and Equations Problems

Exercise 1

1   **a)** Plot the points $A(0, 4)$, $B(2, 6)$, $C(4, 4)$ and $D(2, 0)$ on a set of axes.
   b) Join the points. What kind of shape have you made?

2   The points A and B have coordinates $A(2, 5)$ and $B(-4, 1)$.
Find the coordinates of the midpoint of the line segment AB.

3   For each of the following equations, write down:
   (i) the gradient of the line
   (ii) the coordinates of the line's y-intercept
   a) $y = 2x + 3$ **b)** $y = 3x + 8$ **c)** $y = 4x - 5$
   d) $y = 3 - x$ **e)** $y = 3x + \frac{1}{2}$ **f)** $y = -\frac{2}{3}x - 1$

4   Find the equation of the line which is parallel to the y-axis which passes through the point $(11, -4)$.

5   A horizontal line is drawn on a coordinate grid. The line passes through the point $(3, 7)$.
What is the equation of the line?

6   Find the gradient of each of the line segments shown in the diagram on the right.

7   Match the graphs shown on the left with the correct equation from the list below.
$y = x$ $x = -5$ $y = x^2$ $y = -4$

8   Find the gradient of the line passing through the following points.
   a) $(0, 0)$ and $(3, 15)$ **b)** $(-4, -5)$ and $(-1, 4)$
   c) $(-7, 2)$ and $(-4, -1)$ **d)** $(5, -2)$ and $(2, 10)$

9   **a)** Write down the coordinates of each of the points A to E.
   b) Find the coordinates of the midpoint of AB.
   c) Find the coordinates of the midpoint of BC.
   d) Write down the equation of the line that passes through points A and E.
   e) Find the gradient of the line BC.

Section 12 — Graphs and Equations

10 Draw each of the following lines on a set of axes.
   a) $x = 1$ **b)** $y = -3$ **c)** $x = -1$ **d)** $y = 5$

11 a) Copy and complete the table to show the value of $y = 8 - x$ for values of x from -3 to 3.
   b) Plot the graph of $y = 8 - x$.

x	-3	-2	-1	0	1	2	3
y							
Coordinates							

12 a) Copy and complete the table to show the value of $y = 2x + 2$ for values of x from -3 to 3.
   b) Plot the graph of $y = 2x + 2$.
   c) Use your graph to find the value of x when $y = 5$.

x	-3	-2	-1	0	1	2	3
y							
Coordinates							

13 a) Draw the line $y = 6 - 3x$ for values of x from -1 to 3.
   b) Find the equation of the line parallel to this one that passes through $(2, -4)$.

14 The gradient of a line is 10%.
   a) Give the gradient of the line as a fraction.
   b) The line goes through points $(1, 1)$ and $(21, y)$. Work out the value of y.

15 Find the equation of the straight line that passes through $(-1, 6)$ and $(5, 18)$.

16 Sketch the general shape of the following:
   a) A quadratic graph where the number in front of the x^2 term is positive.
   b) A cubic graph where the number in front of the x^3 term is negative.
   c) A reciprocal graph of the form $y = \frac{A}{x}$ where A is positive.

17 The graph on the right shows the curve $y = 3 - x - x^2$. Use the graph to estimate the solutions to the equation $3 - x - x^2 = 0$. Give your answers to 1 decimal place.

18 a) Copy and complete this table to show the values of $y = x^2 + 5x$ for values of x from -4 to 2.

x	-4	-3	-2	-1	0	1	2
x^2			4				
$5x$			-10				
$x^2 + 5x$			-6				

   b) Draw the graph of $y = x^2 + 5x$ for values of x from -4 to 2.
   c) Find the coordinates of the turning point of your graph.

19 a) Draw the graph of $y = x^3 - 6x^2 + 12x - 5$ for values of x between -1 and 5.
   b) Estimate the value of x when the graph crosses the x-axis. Give your answer to 1 decimal place.

Section 12 — Graphs and Equations

Section 13 — Real-Life Graphs

13.1 Interpreting Real-Life Graphs

Graphs can be used to represent real-life situations.
For example, straight-line graphs can be used to convert between different units or currencies.

Example 1

The graph shown can be used to convert between pounds (£) and euros (€).

a) Use the graph to change £300 to euros.
Follow the grid upwards from £300 until you reach the line.
Then follow the grid across to find the amount in euros.
£300 = €350

b) Use the graph to change €210 to pounds.
Follow the grid across from €210 until you reach the line. Then follow the grid downwards to find the amount in pounds.
€210 = £180

Exercise 1

The graph on the right can be used to convert between pounds (£) and euros (€).
Use this graph to answer **Questions 1-4**.

1. Use the graph to convert the following amounts from pounds to euros.
   a) £50   b) £250   c) £110   d) £290

2. Use the graph to convert the following amounts from euros to pounds.
   a) €50   b) €200   c) €360   d) €430

3. A dress costs €130. How much is this in pounds?

4. a) A TV costs £420 in the UK. How much is this in euros?
   b) The price of the TV in France is €470. How much is this in pounds?
   c) In which country is the TV cheaper?

Section 13 — Real-Life Graphs

The graph on the right can be used to convert between pounds (£) and Canadian dollars ($). Use this graph to answer **Questions 5-8**.

5 Use the graph to convert the following amounts from pounds to Canadian dollars.
   a) £10   **b)** £30   **c)** £44   **d)** £62

6 Use the graph to convert the following amounts from Canadian dollars to pounds.
   a) $10   **b)** $74   **c)** $54   **d)** $40

7 **a)** A shirt costs $58. How much is this in pounds?
   b) I want to buy two shirts. How much will it cost me in pounds?

8 **a)** Convert £40 into Canadian dollars.
   b) Use your answer to convert £80 into Canadian dollars.

The graph on the left shows the cost of different weights of fudge. Use this graph to answer **Questions 9-12**.

9 Estimate the cost of the following weights of fudge.
   a) 100 g   **b)** 380 g   **c)** 60 g   **d)** 410 g

10 Use the graph to estimate the weight of fudge that could be bought with the following amounts of money.
   a) £5   **b)** £9   **c)** £2.20   **d)** £3.80

11 **a)** Find the cost of 400 g of fudge.
   b) Use your answer to find the cost of 800 g of fudge.

12 How much fudge could I buy for £20?

The graph on the right can be used to convert between kilometres per hour (km/h) and miles per hour (mph). Use this graph to answer **Questions 13-15**.

13 **a)** Convert 38 km/h into miles per hour.
   b) Convert 27 mph into km/h.

14 The speed limit on a particular road is 30 mph. A driver travels at 52 km/h. By how many miles per hour is the driver breaking the speed limit?

15 The maximum speed limit in the UK is 70 mph. The maximum speed limit in Spain is 120 km/h. Which country has the higher speed limit, and by how much?

Section 13 — Real-Life Graphs

Non-Linear Graphs

Graphs describing real-life situations can be almost any shape. Whatever the shape, the gradient shows the rate of change — the change in something per something else.

The gradient is always: *y*-axis units **per** *x*-axis units

Example 2

The graph shows the temperature of an oven as it heats up.

a) Describe how the temperature of the oven changes during the first 10 minutes shown on the graph.

b) What is the temperature of the oven after 7 minutes?

c) How long does it take for the temperature to reach 190 °C?

1. The gradient of the curve shows the change in temperature per unit of time. The curve is very steep at first, then begins to level out as the temperature increases.

2. Follow the grid upwards from 7 minutes until you reach the curve, then read across to find the temperature.

3. Follow the grid across from 190 °C, then read downwards to find the time.

a) The temperature rises quickly at first, but then rises more slowly as the oven heats up.

b) **205 °C**

c) **5 minutes**

Exercise 2

1 Match each graph below to the most accurate description.

a)   b)   c)   d)
Time   Time   Time   Time

A: The temperature rose quickly, and then fell again gradually.

B: The number of people who needed hospital treatment stayed at the same level all year.

C: The cost of gold went up more and more quickly.

D: The temperature fell overnight, but then climbed quickly again the next morning.

2   The graph on the left shows the temperature in two ovens as they warm up.
   a) Which oven reaches 100 °C more quickly?
   b) Which oven reaches a higher maximum temperature?
   c) Estimate how many seconds it takes Oven 1 to reach its maximum temperature.
   d) Estimate how many seconds it takes Oven 2 to reach its maximum temperature.
   e) (i) After how many seconds are the two ovens at the same temperature?
      (ii) What temperature do they both reach at this time?
   f) What do the gradients of the lines represent?

3   The graph shows the depth of water in a harbour one day between the times of 08:00 and 20:00.
   a) Describe how the depth of water changed over this time period.
   b) At approximately what time was the depth of water the greatest?
   c) What was the minimum depth of water during this period?
   d) At approximately what times was the water 3 m deep?
   e) Mike's boat floats when the depth of the water is 1.6 m or over. Estimate the amount of time that his boat was not floating during this period.

4   a) Vase P is 30 cm tall. The depth of water in Vase P as it is filled up with water flowing at a steady rate is shown on the graph on the right. By how much does the depth of water increase:
      (i)   between 0 and 5 seconds?
      (ii) between 10 and 15 seconds?
      (iii) between 25 and 30 seconds?
   b) Vase Q is also 30 cm tall. The depth of water in Vase Q is also shown on the graph. By how much does the depth of water increase:
      (i)   between 0 and 5 seconds?
      (ii) between 10 and 15 seconds?
      (iii) between 25 and 30 seconds?
   c) Describe the difference between how the depth of water increases in Vase P and Vase Q.

158   Section 13 — Real-Life Graphs

13.2 Drawing Real-Life Graphs

To draw a graph representing a real-life situation, you need some points to plot.
Your graph could be either a **straight line** or a **curve**.
- For a **straight line**, you'll need to plot **at least three** points.
- But if the graph is a **curve**, you'll need **more than three** points.

Example 1

A plumber charges customers a standard fee of £40, plus £30 per hour for all work carried out.
a) Draw a graph to show how the plumber's fee varies with the amount of time the job takes.
b) Use the graph to estimate the amount of time taken to do a job costing £250.

1. Make a table showing the fee for different numbers of hours.
   A 1-hour job will cost £40 + £30 = £70.
   A 2-hour job will cost £40 + (2 × £30) = £100.
   A 3-hour job will cost £40 + (3 × £30) = £130.

   a)
Time (hours)	1	2	3	4	5
Fee (£)	70	100	130	160	190

2. Plot the values on a sheet of graph paper and join the points to draw the graph.
   For each extra hour, the fee increases by £30, so this is a straight-line graph.
   This means you only really needed 3 points in your table — but if you're not sure whether it's going to turn out to be a straight line or not, it's always best to plot too many points.

3. Follow the grid across from £250, then read downwards to find the correct time.

   b) **7 hours**

Exercise 1

1 The cost of hiring a digger is £40 per day, plus a fixed cost of £20.

a) Copy and complete the table to show the cost of hiring the digger for different numbers of days.

No. Days	1	2	3	4	5
Cost (£)	60				

b) Copy the coordinate grid on the right, then plot the values from your table and draw a line through the points.

c) Using your graph, find:
   (i) The cost of hiring the digger for 7 days.
   (ii) The number of days the digger was hired for if it cost £260.

Section 13 — Real-Life Graphs

2 The instructions for cooking different weights of chicken are as follows:

   '*Cook for 35 mins per kg, plus an extra 25 minutes.*'

   a) Copy and complete the table to show the cooking times for chickens of different weights.

Weight (kg)	1	2	3	4	5
Time (minutes)					

   b) Draw a set of axes on a sheet of graph paper.
   Plot the weight on the vertical axis and the time on the horizontal axis.
   Then plot the values from your table to draw a graph showing the cooking times for different weights of chicken.

   c) A chicken cooks in 110 minutes. What is the weight of the chicken?

   $T = 35w + 25$

3 The cost of a hotel room is £80 per night for the first 3 nights, then £50 per night for every night after that.

   a) Draw a graph showing how the cost of staying at the hotel varies with the length of stay.

   b) Use your graph to find how much it would cost to stay at the hotel for 6 nights.

   c) A guest was charged £340. How many nights did she stay at the hotel?

4 A delivery company charges £6.40 to deliver the first parcel in an order, plus £1.30 for every additional parcel in the order after that.

   a) Draw a graph showing how the cost of a delivery varies with the number of parcels in the delivery. Plot the number of parcels on the horizontal axis and the cost on the vertical axis.

   b) Use your graph to find the cost of sending 8 parcels.

   c) How many parcels did a customer post if she was charged £14.20?

5 This table shows how the fuel efficiency of a car in miles per gallon (mpg) varies with the speed of the car in miles per hour (mph).

Speed (mph)	55	60	65	70	75	80
Fuel Efficiency (mpg)	32.3	30.7	28.9	27.0	24.9	22.7

   a) Draw a pair of axes with speed on the horizontal axis and fuel efficiency on the vertical axis. Plot the points from the table on your axes and join them up with a smooth curve.

   b) Use your graph to predict the fuel efficiency of the car when it is travelling at 73 mph.

6 Helena is a baby girl. A health visitor records the weight of Helena every two months. The measurements are shown in the table below.

Age (months)	0	2	4	6	8	10	12	14	16
Weight (kg)	3.2	4.6	5.9	7.0	7.9	8.7	9.3	9.8	10.2

   a) Draw a graph to show this information.
   Plot age on the horizontal axis and weight on the vertical axis.
   Join your points with a smooth curve.

   b) Keira is 9 months old and has a weight of 9.1 kg.
   Use your graph to estimate how much heavier Keira is than Helena was at 9 months old.

Section 14 — Proportion

14.1 Direct Proportion

If the **ratio** between two things is always the same, then they're in **direct proportion**.
For example, if 1 item costs £2, then 2 items will cost £4, 3 items will cost £6, etc. The ratio is always 1 item : £2. You can use this relationship between quantities to convert from one to another.

Example 1

If 8 chocolate bars cost £6, calculate the cost of 10 chocolate bars.

1. Calculate the cost of one bar by dividing the total cost by the number of bars.

   8 bars cost £6
   so 1 bar costs £6 ÷ 8 = £0.75

2. Then multiply this by the new number of bars.

   10 bars cost £0.75 × 10 = **£7.50**

Example 2

Oliver has 30 euros (€) left over from a holiday in France. Assuming the exchange rate is £1 = €1.14, how many pounds can he exchange his euros for?

1. Work out how many pounds €1 is worth by dividing both sides of the equation "£1 = €1.14" by 1.14.

   €1.14 = £1
   so €1 = £1 ÷ 1.14 = £0.877...

2. Then multiply this by the number of euros Oliver has.

   €30 = 30 × £0.877... = **£26.32**
   (to the nearest penny)

Exercise 1

1. If 1 pair of jeans costs £35, find the cost of the following:
   a) 2 pairs of jeans
   b) 5 pairs of jeans
   c) 20 pairs of jeans

2. If £1 is worth €1.14, convert the following amounts into euros (€).
   a) £10
   b) £20
   c) £100
   d) £850

3. The cost of 8 identical books is £36. What is the cost of 12 of these books?

4. If it takes 1.8 kg of flour to make 3 loaves of bread, how much flour is needed to make 5 loaves?

5. If 10 litres of paint costs £45, find the cost of: a) 3 litres, b) 14 litres, c) 60 litres.

6. If 1 book costs £7.50, work out how many books you can buy for: a) £22.50 b) £60

7. If 7 of the same DVDs cost £84, how many DVDs can be bought for £48?

8. If 24 houses can be built by 6 builders, how many builders would it take to build 52 houses in the same amount of time?

9. Two-and-a-half kilograms of apples cost £6.85. Leroy bought some of these apples and paid a total of £13.70. How many kilograms of apples did he buy?

10. Grace buys 11 pens for £12.32 and 6 note pads for £5.88.
    How much would she pay altogether for 8 pens and 5 note pads?

Exercise 2

1 A bus travels 50 km in 40 minutes. Assuming the bus continues to travel at the same average speed, calculate the following:
   a) the time it would take to travel 65 km
   b) the distance the bus would travel in 16 minutes

2 A car uses 35 litres of petrol to travel 250 km.
   a) How far, to the nearest km, can the car travel on 50 litres of petrol?
   b) How many litres of petrol would the car use to travel 400 km?

3 Philip changed £50 into Swiss francs before going on holiday to Switzerland. The exchange rate was £1 = 1.47 Swiss francs.
   a) How many Swiss francs did he get?

   At the end of his holiday, Philip changed his remaining 30 Swiss francs back into pounds.
   b) The exchange rate had changed to £1 = 1.50 Swiss francs. How much money did he get back in pounds?

4 The recipe on the right shows the ingredients needed to make 3 servings of scrambled egg.
   a) How many eggs are needed to make 7 servings?
   b) Stacey has 60 g of butter. How many servings can she make?
   c) Joanne uses 220 ml of milk. How many grams of salt should she use?

> **Scrambled Egg** (3 servings)
> 6 Eggs   15 g Butter
> 60 ml Milk   4.5 g Salt

Example 3

A supermarket sells bread buns in packs of 6, 12 and 24.
The pack of 6 costs 78p, the pack of 12 costs £1.44 and the pack of 24 costs £3.00.
Which pack size represents the best value for money?

1. For each pack divide the cost by the pack size to get the price per unit.

   6 pack: 78p ÷ 6 = 13p per bread bun
   12 pack: £1.44 ÷ 12 = 12p per bread bun
   24 pack: £3.00 ÷ 24 = 12.5p per bread bun

2. The pack size with the best value for money is the one with the lowest cost per bread bun.

   The **12 pack** is the best value for money.

Exercise 3

1 A greengrocers sells apples individually, in packs of 6 or in bags of 10. Individually they cost 30p each, the pack of 6 costs £1.50 and the bag of 10 costs £2.40. Which of these options represents the best value for money?

2 A coffee shop sells coffee in small, medium and large cups. A small coffee is 240 ml and costs £2, a medium coffee is 350 ml and costs £3 and a large coffee is 470 ml and costs £4. Which size of cup represents the best value for money?

3 Sausages are sold in packs of 6, 8 or 10. A pack of 6 costs £2.18, a pack of 8 costs £2.80 and a pack of 10 costs £3.46. Which pack of sausages represents the best value for money?

Graphs of Direct Proportions

Two quantities are **directly proportional** if, when you plot them on a graph, you get a **straight line** through the **origin**.

The **general equation** for two quantities in direct proportion is:

$y = \mathbf{A}x$ where y is directly proportional to x and A is just a number.

Example 4

y is directly proportional to x. When $x = 10$, $y = 25$.

Sketch the graph of this direct proportion.

1. A sketch only requires the rough shape of the graph with the important points labelled.
2. As x and y are directly proportional, the graph is a straight line through the origin. You also know that it goes through point (10, 25). So mark these two points and draw a straight line through them.

Exercise 4

1 Which of these graphs shows that y is directly proportional to x? Explain your answer.

2 Sketch the graphs of the following proportions:
  a) y is directly proportional to x. When $x = 20$, $y = 8$.
  b) s is directly proportional to t. When $t = 80$, $s = 15$.

Example 5

y is directly proportional to x. Fill in the gaps in the table.

x	3	5	10	12	
y		25			100

1. From the table you can see that when $x = 5$, $y = 25$.
2. Divide x and y by 5 to find the value of y when $x = 1$. When $x = 5 \div 5 = 1$, $y = 25 \div 5 = 5$.
3. Now multiply each value of x in the table by 5 to get the missing values of y, and divide the value of y by 5 to get the missing value of x.

x	3	5	10	12	$100 \div 5 = \underline{\mathbf{20}}$
y	$3 \times 5 = \underline{\mathbf{15}}$	25	$10 \times 5 = \underline{\mathbf{50}}$	$12 \times 5 = \underline{\mathbf{60}}$	100

Section 14 — Proportion

Exercise 5

1 In each of the following tables, y is directly proportional to x.
   (i) Copy and complete each table.
   (ii) Draw the graph of each direct proportion.

a)
x	8	12
y	2	

b)
x	4	
y	3	6

c)
x	2	7	10	
y			30	36

d)
x	−2	0	3	
y	−10			30

Example 6

y is directly proportional to x. When $y = 42$, $x = 6$.

a) Write an equation in the form $y = Ax$ to represent this direct proportion.

   1. Put the values of x and y into the equation to find A. $42 = A \times 6$
                                                                                                   A = $42 \div 6 = 7$

   2. Write out the equation with your value of A.   **$y = 7x$**

b) Calculate the value of y when $x = 51$.
Put the value of x into your equation from part a). $y = 7 \times 51 =$ **357**

Exercise 6

1 s is directly proportional to t. When $s = 80$, $t = 4$.
   a) Write an equation in the form $s = At$ to represent this direct proportion.
   b) Work out the value of s when $t = 13$.
   c) Sketch the graph of this direct proportion.

2 j is directly proportional to h. When $j = 15$, $h = 5$.
   a) Write an equation to represent this direct proportion.
   b) Work out the value of j when $h = 40$.
   c) Sketch the graph of this direct proportion.

3 r is directly proportional to t. When $r = 9$, $t = 6$.
   a) Write an equation to represent this direct proportion.
   b) Accurately draw the graph of this direct proportion.

4 p is directly proportional to q. When $p = 14$, $q = 4$.
   a) Accurately draw the graph of this direct proportion.
   b) Use your graph to find the value of p when $q = 8$.

5 f is directly proportional to g. When $f = 2.7$, $g = 27$.
   a) Sketch the graph of this direct proportion.   b) What is the value of f when $g = 21$?

Section 14 — Proportion

14.2 Inverse Proportion

If one quantity decreases as another increases, then they're **inversely proportional**.
E.g. if one quantity is doubled then the other is halved.

Example 1

Four people take five hours to dig a hole.
How long would it take ten people to dig the same sized hole at the same rate?

1. Work out how long 1 person will take — the fewer people there are, the longer it will take.

    4 people take 5 hours
    1 person will take 5 × 4 = 20 hours

2. Divide by the new number of people.

    10 people will take 20 ÷ 10 = **2 hours**.

Exercise 1

1. It takes three people two hours to paint a wall.
   How long would it take six people to paint the same wall at the same rate?

2. It takes four teachers three and a half hours to mark a set of test papers.
   How long would it take seven teachers to mark the same set of papers at the same rate?

3. Four chefs can prepare a meal in twenty minutes. They hire an extra chef. How long will it take the five of them to prepare the same meal, if they all work at the same rate as the original four?

4. A journey takes two hours when travelling at an average speed of 30 mph.
   How long would the same journey take when travelling at an average speed of 45 mph?

5. It will take five builders sixty-two days to complete a particular project.
   a) At this rate, how long would the project take if there were only two builders?
   b) If the project needed completing in under forty days, what is the minimum number of builders that would be required?

Example 2

It takes 5 examiners 4 hours to mark 125 exam papers.
How long would it take 8 examiners to mark 200 papers at the same rate?

1. Split the calculation up into stages by keeping one variable constant each time.

    Keeping the number of papers (125) constant:
    5 examiners take 4 hours

2. First find how long it will take 8 examiners to mark 125 papers.

    1 examiner will take 4 × 5 = 20 hours
    8 examiners will take 20 ÷ 8 = 2.5 hours

3. Then find how long it will take 8 examiners to mark 200 papers.

    Keeping the number of people (8) constant:
    1 paper will take 2.5 ÷ 125 = 0.02 hours
    200 papers will take 0.02 × 200 = **4 hours**.

Exercise 2

1. It takes 3 hours for two people to clean six identical rooms.
   How long would it take five people to clean 20 of the same rooms at the same rate?

2. It takes two electricians nine days to rewire two identical houses.
   How long would it take three electricians to rewire three of the same houses at the same rate?

3 It takes 144 minutes for 2 bakers to bake 72 identical buns.
How long would it take for 5 bakers to bake 90 of these buns if they each work at the same rate?

4 It takes twenty minutes for three people to shovel snow from two identical driveways.
At this rate, how long would it take two people to shovel snow from five of the same driveways?

5 Fourteen people can paint 35 identical plates in two hours.
At this rate, how long would it take twenty people to paint 60 identical plates?

6 It will take twelve workers three weeks to complete four projects.
Each project takes the same number of man-hours to complete.

   a) At this rate, how long would it take fifteen workers to complete ten projects?

   b) The ten projects need to be completed in under four weeks. What is the minimum number of workers that would be needed, given that they all work at the same rate as the original workers?

Graphs of Inverse Proportions

When two quantities are **inversely proportional**, plotting them on a graph looks like this.

The **general equation** for an inverse proportion is: $y = \frac{A}{x}$ or $xy = A$

Exercise 3

1 Which of these graphs shows that y is inversely proportional to x? Explain your answer.

2 Which of the equations below show that y is inversely proportional to x?

$y = \frac{4}{x}$ $\quad y = \frac{7}{x} + 3$ $\quad \frac{y}{x} = 8$ $\quad yx = 9$ $\quad y = 3 - \frac{1}{x}$

Example 3

y is inversely proportional to x. Fill in the gaps in the table.

x	1		5	10
y		100		20

1. From the table you can see that when $x = 10$, $y = 20$.

2. Multiply y by 10 to find the value of y when $x = 1$.

   When $x = 10 \div 10 = 1$,
   $y = 20 \times 10 = 200$.

3. Now you can divide 200 by the value of x to get the other missing value of y, and divide 200 by the value of y to get the missing value of x.

x	1	$200 \div 100 = \underline{\mathbf{2}}$	5	10
y	**200**	100	$200 \div 5 = \underline{\mathbf{40}}$	20

Section 14 — Proportion

3 In each of the following tables, y is inversely proportional to x.
Use this information to copy and complete each table.

a)
x	12	6
y	15	

b)
x	11	
y	4	2

c)
x	2	4	8	10
y			20	

d)
x		7
y	25.2	9

e)
x		3	6	30
y	180		15	

f)
x		4	20	100
y	320		4	

4 p is inversely proportional to q.
   a) Copy and complete the table on the right.
   b) Use the table to draw the graph of this inverse proportion.

q	0.2	0.4	0.5	1	2	4	5	10
p					1			

14.3 Proportion Problems

Exercise 1

1 It costs me £20 to put 12.5 litres of petrol in my car. How much will it cost me for a full tank of petrol if the tank holds 60 litres?

2 Emma changed £500 into Rand (R) before going on holiday to South Africa. The exchange rate at the time was £1 = R 17.5.
   a) How many Rand did she get for her £500?

   On holiday Emma spent R 6200. When she got home, she changed the Rand she had left (from her original amount) back into pounds. The exchange rate had changed to £1 = R 16.9.
   b) How much money, in pounds, did she get back?

3 It takes a runner 8 minutes to run 5 laps of a 400 m track. How many minutes will it take the runner, running at the same speed, to complete 9 laps of a 200 m track?

4 8 chickens will lay 20 eggs in 3 days.
If chickens always lay eggs at the same rate,
   a) how many days will it take 12 chickens to lay 100 eggs?
   b) how many chickens would be required if a farmer needed 30 eggs each day?

5
a	2	4	10	80
b	20			

Copy and complete the table above if:
   a) a is directly proportional to b.
   b) a is inversely proportional to b.

6 Sketch a graph to show each of the following proportions:
   a) y is directly proportional to x.
   b) y is inversely proportional to x.

7 The formula below shows how speed, distance and time are related:
$$\text{Speed} = \frac{\text{Distance}}{\text{Time}}$$
For each of the following statements, decide whether they are true or false.
   a) For a fixed distance, speed is inversely proportional to time.
   b) For a fixed speed, distance is inversely proportional to time.
   c) For a fixed speed, time is directly proportional to distance.

8 y is inversely proportional to x and when $y = 30$, $x = 4$.
   a) Find y when $x = 8$.
   b) Find x when $y = 0.5$.
   c) Find an equation in the form $y = \frac{A}{x}$ to represent this inverse proportion.

Section 14 — Proportion

Section 15 — Angles and 2D Shapes

15.1 Basic Angle Properties

Angles at a point on a straight line add up to **180°**.

$a + b + c = 180°$

Angles around a point add up to **360°**.

$a + b + c + d = 360°$

Perpendicular lines meet at 90° to form a **right angle** (shown by the little square).

$a + b = 90°$

Angles within a **right angle** add up to **90°**.

Example 1

Find the size of angle a.

1. Angles on a straight line add up to 180°. Use this to form an equation in terms of a.
2. Simplify the equation.
3. Solve the equation to find a.

$40° + a + 90° = 180°$
$a + 130° = 180°$
$a = 180° - 130°$
$\underline{a = 50°}$

Exercise 1

In **Questions 1-3**, find the missing angles marked with letters.
(The angles aren't drawn accurately, so you shouldn't try to measure them.)

Example 2

Find the value of a in the diagram.

1. Angles around a point add up to 360°. Use this to form an equation in terms of a.
2. Simplify the equation.
3. Then solve your equation to find a.

$a + 2a + 80° + 40° + 90° = 360°$
$3a + 210° = 360°$
$3a = 360° - 210° = 150°$
$a = 150 \div 3 = \underline{\mathbf{50°}}$

Exercise 2

The angles in this Exercise aren't drawn accurately, so don't try to measure them.

1 Find the value of each of the letters in the following diagrams.

2 Using the diagram on the right, state whether the following are true or false. Give a reason for your answer in each case.

a) EB is a straight line
b) AO is perpendicular to EO
c) FC is a straight line
d) the angle $p = 98°$

3 Find the value of each of the letters in the following diagrams.

4 Explain why the line AOB on the right cannot be a straight line.

5 a) Given that $x = 40°$, find the sizes of the three angles involving x in the diagram.
b) Find the value of m.

Section 15 — Angles and 2D Shapes **169**

15.2 Triangles

An **isosceles** triangle has 2 equal sides (shown by the 'tick marks'). It also has 2 equal angles.

An **equilateral** triangle has 3 equal sides. It also has 3 equal angles.

The sides and angles of a **scalene** triangle are all different.

A **right-angled** triangle has 1 right angle.

An **acute-angled** triangle has 3 acute angles.

An **obtuse-angled** triangle has 1 obtuse angle.

The angles in **any** triangle add up to 180°.

$$a + b + c = 180°$$

Example 1

Find the value of x in the triangle shown.

1. The angles in a triangle add up to 180°. Use this to form an equation in terms of x. $\implies$ $x + 60° + 90° = 180°$
   $x + 150° = 180°$
2. Solve your equation to find x. $\implies$ $x = 180° - 150° = \underline{\mathbf{30°}}$

Exercise 1

1   Describe each of these triangles using the above definitions.

a)   b)   c)   d)

In **Questions 2-7**, the angles aren't drawn accurately, so don't try to measure them.

2   Find the missing angles marked with letters.

72°, 55°, a

68°, b

21°, 144°, c

d, 74°

170   Section 15 — Angles and 2D Shapes

3 Find the missing angles marked with letters.

Example 2

Find the value of x in the triangle shown.

1. Form an equation in terms of x.
2. Solve your equation to find x.

$x + 2x + 3x = 180°$
$6x = 180°$
$x = 180° \div 6 = \underline{\mathbf{30°}}$

4 Find the values of the letters shown in the following diagrams.

Example 3

Find the values of j and k in the isosceles triangle shown.

1. The triangle is isosceles, so angle j is the same size as the angle of 35°. $\underline{\mathbf{j = 35°}}$

2. Now use the fact that angles in a triangle add up to 180° to form an equation in terms of k. Then solve your equation to find k.

$35° + 35° + k = 180°$
$70° + k = 180°$
$k = 180° - 70° = \underline{\mathbf{110°}}$

5 Find the values of the letters shown in these diagrams.

6 a) Find the value of x.
b) Find the value of y.

7 a) Find the value of p.
b) Find the value of q.

Section 15 — Angles and 2D Shapes

15.3 Parallel and Intersecting Lines

Opposite Angles

When two straight lines **intersect** (or cross), two pairs of **opposite angles** are formed. Opposite angles are equal.

Example 1

Find the values of a, b and c shown in the diagram.

1. a and 70° are opposite angles, so they are equal. $\underline{a = 70°}$
2. b and the angle marked 70° lie on a straight line, so they add up to 180°. $70° + b = 180°$
   $b = 180° - 70° = \underline{110°}$
3. c and b are opposite angles, so they are equal. $c = b = \underline{110°}$

Exercise 1

In **Questions 1-4**, the angles aren't drawn accurately, so don't try to measure them.

1 Find the missing angles marked by letters.

2 The diagram on the right shows a teepee in the shape of an isosceles triangle.
   a) Find the size of angle v.
   b) Use your answer to write down the value of w. Give a reason for your answer.

3 Find the missing angles marked by letters.

4 The diagram on the right shows two isosceles triangles. Find the missing angles marked by letters.

172   *Section 15 — Angles and 2D Shapes*

Alternate Angles

When a straight line crosses two parallel lines (shown by the arrows), it forms two pairs of **alternate angles** (in a sort of Z-shape). Alternate angles are equal.

Example 2

Find the values of a, b and c in the diagram.

1. a and 43° are alternate angles, so they are equal. $\underline{\boldsymbol{a = 43°}}$
2. b and the angle marked 43° lie on a straight line, so they add up to 180°. $43° + b = 180°$ $b = 180° - 43° = \underline{\boldsymbol{137°}}$
3. c and b are alternate angles, so they are equal. $c = b = \underline{\boldsymbol{137°}}$

Exercise 2

In **Questions 1-3**, the angles aren't drawn accurately, so don't try to measure them.

1 Find the missing angles marked by letters.

2 The diagram on the right shows a staircase between two parallel floors of a building. The staircase makes an angle of 42° with the lower floor.

   a) Write down the angle that the staircase makes with the upper floor, marked x on the diagram.

   b) Give a reason for your answer.

3 Find the missing angles marked by letters.

Section 15 — Angles and 2D Shapes 173

Corresponding Angles and Allied Angles

Corresponding angles formed by parallel lines are equal.

Corresponding angles form a sort of F-shape.

$a + b = 180°$

When a straight line crosses two parallel lines to make a kind of C-shape, the interior angles are known as **allied angles** and add up to 180°.

Example 3

Find the values of a, b and c shown in the diagram.

1. a and 62° are corresponding angles, so they are equal. $\underline{a = 62°}$
2. b and the angle marked 62° lie on a straight line, so they add up to 180°. (Or you could say a and b are allied angles, so they add up to 180°.)
   $62° + b = 180°$
   $b = 180° - 62° = \underline{118°}$
3. c and b are corresponding angles, so they're equal. $c = b = \underline{118°}$

Exercise 3

In **Questions 1-4**, the angles aren't drawn accurately, so don't try to measure them.

1 Find the missing angles marked by letters.

2 Find the missing angles marked by letters.

174   *Section 15 — Angles and 2D Shapes*

3 Two wooden posts stand vertically on sloped ground. The first post makes an angle of 99° with the downward slope, as shown. Find the angle that the second post makes with the upward slope, labelled y on the diagram.

4 Find the missing angles marked by letters.

Exercise 4 — Mixed Exercise

In **Questions 1-2**, the angles aren't drawn accurately, so don't try to measure them.

1 Find the missing angles marked by letters. In each case, give a reason for your answer.

2 The diagram on the right shows some scaffolding. The triangle formed between the two horizontal bars is isosceles.

Find the size of angles w, x, y and z, giving a reason for your answer in each case.

Section 15 — Angles and 2D Shapes **175**

15.4 Quadrilaterals

A **quadrilateral** is a 4-sided shape. The angles in a quadrilateral add up to **360°**.

Example 1
Find the missing angle x in this quadrilateral.

1. The angles in a quadrilateral add up to 360°.
   Use this to write an equation involving x.
2. Then solve your equation to find the value of x.

$79° + 73° + 119° + x = 360°$
$271° + x = 360°$
$x = 360° - 271° = \underline{\mathbf{89°}}$

Exercise 1

1 Find the size of the angles marked by letters in the following quadrilaterals.
   (They're not drawn accurately, so don't try to measure them.)

   Shape 1: a, 93°, 69°, 86°
   Shape 2: 76°, b, 103°, 89°
   Shape 3: c, 129°, 67°, 74°
   Shape 4: 72°, 112°, 106°, d
   Shape 5: 119°, e, 60°, 72°

Squares and Rectangles

A **square** is a quadrilateral with 4 equal sides and 4 angles of 90°.

A **rectangle** is a quadrilateral with 4 angles of 90° and opposite sides of the same length.

Exercise 2

1 Copy the diagram below, then add two more points to form a square. Join the points to complete the square.

2 Copy the diagram below, then add two more points to form a rectangle. Join the points to complete the rectangle.

Section 15 — Angles and 2D Shapes

3 a) Measure the length of the diagonals on the square on the right. What do you notice?
  b) At what angle do the two diagonals cross?
  c) By measuring diagonals, determine which of the following are squares.
   (i)   (ii)   (iii)

Parallelograms and Rhombuses

$a + b = 180°$

A **parallelogram** is a quadrilateral with 2 pairs of equal, parallel sides. Opposite angles of a parallelogram are equal. Neighbouring angles add up to 180°.

A **rhombus** is a quadrilateral with 2 pairs of parallel sides, all of the same length. Opposite angles of a rhombus are equal. Neighbouring angles add up to 180°.

Example 2

Find the size of the angles marked with letters in this rhombus.

1. Opposite angles in a rhombus are equal. Use this fact to find angle x.
2. Neighbouring angles in a rhombus add up to 180°. Use this fact to find angle y.
3. Opposite angles in a rhombus are equal, so z is the same size as y.

$x = \mathbf{60°}$
$60° + y = 180°$
$y = 180° - 60° = \mathbf{120°}$
$z = \mathbf{120°}$

Exercise 3

1 a) Copy the diagram on the right. Add one more point and join the points to form a rhombus.
  b) On a new grid, plot four points to form a parallelogram.

2 Calculate the size of the angles marked by letters in these quadrilaterals. (They're not drawn accurately, so don't try to measure them.)

122°, 72°, 108°, 118°, 51°, 110°

Section 15 — Angles and 2D Shapes

Kites

A **kite** is a quadrilateral with 2 pairs of equal sides and 1 pair of equal angles in opposite corners.

Example 3

Find the size of the angles marked with letters in this kite.

1. a and the 112° angle must be equal.
2. A kite is a quadrilateral, so its angles add up to 360°. Use this to write an equation in terms of b.

$a = \underline{\mathbf{112°}}$
$112° + 112° + 89° + b = 360°$
$313° + b = 360°$
$b = 360° - 313° = \underline{\mathbf{47°}}$

Exercise 4

1 Which letter goes in each box to complete the sentences about this kite?

   a) Angle b is the same size as angle ☐
   b) The length of side P is the same as side ☐
   c) The length of side R is the same as side ☐

2 Find the size of the angles marked by letters in these kites. (They're not drawn accurately, so don't try to measure them.)

Trapeziums

$a + b = 180°$
$c + d = 180°$

A **trapezium** is a quadrilateral with 1 pair of parallel sides.

$a + b = 180°$

An **isosceles trapezium** is a trapezium with 2 pairs of equal angles, and 2 sides of the same length.

178 Section 15 — Angles and 2D Shapes

Example 4

Find the size of the angles marked with letters in this isosceles trapezium.

1. This is an isosceles trapezium, so a must equal 58°.

   $a = \mathbf{58°}$

2. Angle c and the angle of 58° must add up to 180°.

   $c + 58° = 180°$
   $c = 180° - 58° = \mathbf{122°}$

3. Angles a and b must add up to 180°.
   (Or use the fact that b and c must be equal.)

   $a + b = 180°$
   $b = 180° - a = 180° - 58° = \mathbf{122°}$

Exercise 5

1 Choose the correct word from each pair to complete the following sentences.
   a) A trapezium is a quadrilateral with one pair of (**parallel** / **equal**) sides.
   b) An isosceles trapezium has (**one pair** / **two pairs**) of equal angles.
   c) An isosceles trapezium has (**one pair** / **two pairs**) of parallel sides.
   d) An isosceles trapezium has (**one pair** / **two pairs**) of equal sides.
   e) The angles in a trapezium add up to (**180°** / **360°**).

2 Find the size of the angles marked by letters in these trapeziums. (Don't measure them.)

Exercise 6 — Mixed Exercise

1 Match one name from the box to each of the quadrilaterals below.

   square   kite   rectangle   trapezium   parallelogram

   a)   b)   c)   d)   e)

2 Write down all the different types of quadrilaterals which satisfy each of the following properties.
   a) 4 equal sides
   b) 4 angles of 90°
   c) 2 pairs of equal sides
   d) 2 pairs of parallel sides
   e) at least 1 pair of parallel sides
   f) exactly 1 pair of parallel sides

3 Find the size of the angles marked by letters in these diagrams. (Don't measure them.)

4 A quadrilateral has 40°, 83° and 99° angles. Find the size of the fourth angle.

5 A parallelogram has two angles of 100° each. Find the size of the other two angles.

6 An isosceles trapezium has two angles of 53°. Find the size of the other two angles.

7 A kite has exactly one angle of 50° and exactly one angle of 90°. Find the size of the other two angles.

15.5 Interior and Exterior Angles

A **polygon** is a shape whose sides are all straight.

A **regular polygon** has sides of equal length and angles that are all equal.

Polygons have special names depending on the number of sides they have.
For example: (i) A polygon with 3 sides is a **triangle**. (ii) A polygon with 4 sides is a **quadrilateral**.
(iii) A polygon with 5 sides is a **pentagon**. (iv) A polygon with 6 sides is a **hexagon**.

Interior Angles

The **interior angles** of a polygon are the angles inside each corner.

The **sum** of a polygon's interior angles depends on the **number of sides** it has.
For example, the interior angles of a shape with 3 sides (a triangle) always add up to 180°.

Example 1

Find the sum of the interior angles of a pentagon.
1. You can find the sum of a shape's interior angles by splitting it up into triangles. So first draw any pentagon — it doesn't have to be regular.
2. Split the pentagon into triangles by drawing lines from one corner to all the others.
3. Angles in a triangle add up to 180°, and there are 3 triangles.

So the sum of the interior angles of a pentagon is 3 × 180° = **540°**

Section 15 — Angles and 2D Shapes

Exercise 1

1 By dividing each shape into triangles, find the sum of the interior angles of the following:

a)   b)   c)   d)

2 Find the sum of the interior angles of a polygon with:
a) 6 sides   b) 10 sides   c) 12 sides   d) 20 sides

Example 2

A pentagon has four interior angles of 100°. Find the size of the fifth angle.

1. The interior angles of a pentagon add up to 540°. Use this fact to write an equation for the size of the missing angle, x.

    $100° + 100° + 100° + 100° + x = 540°$
    $400° + x = 540°$

2. Solve your equation to find x.

    $x = 540° − 400° = \underline{\mathbf{140°}}$

3 Sketch the polygon shown on the right.
 a) What happens when you try to divide the polygon into triangles by drawing a line from the 65° angle to each of the other corners?
 b) Join the corner marked x to each of the other corners to split the shape into triangles.
 c) Find the sum of the interior angles of the shape.
 d) Find the size of the angle marked x.

4 Find the size of the angles marked by letters in these polygons.

Interior Angle Formula

There's a formula connecting the **sum** of a polygon's **interior angles** (S) and the **number of sides** (n) the polygon has.

$$S = (n − 2) \times 180°$$

Example 3

Find the size of each of the interior angles of a regular hexagon.

1. Use the formula to find the sum of the interior angles of a hexagon.

    $S = (6 − 2) \times 180°$
    $= 4 \times 180° = 720°$

2. All the angles in a regular polygon are equal, so divide the sum by the number of angles.

    So each interior angle of a regular hexagon is $720° \div 6 = \underline{\mathbf{120°}}$

Section 15 — Angles and 2D Shapes

5 A regular heptagon is shown on the right.
   a) Find the sum of the interior angles of a heptagon.
   b) Find the size of each of the interior angles of a regular heptagon.

6 Find the size of each of the interior angles in the following shapes.
   a) Regular octagon (8 sides)
   b) Regular nonagon (9 sides)
   c) Regular decagon (10 sides)

7 Four angles of a pentagon are 110°.
   a) Find the size of the fifth angle.
   b) Is this a regular pentagon? Give a reason for your answer.

Exterior Angles

The **exterior angles** of a polygon are the angles between a side and a line that extends out from one of the neighbouring sides.

The sum of the exterior angles of any polygon is **360°**.

$$a + b + c + d + e = 360°$$

You can use the **exterior angle** to find the corresponding **interior angle** using this formula:

$$\text{Interior angle} = 180° - \text{Exterior angle}$$

In a **regular n-sided polygon**, all the exterior angles are **equal** and their size is given by:

$$\text{Exterior angle} = \frac{360°}{n}$$

Example 4

Find the size of each of the exterior angles of a regular hexagon.

1. A hexagon has 6 sides.
2. The hexagon is regular so use the exterior angle formula.

$360° \div 6 = 60°$
So each exterior angle is **60°**

Exercise 2

1 The diagram on the right shows a regular pentagon with the exterior angles marked on.
   a) Find a, the size of each of the exterior angles of the pentagon.
   b) Hence find b, the size of each of the interior angles of the pentagon.

2 **a)** Find the size of each of the exterior angles of the following polygons.
   (i) regular heptagon   **(ii)** regular octagon   **(iii)** regular nonagon
   b) Use your answers to part **a)** to find the size of each of the interior angles of these polygons.

Section 15 — Angles and 2D Shapes

3 Find the size of the angles marked by letters in these diagrams.

4 Find the size of the unknown exterior angle in a shape whose other exterior angles are:
a) 100°, 68°, 84° and 55°
b) 30°, 68°, 45°, 52°, 75° and 50°
c) 42°, 51°, 60°, 49°, 88° and 35°
d) 19°, 36°, 28°, 57°, 101°, 57° and 22°

Example 5

A regular polygon has exterior angles of 30°.
How many sides does the polygon have?

It's a regular polygon so just put 30° into the exterior angle formula.

$30° = \frac{360°}{n}$

$n = 360° \div 30° = 12$

So the regular polygon has **12 sides**.

5 A regular polygon has exterior angles of 45°.
a) How many sides does the polygon have? What is the name of this kind of polygon?
b) Sketch the polygon.
c) What is the size of each of the polygon's interior angles?
d) What is the sum of the polygon's interior angles?

6 The exterior angles of some regular polygons are given below.
For each exterior angle, find:
  (i) the number of sides the polygon has,
  (ii) the size of each of the polygon's interior angles,
  (iii) the sum of the polygon's interior angles.
a) 60°   b) 90°   c) 40°   d) 120°   e) 10°
f) 9°   g) 6°   h) 5°   i) 4°   j) 3°

7 Find the values of the letters in the following diagrams.

Section 15 — Angles and 2D Shapes

15.6 Symmetry

Line Symmetry

A **line of symmetry** on a shape is a mirror line, where you can fold the shape so that both halves match up exactly. Each side of the line of symmetry is a **reflection** of the other.

Line of Symmetry

Isosceles Triangle

Example 1

How many lines of symmetry does an equilateral triangle have?

An equilateral triangle has three mirror lines, where the shape can be folded perfectly in half.

An equilateral triangle has **3 lines of symmetry**.

Exercise 1

1. Copy each of the shapes below, then draw on any lines of symmetry. State the number of lines of symmetry you have drawn for each shape.

   a)   b)   c)   d)

   e)   f)   g)   h)

2. Sketch each of the shapes below, then draw on any lines of symmetry. State the number of lines of symmetry you have drawn for each shape.

   a) rectangle
   b) rhombus
   c) parallelogram
   d) isosceles trapezium
   e) regular pentagon
   f) regular hexagon
   g) regular heptagon
   h) regular octagon

Section 15 — Angles and 2D Shapes

Rotational Symmetry

The **order of rotational symmetry** of a shape is the number of positions you can rotate (turn) the shape into so that it looks exactly the same.

Equilateral Triangle → → Rotational symmetry of order 3

A shape that only looks the same once every complete turn has rotational symmetry of **order 1** (or **no rotational symmetry**).

Example 2

What is the order of rotational symmetry of a rhombus?

There are two orientations in which a rhombus looks exactly the same.

A rhombus has **rotational symmetry of order 2**.

Exercise 2

1 Find the order of rotational symmetry of each of the following shapes.

a) b) c) d) e)

f) g) h) i) j)

2 Sketch each of the shapes below, then find the order of rotational symmetry for each.

a) square b) isosceles triangle c) scalene triangle d) isosceles trapezium
e) regular pentagon f) regular hexagon g) regular octagon h) regular decagon

Section 15 — Angles and 2D Shapes

Exercise 3 — Mixed Exercise

1 For each of the shapes below, find:
  (i) the number of lines of symmetry,
  (ii) the order of rotational symmetry.

a) equilateral triangle, 3 cm, 3 cm, 3 cm

b) right-angled triangle, 3 cm, 4 cm, 5 cm

c) plus/cross shape, 4 cm, 5 cm, 5 cm, 5 cm, 5 cm, 4 cm

d) kite, 3 cm, 5 cm, 3 cm, 5 cm

2 Decide which of the shapes below matches each of the descriptions.

A, B, C, D

a) 1 line of symmetry, no rotational symmetry.
b) 4 lines of symmetry, rotational symmetry of order 4.
c) No lines of symmetry, rotational symmetry of order 2.
d) 5 lines of symmetry, rotational symmetry of order 5.

3 Copy the diagram below, then shade one more square to make a pattern with 1 line of symmetry.

4 Copy the diagram below, then shade two more squares to make a pattern with 2 lines of symmetry.

5 Copy the diagram below, then shade one more square to make a pattern with rotational symmetry of order 2.

6 Copy the diagram below, then shade two more squares to make a pattern with 4 lines of symmetry and rotational symmetry of order 4.

Section 15 — Angles and 2D Shapes

15.7 Angles and 2D Shapes Problems

Exercise 1

For **Questions 1-3**, find the missing angles marked with letters.
(None of the pictures are drawn accurately, so don't measure them.)

1 162°, a ; 28°, b ; 53°, c, d, e ; f, f, f, f

115°, 59°, g ; 135°, 41°, h ; i, i, i, i, i ; 31°, j ; 58°, 75°, m, l, n, k

2 101°, 87°, r ; s, 95°, 103°, t ; 62°, u, v ; y, 102°, w, x, 71°, 95°

3 124°, o ; p, 62°, q ; r, 108°, 85°

4 This question is about shapes *A-G* below.

A, B, C, D, E, F, G

a) Which of the shapes are polygons?
b) Which of the shapes are hexagons?
c) Which of the shapes are pentagons?
d) Which of the shapes are quadrilaterals?

5 Find the size of the angles marked with letters.

122°, 122°, a, a ; b, 35°, 55° ; 48°, d, c ; 74°, e, 40°, g, f, h

Section 15 — Angles and 2D Shapes

6 Find the size of the angles marked with letters.

7 Are the lines *AB* and *CD* parallel to each other? Explain your answer.

8 a) Calculate the sum of the interior angles of a hexagon.
   b) Use your answer to find angle *x*.

9 a) Calculate the sum of the interior angles of a pentagon.
   b) Use your answer to find the size of angle *y*.

10 Find angles *w* and *z*.

11 Find angle *p* in the diagram below.

12 The diagram below shows a kite and a square.
   a) Write down the value of *a*.
   b) Use your answer to find the size of angles *b* and *c*.

13 a) Find *x* in the diagram below.
   b) Use your answer to find *y*.

14 Find *x* and *y* in the diagram below.

Section 16 — Units, Measuring and Estimating

16.1 Reading Scales

Reading Scales

Some marks on a **scale** have a number written next to them. Usually, other marks don't — you have to work out what they represent.

Example 1

Write down the volume of liquid in the beaker on the right.

1. Write down the interval between the numbered units.   10 ml
2. Divide this interval by the number of smaller divisions between each number to find what each division represents. Here, there are 2 divisions between each number. $10 \div 2 = 5$ ml
3. The amount in the beaker is 20 ml, plus the amount represented by one small division. $20 + 5 = \underline{\textbf{25 ml}}$

Exercise 1

1. Write down the lengths shown by the arrows on the ruler. Give your answers in centimetres.

   a) [ruler 0–10 cm with arrows A, B, C]

   b) [ruler 0–100 cm with arrows A, B, C]

   c) [ruler 20–60 cm with arrows A, B, C]

2. Use the fact that 1 cm = 10 mm to write down the length of each of the bugs in mm.

   a)   b)   c)

Section 16 — Units, Measuring and Estimating

3 Write down the mass shown by the arrow on each scale.

a) b) c) d)

4 Write down the weight of the bananas.

5 Write down the volume of liquid in the bottle.

6 Write down the volume of liquid shown in each of these containers.

a) b) c) d)

Inaccuracy of Measurements

The **accuracy** of a measurement depends on the device being used to make that measurement.

For example, this ruler measures to the nearest millimetre — so both these bugs seem to be 9 mm long.
But using a more precise piece of equipment, you can see the first bug is actually slightly smaller than the second.

When you measure to the nearest millimetre, anything from 8.5 mm up to 9.5 mm would round to 9 mm. We say that 8.5 mm is the **lower bound** and 9.5 mm is the **upper bound**.

Example 2

The length of a pen is measured and found to be 15 cm, to the nearest 1 cm.
Write down the lower bound and the upper bound for the pen's length.

1. The length has been rounded to the nearest cm.
   The smallest value that would round up to 15 cm is 14.5 cm.   Lower bound = **14.5 cm**
2. The biggest value that would round down to 15 cm is 15.5 cm.   Upper bound = **15.5 cm**

Section 16 — Units, Measuring and Estimating

Exercise 2

1 Find the lower and upper bounds for each of these measurements.
   a) A length of 10 cm, which has been measured to the nearest 1 cm.
   b) A mass of 15 g, which has been measured to the nearest 1 g.
   c) A length of 23 km, which has been measured to the nearest 1 km.
   d) A volume of 18 litres, which has been measured to the nearest 1 litre.
   e) A length of 57 mm, which has been measured to the nearest 1 mm.
   f) A volume of 133 ml, which has been measured to the nearest 1 ml.

Example 3
The volume of a teacup is measured and found to be 135 ml, to the nearest 5 ml.
Write down the lower bound and the upper bound for the teacup's volume.

1. The volume has been rounded to the nearest 5 ml.   Lower bound = 135 − (5 ÷ 2)
   Find the lower bound by subtracting <u>half</u> of 5 ml   = **132.5 ml**
   from 135 ml.
2. Find the upper bound by adding <u>half</u> of 5 ml to 135 ml.   Upper bound = 135 + (5 ÷ 2)
3. So values from 132.5 to 137.5 ml would round to 135 ml,   = **137.5 ml**
   when measured to the nearest 5 ml.

2 Find the lower and upper bounds for each of these measurements.
   a) A length of 175 cm, which has been measured to the nearest 5 cm.
   b) A length of 890 km, which has been measured to the nearest 10 km.
   c) A mass of 230 g, which has been measured to the nearest 5 g.
   d) A volume of 65 litres, which has been measured to the nearest 5 litres.
   e) A volume of 2100 litres, which has been measured to the nearest 100 litres.
   f) A length of 20 m, which has been measured to the nearest 2 m.

3 A pipette contains 5.7 cm³ of liquid, measured to the nearest 0.1 cm³.
   What is the greatest amount of liquid that could be in the pipette?

4 A snake is measured to be 10.6 m long to the nearest 0.2 m.
   Write down the lower and upper bound for the snake's length.

5 a) What temperature is shown on the thermometer on the right?
   b) This thermometer is only accurate to the nearest 4 °C. Tom's tomato plants can only survive outside over 22.5 °C. Is it safe for Tom to put his plants outside?

6 Liz's house has a front door which is 96.5 cm wide.
   She wants to buy a table which is given as 95 cm wide, to the nearest 2 cm.
   Can she be sure that the table will fit through her door?

7 A set of kitchen scales can measure masses correct to the nearest 10 g.
   Janek weighs out 100 g of flour. Work out the lower and upper bounds for the mass of the flour.

8 Tanya and Kyle measure their heights. They both say that they are 170 cm to the nearest 10 cm.
   What is the maximum possible difference between their heights?

Section 16 — Units, Measuring and Estimating

16.2 Converting Metric Units — Length, Mass and Volume

To convert between metric units, multiply or divide by the correct **conversion factor**.

Length	Mass	Volume
1 cm = 10 mm	1 g = 1000 mg	1 litre (l) = 1000 ml
1 m = 100 cm	1 kg = 1000 g	1 litre = 100 centilitres (cl)
1 km = 1000 m	1 tonne = 1000 kg	1 ml = 1 cm^3

Example 1

a) Convert 2.5 m into cm.
1. There are 100 cm in 1 m, so the conversion factor is 100.   1 m = 100 cm
2. To convert m into cm you need to multiply by the conversion factor.   So 2.5 m = 2.5 × 100 = **250 cm**

b) Convert 2500 m into km.
1. There are 1000 m in 1 km, so the conversion factor is 1000.   1 km = 1000 m
2. To convert m into km you need to divide by the conversion factor.   So 2500 m = 2500 ÷ 1000 = **2.5 km**

Exercise 1

For **Questions 1-3**, convert each measurement into the units given.

1   a) 2 cm into mm   b) 3 l into ml   c) 4.1 g into mg   d) 15 ml into cm^3
     e) 126.7 cm^3 into ml   f) 2 km into m   g) 2.5 l into cl   h) 2.3 tonnes into kg

2   a) 400 cm into m   b) 3400 m into km   c) 50 cm into m   d) 3000 g into kg
     e) 2000 ml into l   f) 500 ml into l   g) 246 kg into tonnes   h) 500 cl into l

3   a) 2 mm into cm   b) 3 kg into g   c) 12.7 l into ml   d) 379 mm into cm
     e) 3000 kg into tonnes   f) 400 mg into g   g) 123 ml into l   h) 51.16 g into kg
     i) 120 cl into l   j) 271.65 cm into m   k) 22.3 mg into g   l) 105 cm into m

4   a) Convert 1.2 kg to grams.
     b) Use your answer to find how many 30 g servings there are in a 1.2 kg box of cereal.

5   Jane is having a party for 30 guests. Her glasses have a capacity of 400 ml each. If she wants everyone to have a glass of juice, how many 2 litres bottles of juice should she buy?

6   a) Convert 5 m into cm.
     b) Use your answer to **a)** to convert 5 m into mm.

For **Questions 7-8**, convert each measurement into the units given.

7   a) 0.2 km into cm   b) 0.6 tonnes into g   c) 4 km into cm
     d) 0.231 kg into mg   e) 62 m into mm   f) 0.0034 km into mm

8   a) 1 mm into m   b) 3000 mg into kg   c) 150 cm^3 into l
     d) 1532 g into tonnes   e) 1005 cm into km   f) 3023 mg into kg

Section 16 — Units, Measuring and Estimating

9 Jack buys 1.2 kg of flour.
How many pizzas can he make if each pizza needs 200 g of flour?

10 A go-kart has a 5 litre petrol tank.
It uses 10 ml of petrol per lap of a 400 m track.

  a) If James fills up the tank, how many laps of the track can he do?

  b) How many km can James travel on each full tank of petrol?

Example 2
Find the total of 0.2 tonnes, 31.8 kg and 1700 g. Give your answer in kg.

1. Convert all the masses to kilograms.　　0.2 tonnes = 0.2 × 1000 = 200 kg
　　　　　　　　　　　　　　　　　　　　　1700 g = 1700 ÷ 1000 = 1.7 kg

2. Add the masses together.　　　　　　　200 kg + 31.8 kg + 1.7 kg = **233.5 kg**

Exercise 2

1 Complete each calculation.
  a) 3200 ml + 75.3 l = ▢ l
  b) 7.2 tonnes + 340 kg = ▢ tonnes
  c) 681 cm + 51.2 m = ▢ cm
  d) 16.49 km + 6750 m = ▢ m
  e) 3 kg + 375 g + 0.2 kg = ▢ kg
  f) 100 cm + 0.35 m + 12.6 m = ▢ cm
  g) 300 cm^3 + 0.7 l + 250 ml = ▢ ml
  h) 7 m + 20 cm + 35 mm = ▢ cm
  i) 4000 g + 200 kg + 1 tonne = ▢ kg
  j) 12.92 km + 170.6 m + 2050 cm = ▢ m

2 Lucy grows 4.6 kg of potatoes and sells 800 g. What is the mass, in g, of her remaining potatoes?

3 How many metres further is a journey of 3.4 km than a journey of 1800 m?

4 A recipe uses 450 g of flour, 0.2 kg of margarine, 300 g of fruit and 0.1 kg of sugar.
How much more than 1 kg is the total mass of these ingredients? Give your answer in kg.

5 A recycling van collects 3200 g of paper, 15 kg of aluminium, 0.72 tonnes
of glass and 3.2 kg of cardboard. What is the mass of all the recycling in kg?

6 Sharon, Trevor and Elsie get into a cable car while skiing.
Sharon weighs 55.2 kg, Trevor weighs 78.1 kg and Elsie weighs 65.9 kg.
Each person's equipment weighs 9000 g. The cable car is unsafe when carrying
a mass of over a quarter of a tonne. Will Sharon, Trevor and Elsie be safe?

Exercise 3

1 Callum buys 2 tonnes of topsoil for his gardening business.
If he uses 250 kg each day, how long will his supply last?

2 Milly runs a 1500 m fun run, a 100 m sprint and a 13.2 km race.
How many km has she run in total?

3 A café puts two slices of ham into every ham sandwich. A slice of ham weighs 10 g.
If the café expects to sell 500 ham sandwiches, how many 1.5 kg packs of ham should they order?

Section 16 — Units, Measuring and Estimating

4 A reservoir contains 600 000 l of water. A stream flowing into it adds 750 000 ml of water a day.
   a) If no water was removed from the reservoir, how many litres would the volume of water increase by each day?
   b) The reservoir can only hold 800 000 l of water. How many days will it take for the reservoir to start overflowing?

5 a) A recipe for lasagne needs 0.7 kg of minced beef, 400 g of tomato sauce, 300 g of cheese sauce, 0.2 kg of lasagne and 2500 mg of herbs and spices. How many kg do these ingredients weigh?
   b) If 0.2 kg of ingredients will feed one person, how many people can be fed with this recipe?

16.3 Converting Units — Area and Volume

Area

Area is measured in units squared (e.g. m^2, cm^2, mm^2).

To convert between different units of area, multiply or divide by the **square** of the 'length' conversion factor.

For example, the conversion factor between cm and mm is 10. This means the conversion factor between cm^2 and mm^2 is $10^2 = 10 \times 10 = 100$.

$1\ cm^2 = 10 \times 10 = 100\ mm^2$

$1\ cm = 10\ mm$

Example 1

Find the area of this rectangle in mm^2 by:

a) first converting its length and width to mm.
   1. Convert the dimensions to mm.   5 cm = 50 mm
      3 cm = 30 mm
   2. Multiply to get the area. $50 \times 30 = \mathbf{1500\ mm^2}$

b) first finding the area in cm^2, and then using the appropriate conversion factor.
   1. Find the area in cm^2. $5 \times 3 = 15\ cm^2$
   2. Find the conversion factor from cm^2 to mm^2.   1 cm = 10 mm, so $1\ cm^2 = 10 \times 10 = 100\ mm^2$.
   3. Use the conversion factor to convert 15 cm^2 to mm^2. $15\ cm^2 = 15 \times 100 = \mathbf{1500\ mm^2}$

Example 2

Convert an area of 600 cm^2 to m^2.

1. Work out the conversion factor from cm^2 to m^2.   1 m = 100 cm, so $1\ m^2 = 100 \times 100 = 10\ 000\ cm^2$.
2. Divide by the conversion factor. $600\ cm^2 = 600 \div 10\ 000 = \mathbf{0.06\ m^2}$

Section 16 — Units, Measuring and Estimating

Exercise 1

1. Work out the area (in m²) of a field measuring 2 km by 3 km by:
   a) first converting its length and width to m.
   b) first finding the area in km², and then using the appropriate conversion factor.

2. a) Calculate the area (in mm²) of a sticker measuring 20 mm by 40 mm.
   b) Convert this area to cm² by using the appropriate conversion factor.

For **Questions 3-4**, convert each area into the units given.

3. a) 26 cm² into mm²   b) 0.036 km² into m²   c) 1.7 cm² into mm²
   d) 1.05 m² into cm²   e) 0.07 km² into m²   f) 1.2 m² into cm²

4. a) 84 mm² into cm²   b) 1750 cm² into m²   c) 29 000 mm² into cm²
   d) 3 150 000 m² into km²   e) 8500 mm² into cm²   f) 1700 cm² into m²

5. One bottle of weedkiller can treat an area of 16 m². How many bottles of this weedkiller should Ali buy to treat her lawn measuring 990 cm by 430 cm?

6. Sandeesh wants to carpet two rectangular rooms. One of the rooms measures 1.7 m by 3 m, while the other is 670 cm by 420 cm. How many square metres of carpet will she need?

7. a) Convert 8 500 000 mm² to cm².
   b) Use your answer to **a)** to convert 8 500 000 mm² into m².

8. a) Convert 0.00065 m² to cm².
   b) Use your answer to **a)** to convert 0.00065 m² into mm².

9. Convert each of these areas into the units given.
   a) 1.2 m² into mm²   b) 0.001 km² into cm²   c) 60 500 mm² into m²
   d) 673 000 000 cm² into km²   e) 50 million mm² into m²   f) 0.000005 km² into mm²

Volume

Volume is measured in units cubed (e.g. m³, cm³, mm³).

To convert between different units of volume, multiply or divide by the **cube** of the 'length' conversion factor.

For example, the conversion factor between cm and mm is 10. This means the conversion factor between cm³ and mm³ is $10^3 = 10 \times 10 \times 10 = 1000$.

1 cm³ = 10 × 10 × 10 = 1000 mm³

1 cm = 10 mm

Example 3

Convert a volume of 382 000 cm³ to m³.

1. Work out the conversion factor from cm³ to m³.

   1 m = 100 cm, so 1 m³ = 100³ = 100 × 100 × 100 = 1 000 000 cm³.

2. Divide by the conversion factor.

   So 382 000 cm³ = 382 000 ÷ 1 000 000 = **0.382 m³**

Exercise 2

1. Work out the volume (in m³) of the swimming pool shown by:
   a) first converting its length, width and depth to m.
   b) first finding the volume in cm³, and then using the appropriate conversion factor.

2. Convert each of these volumes into the units given.
   a) 0.001 km³ into m³
   b) 15 cm³ into mm³
   c) 0.2 m³ into cm³
   d) 0.055 cm³ into mm³
   e) 1.2 km³ into m³
   f) 17.6 m³ into cm³
   g) 0.435 km³ into m³
   h) 6.7 km³ into m³
   i) 0.000045 cm³ into mm³

3. Convert each of these volumes into the units given.
   a) 134 000 cm³ into m³
   b) 16 000 mm³ into cm³
   c) 3000 cm³ into m³
   d) 453 600 mm³ into cm³
   e) 150 m³ into km³
   f) 91.475 mm³ into cm³
   g) 35.9 cm³ into m³
   h) 131 400 mm³ into cm³
   i) 17 900 m³ into km³

4. A brand of coffee powder is sold in cuboid packets with dimensions 20 cm by 25 cm by 10 cm.
   A volume of 0.003 m³ of coffee powder has already been used.
   What volume (in m³) of coffee powder is left?

5. A carton of apple juice measures 7 cm by 50 mm by 0.17 m, and is completely full.
   a) Find the volume of the carton in cm³.
   b) Hati fills 7 glasses, each of which has a volume of 20 cm³, with juice. How much juice (in cm³) does she use?
   c) How much juice (in mm³) will she have left in the carton?

6. How many of these plastic bricks can be made out of 1 m³ of plastic?

7. A box is 10.5 cm long by 5.3 cm wide by 8.67 cm tall.
   Find the volume of the box in mm³.

8. A 1 litre bottle of orange concentrate says to dilute 25 cm³ of concentrate with 0.5 l of water to make one glass of squash.
   a) How many glasses of squash can you get from this bottle?
   b) What is the total volume of one glass of squash in mm³?

9. A swimming pool measures 3 m deep and has a base with area 375 m².
   a) Work out the volume of the swimming pool in m³.
   b) Find the volume of the pool in cm³.
   c) How many litres of water can the pool hold?

10. a) Convert 0.56 m³ to cm³.
    b) Use your answer to a) to convert 0.56 m³ into mm³.

16.4 Metric and Imperial Units

Imperial units are things like inches, feet and miles for lengths, pounds and ounces for mass, and pints and gallons for volume.

To convert between metric and imperial units, multiply or divide by the **conversion factors** below. (The conversions shown with a wavy equals sign (≈) are not exact, but are very close.)

Length	Mass	Volume
1 inch ≈ 2.5 cm	1 ounce ≈ 28 g	1 pint ≈ 0.57 litres
1 foot = 12 inches ≈ 30 cm	1 pound = 16 ounces ≈ 450 g	1 gallon = 8 pints ≈ 4.5 litres
1 yard = 3 feet ≈ 90 cm	1 stone = 14 pounds ≈ 6400 g	
1 mile ≈ 1.6 km	1 kg ≈ 2.2 pounds	

Example 1

a) Convert 15 miles into km.
   1. 1 mile ≈ 1.6 km so the conversion factor is 1.6.   1 mile = 1.6 km.
   2. Multiply 15 miles by the conversion factor.   So 15 miles = 15 × 1.6 = **24 km**

b) Convert 10 km into miles.
   1. Again, the conversion factor is 1.6.   1 mile = 1.6 km.
   2. Divide by the conversion factor.   So 10 km = 10 ÷ 1.6 = **6.25 miles**

Exercise 1

For **Questions 1-2**, convert the measurements into different imperial units using the conversion factors above.

1. a) 2 feet into inches b) 4 yards into feet c) 0.5 gallons into pints
   d) 4 stone into pounds e) 9 gallons into pints f) 3600 yards into feet

2. a) 32 ounces into pounds b) 56 pounds into stone c) 15 feet into yards
   d) 60 inches into feet e) 32 pints into gallons f) 42 pounds into stone

3. Convert these measurements from imperial units to metric.
   a) 4 inches into cm b) 3 ounces into g c) 2 gallons into l
   d) 10 stone into g e) 5 yards into cm f) 25 miles into km
   g) 2.7 inches into cm h) 4.5 pints into l i) 6.9 feet into cm

4. Convert these measurements from metric units to imperial.
   a) 8 km into miles b) 57 litres into pints c) 12 800 g into stone
   d) 60 cm into feet e) 25 cm into inches f) 16 km into miles
   g) 56 g into ounces h) 7.5 kg into pounds i) 48 km into miles

5. A running track is 400 m long. How many laps of the track make one mile?

Section 16 — Units, Measuring and Estimating

6 A large box of juice holds 3 litres.
   a) How many whole pint jugs can be filled from the box?
   b) Approximately how many litres of juice will be left in the box?

7 Marion is on holiday in Spain. Her car measures speed in mph but the Spanish road signs are in km/h. The speed limit is 90 km/h. What is this in mph?

8 A car manual states that the oil in the car's engine must be changed every 5000 miles. Jack has travelled 3500 miles since the last oil change, driving to and from work. He has also been on two holidays in his car in which he travelled 1000 km and 500 km. How many more miles can Jack travel before he should change the oil?

9 **a)** Convert 18 yards into cm.
   b) Use your answer to part **a)** to convert 18 yards into metres.

For **Questions 10-11** convert each measurement into the units given.

10 **a)** 5 pounds into kg   **b)** 11 feet into m   **c)** 1 stone into kg   **d)** 3 gallons into ml
   e) 20 yards into m   **f)** 330 inches into m   **g)** 16 pints into ml   **h)** 25 stone into kg

11 **a)** 800 ml into pints   **b)** 3.2 kg into stone   **c)** 300 m into miles   **d)** 6.4 kg into stone
   e) 1.35 kg into ounces   **f)** 2800 ml into pints   **g)** 10 kg into ounces   **h)** 0.9 m into feet

Example 2

a) Convert 6 pounds and 2 ounces into kg.
   1. Write the whole mass using the same unit (here, ounces).

   1 pound = 16 ounces,
   so 6 pounds = 6 × 16 = 96 ounces.

   This means 6 pounds and 2 ounces
   = 96 + 2 = 98 ounces

   2. Convert this into grams first. Then convert the result into kg.

   98 ounces = 98 × 28 = 2744 g = **2.744 kg**

b) Convert 35 cm into feet and inches.
   1. Convert 35 cm into inches first.

   35 cm = 35 ÷ 2.5 = 14 inches

   2. Work out how many full feet there are in your answer, and how many inches remaining.

   1 foot = 12 inches,
   so 14 inches = 12 inches + 2 inches
   = **1 foot 2 inches**

Exercise 2

1 For each of the following:
   (i) Convert the mass into ounces, using the conversion factor of 1 ounce ≈ 28 g.
   (ii) Write this in pounds and ounces.
   a) 1904 g   **b)** 840 g   **c)** 2688 g   **d)** 4.9 kg   **e)** 0.98 kg

2 Convert each of the following into feet and inches.
   a) 2 m   **b)** 52.5 cm   **c)** 1.5 km   **d)** 0.75 m   **e)** 50 mm

3 A ride at a theme park states you must be 140 cm or over to ride. Maddie is 4 foot 5 inches and Lily is 4 foot 9 inches. Can they both go on the ride?

4 Jamie and Oliver are cooking. They need 1 pound and 12 ounces of meat for their recipe. They see a 750 g packet of meat in the supermarket. Will this be enough?

Exercise 3 — Mixed Exercise

1 State which is the bigger amount in each of the following pairs.
   a) 10 feet or 3.5 m   b) 1 stone or 7 kg   c) 10 miles or 12 km   d) 15 pints or 9 litres
   e) 3 pounds or 1.5 kg   f) 5 stone or 31 kg   g) 160 stone or 1 tonne h) 2 gallons or 10 litres

2 Julie fills up her car with 6 gallons of petrol.
   How much will she have to pay if petrol costs £1.33 per litre?

3 Jacob's mother asks him to buy 4 pints of milk.
   The shop only sells milk in 1 litre, 2 litre and 4 litre cartons.
   Which of these amounts is closest to what his mother asked for?

4 Lotte's car travels 55 miles to the gallon of petrol.
   If her petrol tank contains 45 litres, how many miles can she travel?

5 Complete each of these calculations.
   a) 2 pints + 400 ml = ◯ ml
   b) 7.2 kg + 2 stone = ◯ kg
   c) 681 cm + 12.4 yards = ◯ m
   d) 16.49 km + 21.5 miles = ◯ km
   e) 3 kg + 1 stone + 1.5 kg = ◯ kg
   f) 100 cm + 2 yards + 15 feet = ◯ cm
   g) 3 l + 4.5 pints + 250 ml = ◯ ml
   h) 7 m + 8 inches + 35 mm = ◯ cm

6 The weights of 10 people getting into a lift are shown below.

11 stone 4 pounds	10 stone	7 stone 2 pounds	13 stone 1 pound	15 stone 4 pounds
12 stone	8 stone 9 pounds	10 stone 3 pounds	16 stone	11 stone 6 pounds

The lift has a weight limit of 1 tonne. Will the total weight of the 10 people exceed this limit?

16.5 Estimating in Real Life

You can **estimate** how big something is by comparing it with something you already know the size of. For example, the average height of a man is approximately 1.8 m, so something half as tall as an average-height man would be just under a metre tall.

Example 1

Estimate the height of this lamp post.
1. Estimate the height of the man. Average height of a man ≈ 1.8 m.
2. Estimate how much taller the lamp post is than the man. The lamp post is roughly twice the height of the man.
3. Estimate the height of the lamp post. Height of the lamp post ≈ 2 × 1.8 m = **3.6 m**

Section 16 — Units, Measuring and Estimating

Example 2

Give sensible units for measuring the height of a room.

When you give a measurement, use units that mean the value isn't too big or too small.

A sensible unit is **metres**.

Most rooms are taller than an average man, but not that much taller — roughly 2 to 3 metres. So it makes sense to measure the height of a room in metres (or possibly cm). You wouldn't use km to measure the height of a room — the number would be very small (0.002 km).

Exercise 1

1   Suggest a sensible metric unit to measure each of the following.
   a) the length of a pencil
   b) the mass of a tomato
   c) the height of a house
   d) the length of an ant
   e) the mass of a bus
   f) the weight of a baby
   g) the distance from Birmingham to Manchester

2   Estimate each of the following, using sensible units.
   a) the height of your bedroom
   b) the length of a family car
   c) the height of a football goal
   d) the arm span of a man
   e) the diameter of a football
   f) the volume of a bath

For **Questions 3-7** give your answer in sensible units.

3   Estimate the height of this house.

4   Estimate the height of this elephant.

5   Estimate the length and height of the bus.

6   Estimate the height and length of this dinosaur by comparing it with a chicken.

7   Estimate the height of this rhino by comparing it with a domestic cat.

Section 16 — Units, Measuring and Estimating

Section 17 — Speed, Density, Pressure

17.1 Speed, Distance, Time Calculations

Finding an Object's Speed

Distance, time and (average) speed are connected by the formula: $\text{Speed} = \dfrac{\text{Distance}}{\text{Time}}$

Example 1

A car travels 150 km in 3 hours. What is the average speed of the car?

1. Substitute the distance and time into the formula.
2. The units of speed are a combination of the units of distance (here, km) and time (here, hours).

$\text{Speed} = \dfrac{\text{Distance}}{\text{Time}}$

$= \dfrac{150}{3} = \underline{\mathbf{50 \text{ km/h}}}$.

Exercise 1

1. Calculate the average speed of each of the following journeys.
   a) distance = 30 km, time = 2 hours
   b) distance = 60 km, time = 3 hours
   c) distance = 150 miles, time = 5 hours
   d) distance = 100 m, time = 25 seconds
   e) distance = 72 000 km, time = 12 hours
   f) distance = 140 miles, time = 4 hours

2. Find the average speed of the following.
   a) a car travelling 80 km in 2 hours
   b) a cyclist travelling 32 km in 2 hours
   c) a cheetah running 100 m in 4 seconds
   d) a snail crawling 50 cm in 500 seconds
   e) a plane flying 1800 miles in 3 hours
   f) a rocket travelling 39 000 m in 5 seconds
   g) an escalator moving 15 m in 10 seconds
   h) a lift travelling 100 m in 80 seconds

3. Find the average speed of the following in km/h.
   You will need to convert the units to kilometres and hours first.
   a) a tractor moving 10 km in 30 minutes
   b) a man walking 1.5 km in 15 minutes
   c) a train travelling 30 000 m in 2.5 hours
   d) a river flowing 2.25 km in 45 minutes
   e) a fish swimming 0.5 km in 12 minutes
   f) a balloon rising 700 m in 3 minutes

Finding Distance and Time

You can rearrange the formula for speed to find distance and time.

$\text{Distance} = \text{Speed} \times \text{Time}$ $\text{Time} = \dfrac{\text{Distance}}{\text{Speed}}$

Example 2

A man runs for 30 minutes with average speed 12 km/h. How far does he run?

1. The speed is in km/h, so convert the time into hours.
2. Substitute the speed and time into the formula.
3. The speed is in km/h, so the distance will be in km.

30 minutes = 0.5 hours
Distance = Speed × Time
= 12 × 0.5 = **6 km**.

Example 3

A train travels 60 miles at a speed of 100 mph. How many minutes will the journey take?

1. Substitute the distance and speed into the formula. $\text{Time} = \dfrac{\text{Distance}}{\text{Speed}} = \dfrac{60}{100} = 0.6$ hours

2. Convert your answer into minutes.

   $0.6 \text{ hours} = 0.6 \times 60 \text{ minutes}$
   $= \mathbf{36 \text{ minutes}}$

Exercise 2

1 For each of the following, use the speed and time given to calculate the distance travelled.
   a) speed = 20 km/h, time = 2 hours
   b) speed = 25 mph, time = 2 hours
   c) speed = 10 m/s, time = 50 seconds
   d) speed = 3 km/h, time = 24 hours
   e) speed = 15 m/s, time = 9 seconds
   f) speed = 70 mph, time = 2.5 hours

2 For each of the following, use the speed and distance given to calculate the time taken.
   a) speed = 2 km/h, distance = 4 km
   b) speed = 3 m/s, distance = 15 m
   c) speed = 15 m/s, distance = 45 m
   d) speed = 60 mph, distance = 150 miles
   e) speed = 18 m/s, distance = 9 m
   f) speed = 24 km/h, distance = 6 km

3 Find the distance travelled by a bus moving at 30 mph for 4 hours.

4 A flight to Spain takes 2 hours. The plane travels at an average speed of 490 mph. How far does the plane travel?

5 A dart is thrown with speed 15 m/s. It hits a dartboard 2.4 m away. How long is the dart in the air?

6 A marathon is approximately 42 km long. How long would it take to complete the marathon at an average speed of 8.4 km/h?

7 A train travels at 56 km/h for 5.6 km. How many minutes does the journey take?

8 A girl skates at an average speed of 7.5 mph. How far does she skate in 15 minutes?

Example 4

A swallow is flying at a speed of 9 m/s. What is its speed in km/h?

1. First convert from m/s to km/s. $9 \text{ m/s} = (9 \div 1000) \text{ km/s} = 0.009 \text{ km/s}$

2. Then convert km/s to km/h. $0.009 \text{ km/s} = (0.009 \times 60 \times 60) \text{ km/h} = \mathbf{32.4 \text{ km/h}}$

9 Convert each of the speeds below into the given units.
   a) 50 m/s into km/h
   b) 72 km/h into m/s
   c) 41.4 km/h into m/s
   d) 26.5 m/s into km/h
   e) 4.35 m/s into km/h
   f) 45.36 km/h into m/s

10 James is cycling at 18 km/h. What is his speed in m/s?

11 A rocket is travelling at 8000 m/s. How fast is it moving in km/h?

12 A slug is moving at 0.5 cm/s. What is its speed in metres per minute (m/min)?

Exercise 3 — Mixed Exercise

1. A football is passed between two players 10 m apart. The ball travels for 2.5 seconds. Find the average speed of the ball in m/s.

2. A man swims one length of a pool in 50 seconds. His speed is 0.5 m/s. Find the length of the pool.

3. A car's average speed is 40 mph. How long will it take the car to travel 100 miles?

4. A bobsleigh covers 1400 m in 50 seconds. Find its average speed in m/s.

5. A tree grows at a rate of 90 cm per year. How much taller does it grow in 4.5 years?

6. A tennis ball moves at an average speed of 48 m/s. How long does it take the tennis ball to travel 36 m?

7. A jogger ran for half an hour at an average speed of 8.1 km/h. How far did he run?

8. A yacht travels 13.5 km in 15 minutes.
   a) What is its average speed in km/h?
   b) What is this speed in m/s?

9. A snail slides 0.8 m in 1 minute 40 seconds.
   a) Find the snail's average speed in m/s.
   b) What is its speed in km/h?

10. A leopard runs 0.25 miles at an average speed of 40 mph. How many seconds does this take the leopard?

17.2 Density, Mass, Volume Calculations

Density is a measure of **mass** per unit **volume**.

Density, mass and volume are connected by this formula:

$$\text{Density} = \frac{\text{Mass}}{\text{Volume}}$$

You can rearrange the formula to find mass and volume.

$$\text{Volume} = \frac{\text{Mass}}{\text{Density}}$$

$$\text{Mass} = \text{Volume} \times \text{Density}$$

Example 1

A 20 g block of wood has a volume of 50 cm^3.

a) Calculate the density of the wooden block in g/cm^3.
   1. Substitute the mass and volume into the formula.
   2. The units of density are a combination of the units of mass (g) and volume (cm^3).

   $$\text{Density} = \frac{\text{Mass}}{\text{Volume}} = \frac{20}{50} = \underline{\mathbf{0.4 \text{ g/cm}^3}}$$

b) What is its density in kg/m^3?
   1. First convert g/cm^3 to kg/cm^3.
      0.4 g/cm^3 = (0.4 ÷ 1000) kg/cm^3 = 0.0004 kg/cm^3
   2. Then convert kg/cm^3 to kg/m^3.
      0.0004 kg/cm^3 = (0.0004 × 100 × 100 × 100) kg/m^3
      = **400 kg/m^3**

Exercise 1

1. For each of the following, use the mass and volume to calculate the density in kg/m^3.
   a) mass = 20 kg, volume = 5 m^3
   b) mass = 300 kg, volume = 5 m^3
   c) mass = 99 kg, volume = 11 m^3
   d) mass = 1000 kg, volume = 4 m^3
   e) mass = 2500 kg, volume = 50 m^3
   f) mass = 63 000 kg, volume = 700 m^3

2 a) Write down the formula to calculate volume from density and mass.
   b) Use your answer to calculate the volume for each of the following.
   (i) density = 8 kg/m^3, mass = 40 kg **(ii)** density = 15 kg/m^3, mass = 750 kg
   (iii) density = 240 kg/m^3, mass = 4800 kg **(iv)** density = 1.25 kg/m^3, mass = 5 kg

3 A limestone statue has a volume of 0.4 m^3. Limestone has a density of 2610 kg/m^3.
   a) Write down the formula to calculate a mass from a volume and a density.
   b) Calculate the mass of the statue.

4 A paperweight has a volume of 8 cm^3 and a density of 11 500 kg/m^3.
   Calculate the mass of the paperweight.

5 Aluminium has a density of 2.7 g/cm^3. What is the density of aluminium in kg/m^3?

17.3 Pressure, Force, Area Calculations

Pressure is the **force** exerted by an object per unit **area**.

Pressure, force and area are connected by these formulas:

$$\text{Pressure} = \frac{\text{Force}}{\text{Area}} \qquad \text{Area} = \frac{\text{Force}}{\text{Pressure}} \qquad \text{Force} = \text{Pressure} \times \text{Area}$$

Pressure is usually measured in **N/m²** (also known as pascals — **Pa**) or **N/cm²**.

Example 1

An object is resting with its base on horizontal ground. The area of the object's base is 20 cm² and the object weighs 60 N. What pressure is the object exerting on the ground?

1. Substitute the force and area into the formula. $\text{Pressure} = \frac{\text{Force}}{\text{Area}} = \frac{60}{20}$
2. The units of pressure are a combination of the units of force (N) and area (cm²).
   $= \underline{\mathbf{3 \text{ N/cm}^2}}$

Exercise 1

1 For each of the following, use the area and force to calculate the pressure.
   a) Area = 3 cm², Force = 27 N **b)** Area = 5 m², Force = 125 N
   c) Area = 4 m², Force = 4800 N **d)** Area = 80 cm², Force = 640 N

2 Calculate the area in each of the following situations.
   a) Pressure = 6 N/cm², Force = 36 N **b)** Pressure = 120 N/m², Force = 840 N
   c) Pressure = 2.5 N/cm², Force = 10 N **d)** Pressure = 180 N/m², Force = 540 N

3 Calculate the force in each of the following situations.
   a) Pressure = 300 N/m², Area = 5 m² **b)** Pressure = 36 N/cm², Area = 30 cm²

4 A cube has edges of length 10 cm. When it rests on horizontal ground it exerts a pressure of 0.02 N/cm². What is its weight?

5 A square-based pyramid is resting with its square face on horizontal ground. The pyramid has a weight of 45 N and its square face has a side length of 3 cm. What pressure is the pyramid exerting on the ground?
   Give your answer in: **a)** N/cm² **b)** N/m²

Section 17 — Speed, Density, Pressure

17.4 Distance-Time Graphs

Representing a Journey on a Distance-Time Graph

A **distance-time** graph shows how the distance of a moving object from its starting position changes.

Example 1

Danny cycles 5 miles in 20 minutes. He stops and rests for 10 minutes, then returns to his starting point in 30 minutes. Copy the axes on the right and use them to draw a graph of Danny's journey.

1. The first part of the graph shows 5 miles being covered in 20 minutes.
2. The second part of the graph shows no distance covered during the next 10 minutes.
3. The final part of the graph shows the 5-mile return journey taking 30 minutes.

Exercise 1

1 Adi is a keen cyclist. The following points describe the different stages of one of her bike rides.
- Adi cycles 30 km in 2 hours.
- She stops and rests for half an hour.
- She then cycles a further 40 km in 2.5 hours.

Copy the coordinate grid on the right.

a) Draw a straight line on the grid to represent the first stage of Adi's journey.

b) The second stage of her ride is represented by a horizontal line. Draw this part of the graph.

c) (i) After the third stage of her ride, how far is Adi from her original starting point?

(ii) Draw the straight line representing the third stage of Adi's ride.

Section 17 — Speed, Density, Pressure

2 The following points describe the different stages of one of James's runs.
- James runs 10 km in 2 hours.
- He stops to rest for an hour.
- He then returns to his starting point in 2.5 hours.

Copy the coordinate grid on the right.
   a) Draw the line representing the first stage of his run.
   b) Draw the line representing his hour of rest.
   c) Draw the line showing his return journey.

Draw a graph representing each of the journeys described in **Questions 3-6**.

3 Yemi drives 50 km in 1 hour, stops at a service station for half an hour, then drives a further 30 km in half an hour.

4 Sandy walks 2 km to the bus stop in 20 minutes. She waits for 10 minutes for a bus to arrive. She then travels a further 5 km on the bus in 15 minutes.

5 Harry walks 3 km in 50 minutes to his friend's house. He stays there for 1 hour.
He then walks back towards home for 30 minutes until he gets to a shop, 1 km from home.
He stays at the shop for 10 minutes before walking home, which takes a further 15 minutes.

6 Josh and Ron live 3.5 miles apart. Josh walks 1 mile to the bus stop in 20 minutes.
He waits 10 minutes for the bus, then travels 2 miles in 5 minutes.
He gets off the bus and walks the rest of the way to Ron's house in 15 minutes.

7 This graph shows a family's car journey. The family left home at 9:00 am.

   a) (i) How long did the family travel for before stopping?
      (ii) How far had they travelled when they stopped?
   b) How long did the family stay at their destination before setting off home?
   c) (i) What time did they start back home?
      (ii) How long did the journey home take?

8 Describe the journey that is represented by each of these distance-time graphs.

Finding Speed from a Distance-Time Graph

The **gradient** of a distance-time graph gives the **speed** of an object.

The **steeper** the graph, the **faster** the object is moving.
A **horizontal** line means the object is **stationary**.

Example 2

Bill left his house at 8:00 am and walked to a bus stop. He waited 15 minutes for the bus, and then travelled to his hospital appointment. After his appointment, he returned home by taxi. The graph shows Bill's journey.

a) (i) How far is the bus stop from Bill's house?
   (ii) How long (in hours) did it take Bill to walk to the bus stop?
   (iii) How fast (in km/h) did Bill walk to the bus stop?
b) (i) How far did Bill travel on the bus?
   (ii) How long did Bill's bus journey take?
   (iii) What was the average speed of the bus?
c) What was the average speed of the taxi?

1. You can read distances and times from the graph.
2. If you know the distance something has travelled and how long it took, then you can work out its speed using 'speed = distance (d) ÷ time (t)'.
3. Notice that the faster an object travels, the steeper the graph is for that section of its journey. For example, the 'bus section' of the graph is steeper than the 'walking section'. But the steepest part is the 'taxi section'.

a) (i) **1 km**
   (ii) 15 minutes = **0.25 hours**
   (iii) Speed = $\frac{d}{t} = \frac{1}{0.25}$ = **4 km/h**
b) (i) **4 km**
   (ii) 30 minutes = **0.5 hours**
   (iii) Speed = $\frac{4}{0.5}$ = **8 km/h**
c) Speed = $5 \div \frac{1}{4} = 5 \times 4$ = **20 km/h**

Exercise 2

1 This graph shows a commuter's journey to work. His journey consisted of two stages of travelling, separated by a break of 30 minutes.

   a) Without carrying out any calculations, state which of the journey's two stages was at a higher speed. Explain your answer.
   b) (i) How far did the commuter travel in stage 1 of his journey (the first 30 minutes)?
      (ii) What was his speed (in km/h) for the first stage?
   c) What was his speed (in km/h) during the second stage of his journey?

Section 17 — Speed, Density, Pressure

2 The graph shows a hill walker's trek. She stopped for a rest at 12:00 and for lunch at 13:00.

a) Without carrying out any calculations, state the times between which she was walking fastest. Explain your answer.
b) (i) For how long did she walk before she first stopped for a rest?
   (ii) How far did she walk during this time?
   (iii) What was her average speed during this first part of her walk?
c) What was her average speed after her rest but before she stopped for lunch?
d) What was her average speed after lunch?

3 Chay is going on a journey. The following points describe his journey.
- Chay travels 40 km by bus, as shown on the graph.
- He gets off the bus and then waits half an hour for a train.
- He gets on the train and travels for a further 1 hour 30 minutes, as shown on the graph.
- He spends 30 minutes at his destination.
- He then returns home by taxi at an average speed of 60 km/h.

a) Find the average speed Chay travelled:
   (i) by bus.   (ii) by train.
b) Copy the above graph, and extend the line to show Chay's 30 minutes at his destination.
c) Find the time it took Chay to travel home by taxi.
d) Show Chay's taxi ride home on your graph.

4 Draw distance-time graphs to show the following journeys.
a) Ash catches a train at 10:00, then travels for 200 miles at an average speed of 100 mph.
b) Corey sets off at 09:00 and drives 120 miles at an average speed of 40 mph.
After 1 hour at his destination, he drives back to his starting point at an average speed of 60 mph.

Section 17 — Speed, Density, Pressure

Section 18 — Scale Drawings and Bearings

18.1 Scale Drawings

Scales with Units

A scale tells you the relationship between distances on a map or plan and distances in real life.
E.g. A map scale of 1 cm : 100 m means that 1 cm on the map represents an actual distance of 100 m.

Example 1

A plan of a garden is drawn to a scale of 1 cm : 5 m.

a) The distance between two trees is measured on the plan as 3 cm. What is the actual distance between the trees?

×3 ⟨ 1 cm represents 5 m / 3 cm represents **15 m** ⟩ ×3

b) The actual distance between the garden shed and the pond is measured as 2.5 m. What would the distance between the shed and the pond be on the plan?

÷2 ⟨ 5 m is shown as 1 cm / 2.5 m is shown as **0.5 cm** ⟩ ÷2

Exercise 1

1 A map scale is given as 2 cm : 1 km.

   a) Convert the following distances on the map to actual distances.
   (i) 4 cm (ii) 6 cm (iii) 22 cm
   (iv) 3 cm (v) 0.5 cm (vi) 0.25 cm

   b) Convert the following actual distances to distances on the map.
   (i) 5 km (ii) 8 km (iii) 14 km
   (iv) 3.5 km (v) 0.5 km (vi) 0.7 km

2 An atlas uses a scale of 1 cm : 100 km.
Find the actual distances represented by:
   a) 7 cm **b)** 1.5 cm **c)** 0.8 cm
   d) 6.22 cm **e)** 3.01 cm **f)** 43 mm

3 The scale on a map of Europe is 1 cm : 50 km. Find the distance used on the map to represent the following actual distances.
   a) 150 km **b)** 600 km **c)** 1000 km
   d) 25 km **e)** 10 km **f)** 15 km

4 The floor plan of a house is drawn to a scale of 1 cm : 2 m. Find the actual dimensions of the rooms if they are shown on the plan as:
   a) 2.7 cm by 1.5 cm
   b) 3.2 cm by 2.2 cm
   c) 1.85 cm by 1.4 cm
   d) 0.9 cm by 1.35 cm

Example 2

The distance between two villages is 12 km. This is represented on a map by a distance of 24 cm. Express the scale of the map in the form 1 cm : n km.

1. Write down the distances you are given as a scale.   24 cm : 12 km
2. Divide both sides by 24 to find the scale in the form 1 cm : n km.
   (24 ÷ 24) cm : (12 ÷ 24) km
   1 cm : 0.5 km

Section 18 — Scale Drawings and Bearings

5 The distance from Madrid to Malaga is shown on a map as 11 cm. The actual distance is 440 km. Express the scale of the map in the form 1 cm : n km.

6 The distance from Thenford to Syresham is 12 km. This is shown on a map as 4 cm.
   a) Express the scale of the map in the form 1 cm : n km.
   b) The same map shows the distance from Chacombe to Badby as 7 cm. What is the actual distance between these two villages?

7 You are asked to draw up the plans for a building using the scale 1 cm : 0.5 m. Find the lengths you should draw on the plan to represent the following actual distances.
   a) 4 m   **b)** 18 m   **c)** 21 m   **d)** 11.8 m

8 A street of length 0.8 km is to be drawn on a map with scale 1 cm : 0.5 km. What length will the street appear on the map?

9 Below is the plan for a kitchen surface.

1 mm : 3 cm

Measure the appropriate lengths on the plan to find the actual dimensions of the following.
   a) The sink area   **b)** The hob area

10 The plan below represents the distances between A, B and C.
The actual distance AB is 150 m.

   a) Measure AB on the plan to find the scale in the form 1 cm : n m.
   b) Use your scale to find:
   (i) the distance AC **(ii)** the distance BC

Scales Without Units

A scale without units (e.g. 1 : 100) means you can use any units.
For example, 1 cm : 100 cm or 1 mm : 100 mm.

Example 3

A map uses a scale of 1 : 200. What is the actual distance between two points which appear 35 cm apart on the map?

1. Write the scale down using centimetres, to match the distance given in the question.

   1 cm : 200 cm

2. Multiply both sides of the equation by the same number.

   1 cm represents 200 cm, so 35 cm represents 35 × 200 = 7000 cm.

3. Give your answer using sensible units.

   So the actual distance is **70 m**.

Exercise 2

1 A map scale is given as 1 : 350.
   a) Convert the following distances on the map to actual distances.
   (i) 2 cm   **(ii)** 7 cm   **(iii)** 22 cm   **(iv)** 9.9 cm   **(v)** 14.5 cm   **(vi)** 25.7 cm
   b) Convert the following actual distances to distances on the map.
   (i) 700 cm   **(ii)** 875 cm   **(iii)** 175 cm   **(iv)** 2.1 m   **(v)** 945 cm   **(vi)** 1.47 m

2 A plan uses the scale 1 : 75. Find the actual distances represented by these lengths on the plan.
   a) 4 cm   **b)** 11 cm   **c)** 5.5 cm   **d)** 7.9 cm   **e)** 24.1 cm   **f)** 17.2 cm

3 Convert these actual distances to the lengths they will appear on a map with scale 1 : 1000.
   a) 300 m   **b)** 1400 m   **c)** 840 m   **d)** 120 m   **e)** 1 km   **f)** 0.43 km

4 Toy furniture is made to a scale of 1 : 40. Find the dimensions of the actual furniture when the toys have the following measurements.
   a) Height of wardrobe: 5 cm
   b) Width of bed: 3.5 cm
   c) Length of table: 3.2 cm
   d) Height of chair: 2.4 cm

6 A model railway uses a scale of 1 : 500. Use the actual measurements given below to find measurements for the model.
   a) Length of carriage: 20 m
   b) Height of coal tower: 30 m
   c) Length of footbridge: 100 m
   d) Height of signal box: 6 m

5 A road of length 6.7 km is to be drawn on a map. The scale of the map is 1 : 250 000. How long will the road be on the map?

7 A map uses the scale 1 : 72. Find the lengths on the map that represent these actual distances.
   a) 5.4 m   **b)** 8.1 m   **c)** 3.24 m

Example 4
The plan of the grounds of a stately home has a scale of 1 : 40 000. Represent this scale in the form 1 cm : n m.

1. Write the scale down using centimetres to match the left-hand side of 1 cm : n m.   1 cm : 40 000 cm
2. Convert the right-hand side to metres by dividing by 100.   1 cm : (40 000 ÷ 100) m

1 cm : 400 m

8 A path of length 4.5 km is shown on a map as a line of length 3 cm.
   a) Express the scale in the form 1 cm : n km.
   b) Express the scale in the form 1 : k.

9 The plan for a school has a scale of 1 : 1500.
   a) Express this scale in the form 1 cm : n m.
   b) The school playground is 60 m in length. Find the corresponding length on the plan.

10 On the plans for a house, 3 cm represents the length of a garden with actual length 18 m.
   a) Find the map scale in the form 1 : n.
   b) On the plan, the width of the garden is 1.2 cm. What is its actual width in metres?
   c) The lounge has a length of 4.5 m. What is the corresponding length on the plan?

11 The grid below shows the main tourist attractions of a major city.

Theatre · Art Gallery · Museum · Park · Cathedral

1 : 120 000

Find the actual distances between:
   a) the museum and the cathedral
   b) the art gallery and the theatre
   c) the cathedral and the park

Example 5

The diagram shows a rough sketch of a garden.
Use the scale 1 : 400 to draw an accurate plan of the garden.

1. Write down the scale in cm. 1 cm : 400 cm
2. Change the right-hand side to metres. 1 cm : 4 m
3. Use the scale to work out the lengths for the plan.
   4 m is shown as 1 cm, so:
   12 m is shown as 3 cm
   8 m is shown as 2 cm
   2 m is shown as 0.5 cm
   3 m is shown as 0.75 cm
4. Use these lengths to draw an accurate plan.

Exercise 3

1 A sketch of the floor plan for a symmetrical squash court is shown below. Use the scale 1 : 50 to draw an accurate plan of the court.

2 Draw an accurate plan of the kitchen shown below using the scale 1 : 20.

3 Below is a rough sketch of a house extension.

   a) Use the scale 1 : 25 to draw an accurate plan for the extension.
   b) Find the door's actual width and height.

4 Below is a sketch of a park lake.

   a) Draw an accurate plan of the lake using the scale 1 cm : 3 m.
   b) There is a duck house at the intersection of AC and BD. Use your plan to find the actual distance from the duck house to point B.

18.2 Bearings

A bearing tells you the direction of one point from another.
Bearings are given as three-figure angles, measured clockwise from north.

Example 1
a) Find the bearing of B from A.
b) Find the bearing of C from A.

1. Find the clockwise angle from north.
2. Give the bearing as three figures.

a) $90° - 27° = 63°$
So the bearing of B from A is **063°**.

b) $360° - 35° = 325°$
So the bearing of C from A is **325°**.

Exercise 1

1 Write these compass directions as bearings.
   a) East   b) Northeast   c) South
   d) West   e) Southwest   f) Northwest

2 Find the bearing of B from A in the following.
   a) through h) [diagrams with angles: 62°, 40°, 47°, 31°, 19°, 67°, 83°, 72°]

3 A ship travels in a direction which is 25° north of east. Write this as a bearing.

4 Find the angle θ in each of the following using the information given.
   a) Bearing of D from C is 111°
   b) Bearing of D from C is 203°
   c) Bearing of D from C is 285°
   d) Bearing of D from C is 243°
   e) Bearing of D from C is 135°
   f) Bearing of D from C is 222°

5 Mark a point O and draw in a north line. Use a protractor to help you draw the points a) to f) with the following bearings from O.
   a) 040°   b) 079°   c) 321°
   d) 163°   e) 007°   f) 263°

Section 18 — Scale Drawings and Bearings   **213**

Example 2

The bearing of X from Y is 244°. Find the bearing of Y from X.

1. Draw a diagram showing what you know.
2. Draw a north line through point X.
3. Find the **alternate angle** to the one you're looking for.
4. Use angle properties to find the bearing.

So the bearing of Y from X is **064°**.

Exercise 2

1 The bearing of B from A is 218°. Find the bearing of A from B.

2 The bearing of D from C is 125°. Find the bearing of C from D.

3 The bearing of F from E is 310°. Find the bearing of E from F.

4 The bearing of H from G is 023°. Find the bearing of G from H.

5 The bearing of K from J is 101°. Find the bearing of J from K.

6 Find the bearing of N from M given that the bearing of M from N is:
   a) 200°   b) 310°   c) 080°
   d) 117°   e) 015°   f) 099°

7
   a) Measure the angle θ in the diagram.
   b) Write down the bearing of R from S.

8 The point Q lies west of point P.
   a) Write down the bearing of Q from P.
   b) Write down the bearing of P from Q.

9 The point Z lies southeast of the point Y.
   a) Write down the bearing of Z from Y.
   b) Find the bearing of Y from Z.

10
   a) Find the bearing of V from U.
   b) Find the bearing of U from V.

11 Find the bearing of:
   a) B from A   b) C from A
   c) D from A   d) E from A
   e) A from B   f) A from C
   g) A from D   h) A from E

214 Section 18 — Scale Drawings and Bearings

Example 3

The points *P* and *Q* are a distance of 75 km apart. *Q* lies on a bearing of 055° from *P*.
Use the scale 1 cm : 25 km to draw an accurate scale diagram of *P* and *Q*.

1. Draw *P* and a north line through it. Measure the required bearing.
2. Use the scale to work out the distance between the two points.

   25 km is shown by 1 cm, so 75 km is shown by 3 cm.
3. Draw *Q* the correct distance and direction from *P*.

Exercise 3

1 Above is a rough map of part of Europe. A pilot flies from Bern to Stuttgart, then on to Munich. This is shown on the enlarged part of the map, which is drawn using a scale of 1 cm : 100 km.

  a) Find the distance and bearings of the following stages of the journey.

   (i) Bern to Stuttgart   **(ii)** Stuttgart to Munich

  b) The pilot returns directly from Munich to Bern. Find the actual distance travelled in this stage.

2 Skopje is 150 km from Tirana, on a bearing of 048°.
 Draw an accurate scale diagram of Skopje and Tirana using the scale 1 cm : 30 km.

3 Salzburg lies 540 km from Bonn, on a bearing of 125°.
 Draw an accurate scale diagram of the two locations using the scale 1 cm : 90 km.

4 A pilot flies 2000 km from Budapest to Madrid, on a bearing of 242°.
 Draw an accurate scale diagram of the journey using the scale 1 : 100 000 000.

5 Use the scale 1 : 22 000 000 to draw an accurate scale diagram of a 880 km journey from Budapest to Bern, on a bearing of 263°.

6 The scale drawing on the right shows three more European cities. The scale of the diagram is 1 : 10 000 000.

  a) Use the diagram to find the following distances.

   (i) *PQ*   **(ii)** *QR*   **(iii)** *PR*

  b) Use a protractor to find the following bearings.

   (i) *Q* from *P*   **(ii)** *R* from *Q*   **(iii)** *P* from *R*

Section 18 — Scale Drawings and Bearings

18.3 Scale Drawings and Bearings Problems

Exercise 1

1. Town *A* is 14 km north of Town *B*, which is 14 km east of Town *C*. Find the following bearings.
   a) Town *B* from Town *A*
   b) Town *C* from Town *B*
   c) Town *C* from Town *A*

2. The diagram shows an accurate scale plan of a circular walk. The actual distance from The Knott to Hartsop Village is 3 km.

   a) Find the scale of the plan in the form 1 cm : *n* km.
   b) Measure the distances on the diagram to find the total length of the walk.

   Point *X* lies between High Street and The Knott. There are two paths leading away from *X*.

   c) What bearing should a walker take at *X* to ensure they take the correct path to the Knott?

3. A jogger runs 230 m on a bearing of 020°, then 390 m on a bearing of 110°.
   a) Use the scale 1 cm : 100 m to draw an accurate scale diagram of the two stages of his run.
   b) Find the angle the jogger changes direction by after the first stage of his run.

4. A boat sails on a bearing of 055° for 2000 m. It then changes course and sails on a bearing of 100° for 1500 m.
   a) Draw a scale diagram of the boat's journey. Use the scale 1 cm : 500 m.

   The boat returns directly to its starting point. Use your scale diagram to find the following:
   b) the direct return distance,
   c) the bearing of the return journey.

5. Arran is at the centre of a maze. He makes the following sequence of moves.
   Walk 10 m, turn right
   Walk 10 m, turn right
   Walk 20 m, turn left
   Walk 10 m, turn left
   Walk 30 m, turn left
   Walk 30 m
   He is now at the exit of the maze.
   a) Using a suitable scale, make a scale drawing of the path that Arran follows to find the exit.
   b) Use your drawing to find the direct distance from the centre of the maze to the exit.

6. Leicester is 100 km south of Doncaster. King's Lynn is 100 km east of Leicester.
   a) Sketch the layout of the three locations.
   b) Find the bearing of King's Lynn from Leicester.
   c) Draw a north line through Doncaster. Find the bearings from Doncaster of:
      (i) Leicester   (ii) King's Lynn
   d) Draw a north line through King's Lynn. Find the bearings from King's Lynn of:
      (i) Leicester   (ii) Doncaster

Section 19 — Pythagoras and Trigonometry

19.1 Pythagoras' Theorem

In a right-angled triangle, the lengths of the sides are connected by Pythagoras' Theorem: $h^2 = a^2 + b^2$

h is the hypotenuse — the longest side, opposite the right angle.
a and b are the shorter sides.

Example 1

Find the length x on the triangle shown. Give your answer to 2 decimal places.

1. x is the hypotenuse, so substitute x for h and replace a and b with 4 and 7.
2. Find x.
3. Round your answer and use the correct units.

$h^2 = a^2 + b^2$
$x^2 = 7^2 + 4^2$
$x^2 = 49 + 16 = 65$
$x = \sqrt{65} = 8.0622...$

So $x = $ **8.06 cm** (to 2 d.p.)

Exercise 1

Unless told otherwise, give any non-exact answers to 2 decimal places.

1 Find the length of the hypotenuse in each of the triangles below.

a) x, 3 cm, 4 cm

b) 12 mm, 5 mm, z

c) q, 18 cm, 24 cm

d) p, 30 m, 16 m

e) 3 cm, y, 6 cm

f) r, 52 m, 52 m

g) 2.4 m, 0.7 m, s

h) 6.7 cm, t, 3.9 cm

i) 5.12 km, u, 3.78 km

j) 7.2 mm, 11.5 mm, v

k) 1.3 m, 0.5 m, w

l) 1.9 m, a, 2.7 m

Section 19 — Pythagoras and Trigonometry **217**

2 Find the length of the longest side of a right-angled triangle if the other sides are 8.7 cm and 6.1 cm in length.

3 Find the length of the hypotenuse of a right-angled triangle if the shorter sides have the following lengths.
   a) $a = 5$ cm, $b = 7$ cm
   b) $a = 4$ cm, $b = 11$ cm
   c) $a = 6.3$ mm, $b = 1.9$ mm

4 In triangle XYZ, angle XYZ is 90°, XY is 4.5 cm and YZ is 4.9 cm. Find the length of XZ.

5 Find the distance PS in the rectangle below.

6 A rectangular field is 20 m long and 15 m wide. What is the distance diagonally across the field?

7 I run 540 m south and then 970 m east. What is my final distance from my starting point? Give your answer to the nearest metre.

8 XYZ is an isosceles triangle. M is the mid-point of YZ. Find the length of XY.

9 The triangle JKL is drawn inside a circle centred on O, as shown. JK and KL have lengths 4.9 cm and 6.8 cm respectively.
   a) Find the length of JL.
   b) Find the radius of the circle.

10 Find the length of the line segment AB.

11 A spaghetti jar is in the shape of a cylinder. The jar has radius 6 cm and height 28 cm. What is the length of the longest stick of dried spaghetti that will fit inside the jar?

Example 2

Find the length a on the triangle shown. Give your answer to 2 decimal places.

1. a is one of the shorter sides, so use Pythagoras' formula with $h = 11$ and $b = 7$.

   $h^2 = a^2 + b^2$
   $11^2 = a^2 + 7^2$

2. Rearrange to find a.

   $a^2 = 11^2 - 7^2$
   $a^2 = 121 - 49 = 72$
   $a = \sqrt{72} = 8.4852...$

3. Round your answer and use the correct units.

   So $a = $ **8.49 m** (to 2 d.p.)

Section 19 — Pythagoras and Trigonometry

Exercise 2

Unless told otherwise, give any non-exact answers to 2 decimal places.

1 Find the lengths of the missing sides in these triangles.

a) 13 cm (hypotenuse), 12 cm, l

b) 2 cm, 6 cm, m

c) 7 mm, 11 mm, n

d) 10 cm, 26 cm, p

e) 9 cm, 41 cm, h

f) 37 mm, 45 mm, i

g) 7.6 m, 6.1 m, j

h) 15.9 km, 21.7 km, k

i) 5.87 cm, 7.04 cm, f

j) 240 mm, 165 mm, g

k) 9.54 m, 3.17 m, b

l) 170 cm, 300 cm, c

2 Find the length b in the right-angled triangle if a and h are as follows.

a) $a = 1$ cm, $h = 8$ cm
b) $a = 6$ m, $h = 13$ m
c) $a = 4.1$ mm, $h = 11.3$ mm
d) $a = 17.7$ cm, $h = 22.9$ cm

3 The lengths of the longest and shortest sides of a right-angled triangle are 17.3 cm and 6.6 cm. Find the length of the third side.

4 Find the horizontal distance from the bottom of the broom to the base of the wall.

(0.9 m, 1.2 m)

5 The end of a ladder of length 3.3 m is placed on the ground 0.8 m from the base of a wall. When leant against the wall, how high up the wall does the ladder reach?

6 A slice of toast is in the shape of a right-angled triangle. The hypotenuse of the triangle has length 14 cm, and a shorter side is of length 11 cm. Find the length of the third side.

7 Find the radius of the base of the cone shown below.

(29.2 cm, 22.4 cm)

8 A kite gets stuck at the top of a tree. The kite's 15 m string is taut, and its other end is held on the ground, 8.5 m from the base of the tree. Find the height of the tree.

Section 19 — Pythagoras and Trigonometry

9 Find the vertical height of the tent shown.

10 A pilot flies 860 km from Lyon to Prague. He then flies 426 km south to Ljubljana, which is directly east of Lyon. Find the distance from Ljubljana to Lyon to the nearest kilometre.

11 Newtown is 88 km northwest of Oldtown. Bigton is 142 km from Newtown, and lies northeast of Oldtown. What is the distance from Bigton to Oldtown? Give your answer to the nearest kilometre.

12 What is the height of the kite below?

Exercise 3 — Mixed Exercise

Unless told otherwise, give any non-exact answers to 2 decimal places.

1 Kevin is mending the battlements on his castle. How long is his ladder?

2 What is the shortest distance from Fishlare to Rossguard?

3 Find the length of the diagonals of a square with sides of length 7.7 m.

4 My favourite twig is 43 cm long. Will it fit on a tray 35 cm long and 25 cm wide?

5 A rectangular wooden frame is supported by a diagonal strut from one corner to the opposite corner. The frame measures 2 m by 0.7 m. Find the length of the strut.

6 A boat is rowed 200 m east and then 150 m south. If it was rowed in a straight line instead, how much shorter would the journey be?

7 A delivery company charges extra if a letter has a diagonal length greater than 25 cm. I want to send a letter that measures 205 mm by 155 mm. Will I have to pay extra?

8 Find the length of corrugated iron needed to make a roof for my bike shed, shown below.

9 An equilateral triangle has sides of length 10 cm. Find the triangle's vertical height.

10 Find the following lengths.
  a) AB **b)** BC **c)** AC

220   Section 19 — Pythagoras and Trigonometry

11 The diagram below shows two triangles, *PRS* and *PQS*. Find the lengths of:
 a) *PQ* b) *PR* c) *QR*

12 A pool is 50 m by 25 m. How many 6 cm goldfish could float head-to-tail in a line across the pool's diagonal?

13 Find the distance between points *P* and *Q* with coordinates (11, 1) and (17, 19) respectively.

14 Is Croughton closer to Dullverston or Marrow? By how far?

15 Find the height of the symmetrical house shown below.

16 Find the side lengths of the rhombus below.

17 The square *PQRS* is drawn inside another square *ABCD*, as shown in the diagram. Find the side length of *ABCD*.

19.2 Trigonometry — Sin, Cos and Tan

The Three Formulas

In a right-angled triangle, the side opposite the right angle is called the **hypotenuse**, the side opposite an angle is called the **opposite** and the side next to an angle is called the **adjacent**.

The three sides are linked by the following formulas:

$$\sin x = \frac{\text{opp}}{\text{hyp}}, \quad \cos x = \frac{\text{adj}}{\text{hyp}}, \quad \tan x = \frac{\text{opp}}{\text{adj}}$$

Example 1

Find the length of side *y*.
Give your answer correct to 3 significant figures.

You are given the hypotenuse and asked to find the adjacent, so use the formula for $\cos x$.

$\cos 29° = \frac{y}{4}$

$4\cos 29° = y$

$y = 3.4984... = \underline{\textbf{3.50 cm}}$ (to 3 s.f.)

Section 19 — Pythagoras and Trigonometry

Exercise 1

1 Find the lengths of the missing sides marked with letters.
Give your answers to 3 significant figures.

a) Triangle with 43° angle, hypotenuse 6 cm, side a opposite.

b) Right triangle with 58° angle, side b opposite, 11 cm adjacent.

c) Right triangle with 12° angle, side c, 5 cm.

d) Right triangle with 63° angle, 9 cm, side d.

e) Right triangle with 37° angle, 6 cm, side p.

f) Right triangle with 20 cm, 34° angle, side q.

g) Right triangle with 48° angle, side r, 7 cm.

h) Right triangle with 11° angle, side s, 4.5 cm.

2 Find the missing length m (to 3 s.f.).

Isosceles triangle with 66° apex angle, equal sides 10 cm, m is half the base.

3 Find the missing length n (to 3 s.f.).

Isosceles triangle with 51° half-apex angle, equal sides 12 cm, base n.

Example 2

Find the size of missing angle x in the triangle to the right.
Give your answer to 1 decimal place.

1. You are given the hypotenuse and the opposite, so use the formula for $\sin x$.
2. Use the inverse to find the angle.

$\sin x = \dfrac{6}{7}$

$x = \sin^{-1}\left(\dfrac{6}{7}\right)$

$x = 58.9972... =$ **59.0°** (to 1 d.p.)

4 Find the sizes of the missing angles marked with letters. Give your answers to 1 decimal place.

a) Right triangle with 3 m, 8 m, angle a.

b) Right triangle with 14 cm, 10 cm, angle b.

c) Right triangle with 11 cm, 12 cm, angle c.

Section 19 — Pythagoras and Trigonometry

5 Find the sizes of the missing angles marked with letters, giving your answers to 1 decimal place.

a) 12 cm, 2 cm, angle d

b) 5 cm, 7.5 cm, angle e

c) 15 mm, 13 mm, angle f

Common Trig Values

The sin, cos and tan of some angles have **exact values** shown in this table:

$\sin 0° = 0$	$\sin 30° = \frac{1}{2}$	$\sin 45° = \frac{1}{\sqrt{2}}$	$\sin 60° = \frac{\sqrt{3}}{2}$	$\sin 90° = 1$
$\cos 0° = 1$	$\cos 30° = \frac{\sqrt{3}}{2}$	$\cos 45° = \frac{1}{\sqrt{2}}$	$\cos 60° = \frac{1}{2}$	$\cos 90° = 0$
$\tan 0° = 0$	$\tan 30° = \frac{1}{\sqrt{3}}$	$\tan 45° = 1$	$\tan 60° = \sqrt{3}$	

Exercise 2

1 Without using your calculator, find the size of the angles marked with letters.

a) $\sqrt{3}$ cm, 2 cm, angle a

b) 1 m, $\sqrt{2}$ m, angle b

c) 1 cm, $\sqrt{3}$ cm, angle c

d) 8 mm, 4 mm, angle d

2 Find the exact length of the sides marked with letters.

a) 1 m, 30°, side e

b) 2 cm, 60°, side f

c) 45°, 8 mm, side g

d) 30°, 2 m, side h

3 Show that:
$\tan 45° + \sin 60° = \frac{2 + \sqrt{3}}{2}$

4 Triangle ABC is an equilateral triangle with side length 2 mm.
What is the exact height of the triangle?
Give your answer in its simplest form.

5 Triangle DEF is isosceles. $DF = 7\sqrt{2}$ cm and angle $DEF = 90°$.
What is the exact length of side DE?

Section 19 — Pythagoras and Trigonometry

19.3 Pythagoras and Trigonometry Problems

Exercise 1

1. A pilot flies 150 km on a bearing of 090°, then 270 km on a bearing of 180°. Find the direct distance from his start point to his end point. Give your answer to the nearest kilometre.

2. Find the lengths of the sides marked with letters in each of the following. Give your answers to 3 significant figures.

   a) 3 cm, 5 cm, a
   b) b, 28 cm, 32°
   c) 17 cm, 62°, c
   d) d, 29°, 2.1 m

3. Melissa is building a slide for an adventure playground. The first slide she builds has an 8 m high vertical ladder and a slide of 24 m. Find m, the angle of elevation the slide makes with the ground, to 1 d.p.

4. A ladder is leaning against the side of a tower. The base of the ladder is placed 8 m away from the bottom of the tower, making an angle of 68° with the ground. It reaches a window h m above the ground. Find the value of h, giving your answer to 1 decimal place.

5. The points P and R have coordinates $P(1, 3)$ and $R(7, 8)$. Find the length of the line segment PR, correct to 1 d.p.

6. Find the exact lengths of the sides marked with letters in each of the following.

   a) 45°, 3 cm, 30°, a
   b) 60°, 12 cm, b

7. The shape shown is made up of two right-angled triangles. Find the value of x. (1 cm, 8 cm, 7 cm, x)

8. A kite with taut string of length 5.8 m is flying in the air. The kite is 4.1 m vertically higher than the other end of the string. Find the angle between the string and the horizontal, to 1 d.p.

9. Town W is 25 km due south of Town X. Town Y is 42 km due east of Town W. Find the bearing of Town Y from Town X, to 1 d.p.

Section 19 — Pythagoras and Trigonometry

Section 20 — Vectors

20.1 Column Vectors

A **vector** has **length** and **direction**.
A vector can be written as a **column vector** or drawn as an **arrow**.

Column vector: $\vec{AB} = \mathbf{a} = \begin{pmatrix} 3 \\ 2 \end{pmatrix}$ ← x-component: 3 units right
← y-component: 2 units up

Example 1

Draw the vector $\mathbf{m} = \begin{pmatrix} -3 \\ 2 \end{pmatrix}$.

The positive and negative directions in column vectors are the same as they are for coordinates.

So –3 in the x-component means '3 units left', and 2 in the y-component means '2 units up'.

Exercise 1

1 Draw arrows to represent the following vectors.

a) $\begin{pmatrix} 1 \\ 4 \end{pmatrix}$
b) $\begin{pmatrix} 3 \\ 5 \end{pmatrix}$
c) $\begin{pmatrix} -2 \\ 4 \end{pmatrix}$
d) $\begin{pmatrix} 0 \\ 5 \end{pmatrix}$
e) $\begin{pmatrix} -3 \\ -5 \end{pmatrix}$
f) $\begin{pmatrix} 3 \\ 0 \end{pmatrix}$
g) $\begin{pmatrix} -3 \\ -3 \end{pmatrix}$
h) $\begin{pmatrix} 2.5 \\ 4 \end{pmatrix}$
i) $\begin{pmatrix} 0 \\ -3 \end{pmatrix}$
j) $\begin{pmatrix} 1.5 \\ -2 \end{pmatrix}$
k) $\begin{pmatrix} 7 \\ 1 \end{pmatrix}$
l) $\begin{pmatrix} -3.5 \\ 3.5 \end{pmatrix}$

2 Write down the column vectors represented by these arrows:

Section 20 — Vectors

A vector can be **multiplied** by a scalar (number) to give another vector.
The resulting vector is **parallel** to the original vector.
If the scalar is **negative**, the direction of the vector is **reversed**.

Example 2

If $\mathbf{p} = \begin{pmatrix} 2 \\ -3 \end{pmatrix}$, write the following as column vectors: a) $2\mathbf{p}$ b) $\frac{1}{2}\mathbf{p}$ c) $-\mathbf{p}$

Multiply a vector by a scalar by multiplying the x-component and the y-component separately.

a) $2\mathbf{p} = \begin{pmatrix} 2 \times 2 \\ 2 \times -3 \end{pmatrix} = \begin{pmatrix} 4 \\ -6 \end{pmatrix}$ b) $\frac{1}{2}\mathbf{p} = \begin{pmatrix} \frac{1}{2} \times 2 \\ \frac{1}{2} \times -3 \end{pmatrix} = \begin{pmatrix} 1 \\ -1.5 \end{pmatrix}$ c) $-\mathbf{p} = \begin{pmatrix} -1 \times 2 \\ -1 \times -3 \end{pmatrix} = \begin{pmatrix} -2 \\ 3 \end{pmatrix}$

3 If $\mathbf{q} = \begin{pmatrix} -1 \\ 3 \end{pmatrix}$, find and draw the following vectors.
   a) $3\mathbf{q}$ b) $5\mathbf{q}$ c) $\frac{3}{2}\mathbf{q}$ d) $-2\mathbf{q}$

4 $\mathbf{a} = \begin{pmatrix} 4 \\ -2 \end{pmatrix}$ $\mathbf{b} = \begin{pmatrix} -1 \\ 4 \end{pmatrix}$ $\mathbf{c} = \begin{pmatrix} 3 \\ 12 \end{pmatrix}$ $\mathbf{d} = \begin{pmatrix} 8 \\ -4 \end{pmatrix}$ $\mathbf{e} = \begin{pmatrix} 1 \\ 4 \end{pmatrix}$ $\mathbf{f} = \begin{pmatrix} 0 \\ 3 \end{pmatrix}$ $\mathbf{g} = \begin{pmatrix} 3 \\ -12 \end{pmatrix}$ $\mathbf{h} = \begin{pmatrix} 6 \\ 0 \end{pmatrix}$

From the list of vectors above:
a) Which vector is equal to $2\mathbf{a}$?
b) Which vector is equal to $-3\mathbf{b}$?
c) Which vector is the same length as $\mathbf{e}$?
d) Which vector is parallel to $\mathbf{c}$?

Adding and Subtracting Vectors

To **add** or **subtract** vectors, add or subtract the x-components and y-components separately.
The sum of two vectors is called the **resultant vector**.

Vectors can also be added by drawing them in a chain, nose-to-tail.
The resultant vector goes in a straight line from the start to the end of the chain of vectors.

Example 3

$\mathbf{p} = \begin{pmatrix} 3 \\ 1 \end{pmatrix}$ $\mathbf{q} = \begin{pmatrix} -2 \\ 0 \end{pmatrix}$ $\mathbf{r} = \begin{pmatrix} 1 \\ -3 \end{pmatrix}$

Work out the following and draw the resultant vectors:
a) $\mathbf{p} + \mathbf{q}$
b) $\mathbf{r} - \mathbf{q}$
c) $2\mathbf{q} + \mathbf{p} - \mathbf{r}$

$= \begin{pmatrix} 3 + (-2) \\ 1 + 0 \end{pmatrix} = \begin{pmatrix} 1 \\ 1 \end{pmatrix}$ $= \begin{pmatrix} 1 - (-2) \\ -3 - 0 \end{pmatrix} = \begin{pmatrix} 3 \\ -3 \end{pmatrix}$ $= \begin{pmatrix} 2 \times (-2) + 3 - 1 \\ 2 \times 0 + 1 - (-3) \end{pmatrix} = \begin{pmatrix} -2 \\ 4 \end{pmatrix}$

Exercise 2

1 Write the answers to the following calculations as column vectors.
For each expression, draw arrows to represent the two given vectors and the resultant vector.

a) $\begin{pmatrix} 5 \\ 2 \end{pmatrix} + \begin{pmatrix} 3 \\ 4 \end{pmatrix}$
b) $\begin{pmatrix} 4 \\ -1 \end{pmatrix} + \begin{pmatrix} 1 \\ 6 \end{pmatrix}$
c) $\begin{pmatrix} 0 \\ 5 \end{pmatrix} + \begin{pmatrix} -3 \\ 4 \end{pmatrix}$
d) $\begin{pmatrix} -2 \\ 6 \end{pmatrix} + \begin{pmatrix} -3 \\ 1 \end{pmatrix}$

e) $\begin{pmatrix} 7 \\ 6 \end{pmatrix} - \begin{pmatrix} 3 \\ 4 \end{pmatrix}$
f) $\begin{pmatrix} 5 \\ -1 \end{pmatrix} - \begin{pmatrix} 1 \\ 3 \end{pmatrix}$
g) $\begin{pmatrix} 2 \\ -1 \end{pmatrix} - \begin{pmatrix} -2 \\ 2 \end{pmatrix}$
h) $\begin{pmatrix} -3 \\ 0 \end{pmatrix} - \begin{pmatrix} 6 \\ 2 \end{pmatrix}$

2 If $\mathbf{a} = \begin{pmatrix} 2 \\ 3 \end{pmatrix}$, $\mathbf{b} = \begin{pmatrix} 0 \\ -2 \end{pmatrix}$ and $\mathbf{c} = \begin{pmatrix} -1 \\ 4 \end{pmatrix}$, work out:

a) $\mathbf{b} + \mathbf{c}$
b) $\mathbf{c} - \mathbf{a}$
c) $2\mathbf{c} + \mathbf{a}$
d) $3\mathbf{a} + \mathbf{b}$
e) $\mathbf{a} - 2\mathbf{c}$
f) $\mathbf{a} + \mathbf{b} - \mathbf{c}$
g) $5\mathbf{b} + 4\mathbf{c}$
h) $4\mathbf{a} - \mathbf{b} + 3\mathbf{c}$

3 If $\mathbf{p} = \begin{pmatrix} 5 \\ 0 \end{pmatrix}$, $\mathbf{q} = \begin{pmatrix} -3 \\ -1 \end{pmatrix}$ and $\mathbf{r} = \begin{pmatrix} 2 \\ 7 \end{pmatrix}$, work out:

a) $\mathbf{p} + \mathbf{r}$
b) $\mathbf{p} - \mathbf{q}$
c) $3\mathbf{q} + \mathbf{r}$
d) $4\mathbf{r} - 2\mathbf{q}$
e) $3\mathbf{p} + 2\mathbf{r}$
f) $\mathbf{p} + \mathbf{r} - \mathbf{q}$
g) $6\mathbf{r} - 3\mathbf{q}$
h) $2\mathbf{p} - 3\mathbf{q} + \mathbf{r}$

4 $\mathbf{u} = \begin{pmatrix} 6 \\ -2 \end{pmatrix}$, $\mathbf{v} = \begin{pmatrix} -2 \\ 3 \end{pmatrix}$ and $\mathbf{w} = \begin{pmatrix} 1 \\ 2 \end{pmatrix}$

a) Work out $\mathbf{u} + 2\mathbf{v}$
b) Draw the vectors $\mathbf{u} + 2\mathbf{v}$ and $\mathbf{w}$
c) What do you notice about the directions of the vectors $\mathbf{u} + 2\mathbf{v}$ and $\mathbf{w}$?

Example 4

Describe the following vectors in terms of **a** and **b**.

a) $\overrightarrow{RS}$

1. Find a route from R to S using just vectors **a** and **b**.
2. You can check the answer by doing the vector addition — from the diagram, $\overrightarrow{RS} = \begin{pmatrix} 5 \\ 2 \end{pmatrix}$, $\mathbf{a} = \begin{pmatrix} 2 \\ 0 \end{pmatrix}$ and $\mathbf{b} = \begin{pmatrix} 1 \\ 2 \end{pmatrix}$.

$\overrightarrow{RS} = 2\mathbf{a} + \mathbf{b}$

Check: $2\mathbf{a} + \mathbf{b} = 2\begin{pmatrix} 2 \\ 0 \end{pmatrix} + \begin{pmatrix} 1 \\ 2 \end{pmatrix}$
$= \begin{pmatrix} 4 \\ 0 \end{pmatrix} + \begin{pmatrix} 1 \\ 2 \end{pmatrix} = \begin{pmatrix} 5 \\ 2 \end{pmatrix} = \overrightarrow{RS}$

b) $\overrightarrow{TU}$

1. Find a route from T to U using just vectors **a** and **b**.
2. Remember to check the answer by doing the vector addition — from the diagram, $\overrightarrow{TU} = \begin{pmatrix} 0 \\ 4 \end{pmatrix}$.

$\overrightarrow{TU} = -\mathbf{a} + 2\mathbf{b}$

Check: $-\mathbf{a} + 2\mathbf{b} = -\begin{pmatrix} 2 \\ 0 \end{pmatrix} + 2\begin{pmatrix} 1 \\ 2 \end{pmatrix}$
$= \begin{pmatrix} -2 \\ 0 \end{pmatrix} + \begin{pmatrix} 2 \\ 4 \end{pmatrix} = \begin{pmatrix} 0 \\ 4 \end{pmatrix} = \overrightarrow{TU}$

Exercise 3

1

Write the following vectors in terms of **a** and **b**.

a) $\overrightarrow{WH}$ b) $\overrightarrow{ZH}$ c) $\overrightarrow{FX}$ d) $\overrightarrow{UD}$
e) $\overrightarrow{DU}$ f) $\overrightarrow{FZ}$ g) $\overrightarrow{CZ}$ h) $\overrightarrow{DW}$

20.2 Vectors Problems

Exercise 1

1 a) Match the following column vectors to the correct vectors in the diagram below.

$\begin{pmatrix} 1 \\ 4 \end{pmatrix}$ $\begin{pmatrix} -2 \\ -4 \end{pmatrix}$

$\begin{pmatrix} -4 \\ -1 \end{pmatrix}$ $\begin{pmatrix} 4 \\ -2 \end{pmatrix}$

$\begin{pmatrix} 0 \\ -5 \end{pmatrix}$ $\begin{pmatrix} 3 \\ 4 \end{pmatrix}$

$\begin{pmatrix} 4 \\ -1 \end{pmatrix}$ $\begin{pmatrix} 1 \\ -4 \end{pmatrix}$

b) Which vector has the same length as **c**?
c) Which vector has the same length as **a**?
d) Four of the vectors have the same length. Which vectors are these?

2 If $\mathbf{p} = \begin{pmatrix} 4 \\ -3 \end{pmatrix}$, $\mathbf{q} = \begin{pmatrix} 0 \\ 2 \end{pmatrix}$ and $\mathbf{r} = \begin{pmatrix} -1 \\ 5 \end{pmatrix}$, find:

a) 3**p**   b) 2**q** + **r**   c) **r** − 2**p**   d) **p** + 5**r** − 3**q**

3 $\mathbf{a} = \begin{pmatrix} 6 \\ -4 \end{pmatrix}$ $\mathbf{b} = \begin{pmatrix} -2 \\ 3 \end{pmatrix}$ $\mathbf{c} = \begin{pmatrix} 1 \\ 2 \end{pmatrix}$ $\mathbf{d} = \begin{pmatrix} 4 \\ -2 \end{pmatrix}$ $\mathbf{e} = \begin{pmatrix} 3 \\ 6 \end{pmatrix}$ $\mathbf{f} = \begin{pmatrix} 4 \\ -6 \end{pmatrix}$

a) Draw the vector **a** + **b** and write down the resultant vector as a column vector.
b) Draw the vector **e** − **d** and write down the resultant vector as a column vector.
c) Which two vectors above give the resultant vector $\begin{pmatrix} 10 \\ -10 \end{pmatrix}$ when they are added together?
d) Which two vectors above can be added to give the resultant vector $\begin{pmatrix} 1 \\ 9 \end{pmatrix}$?
e) Which vector above is parallel to **c**?   **f)** Which vector above is parallel to **b**?

Vector Geometry

Example 1

In triangle OAB, $\vec{OA} = \mathbf{a}$ and $\vec{OB} = \mathbf{b}$.

Write down, in terms of **a** and **b**,   a) $\vec{AO}$ b) $\vec{AB}$ c) $\vec{BA}$

To get from A to O, you go
backwards along the vector **a**.   a) $\vec{AO} = -\mathbf{a}$

To get from A to B, you go
backwards along **a** and then along **b**.   b) $\vec{AB} = -\mathbf{a} + \mathbf{b}$

To get from B to A, you go
backwards along **b** and then along **a**.   c) $\vec{BA} = -\mathbf{b} + \mathbf{a}$

Exercise 2

1   ABCD is a trapezium. $\vec{AB} = 4\mathbf{p}$, $\vec{AD} = \mathbf{q}$ and $\vec{DC} = \mathbf{p}$.
Write the following vectors in terms of **p** and **q**:

   a) $\vec{BA}$ b) $\vec{CD}$ c) $\vec{AC}$
   d) $\vec{CA}$ e) $\vec{CB}$ f) $\vec{BD}$

2   In the diagram on the left, $\vec{OA} = \mathbf{a}$ and $\vec{OB} = \mathbf{b}$.
Point C is added such that $\vec{OC} = \mathbf{a} + \mathbf{b}$.

   a) Write down, in terms of **a** and **b**:   (i) $\vec{CO}$ (ii) $\vec{AB}$
   b) What type of shape is OACB?

3   In the triangle OBD, $\vec{OA} = \mathbf{a}$ is $\frac{1}{4}$ of the length of $\vec{OB}$
and $\vec{OC} = \mathbf{c}$ is $\frac{1}{3}$ of the length of $\vec{OD}$.

Write down, in terms of **a** and **c**:

   a) $\vec{OB}$ b) $\vec{OD}$ c) $\vec{AB}$
   d) $\vec{CD}$ e) $\vec{DB}$ f) $\vec{BD}$

4   ABCDEF is a regular hexagon. M is the centre of the hexagon.
$\vec{AB} = \mathbf{p}$ and $\vec{BC} = \mathbf{q}$ and $\vec{CD} = \mathbf{r}$.

The following vectors can all be written, in terms of **p**, **q** and **r**,
in multiple different ways. For each vector, write down two ways.

   a) $\vec{ED}$ b) $\vec{FE}$ c) $\vec{AF}$
   d) $\vec{EF}$ e) $\vec{MF}$ f) $\vec{EM}$

Section 20 — Vectors

Section 21 — Constructions

21.1 Circles

Radius and Diameter

Radius: a line from the centre of a circle to the edge. The circle's centre is the same distance from all points on the edge.

Diameter: a line from one side of a circle to the other through the centre.
The diameter is twice the radius: $d = 2r$

Example 1

a) A circle has radius 4 cm. What is its diameter?
b) A circle has diameter 7 m. What is its radius?

1. Use the formula $d = 2r$.
2. Remember to use the correct units.

a) $d = 2r$
$d = 2 \times 4$
= **8 cm**

b) $7 = 2r$
So $r = 7 \div 2$
= **3.5 m**

Exercise 1

1 Find the diameter of each of the following circles.
   a) 3 cm   b) 2 cm   c) 35 mm   d) 28 mm

2 Find the radius of each of the following circles.
   a) 8 cm   b) 10 mm   c) 19 mm   d) 4.8 cm

3 Find the diameter of a circle with radius:
   a) 4 cm   b) 6 cm   c) 30 mm   d) 25 m   e) 2.8 m
   f) 4.6 mm   g) 3.7 m   h) 49 mm   i) 55 m   j) 4.2 mm

4 Find the radius of a circle with diameter:
   a) 2 cm   b) 12 cm   c) 14 m   d) 28 mm   e) 1.4 cm
   f) 2.8 m   g) 57 mm   h) 4.3 cm   i) 0.8 m   j) 0.02 cm

5 Use a compass to draw a circle with:
   a) a radius of 4 cm   b) a radius of 5 cm   c) a diameter of 80 mm
   d) a diameter of 6 cm   e) a diameter of 7 cm   f) a diameter of 23 mm

Section 21 — Constructions

More Parts of Circles

Circumference: the distance around the outside of a circle.

Tangent: a straight line that just touches the circle.

Arc: a part of the circumference.

Chord: a line between two points on the circle **not** through the centre.

Sector: an area of a circle like a "slice of pie".

Segment: the area of a circle between an arc and a chord.

Exercise 2

1 Name the feature highlighted in each diagram below.

a) b) c) d)

e) f) g) h)

2 What do the labels *A-F* show in the diagrams below?

3 Draw a circle. Then draw and label the following features.

    a) a chord   **b)** an arc   **c)** a tangent   **d)** a diameter

Section 21 — Constructions

21.2 Lines, Angles and Triangles

For this topic, you'll need to know how to use a **ruler** to measure lengths...

...and a **protractor** to measure angles.

Make sure you know how to use both scales on your protractor.

Example 1

Measure the size of angle a.

1. Put the protractor's cross exactly where the two lines meet.
2. Use the correct scale — this is an acute angle, so use the scale showing angles less than 90°.

$a = \underline{\mathbf{24°}}$

Exercise 1

1 In each diagram below, measure the size of the angle and the length of the lines.

2 Draw a line 6 cm long.
   a) On one end of your line, draw an angle of 70°.
   b) On the other end of your line, draw an angle of 30°.

3 Draw a line 8.5 cm long.
   a) On one end of your line, draw an angle of 130°.
   b) On the other end of your line, draw an angle of 170°.

4 Measure all the angles in these triangles.
   Make sure your answers add up to 180°.
   a)
   b)

Section 21 — Constructions

Example 2

Draw triangle *ABC*, where side *AB* is 4 cm, angle *BAC* is 55°, and angle *ABC* is 35°.

1. Draw and label the side you know the length of.
2. Use your protractor to draw the first angle. Angle *BAC* is at point *A*.
3. Draw the second angle, and complete the triangle.

Exercise 2

1 Draw the following triangles accurately, then measure the lengths marked *l*.

a) 37°, 4 cm

b) 25°, 80°, 6 cm

c) 38°, 110°, 5 cm

d) 72°, 41°, 5.5 cm

2 a) Draw each of the triangles *ABC* described below.
   (i) *AB* = 4 cm, angle *BAC* = 55°, angle *CBA* = 35°.
   (ii) *AB* = 8 cm, angle *BAC* = 22°, angle *CBA* = 107°.
   (iii) *AB* = 6.5 cm, angle *BAC* = 65°, angle *CBA* = 30°.
   (iv) *AB* = 7.2 cm, angle *BAC* = 120°, angle *CBA* = 28°.

b) Measure the length of side *BC* in each of your triangles in part **a)**.

3 Draw an equilateral triangle with sides of length 4 cm.

4 Alec is standing 5 km directly west of Brenda. At noon, Alec starts to walk northeast, while Brenda starts to walk at the same speed northwest.

By carefully drawing their paths on a scale drawing using 1 cm to represent 1 km, find how far from their starting points they eventually meet.

Section 21 — Constructions

Example 3

Draw triangle *ABC*, where *AB* is 4 cm, *BC* is 4 cm, and angle *ABC* is 25°.

1. Draw and label a side you know the length of.
2. Use your protractor to draw the angle you know. Point *C* is 4 cm from *B* along this line.
3. Complete the triangle by drawing the line *AC*.

Exercise 3

1 Draw the following triangles accurately, then measure the lengths marked *l*.

a) 5 cm, 12 cm, *l* (right angle)

b) 7 cm, 6 cm, 50°, *l*

c) 4 cm, 4.5 cm, 70°, *l*

d) 69 mm, 61 mm, 115°, *l*

2 a) Draw each of the triangles *ABC* described below.
  (i) *AB* = 6 cm, *BC* = 7 cm, angle *ABC* = 40°.
  (ii) *AB* = 4 cm, *BC* = 3 cm, angle *ABC* = 110°.
  (iii) *AB* = 65 mm, *BC* = 53 mm, angle *ABC* = 20°.
  (iv) *AB* = 45 mm, *BC* = 45 mm, angle *ABC* = 45°.

  b) Measure the length of side *AC* in each of your triangles in part **a)**.

3 Draw an isosceles triangle with an angle of 50° between its two 5 cm long sides.

4 A rhombus *PQRS* has sides of length 5 cm and two angles of 60°.
  a) Draw the side *SR* accurately.
  b) Draw accurately **(i)** the angle *PSR*, which measures 60° and **(ii)** side *PS*.
  c) Angles *SPQ* and *QRS* are equal.
    By considering the angles in a quadrilateral, find the size of angles *SPQ* and *QRS*.
  d) Complete your accurate drawing of the rhombus.

5 a) Draw a rhombus with sides measuring 6 cm and two angles of 40°.
  b) Draw a rhombus with sides measuring 4.5 cm and two angles of 110°.

Section 21 — Constructions

Example 4

Draw triangle *ABC*, where *AB* is 3 cm, *BC* is 2.5 cm, and *AC* is 2 cm.

1. Draw and label one of the sides.

2. Set your compass to 2.5 cm. Draw an arc 2.5 cm from *B*.

3. Now set your compass to 2 cm. Draw an arc 2 cm from *A*.

4. *C* is where your arcs cross.

Exercise 4

1 These triangles are not drawn accurately. Draw them accurately using the measurements given.

a) 6 cm, 10 cm, 8 cm
b) 4.5 cm, 3 cm, 5 cm
c) 40 mm, 88 mm, 72 mm
d) 7 cm, 6.5 cm, 11 cm
e) 5.8 cm, 4.1 cm, 6.9 cm
f) 102 mm, 69 mm, 52 mm

2 Draw each of the triangles *ABC* described below.
a) *AB* is 5 cm, *BC* is 6 cm, *AC* is 7 cm.
b) *AB* is 4 cm, *BC* is 7 cm, *AC* is 9 cm.
c) *AB* is 8 cm, *BC* is 8 cm, *AC* is 4 cm.
d) *AB* is 4.6 cm, *BC* is 5.4 cm, *AC* is 8.4 cm.

3 Draw an isosceles triangle with two sides of length 5 cm and a side of length 7 cm.

4 Using a scale of 1 cm : 10 miles, draw a map showing the layout of the following three towns. (All distances are 'as the crow flies'.)
- Weymouth is 54 miles from Exeter.
- Exeter is 47 miles from Yeovil.
- Yeovil is 27 miles from Weymouth.

Section 21 — Constructions

21.3 Constructions

For the constructions in this topic, the only things you can use are a **ruler** and **compass**.

Constructing a Perpendicular Bisector

The **perpendicular bisector** of a line between points A and B:
- is at right angles to the line AB
- cuts the line AB in half.

All points on the perpendicular bisector are the same distance from both A and B.

Example 1

Draw a line AB 3 cm long. Construct its perpendicular bisector using a ruler and compass only.

1. Draw points A and B 3 cm apart. Join them with the line AB.
2. Place compass point at A, with the radius more than half of the length AB. Draw two arcs as shown.
3. Keep the radius the same and put the compass point at B. Draw two more arcs.
4. Use a ruler to draw a straight line through the points where the arcs meet. This is the perpendicular bisector.

Exercise 1

1. Draw a horizontal line PQ 5 cm long.
   Construct its perpendicular bisector using a ruler and compass only.

2. Draw a vertical line XY 9 cm long.
   Construct its perpendicular bisector using a ruler and compass only.

3. Draw a line AB 7 cm long.
   Construct its perpendicular bisector using a ruler and compass only.

4. a) Draw a line AB 6 cm long. Construct the perpendicular bisector of AB.
   b) Draw the rhombus $ACBD$ with diagonals 6 cm and 8 cm.

5. a) Draw a circle with radius 5 cm, and draw <u>any</u> two chords. Label your chords AB and CD.
   b) Construct the perpendicular bisector of chord AB.
   c) Construct the perpendicular bisector of chord CD.
   d) Where do the two perpendicular bisectors meet?

Section 21 — Constructions

Constructing an Angle Bisector

An **angle bisector** cuts an angle in half.

Example 2

Draw an angle of 60° using a protractor.
Construct the angle bisector using only a ruler and compass.

1. Place the point of the compass on the angle...
2. ...and draw arcs crossing both lines...
3. ...using the same radius.
4. Now place the point of the compass where your arcs cross the lines, and draw two more arcs — using the same radius.
5. Draw the angle bisector.

Exercise 2

1 Draw the following angles using a protractor.
For each angle, construct the angle bisector using a ruler and compass.
- a) 100°
- b) 140°
- c) 96°
- d) 44°
- e) 50°
- f) 70°
- g) 20°
- h) 65°

Check each of your angle bisectors with a protractor.

2 a) Draw any triangle. Use a ruler to make sure all the sides are straight.
b) Construct the bisectors of each of the angles.
What do you notice about these bisectors?

3 a) Use a protractor to draw an angle ABC of 110°, with $AB = BC = 5$ cm.
Construct the bisector of angle ABC.

b) Mark point D on your drawing, where D is the point on the angle bisector with $BD = 8$ cm.
What kind of quadrilateral is $ABCD$?

Section 21 — Constructions

Constructing a Perpendicular from a Point to a Line

The **perpendicular** from a point to a line:
- passes through the point, and
- meets the line at 90°.

The perpendicular from a point to a line is the **shortest distance** to the line.

perpendicular from the point X to the line AB

Example 3

Construct the perpendicular from the point X to the line AB using only a ruler and compass.

1. Draw an arc centred on X cutting the line twice.
2. Draw an arc centred on one of the points where your arc meets the line.
3. Do the same for the other point, keeping the radius the same.
4. Draw the perpendicular to where the arcs cross.

Exercise 3

1. Use a ruler to draw a triangle like the one on the right. Construct the perpendicular from X to the line YZ.

2. Draw three points not on a straight line. Label your points P, Q and R. Draw a long straight line passing through your points P and Q. Construct the perpendicular from R to this line.

3. a) On squared paper draw axes with x-values from 0 to 10 and y-values from 0 to 10.
   b) Plot the points $A(1, 2)$, $B(9, 1)$ and $C(6, 8)$.
   c) Construct the perpendicular from point C to the line AB.

4. a) Draw any triangle. Use a ruler to make sure all the sides are straight.
   b) Construct a perpendicular from each of the triangle's corners to the opposite side. What do you notice about these lines?

5. a) Construct triangle DEF, where DE = 5 cm, DF = 6 cm and angle FDE = 55°.
   b) Construct the perpendicular from F to DE. Label the point where the perpendicular meets DE as point G.
   c) Measure the length FG. Use your result to work out the area of the triangle to 1 decimal place.

Constructing an Angle of 60°

You'd need to construct an angle of 60° to draw an accurate equilateral triangle.

Example 4

Draw a line *AB* and construct an angle of 60° at *A*.

1. Place the compass point on *A* and draw a long arc that crosses the line *AB*.
2. Place the compass point where the arc meets the line, and draw another arc of the same radius.
3. Draw a straight line through *A* and the point where your arcs cross. The angle will be 60°.

Exercise 4

1. Draw a line *AB* measuring 5 cm. Construct an angle of 60° at *A*.
2. a) Draw a line measuring 6 cm.
   b) Construct an angle of 60° at each end of the line. Join your lines to form a triangle.
   c) By measuring the lengths of the sides, check that your triangle is equilateral.

Constructing an Angle of 30°

Construct an angle of 30° by bisecting an angle of 60°.

Example 5

Draw a line *AB* and construct an angle of 30° at *A*.

1. Construct an angle of 60° at *A*...
2. ...then form the angle bisector to make an angle of 30°.

Exercise 5

1. Draw a line *AB* measuring 6 cm. Construct an angle of 30° at *A*.
2. a) Construct the triangle *ABC* where *AB* = 7 cm, angle *CAB* = 60° and angle *CBA* = 30°.
   b) Check that angle *ACB* is a right angle using a protractor.
3. Construct an isosceles triangle *PQR* where *PQ* = 8 cm and the angles *RPQ* and *RQP* are both 30°.

Section 21 — Constructions

Constructing an Angle of 90°

Remember, an angle of 90° is called a right angle.

Example 6
Construct an angle of 90°.

1. Draw a straight line, and mark the point where you want to form the right angle.
2. Draw arcs of the same radius on either side of your point.
3. Increase the radius of your compass, and draw two arcs of the same radius — one arc centred on each of the intersections.
4. Draw a straight line to complete the right angle.

Exercise 6

1 a) Draw a straight line, and mark a point roughly halfway along it. Label the point X.
   b) Construct a right angle at X using only a ruler and compass.

2 Using a ruler and compass only, construct a rectangle with sides of length 5 cm and 7 cm.

Constructing an Angle of 45°

Construct an angle of 45° by bisecting an angle of 90°.

Example 7
Construct an angle of 45°.

1. Construct an angle of 90°.
2. ...then form the angle bisector to make an angle of 45°.

Exercise 7

1 a) Draw a straight line, and mark a point roughly halfway along it. Label the point X.
   b) Construct an angle of 45° at X using only a ruler and compass.

2 Construct an isosceles triangle ABC where AB = 8 cm and the angles CAB and CBA are both 45°.

Section 21 — Constructions

Constructing Parallel Lines

Construct parallel lines by making two angles of 90°.

Example 8

Construct a line parallel to AB through the point P.

1. Construct the line perpendicular to AB passing through P.
2. Construct a right angle to the line you've drawn at point P.
   This will be parallel to AB.

Exercise 8

1. Draw a line AB, and mark a point P approximately 4 cm from your line. Construct a line parallel to AB through the point P.

2. Draw two straight lines that cross each other at a single point. By adding two parallel lines, construct a parallelogram.

3. Draw a line AB 10 cm long.
   a) Construct angles of 60° at points A and B, as shown.
   b) Mark point C on the line 3 cm from B.
   c) By drawing a line parallel to AB, complete the trapezium $ABCD$.

Exercise 9 — Mixed Exercise

1. Draw a line AB 8 cm long.
   a) Construct an angle of 60° at A.
   b) Complete the construction of a rhombus $ABCD$ with sides of length 8 cm.

2. a) Construct an equilateral triangle with sides of 5.8 cm.
   b) Construct a line through one of the vertices that is parallel to the opposite side.

3. a) Construct the triangle ABC with $AB = 7.4$ cm, angle $CAB = 60°$ and angle $ABC = 45°$.
   b) Calculate the size of angle ACB.
      Check the angle in your drawing using a protractor.

4. Using a ruler and compass only, construct an angle of 15°.

Section 21 — Constructions

21.4 Loci

A **locus** (plural = 'loci') is a set of points which satisfy a particular condition.

The locus of points 1 cm from a point P is a **circle** with radius 1 cm centred on P.

The locus of points 1 cm from a line AB is a 'sausage shape'.

The locus of points **equidistant** (the same distance) from points A and B is the **perpendicular bisector** of AB.

The locus of points equidistant from two lines is their **angle bisector**.

Example 1

Construct the locus of points that satisfy all the following conditions:
(i)   inside rectangle $ABCD$,
(ii) more than 2 cm from point A,
(iii) less than 1 cm from side CD.

(i) and (ii) — these are all the points inside rectangle $ABCD$ more than 2 cm from point A.

(iii) — these are all the points that are also less than 1 cm from CD.

Exercise 1

1. Draw a 7 cm long line AB. Construct the locus of all the points 2 cm from the line.

2. a) Mark a point X on your page. Draw the locus of all points which are 3 cm from X.
   b) Shade the locus of all points that are less than 3 cm from X.

Section 21 — Constructions

3 Mark two points *A* and *B* on your page 6 cm apart.
Construct the locus of all points which are equidistant from *A* and *B*.

4 Draw two lines that meet at an angle of 50°.
Construct the locus of all points which are equidistant from the two lines.

5 Draw a line *AB* 6 cm long. Draw the locus of all points which are 3 cm from *AB*.

6 a) Mark points *P* and *Q* on your page 5 cm apart.
b) Draw the locus of points which are 3 cm from *P*.
c) Draw the locus of points which are 4 cm from *Q*.
d) Show clearly which points are both 3 cm from *P* and 4 cm from *Q*.

7 a) Draw axes on squared paper with *x*- and *y*-values from 0 to 10.
Plot the points *P*(2, 7) and *Q*(10, 3).
b) Construct the locus of points which are equidistant from *P* and *Q*.

8 a) Construct a triangle with sides 4 cm, 5 cm and 6 cm.
b) Draw the locus of all points which are exactly 1 cm from any of the triangle's sides.

9 a) Construct an isosceles triangle *DEF* with *DE* = *EF* = 5 cm and *DF* = 3 cm.
b) Draw the locus of points which are equidistant from *D* and *F* and less than 2 cm from *E*.

Exercise 2

1 A ship sails so that it is always the same distance from a port *P* and a lighthouse *L*. The lighthouse and the port are 3 km apart.
a) Draw a scale diagram showing the port and lighthouse. Use a scale of 1 cm : 1 km.
b) Show the path of the ship on your diagram.

2 Some students are doing a treasure hunt. They know the treasure is:
- located in a square region *ABCD*, which measures 10 m × 10 m
- the same distance from *AB* as from *AD*
- 7 m from corner *C*.

Draw a scale diagram to show the location of the treasure. Use a scale of 1 cm : 1 m.

3 Two edges of a field meet at an angle of 80°. A bonfire has to be the same distance from each edge and 3 m from the corner.
Copy and complete the diagram below to show the position of the fire.

Scale 1 cm : 1 m

80°

4 Two camels set off at the same time from towns *A* and *B*, located 50 miles apart in the desert.
a) Draw a scale diagram showing towns *A* and *B*. Use a scale of 1 cm : 10 miles.
b) If a camel can walk up to 40 miles in a day, show on your diagram the region where the camels could possibly meet each other after walking for one day.

5 A walled rectangular yard has length 4 m and width 2 m. A dog is secured by a lead of length 1 m to a post in the corner of the yard.
a) Show on an accurate scale drawing the area in which the dog can move.
Use the scale 1 cm : 1 m.
b) The post is replaced with a 3 m rail mounted horizontally along one of the long walls, with one end in the corner.
If the end of the lead attached to the rail is free to slide, show the area in which the dog can move.

3 m

rail

Section 21 — Constructions **243**

Section 22 — Area and Perimeter

22.1 Rectangles and Triangles

Perimeter

Perimeter (P) is the distance around the outside of a shape.

Square: $P = 4l$

Rectangle: $P = 2l + 2w$

Triangle: $P = a + b + c$

Example 1

Find the perimeter of each of these shapes:

a) Rectangle 5 cm by 3 cm

1. Write down the formula for perimeter.
2. Substitute in the lengths of the sides.

$P = 2l + 2w$
$= (2 \times 5) + (2 \times 3)$
$= 10 + 6$
= **16 cm**

b) Triangle with sides 4.1 m, 6.2 m, 8.3 m

$P = a + b + c$
$= 4.1 + 8.3 + 6.2$
= **18.6 m**

Exercise 1

1. Find the perimeters of the shapes below.

   a) Right triangle with sides 3 cm, 4 cm, 5 cm

   b) Rectangle 11 m by 3 m

   c) Square with side 5 cm

   d) Rectangle 6 cm by 4 cm

   e) Triangle with sides 18 m, 14 m, 11 m

   f) Rectangle 30 mm by 15 mm

   g) Square with side 4.2 cm

   h) Triangle with sides 5.2 mm, 13.8 mm, 12.8 mm

   i) Triangle with sides 10.8 m, 6.6 m, 8.5 m

244 Section 22 — Area and Perimeter

Area

Area (*A*) is the amount of space inside a shape.

Area = (side length)²
$A = l^2$

Area = length × width
$A = lw$

Area = ½ × base × perpendicular height
$A = \tfrac{1}{2}bh$

Example 2

Find the area of each of these shapes:

1. Write down the formula for area.
2. Substitute in the lengths needed.
3. It's an area, so use 'squared' units.

a) 3.2 m

$A = l^2$
$= 3.2^2$
$= \underline{\mathbf{10.24\ m^2}}$

b) 9 mm, 16 mm

$A = \tfrac{1}{2}bh$
$= \tfrac{1}{2} \times 16 \times 9$
$= \underline{\mathbf{72\ mm^2}}$

Exercise 2

1 Find the areas of the shapes below.

a) 5 cm, 10 cm

b) 9 m, 4 m

c) 4 mm

d) 11 m, 3 m

e) 11 cm

f) 2 mm, 10 mm

g) 4 cm, 3 cm

h) 22 cm, 8 cm

i) 10 cm, 5 cm

Section 22 — Area and Perimeter

Exercise 3 — Mixed Exercise

1 For each shape below, find: **(i)** its perimeter, **(ii)** its area.

a) 3.1 cm × 1.4 cm rectangle

b) 3.1 mm × 1.1 mm rectangle

c) 1.8 cm square

2 For each shape described below, find: **(i)** its perimeter, **(ii)** its area.
  a) a square with sides of length 4 cm.
  b) a rectangle of width 6 m and length 8 m.
  c) a rectangle 23 mm long and 15 mm wide.
  d) a square with 17 m sides.
  e) a rectangle 22.2 m long and 4.3 m wide.
  f) a rectangle of length 9 mm and width 2.4 mm.

3 For each of the triangles below, find: **(i)** its perimeter, **(ii)** its area.

a) triangle with sides 7 cm, 9 cm, 8 cm and height 6.7 cm

b) triangle with sides 9 m, 6 m, 11 m and height 4.9 m

c) triangle with base 18.8 m, sides 8.9 mm and 15.1 mm, height 7 mm

d) triangle with base 12.8 mm, side 13 mm, height 4 mm

e) triangle with sides 12.5 m, 10.9 m, 8.1 m and height 8 m

f) triangle with sides 7.3 m, 10 m, 15 m, 11 m

4 Barbie has a rectangular lawn 23.5 m long by 17.3 m wide. She is going to mow the lawn and then put edging around the outside.
  a) What area will Barbie have to mow (to the nearest m²)?
  b) How much lawn edging will she need?

5 The police need to cordon off and then search a rectangular crime scene measuring 2.1 m by 2.8 m.
  a) What area do the police need to search?
  b) What is the perimeter of the crime scene?

6 A rectangular garden 24 m long and 5.4 m wide is to be re-turfed. Turf is bought in rolls that are 60 cm wide and 8 m long.
How many rolls of turf are needed to cover the garden?

7 A rectangular floor measures 9 m by 7.5 m. It is to be tiled using square tiles with sides of length 0.5 m.
  a) What is the area of the floor?
  b) What is the area of one of the tiles?
  c) How many tiles will be needed to cover the floor?

8 Ali bakes the cake shown below.

28 cm × 22 cm × 8 cm cake

  a) What length of ribbon is needed to go around the outside of the cake?
  b) If the top and the four sides are to be iced, what area of icing will be needed?

246   *Section 22 — Area and Perimeter*

Composite Shapes involving Rectangles and Triangles

A composite shape is one that's made out of simpler shapes joined together.

Example 3
Find this shape's: a) perimeter, b) area.

a) perimeter
1. Label the missing sides, and find their lengths.
2. Add the lengths of all the sides.

$P = 10 - 4 = 6$ cm
$Q = 7 + 11 = 18$ cm

perimeter = 7 + 6 + 11 + 4 + 18 + 10
= **56 cm**

b) area
1. Split the shape into rectangles A and B, and find their areas.
2. Add these to find the total area.

Area of rectangle A = 10×7
= 70 cm²
Area of rectangle B = 11×4
= 44 cm²
Total area of shape = 70 + 44
= **114 cm²**

Exercise 4

1 Find the area of each shape below.

a) [8 m, 4 m, 4 m, 9 m]

b) [6 m, 4 m, 10 m, 8 m]

c) [5 mm, 8 mm, 14 mm, 12 mm]

2 For each shape below, find: **(i)** its perimeter, **(ii)** its area.

a) [8 cm, 5 cm, 13 cm, 12 cm]

b) [5 cm, 3 cm, 7 cm, 4 cm]

c) [10 mm, 15 mm, 8 mm, 23 mm]

3 Find the area of the shapes below by splitting them into a rectangle and a triangle.

a) [8 m, 4 m, 20 m]

b) [21 cm, 9 cm, 5 cm]

Section 22 — Area and Perimeter 247

22.2 Other Quadrilaterals

Parallelograms

Parallelograms have two pairs of parallel sides, with opposite sides being the same length. Parallel sides are shown with matching arrows.

The **area** of a parallelogram is given by the formula: $A = bh$

Here, h is the perpendicular height — it's measured at right angles to the base.

Example 1

Find the area of the parallelogram on the right.

1. Write down the formula for the area of a parallelogram. $A = bh$
2. Substitute in the values for b and h. $= 8 \times 3$
3. Use 'squared' units — here, it's cm². $= \underline{\mathbf{24 \text{ cm}^2}}$

Exercise 1

1 Find the area of each parallelogram below.

a) 4 cm, 7 cm
b) 2 m, 4 m
c) 8 mm, 6 mm
d) 6 mm, 9 mm
e) 35 m, 18 m
f) 8.2 mm, 5.8 mm

2 The logo of a company that designs rockets consists of two identical parallelograms. Find the total area of the logo.

3.1 cm, 8.2 cm

3 Without doing any calculations, explain which of the shapes below has the larger area.

6 cm × 6 cm square; parallelogram with 6 cm sides

248   *Section 22 — Area and Perimeter*

Trapeziums

The shape on the right is a trapezium. It has one pair of parallel sides.

The **area** of a trapezium is given by the formula: $A = \frac{1}{2}(a + b) \times h$

Remember, a and b are the parallel sides, and h is the perpendicular height.

Example 2

Find the area of the trapezium on the right.

1. Write down the formula for the area of a trapezium.
2. Substitute in the values for a, b and h.
3. Use 'squared' units — here, it's cm².

$$A = \frac{1}{2}(a + b) \times h$$
$$= \frac{1}{2}(6 + 8) \times 3$$
$$= \frac{1}{2} \times 14 \times 3$$
$$= 7 \times 3 = \underline{\mathbf{21\ cm^2}}$$

Exercise 2

1 Find the area of each trapezium below.

a) 4 m, 4 m, 10 m

b) 12 mm, 9 mm, 8 mm

c) 3 mm, 5 mm, 13 mm

d) 4.1 cm, 3.2 cm, 6.3 cm

e) 23.4 mm, 19.5 mm, 8.8 mm

f) 0.6 cm, 0.2 cm, 0.25 cm, 0.9 cm, 0.3 cm

2 The picture below shows the end of a barn. Find its total area.

7 m, 4 m, 3 m, 10 m, 10 m

3 What can you say about the area of these two shapes? Explain your answer.

6 cm; 3 cm, 9 cm

Section 22 — Area and Perimeter **249**

Exercise 3 — Mixed Exercise

1 Find the area of each shape below.

a) 8 cm (top), 3 cm (bottom), 4 cm (height)

b) 21 m (base), 10 m (height)

c) 20 mm (top), 55 mm (bottom), 25 mm (height)

d) 16 mm (base), 18 mm (height)

e) 9.2 cm (base), 5.5 cm (height)

f) 2.5 m, 3 m, 1 m

2 The picture below shows part of a tiled wall. All the tiles are parallelograms.

66 cm, 44 cm

Find the area of one tile.

3 The flag below is in the shape of a trapezium. The coloured strips along the top and bottom edges are parallelograms.

40 cm, 20 cm, 60 cm

a) Find the total area of the flag.
b) Find the total area of the coloured strips.

Composite Shapes involving Parallelograms and Trapeziums

The area of a composite shape can be found by adding or subtracting the areas of simpler shapes.

Example 3

For the composite shape on the right, find:
(i) its area,
(ii) its perimeter.

8 cm, 3.3 cm, 4.4 cm, 3 cm, 4 cm

Parallelogram A: 8 cm, 3 cm
Parallelogram B: 4 cm

1. Find the areas of parallelograms A and B.
2. Add these areas to find the total area.

(i) Area of A = bh
    $= 8 \times 3 = 24$ cm²
    Area of B = bh
    $= 8 \times 4 = 32$ cm²
    Total area = 24 + 32
    = **56 cm²**

The perimeter is the distance around the outside of the shape.

(ii) $P = 8 + 3.3 + 4.4 + 8 + 4.4 + 3.3$
    = **31.4 cm**

Section 22 — Area and Perimeter

Example 4

Find the area of the shape on the right.

1. Form a parallelogram (A) by adding a trapezium (B) to the corner of the original shape.

2. Find the areas of parallelogram A and trapezium B.

3. Subtract to find the original shape's area.

Area of A = bh
= 12 × 6 = __72 m²__

Area of B = $\frac{1}{2}(a + b) \times h$
= $\frac{1}{2}(6 + 4) \times 2$ = __10 m²__

Total area = 72 − 10 = __**62 m²**__

Exercise 4

1 Find each shaded area below.

a)

b)

2 For each shape below, find: **(i)** the area, **(ii)** the perimeter.
The dotted lines show lines of symmetry.

a)

b)

c)

d)

Section 22 — Area and Perimeter

22.3 Circumference of a Circle

The diameter (d) of a circle is always twice as long as the radius (r): $d = 2r$

The **circumference** (C) of a circle is given by the formula: $C = \pi d = 2\pi r$

Calculators usually have a special button for the number π.
If your calculator doesn't have a button for π, use the value 3.142.

Example 1

Find the circumference of the circle shown. Give your answer to 1 decimal place.

1. Write down the diameter. $d = 8$ cm
2. Use the formula $C = \pi d$.
$C = \pi d$
$C = \pi \times 8$
$C = 25.1327...$
3. Round your answer. And use the correct units. $C = \underline{\mathbf{25.1\ cm}}$ (to 1 d.p.)

Example 2

Find the circumference of a circle which has radius 6 m. Give your answer to 1 decimal place.

1. Write down the radius. $r = 6$ m
2. Use the formula $C = 2\pi r$.
$C = 2\pi r$
$C = 2 \times \pi \times 6$
$C = 37.6991...$
3. Round your answer. And use the correct units. $C = \underline{\mathbf{37.7\ m}}$ (to 1 d.p.)

Exercise 1

1 Find the circumference of each circle. Give your answers to 1 decimal place.

a) 8 cm
b) 12 cm
c) 2 cm
d) 10 cm
e) 30 mm
f) 5 mm
g) 7 m
h) 9 cm

Section 22 — Area and Perimeter

2 For each circle below, write down the diameter and then find its circumference. Give your answers to 1 decimal place.

a) 2 cm
b) 1.5 mm
c) 2.5 cm
d) 0.5 m
e) 1.7 cm
f) 1.3 mm
g) 2.6 m
h) 11.1 mm

3 Find the circumference of the circles with the diameter (d) or radius (r) given below. Give your answers to 1 decimal place.

a) $d = 4$ cm
b) $d = 8$ mm
c) $d = 9$ m
d) $d = 6$ cm
e) $r = 11$ m
f) $r = 22$ cm
g) $r = 14$ km
h) $r = 35$ mm
i) $d = 2.5$ m
j) $r = 1.9$ cm
k) $r = 0.1$ km
l) $d = 6.3$ mm

Example 3

The shape on the right consists of a semicircle on top of a rectangle. Find the perimeter of the shape.

1. Find the curved length. This is half the circumference of a circle with diameter 6 cm.

   Curved length = $\pi d \div 2$
   $= \pi \times 6 \div 2$
   $= 9.42$ cm (to 2 d.p.)

2. Find the total length of the straight sides.

   Total of straight sides = $4 + 6 + 4$
   $= 14$ cm

3. Add the two parts.

   Total length = curved length + straight length
   $= 9.42 + 14$
   $= \underline{\mathbf{23.4 \text{ cm}}}$ (to 1 d.p.)

Exercise 2

1 Find the perimeter of each shape below. Give your answers to 1 decimal place.

a) 4 cm
b) 26 mm
c) 2 m
d) 7 cm

Section 22 — Area and Perimeter 253

2 Find the perimeter of each shape below. Give your answers to 1 decimal place.

a) 4 cm, 3 cm

b) 10 mm, 8 mm

c) 5 cm, 4 cm, 4 cm

d) 9 mm

e) 9 mm, 9 mm

f) 3 cm, 2 cm

Exercise 3

In the following questions, give your answers to 1 decimal place unless the question tells you otherwise.

1 What is the circumference of a circular flower bed with a diameter of 3 m?

2 A circular table mat has a radius of 10 cm. What is the circumference of the mat?

3 Find the circumference of this circular cake.

25 cm

4 An archaeologist plans to excavate a circular burial mound with radius 23 m. What is the circumference of the mound?

5 A circular pond has a diameter of 84 cm. What is the circumference of the pond to the nearest cm?

6 Measure the diameter of the circle below, and then calculate its circumference.

7 A volcanic crater has a radius of 5.7 km. Kate and William walked all the way around the outside. How far did they walk?

8 A craftsman makes a circular table with a radius of 55 cm.

   a) What is the circumference of the table?

   b) A customer orders a smaller circular table with a diameter only half as big. Find the circumference of the smaller table.

9 A lake is in the shape of a quarter-circle, as shown. How long would a footpath around the lake be?

800 m

10 A running track consists of two semicircles of radius 80 m, joined together by two straight sections, each with length 100 m. Calculate the length of the running track.

80 m, 100 m

11 Alec used wooden fencing to build a semicircular sheep pen, with a wall forming the straight side. If the radius of the semicircle is 16 m, how many metres of fencing did Alec have to use?

Section 22 — Area and Perimeter

12 A window consists of a rectangle 1.5 m wide and 2.1 m high with a semicircle on top. Calculate the perimeter of the window.

13 A company's logo consists of a rectangle measuring 5 cm by 3 cm, with a semicircle on each side.

Calculate the length of the logo's perimeter to 1 decimal place.

22.4 Area of a Circle

The area (A) of a circle is given by the formula: $A = \pi r^2$

Example 1

Find the area of the circle below. Give your answer to 1 decimal place.

1. Write down the radius. $r = 3$

2. Use the formula $A = \pi r^2$.
   (Remember: $r^2 = r \times r$)

   $A = \pi r^2$
   $= \pi \times 3 \times 3$
   $= 28.274...$

3. Round your answer.
   And use 'squared' units — here, it's cm².

   $A = \underline{\mathbf{28.3 \text{ cm}^2}}$ (to 1 d.p.)

Exercise 1

In the following questions, give your answers to 1 decimal place unless told otherwise.

1 Find the area of each circle.

a) 2 cm   b) 10 mm   c) 3 m   d) 30 mm

2 Write down the radius of each circle, and then find its area.

a) 8 cm   b) 50 mm   c) 7 m   d) 12 mm

Section 22 — Area and Perimeter

3 Find the areas of the circles with the diameter (*d*) or radius (*r*) given below.
Give your answers to 1 decimal place.
a) *r* = 6 mm
b) *r* = 5 cm
c) *r* = 4 m
d) *r* = 6.5 cm
e) *d* = 8.5 mm
f) *d* = 3.5 m
g) *d* = 12 km
h) *d* = 22 cm
i) *r* = 1.3 m
j) *d* = 44 mm
k) *d* = 1.2 mm
l) *r* = 1.05 m

4 What is the area of a circular rug whose radius is 3.5 m?

5 What is the area of the following badge?

◄— 8 cm —►

6 A drinks coaster has a diameter of 13 cm. What is its area?

7 A circular pond has diameter 7.2 m. What is its area?

8 What is the area of a circular reservoir of radius 0.8 km?

9 Find the coloured area in the diagram below.

↕ 3 cm

10 a) A 2p coin has a radius of 1.3 cm. What is its area?

b) A 5p coin has a diameter of 1.8 cm. Which has the greater area: a 2p coin or two 5p coins?

11 Which of these shapes has the greater area?

◄— 22 mm —►   ↕ 20 mm   ◄— 24 mm —►

12 Find the area of the semicircle below.

◄— 10 cm —►

13 What is the area of this quarter-circle?

↕ 2 cm

Example 2

Find the total area of the shape on the right.

3 cm

2 cm

1. Divide the shape into a rectangle and a semicircle.

2. Find the area of the rectangle.   Area of rectangle = 3 × 2
= 6 cm²

3. Find the area of the semicircle. (Since its diameter is 2 cm, its radius must be 1 cm.)
Area of semicircle = (area of circle of radius 1 cm) ÷ 2
= (πr^2) ÷ 2
= ($\pi \times 1^2$) ÷ 2
= 1.6 cm² (to 1 d.p.)

4. Add the two areas.   Total area = area of rectangle + area of semicircle
= 6 + 1.6
= **7.6 cm²** (to 1 d.p.)

Section 22 — Area and Perimeter

Exercise 2

1 Find the area of each shape below. Give your answers to 1 decimal place.

a) 7 cm

b) 5 mm, 10 mm

c) 5 cm, 2 cm

d) 4 cm, 4 cm

e) 6 cm, 5 cm

f) 4 mm, 20 mm

g) 5 cm, 8 cm

h) 10 mm, 10 mm

i) 2 cm, 2 cm

2 A flower bed is in the shape of a semicircle of radius 2.5 m. What is its area?

3 A church window is in the shape of a rectangle 1 m wide and 2 m high, with a semicircle on top. What is its area?

4 A cookie cutter is in the shape of a quarter circle of radius 6 cm. What is the area of each biscuit made with the cutter?

5 Find the area of the sports field below.
70 m, 20 m

6 Find the coloured area in the diagram below.
3 cm

7 A circular pond of diameter 4 m is surrounded by a path 1 m wide, as shown below. What is the area of the path?
4 m, 1 m

8 Timi made an apron from a rectangle of material 50 cm wide and 80 cm high. She cut out a quarter circle of radius 15 cm from the top two corners.
   a) What area did Timi cut away?
   b) What was the area of the finished apron?

Section 22 — Area and Perimeter

22.5 Arcs and Sectors of Circles

Length of arc = $\frac{\theta}{360} \times$ **circumference of circle** = $\frac{\theta}{360} \times 2\pi r$

Area of sector = $\frac{\theta}{360} \times$ **area of circle** = $\frac{\theta}{360} \times \pi r^2$

Example 1

For the circle below, calculate the exact area of the minor sector and the exact length of the minor arc.

Put $\theta = 60°$ and $r = 3$ cm into the formulas.

For exact solutions, leave the answers in terms of π.

Area of sector = $\frac{60}{360} \times \pi \times 3^2 = \frac{1}{6} \times 9\pi = \frac{3}{2}\pi$ cm²

Length of arc = $\frac{60}{360} \times (2 \times \pi \times 3) = \frac{1}{6} \times 6\pi = \pi$ **cm**

Exercise 1

1 For each of the circles below, find the exact minor arc length and exact minor sector area.

a) 3 cm, 15°
b) 100°, 4 cm
c) 45°, 10 cm
d) 10 cm, 120°

2 For the circles below, find the major sector area and major arc length to 2 decimal places.

a) 5.5 cm, 311°
b) 10.5 in, 206°
c) 39°, 12 in
d) 6.5 m, 172°

22.6 Area and Perimeter Problems

Exercise 1

Where necessary, give your answers to 1 decimal place.

1 Find the shaded area in each of the following.

a) 1 m (top), 4 m, 1.5 m, 6 m, 1.5 m (height)

b) 20 mm (top), 50 mm, 40 mm

c) *All 4 parallelograms are identical.* 9 mm, 6 mm

Section 22 — Area and Perimeter

2 Find the perimeter and area of the following shapes. Give your answers to 1 decimal place.

a) *Curved sections are semicircles.* (1 cm, 1 cm)

b) (80 m, 80 m, 80 m)

c) *Curved sections are quarter-circles.* (1 cm, 6 cm, 1 cm, 1 cm)

3 A circular gasket is a ring of material with a hole in the centre.

a) Find the area of the gasket below. (1.8 cm, 8.2 cm)

b) A different circular gasket has a diameter of 10.1 cm. The hole in the centre has a radius of 3.8 cm. Find the area of the gasket.

4 A circular tower has a radius of 8 m, and is surrounded by a moat that is 16 m wide.

What is the area of the moat's surface? (16 m, 8 m)

5 Raheel assembled the four pieces of wood shown below to make a photo frame. Each piece of wood is in the shape of a trapezium. Find the total area of wood.

(22 cm, 2 cm, 16 cm, 2 cm, 2 cm, 8 cm, 2 cm, 14 cm, 2 cm)

7 Tyler makes some circular soap, and cuts it into 10 segments wrapped in ribbon, as shown on the right. What length of ribbon is needed to wrap once around one segment? Give your answer to 1 decimal place. (36°, 7 cm)

8 Find the exact minor arc length and sector area for a circle with diameter 10 m and major sector angle 320°.

9 What can you say about the areas of these two shapes? Explain your answer.

(①, ②, a, a)

Section 22 — Area and Perimeter

Example 1

What is the diameter of a circle which has circumference 26 cm?

1. Write down the formula linking the diameter and circumference. $C = \pi d$
2. Substitute in the numbers from the question. $26 = \pi \times d$
   $d = \dfrac{26}{\pi}$
3. Rearrange to find the diameter. And remember the units. $d = \underline{\mathbf{8.28\ cm}}$ (to 2 d.p.)

Exercise 2

Where necessary, give your answers to 1 decimal place.

1. The circumference of a circle is 128 m. What is its diameter?
2. The circumference of a circle is 45 cm. What is its diameter?
3. The circumference of a circle is 18.9 cm. What is its radius?
4. A tree measures 29 feet around its base. What is its diameter?
5. Jo walked all the way round a circular lake, a distance of 16 km. Find the lake's diameter.
6. Fifty people stand in a circle with their arms stretched out so their fingertips just touch. The average fingertip-to-fingertip distance is measured as 1.6 m.

   What is the diameter of the circle made by the 50 people?

Example 2

What is the radius of a circle which has area 50 m²?

1. Write down the formula linking the radius and area. $A = \pi r^2$
2. Substitute in the numbers from the question. $50 = \pi \times r^2$
3. Rearrange to find r^2. $r^2 = 50 \div \pi = 15.915$
4. Take the square root ($\sqrt{\ }$) to find r. $r = \sqrt{15.915}$
   $= \underline{\mathbf{4.0\ m}}$ (to 1 d.p.)

Exercise 3

Where necessary, give your answers to 1 decimal place.

1. The area of a circle is 75 cm². What is its radius?
2. What's the radius of a circle with area 29 m²?
3. A park's population of frogs lives in a circular pond covering an area of 125 m². What is the radius of the pond?
4. A circular pool for sailing model yachts is to be built. Each model yacht will need 20 m² of water.

   What is the smallest possible diameter of the pool if it must be able to accommodate at least 12 yachts?

Section 22 — Area and Perimeter

Section 23 — 3D Shapes

23.1 Nets

Faces, Vertices and Edges

You need to know how to describe the different parts of a three-dimensional (3D) object.

Face: one of the flat surfaces of a 3D object.

Edge: where two faces (or surfaces) meet — edges are usually straight.

Vertex (plural = '**vertices**'): a corner.

A cylinder has 2 circular faces...
...1 curved surface...
...and 2 curved edges.

Example 1

How many faces, vertices and edges does a cube have?

1. Count the number of flat surfaces.
2. Count the number of corners.
3. Count how many places two faces meet.

So a cube has **6 faces**, **8 vertices** and **12 edges**.

Prisms

A **prism** is a 3D shape which has a **constant cross-section** — this means it's the "same all the way through".

Exercise 1

1. Write down the number of faces, vertices and edges in the following 3D shapes.

   a) Cuboid   b) Triangular Prism   c) Tetrahedron   d) Square-based Pyramid

2. Name the 3D shapes described below.

   a) 6 identical faces, 8 vertices and 12 edges
   b) 2 parallel triangular faces, 3 rectangular faces
   c) 4 triangular faces, 6 edges
   d) 1 square face, 4 identical triangular faces
   e) 2 circular faces, 1 curved surface and 2 curved edges

3. Which of the following 3D shapes are prisms?

   A   B   C   D   E

Section 23 — 3D Shapes **261**

Nets

A net of a 3D object is a 2D (two-dimensional, or 'flat') shape that can be folded to make the 3D object.

Net of a cube → → → Cube

Net of a cylinder → → → Cylinder

Example 2

How many a) triangles and b) rectangles are there in the net of a triangular prism?

1. Sketch a triangular prism.
2. Count the triangular faces — this will be the number of triangles in the net.
3. Count the rectangular faces — this will be the number of rectangles in the net.

So the net will have a) **2 triangles** and b) **3 rectangles**.

Exercise 2

1 State how many **(i)** squares and **(ii)** triangles there will be in the nets of the following.
   a) tetrahedron   b) cube
   c) square-based pyramid

2 How many faces will the 3D shape with this net have?

3 Is the net on the right the net of a cuboid? Explain your answer.

4 Is the net on the right the net of a cube? Explain your answer.

5 Name and sketch the 3D objects with the following nets. Mark the edge lengths on your sketches.

a) 4 cm, 4 cm, 4 cm, 4 cm

b) 2 cm, 6 cm, 3 cm, 2 cm, 2 cm, 6 cm, 2 cm

c) 3 cm, 6 cm, 4 cm, 5 cm, 3 cm, 4 cm

262 Section 23 — 3D Shapes

6 How many rectangles with the following dimensions will the net of this cuboid have?
   a) 2 cm × 3 cm
   b) 2 cm × 4 cm
   c) 3 cm × 4 cm
   d) 2 cm × 2 cm

7 How many rectangles with the following dimensions will the net of this triangular prism have?
   a) 4 cm × 6 cm
   b) 5 cm × 6 cm
   c) 3 cm × 6 cm
   d) 3 cm × 4 cm

8 Which of the nets *A*, *B* or *C* is the net of the triangular prism shown below?

Example 3
Draw a net for a cuboid with dimensions 2 cm × 2 cm × 3 cm. Label the net with its dimensions.

1. Sketch the cuboid.
2. Draw it 'unfolded' — there could be several ways of doing this.

Example 4
Draw a net for a cylinder with length 6 cm and radius 1 cm. Label the net with its dimensions.

1. Sketch the cylinder.
2. Draw it 'unfolded'.
3. Find the missing length, *l*, of the rectangle — it's equal to the circumference of the circle.

$l = 2\pi r$
$= 2 \times \pi \times 1$
$= \mathbf{6.28\ cm}$ (to 2 d.p.)

Exercise 3

1 Copy and complete the unfinished nets of the objects shown below.
   a)
   b)

Section 23 — 3D Shapes   263

2 Draw a net of each of the following objects. Label each net with its dimensions.

a) 1 cm × 1 cm × 1 cm
b) 3 cm × 1 cm × 1.5 cm
c) triangular prism with 1.5 cm sides and 3.5 cm length
d) trapezoidal prism with 5 cm, 8 cm, 4 cm, 3 cm
e) pyramid with 2 cm × 2 cm base and 5 cm slant
f) tetrahedron with 5 cm edges
g) cylinder, radius 2 cm, length 7 cm
h) cylinder, diameter 6 cm, height 3 cm

3 Draw a net of each of the following objects. Label each net with its dimensions.
   a) a cube with 2 cm edges
   b) a 1.5 cm × 2 cm × 2.5 cm cuboid
   c) a tetrahedron with 3.5 cm edges
   d) a cylinder of length 4 cm and radius 2.5 cm
   e) a prism of length 3 cm whose cross-section is an equilateral triangle of side 2 cm
   f) a pyramid with square base of side 5 cm and slanted edge of length 4 cm

23.2 Plans and Elevations

Plans and elevations are two-dimensional (flat) pictures of three-dimensional objects, viewed from particular directions. The view looking vertically downwards from above is the **plan**. The views looking horizontally from the front and side are called the **front** and **side elevations**.

Example 1

Draw the plan and elevations of this shape from the directions indicated.

1. Split the shape into rows and columns.
2. Viewed from above, there are 4 blocks in row 1, 1 block in row 2 and 1 block in row 3.
3. Viewed from the front, there are 3 blocks in row 1, 1 block in row 2 and 1 block in row 3.
4. Viewed from the side, there are 3 blocks in column 3 and 1 block in the other columns.

264   *Section 23 — 3D Shapes*

Exercise 1

1 Below are the front and side elevations of the given objects. Draw the plan view for each.

a) Front Elevation Side Elevation

b) Front Elevation Side Elevation

2 Below are the plan view and front elevation of the given objects. Draw the side elevation for each.

a) Plan View Front Elevation

b) Plan View Front Elevation

3 For each of the following, draw: **(i)** the plan view,
(ii) the front and side elevations, using the directions shown in **a)**.

a)   b)   c)   d)

4 Which of the solid objects A, B or C below corresponds to the plan and elevations shown?

Plan View
Front Elevation   Side Elevation

A B C

5 Which of the solid objects P, Q or R below corresponds to the plan and elevations shown?

Plan View
Front Elevation   Side Elevation

P Q R

Section 23 — 3D Shapes

6 Use a square grid to draw: **(i)** the plan view,
(ii) the front and side elevations, using the directions shown in **a)**.
(The distance between neighbouring dots is 1 cm.)

a) Front, Side
b)
c)
d)
e)
f)
g)
h)

Example 2

Draw the plan and elevations of this cuboid.
Label the plan and elevations with their dimensions.

3 cm, 1 cm, 5 cm, Front, Side

1. Viewed from above, the cuboid appears as a 5 cm × 1 cm rectangle.

2. Viewed from the front, the cuboid appears as a 1 cm × 3 cm rectangle.

3. Viewed from the side, the cuboid appears as a 5 cm × 3 cm rectangle.

Plan View — 5 cm × 1 cm

Front Elevation — 1 cm × 3 cm   **Side Elevation** — 5 cm × 3 cm

Exercise 2

1 For each of the following, draw the plan, front elevation and side elevation from the directions indicated in part **a)**. Label the plan and elevations with their dimensions.

a) 1 cm, 1 cm, 1 cm, Front, Side
b) 1 cm, 3 cm, 1 cm
c) 5 cm, 2 cm, 2 cm
d) 5 cm, 2 cm, 6 cm
e) 3 cm, 1 cm, 4 cm
f) 3 cm, 2 cm, 2 cm

Section 23 — 3D Shapes

2 For each of the following, draw the plan, front elevation and side elevation from the directions indicated in part **a)**. Label the plan and elevations with their dimensions.

a) 5 cm, 2 cm, Side, Front

b) 2 cm, 6 cm

c) 6 cm, 3 cm

3 Draw the plan, front elevation and side elevation for each of the following. Label the plan and elevations with their dimensions.

a) a cube of side 2 cm
b) a 2 cm × 1 cm × 5 cm cuboid
c) a cylinder of radius 3 cm and length 4 cm
d) a cone of height 4 cm and base radius 1 cm
e) a 4 cm long prism whose cross-section is an isosceles triangle of height 5 cm and base 3 cm
f) a pyramid of height 5 cm whose base is a square of side 3 cm

23.3 Isometric Drawings

Pictures of 3D shapes drawn on a grid of dots or lines arranged in a pattern of equilateral triangles are called **isometric drawings**.

Example 1

Draw this triangular prism on isometric paper.

3 cm, 4 cm, 3 cm

1. Vertical lines stay vertical on isometric drawings, while horizontal lines appear at an angle. Draw the vertical height (3 cm) and base width (4 cm) of the triangular face, then complete the triangle.

2. Draw the 3 cm edges of the prism.

3. Complete the drawing by adding in the final edge.

Exercise 1

1 Draw the following cuboids on isometric paper.

a) 2 cm, 2 cm, 4 cm
b) 1 cm, 2 cm, 3 cm
c) 3 cm, 4 cm, 2 cm
d) 3 cm, 3 cm, 1 cm

Section 23 — 3D Shapes

2 Draw the following triangular prisms on isometric paper.

a) 3 cm, 2 cm, 5 cm
b) 4 cm, 6 cm, 2 cm
c) 4 cm, 2 cm, 4 cm
d) 4 cm, 4 cm, 3 cm

3 Draw the following 3D objects on isometric paper.
a) a cube with 2 cm edges
b) a cube with 3 cm edges
c) a 2 cm × 2 cm × 3 cm cuboid
d) a 1 cm × 2 cm × 4 cm cuboid
e) a prism of length 3 cm whose cross-section is a right-angled triangle of base 3 cm and vertical height 2 cm
f) a prism of length 2 cm whose cross-section is an isosceles triangle of base 4 cm and vertical height 4 cm

4 Draw the following prisms on isometric paper.

a) 2 cm, 2 cm, 4 cm, 2 cm, 2 cm, 4 cm
b) 4 cm, 3 cm, 4 cm, 1 cm, 1 cm, 5 cm
c) 1 cm, 1 cm, 1 cm, 1 cm, 3 cm
d) 3 cm, 2 cm, 1 cm, 1 cm, 1 cm, 3 cm
e) 5 cm, 4 cm, 1 cm
f) 4 cm, 2 cm, 3 cm, 4 cm

Example 2

The diagram shows the plan and front and side elevations of a prism. Draw the prism on isometric paper.

1. Transfer the front elevation onto isometric paper, using the dots to measure the dimensions.
2. Use the side elevation to draw in the side of the prism.
3. Use the plan view to complete the drawing.

Section 23 — 3D Shapes

Exercise 2

1. The following diagrams show the constant cross-section of prisms of length 3 cm. Draw each prism on isometric paper.

   a)   b)   c)   d)   e)

2. The following diagrams show the constant cross-section of prisms of length 2 cm. Draw each prism on isometric paper.

   a)   b)   c)   d)   e)

3. The following diagrams show the plan, and front and side elevations of different 3D objects. Draw each object on isometric paper.

   a)   b)   c)

   d)   e)   f)

Section 23 — 3D Shapes

23.4 Volume

Cubes and Cuboids

The volume of a cuboid is given by the following formula.

Volume = Length × Width × Height

Example 1

Find the volume of the cuboid shown.

Substitute the values of the length, width and height of the cuboid into the equation — give your answer with correct units.

Volume = Length × Width × Height
= 5 × 2 × 3 = **30 cm³**

Exercise 1

1. The following shapes are made up of cubes with edges of length 1 cm. Find the volumes of the shapes.

   a)   b)   c)   d)

2. Find the volumes of the following cuboids.

   a) 1 cm, 5 cm, 6 cm
   b) 1 m, 2 m, 5 m
   c) 7 cm, 2 cm, 2 cm
   d) 6 mm, 2 mm, 7 mm
   e) 9 cm, 2 cm, 1.5 cm
   f) 4 m, 4 m, 4 m

3. Find the volumes of the cuboids with the following dimensions.
   a) 1 cm × 2 cm × 3 cm
   b) 3 cm × 2 cm × 4 cm
   c) 5 m × 2 m × 7 m
   d) 20 cm × 10 cm × 8 cm
   e) 2.5 cm × 3.0 cm × 4.2 cm
   f) 18 m × 14 m × 3 m
   g) 2 mm × 13 mm × 5 mm
   h) 1.8 mm × 3.2 mm × 6.1 mm
   i) 9.1 cm × 2.9 cm × 7.6 cm

4. Find the volume of a cube whose edges are 3.2 mm long.

5. Box *A* measures 1 m × 0.3 m × 2.4 m. Box *B* measures 2 m × 0.3 m × 1.1 m. By how much do their volumes differ?

6. Will 3.5 m³ of sand fit in a cuboid-shaped box with dimensions 1.7 m × 1.8 m × 0.9 m?

7. A cereal box is 9 cm long, 23 cm wide and 32 cm high. The box is half full of cereal. What is the volume of cereal in the box?

Section 23 — 3D Shapes

8 Split the following 3D objects into cuboids to find their volumes.
   a)
   b)

9 A matchbox is 5 cm long and 3 cm wide and has a volume of 18 cm³. What is its height?

10 A bath can be modelled as a cuboid with dimensions 1.5 m × 0.5 m × 0.6 m, as shown.
   a) What is the maximum volume of water that the bath will hold?
   b) Find the volume of water needed to fill the bath to a height of 0.3 m.
   c) Find the height of the water if the volume of water in the bath is 0.3 m³.

Prisms

The volume of a prism is given by the following formula.

Volume = Area of Cross-Section × Length

Example 2

Find the volume of each of the shapes on the right.

1. Find the area of the cross-section.
2. Substitute the values of the cross-sectional area and length into the volume formula.
3. Give your answer with correct units.

a) Area of Cross-section = $\frac{1}{2}$ × base × height
   = $\frac{1}{2}$ × 4 × 5 = 10 cm²

   Volume = Area of Cross-section × Length
   = 10 × 6 = **60 cm³**

b) Area of Cross-section = πr^2 = $\pi × 2^2$ = 12.57 cm²

   Volume = Area of Cross-section × Length
   = 12.57 × 7 = **88.0 cm³** (to 1 d.p.)

Exercise 2

1 Find the volumes of the prisms with the following cross-sectional areas and lengths.
   a) area = 2 cm², length = 3 cm
   b) area = 6 cm², length = 9 cm
   c) area = 1.5 m², length = 6 m
   d) area = 3.5 cm², length = 3.5 cm
   e) area = 9.25 mm², length = 1.75 mm
   f) area = 11.6 mm², length = 9.1 mm

2 Find the volumes of the following prisms.
   a)
   b)
   c)
   d)

Section 23 — 3D Shapes

3 The following diagrams show the cross-sections of prisms of the length shown.
Find the volume of each prism. The grid spacing is 1 cm.

a) Length = 2 cm
b) Length = 3 cm
c) Length = 1.2 cm
d) Length = 4.6 cm

4 Find the volumes of the following prisms.
a) a triangular prism of base 13 cm, vertical height 12 cm and length 8 cm
b) a triangular prism of base 4.2 m, vertical height 1.3 m and length 3.1 m
c) a cylinder of radius 4 m and length 18 m
d) a cylinder of radius 6 mm and length 2.5 mm
e) a prism with parallelogram cross-section of base 3 m and vertical height 4.2 m, and length 1.5 m

5 By first calculating their cross-sectional areas, find the volumes of the following prisms.

a) 3.6 m, 1.2 m, 1.2 m, 2.4 m, 2.5 m
b) 6 cm, 2 cm, 5 cm, 4 cm
c) 2 mm, 2 mm, 4 mm, 5.5 mm
d) 1 m, 1.5 m, 1 m, 1 m, 1 m, 3 m, 2 m

6 The following diagrams show prisms drawn on isometric paper with grid spacing 1 cm.
Find the volume of each prism.

a) b) c) d)

Spheres

For a sphere of radius r: **Volume = $\frac{4}{3}\pi r^3$**

Example 3

Find the exact volume of a sphere with radius 6 cm.
'Exact' means you should leave your answer in terms of π.

Volume = $\frac{4}{3} \times \pi \times 6^3$ = **288π cm³**

Exercise 3

1. For each of the following, find the exact volume of the sphere with the given radius, r.
   a) $r = 3$ cm   b) $r = 9$ cm   c) $r = 15$ m   d) $r = 21$ mm   e) $r = 1.5$ m

2. For each of the following, find the volume of the sphere with the given radius, r.
   Give your answers to 2 d.p.
   a) $r = 2$ cm   b) $r = 8$ m   c) $r = 9.6$ mm   d) $r = 15.7$ m   e) $r = 6.32$ cm

3. Find the radius of the sphere with volume 24 429 cm³. Give your answer correct to 1 d.p.

Cones and Frustums

For a **cone** with base radius r and vertical height h:

Volume $= \frac{1}{3}\pi r^2 h$

A **frustum** of a cone is what is left when you **remove** the top part of the cone. Its volume is found using:

volume of frustum = volume of original cone − volume of removed cone

Example 4

Find the exact volume of the frustum shown on the right.

Volume of original cone = $\frac{1}{3} \times \pi \times 15^2 \times 20 = 1500\pi$ cm³

Volume of removed cone = $\frac{1}{3} \times \pi \times 6^2 \times 8 = 96\pi$ cm³

Volume of frustum = 1500π cm³ − 96π cm³ = **1404π cm³**

Exercise 4

1. Find the exact volume of the cones with the given properties.
   a) base radius = 5 m, height = 12 m
   b) base radius = 7 cm, height = 24 cm
   c) base radius = 15 m, height = 8 m
   d) base radius = 30 mm, height = 5.5 mm

2. A cone of height 4 cm and base radius 3 cm is removed from a cone of height 16 cm and base radius 12 cm, as shown in the sketch on the right.
   a) Find the exact volume of the original cone.
   b) Find the exact volume of the removed cone.
   c) Hence find the exact volume of the frustum.

3. The frustum on the left is what remains after the top 12 cm is removed from a 24 cm tall cone. What is the volume of the frustum? Give your answer to 2 d.p.

Pyramids

Find the volume of a pyramid using the formula: **Volume = $\frac{1}{3}$ × base area × height**

Example 5
Find the volume of the rectangular-based pyramid shown.
Volume = $\frac{1}{3}$ × (5 × 3) × 7 = **35 cm³**

Exercise 5

1. Find the volumes of triangular-based pyramids with the following dimensions.
   a) base area = 18 cm², height = 10 cm
   b) base area = 8 m², height = 3 m

2. Find the volume of a rectangular-based pyramid of height 10 cm with base dimensions 4 cm × 9 cm.

3. A hexagon-based pyramid is 15 cm tall. The area of its base is 18 cm². Calculate its volume.

4. Just to be controversial, Pharaoh Tim has decided he wants a pentagon-based pyramid. The area of the pentagon is 27 m² and the height of the pyramid is 12 m. What is the volume of Tim's pyramid?

5. A square-based pyramid has height 13.5 cm and volume 288 cm³. Find the side length of its base.

Rates of Flow

Rates of flow are measured as a **volume** per unit of **time** (e.g. litres per minute or cm³ per second).

Rate of flow = $\frac{\text{Volume}}{\text{Time taken}}$

Example 6
Water flows into this cuboid shaped tank at a rate of 150 cm³ per second. How long does it take to fill the tank?

1. Calculate the volume of the cuboid.
   Volume of cuboid = 20 × 30 × 50 = 30 000 cm³

2. Divide volume by rate of flow to get the time taken.
   Time to fill the tank = 30 000 ÷ 150 = **200 seconds**

Exercise 6

1. Work out the average rates of flow when these volumes are completely filled in the given time:
   a) Volume = 600 cm³, Time = 15 seconds
   b) Volume = 7200 litres, Time = 40 minutes
   c) Volume = 385 m³, Time = 5 minutes
   d) Volume = 150 litres, Time = 8 hours

2. A cube with a side length of 30 cm is filled with sand at a rate of 15 cm³ per second. How many minutes does it take to fill the cube?

3. Grain is being poured into the empty cylindrical tank shown on the right. The grain is flowing at a rate of 12 m³ every minute.

   How long will it take to fill the tank? Give your answer to the nearest minute.

23.5 Surface Area

Find the surface area of a 3D shape by adding together the areas of all its faces.

Example 1

Find the surface area of the cuboid shown.

1. Find the area of each face of the shape.
   2 faces of area 8 × 5 = 40 cm²
   2 faces of area 8 × 3 = 24 cm²
   2 faces of area 5 × 3 = 15 cm²

2. Add together the areas of the faces.
   So the total surface area is
   (2 × 40) + (2 × 24) + (2 × 15) = 80 + 48 + 30

3. Give your answer with correct units.
   = **158 cm²**

Example 2

Find this prism's surface area by considering its net.

1. Draw the net of the triangular prism.

2. Find the area of each face.
   Area of 1 triangular face = $\frac{1}{2}$ × 12 × 8 = 48 cm²
   Area of 'base' rectangle = 12 × 13 = 156 cm²
   Area of 'slanted' rectangle = 10 × 13 = 130 cm²

3. Add the different areas to find the total surface area.

4. Give your answer with correct units.
   Total surface area of triangular prism
   = (2 × 48) + 156 + (2 × 130) = **512 cm²**.

Exercise 1

1 A cube has 6 faces, each of area 2 cm². Find the total surface area of the cube.

2 a) Find the area of one face of the cube shown.
   b) Find the total surface area of the cube.

3 a) Find the area of one face of a cube with edges of length 2 m.
   b) Find the total surface area of the cube.

4
   a) Find the area of face *A* of the cuboid shown.
   b) Find the area of face *B*.
   c) Find the area of face *C*.
   d) Find the total surface area of the cuboid.

Section 23 — 3D Shapes

5 Find the surface area of the following cubes and cuboids.

a) 3 cm × 3 cm × 3 cm
b) 4 cm × 3 cm × 1 cm
c) 1.5 m × 1 m × 4 m
d) 2.5 m × 2.5 m × 4.5 m

6 By considering their nets, find the surface area of these shapes.

a) triangular prism with sides 12 mm, 5 mm, 13 mm and length 11 mm
b) triangular prism with slant sides 2 m and 2.5 m, base 3 m and length 3.2 m
c) square-based pyramid with base 4 cm and slant edges 7 cm
d) rectangular-based pyramid with base 6 cm × 8 cm and slant edges 9 cm

7 Find the surface area of the following shapes.
a) a cube with edges of length 5 m
b) a cube with edges of length 6 mm
c) a 1.5 m × 2 m × 6 m cuboid
d) a 7.5 m × 0.5 m × 8 m cuboid
e) a prism of length 2.5 m whose cross-section is an isosceles triangle of height 4 m, slant edge 5 m and base 6 m

8 The local boy scouts are waterproofing their tent, shown.

a) Find the surface area of the outside of the tent.

b) How many tins of waterproofing spray will they need to buy to cover the outside of their tent if each tin covers an area of 4 m²?

Tent dimensions: 1.4 m, 1.75 m, 2.1 m, 2.5 m

Cylinders

Example 3

Find this cylinder's surface area by considering its net.

Cylinder: radius 2 cm, length 8 cm

1. Draw the net of the cylinder.
2. Find the missing length, l, of the rectangle — it's equal to the circumference of the circle.

   $l = 2\pi r$
   $= 2 \times \pi \times 2$
   $= 4\pi$

3. Find the area of each face.

   Area of circle $= \pi r^2 = \pi \times 2^2 = 4\pi$
   $= 12.566...$ cm²

   Area of rectangle $= 8 \times 4\pi$
   $= 100.530...$ cm²

4. Add together the individual areas.
5. Give your answer with correct units.

   So total surface area $= (2 \times 12.566...) + 100.530...$
   $= \underline{\mathbf{125.7 \text{ cm}^2}}$ (to 1 d.p.)

276   Section 23 — 3D Shapes

Exercise 2

Round any inexact answers to 2 decimal places unless told otherwise.

1

a) Draw the net of the cylinder shown above.
b) Find the area of each surface of the cylinder.
c) Find the surface area of the cylinder, correct to 1 decimal place.

2

a) Draw the net of the cylinder shown above.
b) Find the area of each surface of the cylinder.
c) Find the surface area of the cylinder, correct to 1 decimal place.

3 Find the surface area of the following cylinders.

a) 1 cm, 4 cm
b) 3 m, 9 m
c) 8 mm, 7 mm
d) 3.5 m, 2.5 m
e) 2.8 m, 1.2 m
f) 11.1 mm, 1.4 mm
g) 1 m, 2.1 m
h) 6 m, 8 m

4 Find the surface area of the cylinders with the following dimensions. Give your answers correct to 1 decimal place.

a) radius = 2 m, length = 7 m
b) radius = 7.5 mm, length = 2.5 mm
c) radius = 12.2 cm, length = 9.9 cm
d) diameter = 22.1 m, length = 11.1 m
e) diameter = 0.8 m, length = 0.6 m

5 Ian is painting his cylindrical gas tank. The tank has radius 0.8 m and length 3 m. He uses tins of paint which cover an area of 14 m².

a) What is the surface area of the tank?
b) How many tins of paint will Ian need?

6 A cylindrical metal pipe has radius 2.2 m and length 7.1 m. The ends of the pipe are open.

a) Find the curved surface area of the outside of the pipe.
b) A system of pipes consists of 9 of the pipes described above. What area of metal is required to build the system of pipes? Give your answer correct to 1 decimal place.

7 The diagram shows a cylindrical bin which is closed at one end and open at the other. Find the total surface area of the outside of the bin.

0.4 m, 1.1 m

Section 23 — 3D Shapes

Spheres and Cones

The **surface areas** of spheres and cones can be found using the following formulas:

Surface area of a sphere = $4\pi r^2$ Where r is the radius of the sphere.

Surface area of a cone = $\pi r l + \pi r^2$ Where r is the radius at the base of the cone and l is the slant height.

Example 4

Find the exact surface area of:

a) a sphere with radius 3 cm.

Put $r = 3$ into the formula — leave your answer in terms of π.

Surface area = $4 \times \pi \times 3^2 =$ **36π cm²**

b) a cone with base radius 4 cm and a slant height of 10 cm.

Put $r = 4$ and $l = 10$ into the formula — leave your answer in terms of π.

Surface area = $(\pi \times 4 \times 10) + (\pi \times 4^2)$
= $40\pi + 16\pi =$ **56π cm²**

Exercise 3

1 For each of the following, find the exact surface area of the sphere with the given radius, r.
  a) $r = 2$ cm
  b) $r = 5$ cm
  c) $r = 7$ m
  d) $r = 9$ mm
  e) $r = 10.5$ m

2 For each of the following, find the surface area of the sphere with the given radius, r. Give your answers to 2 d.p.
  a) $r = 2.5$ cm
  b) $r = 7.1$ m
  c) $r = 11.2$ mm
  d) $r = 19.3$ m
  e) $r = 4.88$ cm

3 Find the exact surface area of the cones with the given properties.
  a) $r = 5$ m, $l = 13$ m
  b) $r = 7$ cm, $l = 25$ cm
  c) $r = 15$ m, $l = 17$ m

4 Find the surface area of each of the following, giving your answers to 2 d.p.
  a) sphere, 8 m
  b) cone, slant height 8 cm, base 5 cm
  c) sphere, 1.1 m
  d) cone, slant height 7.1 cm, base 3 cm

5 Find the radius of the sphere with surface area 265.9 cm². Give your answer correct to 1 d.p.

Exercise 4 — Mixed Exercise

Give any inexact answers correct to 2 decimal places unless told otherwise.

1. The diagram on the right shows part of a net of a triangular prism of width 6 cm, vertical height 4 cm, and length 3 cm.
   a) Copy the diagram. After measuring an appropriate length, add the remaining faces to the net.
   b) Use the net to find the surface area of the triangular prism.

2. A cylindrical disc has a radius of 4 cm and a height of 0.5 cm.
   a) Find the surface area of the disc.
   b) Find the surface area of a stack of 10 discs, assuming there are no gaps between each disc.

3. The following shapes are drawn on isometric paper with grid spacing 1 cm. Find the surface area of each shape.
   a)   b)   c)   d)

4. a) Find the surface area of the square based pyramid on the right.
   b) A company wants to paint the triangular faces of the pyramid. 1 litre of paint costs £9 and covers 12 square metres. How much will the company have to spend on paint?

5. a) Use Pythagoras' formula $h^2 = a^2 + b^2$ to find the vertical height, b, of the triangular prism shown.
   b) Draw a net of the prism.
   c) Find the surface area of the prism.

6. The cone on the right has base radius 56 cm and perpendicular height 33 cm.
   a) Use Pythagoras' theorem $h^2 = a^2 + b^2$ to find the slant height of the cone.
   b) Find the exact surface area of the cone.

7. A sphere has a radius of 10 cm.
   A cone has a base radius of 5 cm and a slant height of 15 cm.
   Find the ratio of the surface area of the sphere to the surface area of the cone.
   Give your answer in its simplest form.

Section 23 — 3D Shapes

8 The diagram on the right shows a conservatory in the form of a prism, made up of three glass walls and a glass roof.
  a) Make an accurate scale drawing of a side elevation of the conservatory. Use the scale 1 cm : 1 m.
  b) Use your drawing to find the actual length marked *l* in the diagram. Give your answer to the nearest tenth of a metre.
  c) Calculate the total surface area of the outside of the conservatory. Give your answer to the nearest square metre.

A window cleaner charges £5 plus £0.50 per square metre (rounded up to the next whole number of m²) to clean windows.
  d) How much would it cost to have the outside of the conservatory cleaned?
  e) How much would it cost to have the inside of the conservatory cleaned as well as the outside?

23.6 3D Shapes Problems

Exercise 1

Where appropriate, give your answers to these questions to 2 decimal places.

1 For each of the shapes *P* and *Q* above, complete the following.
  a) Draw a net of the shape.
  b) Draw the plan, and front and side elevations of the shape from the directions indicated.
  c) Draw the shape on isometric paper.
  d) Calculate the shape's volume.
  e) Calculate the shape's surface area.

2 a) Draw an accurate net of a cylinder of length 3 cm and radius 1.5 cm. Label your diagram with the net's dimensions.
  b) Use the net to find the cylinder's surface area.

3 24 cubes with edges of length 8 cm fit exactly in a tray of depth 8 cm, as shown.
  a) Find the volume of one cube.
  b) Find the volume of the tray.

4 **a)** Sketch the 3D shape with the net shown.
   b) Use isometric paper to accurately draw the shape.

5 **a)** Draw an accurate, full-sized net of the triangular prism shown.
   b) Measure the appropriate length on your drawing to find the vertical height, h, of the prism.
   c) Draw the plan, and front and side elevations of the prism.
   d) Draw the triangular prism on isometric paper.

6 Karl is making jam for the summer fete. His jam pan is cylindrical with radius 20 cm. The jam in his pan is 18 cm deep.
   a) Find the volume of jam in Karl's pan to the nearest cm^3.

   Jam jars are cylindrical with radius 3 cm and can be filled to a depth of 10 cm.
   b) Find the volume of one jar to the nearest cm^3.
   c) How many jars can Karl fill with the amount of jam he has made?

7 A cube has a total surface area of 54 cm^2.
   a) Find the area of one face of the cube.
   b) Find the length of the edges of the cube.
   c) Find the cube's volume.
   d) How long will it take to fill the cube with water flowing at a rate of 2.5 cm^3 per second?
   e) Draw the cube on isometric paper.

8 Beans are sold in cylindrical tins of diameter 7.4 cm and height 11 cm.
   a) Find the volume of one tin.

   The tins are stored in boxes which hold 12 tins in three rows of 4, as shown
   b) Find the dimensions of the box.
   c) Find the volume of the box.
   d) Calculate the volume of the box that is not taken up by tins when it is fully packed. Give your answer correct to 1 decimal place.

9 Two cuboids, A and B, are shown in the diagram on the right.
   a) Find the ratio of the volume of cuboid A to the volume of cuboid B. Give your answer in its simplest form.
   b) Find the ratio of the surface area of cuboid A to the surface area of cuboid B. Give your answer in its simplest form.

Section 23 — 3D Shapes

10 The shape on the right is made by joining together
the bases of two identical square-based pyramids.
Each pyramid has height 9 cm and base side length 7 cm.
Find the volume of this shape.

11 Katie is comparing two spheres, A and B.
Sphere A has a radius of 2 cm and sphere B has a radius of 3 cm.
  a) What is the ratio of the radius of sphere A to the radius of sphere B?
  b) Work out the ratio of the surface area of sphere A to the surface area of sphere B.
     Give your answer in its simplest form.
  c) Work out the ratio of the volume of sphere A to the volume of sphere B.
     Give your answer in its simplest form.

12 Toilet paper is sold in cylindrical rolls of diameter 12 cm and height 11 cm.
The card tube at the centre of the roll is 5 cm in diameter.
  a) Find the total volume of one roll of toilet paper,
     including the card tube.
  b) Find the volume of the card tube.
  c) Hence find the volume of the paper.
     Give your answer correct to 1 decimal place.

Each rectangular sheet of paper measures 11 cm × 13 cm and is 0.03 cm thick.
  d) Find the volume of one sheet of paper.
  e) Hence find the number of sheets of paper in one roll, to the nearest sheet.

13 A cylinder of diameter 25 mm has volume 7854 mm³.
  a) Find the length of the cylinder.
  b) Find the surface area of the cylinder to the nearest mm².

The cylinder is enclosed in a cuboid, as shown.
  c) Find the volume of the cuboid to the nearest mm³.
  d) Find the volume of the empty space between the cylinder and the cuboid to the nearest mm³.

14 a) Find the exact volume of the cone shown on the right.
  b) (i) Use Pythagoras' theorem $h^2 = a^2 + b^2$ to find h,
         the slant height of the cone.
     (ii) Find the exact surface area of the cone.

The cone is cut parallel to the circular face and a cone of height 8 m
and base radius 6 m is removed to leave a frustum.
  c) Find the exact volume of the frustum.

Section 24 — Transformations

24.1 Reflection

When an object is **reflected** in a line, its size, shape and distance from the line all stay the same.

Example 1

Copy the first diagram below, then reflect the shape in the mirror line.

1. Reflect one corner at a time.
2. The image of each point is the same distance from the mirror line as the original.
3. Join up the corners to create the image.

Exercise 1

1 Copy the diagrams below, and reflect each of the shapes in the mirror line.

a)
b)
c)
d)
e)
f)
g)
h)

2 Copy the diagrams below, and reflect each of the shapes in the mirror line.

a) b) c) d) e)

3 Copy the diagram, and reflect the shape in the mirror line.

Example 2

a) Copy the axes shown, then reflect the shape ABCDE in the y-axis.
b) Label the image points A_1, B_1, C_1, D_1 and E_1 with their coordinates.

1. This time, the y-axis is the mirror line.
2. Reflect the shape — one point at a time.
3. Write down the coordinates of each of the image points.

Exercise 2

1. a) Copy the diagram on the right, and reflect the shape in the y-axis.
   b) Label the image points A_1, B_1, C_1, D_1 and E_1 with their coordinates.
   c) Describe a rule connecting the coordinates of A, B, C, D and E and the coordinates of A_1, B_1, C_1, D_1 and E_1.

2. Copy each of the diagrams below, and reflect the shapes in the y-axis.
   a)
   b)

3. a) Copy each of the diagrams below, and reflect the shapes in the x-axis. The first shape has been done for you.
   (i)
   (ii)

   b) Describe a rule connecting the coordinates of a point and its reflection in the x-axis.

Section 24 — Transformations

4 The following points are reflected in the *x*-axis. Find the coordinates of the image points.
   a) (1, 2)   b) (3, 0)   c) (–2, 4)   d) (–1, –3)   e) (–2, –2)

5 The following points are reflected in the *y*-axis. Find the coordinates of the image points.
   a) (4, 5)   b) (7, 2)   c) (–1, 3)   d) (–3, –1)   e) (–4, –8)

6 Copy the diagram shown on the right.
   a) Reflect shape *P* in the *y*-axis. Label the image *Q*.
   b) Reflect shape *P* in the *x*-axis. Label the image *R*.
   c) Reflect shape *Q* in the *x*-axis. Label the image *S*.
   d) In which line would you reflect shape *R* to get shape *S*?

Example 3

Copy the diagram shown, then reflect the shape in the line $x = 5$.

1. Draw in the mirror line, $x = 5$.
2. Reflect the shape in the line as usual, one point at a time. The image of each point should be the same distance from the mirror line as the original point.

Exercise 3

1 Copy the diagram shown on the right.
   a) Reflect shape *A* in the line $x = 2$. Label the image A_1.
   b) Reflect shape *B* in the line $x = -1$. Label the image B_1.
   c) Reflect shape *C* in the line $x = 1$. Label the image C_1.
   d) Complete the following: *Shape B_1 is the reflection of shape A using the mirror line* $y = \boxed{}$

2 Copy the diagram shown on the right.
   a) Reflect shape *A* in the line $y = 6$. Label the image A_1.
   b) Reflect shape *B* in the line $y = 4$. Label the image B_1.
   c) Reflect shape *C* in the line $y = 5$. Label the image C_1.
   d) Reflect shape *D* in the line $y = 3$. Label the image D_1.
   e) Shape C_1 is the reflection of shape *B* in which mirror line?

Example 4

Copy the diagram below, then reflect the shape in the line $y = x$.

1. Reflect each corner in the mirror line. The image should be the same distance from the mirror as the point, and the line joining a point to its image should be perpendicular to the mirror line.

2. Join up the vertices to create the image.

Exercise 4

1 a) Copy the diagram on the right, and reflect the shape $ABCD$ in the line $y = x$.

b) Label the image points A_1, B_1, C_1 and D_1 with their coordinates.

c) Describe a rule connecting the coordinates of a point and the coordinates of its image after reflection in the line $y = x$.

2 Copy each of the diagrams below, and reflect the shapes in the line $y = x$.

a)

b)

3 The points with the following coordinates are reflected in the line $y = x$. Find the coordinates of the reflections.

 a) (1, 2)   **b)** (3, 0)   **c)** (−2, 4)   **d)** (−1, −3)   **e)** (−2, −2)

286   *Section 24 — Transformations*

24.2 Rotation

When an object is **rotated** about a point, its size, shape and distance from the point all stay the same.
You need three pieces of information to describe a rotation:
  (i) the **centre** of rotation   (ii) the **direction** of rotation   (iii) the **angle** of rotation
(But a rotation of 180° is the same in both directions, so you don't need to state the direction.)

Remember, 90° = $\frac{1}{4}$ turn, 180° = $\frac{1}{2}$ turn, 270° = $\frac{3}{4}$ turn.

Example 1

Copy the first diagram below, then rotate the shape 180° about point *P*.

1. Draw the shape on a piece of tracing paper. (Or imagine a drawing of it.)
2. Rotate the tracing paper half a turn about *P*, the centre of rotation. ('About *P*' means *P* doesn't move.)
3. Draw the image in its new position.

Exercise 1

1 Copy the diagrams below, then rotate the shapes 180° about *P*.
  a)   b)

2 Copy the diagrams below, then rotate the shapes 90° clockwise about *P*.
  a)   b)

Example 2

Copy the first diagram below, then rotate the shape 90° clockwise about point *P*.

1. This time the centre of rotation is not a point on the shape.
2. Draw the shape on a piece of tracing paper. (Or imagine a drawing of it.)
3. Rotate the tracing paper 90° clockwise about *P*.
4. Draw the image.

Section 24 — Transformations

3 Copy the diagrams below, then rotate the shapes 90° anticlockwise about P.

a) b) c) d)

4 Copy the diagram above, then rotate the shape by the following angles about P.
a) 90° clockwise
b) 270° clockwise

5 On separate copies of the diagram above, rotate the shape as follows.
a) 90° clockwise about P
b) 270° clockwise about Q
c) 180° about R

6 Copy the diagram above, then rotate the shape as follows.
a) 90° anticlockwise about P.
b) 90° clockwise about Q.

7 Copy the diagram above, then complete the following.
a) Rotate A 90° clockwise about the origin.
b) Rotate B 270° anticlockwise about the origin.

8 Copy the diagram above, then complete the following.
a) Rotate A 90° clockwise about (–8, 5).
b) Rotate B 90° clockwise about (1, 4).
c) Rotate C 90° clockwise about (8, –4).
d) Rotate D 180° about (–2, –5).

Section 24 — Transformations

9

Copy the diagram above, then complete the following.
a) Rotate A 180° about (−5, 6).
b) Rotate B 90° anticlockwise about (5, 9).
c) Rotate C 180° about (−3, −5).
d) Rotate D 180° about (3, −1).

10 The point X has coordinates (4, 2).
  a) Plot X on a pair of axes.
  b) Rotate X 180° about the origin. Label the image Y.
  c) Write down the coordinates of Y.

11 The triangle ABC has vertices A(−2, 1), B(−2, 6) and C(4, 1).
  a) Draw the triangle on a pair of axes.
  b) Rotate the triangle 90° anticlockwise about (5, 4). Label the image $A_1B_1C_1$.
  c) Write down the coordinates of A_1, B_1 and C_1.

12 The triangle DEF has coordinates D(−2, −2), E(−2, 5) and F(3, 5). DEF is rotated 180° about (2, 0) to create the image $D_1E_1F_1$. Find the coordinates of D_1, E_1 and F_1.

Example 3

Describe fully the rotation that transforms shape A to shape B.

1. The shape looks like it has been rotated clockwise by 90°.

2. Rotate the shape 90° clockwise about different points until you get the correct image — tracing paper will help if you have some.

3. Write down the centre, direction and angle of rotation.

So A is transformed to B by a rotation of **90° clockwise** (or **270° anticlockwise**) about **the origin**.

Section 24 — Transformations

Exercise 2

1

a) Describe fully the rotation that transforms shape *A* to shape *B*.
b) Describe fully the rotation that transforms shape *C* to shape *D*.

2

a) Describe fully the rotation that transforms shape *E* to shape *F*.
b) Describe fully the rotation that transforms shape *G* to shape *H*.

3

a) Describe fully the rotation that transforms shape *I* to shape *J*.
b) Describe fully the rotation that transforms shape *K* to shape *L*.

4

a) Describe fully the rotation that transforms shape *M* to shape *N*.
b) Describe fully the rotation that transforms shape *P* to shape *Q*.

5

a) Describe fully the rotation that transforms shape *R* to shape *S*.
b) Describe fully the rotation that transforms shape *R* to shape *T*.
c) Describe fully the rotation that transforms shape *S* to shape *T*.

6 The triangle *UVW* has vertices *U*(1, 1), *V*(3, 5) and *W*(–1, 3).
The triangle *XYZ* has vertices *X*(–2, 4), *Y*(–6, 6) and *Z*(–4, 2).

a) Draw the two triangles on a pair of axes.
b) Describe fully the rotation that transforms *UVW* to *XYZ*.

24.3 Translations

When an object is **translated**, its size and shape stay the same, but its position changes.

A translation can be described by the vector $\begin{pmatrix} a \\ b \end{pmatrix}$ — where the shape moves a units right and b units up.

Example 1

Copy the diagram below, then translate the shape by the vector $\begin{pmatrix} 5 \\ -3 \end{pmatrix}$.

$\begin{pmatrix} 5 \\ -3 \end{pmatrix}$ is a translation of:

(i) 5 units to the right,
(ii) 3 units down (which is the same as –3 units up).

Exercise 1

1 Write down in words the translations described by the following vectors.

a) $\begin{pmatrix} 1 \\ 1 \end{pmatrix}$ b) $\begin{pmatrix} 2 \\ 0 \end{pmatrix}$ c) $\begin{pmatrix} 3 \\ -1 \end{pmatrix}$ d) $\begin{pmatrix} -2 \\ 6 \end{pmatrix}$ e) $\begin{pmatrix} -3 \\ -2 \end{pmatrix}$ f) $\begin{pmatrix} -5 \\ 0 \end{pmatrix}$

2 Copy the diagrams below, then translate each shape by the vector written next to it.

a)

b)

3 a) Copy the diagram on the right, then translate the triangle ABC by the vector $\begin{pmatrix} -10 \\ -1 \end{pmatrix}$. Label the image $A_1B_1C_1$.

b) Label A_1, B_1 and C_1 with their coordinates.

c) Describe a rule connecting the coordinates of A, B and C and the coordinates of A_1, B_1 and C_1.

Section 24 — Transformations

Example 2
Find the coordinates of the point (2, –5) after it has been translated by $\begin{pmatrix} 6 \\ -4 \end{pmatrix}$.

The x-coordinate increases by 6, while the y-coordinate decreases by 4.

$(2 + 6, -5 - 4) =$ **(8, –9)**

4 Find the coordinates of the image of the point (3, –4) after it has been translated by:
   a) $\begin{pmatrix} 0 \\ 1 \end{pmatrix}$
   b) $\begin{pmatrix} 3 \\ 0 \end{pmatrix}$
   c) $\begin{pmatrix} 4 \\ -2 \end{pmatrix}$
   d) $\begin{pmatrix} -1 \\ -5 \end{pmatrix}$
   e) $\begin{pmatrix} -3 \\ 5 \end{pmatrix}$
   f) $\begin{pmatrix} 2 \\ -2 \end{pmatrix}$

5 Find the coordinates of the following points after they have been translated by $\begin{pmatrix} -3 \\ 4 \end{pmatrix}$.
   a) (1, 0)
   b) (2, 5)
   c) (–3, 1)
   d) (6, –2)
   e) (–2, –7)
   f) (–4, 4)

6 The triangle DEF has corners D(1, 1), E(3, –2) and F(4, 0). After the translation $\begin{pmatrix} -2 \\ 2 \end{pmatrix}$, the image of DEF is $D_1E_1F_1$. Find the coordinates of D_1, E_1 and F_1.

7 The quadrilateral PQRS has corners P(0, 0), Q(4, 1), R(2, 3), S(–1, 2). After the translation $\begin{pmatrix} -3 \\ -4 \end{pmatrix}$, the image of PQRS is $P_1Q_1R_1S_1$. Find the coordinates of P_1, Q_1, R_1 and S_1.

Example 3
Describe fully the translation that maps A onto B.

1. Count how many units horizontally and vertically the shape has moved.

2. Giving the translation vector is a way to describe it fully.

The image is 8 units to the left and 3 units down, so the translation is described by the vector $\begin{pmatrix} -8 \\ -3 \end{pmatrix}$.

Exercise 2

1 Write the following translations in vector form.
   a) 1 unit to the right, 2 units up
   b) 1 unit to the right, 2 units down
   c) 2 units to the left
   d) 3 units down
   e) 4 units to the left, 3 units down
   f) 6 units to the right, 7 units up
   g) 5 units to the left, 2 units up
   h) 6 units up

2

a) Write down in words the translation that maps W onto X.

b) Write the vector describing the translation that maps W onto X.

c) Describe fully the translation that maps Y onto Z.

3

Describe fully the translation that maps:
a) A to B
b) A to C
c) C to B
d) C to D
e) D to A
f) D to B

4

Describe fully the translation that maps:
a) P to R
b) R to S
c) P to Q
d) S to R
e) Q to R
f) S to P

5 The triangle DEF has vertices D(–3, –2), E(1, –1) and F(0, 2). The triangle GHI has vertices G(0, 2), H(4, 3) and I(3, 6).

a) Sketch triangles DEF and GHI.

b) Describe fully the translation that maps DEF onto GHI.

6 The triangle JKL has vertices J(1, 0), K(–2, 4) and L(–4, 7). The triangle MNP has vertices M(0, 2), N(–3, 6) and P(–5, 9).

a) Describe fully the translation that maps JKL onto MNP.

b) Describe fully the translation that maps MNP onto JKL.

Example 4

Shape B is the image of shape A after the translation $\begin{pmatrix} 7 \\ -3 \end{pmatrix}$.
Draw shape A.

1. Find the vector that maps B onto A — it's the negative of the vector that maps A to B.

   A to B is given by $\begin{pmatrix} 7 \\ -3 \end{pmatrix}$.
   So B to A must be given by $\begin{pmatrix} -7 \\ 3 \end{pmatrix}$.

2. So shape A must be 7 units to the left and 3 units up from shape B.

Section 24 — Transformations

Exercise 3

1 This question is about the diagram on the right.
   a) Describe fully the transformation that maps X onto Y.
   b) Describe fully the transformation that maps Y onto X.
   c) What do you notice about your answers to **a)** and **b)**?

2 Shape Z is the image of shape W after the translation $\begin{pmatrix} 1 \\ -4 \end{pmatrix}$.
Write down the translation that maps Z onto W.

3 Copy the diagram on the left.
   a) W is the image of A after the translation $\begin{pmatrix} 0 \\ 2 \end{pmatrix}$. Draw A.
   b) Draw B, given that X is the image of B after the translation $\begin{pmatrix} 5 \\ 0 \end{pmatrix}$.
   c) Y is the image of C after the translation $\begin{pmatrix} -1 \\ -5 \end{pmatrix}$. Draw C.
   d) Draw D, given that Z is the image of D after the translation $\begin{pmatrix} 3 \\ 2 \end{pmatrix}$.

4 The triangle PQR has vertices P(–1, 0), Q(–4, 4) and R(3, 2). PQR is the image of the triangle DEF after the translation $\begin{pmatrix} -1 \\ 4 \end{pmatrix}$. Find the coordinates of D, E and F.

24.4 Enlargements

Scale Factors

When an object is **enlarged**, its shape stays the same, but its size changes (and can be either bigger or smaller). The **scale factor** of an enlargement tells you how much the size changes.

Example 1

Copy the diagram on the right, then enlarge the shape anywhere on the grid by scale factor 2.

1. Find the dimensions of the shape you're enlarging.
2. Multiply these by the scale factor to find the dimensions of the image.
3. Draw the image using the dimensions you've found.

The original shape is 4 units wide and 3 units tall. So the enlargement will be 4 × 2 = 8 units wide and 3 × 2 = 6 units tall.

Section 24 — Transformations

Exercise 1

1 Copy the diagram below, then enlarge the shapes by scale factor 2.

a)
b)
c)
d)

2 Copy the diagram below, then enlarge the shapes by scale factor 3.

a)
b)
c)

3 Sketch the following shapes after they have been enlarged by scale factor 5.

a) 1 cm × 1 cm square

b) 2 cm × 1 cm rectangle

c) right triangle, 1.5 cm and 2 cm

d) L-shape, 1 cm, 2 cm, 1 cm, 2 cm

Example 2

Copy the diagram on the right, then enlarge the shape anywhere on the grid by scale factor $\frac{1}{2}$.

1. Again, multiply the dimensions of the shape by the scale factor: $6 \times \frac{1}{2} = 3$ and $4 \times \frac{1}{2} = 2$.
2. Draw the image using the new dimensions — this time, the image will be smaller than the original.

Exercise 2

1 Copy the diagram below, then enlarge the shapes by scale factor $\frac{1}{2}$.

a)
b)
c)

2 Copy the diagram below, then enlarge the shapes by scale factor $\frac{1}{3}$.

a)
b)
c)

Section 24 — Transformations **295**

3 A square with sides of length 16 cm is enlarged by scale factor $\frac{1}{4}$. How long are the square's sides after the enlargement?

4 A 15 cm × 35 cm rectangle is enlarged by scale factor $\frac{1}{5}$. What are the dimensions of the rectangle after the enlargement?

Centres of Enlargement

The **centre of enlargement** tells you where the enlargement is measured from.

Example 3

Copy the first diagram below, then enlarge the shape by scale factor 2 with centre of enlargement (2, 2).

1. Draw a line from (2, 2) through each corner of the shape. Continue each line until it is twice as far away from (2, 2) as the original corner.
2. Join up the ends of the lines to create the image.

Exercise 3

1 Copy each of the following diagrams, then enlarge each shape by scale factor 2 with centre of enlargement (0, 0).

a)   b)   c)   d)

2 Copy the diagram on the right.
  a) Enlarge A by scale factor 2 with centre of enlargement (–8, 9).
  b) Enlarge B by scale factor 2 with centre of enlargement (9, 9).
  c) Enlarge C by scale factor 3 with centre of enlargement (9, –8).
  d) Enlarge D by scale factor 4 with centre of enlargement (–8, –8).

3 The triangle PQR has corners at P(1, 1), Q(1, 4) and R(4, 2).
  a) Draw PQR on a pair of axes.
  b) Enlarge PQR by scale factor 2 with centre of enlargement (–1, 1).

Section 24 — Transformations

4   The square *ABCD* is shown on the left. $A_1B_1C_1D_1$ is the image of *ABCD* after it has been enlarged by scale factor 2 with centre of enlargement (0, 0).

   a) Find the distance of each of the following corners from (0, 0).
      (i) *A*   (ii) *B*   (iii) *C*   (iv) *D*
   b) What will the distance of the following corners be from (0, 0)?
      (i) A_1 (ii) B_1 (iii) C_1 (iv) D_1
   c) Copy the diagram and draw a line from (0, 0) through each corner of *ABCD*. Mark the points A_1, B_1, C_1 and D_1 on these lines. Join up the points A_1, B_1, C_1 and D_1 to draw $A_1B_1C_1D_1$.

5   Copy the diagram on the right, then enlarge each shape by scale factor 2, using the centre of enlargement marked inside the shape.

6   The shape *WXYZ* has corners at *W*(0, 0), *X*(1, 3), *Y*(3, 3) and *Z*(4, 0).
   a) Draw *WXYZ* on a pair of axes.
   b) Enlarge *WXYZ* by scale factor 3 with centre of enlargement (2, 2).

7   The triangle *PQR* is shown on the left. $P_1Q_1R_1$ is the image of *PQR* after it has been enlarged by scale factor 2 with centre of enlargement (2, 2).
   a) Find the distance of each of the following corners from (2, 2).
      (i) *P*   (ii) *Q*   (iii) *R*
   b) What will the distance of the following corners be from (2, 2)?
      (i) P_1 (ii) Q_1 (iii) R_1
   c) Copy the diagram and draw a line from the point (2, 2) through *P* and *Q*. Mark the points P_1, Q_1 and R_1 on your diagram. Join up the points P_1, Q_1 and R_1 to draw $P_1Q_1R_1$.

8   Copy the diagram on the right, then enlarge each shape by scale factor 2, using the centre of enlargement marked on the shape's corner.

9   The shape *KLMN* has corners at *K*(3, 4), *L*(3, 6), *M*(5, 6) and *N*(5, 5).
   a) Draw *KLMN* on a pair of axes.
   b) Enlarge *KLMN* by scale factor 3 with centre of enlargement (3, 6). Label the shape $K_1L_1M_1N_1$.
   c) Enlarge *KLMN* by scale factor 2 with centre of enlargement (5, 6). Label the shape $K_2L_2M_2N_2$.

Section 24 — Transformations

Example 4

Copy the first diagram below, then enlarge the shape by scale factor $\frac{1}{2}$ with centre of enlargement (2, 7).

1. Draw lines from (2, 7) to each corner. The image points will lie $\frac{1}{2}$ as far from the centre of enlargement as the original corner.
2. Join up the image points.

Exercise 4

1 Copy the diagram on the left.

a) Enlarge A by scale factor $\frac{1}{2}$ with centre of enlargement (–8, 9).
b) Enlarge B by scale factor $\frac{1}{3}$ with centre of enlargement (0, 1).
c) Enlarge C by scale factor $\frac{1}{4}$ with centre of enlargement (–1, –8).
d) Enlarge D by scale factor $\frac{1}{5}$ with centre of enlargement (2, 3).

2 Copy the diagram on the right.

a) Enlarge A by scale factor $\frac{1}{2}$ with centre of enlargement (–4, 5).
b) Enlarge B by scale factor $\frac{1}{3}$ with centre of enlargement (7, 7).
c) Enlarge C by scale factor $\frac{1}{4}$ with centre of enlargement (6, –4).
d) Enlarge D by scale factor $\frac{1}{5}$ with centre of enlargement (–3, –2).

Example 5

Describe the enlargement that maps shape X onto shape Y.

1. Pick any side of the shape, and see how many times bigger this side is on the image than the original. This is the scale factor.
2. Draw a line from each corner on the image through the corresponding corner on the original shape. The point where these lines meet is the centre of enlargement.

An enlargement by scale factor **2**, centre **(11, 10)**.

298 Section 24 — Transformations

Exercise 5

1 For each of the following, describe the enlargement that maps shape A onto shape B.

a)   b)   c)

2 For each of the following, describe the enlargement that maps shape B onto shape A.

a)   b)   c)

Perimeter, Area and Volume

When a 2D shape is enlarged, **lengths** (such as the lengths of sides, or the shape's **perimeter**) are multiplied by the scale factor. But the shape's **area** is multiplied by the **square of the scale factor**. When a 3D object is enlarged, its **volume** is multiplied by the **scale factor cubed**.

Example 6

Find the perimeter of this triangle after it has been enlarged by scale factor 4.

3 cm, 4 cm, 5 cm

1. Find the perimeter of the original triangle.   Perimeter = 3 + 4 + 5 = 12 cm
2. The perimeter of the enlarged triangle will be 12 + 16 + 20 = 48 cm. This is the same as the original perimeter multiplied by the scale factor.   Perimeter after enlargement = 12 × 4 = 48
3. Give your answer with the correct units.   So the perimeter of the image is **48 cm**.

Exercise 6

1 The rectangle WXYZ has vertices W(1, 1), X(1, 2), Y(4, 2) and Z(4, 1).
  a) Draw WXYZ on a pair of axes, and find the perimeter of WXYZ.
  b) Enlarge WXYZ by scale factor 2 with centre of enlargement (0, 0). Label the image $W_1X_1Y_1Z_1$.
  c) Find the perimeter of $W_1X_1Y_1Z_1$.

2 The shapes below are enlarged by the given scale factor. Find the perimeter of each image.
  a) a square of side 3 cm; scale factor 3
  b) a 2 m × 8 m rectangle; scale factor 5
  c) a triangle with sides of length 5 m, 12 m and 13 m; scale factor 6

Section 24 — Transformations

Example 7

Find the area of this rectangle after it has been enlarged by scale factor 3.

4 cm, 2 cm

1. Find the area of the original rectangle.
   Area = 4 × 2 = 8 cm²
2. The image will have sides of length 12 cm and 6 cm. So the area of the image will be 12 × 6 = 72 cm², the same as the original area multiplied by the square of the scale factor.
   Area after enlargement = 8 × 3² = 8 × 9 = 72
3. Give your answer with the correct units.
   So the area of the image is **72 cm²**.

3 The square $ABCD$ has vertices $A(0, 0)$, $B(0, 3)$, $C(3, 3)$ and $D(3, 0)$.
   a) Draw $ABCD$ on a pair of axes, and find the area of $ABCD$ in square units.
   b) Enlarge $ABCD$ by scale factor 2 with centre of enlargement $(0, 0)$. Label the image $A_1B_1C_1D_1$.
   c) Find the area of $A_1B_1C_1D_1$ in square units.

4 The shapes below are enlarged with the given scale factors. Find the area of each image.
   a) a shape with area 4 cm²; scale factor 2
   b) a square of side 2 cm; scale factor 3
   c) a 5 m × 3 m rectangle; scale factor 3
   d) a triangle with base 5 cm and vertical height 1 cm; scale factor 4

Example 8

Find the volume of this cube after it has been enlarged by scale factor 4.

2 cm, 2 cm, 2 cm

1. Find the volume of the original cube.
   Volume = 2 × 2 × 2 = 8 cm³
2. The volume of the enlarged cube will be 8 × 8 × 8 = 512 cm³. This is the same as the original volume multiplied by the scale factor cubed.
   Volume after enlargement = 8 × 4³ = 8 × 64 = 512
3. Give your answer with the correct units.
   So the volume of the cube after it has been enlarged is **512 cm³**.

5 A cuboid has dimensions 1 cm × 4 cm × 3 cm.
   a) Find the volume of the cuboid.
   The cuboid is enlarged by scale factor 2.
   b) Sketch the image of the cuboid, labelling the edges with their dimensions.
   c) Find the volume of the cuboid's image.

6 The objects below are enlarged with the given scale factors. Find the volume of each image.
   a) an object with volume 5 cm³; scale factor 2
   b) an object with volume 1 cm³; scale factor 4
   c) a cube of edge 1 cm; scale factor 3
   d) a cube of edge 3 m; scale factor 2
   e) a 2 m × 2 m × 1 m cuboid; scale factor 5

24.5 Combinations of Transformations

Transformations can be **combined** (performed one after another). But the **order** in which you combine them is important — for example, a reflection followed by a rotation won't necessarily give the same result as the rotation followed by the reflection.

Example 1

Copy the first diagram below and then: (i) reflect the shape in the line $x = 1$,
(ii) rotate the image 90° anticlockwise about the origin.

1. First reflect the shape in the line $x = 1$.
2. Then rotate the image 90° anticlockwise about the origin.

Example 2

Copy the first diagram below and then: (i) rotate the shape 90° anticlockwise about the origin,
(ii) reflect the image in the line $x = 1$.

1. First rotate the shape 90° anticlockwise about the origin.
2. Then reflect the image in the line $x = 1$.

Exercise 1

1 Copy the diagram on the right.
   a) (i) Reflect shape A in the line $y = -1$. Label the new image B.
      (ii) Rotate B 90° clockwise about the origin. Label the final image C.
   b) (i) Rotate shape A 90° clockwise about the origin. Label the new image D.
      (ii) Reflect this new image in the line $y = -1$. Label the final image E.

Section 24 — Transformations

2 Copy the diagram on the right.
  a) (i) Translate A by $\begin{pmatrix} 0 \\ -2 \end{pmatrix}$. Label the new image A_1.
     (ii) Enlarge A_1 by scale factor 3 with centre of enlargement (9, −7). Label the final image A_2.
  b) (i) Translate B by $\begin{pmatrix} -2 \\ -1 \end{pmatrix}$. Label the new image B_1.
     (ii) Reflect B_1 in the y-axis. Label the final image B_2.
  c) (i) Rotate C 90° clockwise about (−5, −5). Label the new image C_1.
     (ii) Translate C_1 by $\begin{pmatrix} 3 \\ -1 \end{pmatrix}$. Label the final image C_2.

3 Copy the diagram on the right.
  a) (i) Enlarge A by scale factor 3 with centre of enlargement (9, −7). Label the new image A_1.
     (ii) Translate A_1 by $\begin{pmatrix} 0 \\ -2 \end{pmatrix}$. Label the final image A_2.
  b) (i) Reflect B in the y-axis. Label the new image B_1.
     (ii) Translate B_1 by $\begin{pmatrix} -2 \\ -1 \end{pmatrix}$. Label the final image B_2.
  c) (i) Translate C by $\begin{pmatrix} 3 \\ -1 \end{pmatrix}$. Label the new image C_1.
     (ii) Rotate C_1 90° clockwise about (−5, −5). Label the final image C_2.

4 a) Triangle DEF has corners at $D(-3, -2)$, $E(0, -2)$ and $F(-1, 3)$. Draw DEF on a pair of axes.
   b) (i) Reflect DEF in the line $x = 1$. Label the image $D_1E_1F_1$.
      (ii) Rotate $D_1E_1F_1$ 90° clockwise about (7, 1). Label the image $D_2E_2F_2$.
   c) (i) Rotate the original shape DEF 90° clockwise about (7, 1). Label the image $D_3E_3F_3$.
      (ii) Reflect $D_3E_3F_3$ in the line $x = 1$. Label the image $D_4E_4F_4$.

5 a) Triangle PQR has corners at $P(0, 0)$, $Q(4, 2)$ and $R(4, 0)$. Draw PQR on a pair of axes.
   b) (i) Rotate PQR 90° clockwise about the point (4, 2). Label the image $P_1Q_1R_1$.
      (ii) Enlarge $P_1Q_1R_1$ using a scale factor 1.5 and centre of enlargement (2, 6). Label the image $P_2Q_2R_2$.
   c) (i) Enlarge the original shape PQR using a scale factor 1.5 and centre of enlargement (2, 6). Label the image $P_3Q_3R_3$.
      (ii) Rotate $P_3Q_3R_3$ 90° clockwise about the point (4, 2). Label the image $P_4Q_4R_4$.

Example 3
Draw triangle *ABC*, which has its corners at *A*(2, 2), *B*(6, 5) and *C*(6, 2).
a) Rotate *ABC* 180° about the point (1, 1), then translate the image by $\begin{pmatrix} -2 \\ -2 \end{pmatrix}$.
   Label the image $A_1B_1C_1$.
b) Find a **single** rotation that transforms triangle *ABC* onto the image $A_1B_1C_1$.

a) Rotate *ABC* 180° about (1, 1)...

... then translate by $\begin{pmatrix} -2 \\ -2 \end{pmatrix}$.

b) A rotation of 180° about the origin maps *ABC* onto $A_1 B_1 C_1$.

Exercise 2

1 Copy the diagram below.

a) (i) Rotate shape *P* 180° about (4, 5). Label the image P_1.
   (ii) Translate the image by $\begin{pmatrix} 2 \\ 2 \end{pmatrix}$. Label the final image P_2.
b) Rotate shape *P* 180° about (5, 6). Label the final image P_3.
c) (i) Rotate shape *Q* 180° about (4, 5). Label the image Q_1.
   (ii) Translate the image by $\begin{pmatrix} 2 \\ 2 \end{pmatrix}$. Label the final image Q_2.
d) Rotate shape *Q* 180° about (5, 6). Label the final image Q_3.
e) What do you notice about images P_2 and P_3 and about images Q_2 and Q_3?

2 Triangle *ABC* has its corners at *A*(2, 1), *B*(6, 4) and *C*(6, 1).
a) Draw triangle *ABC* on a pair of axes, where both the *x*- and *y*-axes are labelled from −6 to 6.
b) Reflect *ABC* in the *y*-axis. Label the image $A_1B_1C_1$.
c) Reflect the image $A_1B_1C_1$ in the *x*-axis. Label the image $A_2B_2C_2$.
d) Find a **single** rotation that transforms triangle *ABC* onto the image $A_2B_2C_2$.

3 Draw triangle *PQR* with corners at *P*(2, 3), *Q*(4, 3) and *R*(4, 4).
a) Rotate *PQR* 90° clockwise about the point (2, 3). Label the image $P_1Q_1R_1$.
b) Translate $P_1Q_1R_1$ by $\begin{pmatrix} 1 \\ -5 \end{pmatrix}$. Label the new image $P_2Q_2R_2$.
c) Describe a **single** transformation that transforms triangle *PQR* onto the image $P_2Q_2R_2$.

4 By considering triangle *STU* with corners at *S*(1, 1), *T*(3, 1) and *U*(1, 2), find the single transformation equivalent to a rotation of 180° about the origin, followed by a translation by $\begin{pmatrix} 6 \\ 2 \end{pmatrix}$.

Section 24 — Transformations

24.6 Congruence and Similarity

Congruence

Two shapes are **congruent** if they are exactly the **same shape** and **size**.
The images of rotated and reflected shapes are congruent to the original shapes.

Example 1

Which two of the shapes *A*, *B* and *C* are congruent?

Compare each shape to see if they are the same shape and size. Tracing paper may help with this.

1. *A* and *B* are different sizes.
2. *A* and *C* are different sizes.
3. *B* and *C* are the same size and shape, just in different orientations.

The two congruent shapes are **_B_ and _C_**.

Exercise 1

1 Write down the letters of the congruent pairs of shapes shown in the box below. For example, *A* is congruent to *G*.

2 For each of the following, decide which shape is **not** congruent to the others.

a)
b)
c)
d)
e)
f)

Section 24 — Transformations

Congruent Triangles

Two triangles are congruent if they satisfy any of the following '**congruence conditions**'.

Side, Angle, Side:
Two sides and the angle between on one triangle are the same as two sides and the angle between on the other triangle.

Side, Side, Side:
The three sides on one triangle are the same as the three sides on the other triangle.

Angle, Angle, Side:
Two angles and a side on one triangle are the same as two angles and the corresponding side on the other triangle.

Right angle, Hypotenuse, Side:
Both triangles have a right angle, both triangles have the same hypotenuse and one other side is the same.

Example 2

Are these two triangles congruent? Give a reason for your answer.

Two of the sides and the angle between them are the same on both triangles. So the triangles **are congruent**.

Exercise 2

1 For each pair of triangles, write down whether the triangles are congruent and explain why.

a) 4 cm, 50°, 4 cm ; 4 cm, 50°, 4 cm

b) 5 cm, 50°, 55° ; 3 cm, 50°, 55°

c) 2 cm, 3 cm, 4 cm ; 2 cm, 3 cm, 4 cm

d) 10 cm, 29 cm ; 26 cm, 10 cm

2 Show that each pair of triangles below is congruent.

a) 3 cm, 75°, 50° ; 3 cm, 75°, 55°

b) 5 cm, 4 cm ; 4 cm, 3 cm

Section 24 — Transformations 305

Similarity

Two shapes are **similar** if they are exactly the **same shape**, but they can be **different sizes**. The image of a shape after it has been enlarged is similar to the original shape.

Example 3

Which two of the shapes P, Q and R are similar?

1. Compare P and Q — they are the same shape, but different sizes.
2. Compare P and R — they are different shapes.
3. Compare Q and R — they are different shapes.

The two similar shapes are ***P* and *Q***.

Exercise 3

1 Write down the letters of the similar shapes shown in the box below. For example, A, C and F are similar.

2 For each of the following, decide which two shapes are similar.

a)

b)

c)

d)

e)

f)

306 *Section 24 — Transformations*

Similar Triangles

Two triangles are similar if they satisfy **any** of the following conditions.
And if two triangles *are* similar, then **all** of the conditions are true.

The angles in one triangle are the same as the angles in the other triangle.

All corresponding sides of the two triangles are in the same ratio.

Two sides of the triangles are in the same ratio, and the angle between them is the same for both triangles.

Example 4

Are these two triangles similar? Give a reason for your answer.

Look to see whether the triangles satisfy any of the conditions for similarity. The orientation of the triangles doesn't matter.

The angles in one triangle are the same as the angles in the other triangle. So the triangles **are similar**.

Example 5

Explain why these two triangles are similar.

Look to see which condition for similarity the triangles satisfy. Again, the orientation of the triangles doesn't matter.

All the sides in the first triangle are twice the length of those in the second triangle. So **corresponding sides are in the same ratio**.

Exercise 4

1. Explain why each of the following pairs of triangles are similar.

   a)

   b)

   c)

   d)

Section 24 — Transformations

2 Decide whether each of the following pairs of triangles are similar.

a) b)

c) d)

e) f)

Example 6

Triangles *ABC* and *DEF* are similar. Find the lengths of *DE* and *AC*.

1. The triangles are similar, so the side lengths must be in the same ratio from one triangle to the other.
2. Compare the lengths of corresponding sides to find the ratio.
3. Use this ratio to find the missing side lengths.
4. Give your answers with the correct units.

$EF = 2 \times BC$
So $DE = 2 \times AB$
$= 2 \times 7 =$ **14 cm**
And $DF = 2 \times AC$
So $AC = DF \div 2$
$= 18 \div 2 =$ **9 cm**

Example 7

Triangles *PQR* and *UVW* are similar. Find angle *x*.

Drawn to scale

1. Find the missing angle in triangle *PQR*.

   Angle $QRP = 180° - (110° + 30°)$
   $= 40°$

2. Work out which angles in the triangles correspond to each other.

   The diagrams are drawn to scale, so the obtuse angle *PQR* corresponds to angle *UVW*. And angle *QPR* corresponds to angle *VWU*.

3. Use the properties of similar triangles to determine the required angle.

   So angle *QRP* must correspond to angle *VUW*, which means **x = 40°**

308 *Section 24 — Transformations*

Exercise 5

1 The triangles in each pair below are similar.
   a) **(i)** Write down the value of x.
   (ii) Find the value of y.
   b) Find the value of z.

In **Questions 2-6**, the lines marked with arrows are parallel.

2 The diagram shows two similar triangles, ABC and ADE.

   a) State which angle in triangle ABC corresponds to:
   (i) angle ADE
   (ii) angle AED
   (iii) angle DAE
   b) Find the ratio of the length of AB to the length of AD.
   c) Find the length of: **(i)** AE **(ii)** BC

3 The diagram shows two similar triangles, QRU and QST.

   a) Find the length of ST.
   b) Find the length of QT.
   c) Find the length of UT.

4 The diagram shows two similar triangles, STW and SUV.

   a) Find the length of TW.
   b) Find the length of SU.
   c) Find the length of TU.

5 Triangles XRQ and XYZ are similar.

   a) State the size of angle QXR. Explain your answer.
   b) Use alternate angles to state which angle in triangle XRQ is equal to angle XYZ.
   c) Find the ratio of the length of RX to the length of YX.
   d) Use your answers to find the length of:
   (i) YZ **(ii)** XQ

6 Find the missing angles and lengths marked a-f in the diagram below.

Section 24 — Transformations

Section 25 — Collecting Data

25.1 Using Different Types of Data

The first stage in the data-handling cycle is to decide **what data** you need to collect and **how** you're going to get it.

Primary data is data you **collect yourself**, e.g. by doing a survey or experiment. **Secondary data** is data that has been **collected by someone else**. You can get secondary data from things like newspapers or the internet.

Example 1

Marya wants to know if there's a link between area and population in 10 African countries.

a) What pieces of data does Marya need to find?
This is the information she needs to answer her question. ⟹ The **areas and populations** of the 10 countries she's interested in.

b) Where could Marya get the data from? ⟹ E.g. she could find it on the **internet**.

c) Is Marya's data primary or secondary data?
The data has been collected by someone else, so... ⟹ It's **secondary** data.

Example 2

Jon wants to test whether a six-sided dice has an equal chance of landing on each of its sides. Explain how he could collect data for the test. Is his data primary or secondary data?

1. Jon needs to do an experiment. ⟹ He could roll the dice lots of times and record how many times it lands on each side using a tally chart.

2. He collects the data himself, so... ⟹ His data is **primary** data.

Exercise 1

Will the data collected in **Questions 1-4** be primary or secondary data?

1. Megan and Jane want to find out the types of music that students like.
   a) Megan plans to send a questionnaire to students from her college.
   b) Jane plans to use the results of an online music survey on the college's website.

2. James plans to interview people as they leave a supermarket to find out how often they shop there.

3. Faheem is going to use the data on election results that appeared in his local newspaper.

4. Nancy is going to time how long it takes her friends to run 100 metres.

For each investigation in **Questions 5-9**:
  a) Describe what data is needed and suggest a suitable method for collecting it.
  b) Say whether the data will be primary or secondary data.

5 Nikita wants to know what the girls in her class think about school dinners.

6 Dan wants to find the most common colour of car passing his house in a 30-minute interval.

7 Anne wants to compare the daily rainfall in London and Manchester last August.

8 Rohan wants to test his theory that the boys in his class can throw a ball further than the girls.

9 Jim wants to find out how the temperature in his garden at 10 am each morning compares with the temperature recorded by the Met Office for his local area.

Discrete and Continuous Data

Data can be **qualitative** (in the form of **words**), or **quantitative** (**numbers**).

Quantitative data can be **discrete** or **continuous**. **Discrete data** can only take certain values (usually whole numbers). It's often things you can count, e.g. the number of goals scored in a football match. **Continuous data** can take any value in a range. It's always measured, e.g. the height or weight of something.

Example 3
Say whether the following data is qualitative, discrete or continuous.
  a) The hometowns of 10 people.
     This data is in the form of words, so... ⟹ It's **qualitative** data.
  b) The weights of the bags of potatoes on sale in a greengrocer's.
     This data is numerical and has to be measured, so... ⟹ It's **continuous** data.
  c) The number of students in each class at a school.
     This data is numerical and can be counted, so... ⟹ It's **discrete** data.

Exercise 2

Will the data in **Questions 1-10** be qualitative, discrete or continuous?

1 The number of words in your favourite song.
2 Your favourite food.
3 The numbers of pets in 20 households.
4 The sizes of the crowds at 10 rugby matches.
5 The heights of 100 tomato plants.
6 The time it takes Matt to walk to school.
7 The nationalities of the people in a park.
8 The lengths of 30 worms.
9 The distances of planets from the Sun.
10 The hair colours of 50 people.

11 Gemma thinks there is a link between the average number of chocolate bars eaten each week by pupils in her class and how fast they can run 100 metres.
  a) Describe two sets of data Gemma should collect to investigate this link.
  b) Describe suitable methods for collecting the data.
  c) Say whether each set of data is discrete data or continuous data.
  d) Say whether each set of data is primary data or secondary data.

25.2 Data-Collection Sheets and Questionnaires

Data-Collection Sheets

Data-collection sheets vary with the type of data being collected. Simple **tally charts** can be used to record data as you collect it. If there's a **large range** of data values, you need to **group** them into classes. If **two variables** are being recorded, you can use a **two-way table**.

Example 1

A restaurant manager asks 50 customers to choose their favourite way to eat potatoes from the following four options: boiled, mashed, baked and roast.

Design a tally chart that could be used to record the data.

Column for data names... — with a row for every possible answer

Potato type	Tally	Frequency
Boiled		
Mashed		
Baked		
Roast		

Frequency column for adding up the tally marks

Tally column with plenty of space to record the marks

Exercise 1

1 Give **two** things that are wrong with this tally chart for recording the colours of cars in a car park.

Car colour	Frequency
Red	
Black	
Blue	
Silver	

2 Design a tally chart that could be used to record the answers to each of the questions below. In each case, all the possible answers are listed.

   a) How many times a week do you go to the supermarket? Choose from: 0, 1, 2, 3, more than 3.

   b) Where did you go for your last holiday? Choose from: UK, Europe, USA, Asia, other.

3 Design a tally chart that could be used to record the answers to each of these questions.

   a) What's the main method of transport you use to get to work?

   b) How many days were there in the month you were born?

Example 2

A group of students take a test. The tests are marked and given a score out of 50. Design a tally chart to record the students' scores. (You can assume that all scores are whole numbers.)

1. This is discrete data, but a large range of scores are possible, so group them into a sensible number of classes.
2. Make sure the classes cover all possible scores between 0 and 50.
3. Make sure the classes don't overlap — each score should only be able to go into one class.

Test Score	Tally	Frequency
0 – 10		
11 – 20		
21 – 30		
31 – 40		
41 – 50		

Section 25 — Collecting Data

Example 3

An assault course is designed to take about 10 minutes to complete.
Design a tally chart that could be used to record the times taken by a group of people.

1. The data is continuous, so describe the classes using inequalities.
2. Make sure there are no gaps between classes and that classes don't overlap.
3. Leave the last class open-ended to make sure all possible times are covered.

Time (t mins)	Tally	Frequency
$0 < t \leq 5$		
$5 < t \leq 10$		
$10 < t \leq 15$		
$15 < t \leq 20$		
$t > 20$		

Exercise 2

1 Give **two** things that are wrong with each of these tally charts and design an improved version.

   a) Chart for recording the number of times people went to the cinema last year.

No. of cinema trips	Tally	Frequency
1 – 10		
10 – 20		
20 – 30		
30 – 40		
40 or more		

   b) Chart for recording the number of people watching a band play at each venue on their tour (max. venue capacity = 25 000).

No. of people	Tally	Frequency
0 – 5000		
6000 – 10 000		
11 000 – 15 000		
16 000 – 20 000		

   c) Chart for recording the length of time people can hop on one leg for.

Time (t mins)	Tally	Frequency
$t \leq 5$		
$t \geq 5$		

   d) Chart for recording weights of pumpkins.

Weight (w kg)	Tally	Frequency
$w < 3$		
$3 < w < 3.5$		
$3.5 < w < 4$		

2 Write down five classes that could be used in a tally chart for recording each set of data below.

   a) The heights of 50 plants, which range from 5 cm to 27 cm.
   b) The number of quiz questions, out of a total of 20, answered correctly by some quiz teams.
   c) The weights of 30 bags of apples, where each bag should weigh roughly 200 g.
   d) The volumes of tea in 50 cups of tea as they're served in a cafe. Each cup can hold 300 ml.

3 Design a tally chart that could be used to record the following data.

   a) The average lengths of time 100 people spend watching TV each week.
   b) The numbers of pairs of socks owned by 50 students.
   c) The lengths of 20 people's feet.
   d) The distances that 30 people travel to get to work and back each day.

Section 25 — Collecting Data

Example 4

Raymond is investigating how fast the players at a tennis club can serve.
He's interested in whether being right-handed or left-handed has any effect on average speed.

Design a two-way table he could use to record the data he needs.

One variable goes down the side and the other goes across the top

	Average serve speed (s mph)				
	$s < 40$	$40 \leq s < 50$	$50 \leq s < 60$	$60 \leq s < 70$	$s \geq 70$
Right-handed					
Left-handed					

Use inequalities for continuous data

Make sure there are no gaps and classes don't overlap

Rows and columns should cover every possible result

Space for tally marks

Exercise 3

1 This table has been designed to record the hair colour and age (in whole years) of 100 adults.

	Age in whole years					
	0 – 15	15 – 30	30 – 45	45 – 60	60 – 75	75 or older
Blonde						
Light brown						
Dark brown						

  a) Give three criticisms of the table.
  b) Design an improved version of the table.

2 Design two-way tables that could be used to record the following data.

  a) The favourite season of the year of 50 men and 50 women.
  b) The type of music adults and children prefer listening to out of pop, classical and rock.
  c) The average length of time spent doing homework each evening by pupils in each of the school years 7-11. Assume no one spends more than an average of 4 hours an evening on homework.

3 For each investigation below, design a two-way table for recording the data.

  a) Nathan wants to find out whether children watch more TV on average each day than adults.
  b) Felicity is investigating whether pupils in different school years use different methods of transport to get to school.
  c) Chloe is going to ask people how tall they are and how many portions of fruit they eat on average each week.

Exercise 4

For each investigation below, design a data-collection sheet to record the data.

1 Camilla plans to count the number of people in each of 50 cars driving into a car park.

2 Theo is going to ask 100 people to rate his new hairstyle from 1 to 5.
He's interested in whether children give him higher scores than adults.

3 Greg is investigating how much pocket money everyone in his class gets.

4 Simran wants to test her theory that people who play a lot of sport don't watch much TV.

Questionnaires

Questionnaires need to be **easy to use** — e.g. the questions should be clear and easy to answer accurately. It's also important to design the questions so that the answers will be **easy to analyse** and will give relevant and unbiased information.

Example 5

John and Carly are both investigating how people spend their pocket money.

John's questionnaire includes the following question. | *How much do you spend on sweets?*

Carly's questionnaire includes this question:

| *How much money do you spend on sweets each week on average?* |
| **None** ☐   **Less than £1** ☐   **£1–£2** ☐   **More than £2** ☐ |

Explain why Carly's question is better than John's question.

1. Look at how easy the questions are to answer.

   Carly's question is **easier to answer** because she's given a **specific time span** and a **range of options** to tick.

2. Look at how easy the answers will be to analyse.

   It will be **easier to analyse** Carly's data because there are **only 4 options** to choose from, whereas the answers to John's question could all be different.

Example 6

Give two criticisms of the following question.

| *How many hours of TV do you watch each day on average?* |
| 0–1 ☐   1–2 ☐   2–3 ☐   3–4 ☐ |

Look closely at the tick boxes.
The **tick boxes overlap** — e.g. if you watch 1 hour of TV, you don't know whether to tick the first or second box. And the **boxes don't cover all possible options**.

Example 7

The following questions are from a questionnaire. Give one criticism of each question.

a) *How old are you?*

   Think about the people answering the question.

   This could be a **sensitive question**, so it would be better to have a range of options to tick.

b) *Do you agree that it's important to follow the latest fashions?*

   Think about whether the question is fair or biased.

   This is a **leading question**. It encourages people to give a certain opinion, so the results might be **biased**.

Section 25 — Collecting Data

Exercise 5

Give one criticism of each of the following questions.

1. How often do you go to the cinema?
2. Do you agree that the best superhero is *Super-Invisible-Wonder-Penguin*?
3. How much do you weigh?
4. How many pets does your family have?
   1 ☐   2 ☐   3 ☐   More than 3 ☐
5. How tall are you?   150 cm or less ☐
   150–180 cm ☐   180 cm or more ☐

Exercise 6

Write an improved version of each of the questions below.

1. How much time do you spend reading each week on average?
   0–1 hours ☐   1–2 hours ☐   2–3 hours ☐   3–4 hours ☐   4 or more hours ☐
2. What's your favourite type of TV programme? Tick one box.
   Comedy ☐   Soap ☐   Reality ☐   Sport ☐
3. Do you agree that the gym should open a new tennis court rather than a new squash court?

Exercise 7

Write a question to find out each of the following pieces of information. Use suitable tick boxes.

1. How often the members of a gym use the facilities.
2. Which days of the week people usually shop at the supermarket (allow more than one day).
3. What the people who attend a dance class think of the length of the class.

25.3 Sampling and Bias

The group of people or things you want to find out about is called the **population**. Usually, it's quicker, cheaper and more practical to collect data from a **sample** of the population, rather than the whole thing.

Different samples will give different results, but the **bigger** the sample, the more reliable they should be.

Example 1

Michael and Tina have written a questionnaire to find out what students at their college think about public transport. Michael gives the questionnaire to 10 students and Tina gives the questionnaire to 50 students. Michael concludes that 50% of students are happy with public transport, whereas Tina concludes that only 30% are happy.

a) Why have Michael and Tina only given the questionnaire to some of the students?
   Think about the advantages of sampling...
   E.g. there are fewer copies to print, so **print costs will be lower**.
   Also, it will take them **much less time** to collect and analyse the results.

b) Whose results are likely to be more reliable? Explain your answer.
   Think about the size of the sample...
   Tina's results are likely to be more reliable because she has used a **bigger sample**.

Exercise 1

1. Identify the population and the sample in the following scenario:
   A university wants to find out how its students feel about plans to build a new library. It randomly distributes a survey to 800 of its students.

2. Jenny wants to know how long it takes the pupils in Year 7 to type out a poem. She plans to time a sample of 30 out of the 216 Year 7 pupils. Give two advantages for Jenny of using a sample.

3. A supermarket chain wants to know what people in a town think of their plan to build a new supermarket there. They've hired a team of researchers to interview a sample of 500 people. Give one reason why they wouldn't want to interview everyone in the town.

4. Jim is testing a box of matches to see how long they burn for. He does this by lighting 10 of the matches. Explain why Jim doesn't test all the matches.

5. An audience of 1000 people are watching a musical. Kelly wants to know what they think about it and plans to interview 5 of the audience afterwards. What's wrong with Kelly's plan?

6. Melissa and Karen are doing an experiment to see if a coin is fair. They each toss the coin 100 times and record the number of heads. 52% of Melissa's tosses are heads and 47% of Karen's tosses are heads. Explain why Melissa and Karen get different results.

7. Alfie and Lisa want to find out what the most popular flavour of ice cream is. Alfie asks 30 people and finds that 'chocolate' is the most popular. Lisa asks 15 people and finds that it's 'strawberry'. Based on this information, what would you say is the most popular flavour? Explain your answer.

8. Jack, Nikhil and Daisy bake a batch of 200 cupcakes to sell on their market stall. Jack thinks they should taste one cake to check the quality is OK. Nikhil thinks they should taste 10 cakes and Daisy thinks they should taste 50 cakes. Say who you agree with and explain why.

Choosing a Fair Sample

When you're choosing a sample, it's important to make sure that it **fairly represents** the **population**. If it's **biased**, the data you get will be different from the data you'd get if you asked everyone.

To **avoid bias**, you need to choose the items or people to include in your sample carefully. If possible, it's a good idea to select your sample at **random** — which means that everything or everyone in the population has an equal chance of being selected.

Example 2

Gina plans to sample 50 shoppers at a supermarket to see what they think about the supermarket's decision to close earlier in the evenings. She decides to stand outside the supermarket on a Wednesday morning and ask the first 50 people she sees leaving the shop.

a) Explain why this will give her a biased sample.

   Think about when she selects the sample...

   E.g. Gina is only asking people who are free to shop on a Wednesday morning, so she's excluding all the shoppers who are at work or school. She's also excluding people who only shop in the evening, who will probably be more affected by the earlier closing.

b) Suggest how Gina could choose a fairer sample.

   Think about how she could include more groups of shoppers...

   E.g. Gina should ask people on different days of the week and at different times of day.

Section 25 — Collecting Data

Exercise 2

Explain why the following methods of selecting a sample will each result in a biased sample.

1 Barry wants to know what people at his college think about a particular film, so he asks 10 of his friends for their opinions.

2 A school cook wants to know whether the pupils want all school dinners to be vegetarian. He asks all the members of the school's animal rights group.

3 A library needs to reduce its opening hours. The librarian asks 20 people on a Monday morning whether the library should close on a Monday or a Friday.

4 A market research company wants to find out about people's working hours. They select 100 home telephone numbers and call them at 2 pm one afternoon.

Example 3

Adam wants to choose 20 of the 89 members of his choir to fill in a questionnaire.
Explain how he could select a random sample.

Everyone should have the same chance of being chosen,
so he needs to start with a list of everyone in the population...

1. First, he should make a list of all the people in the choir and assign everyone a number.
2. Then he could use a calculator or computer to generate 20 random numbers.
3. Finally, he needs to match these numbers to the people on the list to create the sample.

Exercise 3

1 A dentist wants his patients to test a new type of toothbrush.
How could he select a random sample of 20 of his adult patients?

2 A head teacher wants to know what pupils in Year 7 think about after-school clubs.
Explain how he could select a random sample of 50 Year 7 pupils.

3 The manager of a health club wants to survey a random sample of 40 female members.
Explain how she could do this.

Exercise 4

1 George and Stuart want to find out which football team is most popular at their school.
George asks a random selection of 30 pupils and Stuart asks the first 5 pupils he sees at lunchtime.
Give two reasons why George's sample will be more representative of the whole school.

2 Seema wants to find out about the religious beliefs of people in her street, so she stands outside her house on a Sunday morning and interviews the first 20 people she sees. Explain why her sample will be biased, and suggest a better method for selecting her sample.

3 A company has 5 branches across the country. Describe how the management team could select a representative sample of 100 employees to question about pay and working conditions.

4 A factory makes hundreds of the same component each day. Describe how a representative sample of 50 components could be tested each day to make sure the machinery is working properly.

Section 25 — Collecting Data

Section 26 — Analysing Data

26.1 Using Lists and Tables

Tally Charts and Frequency Tables

The **frequency** of a data value is the number of times it occurs in a data set.

Sometimes data values are put into **groups** (e.g. values from 0 to 5, values from 6 to 10, and so on). **Grouped frequency tables** can make complex data sets easier to understand, but they don't show the exact data values.

Example 1

A mathematics test is marked out of 40. Here are the marks for 20 students.

| 10 | 18 | 28 | 38 | 40 | 40 | 29 | 11 | 13 | 16 |
| 18 | 20 | 31 | 40 | 27 | 25 | 22 | 40 | 9 | 34 |

a) Complete the grouped frequency table to show the marks.
   1. Add a tally mark (|) in the Tally column for every test score. Write the tally marks in groups of 5, with the fifth tally mark across the others to make a '5-bar gate'.
   2. Find each frequency by counting the tally marks.

Mark	Tally	Frequency
0-10	||	2
11-20	|||||		6
21-30	|||||	5
31-40	||||| ||	7

b) The pass mark for this test was 21 out of 40.
   How many students passed the test?
   Add the frequencies for the bottom two rows.   5 + 7 = **12**

Exercise 1

1 Ben asks a group of people what type of music they like most. Here are their responses.

| Pop | R&B | Rock | Indie | Pop | R&B | Indie | Pop | Jazz | Pop |
| Pop | Rock | Pop | Pop | Jazz | Pop | Pop | Classical | Indie | Rock |

a) Copy and complete the frequency table on the right.
b) Use your table to answer the following.
   (i) How many people like classical music most?
   (ii) What is the most popular type of music?
   (iii) How many people does Ben ask?

Type of Music	Tally	Frequency
Classical		
Indie		
Pop		
Rock		
Other		

2 The weights (in g) of 16 bananas from a bunch are shown below.

| 118 | 119 | 117 | 120 | 122 | 121 | 117 | 120 |
| 120 | 119 | 117 | 120 | 121 | 121 | 118 | 121 |

a) Copy and complete the frequency table on the right.
b) Use your table to find the most common weight(s) for a banana in this bunch.

Weight (g)	Tally	Frequency
117		
118		
119		
120		
121		
122		

3 Here are the ages of 50 guests at a party.

30	56	4	18	19	35	65	79	54	54
45	32	36	39	26	27	1	3	51	56
19	23	9	11	23	45	41	48	23	32
39	43	44	5	77	61	62	78	39	47
52	56	1	2	80	21	48	54	55	78

a) Copy and complete this grouped frequency table. Continue using groups of 10 years for the rest of the table.

b) Use your table to find which of these age groups is the most common.

Age (years)	Tally	Frequency
0-9		
10-19		
20-29		

4 A mathematics test is marked out of 100. The marks for 50 students are in the box on the right.

20	90	64	35	44	62	29	30	68	69
73	88	80	45	55	61	39	29	47	91
38	65	66	42	81	92	99	33	81	88
45	56	65	65	78	91	95	36	56	27
65	98	39	79	81	82	31	31	98	92

a) Complete this grouped frequency table to show the students' marks.

b) The pass mark for this test was 60 out of 100. Use your table to find how many students passed the test.

c) Could you use your table to find out how many students had passed the test if the pass mark was reduced to 55 out of 100? Explain your answer.

Mark
20-29
30-39
40-49

26.2 Averages and Range

Averages: Mean, Median and Mode

An **average** is a way of representing the value of a whole set of data using just one number. The **mode**, **median** and **mean** are three different types of average.

> **mode** (or **modal value**) = the **most common** value
>
> **median** = **middle value** once the items have been put **in order** from smallest to largest
>
> **mean** = the **total** of all the values ÷ the **number** of values

Example 1

Find the mode of these numbers: 3   7   4   8   3

The mode is the most common number.   Mode = **3**

Exercise 1

1 Find the mode of the following sets of data.

a) 8, 5, 3, 8, 4

b) 6, 9, 2, 7, 7, 6, 5, 9, 6

c) 16, 8, 12, 13, 13, 8, 8, 17

Section 26 — Analysing Data

2 Nine students score the following marks on a test: 34   67   86   58   51   52   71   65   58
Find the mode.

3 The times (to the nearest second) of nine athletes running the 400 m hurdles are:
78   78   84   81   90   79   84   78   95
Find the modal time.

4 Find the modal value of the following: red, yellow, red, black, orange, purple, red, green, black

Example 2

a) Find the median of these numbers: 3   7   4   8   3

1. Put the numbers in order first.
   From smallest to largest, the numbers are: 3   3   4   7   8
2. If there's an odd number of values, then there will be just one value in the middle.
   The median is the value in the middle, so the median = **4**

b) The number 5 is added to the list. Find the new median.

1. If there's an even number of values, then there are two values in the middle.
   From smallest to largest, the list is now: 3   3   4   5   7   8
2. The median will be halfway between the two middle numbers. Find it by adding them together and dividing by 2.
   The two middle values are 4 and 5, so the median = $\frac{4+5}{2}$ = **4.5**

Exercise 2

1 Find the median of the following sets of data.
   a) 8, 5, 3, 8, 4
   b) 6, 9, 2, 7, 7, 6, 5, 9, 6
   c) 16, 18, 12, 13, 13, 8, 8, 17

2 Find the median of the following sets of data.
   a) 1.5, 2.7, 3.8, 4.8, 5.6
   b) 15, 16, 22, 17
   c) 3, 3, 3, 3, 3, 3, 3, 4

3 Nine students score the following marks on a test: 34   67   86   58   51   52   71   65   58
Find the median mark.

4 The times (to the nearest second) of nine athletes running the 400 m hurdles are:
78   78   84   81   90   79   84   78   95
Find the median time.

5 The median of the following data set is 7, but one value is missing.   6, 5, ?, 9, 10
What is the missing value?

6 The median of the following data set is 16.7, but one value is missing.   16.5, 16.9, 15.8, 14.3, 18.9, ?
What is the smallest that the missing number could be?

Section 26 — Analysing Data

Example 3

Find the mean of these numbers: 3 7 4 8 3
1. Find the total of the values.   The total is 3 + 7 + 4 + 8 + 3 = 25.
2. Divide the total by the number of values.   So the mean = 25 ÷ 5 = **5**

Exercise 3

1 Find the mean of the following sets of data.
  a) 8, 5, 3, 8, 4
  b) 6, 9, 2, 7, 7, 6, 5, 9, 6
  c) 16, 18, 12, 13, 13, 8, 8, 17

2 Find the mean of the following sets of data.
  a) 1.5, 2.7, 3.8, 4.8, 5.6
  b) 15.85, 16.96, 22.04, 17.45
  c) 3, 3, 3, 3, 3, 3, 3, 4

3 Nine students score the following marks on a test: 34 67 86 58 51 52 71 65 58
   Find the mean.

4 The times (to the nearest second) of nine athletes running the 400 m hurdles are:
   78 78 84 81 90 79 84 78 95
   Find the mean time.

5 Find the mean, median and mode for each of the following two sets of data.
  a) 1, 2, 2, 2, 3, 3, 5, 8
  b) 1, 2, 3, 3, 3, 3, 4, 5

6 If the mean of the following data set is 7, find the missing value. [6, 5, 8, 8, 5, ?]

7 If the mean of the following data set is 16.3, find the missing value. [16.6, 16.9, 15.8, 14.3, 18.9, ?]

The Range

The **range** tells you how spread out your values are: **range = largest value − smallest value**

Example 4

Find the range of these numbers: 3 7 4 8 3
Subtract the lowest value from the highest.   Range = 8 − 3 = **5**

Exercise 4

1 Find the range of the following sets of data.
  a) 8, 5, 3, 8, 4
  b) 6, 9, 2, 7, 7, 6, 5, 9, 6
  c) 16, 8, 12, 13, 13, 8, 8, 17

2 Find the range of the following sets of data.
  a) 1.5, 2.7, 3.8, 4.8, 5.6
  b) 15.85, 16.96, 22.04, 17.45
  c) 3, 3, 3, 3, 3, 3, 3, 4

3 Nine students score the following marks on a test: 34 67 86 58 51 52 71 65 58
   Find the range of the marks.

4 The times (to the nearest second) of nine athletes running the 400 m hurdles are:
   78 78 84 81 90 79 84 78 95
   Find the range of these times.

5 The range of the following data set is 6. [6, 5, 8, 8, 5, ?]
   What are the two possible values for the missing number?

Finding Averages and the Range from a Frequency Table

Example 5

This frequency table shows the number of mobile phones owned by a group of people.

Number of mobile phones	0	1	2	3
Frequency	4	9	5	2

a) Find the modal number of phones owned.
This is the number with the highest frequency.   Modal number of phones owned = **1**

b) What is the median number of mobile phones owned?
1. The frequencies tell you that the list of all the individual data values would be:
0, 0, 0, 0, 1, 1, 1, 1, 1, 1, 1, 1, 1, 2, 2, 2, 2, 2, 3, 3
2. There are 20 values, so the median is halfway between the 10th and the 11th values. Both these values are 1.

$$\text{Median} = \frac{\text{10th value} + \text{11th value}}{2} = \frac{1+1}{2} = \mathbf{1}$$

c) What is the range of mobile phones owned?   Range = largest value – smallest value
= 3 – 0 = **3**

Example 6

This frequency table shows the number of mobile phones owned by a group of people.

Number of mobile phones	0	1	2	3
Frequency	4	9	5	2

a) How many people were in the group altogether?
This is the total of the frequencies.   Total number of people = 4 + 9 + 5 + 2 = **20**

b) What is the total number of mobile phones owned by this group of people?
You could use the list of values, like in the previous example. But there's another way.

1. First multiply the number of mobile phones by its frequency.

Number of mobile phones	0	1	2	3
Frequency	4	9	5	2
Phones × frequency	0	9	10	6

2. Then add the results together.   Total number of mobile phones = 0 + 9 + 10 + 6 = **25**

c) Find the mean number of mobile phones owned by each person.
Divide the total number of phones by the number of people.

$$\text{Mean of mobile phones owned} = \frac{\text{Total number of mobile phones}}{\text{Total number of people}} = \frac{25}{20} = \mathbf{1.25 \text{ phones}}$$

Exercise 5

1. This frequency table shows the number of pets the students in a class have.

Number of pets	0	1	2	3	4
Frequency	5	8	7	5	2

a) What is the modal number of pets owned?
b) What is the median number of pets owned?
c) How many students had: **(i)** no pets? **(ii)** 1 pet? **(iii)** 2 pets? **(iv)** 3 pets? **(v)** 4 pets?
d) Use your answer to **c)** to find the total number of pets owned by the students.
e) How many students are in the class altogether?
f) Use your answers to **d)** and **e)** to find the mean number of pets owned by each student.

Section 26 — Analysing Data

2 The table shows the number of people living in each of 30 houses.

Number of people	1	2	3	4	5
Frequency	4	6	7	10	3

   a) Write down the modal number of people living in a house.
   b) Find the median number of people living in a house.
   c) Calculate the mean number of people living in a house.
   d) Work out the range of the data.

3 During June, a student wrote down the temperature in his garden in degrees Celsius (°C) every day at noon, as shown in the table.
   a) Find the median noon temperature.
   b) Find the mean noon temperature (correct to 1 decimal place).
   c) The average noon temperature in June in the UK is approximately 18.5 °C. What does this suggest about these results?

Temperature (°C)	Frequency
16	4
17	9
18	2
19	5
20	4
21	6

Finding Averages from a Grouped Frequency Table

If your data is **grouped**, then you can only **estimate** the mean using the **midpoint** of each group.
For the median, you can only say **which group** it lies in — not the exact value.
Instead of a mode, you can only find a **modal group**.
The range is the difference between the **highest** and **lowest** group boundaries.

Example 7

This grouped frequency table shows the number of hours that 20 people spent exercising one week.

Hours, h	$0 \leq h < 4$	$4 \leq h < 8$	$8 \leq h < 12$	$12 \leq h < 16$	$16 \leq h < 20$	$20 \leq h < 24$
Frequency	2	3	6	4	4	1

a) Write down the modal group.
   The modal group is the one with the highest frequency.   Modal group is **$8 \leq h < 12$**.

b) Which group contains the median?
   Both the 10th and 11th values are in the group for $8 \leq h < 12$ hours. So the median must lie in that group too.
   There are 20 values, so the median lies halfway between the 10th and 11th values. This means the median is in the group **$8 \leq h < 12$**.

c) Find an estimate for the mean.
   Find the midpoint for each group by adding together the group boundaries, and dividing by 2.

Hours, h	$0 \leq h < 4$	$4 \leq h < 8$	$8 \leq h < 12$	$12 \leq h < 16$	$16 \leq h < 20$	$20 \leq h < 24$
Frequency	2	3	6	4	4	1
Midpoint of group	$\frac{0+4}{2}=2$	$\frac{4+8}{2}=6$	$\frac{8+12}{2}=10$	$\frac{12+16}{2}=14$	$\frac{16+20}{2}=18$	$\frac{20+24}{2}=22$

Now find the mean as before, using the midpoints instead of the actual data values.

| Frequency × midpoint | 2 × 2 = 4 | 3 × 6 = 18 | 6 × 10 = 60 | 4 × 14 = 56 | 4 × 18 = 72 | 1 × 22 = 22 |

Divide the total of this new row by the total of the frequencies.

Mean $= \frac{4+18+60+56+72+22}{2+3+6+4+4+1} = \frac{232}{20} =$ **11.6 hours**

d) Estimate the range.
   24 is the highest group boundary and 0 is the lowest group boundary.   Range = 24 − 0 = **24 hours**

Section 26 — Analysing Data

Exercise 6

1 The test results of 25 people are shown in this grouped frequency table.

Marks scored	1-5	6-10	11-15	16-20
Frequency	4	5	7	9

   a) Write down the modal group.
   b) Which group contains the median?
   c) Find an estimate for the mean.
   d) Estimate the range of marks.

2 The table on the right shows some information about the weights of some tangerines in a supermarket.

Weight in grams, w	Frequency
$0 \leq w < 20$	1
$20 \leq w < 40$	6
$40 \leq w < 60$	9
$60 \leq w < 80$	24

   a) Find an estimate for the mean.
   b) Find an estimate for the range of weights.
   c) Explain why your answer to part **b)** might be very different from the actual range.

3 Troy collected some information about the number of hours (to the nearest whole hour) students spent watching television over a week.

Time in hours	Frequency
0-5	3
6-10	8
11-15	11
16-20	4

   a) Write down the modal group.
   b) Which group contains the median?
   c) Find an estimate for the mean to 1 decimal place.

Exercise 7 — Mixed Exercise

1 The heights of some sunflowers (to the nearest cm) are shown below.
   132   142   126   142   159   127   148   128
   a) Find: **(i)** the mean,   **(ii)** the median,   **(iii)** the mode.
   b) Find the range.

2 The prices (in £) charged by a selection of stores for the same item are shown below.
   5.00   4.21   4.97   5.00   5.00   5.29   5.05   5.50   5.79   5.00   5.40
   5.20   5.10   5.06   4.50   4.50   5.50   4.50   5.00   5.00   5.50   4.82
   a) Find: **(i)** the mean,   **(ii)** the median,   **(iii)** the mode.
   b) Find the range.

3 The lengths (in cm) of some blades of grass are:
   6.5   7.8   4.3   8.5   4.3   5.9   6.2   9.0   5.7   6.7
   a) Find: **(i)** the mean,   **(ii)** the median,   **(iii)** the mode.
   b) Find the range.

4 This table shows how many customers bought different numbers of cakes from a bakery one day.
   a) Write down the modal number of cakes bought.
   b) Work out the number of customers served.
   c) Find the median number of cakes bought.
   d) **(i)** Calculate the total number of cakes bought.
      (ii) Work out the mean number of cakes bought.
   e) Work out the range of the number of cakes bought.

Number of cakes bought	Frequency
0	8
1	6
2	4
3	2

5 This table shows the number of goals scored one week by 18 teams in the premier division.

Number of goals	0	1	2	3	4	5
Number of teams	1	3	4	5	3	2

   a) Find the median number of goals.
   b) Find the mean number of goals. Give your answer to 1 decimal place.
   c) Write down the mode.
   d) The mean, median and modal numbers of goals scored in the same week of the previous year were all 2. How do these results compare?

6 This table shows the heights (in metres) of 20 people.

Height in metres, h	Frequency
$1.5 < h \leq 1.6$	2
$1.6 < h \leq 1.7$	9
$1.7 < h \leq 1.8$	7
$1.8 < h \leq 1.9$	2

   a) Write down the modal group.
   b) Which group contains the median?
   c) Find an estimate for the mean.
   d) Estimate the range.

7 Susie buys a bag of 5 apples. The weights of the apples are 57 g, 60 g, 69 g, 72 g and 75 g. After Susie has eaten two of the apples, the mean weight of the three that remain is 62 g. What were the weights of the two apples that she ate?

8 The data below shows how long in days it took for 10 tomato seeds to germinate.
   3, 6, 17, 4, 3, 6, 6, 5, 4, 3
   a) What is the range of the data?
   b) Do you think the range is a good measure of the spread of this data?
   c) Is the mode a suitable measure of average for this data?

9 Eight students sat two maths tests. Their scores out of 20 are shown below.
   Test 1: 19, 14, 8, 17, 17, 20, 6, 13
   Test 2: 7, 14, 16, 7, 10, 8, 10, 12
   a) Calculate the mean score for each test.
   b) Find the range for each test.
   c) Use your results from parts **a)** and **b)** to compare the distributions of the scores in the two tests.

10 The vertical line graph shows information on the number of washing machines sold by an electrical shop each day for 40 days.
   a) What is the median number of washing machines sold each day?
   b) What is the modal number sold each day?
   c) Calculate the mean number of machines sold each day.
   d) Find the range of the number of machines sold each day.

Section 26 — Analysing Data

26.3 Two-Way Tables

A **two-way table** shows two variables at the same time.

Example 1

This table shows how students in a class travel to school.

	Walk	Bus	Car	Total
Boys	8	7		19
Girls	6		2	
Total		12		

a) Complete the table.
   Add entries to find row/column totals.
   Subtract from row/column totals to find other entries.

	Walk	Bus	Car	Total
Boys	8	7	19 − 8 − 7 = **4**	19
Girls	6	12 − 7 = **5**	2	6 + 5 + 2 = **13**
Total	8 + 6 = **14**	12	4 + 2 = **6**	19 + 13 = **32**

b) How many girls take the bus to school?
   Find the entry in the Bus column and the Girls row.   **5**

c) How many students walk to school?
   This is the total of the Walk column.   **14**

d) What percentage of students take the bus to school?
   Divide the total of the Bus column by the overall total. $\frac{12}{32} = 0.375 =$ **37.5%**

Exercise 1

1 Copy and complete these two-way tables, showing how groups of students travel to school.

a)
	Walk	Car	Total
Boys	12	6	
Girls	16	3	
Total			

b)
	Walk	Car	Total
Boys	16		25
Girls		4	
Total	34		

c)
	Walk	Bus	Car	Total
Boys	9	5	3	
Girls	5	8	6	
Total				

d)
	Walk	Bus	Car	Total
Boys			8	
Girls	11		4	30
Total	21			60

2 This two-way table shows how many male and female language students from a university Languages department went to study in Germany, France or Spain.

	Germany	France	Spain	Total
Male	16	7	12	
Female	18	4	16	
Total				

a) Copy the table and fill in the entries in the final row and final column.
b) How many female students went to France?
c) How many male students went to Germany?
d) How many students in total went to Spain?
e) How many female students went to either Germany, France or Spain to study?
f) What was the total number of students from this department that went to either Germany, France or Spain to study?

Section 26 — Analysing Data

3   This two-way table gives information about some students' favourite type of snack.
   a) Copy and complete the two-way table.
   b) How many students preferred crisps?
   c) How many females preferred jellies?
   d) What percentage of males preferred chocolate?

	Chocolate	Crisps	Jellies	Total
Male	3			
Female		7	2	
Total	6	12		30

4   This two-way table gives information about the colours of the vehicles in a car park.
   a) Copy and complete the two-way table.
   b) How many motorbikes were blue?
   c) How many vans were there?
   d) What percentage of vehicles were:
      (i) cars?   (ii) vans?   (iii) red?

	Red	Black	Blue	White	Total
Cars	8	7	4		22
Vans		2	1	10	
Motorbikes	2	1		2	
Total	12		6		

26.4 Bar Charts and Pictograms

Bar Charts

Bar charts show how many items fall into different categories.
A **dual bar chart** shows the same categories for two different people or things.

Example 1
The eye colour of 50 students is shown in the frequency table below.

Eye colour	Blue	Brown	Green	Other
Frequency	15	19	10	6

Draw a bar chart to display this information.
Draw a bar of equal width for each eye colour, with a space between each bar.

Exercise 1

1   Arthur asked some students in the canteen which meal they had bought at lunchtime.
   His results are in the table below. Draw a bar chart to show this information.

Meal	Pie & Chips	Pasta	Baked potato	Baguette	Salad
Frequency	11	3	7	10	4

2   Some people at a bus stop were asked which bus they were waiting for.
   Their responses are shown in this frequency table.

Bus	Number 7	Number 23	Coastlander	X94	12a
Frequency	6	5	2	3	2

Draw a bar chart to show this information.

3   One morning a coffee shop recorded the first 100 drinks that were ordered.
   Their results are in the frequency table below. Draw a bar chart to show this information.

Drink	Espresso	Latte	Cappuccino	Mocha	Tea	Other
Frequency	23	19	12	15	22	9

Section 26 — Analysing Data

Example 2

Manpreet and Parminder recorded how many TV programmes they watched each day for a week. Their results are in the table below. Draw a dual bar chart to display this information.

Day	Mon	Tues	Wed	Thur	Fri	Sat	Sun
Number of programmes watched by Manpreet	1	2	4	2	3	7	4
Number of programmes watched by Parminder	2	1	0	2	3	4	0

1. Each day will have two bars — one for Manpreet and one for Parminder.

2. Use different colours or shades for Manpreet and Parminder's bars — and include a key to show which is which.

4 The people in an office were asked how many cups of tea they drank each morning and afternoon. The results are in this table.

Name	Nigel	Ali	Raul	Kate	Ailsa	Jan
Cups (Morning)	3	2	1	3	0	2
Cups (Afternoon)	2	1	4	3	0	2

a) Draw a dual bar chart to show this information.

b) What fraction of the cups of tea drank by Nigel were in the afternoon?

5 The number of rainy days each season in Plymouth and Aberdeen is shown in the table.

Season	Spring	Summer	Autumn	Winter
Rainy days (Plymouth)	38	40	48	52
Rainy days (Aberdeen)	45	47	53	53

a) Draw a dual bar chart to show this information.

b) Use your graph to compare the number of rainy days per season in each city.

Pictograms

A **pictogram** uses symbols to represent a certain number of items.

Example 3

This table shows the number of TVs in four secondary schools.

School	Long Beck	Tudor Hall	Alderbrook	Lode Heath
TVs	20	10	8	13

Using the symbol ▢ to represent 4 TVs, draw a pictogram to show this information.

1. Work out how many symbols you need to draw for each school.
   For example, for Tudor Hall:
   × 2.5 (4 TVs = ▢
   10 TVs = ▢▢⊏) × 2.5

   Long Beck ▢▢▢▢▢
   Tudor Hall ▢▢⊏
   Alderbrook ▢▢
   Lode Heath ▢▢▢⊏

2. Include a key to show what one symbol represents. ⟹ Key: ▢ represents 4 TVs.

Exercise 2

1 Members of a hockey club were asked which activity they would like to do on a team day out. The results are in this frequency table.

Activity	Theme Park	Bowling	Cinema	Boat Trip
Frequency	14	10	5	3

Draw a pictogram to show this information. Represent 2 club members using the symbol: 👤

2 The incomplete pictogram on the right shows the number of packets of sweets a shop sold on Monday, Tuesday and Wednesday.

a) How many packets of sweets were sold on:
   (i) Tuesday?   (ii) Wednesday?

b) Copy the pictogram, and use the information below to complete it.
   - On Thursday the shop sold 20 packets.
   - On Friday they sold 50 packets.
   - On Saturday they sold 65 packets.
   - On Sunday the shop was closed.

3 This pictogram shows the number of letters that were delivered to each of the 6 houses in a street one week.

a) How many letters were delivered to Number 4?
b) Which house received fewest letters during the week?
c) How many letters in total were delivered to the 6 houses?

Key: ✉ represents 4 letters

26.5 Stem and Leaf Diagrams

Building Stem and Leaf Diagrams

Stem and leaf diagrams are a bit like bar charts, but the bars are made out of the actual data. A stem and leaf diagram always needs a **key** to show someone how to read it.

Example 1

Here are the marks scored by pupils in a class test.

56, 52, 82, 65, 76, 82, 57, 63, 69, 73, 58, 81, 73, 52, 73, 71, 67, 59, 63

Use this data to build an ordered stem and leaf diagram.

1. Write down the 'stems' — here use the first digit of the marks.

   5 | 6 2 7 8 2 9
   6 | 5 3 9 7 3
   7 | 6 3 3 3 1
   8 | 2 2 1

2. Next, make a 'leaf' for each data value by adding the second digit to the correct stem.

3. Put the leaves in each row in order — from lowest to highest.

4. Always include a key.

   Key: 2 | 1 means 21

   5 | 2 2 6 7 8 9
   6 | 3 3 5 7 9
   7 | 1 3 3 3 6
   8 | 1 2 2

Section 26 — Analysing Data

Exercise 1

1 Use the data sets below to make ordered stem and leaf diagrams.
   a) 41, 48, 51, 54, 59, 65, 65, 69, 74, 80, 86, 89
   b) 12, 15, 26, 15, 39, 24, 41, 41, 27, 17, 36, 31
   c) 46, 87, 42, 94, 67, 54, 59, 63, 83, 71, 66, 74

2 Only some of the values from the data sets have been added to the stem and leaf diagrams below. Copy and complete the diagrams by adding the rest of the data values. Use the keys to help.

a)

3	1
4	0 4
5	3 7 9
6	0
7	7

Key: 3 | 1 means 3.1

3.1	4.0	4.4	5.3
5.7	5.9	6.0	7.7
3.4	4.9	5.4	5.1
6.1	5.7	7.1	4.4

b)

20	3 5
30	1
40	2 9
50	0
60	6 8

Key: 20 | 1 means 201

203	205	301	402
409	500	606	608
304	409	404	501
403	601	503	402

3 The amount of rainfall in cm over Morecambe Bay was recorded every week for 16 weeks. The measurements are shown below. Use this data to make an ordered stem and leaf diagram.

| 0.0 | 3.8 | 3.6 | 0.1 | 2.7 | 0.6 | 0.3 | 1.1 |
| 2.0 | 1.3 | 0.0 | 1.6 | 4.1 | 0.0 | 2.5 | 3.1 |

Using Stem and Leaf Diagrams

You can find the mode, median and range from a stem and leaf diagram.
You can also quickly see how many values fall between certain limits — 'between 2 and 8', for example.

Example 2

The stem and leaf diagram below shows the number of seconds 19 children took to open a jar of jam. Use it to find:
a) the mode of the data   b) the median of the data   c) the range of the data

0	6 8 8
1	0 2 4 4 4 5 5 7
2	0 4 5 6 6 7
3	1 3

Key: 2 | 1 means 21 seconds

1. Find the mode by looking for the number that repeats most often in one of the rows — here, there are three 4's in the second row. Use the key to work out what it represents.   a) **14 seconds**

2. There are 19 data values, so the median is the 10th value. Count along the 'leaves' to find it, starting with the first row.   b) **15 seconds**

3. Find the range by subtracting the first number from the last.   c) 33 − 6 = **27 seconds**

Exercise 2

1 Use the stem and leaf diagram on the right to find:
   a) the mode of the data
   b) the median of the data
   c) the range of the data

0	5 8
1	2 3 7 9
2	0 1 3 9
3	2 2 2

Key: 2 | 1 means 21

Section 26 — Analysing Data 331

2 Use this diagram showing 12 pupils' test marks to find:
   a) the median mark
   b) the number of marks above 60
   c) the number of marks between 53 and 63

Key: 2 | 1 means 21

```
5 | 2 5 5 7 8
6 | 1 1 8 9
7 | 1 7 7
```

3 The times in seconds that 16 people took to run a 100 m race are shown in the box.
   a) Use these times to create an ordered stem and leaf diagram.
   b) Find the mode of the times.
   c) Find the range of the times.
   d) To qualify for the final, a contestant had to finish in under 13 seconds. How many of those who took part qualified?

10.2	13.1	13.9	14.2
17.3	11.7	11.4	12.9
15.4	13.6	13.9	10.6
12.8	13.9	12.4	13.3

4 Ed measured the heart rates (in beats per minute, bpm) of 15 people at rest, and then again after they'd exercised. He presented the results in a back-to-back stem and leaf diagram.

Key: 7 | 6 at rest means 67 bpm
7 | 6 after exercise means 76 bpm

   a) Calculate the median of:
   (i) the 'at rest' data
   (ii) the 'after exercise' data
   b) What conclusion can you draw from your answers to **a)**?

```
       heart rate at rest  |   heart rate after exercise
       8 7 6 4 3 2 2 | 6 | 5 8 8 9
             9 8 6 3 2 2 | 7 | 4 5 7 7 8
                     4 1 | 8 | 5 6 7
                         | 9 | 1 3 7
```

26.6 Pie Charts

In a **pie chart**, the size of the **angle** of each sector represents the **frequency** of a data value.

Example 1

Jack asked everyone in his class to name their favourite colour. The frequency table on the right shows his results.

Colour	Red	Green	Blue	Pink
Frequency	12	7	5	6

Draw a pie chart to show his results.

1. Calculate the total frequency. This is the number of people in Jack's class.

   Total frequency = 12 + 7 + 5 + 6 = 30

2. Divide 360° by the total frequency to find the number of degrees needed to represent each person.

   Each person represented by 360° ÷ 30 = 12°

3. Multiply each frequency by the number of degrees for one person. This tells you the angle for each colour. (These should add up to 360°. Here: 144° + 84° + 60° + 72° = 360°)

Colour	Red	Green	Blue	Pink
Frequency	12	7	5	6
Angle	144°	84°	60°	72°

4. Draw a pie chart — the sizes of the sectors are the angles you've just calculated.

332   *Section 26 — Analysing Data*

Exercise 1

1 Albert recorded the colours of cars that passed his school.
His results are shown in the table on the right.

Colour	Black	Silver	Red	Other
Frequency	25	17	8	10

   a) Find the total number of cars Albert recorded.
   b) Find how many degrees represent one car.
   c) Calculate the angle needed to represent each colour.
   d) Draw a pie chart to illustrate this data.

2 Becky asked her friends which football team they support.
Their answers are shown in the table below.

Team	Carlisle United	Kendal Town	Millom Reds	Bristol
Frequency	13	9	8	6

   a) Find the total frequency.
   b) Calculate the angle needed to represent each of the four football teams.
   c) Draw a pie chart showing Becky's results.

3 Clive carried out a survey to find how many brothers or sisters the pupils in his school have. His results are in the frequency table on the right.

Number of brothers or sisters	1	2	3	4 or more
Frequency	67	24	19	10

Draw a pie chart to display Clive's results.

4 Daisy asked a group of people where they went on holiday last year.
Her results are in the table below. Draw a pie chart to show her data.

Holiday destination	UK	Europe	USA	Other	Did not go on holiday
Frequency	22	31	8	11	18

5 Vicky asked people entering a sports centre what activity they were going to do.
   • 33 were going to play squash
   • 21 were going swimming
   • 52 were going to use the gym
   • 14 had come to play table tennis.
Draw a pie chart to show this data.

6 Mina recorded the favourite flavour of crisps of each of the pupils at her school.

Flavour	Plain	Salt and Vinegar	Cheese and Onion	Other
Frequency	18	13	10	7

   a) Calculate the total frequency.
   b) Calculate the size of the angle needed to represent each flavour in a pie chart.
   c) Draw a pie chart to represent Mina's data.

Section 26 — Analysing Data

7 Peter surveyed his friends to find out how they travelled to school. He recorded the results in the table on the right.

Method of transport	Walking	Bus	Car	Bike
Frequency	36	16	12	16

Draw a pie chart to represent Peter's data.

8 Oliver recorded the types of vehicle he saw on a busy road using the tally chart below. Show Oliver's data in a pie chart.

Car	Van	Lorry	Bicycle	Other

9 Basil used a questionnaire to find out which subject pupils at his school enjoyed the most. His data is shown in the frequency table below. Show this data in a pie chart.

Subject	Maths	Art	PE	English	Science	Other
Frequency	348	297	195	87	108	45

Interpreting Pie Charts

Pie charts let you compare the frequencies of different items, and say which ones occurred more often, and which ones occurred less often. However, pie charts **don't** show the frequencies themselves.
To work out the frequencies from a pie chart, you need to know the sizes of the **angles** of the sectors.

Example 2

A headteacher carries out a survey to find out how pupils travel to school. The pie chart on the right shows the results of the survey.

a) What is the most popular way to travel to school?
The most popular way to travel is the one represented by the largest sector. **Walking**

b) Which method of transport is twice as common as cycling?
Cycling is represented by a sector with an angle of 45°.
Travelling by car is represented by a sector with an angle of 90°. **Travelling by car**

c) 280 pupils walk to school. How many pupils took part in the survey altogether?
 1. The 280 pupils who walk are represented by an angle of 140°.
 2. Use this to work out how many pupils the whole pie chart represents.

 140° represents 280 pupils
 So 1° represents 280 ÷ 140 = 2 pupils.
 This means 360° represents 360 × 2 = **720 pupils**.

d) How many pupils cycle to school?
 1. You already know what 1° of the pie chart represents.
 2. Multiply this by the 'Cycle' sector angle to find how many pupils cycle to school.

 1° represents 2 pupils.
 So 45° represents **90 pupils**.

334 *Section 26 — Analysing Data*

Exercise 2

1 Match pie charts P, Q, R and S to the correct data set.

Data Set 1	A	B	C	D
Frequency	10	10	5	5

Data Set 2	A	B	C	D
Frequency	24	12	6	6

Data Set 3	A	B	C	D
Frequency	25	20	10	5

Data Set 4	A	B	C	D
Frequency	25	25	5	5

2 Jennifer asked pupils in her school to name their favourite type of pizza. The pie chart on the right shows the results.
   a) Which was the most popular type of pizza?
   b) What fraction of the pupils said cheese and tomato was their favourite type of pizza?
   c) 17 pupils said that vegetable was their favourite type of pizza. Calculate the total number of pupils that Jennifer asked.
   d) Use your answer to part **c)** to calculate the number of pupils that said spicy chicken was their favourite type of pizza.

3 Andy and Beth record the number of homework tasks they are set in their Maths, English and Science lessons during one term.

Their data is displayed in the pie charts on the right.
   a) Andy says: "Half of all the homework tasks I recorded were for Maths." Is he correct?
   b) Beth says: "I got the same number of Maths tasks and English tasks." Is she correct?
   c) Beth says: "I have a smaller proportion of English homework than Andy." Is she correct?
   d) Do the pie charts tell you who spent more time on their English homework? Explain your answer.

4 The company that produces Pixie washing-up liquid carries out a survey of 600 people. It finds that 120 of the people surveyed use Pixie. It uses the diagram on the right to show this information in its advertising.
   a) Explain why the diagram is misleading.
   b) Draw an accurate pie chart to represent the results of the survey.

Section 26 — Analysing Data

5) A librarian carried out a survey of the ages of people using the library.
The results are shown in the pie chart on the right.

   a) Which age group used the library most?
   b) What fraction of the library users were aged 11-16?
   c) There were 18 people aged 17-29 who took part in the survey.
   How many people took part in the survey altogether?
   d) How many of the people in the survey were:
      (i) Under 11?   **(ii)** 11-16?

Leaflets were handed out to persuade more young people to use the library.
Another survey was then carried out to find the ages of library users.
The results are shown in the pie chart on the right.

   e) The second survey was smaller than the original one.
   If 6 people aged 17-29 took part in this second survey,
   how many people took part altogether?
   f) How many people who took part in the new survey were aged 16 or under?

26.7 Time Series

A **time series** is a set of data collected at regular intervals over a period of time.
Time series are usually shown as a line graph.
You can use time series graphs to find **trends** in the data.

Example 1

The data below shows the total rainfall in Jack's garden each season for three years.

Season	Spr	Sum	Aut	Win	Spr	Sum	Aut	Win	Spr	Sum	Aut	Win
Rainfall (mm)	225	200	275	375	250	225	300	425	300	250	325	475

a) Draw a line graph to display this data.
Plot the points from the table and
join them up with straight lines.

b) Describe and interpret the
repeating pattern in the data.
You need to interpret what you see on the
graph in the context of the data.
Each year the rainfall is lower in summer
than spring. It increases in the autumn, and is
even higher in the winter, then drops again the following spring.

c) Describe the overall trend in the data.
Look at what's happening to the peaks and troughs of the graph.
There is an upward trend in the amount of rainfall.

336   *Section 26 — Analysing Data*

Exercise 1

1 This table shows the amount of gas used (in m³) by a family over a period of three years.

Season	Spring	Summer	Autumn	Winter
2012	202	80	170	298
2013	196	76	161	283
2014	183	69	149	259

a) Copy the axes on the right, and draw a graph to show how the amount of gas used varied over the three years.

b) Describe and interpret the repeating pattern seen on the graph.

c) Describe the overall trend seen in the data.

2 This table shows the highest temperature, in °C, recorded in London and Sydney each month during one year.

Month	Jan	Feb	Mar	Apr	May	Jun	Jul	Aug	Sep	Oct	Nov	Dec
London	7	8	11	13	17	20	23	22	19	15	11	8
Sydney	26	27	25	22	20	17	16	18	19	22	24	25

a) Draw a line graph to show the highest monthly temperature in London during the year.

b) On the same axes, draw a line graph to show the highest monthly temperature in Sydney during the year.

c) Describe the shapes of your two lines. What does this tell you about the way the temperature changes in the two cities during the year?

3 The line graph shows the number of pairs of sunglasses sold by a shop over four years.

a) Describe and interpret the repeating pattern seen in the graph.

b) Describe the overall trend shown by the graph.

c) Give a reason why the graph might be misleading.

Section 26 — Analysing Data

26.8 Scatter Graphs

Drawing Scatter Graphs

A **scatter graph** shows two variables plotted against each other.
These variables are often the results from a survey or an experiment.

Example 1

Jeremy measured the height and shoe size of 10 people.
Use his results to plot a scatter graph of shoe size against height in cm.

Height (cm)	165	159	173	186	176	172	181	169	179	194
Shoe size	6	5	8	9	8.5	7	8	6	8	11

1. Draw and label your axes.
   Here, height has been plotted along the horizontal axis and shoe size up the vertical axis.
2. Plot each point carefully.
3. Don't join the points up on a scatter graph.

Exercise 1

1 The scatter graph on the right shows the number of flags a shop sold each day of a football tournament.

   a) How many flags were sold on the 3rd day of the tournament?

   b) On which day of the tournament were most flags sold?

   c) On how many days did the shop sell 7 flags?

2 The outside temperature and the number of ice creams sold in a cafe were recorded for six days. The results are shown in the table below.

Temp (°C)	28	25	26	21	23	29
Ice creams sold	30	22	27	5	13	33

Copy the axes on the right, then use the data from the table to plot the scatter graph.

3 Ten children of different ages were asked how many baby teeth they still had.
Use the results below to plot a scatter graph.
Plot age on the horizontal axis and the number of baby teeth on the vertical axis.

Age (years)	5	6	8	7	9	7	10	6	8	9
Baby teeth	20	17	11	15	7	17	5	19	13	8

Correlations and Lines of Best Fit

Two variables are **correlated** if they are related to each other.
- A **positive correlation** means that the variables increase and decrease together.
- A **negative correlation** means that as one variable increases, the other decreases.

Correlation is easy to see on a scatter graph.
The closer the points are to being in a straight line, the **stronger** the correlation of the graph.

If two variables are correlated, then you can draw a **line of best fit** on their scatter graph.
This is a straight line that passes close to most of the points.

Example 2

Describe the strength and type of correlation shown by each scatter graph.

a) **Strong positive correlation**

b) **Moderate negative correlation**

c) **Weak positive correlation**

d) There's no pattern here.
No correlation

Exercise 2

1 Describe the strength and type of correlation seen in the scatter graphs below.

a) b) c)

2 Are the following pairs of variables likely to show positive correlation, negative correlation or no correlation? Explain your answers.
   a) Outside temperature and ice cream sales
   b) Outside temperature and hot chocolate sales
   c) Outside temperature and bread sales
   d) Age of a child and his or her height
   e) Speed limit in a street and the average speed of cars as they drive down that street

Section 26 — Analysing Data

Example 3

The scatter graph on the right shows the marks a class of pupils achieved in a Maths test plotted against the marks they achieved in an English test.

a) Draw a line of best fit on the graph.
b) Jimmy was ill on the day of the Maths test. If he scored 75 in his English test, predict what his Maths mark would have been.
c) Elena was ill on the day of the English test. If she scored 35 on her Maths test, predict what her English result would have been.

This point is an <u>outlier</u> - it doesn't fit with the general pattern, so ignore it when you draw your line.

a) The marks are positively correlated, so you can draw a line passing close to all the points. It doesn't have to actually go through any of the points or the origin.

b) Draw a line up from 75 on the 'English' axis to the line of best fit, then across to the 'Maths' axis.
Predicted Maths mark for Jimmy = **56**

c) Draw a line across from 35 on the 'Maths' axis to the line of best fit, and then down.
Predicted English mark for Elena = **51**

Exercise 3

1 Could a line of best fit be drawn on each of these graphs? Explain your answers.

a)   b)   c)

2 Pupils in a class were asked how many hours at the weekend they spent doing homework and watching television. The results are shown on this scatter graph.

a) Describe the correlation between time spent watching TV and time spent doing homework.
b) Use the line of best fit to predict how long a pupil spends on homework if they watch 5.5 hours of TV at the weekend.
c) Amelia did 3.5 hours of homework at the weekend. Predict how many hours she spent watching TV.

340   *Section 26 — Analysing Data*

3 The graph on the right shows the height of various types of tree plotted against the width of their trunks.

   a) Describe the correlation between the width of the trunks and the height of the trees.
   b) Give the width and the height of the tree that appears as an outlier on the graph.
   c) Use the graph to predict the width of a tree's trunk if it is 13 m tall.
   d) A tree has grown into power lines, meaning that measuring its height would be dangerous. If the trunk is 100 cm wide, predict the tree's height.

4 Anton wants to buy a particular model of car. The table below shows the cost of several of these cars that are for sale, as well as their mileage.

Mileage	5000	20 000	10 000	12 000	5000	25 000	27 000
Cost (£)	3500	2000	3000	2500	3900	1000	500

   a) The first two points have already been plotted on the scatter graph on the right. Copy and complete the graph.
   b) Draw a line of best fit through your points.
   c) Thelma has seen a car of this model with a mileage of 15 000. Predict the cost of this car.
   d) A car costs £1500. Predict the mileage of the car.

5 The outside temperature and the number of drinks sold by two vending machines were recorded over a 10-day period. The results are shown in these tables.

Temperature (°C)	14	29	23	19	22	31	33	18	27	21
Drinks sold from Machine 1	6	24	16	13	15	28	31	13	22	14

Temperature (°C)	14	29	23	19	22	31	33	18	27	21
Drinks sold from Machine 2	7	25	18	15	17	32	35	14	24	17

For each machine:
   a) Draw a scatter graph to represent the data.
   b) Draw a line of best fit.
   c) Predict the number of drinks that would be sold if the outside temperature was 25 °C.
   d) Explain why it might not be appropriate to use your lines of best fit to estimate the number of drinks sold from each machine if the outside temperature was 3 °C.
   e) Lucas says, "An increase in temperature causes more vending machine drinks to be sold." Do you agree with Lucas's statement? Explain your answer.

Section 26 — Analysing Data

Section 27 — Probability

27.1 Probability — The Basics

Probability is all about **how likely** events are to happen. The probability of any event happening is between **impossible** (definitely won't happen) and **certain** (definitely will happen). So events can be put on a **probability scale** like this.

|—————|—————|—————|—————|
Impossible   Unlikely   Evens   Likely   Certain

Example 1

One of these four cards is chosen at random. ⟹ 1 2 3 4

Mark each of statements A-C in the correct place on the scale below.

- A — the card is a 1   There's one 1, so it's not impossible, but it's less than 50/50.
- B — the card is 4 or less   All the cards are 4 or less.
- C — the card is a 5   None of the cards is a 5.

          C   A   B
|—————|—————|—————|—————|
Impossible   Unlikely   Evens   Likely   Certain

Exercise 1

1 Choose from the words: *impossible, unlikely, evens, likely* and *certain* to describe the following.
   a) Tossing a coin and getting tails.
   b) Rolling a '9' on a normal six-sided dice.
   c) A person growing to be 10 metres tall.
   d) Rolling an even number on a fair dice.
   e) Rolling 1 or more on a normal dice.
   f) Spinning '6' on a spinner labelled 5, 6, 7, 8.
   g) Picking a red card from a pack of 52 cards.
   h) Spinning 2 or more on a spinner labelled 1-4.

2 One card is picked at random from eight cards numbered 1 to 8.
   Make a copy of this probability scale and add arrows to show the probability of each of the events described below. Each arrow should match one of the words.

|—————|—————|—————|—————|
Impossible   Unlikely   Evens   Likely   Certain

   a) The card is less than 9.
   b) The card is an odd number.
   c) The card is greater than 2.
   d) The card is greater than or equal to 7.
   e) The card is 6 or less.
   f) The card is a zero.

3 These eight cards are placed face down on a table and one is selected at random.

P A R A L L E L

a) Which letter is twice as likely to be on the selected card as the letter P?
b) Which letter is three times as likely to be on the selected card as the letter E?
c) The three arrows below show the probability of selecting each of the letters P, A, R, L and E. Match each letter to one of the arrows. (You can use each arrow for more than one letter.)

Impossible   Unlikely   Evens   Likely   Certain

Writing Probabilities as Numbers

All probabilities can be written as a number between **0 and 1**.
An event that's **impossible** has a probability of **0**
and an event that's **certain** has a probability of **1**.

So, using **fractions**, the probability scale looks like this: 0 — ¼ — ½ — ¾ — 1

You can also write probabilities as **decimals** or **percentages**.

Example 2

A fair, six-sided dice is rolled. This scale shows the probabilities of three possible results.

Match each letter on the scale to the correct result.

a) 6 or less is rolled — All possible rolls are 6 or less, so this is certain. ⟹ C
b) 1 is rolled — There's one 1 but six numbers altogether. So the probability of rolling 1 is a sixth of the way along the scale. ⟹ A
c) 1 or 2 is rolled — There are two possibilities for this, meaning it's twice as likely as rolling a 1. This means the probability is twice as big. ⟹ B

Exercise 2

1 Match each letter on this scale to the correct probability.

a) 0.5   b) 25%   c) $\frac{1}{6}$ d) 0.4   e) $\frac{2}{3}$

2 Match each letter on this probability scale to one of the events below.

```
        A   B         C             D
        ↓   ↓         ↓             ↓
├───────┼─────────────┼─────────────┼───────┤
0       ¼             ½             ¾       1
```

  a) Rolling an odd number on a fair dice.
  b) Selecting a card at random from a pack of 52 cards and getting a diamond.
  c) Selecting a card at random from a pack of 52 cards and not getting a diamond.
  d) Spinning blue on a fair, three-sided spinner with 1 blue section and 2 orange sections.

3 Draw a probability scale from 0 to 1 and mark on the probabilities of the events below.
  a) Tossing a fair coin and getting heads or tails.
  b) Rolling a fair, six-sided dice and getting a 4, 5 or 6.
  c) Selecting one card at random from cards numbered 1 to 10, and getting:
   (i) the number 7, **(ii)** either the number 9 or the number 10.

27.2 Calculating Probabilities

The **probability** of something happening depends on the **total number of possible outcomes**. When **all** the possible outcomes are **equally likely**, you can work out probabilities using this formula:

$$\text{Probability of event} = \frac{\text{number of ways event can happen}}{\text{total number of possible outcomes}}$$

The probability of event A happening is often written as **P(A)**.

Example 1

A box contains 20 coloured counters, numbered 1 to 20.
11 of the counters are blue, 7 of the counters are purple and 2 of the counters are yellow.
If one counter is selected at random, work out the following probabilities.

  a) The counter is the number 12.
   1. Find the total number of outcomes — there are 20 counters, so... ⟶ Total outcomes = 20
   2. Count the number of outcomes that are 12. There's 1 counter numbered 12, so... ⟶ There's 1 way of getting 12.
   3. Put the numbers into the formula. $P(12) = \frac{1}{20}$

  b) The counter is yellow.
   1. Count the number of outcomes that are yellow. There are 2 yellow counters, so... ⟶ There are 2 ways of getting yellow.
   2. Put the numbers into the formula. $P(\text{yellow}) = \frac{2}{20} = \frac{1}{10}$
      (You already know there are 20 outcomes in total.)

  c) The counter is either blue or yellow.
   Count how many counters are either blue or yellow, and then divide by 20.   13 counters are either blue or yellow.
   $P(\text{blue or yellow}) = \frac{13}{20}$

Section 27 — Probability

Exercise 1

1 State the total number of possible outcomes in each of the following situations.
  a) A coin is tossed.
  b) One card is selected from a pack of 52.
  c) A ten-sided dice is rolled.
  d) A fair spinner with 8 sections is spun.
  e) One day of the week is chosen at random.
  f) One day of the year is chosen at random.

2 This fair spinner is spun once.
  a) How many possible outcomes are there?
  b) What is the probability of spinning a 1?
  c) What is the probability of spinning a 3?

3 Calculate the probability of rolling a fair, six-sided dice and getting each of the following.
  a) 6
  b) 2
  c) 7
  d) 4 or 5
  e) a multiple of 3
  f) a factor of 6

4 Nine cards numbered 1 to 9 are face down on a table. If one of the cards is selected at random, find the probability of selecting each of the following.
  a) card 4
  b) card 1 or 2
  c) an even number
  d) a number less than 6

5 A fair spinner has 12 equal sections. 5 are yellow, 3 are green and the rest are purple. Find the probability that the spinner lands on the following colours.
  a) green
  b) purple
  c) yellow or green
  d) not green

6 A bag contains some coloured balls — 2 black, 4 blue, 2 green, 3 red, 2 yellow, 1 orange, 1 brown and 1 purple. If a ball is selected at random, find the probabilities of getting the following colours.
  a) green
  b) red
  c) orange
  d) black
  e) blue or green
  f) red, green or brown
  g) not purple
  h) white

7 A pack of 52 playing cards is shuffled and one card is selected at random. Find the probability of selecting each of the following.
  a) a club
  b) an ace
  c) a red card
  d) the two of hearts
  e) not a spade
  f) a 4 or a 5

8 For each of the following, draw a copy of the spinner on the right and then number the sections to fit the rule.
  a) The probability of getting 2 is $\frac{3}{8}$.
  b) The probability of getting 3 is $\frac{1}{2}$.
  c) The probability of getting 5 and the probability of getting 6 are both $\frac{1}{4}$.

Exercise 2

1 John was born in 1996 (a leap year). A friend tries to guess John's birthday. What is the probability that he guesses:
  a) the correct month?
  b) the exact date?

2 Diane has 20 different pairs of socks. She picks 1 sock at random. If she then picks another sock at random from the remaining socks, what is the probability that the 2 socks make a pair?

3 A box of chocolates contains 8 caramels, 6 truffles and 4 pralines.
Half of each type of chocolate are coated in milk chocolate and half are coated in white chocolate.
All the chocolates are individually wrapped in identical paper.

Chelsea selects a chocolate at random. She doesn't like pralines or white chocolate.

a) What is the probability that she gets a white-chocolate-coated praline?

b) (i) How many chocolates are <u>neither</u> praline <u>nor</u> coated in white chocolate?

(ii) What is the probability that Chelsea gets a chocolate she likes?

4 At a summer fair, 100 raffle tickets are sold. Each ticket is bought by a different person.
The winning number is drawn at random.

a) What is the probability that the first person to buy a ticket wins the first prize to be drawn?

b) What is the probability that the last person to buy a ticket wins the first prize to be drawn?

5 Explain why the following statement is false.
"When a football team plays a match there are 3 possible outcomes for the team — win, draw and lose. So the probability that they win the match is always $\frac{1}{3}$."

Mutually Exclusive Events

Events that can't happen at the same time are called **mutually exclusive**.
For example, rolling a 1 and rolling a 3 in the same dice roll are mutually exclusive events.

- The probabilities of mutually exclusive events covering **all possible outcomes** always **add up to 1**.
- The probability of something happening and the probability of that thing **not** happening must always add up to 1, because these are mutually exclusive events. This means:

Probability something <u>doesn't</u> happen = 1 – Probability it <u>does</u> happen

Example 2

Jim gets the train to work every day. The probability that his train is late on any day is 0.05.

a) Explain whether the events 'train is late' and 'train is not late' are mutually exclusive.
The train can't be both late and not late, so the events **are mutually exclusive**.

b) Work out the probability that Jim's train is not late.
The train is either late or not late, so... ⟹ P(not late) = 1 – 0.05 = **0.95**

Exercise 3

1 A fair, six-sided dice is rolled. Here are three possible events:

A — a 5 is rolled,   **B** — a number less than 3 is rolled,   **C** — an odd number is rolled

Say whether these pairs of events are mutually exclusive.

a) A and B   b) A and C   c) B and C

2 Charlie chooses one month of the year at random. Here are four possible events.

A — the name begins with J   **B** — the name begins with M
C — the name ends in Y   **D** — it's one of the first four months

Say whether these pairs of events are mutually exclusive.

a) A and B   b) A and C   c) A and D   d) B and C   e) B and D

3 The probability that Jake's school bus is late is 0.2. What is the probability that it's not late?

4 The probability that it will snow in a particular Canadian town on a particular day is $\frac{5}{8}$. What is the probability that it won't snow there on that day?

5 The probability that Clara wins a raffle prize is 25%.
Find the probability that she doesn't win a prize.

6 Gary and Phil have worked out that the probability that Gary beats Phil at tennis is 0.45.
Find the probability that Phil beats Gary at tennis.

7 If the probability that Jed doesn't finish a crossword is 0.74, what's the probability he does finish it?

8 In a class, the probability that a randomly selected pupil is a boy is 0.45, and the probability that the pupil has blonde hair is 0.2. Find the probability that a randomly selected pupil:
   a) is a girl
   b) doesn't have blonde hair

Example 3

A bag contains red, green, blue and white counters.
The table opposite shows the probabilities of randomly selecting a red, green or white counter.
Work out the probability of selecting a blue counter.

Colour	Red	Green	Blue	White
Probability	0.2	0.1		0.5

These are mutually exclusive events, so the probabilities must add up to 1. This means the probability of selecting blue is 1 minus the other 3 probabilities added together.

Probability = 1 – (0.2 + 0.1 + 0.5)
= 1 – 0.8 = **0.2**

Exercise 4

1 This table shows the probabilities of winning the four possible prizes in a lucky dip.
Find the missing probability.

Prize	Lollipop	Pen	Cuddly toy	Gift voucher
Probability	0.4	0.1		0.2

2 This table shows the probabilities of getting each of the five possible colours on a spinner.
   a) Find the missing probability.
   b) Find the probability of spinning 'not pink'.

Colour	Red	Blue	Green	Pink	Black
Probability		0.2	0.1	0.1	0.3

3 When two football teams play each other the probability that Team A wins is 0.4 and the probability that Team B wins is 0.15. What is the probability that the match is a draw?

4 A bag contains some equal-sized discs. The discs are either yellow, orange or red.
If Jack takes out one disc without looking, the probability it's yellow is $\frac{1}{4}$ and the probability it's orange is $\frac{3}{8}$.
Work out the probability that Jack takes a red disc.

5 One counter is selected at random from a box containing blue, green and red counters.
The probability that it's a blue counter is 0.5 and the probability that it's a green counter is 0.4.
If there are 4 red counters in the box, how many counters are there altogether?

Exercise 5 — Mixed Exercise

1 This table shows the number of sweets of various colours in a bag.

Yellow	Orange	Red
6	4	5

  a) If one sweet is chosen at random, find the probability that the sweet:
   (i) is yellow   (ii) is red   (iii) is not red
  b) Three white sweets are added to the bag. Find the probability that a randomly selected sweet:
   (i) is red   (ii) is not red   (iii) is not yellow

2 A game of chance involves spinning the pointer on this circular disc.
  a) What is the probability that the pointer stops on A?
  b) What is the probability that the pointer doesn't stop on C?

3 A fair, six-sided dice is rolled.
  a) What is the probability of rolling an even number?
  b) What is the probability of rolling a multiple of 3?
  c) Explain why your answers to parts **a)** and **b)** don't add up to 1.

27.3 Listing Outcomes

When **two things** are happening at once (for example, tossing a coin and rolling a dice) it's much easier to work out probabilities if you **list all the possible outcomes** in a logical way.

Example 1

Anne has three tickets for a theme park. She chooses two friends at random to go with her. She chooses one girl from Belinda, Claire and Dee, and one boy from Fred and Greg.

a) List all the possible combinations of friends she could choose.

  1. Make a simple two-column table — 1 column for the girls and 1 for the boys.
  2. Write in the first girl and then fill in all the possibilities for the boys.
  3. Repeat for the other 2 girls.
  4. Each row of the table is a possible outcome.

Girls	Boys
Belinda	Fred
Belinda	Greg
Claire	Fred
Claire	Greg
Dee	Fred
Dee	Greg

b) What is the probability that Anne chooses Claire to go with her?

  1. Count the number of rows that Claire's name appears in.   There are 2 outcomes that include Claire.
  2. The total number of rows is the total number of outcomes.   And there are 6 possible outcomes in total.
  3. Divide the two numbers to find the probability.   So probability = $\frac{2}{6}$ or $\frac{1}{3}$

Exercise 1

1 Use a two-column table to list all the possible outcomes when:
   a) two coins are tossed
   b) a six-sided dice is rolled and a coin is tossed

2 A bag contains two balls — one green and one blue. One ball is selected at random, then replaced before a second ball is selected at random. List all the possible combinations of colours.

3 A spinner has three equal sections coloured blue, purple and orange.
List all the possible outcomes if this spinner is spun twice.

4 A burger bar offers the meal deal shown here.
   a) List all the different combinations available.

   Jana picks one combination at random.
   b) What is the probability she chooses a veggie burger and cola?
   c) What is the probability she chooses a cheeseburger?

Choose 1 burger and 1 drink

Burgers	Drinks
Hamburger	Cola
Cheeseburger	Lemonade
Veggie burger	Coffee

5 The spinner on the right is spun twice.
   a) Copy and complete the table to list all the possible combinations of scores.
   b) What is the probability of spinning 3 on each spin?
   c) What is the probability of getting a total of 3 or less over two spins?

1st spin	2nd spin
1	1
1	2

6 a) A coin is tossed three times. List all the possible outcomes.
   b) Work out the probability of getting:
      (i) three tails
      (ii) one head and two tails

Using Two-Way Tables

If there are lots of possible outcomes from **two experiments**, you can use a **two-way table** to record them all.

Example 2

A white four-sided dice and a blue four-sided dice, both numbered 1-4, are rolled together.
a) Draw a two-way table to show all the possible total scores.
   1. Put the outcomes for one dice across the top and those for the other dice down the side.
   2. Fill in each square with the score for the row and the score for the column added together.

	White dice			
	1	2	3	4
Blue dice 1	2	3	4	5
2	3	4	5	6
3	4	5	6	7
4	5	6	7	8

b) What is the probability of scoring a total of 4?
   1. Count how many times a total of 4 appears in the table.
   2. Then divide by the total number of outcomes.

3 of the outcomes are 4 and there are 16 outcomes in total.

So probability = $\frac{3}{16}$

Section 27 — Probability

Exercise 2

1 Copy and complete each of the tables below to show all the possible outcomes.

a) A coin is tossed and a six-sided dice is rolled.

	1	2	3	4	5	6
H	H1	H2				
T						T6

b) A spinner with 3 equal sections, coloured red, white and blue, is spun twice.

	Red	White	Blue
Red	RR		
White			
Blue			

2 Two six-sided dice are rolled.

a) Copy and complete this table to show all the possible total scores.
b) How many possible outcomes are there?
c) Find the probability of each of the following total scores.
  - **(i)** 6
  - **(ii)** 12
  - **(iii)** 1
  - **(iv)** less than 8
  - **(v)** more than 8
  - **(vi)** an even number

	1	2	3	4	5	6
1						
2						
3						
4						
5						
6						

3 A bag contains 3 balls — 1 blue, 1 green and 1 yellow.
A second bag contains 4 balls — 1 blue, 2 green and 1 yellow.
One ball is taken at random from each bag.

a) Copy and complete this table to show all the possible outcomes.
b) Find the probability of selecting:
  - **(i)** 2 blue balls
  - **(ii)** 2 green balls
  - **(iii)** 2 balls the same colour
  - **(iv)** at least 1 yellow ball

	B	G	G	Y
B				
G				
Y				

Exercise 3

1 Tom rolls a six-sided dice and spins a spinner with four equal sections labelled A, B, C and D.

a) Draw a two-way table to show all the possible outcomes.
b) Find the probability that Tom gets each of the following.
  - **(i)** 6 and A
  - **(ii)** C and 5
  - **(iii)** B and less than 3
  - **(iv)** an odd number and B
  - **(v)** C and an even number
  - **(vi)** A or B and more than 4

2 Hayley and Asha are playing a game. In each round they both spin a spinner with five equal sections labelled 1 to 5.

a) Copy and complete this two-way table to show all the possible outcomes for the girls' spins.
b) What is the probability that Hayley gets a higher score than Asha in a round?
c) What is the probability that Asha scores 5 and Hayley scores less than 5 in a round?

Asha's score (2nd number)

Hayley's score (1st number)	1	2	3	4	5
1	1, 1	1, 2			
2	2, 1				
3	3, 1				
4					
5					

27.4 Probability from Experiments

Estimating Probabilities

You can **estimate** probabilities using the results of an experiment or what you know has already happened. Your estimate is called a **relative frequency** (or an **experimental probability**). Work out relative frequency using this formula:

$$\text{Relative Frequency} = \frac{\text{Number of times the result has happened}}{\text{Number of times the experiment has been carried out}}$$

The **more times** you do the experiment, the **more accurate** the estimate should be.

Example 1

A biased dice is rolled 100 times. Here are the results.

Score	1	2	3	4	5	6
Frequency	11	14	27	15	17	16

a) Estimate the probability of rolling a 1.
  1. Find the number of times 1 was rolled.
  2. Divide by the total number of rolls.

1 was rolled 11 times.
So probability $= \frac{11}{100}$

b) Estimate the probability of rolling a 3.
  1. Find the number of times 3 was rolled.
  2. Divide by the total number of rolls.

3 was rolled 27 times.
So probability $= \frac{27}{100}$

Exercise 1

1 Ken wants to estimate the probability that a drawing pin lands with its point up when it's dropped. He drops the drawing pin 50 times and finds that it lands with its point up 17 times.
  a) Use these results to estimate the probability that the drawing pin lands with its point up.
  b) Estimate the probability that the drawing pin lands with its point down.

2 A spinner with four sections is spun 100 times. The results are shown in the table below.

Colour	Red	Green	Yellow	Blue
Frequency	49	34	8	9

  a) Find the relative frequency of each colour.
  b) Sam uses these relative frequencies to estimate the probability of spinning each colour. How could these estimates be made more accurate?

3 Stacy rolls a six-sided dice 50 times, and 2 comes up 13 times.
Jason rolls the same dice 100 times, and 2 comes up 18 times.
  a) Use Stacy's results to estimate the probability of rolling a 2 on this dice.
  b) Use Jason's results to estimate the probability of rolling a 2 on this dice.
  c) Explain whose estimate should be more accurate.

4 Jamal records the colours of the cars passing his school.

Colour	Silver	Black	Red	Blue	Other
Frequency	452	124	237	98	89

  a) Find the relative frequency (as a decimal) of:
   (i) silver   **(ii)** red
  b) Estimate the probability that the next car passing Jamal's school will not be silver, black, red or blue.

Section 27 — Probability

5 Sue wants to know how likely it is that her school bus will arrive on time.
She keeps a record for 6 weeks and finds that the bus is on time 25 times out of 30 days.
Estimate the probability that the next time Sue gets the bus, it will arrive on time.

6 Jack and his dad have played golf against each other 15 times.
Jack has won 8 times, and there have been no draws.
   a) Estimate the probability that Jack will win the next time they play.
   b) Estimate the probability that Jack's dad will win the next time they play.

7 George has burnt 12 of the last 20 cakes he's baked.
Estimate the probability that the next cake he bakes won't be burnt.

8 Lilia wants to estimate the probability that the football team she supports will win a match.
Describe how she could do this.

Expected Frequency

You can **estimate** the **number of times** an event will happen by working out its **expected frequency**.

Expected frequency of an event = probability of the event × number of trials

Here, 'trial' just means an action that could lead to the event happening
— for example, a toss of a coin or a spin of a dice.

Example 2

The probability that a biased dice lands on 1 is 0.3.
How many times would you expect to roll a 1 if you rolled the dice 50 times?

Multiply the probability of rolling a 1 by the number of rolls. ⟹ 0.3 × 50 = **15 times**

Exercise 2

1 The probability that a biased dice lands on 4 is 0.75.
How many times would you expect the dice to land on 4 if it's rolled:
   a) 20 times?   b) 60 times?   c) 100 times?   d) 1000 times?

2 A fair, six-sided dice is rolled 120 times. How many times would you expect to roll:
   a) a 5?   b) a 6?   c) an even number?   d) higher than 1?

3 This spinner on the right has 3 equal sections.
How many times would you expect to spin 'penguin' in:
   a) 60 spins?   b) 300 spins?   c) 480 spins?

4 60% of the people who buy bread from a bakery buy brown bread. If 20 people buy bread from the bakery tomorrow, how many of them would you expect to buy brown bread?

Section 27 — Probability

Frequency Trees

When an experiment has two or more steps, you can record your results in a **frequency tree**.

Example 3 James asks 200 people of various ages to roll a dice.
There were 120 people under the age of 20 and 16 of them rolled a six.
Of the people aged 20 and over, 18 rolled a six.
Fill in the frequency tree below to show this information.

Fill in the bits of the tree given in the question first — the total number of people goes in this box.

The numbers at the end of a set of branches should always add up to the number at the start of the branches.

200 − 120 = 80 people are aged 20 and over
120 − 16 = 104 people under 20 didn't roll a six
80 − 18 = 62 people aged 20 and over didn't roll a six

Exercise 3

1 Copy and complete the frequency trees below:

a) [Frequency tree: 100 → Male (60) → Yes (22), No; Female → Yes (6), No. Labels: Gender, Over 6 foot tall?]

b) [Frequency tree: 500 → Yes → Yes (240), No; No (120) → Yes, No (98). Labels: Travel to work by train?, Late for work?]

2 720 truck drivers were asked to do an eye test. 640 said their vision was fine.
180 of the drivers who said their vision was fine failed the eye test.
30 of the drivers who said their vision wasn't fine passed the eye test.

a) Draw and complete a frequency tree to represent this information.
b) A driver that said their vision wasn't fine is selected at random.
   What is the probability that they failed the eye test?
c) Use your frequency tree to estimate the probability that a randomly selected truck driver says their vision is fine and passes the eye test. Give your answer as a fraction in its simplest form.

Fair or Biased?

Things like dice and spinners are **fair** if they have the same chance of landing on each side or section.
To decide whether something is fair or biased, you need to do an experiment. Then you can compare the **theoretical probability** of each outcome with the **relative frequency** from your experiment.

For example, if you rolled a six-sided dice 100 times, you'd expect it to land on 6 about $\frac{1}{6}$ of the time. But if $\frac{1}{2}$ of the rolls were 6, you'd say the dice was **biased**.

Or you can compare the **frequency** of each outcome in your experiment with the **expected frequency**.

For example, if in 100 trials the expected frequency was 17, but the actual frequency was 50, then you'd say the dice was biased.

Section 27 — Probability **353**

Example 4

Amir thinks his dice is biased. He rolls it 60 times and records the results shown in this table.

Score	1	2	3	4	5	6
Frequency	12	3	9	10	14	12

a) Work out the relative frequencies of each score.
   1. For each score, work out frequency ÷ total number of rolls.
   2. Write the probabilities as decimals so they're easier to compare.

1: $\frac{12}{60} = \mathbf{0.2}$ 2: $\frac{3}{60} = \mathbf{0.05}$

3: $\frac{9}{60} = \mathbf{0.15}$ 4: $\frac{10}{60} = \mathbf{0.17}$

5: $\frac{14}{60} = \mathbf{0.23}$ 6: $\frac{12}{60} = \mathbf{0.2}$

b) Do you think the dice is fair or biased? Explain your answer.
Compare the relative frequencies to the theoretical probability of $\frac{1}{6} = 0.17$ for each score.
The relative frequency of a score of 2 is very different from the theoretical probability, so the experiment suggests that the dice is **biased**.

Exercise 4 — Mixed Exercise

1 A spinner has four sections coloured blue, green, white and pink.
This table shows the results when the spinner is spun 100 times.

a) Work out the relative frequencies of the four colours.
b) Write down the theoretical probability of getting each of the colours, assuming the spinner is fair.
c) Explain whether you think the spinner is fair or biased.

Colour	Blue	Green	White	Pink
Frequency	22	21	18	39

2 A six-sided dice is rolled 120 times and 4 comes up 32 times.

a) How many times would you expect 4 to come up in 120 rolls if the dice is fair?
b) Use your answer to part **a)** to explain whether you think the dice is fair or biased.
c) Explain how you could find a more accurate estimate for the probability of rolling a 4.

3 Three friends each toss a coin and record the number of heads they get.
The table on the right shows their results.

a) Copy and complete the table.
b) Explain whose results should be the most accurate.
c) Explain whether you think the coin is fair or biased.

	Amy	Steve	Hal
No. of tosses	20	60	100
No. of heads	12	33	49
Relative frequency of heads			

4 Information on 800 UK residents' hair and eye colour was collected. The data was recorded in the two-way table shown on the right.

a) Show the information from this two-way table on a frequency tree.
b) Find the relative frequency of someone having brown hair and brown eyes.
c) If you collected the same data on another group of 2000 UK residents, how many would you estimate have brown hair and brown eyes?

		Has brown hair?	
		Yes	No
Has brown eyes?	Yes	220	105
	No	335	140

Section 27 — Probability

27.5 The AND / OR Rules

The AND Rule

The probability of event A **AND** event B both happening is equal to the probability of event A **multiplied** by the probability of event B.

$P(A \text{ and } B) = P(A) \times P(B)$

The AND rule only works when events A and B are **independent** — one event happening does not affect the other happening.

Example 1

A biased dice has a probability of 0.2 of landing on 6. The dice is rolled twice. What is the probability that two sixes are rolled?

The first roll has no effect on the second roll, so the events '6 on first roll' and '6 on second roll' are independent.

P(6 on 1st roll and 6 on 2nd roll)
= P(6 on 1st) × P(6 on 2nd)
= 0.2 × 0.2 = **0.04**

Exercise 1

1. A fair coin is tossed and a fair, six-sided dice is rolled. Find the probability that the results are:
   a) a head and a 6
   b) a head and an odd number
   c) a tail and a square number
   d) a tail and a prime number
   e) a head and a multiple of 3
   f) a tail and a factor of 5

2. 10% of the pupils in a school are left-handed and 15% wear glasses. Assuming that the hand they write with and glasses wearing are independent, find the probability that a pupil picked at random:
   a) is right-handed
   b) doesn't wear glasses
   c) wears glasses and is left-handed
   d) doesn't wear glasses and is right-handed

3. A bag contains ten coloured balls. Five of them are red and three of them are blue. A ball is taken from the bag at random, then replaced. A second ball is then selected at random. Find the probability that:
   a) both balls are red
   b) both balls are blue
   c) neither ball is blue

The OR Rules

If A and B are **mutually exclusive** events: $P(A \text{ or } B) = P(A) + P(B)$

If A and B are **not mutually exclusive** events: $P(A \text{ or } B) = P(A) + P(B) - P(A \text{ and } B)$

Example 2 The fair spinner shown is spun once. What is the probability that it lands on a 2 or a shaded sector?

The spinner can land on both 2 and a shaded sector at the same time so they are <u>not</u> mutually exclusive.

P(2 or shaded)
= P(2) + P(shaded) − P(2 and shaded)
= $\frac{6}{10} + \frac{5}{10} - \frac{2}{10} = \frac{9}{10}$ = **0.9**

Section 27 — Probability

Exercise 2

1 A bag contains some coloured balls. The probability of randomly selecting a pink ball is 0.5, a red ball is 0.4 and an orange ball is 0.1. Find the probability that a randomly selected ball will be:
   a) pink or orange   **b)** pink or red   **c)** red or orange

2 Chocolates in a box are wrapped in four different colours of foil — gold, silver, red or blue. The table shows the probabilities of randomly picking a chocolate wrapped in each colour.

Colour	Gold	Silver	Red	Blue
Probability	0.4	0.26	0.14	0.2

Find the probability of picking a chocolate wrapped in:
   a) red or gold foil   **b)** silver or red foil   **c)** gold or blue foil   **d)** silver or gold foil

3 On sports day, pupils are split into three equal teams — the Eagles, the Falcons and the Ospreys. What is the probability that a pupil picked at random belongs to:
   a) the Eagles?   **b)** the Eagles or the Falcons?   **c)** the Falcons or the Ospreys?

4 A fair 20-sided dice, numbered 1-20, is rolled. What is the probability that it lands on:
   a) a multiple of 3 or an odd number?   **b)** a factor of 20 or a multiple of 4?

5 A card is randomly chosen from a standard pack of 52 playing cards.
   a) What's the probability that it's a red suit or a queen?
   b) What's the probability that it's a club or a picture card?

6 Jane is told that in a class of 30 pupils, 4 wear glasses and 10 have blonde hair.
She says that the probability that a pupil picked at random from the class will have blonde hair or wear glasses is $\frac{10}{30} + \frac{4}{30} = \frac{14}{30}$. Say whether you agree with Jane and explain why.

27.6 Tree Diagrams

Tree diagrams show **all** the possible results for a series of experiments or situations.
They're really useful for working out **probabilities** of combinations of events.

Example 1

A fair coin is tossed twice.
   a) Draw a tree diagram showing all the possible results for the two tosses.
   1. Draw a set of branches for the first toss. You need 1 branch for each of the 2 results.
   2. Draw a set of branches for the second toss. Again, there are two possible results.
   3. Write on the probability for each branch.

   b) Find the probability of getting heads then tails.
   Multiply along the branches for Heads and Tails.   P(H then T) = 0.5 × 0.5 = **0.25**

Exercise 1

1 Copy and complete the following tree diagrams.

   a) A fair spinner has five equal sections — three are red and two are blue. The spinner is spun twice.

   b) A bag contains ten coloured balls — five red, three blue and two green. A ball is selected at random and replaced, then a second ball is selected.

2 For each of these questions, draw a tree diagram showing all the possible results. Write the probability on each branch.

   a) A biased coin lands on heads with a probability of 0.65. The coin is tossed twice.

   b) A spinner with pink and blue sections is spun twice. The probability it lands on pink is 0.3.

   c) The probability a football team wins is 0.7, draws is 0.1 and loses is 0.2. The team plays two matches.

3 The probability that Freddie beats James at snooker is 0.8. They play two games of snooker.

   a) Draw a tree diagram to show all the possible results for the two games.

   b) Find the probability that Freddie wins both games.

4 Sally owns 12 DVDs, four of which are comedies, and Jesse owns 20 DVDs, eight of which are comedies. They each select one of their DVDs at random to watch over the weekend.

   a) Draw a tree diagram showing the probabilities of each choice being 'comedy' or 'not a comedy'.

   b) Find the probability that neither of them chooses a comedy.

   c) Find the probability that at least one of them chooses a comedy.

5 The probability that Alex goes to the cinema on Saturday is 0.7. The probability that Alex goes to the cinema on Sunday is 0.2 if he went on Saturday, and 0.6 if he didn't go on Saturday.

   a) Draw a tree diagram showing the probabilities of Alex going and not going to the cinema on Saturday and Sunday.

   b) What is the probability that Alex goes to the cinema on both days?

   c) What is the probability that Alex goes to the cinema on exactly one of the two days?

6 In a Year 11 class there are 16 boys and 14 girls. They all put their names into a box. One name is selected at random and not replaced, then another name is selected at random.

   a) Draw a tree diagram showing the probabilities of each name selected being a boy or a girl.

   b) What is the probability that two boys are picked?

   c) What is the probability that exactly one girl is picked?

Section 27 — Probability

27.7 Sets and Venn Diagrams

Sets

A **set** is a specific group of items or numbers. The items in a set are called **elements** of the set.
Sets can be written in a number of different ways — e.g. A = {1, 4, 9, 16}, A = {square numbers < 20} and A = { $x : x$ is a square number less than 20} all represent the same set A.

Set Notation

$x \in A$	x is an **element** of A
n(A)	the **number** of elements in A
ξ	the **universal set** (the set containing **all** the elements)
A ∪ B	the **union** of sets A and B (all elements in **either** set)
A ∩ B	the **intersection** of sets A and B (all elements in **both** sets)
A'	the **complement** of set A (all elements **not** in set A)

Example 1

Given that ξ = {positive integers less than 20}, list the elements of the following sets:
a) A = {multiples of 2}   **A = {2, 4, 6, 8, 10, 12, 14, 16, 18}**
b) B = {$x : x$ is a factor of 40}   **B = {1, 2, 4, 5, 8, 10}**
c) A ∪ B   **A ∪ B = {1, 2, 4, 5, 6, 8, 10, 12, 14, 16, 18}**
d) A ∩ B   **A ∩ B = {2, 4, 8, 10}**

Exercise 1

1. a) List the elements of the following sets.
   (i) A = {even numbers between 11 and 25}   (ii) B = {prime numbers less than 30}
   (iii) C = {$x : x$ is a square number < 200}   (iv) D = {factors of 30}
   b) Write down: (i) n(A)   (ii) n(B)   (iii) n(C)   (iv) n(D)

2. A = {1, 2, 4, 5, 7, 8}, B = {2, 4, 6, 8}. Find the following: a) A ∪ B   b) A ∩ B

3. ξ = {positive integers less than 10}, A = {1, 3, 7, 9}, B = {2, 3, 5, 6, 8, 9}. Find the following:
   a) n(A)   b) n(B)   c) A'   d) A ∪ B   e) B'
   f) A ∩ B   g) n(A ∪ B)   h) A' ∪ B   i) A ∩ B'   j) A' ∪ B'

Venn Diagrams

Venn diagrams are used to display **sets** and to show when they overlap.

- The whole diagram represents all the elements of the **universal set**, ξ.
- Elements in this circle are in set A. Any elements **not** in this circle are in the **complement** of set A.
- The entire shaded area represents the **union** of sets A and B (elements in either set A **or** set B).
- The overlap contains all the elements in both set A **and** set B (the **intersection**).

Section 27 — Probability

Example 2

a) Given that ξ = {positive integers less than or equal to 12}, draw a Venn diagram for the sets A = $\{x : x$ is a multiple of 3$\}$ and B = $\{x : x$ is a factor of 30$\}$.

1. Write out sets A and B:
   A = {3, 6, 9, 12}   B = {1, 2, 3, 5, 6, 10}
2. A ∩ B = {3, 6} so these elements go in the overlap (intersection) of the two circles.
3. The elements of ξ that aren't in either set go outside the circles.

b) What is the probability that a randomly selected element is in set A?

Divide the number of elements of set A by the total number of elements.
$$\frac{n(A)}{n(\xi)} = \frac{4}{12} = \frac{1}{3}$$

Exercise 2

1 Draw Venn diagrams to show the following sets, where ξ = {positive integers ≤ 10}.
  a) A = {1, 3, 5}   B = {1, 3, 7}
  b) A = {2, 3, 4, 5}   B = {1, 3, 5, 7, 9}
  c) A = {2, 6, 10}   B = {1, 3, 6, 9}
  d) A = {2, 3, 4, 5, 6}   B = {1, 3, 7}

2 At a fast food restaurant there are two options for side dishes — fries or salad. The number of customers (out of a total of 200) who chose each side dish is recorded in the Venn diagram on the right. What is the probability that a randomly chosen customer:
  a) only had salad?
  b) only had fries?
  c) didn't have a side?
  d) had salad?
  e) had fries?
  f) had fries and salad?

(Fries: 87, intersection: 27, Salad: 76, outside: 10)

3 A survey was taken at a hotel in a ski resort which asked people if they could ski and if they could snowboard. The number of people who could do each activity is shown in the Venn diagram on the right. What is the probability that a randomly chosen hotel guest:
  a) can ski?
  b) can snowboard?
  c) can ski and can snowboard?

(Ski: 118, intersection: 32, Snowboard: 88, outside: 36)

4 a) Given that ξ = {positive integers ≤ 10}, draw a Venn diagram for the sets A = $\{x : x$ is an odd number$\}$ and B = $\{x : x$ is a prime number$\}$.
   b) What is the probability that a randomly chosen element is:
   (i) in B?
   (ii) in A ∩ B?
   (iii) in A ∩ B'?

5 In a class of 30 pupils: 23 like Maths (M), 18 like English (E) and 15 like Maths and English.
   a) Draw a Venn diagram to show this information.
   b) What is the probability that a randomly selected pupil:
   (i) likes Maths and English?
   (ii) only likes Maths?
   (iii) only likes English?
   (iv) doesn't like Maths or English?

Answers and Index

Section 1 — Non-Calculator Arithmetic

1.1 Negative Numbers

Page 1   Exercise 1

1. a) −1   b) 4   c) −1   d) −4
   e) 4   f) −8   g) −11   h) −4
   i) 3   j) −11   k) 5   l) −8
2. a) −2   b) 1   c) 0   d) 5
   e) −12   f) −9   g) 15   h) 0
3. a) −4 °C   b) 3 °C   4. a) 9 °C   b) 3 °C
5. −1 °C   6. 5 °C

Page 2   Exercise 2

1. a) 6   b) 2   c) −9   d) −4
   e) −10   f) 0   g) 7   h) 10
   i) −10   j) 6   k) −9   l) 13
2. a) −6   b) −4   c) 5   d) 9
   e) 8   f) −4   g) 20   h) −20
3. a) 11   b) 4   c) 12   d) 7
4. a) −3 + (−2) = −5   b) 5 − (−5) = 10
   c) 11 + (−7) = 4   d) −8 − (−2) = −6

Page 3   Exercise 3

1. a) −12   b) 5   c) −3   d) −16
   e) −1   f) −5   g) −54   h) 88
   i) 12   j) −7   k) 21   l) 9
   m) −6   n) 9   o) −18   p) 8
   q) 36   r) −42   s) −5   t) −24
2. a) −3 × 2 = −6   b) −14 ÷ 7 = −2
   c) −4 × 4 = −16   d) 10 ÷ (−2) = −5
   e) −8 × 3 = −24   f) −18 ÷ (−6) = 3
   g) −12 × (−3) = 36   h) −77 ÷ 11 = −7
3. a) −6   b) −4   c) 1   d) 10
   e) 15   f) −90   g) −14   h) 72
   i) 50   j) 40   k) 45   l) −1

1.2 Whole Number Arithmetic

Page 3   Exercise 1

1. a) 79   b) 83   c) 219   d) 421
2. a) 63   b) 46   c) 146   d) 46
3. a) 93   b) 568   c) 1021   d) 902
   e) 112   f) 208   g) 495   h) 179
   i) 2754   j) 2654   k) 2618   l) 2768
4. a) 366   b) 816   c) 358   d) 557
   e) 249   f) 917   g) 1636   h) 757
5. 155   6. £1922   7. 588

Page 5   Exercise 2

1. a) 520   b) 187   c) 156   d) 384
   e) 703   f) 645   g) 1696   h) 2088
   i) 4288   j) 3479   k) 6688   l) 9114
   m) 4752   n) 6794   o) 8428   p) 6723

2. a) 2600   b) 3420   c) 8875   d) 11 664
   e) 7595   f) 18 349   g) 25 767   h) 17 015
   i) 22 754   j) 34 362   k) 28 105   l) 42 032
3. 1104   4. £396   5. £12 636
6. 3220 tonnes   7. 13 600 matches
8. a) 26 940   b) 56 775   c) 77 049   d) 236 208
   e) 63 000   f) 41 174   g) 110 166   h) 85 994

Page 6   Exercise 3

1. a) 51   b) 34   c) 67   d) 452
   e) 328   f) 225   g) 560   h) 622
2. a) $72\frac{1}{5}$ b) $1737\frac{2}{3}$ c) $839\frac{3}{5}$ d) $512\frac{1}{9}$
   e) $42\frac{6}{7}$ f) $74\frac{5}{9}$ g) $424\frac{1}{6}$ h) $334\frac{1}{4}$ or $334\frac{2}{8}$
3. a) 28   b) 32   c) 41   d) 48
   e) 206   f) 201   g) 401   h) 256
   i) 311   j) 269   k) 310   l) 352
4. a) 21   b) $26\frac{7}{16}$ or $26\frac{14}{32}$ c) $33\frac{6}{7}$ or $33\frac{18}{21}$
   d) 36   e) 38   f) 61
   g) 58   h) $47\frac{1}{33}$ i) $396\frac{1}{6}$ or $396\frac{3}{18}$
   j) $268\frac{18}{25}$ k) $268\frac{15}{31}$ l) $194\frac{3}{44}$
5. 12 stamps, 8 pence change.
6. 28 people   7. 225 boxes   8. £347
9. a) £432   b) £2053   10. 1256 people

1.3 Decimals

Page 7   Exercise 1

1. $\frac{7}{100}$ 2. $\frac{3}{10}$ 3. $\frac{8}{1000}$ 4. $\frac{1}{10\,000}$
5. 2   6. $\frac{6}{1000}$
7. a) 0.1   b) 0.02   c) 0.005   d) 0.7
   e) 0.07   f) 0.001   g) 0.09   h) 0.8

Page 8   Exercise 2

1. a) 0.31   b) 0.21   c) 0.09   d) 0.472
   e) 8.3   f) 0.05   g) 0.1   h) 0.11
   i) 3.7   j) 7.19   k) 12.1   l) 18.07
2. a) 0.02, 0.15, 0.2   b) 0.16, 0.51, 0.61
   c) 0.559, 0.59, 0.591   d) 0.03, 0.035, 0.04
   e) 0.007, 0.017, 0.07, 0.7   f) 0.41, 1.14, 1.4, 1.41
   g) 0.09, 0.75, 2.03, 2.3   h) 0.078, 0.708, 0.78, 0.782
   i) 0.09, 0.1, 0.101, 0.11   j) 0.61, 1.09, 1.6, 1.66
   k) 0.3, 0.31, 3.01, 3.1   l) 4.05, 4.5, 5.04, 5.4
3. a) −1.5, 1.05, 1.5, 1.55   b) −6, −0.6, 0.6, 6.1
   c) −0.1, −0.09, −0.01, 0.1   d) −5, −0.55, −0.5, −0.45
   e) −7.1, −7.07, −7, 0.007
   f) −0.095, −0.09, −0.05, 0.9

1.4 Adding and Subtracting Decimals

Page 9   **Exercise 1**

1. a) 6.9   b) 11.7   c) 19.9   d) 6.6
   e) 1.1   f) 12.1   g) 18.3   h) 10.1
2. a) 5.3   b) 5.7   c) 9.3   d) 1.6
   e) 3.22   f) 1.86   g) 2.5   h) 6.6
3. a) 18.23   b) 1.829   c) 92.192   d) 7.394
   e) 6.291   f) 14.879   g) 17.381   h) 24.002
   i) 12.679   j) 1.908   k) 1.011   l) 25.579
4. a) 17.13   b) 1.18   c) 6.215   d) 64.96
   e) 63.19   f) 11.14   g) 6.441   h) 0.876
   i) 3.394   j) 2.08   k) 9.31   l) 0.261
5. a) 13.35   b) 12.2   c) 9.62   d) 2.65
   e) 2.15   f) 2.78   g) 0.48   h) 5.95
   i) 12.72   j) 2.08   k) 1.18   l) 2.31
   m) 3.21   n) 15.02   o) 11.85   p) 23.67
6. a) 0.9   b) 4.49   c) 6.972   d) 6.547
7. a) 3.8   b) 9.7   c) 20.04   d) 22.49
   e) 44.92   f) 4.2   g) 4.8   h) 18.3
8. a) 8.494   b) 11.45   c) 17.14   d) 22.12
   e) 7.983   f) 22.97   g) 16.652   h) 1.082
9. a) 7.61 + 0.60 = 8.21   b) 5.98 + 0.42 = 6.40
   c) 6.75 + 2.48 = 9.23   d) 5.43 − 2.12 = 3.31

Page 11   **Exercise 2**

1. 6.9 km   2. £49.50   3. 1.25 m
4. £51.50   5. £83.21   6. 14.85 seconds

1.5 Multiplying and Dividing Decimals

Page 12   **Exercise 1**

1. a) 9.2   b) 141   c) 725   d) 2.3
   e) 19   f) 1460   g) 6070   h) 990
   i) 130.4   j) 7800   k) 0.6   l) 230
2. a) 2.59   b) 8.615   c) 38.17   d) 0.5491
   e) 9.015   f) 0.63   g) 0.0051   h) 0.0094
   i) 0.008   j) 0.0232   k) 6.012   l) 0.017

Page 12   **Exercise 2**

1. a) 3141.6   b) 31.416   c) 0.31416   d) 0.031416
2. a) 477.19   b) 4.7719   c) 0.47719   d) 0.047719
3. a) 126   b) (i) 12.6   (ii) 1.26   (iii) 0.0126
4. a) 253   b) (i) 2.53   (ii) 0.253   (iii) 0.0253
5. a) 53.6   b) 19.2   c) 26.4   d) 44.8
   e) 5.85   f) 19.4   g) 10.8   h) 46.5
6. a) 0.18   b) 0.72   c) 0.006   d) 0.002
   e) 0.04   f) 0.006   g) 0.0008   h) 0.000042
7. a) 1.26   b) 1.4   c) 4.05   d) 0.66

    e) 1.08   f) 0.153   g) 0.064   h) 0.0656
    i) 0.366   j) 0.0066   k) 0.468   l) 0.0094

8. a) 13.23   b) 3.22   c) 4.05   d) 4.32
   e) 32.37   f) 59.34   g) 0.528   h) 1.173
   i) 0.0624   j) 0.2688   k) 0.01769   l) 0.000578

Page 13   **Exercise 3**

1. a) 25.648
   b) (i) 256.48   (ii) 2564.8   (iii) 25 648
2. a) 124   b) 420   c) 363   d) 884.8
   e) 122   f) 402.8   g) 6108   h) 4515
   i) 370.08   j) 24   k) 855.75   l) 606.06

Page 14   **Exercise 4**

1. a) 2.7   b) 3.2   c) 1.54   d) 0.53
   e) 1.03   f) 0.45   g) 14.1   h) 0.231
2. a) 2.13   b) 0.0102   c) 28.2   d) 0.34
   e) 0.535   f) 1.724   g) 2.85   h) 0.009
   i) 0.168   j) 7.05   k) 0.3125   l) 44.55
   m) 0.7025   n) 0.0104   o) 1.5075   p) 0.6122
3. a) 64 ÷ 4   b) 16
4. a) 38.4 ÷ 12   b) 3.2
5. a) 3800 ÷ 8   b) 475
6. a) 32   b) 7.8   c) 2.08   d) 44
   e) 8.85   f) 9.435   g) 11.5   h) 0.55
7. a) 752   b) 821   c) 0.4   d) 5.14
   e) 13.5   f) 255.5   g) 5.04   h) 0.65
8. a) 90   b) 780   c) 1500   d) 7200
9. a) 30   b) 355   c) 700   d) 270
   e) 220   f) 5.93   g) 219   h) 40.03
   i) 2880   j) 0.02   k) 0.0125   l) 1.2
10. a) 1.46   b) 0.146
11. a) 0.6025   b) 0.006025
12. a) 0.152   b) 0.0082   c) 0.0444
    d) 0.004574   e) 0.0283   f) 0.005618
    g) 0.1168   h) 0.0022

1.6 Order of Operations

Page 16   **Exercise 1**

1. a) 8   b) 1   c) 17   d) 16
   e) 8   f) 9   g) 22   h) 33
2. a) 28   b) 15   c) 10   d) 26
   e) 7   f) 25   g) 6   h) 10
   i) 42   j) 6   k) 11   l) 21
3. a) 17   b) 26   c) 3   d) 5
   e) 14   f) 3   g) 2   h) 13
4. a) 9 × (7 − 5) = 18   b) (18 − 6) ÷ 3 = 4
   c) 21 ÷ (4 + 3) = 3   d) (5 + 2) × (6 − 2) = 28
   e) (13 − 5) × (13 − 1) = 96   f) (6 + 8 − 7) × 5 = 35
5. a) 6 + 7 × 2 = 20   b) 16 − 6 ÷ 3 = 14
   c) 11 × 3 + 5 = 38   d) 5 + 16 ÷ 2 = 13
   e) 3 × 6 − 9 = 9
   f) 18 − 4 − 6 = 8 <u>or</u> 18 − (4 + 6) = 8

g) $8 \div 2 + 6 = 10$ or $8 \times 2 - 6 = 10$
h) $(35 - 7) \times 2 = 56$ **i)** $(3 + 7) \times 4 = 40$
j) $13 - 4 + 1 = 10$ or $13 - (4 - 1) = 10$
k) $14 \div (6 + 8) = 1$ **l)** $45 \div (6 + 3) = 5$

Page 16   Exercise 2
1 a) 3 **b)** 4 **c)** 2 **d)** 1
  e) 2 **f)** 2 **g)** 4 **h)** $\frac{9}{2}$
  i) $\frac{3}{5}$ **j)** $\frac{2}{3}$ **k)** 3 **l)** 1

1.7 Non-Calculator Arithmetic Problems

Page 17   Exercise 1
1 a) 3 **b)** –21 **c)** –13 **d)** –16
  e) 8 **f)** 40 **g)** –6 **h)** –14
2 –11 °C   **3** 860 °C   **4** 450 tins
5 95 tickets   **6** £728   **7** 9 coaches
8 a) –4.76 **b)** 3.78 **c)** 24.74 **d)** 7.43
9 a) 0.034 **b)** 34.8 **c)** –10.83 **d)** –2155
10 a) –0.102 **b)** –0.738 **c)** 0.4 **d)** 0.036
11 £1.46   **12** 8.8 pints   **13** £60.75
14 £137.62   **15** £66.75   **16** £27.65
17 a) 3.7128 **b)** 0.37128 **c)** 37.128 **d)** 371.28
18 £2.95   **19** 34 pieces
20 a) –13 **b)** –4 **c)** –2 **d)** 0.3
  e) 0 **f)** 0.08 **g)** –9.6 **h)** 3.2

Section 2 — Approximations

2.1 Rounding — Whole Numbers

Page 18   Exercise 1
1 14.1, 14.02, 13.7, 14.09, 14.4999, 13.901
2 a) 10 **b)** 8 **c)** 12 **d)** 8 **e)** 40
  f) 8 **g)** 46 **h)** 1 **i)** 117 **j)** 663
3 a) 12 **b)** 7 **c)** 25 **d)** 46 **e)** 11
4 a) 30 **b)** 30 **c)** 80 **d)** 70 **e)** 50
  f) 60 **g)** 50 **h)** 490 **i)** 660 **j)** 187 520
5 a) 200 **b)** 600 **c)** 700 **d)** 400
  e) 500 **f)** 5700 **g)** 6300 **h)** 4700
  i) 2400 **j)** 12 300
6 a) 3000 **b)** 9000 **c)** 7000 **d)** 10 000
  e) 9000 **f)** 2000 **g)** 4000 **h)** 0
  i) 3000 **j)** 57 000
7 a) (i) 18 **(ii)** 20 **b) (i)** 16 **(ii)** 20
  c) (i) 202 **(ii)** 200 **d) (i)** 1 **(ii)** 0

Page 19   Exercise 2
1 380   **2** 420
3 301 000 km^2
4 a) 7452 **b) (i)** 7450 **(ii)** 7500 **(iii)** 7000
5 391 000 000 miles
6 a) 674 **b)** 665   **7** 1649

2.2 Rounding — Decimal Places

Page 20   Exercise 1
1 0.41, 0.405, 0.35, 0.4295, 0.4124
2 a) 0.2 **b)** 0.7 **c)** 2.7 **d)** 7.1
  e) 13.6 **f)** 1.3 **g)** 72.4 **h)** 8.4
  i) 0.0 **j)** 5.6 **k)** 1.9 **l)** 4.7

Page 20   Exercise 2
1 0.345, 0.3493, 0.3509, 0.3498, 0.3545
2 a) 4.57 **b)** 0.04 **c)** 6.26 **d)** 0.35
  e) 3.10 **f)** 23.75 **g)** 0.34 **h)** 0.67
  i) 0.08 **j)** 10.30 **k)** 1.17 **l)** 0.09
3 a) 0.967 **b)** 0.255 **c)** 2.437 **d)** 6.533
  e) 0.031 **f)** 3.638 **g)** 5.684 **h)** 3.269
  i) 0.009 **j)** 13.685 **k)** 5.855 **l)** 4.570
4 a) 0.13 **b)** 0.7 **c)** 5.732 **d)** 0.001
  e) 21.35 **f)** 0.3 **g)** 0.40 **h)** 3.30
  i) 0.01 **j)** 3.260 **k)** 11.400 **l)** 29.54
  m) 6.00 **n)** 0.0046
5 0.04 kg   **6** 1.2 metres   **7** 2.458 km   **8** 0.395

2.3 Rounding — Significant Figures

Page 21   Exercise 1
1 a) 500 **b)** 30 **c)** 7000 **d)** 900
  e) 4000 **f)** 80 000 **g)** 100 000 **h)** 1000
2 a) 740 **b)** 6600 **c)** 7100 **d)** 2600
  e) 12 **f)** 670 **g)** 140 000 **h)** 970
3 a) 4760 **b)** 46.9 **c)** 5070 **d)** 595
  e) 35 700 **f)** 694 000 **g)** 80.6 **h)** 925 000
4 a) 50 **b)** 5690 **c)** 7 **d)** 360
  e) 6500 **f)** 757 000 **g)** 100 **h)** 380
  i) 79 000 **j)** 600 000 **k)** 600 **l)** 4 570 000
5 1200 km/h   **6** 121 000 km   **7** 260 cm
8 Austria: 84 000 km^2 Greece: 130 000 km^2
  Italy: 300 000 km^2 Luxembourg: 2600 km^2
  Sweden: 450 000 km^2

Page 22   Exercise 2
1 a) 0.07 **b)** 0.3 **c)** 0.0006 **d)** 0.02
  e) 0.5 **f)** 0.0008 **g)** 0.1 **h)** 0.008
2 a) 0.0038 **b)** 0.026 **c)** 0.00018 **d)** 0.087
  e) 3600 **f)** 0.56 **g)** 0.00070 **h)** 170 000
3 a) 0.579 **b)** 0.0852 **c)** 0.107 **d)** 0.000418
  e) 147 **f)** 34.7 **g)** 0.00845 **h)** 0.438
4 a) 0.005 **b)** 0.19 **c)** 0.00439
  d) 0.006 **e)** 0.0096 **f)** 0.000604
  g) 1600 **h)** 2000 **i)** 0.579
  j) 0.03 **k)** 0.03487 **l)** 0.050
  m) 0.360 **n)** 0.1 **o)** 0.069
5 Common vole: 0.028 kg   Gerbil: 0.15 kg
  Meerkat: 0.78 kg   Red squirrel: 0.20 kg
  Shrew: 0.0061 kg
6 0.09 kg/m^3

2.4 Estimating Answers

Page 23   Exercise 1

1. a) 600 b) 1200 c) 500 d) 0.2 e) 900 f) 700
2. a) (i) 800 (ii) underestimate
   b) (i) 360 (ii) overestimate
   c) (i) 200 (ii) underestimate
   d) (i) 1600 (ii) overestimate
   e) (i) 6000 (ii) overestimate
   f) (i) 5400 (ii) overestimate
3. a) 1800
   b) Yes; the answer on the calculator is approximately 10 times the estimate from part a).
4. a) C: 11.088 b) B: 1222.2 c) C: 13.5
5. a) 4 b) 3 c) 6 d) 4 e) 3 f) 8 g) 10 h) 5 i) 40 j) 3
6. a) 5 b) 1 c) 12 d) 5
7. a) 59.2 b) 62.55 c) 147.96 d) 198.85 e) 496.8 f) 42.68 g) 7.426 h) 21.42 i) 8.225 j) 164.4 k) 142.12 l) 4.125
8. £6.00   9. £100   10. £280
11. a) £70 000 b) £1 400 000
12. £20   13. 360 000

2.5 Rounding Errors

Page 25   Exercise 1

1. a) Minimum = 79.5 Maximum = 80.5
   b) Minimum = 350 Maximum = 450
2. a) $55 \leq a < 65$ b) $8.5 \leq b < 9.5$
   c) $450 \leq c < 550$ d) $14\,500 \leq d < 15\,500$
3. a) $45 \leq e < 55$ b) $0.25 \leq f < 0.35$
   c) $535 \leq g < 545$ d) $13.5 \leq h < 14.5$
4. a) $7.55 \leq i < 7.65$ b) $109.85 \leq j < 109.95$
   c) $2.545 \leq k < 2.555$ d) $1.3325 \leq l < 1.3335$

Page 25   Exercise 2

1. a) 1.3 b) 19.13 c) 55.7 d) 103.671
2. a) $1.3 \leq x < 1.4$ b) $5.13 \leq y < 5.14$
   c) $7.731 \leq z < 7.732$

Section 3 — Powers and Roots

3.1 Squares, Cubes and Roots

Page 26   Exercise 1

1.

x	1	2	3	4	5
x^2	1	4	9	16	25

x	6	7	8	9	10
x^2	36	49	64	81	100

2. a) 121 b) 144 c) 225 d) 400 e) 900

3. a) 16 b) 0.01 c) 100 d) 0.09 e) 0.64 f) 0.36 g) 9 h) 0.04 i) 0.16 j) 225

4.

x	1	2	3	4	5
x^3	1	8	27	64	125

5. a) 216 b) 1000 c) 1331 d) 8000 e) 27 000
6. a) −27 b) −125 c) −1000 d) 0.064 e) 0.125 f) −0.125 g) −216 h) −0.027 i) −0.512 j) −1728
7. a) 4 b) −8 c) 0.01 d) 64 e) 64

Page 27   Exercise 2

1.

x	1	4	9	16
$\sqrt{x}$	1	2	3	4
$-\sqrt{x}$	−1	−2	−3	−4

x	25	36	100
$\sqrt{x}$	5	6	10
$-\sqrt{x}$	−5	−6	−10

2. a) 7 b) −7 c) 9 d) −9 e) 11 f) 13 g) −12 h) 20
3. a) 8, −8 b) 11, −11 c) 13, −13 d) 100, −100 e) 14, −14

Page 27   Exercise 3

1.

x	1	8	27	1000
$\sqrt[3]{x}$	1	2	3	10

x	−1	−8	−27	−1000
$\sqrt[3]{x}$	−1	−2	−3	−10

2. a) 4 b) 5 c) 11 d) −4 e) −5 f) 8 g) 6 h) −9

Page 28   Exercise 4 — Mixed Exercise

1. a) 256 b) 1728 c) 9 d) 100 e) −7 f) 169 g) 3375 h) −100
2. a) 19.683 b) 3.61 c) 3.16 (to 2 d.p.) d) 4.31 (to 2 d.p.) e) 0.01 f) 0.001 g) 0.001 h) −0.01
3. a) 5^2 b) $\sqrt{0.5}$ c) $\sqrt{27}$ d) 5^3 e) 0.5^2 f) $\sqrt{200}$ g) 100^2 h) $\sqrt{1000}$ i) 4^3
4. a) 3 b) 5 c) 2 d) 7

3.2 Indices

Page 28   Exercise 1

1. a) 3^2 b) 2^3 c) 7^5 d) 9^6 e) 12^4 f) 17^3
2. a) 16 b) 32 c) 81 d) 4096 e) 1296 f) 4913 g) 3125 h) 243
3. a) (i) 100 (ii) 1000
      (iii) 10 000 (iv) 100 000
      (v) 1 000 000 (vi) 10 000 000
      (vii) 100 000 000 (viii) 1 000 000 000

b) (i) "10^{15} can be written as a '1' followed by 15 zeros."
(ii) "10^n can be written as a '1' followed by n zeros."

4 a) 10^2 b) 10^3 c) 10^4 d) 10^5
   e) 10^6 f) 10^7 g) 10^9 h) 10^{12}

5 a) 17 b) 35 c) 65 d) 61
   e) 964 f) 1064 g) 118 h) 9657
   i) 0 j) 100 128

6 a) 1 b) –11 c) –36 d) 768
   e) 5000 f) 40 g) 69 h) 1 000 128
   i) 2592 j) 20 903 k) 512 l) 10 000 000
   m) 64 n) 745 o) 0.1296

7 a) 27 b) 1 c) 16 d) 81
   e) 81 f) 100 000 g) 1247 h) 100 002
   i) 1944 j) 1 000 000 000 000

Page 29 Exercise 2

1 a) h^4 b) t^5 c) s^7
   d) k^6 e) y^4 f) m^5

2 a) $a^2 \times b^3$ b) $k^4 \times f^3$ c) $m^4 \times n^2$
   d) $s^4 \times t$ e) $w^3 \times v^3$ f) $p^2 \times q^5$

3 a) 100 b) 200 c) 500
   d) 800 e) 2000 f) 10 000

3.3 Laws of Indices

Page 30 Exercise 1

1 a) 3^8 b) 10^{10} c) 4^{11} d) 7^7 e) 2^{13}

2 a) 6^3 b) 8^3 c) 5^5 d) 6^2 e) 2^7

3 a) 4^9 b) 11^{10} c) 100^{69} d) 14^{28} e) 9^{88}

4 a) $\frac{1}{64}$ b) $\frac{1}{8}$ c) $\frac{1}{25}$ d) $\frac{1}{27}$ e) $\frac{1}{16}$
   f) $\frac{1}{8}$ g) $\frac{16}{9}$ h) $\frac{1}{27}$ i) 81 j) $\frac{25}{16}$

5 a) 4^{16} b) 12^4 c) 8^{11} d) 6^{32} e) 3^{48}
   f) 7^5 g) 4^8 h) 11^{18} i) 8^4 j) 15^{26}
   k) 29^{-7} l) 72^{-20} m) 45^{-18} n) 18^{-4} o) 20^{12}

6 a) 9 b) 2 c) 40 d) 4
   e) 3 f) 13 g) 7 h) 6
   i) 11 j) –7 k) –8 l) –41

7 a) a^{10} b) e^9 c) c^{20} d) b^3 e) m^{48}
   f) y^6 g) h^{19} h) g^{12} i) k^{18} j) b^3
   k) d^{-5} l) j^{-20} m) n^{-21} n) p^{-14} o) x^{68}

8 a) 5 b) 2 c) 6 d) 7
   e) 8 f) 8 g) 3 h) 5
   i) 11 j) –3 k) 23 l) –4

Page 31 Exercise 2

1 a) 3^{14} b) 5^{13} c) 8^{17} d) 9^{35}
   e) 7^2 f) 8 g) 12^{12} h) 4^{14}

2 a) 3^3 b) 8^4 c) 2^7 d) 4
   e) 7^4 f) 5^5 g) 10^5 h) 8^7

3 a) 6^{15} b) 2^3 c) 8^7 d) 5^6

4 $\dfrac{4^4 \div 4^3}{4}$, $\dfrac{5^5 \times 5^9}{(5^2)^7}$

5 a) 2^{-5} b) 7^4 c) 9^6 d) 3^{-12}

6 a) a^7 b) z^7 c) m^{15} d) p^{12}

7 a) r^3 b) s^5 c) y^5 d) t^7

8 a) b^{13} b) x^{-30} c) 1 d) n^{54}

3.4 Standard Form

Page 32 Exercise 1

1 a) 2.5×10^2 b) 1.1×10^3 c) 3.3×10^2
   d) 4.8×10^4 e) 5.9×10^6 f) 2.75×10^6
   g) 8.56×10^3 h) 7.34×10^3 i) 8.0808×10^5
   j) 7.45×10^3

2 a) 2.5×10^{-3} b) 6.7×10^{-3} c) 3.03×10^{-2}
   d) 4.8×10^{-4} e) 5.6×10^{-5} f) 3.75×10^{-1}
   g) 7.8×10^{-5} h) 7.07×10^{-2} i) 2.1×10^{-7}
   j) 5.002×10^{-4}

Page 33 Exercise 2

1 a) 3 000 000 b) 400 c) 94 000
   d) 880 000 e) 4090 f) 198 900 000
   g) 66.9 h) 7.2 i) 0.00000356
   j) 0.0423 k) 0.000945 l) 0.0000888
   m) 0.000000019 n) 0.669 o) 0.00000705

Page 33 Exercise 3

1 a) 3.4×10^2 b) 5.67×10^6 c) 5.05×10^1
   d) 9.07×10^7 e) 9.532×10^3 f) 3.4×10^{-6}
   g) 5.05×10^{-5} h) 5.67×10^{-3}

2 a) 6×10^{11} b) 8×10^5 c) 8.4×10^7
   d) 6.8×10^{-2} e) 1.7×10^1 f) 1.47×10^{11}

3 a) 3×10^2 b) 4×10^3 c) 1.2×10^{-4}
   d) 3×10^3 e) 2×10^{-12} f) 9×10^1

4 a) 8×10^3 b) 9.6×10^2 c) 5×10^5
   d) 1.54×10^9 e) 8.1×10^{-2} f) 1.07×10^{-3}

5 a) 1.9×10^4 b) 5.7×10^{-3} c) 2.2×10^7
   d) 1.2×10^{-2} e) 6×10^3 f) 1×10^1

6 3.2×10^3

Section 4 — Multiples and Factors

4.1 Finding Multiples and Factors

Page 34 Exercise 1

1 a) 4, 8, 12, 16, 20 b) 10, 20, 30, 40, 50
   c) 3, 6, 9, 12, 15 d) 6, 12, 18, 24, 30
   e) 7, 14, 21, 28, 35

2 a) 9, 12, 15, 18, 21 b) 8, 12, 16, 20
   c) 5, 15, 20

3 a) 16 b) 27, 36, 45 c) 30

4 a) 10, 20, 30, 40, 50, 60, 70, 80, 90, 100
   b) 15, 30, 45, 60, 75, 90, 105 c) 30, 60, 90

5 a) 21, 24, 27, 30, 33 b) 20, 24, 28, 32
   c) 24

6 30   7 40, 80

Answers 365

Page 35   Exercise 2

1. a) 1, 4, 8   b) 1, 3   c) 1, 3, 7
   d) 1, 4, 8, 20   e) 1, 4, 7   f) 1
2. a) 2, 3, 6   b) 2, 3, 6, 12   c) 2, 3, 5, 6, 15
   d) 2, 3, 6, 12   e) 2, 5   f) 3, 5, 15
3. a) 1, 2, 5, 10   b) 1, 2, 4
   c) 1, 13   d) 1, 2, 4, 5, 10, 20
   e) 1, 5, 25   f) 1, 2, 3, 4, 6, 8, 12, 24
   g) 1, 5, 7, 35   h) 1, 2, 4, 8, 16, 32
   i) 1, 2, 4, 5, 8, 10, 20, 40
   j) 1, 2, 5, 10, 25, 50
   k) 1, 3, 9   l) 1, 3, 5, 15
   m) 1, 2, 3, 4, 6, 9, 12, 18, 36
   n) 1, 7, 49   o) 1, 2, 3, 4, 6, 8, 12, 16, 24, 48
4. a) 1   b) 1, 2   c) 1, 5   d) 1, 2, 5, 10
5. a) 1, 3, 5, 15   b) 1, 3, 7, 21   c) 1, 3
6. a) 1, 5   b) 1, 3   c) 1, 3, 5, 15
   d) 1, 2, 5, 10   e) 1, 5, 25
7. a) 1, 5   b) 1, 2   c) 1, 5   d) 1

4.2 Prime Numbers

Page 36   Exercise 1

1. a) 15   b) 3, 5
2. a) 33, 35, 39
   b) $33 = 3 \times 11$, so 3 and 11 are factors
   $35 = 5 \times 7$, so 5 and 7 are factors
   $39 = 3 \times 13$, so 3 and 13 are factors
3. 5, 47 and 59
4. a) 2, 3, 5, 7   b) 23, 29
5. a) (i) 2   (ii) 2 or 7
   (iii) 2 or 17   (iv) 2 or 37
   b) Because 2 will always be a factor.
6. They all end in zero, so 10 is a factor of all of them.
   Or: They are all even, so 2 is a factor of all of them.

Page 37   Exercise 2

1. a) (i) 14 → 2, 7   (ii) 33 → 11, 3
   (iii) 10 → 2, 5   (iv) 25 → 5, 5
   b) (i) $14 = 2 \times 7$ (ii) $33 = 11 \times 3$
   (iii) $10 = 2 \times 5$ (iv) $25 = 5^2$
2. a) $15 = 3 \times 5$ b) $21 = 3 \times 7$ c) $22 = 2 \times 11$
   d) $35 = 5 \times 7$ e) $39 = 3 \times 13$
3. a) (i) 30 → 2, 15 → 3, 5   (ii) 44 → 2, 22 → 2, 11
   (iii) 24 → 3, 8 → 2, 4 → 2, 2   (iv) 72 → 9, 8; 9 → 3, 3; 8 → 2, 4 → 2, 2
   b) (i) $30 = 2 \times 3 \times 5$ (ii) $44 = 2^2 \times 11$
   (iii) $24 = 2^3 \times 3$ (iv) $72 = 2^3 \times 3^2$
4. a) $42 = 2 \times 3 \times 7$ b) $66 = 2 \times 3 \times 11$
   c) $70 = 2 \times 5 \times 7$ d) $190 = 2 \times 5 \times 19$
   e) $210 = 2 \times 3 \times 5 \times 7$
5. a) $18 = 2 \times 3^2$ b) $50 = 2 \times 5^2$
   c) $36 = 2^2 \times 3^2$ d) $150 = 2 \times 3 \times 5^2$
   e) $32 = 2^5$
6. a) (i), (ii), (iii) factor trees of 64
   b) $64 = 2^6$. The prime factors are the same whichever factor tree you use.
7. a) $8 = 2^3$ b) $6 = 2 \times 3$
   c) $28 = 2^2 \times 7$ d) $27 = 3^3$
   e) $16 = 2^4$ f) $60 = 2^2 \times 3 \times 5$
   g) $40 = 2^3 \times 5$ h) $98 = 2 \times 7^2$
   i) $24 = 2^3 \times 3$ j) $128 = 2^7$
   k) $168 = 2^3 \times 3 \times 7$ l) $225 = 3^2 \times 5^2$
   m) $325 = 5^2 \times 13$ n) $1000 = 2^3 \times 5^3$
   o) $46 = 2 \times 23$
8. a) $75 = 3 \times 5^2$
   b) 3. This is because $75 \times 3 = 3^2 \times 5^2$ — which is a square number because 3 and 5 are both raised to an even power (2).

366 *Answers*

4.3 LCM and HCF

Page 38   Exercise 1

1. a) 12   b) 15   c) 24   d) 10
   e) 42   f) 36   g) 30   h) 60
2. a) 24   b) 30   c) 30
   d) 36   e) 70   f) 90

Page 39   Exercise 2

1. a) 8, 16, 24, 32, 40, 48, 56, 64, 72, 80
   b) 12, 24, 36, 48, 60, 72, 84, 96, 108, 120
   c) After 24 minutes
2. 20 days   3. 35 sweets
4. a) 330   b) 420   c) 48   d) 90
   e) 1248 f) 143   g) 68   h) 924
5. 299   6. 36

Page 40   Exercise 3

1. a) 1, 2, 4   b) 4
2. a) 1, 2, 5, 10 b) 10
3. a) 4   b) 8   c) 6   d) 12
   e) 1   f) 12 g) 7   h) 7
4. a) 1   b) 1   c) 1
5. a) 2   b) 3   c) 6
   d) 18 e) 12 f) 25
6. a) 2   b) 14 c) 2   d) 6
   e) 6   f) 13 g) 17 h) 12
   i) 9   j) 18

Page 41   Exercise 4 — Mixed Exercise

1. a) (i) 1   (ii) 3   (iii) 5   (iv) 4
   b) (i) 45 (ii) 36 (iii) 30 (iv) 60
2. a) 18
   b) No, because 5 isn't a factor of 36 (or 36 isn't a multiple of 5).
   c) 9 ways:
      1 pile of 36 sweets;   2 piles of 18 sweets
      3 piles of 12 sweets;   4 piles of 9 sweets
      6 piles of 6 sweets;   9 piles of 4 sweets
      12 piles of 3 sweets;   18 piles of 2 sweets
      36 piles of 1 sweet
3. 6 ways
   1 packet of 12 cakes;   2 packets of 6 cakes
   3 packets of 4 cakes;   4 packets of 3 cakes
   6 packets of 2 cakes;   12 packets of 1 cake
4. 9 ways
   1 row of 100 chairs;   2 rows of 50 chairs
   4 rows of 25 chairs;   5 rows of 20 chairs
   10 rows of 10 chairs;   20 rows of 5 chairs
   25 rows of 4 chairs;   50 rows of 2 chairs
   100 rows of 1 chair
5. a) 100, 120, 140   b) 120, 150   c) 120
6. 150   7. 280

8. a) (i) 4   (ii) 72   b) (i) 3   (ii) 300
   c) (i) 6   (ii) 864   d) (i) 4   (ii) 3348
   e) (i) 40   (ii) 1200   f) (i) 28 (ii) 588
   g) (i) 28   (ii) 1540   h) (i) 30 (ii) 900
9. a) $78 = 2 \times 3 \times 13$ $92 = 2^2 \times 23$
   b) LCM = 3588   HCF = 2

Section 5 — Fractions

5.1 Equivalent Fractions

Page 42   Exercise 1

1. a) 2, 3, 4   b) $\frac{2}{4}, \frac{3}{6}, \frac{4}{8}$
2. $\frac{2}{6}, \frac{3}{9}, \frac{4}{12}$
3. a) 2   b) 3   c) 12   d) 3
   e) 25   f) 18   g) 60   h) 90
4. a) 3   b) 5   c) 2   d) 3
   e) 5   f) 27   g) 16   h) 11

Page 43   Exercise 2

1. a) 2   b) $\frac{1}{5}$
   c) Yes. There are no further common factors of the numerator and denominator.
2. a) 5
   b) i) $\frac{9}{15}$
      ii) No. It can be simplified further by dividing numerator and denominator by 3, to get $\frac{3}{5}$
3. a) $\frac{1}{3}$ b) $\frac{1}{4}$ c) $\frac{1}{2}$ d) $\frac{1}{8}$
   e) $\frac{1}{5}$ f) $\frac{5}{12}$ g) $\frac{3}{4}$ h) $\frac{4}{5}$
   i) $\frac{3}{5}$ j) $\frac{3}{8}$ k) $\frac{3}{4}$ l) $\frac{1}{4}$
4. a) $\frac{1}{3}, \frac{1}{4}, \frac{1}{3} - \frac{5}{20}$ b) $\frac{3}{4}, \frac{3}{5}, \frac{3}{5} - \frac{6}{8}$
   c) $\frac{2}{9}, \frac{2}{11}, \frac{2}{9} - \frac{6}{33}$ d) $\frac{3}{4}, \frac{3}{4}, \frac{3}{5} - \frac{24}{40}$
5. a) $\frac{7}{10}$ b) $\frac{35}{46}$ c) $\frac{17}{29}$ d) $\frac{49}{166}$
6. a) $\frac{1}{6}$ b) $\frac{1}{8}$ c) $\frac{10}{27}$ d) $\frac{2}{11}$ e) $\frac{7}{30}$
   f) $\frac{27}{64}$ g) $\frac{3}{4}$ h) $\frac{1}{8}$ i) $\frac{9}{19}$

5.2 Mixed Numbers

Page 44   Exercise 1

1. a) $\frac{6}{3}$ b) $\frac{12}{4}$
2. a) $\frac{12}{6}$ b) $\frac{25}{5}$ c) $\frac{30}{5}$ d) $\frac{65}{5}$
3. a) 12   b) $\frac{13}{3}$
4. a) 15   b) $\frac{17}{5}$
5. a) $\frac{4}{3}$ b) $\frac{9}{7}$ c) $\frac{5}{2}$ d) $\frac{25}{7}$

Answers

6 a) $\frac{9}{5}$ b) $\frac{17}{12}$ c) $\frac{29}{10}$ d) $\frac{53}{10}$
   e) $\frac{19}{4}$ f) $\frac{59}{6}$ g) $\frac{62}{5}$ h) $\frac{110}{7}$
   i) $\frac{41}{6}$ j) $\frac{28}{9}$ k) $\frac{103}{10}$ l) $\frac{23}{3}$

Page 45 Exercise 2

1 a) 7   b) 2   c) 9   d) 6
2 a) 4   b) $1\frac{4}{7}$
3 a) 15   b) $5\frac{2}{3}$
4 a) $1\frac{2}{3}$ b) $1\frac{4}{5}$ c) $1\frac{7}{10}$ d) $1\frac{5}{7}$ e) $1\frac{2}{11}$
   f) $2\frac{1}{4}$ g) $2\frac{1}{6}$ h) $3\frac{1}{5}$ i) $2\frac{2}{9}$ j) $3\frac{2}{3}$
5 a) $\frac{13}{2}$ b) $6\frac{1}{2}$
6 a) $1\frac{1}{2}$ b) $2\frac{1}{2}$ c) $3\frac{1}{3}$ d) $4\frac{1}{2}$ e) $1\frac{1}{3}$
   f) $1\frac{2}{5}$ g) $2\frac{1}{4}$ h) $4\frac{1}{4}$ i) $5\frac{2}{3}$ j) $12\frac{1}{4}$
7 a) $\frac{5}{2}$ b) $3\frac{1}{2}$ c) $\frac{15}{4}$ d) $\frac{11}{3}$

5.3 Ordering Fractions

Page 46 Exercise 1

1 a) $\frac{2}{6}, \frac{1}{6}$ b) $\frac{2}{10}, \frac{3}{10}$ c) $\frac{4}{16}, \frac{5}{16}$
   d) $\frac{8}{20}, \frac{7}{20}$ e) $\frac{3}{8}, \frac{2}{8}$ f) $\frac{1}{12}, \frac{8}{12}$
   g) $\frac{5}{18}, \frac{4}{18}$ h) $\frac{8}{28}, \frac{5}{28}$
2 a) $\frac{5}{10}, \frac{2}{10}$ b) $\frac{4}{12}, \frac{3}{12}$ c) $\frac{10}{70}, \frac{7}{70}$
   d) $\frac{7}{21}, \frac{3}{21}$ e) $\frac{5}{40}, \frac{16}{40}$ f) $\frac{3}{12}, \frac{1}{12}$
   g) $\frac{2}{12}, \frac{3}{12}$ h) $\frac{3}{24}, \frac{4}{24}$
3 a) $\frac{2}{9}, \frac{3}{9}$ b) $\frac{8}{12}, \frac{9}{12}$ c) $\frac{35}{42}, \frac{6}{42}$
   d) $\frac{4}{18}, \frac{9}{18}$ e) $\frac{15}{40}, \frac{32}{40}$ f) $\frac{10}{12}, \frac{7}{12}$
   g) $\frac{35}{40}, \frac{12}{40}$ h) $\frac{18}{45}, \frac{20}{45}$
4 a) $\frac{18}{24}, \frac{15}{24}, \frac{14}{24}$ b) $\frac{4}{20}, \frac{14}{20}, \frac{9}{20}$ c) $\frac{6}{42}, \frac{8}{42}, \frac{15}{42}$
   d) $\frac{12}{24}, \frac{9}{24}, \frac{16}{24}$ e) $\frac{24}{60}, \frac{25}{60}, \frac{22}{60}$ f) $\frac{5}{40}, \frac{14}{40}, \frac{24}{40}$
   g) $\frac{28}{42}, \frac{30}{42}, \frac{35}{42}$ h) $\frac{100}{360}, \frac{105}{360}, \frac{132}{360}$

Page 47 Exercise 2

1 a) $\frac{5}{6}, \frac{4}{6}$ b) $\frac{5}{6}$
2 a) $\frac{16}{40}, \frac{15}{40}$ b) $\frac{2}{5}$
3 a) $\frac{5}{8}$ b) $\frac{7}{10}$ c) $\frac{9}{14}$ d) $\frac{2}{3}$
   e) $\frac{5}{6}$ f) $\frac{2}{3}$ g) $\frac{3}{4}$ h) $\frac{3}{4}$
4 a) $\frac{15}{45}, \frac{12}{45}, \frac{10}{45}$ b) $\frac{2}{9}, \frac{4}{15}, \frac{1}{3}$
5 a) $\frac{7}{16}, \frac{1}{2}, \frac{5}{8}$ b) $\frac{3}{10}, \frac{7}{20}, \frac{2}{5}$

   c) $\frac{7}{12}, \frac{5}{8}, \frac{3}{4}$ d) $\frac{19}{24}, \frac{5}{6}, \frac{11}{12}$
6 a) $\frac{5}{12}, \frac{4}{9}, \frac{2}{3}$ b) $\frac{4}{5}, \frac{9}{10}, \frac{11}{12}$
   c) $\frac{5}{22}, \frac{1}{4}, \frac{3}{11}$ d) $\frac{7}{9}, \frac{4}{5}, \frac{13}{15}$
7 a) $\frac{13}{16}, \frac{5}{6}, \frac{7}{8}$ b) $\frac{7}{27}, \frac{4}{15}, \frac{13}{45}$
   c) $\frac{5}{16}, \frac{7}{20}, \frac{9}{25}$ d) $\frac{4}{15}, \frac{11}{36}, \frac{9}{24}$
8 Ben   9 Charlene

5.4 Adding and Subtracting Fractions

Page 48 Exercise 1

1 a) $\frac{2}{3}$ b) $\frac{2}{5}$ c) $\frac{2}{11}$ d) $\frac{2}{5}$
   e) $\frac{1}{2}$ f) $\frac{2}{3}$ g) $\frac{1}{2}$ h) $\frac{3}{8}$
2 a) $1\frac{1}{2}$ b) $1\frac{1}{2}$ c) $1\frac{3}{5}$ d) $1\frac{1}{5}$
   e) $1\frac{9}{11}$ f) $2\frac{1}{7}$ g) $1\frac{4}{15}$ h) $1\frac{9}{20}$
3 a) $\frac{2}{4}$ and $\frac{1}{4}$ b) $\frac{3}{4}$
4 a) $\frac{7}{10}$ b) $\frac{5}{8}$ c) $\frac{2}{3}$ d) $\frac{1}{2}$
   e) $\frac{1}{9}$ f) $\frac{3}{8}$ g) $\frac{3}{10}$ h) $\frac{1}{18}$
5 a) $\frac{27}{30}$ and $\frac{25}{30}$ b) $\frac{1}{15}$
6 a) $\frac{8}{15}$ b) $\frac{1}{15}$ c) $1\frac{1}{10}$ d) $\frac{5}{12}$
   e) $1\frac{7}{15}$ f) $1\frac{11}{15}$ g) $\frac{3}{28}$ h) $1\frac{32}{99}$
   i) $\frac{31}{120}$ j) $1\frac{29}{63}$ k) $\frac{6}{35}$ l) $1\frac{43}{80}$
7 a) $1\frac{5}{18}$ b) $\frac{7}{16}$ c) $\frac{3}{7}$ d) $1\frac{3}{4}$

Page 49 Exercise 2

1 $\frac{5}{9}$ 2 $\frac{2}{7}$ 3 $\frac{1}{2}$ 4 $\frac{7}{20}$ 5 $\frac{3}{10}$

Page 50 Exercise 3

1 a) $\frac{9}{5}$ b) $2\frac{2}{5}$
2 a) 2   b) $3\frac{1}{4}$ c) $3\frac{3}{5}$
   d) 3   e) $\frac{6}{7}$ f) $1\frac{2}{3}$
3 a) (i) $\frac{11}{5}$ (ii) $\frac{8}{5}$ b) $\frac{3}{5}$
4 a) $3\frac{4}{5}$ b) $1\frac{1}{2}$ c) $6\frac{1}{11}$
   d) $2\frac{3}{5}$ e) 5   f) $5\frac{1}{2}$
5 a) (i) $\frac{11}{4}$ (ii) $\frac{3}{2}$
   b) (i) $\frac{11}{4}$ (ii) $\frac{6}{4}$ c) $4\frac{1}{4}$
6 a) $3\frac{7}{10}$ b) $2\frac{8}{9}$ c) $5\frac{1}{4}$ d) $6\frac{3}{8}$
   e) $1\frac{5}{8}$ f) $1\frac{7}{12}$ g) $2\frac{5}{14}$ h) $5\frac{17}{18}$
7 a) (i) $\frac{7}{6}$ (ii) $\frac{25}{8}$
   b) (i) $\frac{28}{24}$ (ii) $\frac{75}{24}$ c) $4\frac{7}{24}$

8 a) $2\frac{7}{20}$ b) $3\frac{7}{24}$ c) $5\frac{22}{35}$ d) $5\frac{19}{30}$
   e) $3\frac{1}{28}$ f) $1\frac{28}{45}$ g) $\frac{11}{28}$ h) $6\frac{4}{33}$
   i) $8\frac{59}{60}$ j) $3\frac{11}{72}$ k) $5\frac{8}{63}$ l) $3\frac{17}{30}$

5.5 Multiplying and Dividing Fractions

Page 51   Exercise 1

1 a) 2   b) 2   c) 3   d) 15
   e) 3   f) 5   g) 4   h) 7
   i) 13   j) 6   k) −8   l) −8

2 a) $4\frac{1}{2}$ b) $2\frac{1}{2}$ c) $8\frac{1}{2}$ d) $2\frac{1}{2}$
   e) $3\frac{1}{5}$ f) $5\frac{1}{4}$ g) $9\frac{3}{4}$ h) $5\frac{4}{5}$
   i) $3\frac{1}{3}$ j) $-2\frac{2}{9}$ k) $-4\frac{1}{6}$ l) $-13\frac{1}{3}$

Page 52   Exercise 2

1 a) 8   b) 21   c) 12   d) 18
   e) 25   f) 14   g) 15   h) 36
   i) 4   j) −20 k) −28 l) 56

2 a) $11\frac{1}{4}$ b) $8\frac{4}{5}$ c) $12\frac{3}{5}$ d) $22\frac{4}{5}$
   e) $13\frac{5}{7}$ f) $22\frac{1}{2}$ g) $21\frac{1}{3}$ h) $27\frac{1}{2}$
   i) $17\frac{7}{9}$ j) $18\frac{3}{4}$ k) $-19\frac{7}{11}$ l) $-38\frac{3}{4}$

3 a) 27   b) 22   c) 24   d) 30
   e) 15   f) 9   g) $27\frac{1}{2}$ h) $26\frac{1}{4}$

4 a) 27   b) 35   c) 88   d) 180

Page 53   Exercise 3

1 a) $\frac{1}{18}$ b) $\frac{2}{15}$ c) $\frac{3}{28}$ d) $\frac{3}{25}$
   e) $\frac{5}{24}$ f) $\frac{8}{35}$ g) $-\frac{10}{49}$ h) $\frac{21}{80}$

2 a) $\frac{1}{6}$ b) $\frac{1}{10}$ c) $\frac{1}{9}$ d) $\frac{5}{16}$
   e) $\frac{3}{14}$ f) $\frac{3}{8}$ g) $\frac{3}{4}$ h) $-\frac{1}{4}$

3 a) $\frac{10}{7}$ b) $\frac{20}{21}$

4 a) $\frac{1}{2}$ b) $1\frac{13}{20}$ c) $1\frac{2}{9}$ d) $1\frac{1}{2}$
   e) $\frac{10}{21}$ f) $\frac{23}{48}$ g) $3\frac{17}{25}$ h) $\frac{11}{12}$

5 a) $\frac{17}{5}$ b) $\frac{3}{2}$ c) $5\frac{1}{10}$

6 a) $1\frac{1}{2}$ b) 4   c) $2\frac{26}{27}$ d) $2\frac{4}{5}$
   e) $7\frac{29}{42}$ f) $6\frac{11}{24}$ g) $6\frac{2}{63}$ h) $16\frac{29}{60}$

Page 54   Exercise 4

1 a) 3   b) 7   c) $\frac{5}{4}$ d) $\frac{8}{5}$
   e) $\frac{27}{12}$ f) $\frac{10}{9}$ g) $\frac{19}{6}$ h) $\frac{107}{84}$

2 a) $\frac{1}{5}$ b) $\frac{1}{12}$ c) $\frac{1}{9}$ d) $\frac{1}{27}$

3 a) $\frac{5}{4}$ b) $\frac{4}{5}$

4 a) $\frac{5}{8}$ b) $\frac{7}{15}$ c) $\frac{9}{13}$ d) $\frac{4}{11}$
   e) $\frac{12}{23}$ f) $\frac{4}{13}$ g) $\frac{3}{17}$ h) $\frac{7}{30}$

Page 55   Exercise 5

1 a) $\frac{3}{10}$ b) $\frac{5}{12}$ c) $\frac{7}{12}$ d) $\frac{14}{15}$
   e) $\frac{25}{48}$ f) $\frac{12}{35}$ g) $-\frac{15}{16}$ h) $-\frac{49}{50}$

2 a) $\frac{4}{9}$ b) $\frac{1}{2}$ c) $\frac{4}{7}$ d) $1\frac{1}{2}$
   e) $\frac{11}{24}$ f) $1\frac{1}{3}$ g) $-1\frac{1}{3}$ h) $\frac{10}{11}$

3 a) 2   b) 3   c) 5   d) $4\frac{4}{7}$
   e) $\frac{1}{6}$ f) $\frac{2}{15}$ g) $\frac{1}{16}$ h) $\frac{1}{14}$

4 a) $\frac{7}{4}$ b) $\frac{4}{7}$ c) $\frac{8}{35}$

5 a) $\frac{3}{8}$ b) $\frac{5}{9}$ c) $\frac{17}{21}$ d) $\frac{20}{27}$
   e) $3\frac{1}{8}$ f) $1\frac{1}{15}$ g) $2\frac{4}{7}$ h) $\frac{20}{21}$

6 a) $\frac{7}{3}$ and $\frac{9}{5}$ b) $\frac{5}{9}$ c) $1\frac{8}{27}$

7 a) $3\frac{1}{3}$ b) $7\frac{1}{2}$ c) $4\frac{2}{3}$ d) $4\frac{4}{5}$
   e) $\frac{10}{51}$ f) $\frac{9}{28}$ g) $\frac{8}{49}$ h) $\frac{5}{18}$
   i) $1\frac{1}{24}$ j) $2\frac{2}{15}$ k) $2\frac{1}{14}$ l) $-1\frac{47}{63}$
   m) $4\frac{1}{14}$ n) $-2\frac{18}{23}$ o) $2\frac{6}{7}$ p) $-1\frac{27}{50}$

5.6 Fractions and Decimals

Page 56   Exercise 1

1 a) Terminating   b) Terminating
   c) Recurring   d) Terminating
   e) Recurring   f) Terminating
   g) Recurring   h) Terminating
   i) Terminating   j) Recurring
   k) Terminating   l) Recurring

2 a) 0.75   b) 0.8   c) 0.625   d) 0.35
   e) 0.4375   f) 0.15625 g) 0.175   h) 0.46
   i) 0.88   j) 0.828125 k) 0.658   l) 0.7578125

3 a) 1.6   b) 2.125   c) 6.35   d) 2.37
   e) 4.719   f) 5.76   g) 7.34375 h) 8.4375

4 a) $0.\dot{3}$ b) $0.\dot{1}\dot{8}$ c) $0.8\dot{3}$ d) $0.\dot{4}$

5 a) $\frac{1}{4}, \frac{3}{10}, \frac{7}{16}$ b) $\frac{5}{6}, \frac{17}{20}, \frac{7}{8}$ c) $\frac{9}{25}, \frac{3}{8}, \frac{4}{10}$

6 a) $0.\dot{6}0\dot{3}$ b) $0.12\dot{3}\dot{4}$ c) $0.2\dot{6}$ d) $0.\dot{1}23\dot{4}$

Page 58   Exercise 2

1 a) 0.9   b) 0.2   c) 0.3   d) 0.8
2 a) 0.91   b) 0.42   c) 0.99   d) 0.08
3 a) 0.007   b) 0.201   c) 0.041   d) 0.027
4 a) 0.52   b) 0.6   c) 0.635   d) 0.34
   e) 0.086   f) 0.46   g) 0.9   h) 0.492
5 a) 65   b) 0.65
6 a) $\frac{32}{100}$ b) 0.32
7 a) 0.2   b) 0.3   c) 0.9   d) 0.6
8 a) 0.34   b) 0.88   c) 0.86   d) 0.32
9 a) 0.002   b) 0.132   c) 0.515   d) 0.102

10 a) 0.4 **b)** 0.48 **c)** 0.666 **d)** 0.48
  e) 0.09 **f)** 0.86 **g)** 0.35 **h)** 0.615

Page 59   Exercise 3

1 a) 0.375 **b)** 0.3125
2 a) 0.25 **b)** 0.75 **c)** 0.05 **d)** 0.025
  e) 0.0625 **f)** 0.875 **g)** 0.175 **h)** 0.1625

Page 59   Exercise 4

1 a) $\frac{7}{10}$ **b)** $\frac{9}{10}$ **c)** $\frac{1}{10}$ **d)** $\frac{2}{5}$
2 a) $\frac{93}{100}$ **b)** $\frac{7}{100}$ **c)** $\frac{23}{100}$ **d)** $\frac{47}{100}$
3 a) $\frac{1}{250}$ **b)** $\frac{801}{1000}$ **c)** $\frac{983}{1000}$ **d)** $\frac{49}{500}$
4 a) $\frac{3}{5}$ **b)** $\frac{3}{25}$ **c)** $\frac{59}{250}$ **d)** $\frac{7}{20}$
  e) $\frac{1}{20}$ **f)** $\frac{21}{250}$ **g)** $\frac{6}{25}$ **h)** $\frac{7}{40}$
  i) $\frac{7}{500}$ **j)** $\frac{2}{25}$ **k)** $\frac{1}{8}$ **l)** $\frac{3}{8}$

Page 60   Exercise 5

1 $0.5\dot{4}$
2 a) $0.\dot{3}$ **b)** $0.\dot{1}$ **c)** $0.08\dot{3}$ **d)** $0.\dot{4}$
  e) $0.1\dot{6}$ **f)** $0.0\dot{9}$ **g)** $0.\dot{6}$ **h)** $0.3\dot{6}$
  i) $0.4\dot{6}$ **j)** $0.8\dot{3}$ **k)** $0.2\dot{6}$ **l)** $0.\dot{7}$
3 a) $0.3\dot{6}$ **b)** $0.6\dot{2}$ **c)** $0.5\dot{2}$ **d)** $0.2\dot{4}\dot{5}$
4 a) (i) $0.\dot{1}4285\dot{7}$ **(ii)** $0.\dot{2}8571\dot{4}$ **(iii)** $0.\dot{4}2857\dot{1}$
  (iv) $0.\dot{5}7142\dot{8}$ **(v)** $0.\dot{7}1428\dot{5}$
  b) The same pattern of 6 numbers in each.
  c) $0.\dot{8}5714\dot{2}$

5.7 Fractions Problems

Page 60   Exercise 1

1 $\frac{18}{27}, \frac{40}{60}, \frac{12}{18}$ **2** $\frac{10}{8}, \frac{25}{20}$
3 a) 0.35 **b)** 0.084 **c)** 0.075 **d)** 0.875
4 $\frac{2}{3}, \frac{11}{16}, \frac{3}{4}, \frac{5}{6}$
5 a) 0.39, 0.35, 0.32, 0.3
  b) $\frac{3}{10}, \frac{8}{25}, \frac{7}{20}, \frac{39}{100}$
6 (number line with arrows: **a)** $\frac{1}{3}$ **c)** $\frac{5}{12}$ **b)** $\frac{5}{8}$ **d)** $\frac{5}{6}$)
7 a) $1\frac{8}{21}$ **b)** $\frac{11}{72}$ **c)** $1\frac{1}{10}$ **d)** $\frac{11}{40}$
8 a) $\frac{7}{22}$ **b)** $1\frac{2}{7}$ **c)** $\frac{3}{7}$ **d)** $\frac{8}{9}$
9 a) $5\frac{21}{40}$ **b)** $\frac{17}{40}$ **c)** $7\frac{13}{20}$ **d)** $2\frac{1}{8}$
10 a) $2\frac{13}{18}$ **b)** $2\frac{1}{2}$ **c)** $24\frac{1}{16}$ **d)** $4\frac{2}{5}$
11 $4\frac{13}{16}$ inches
12 a) $\frac{7}{12}$ **b)** $\frac{23}{30}$ **c)** $\frac{3}{5}$ **d)** $-\frac{3}{16}$

  e) $1\frac{4}{5}$ **f)** $1\frac{7}{20}$ **g)** $-8\frac{5}{6}$ **h)** $2\frac{47}{56}$
13 a) (i) $2\frac{1}{2}$ **(ii)** 3 **(iii)** $1\frac{1}{4}$
  b) The answer is always 1.
14 a) $\frac{1}{6}, \frac{2}{7}, \frac{1}{3}, \frac{4}{5}$
  b) 6, $3\frac{1}{2}$, 3, $1\frac{1}{4}$ (in the order from **a)**)
  c) 6, $3\frac{1}{2}$, 3, $1\frac{1}{4}$
    They are in the same order as the fractions in **a)**, because the smaller a fraction, the larger its reciprocal.
15 a) Terminating **b)** Recurring **c)** Recurring
  d) Recurring **e)** Terminating
16 $\frac{5}{6}$ and $\frac{2}{9}$ **17 a)** $10\frac{9}{20}$ cm **b)** $5\frac{17}{20}$ cm²
18 a) $\frac{2}{5}$ **b)** $\frac{1}{10}$
19 10
  (The cat will eat $9\frac{1}{3}$ tins, but you can't buy $\frac{1}{3}$ of a tin.)
20 16 questions
21 a) $\frac{4}{15}$ **b)** 20 red, 24 blue and 16 yellow.
22 $\frac{11}{15}$
23 a) 40 **b)** $\frac{4}{5}$ **c)** 80
24 a) $\frac{7}{10}$ **b)** $\frac{5}{12}$ **c)** $\frac{41}{42}$
25 a) $\frac{21}{64}$ **b)** E.g.

26 $\frac{17}{35}$

Section 6 — Ratios

6.1 Ratios and Simplifying

Page 63   Exercise 1

1 3 : 1   **2** 1 : 3   **3** 1 : 6   **4** 17 : 14
5 23 : 15   **6** 2 : 6 = 1 : 3   **7** 4 : 2 = 2 : 1
8 a) 1 : 4 **b)** 1 : 3 **c)** 4 : 1 **d)** 2 : 3
  e) 4 : 1 **f)** 5 : 2 **g)** 1 : 4 **h)** 5 : 3
  i) 4 : 3 **j)** 25 : 3 **k)** 2 : 3 **l)** 3 : 5
  m) 11 : 1 **n)** 2 : 5 **o)** 2 : 3 **p)** 4 : 3
  q) 1 : 4 **r)** 5 : 2 **s)** 3 : 7 **t)** 11 : 3
9 a) 3 : 1 : 2 **b)** 5 : 4 : 1 **c)** 7 : 5 : 1 **d)** 6 : 3 : 5
  e) 2 : 1 : 5 **f)** 6 : 2 : 5 **g)** 2 : 3 : 10 **h)** 3 : 7 : 6
  i) 3 : 8 : 4 **j)** 9 : 10 : 18
10 3 : 1   **11** 4 : 3   **12** 2 : 7   **13** 6 : 5   **14** 13 : 8

Page 64   Exercise 2

1 a) 1 : 10 **b)** 1 : 2 **c)** 1 : 100 **d)** 2 : 1
  e) 2 : 5 **f)** 3 : 20 **g)** 3 : 10 **h)** 2 : 7

2 **a)** 20:3
b) 3:13 (using weeks) or 84:365 (using days)
c) 4:55 **d)** 3:100 **e)** 15:2
f) 5:3 **g)** 1:20 **h)** 5:2
3 1:20 **4** 1:40 **5** 1:9
6 3:14 **7** 4:11 **8** 2:5

Page 65 Exercise 3
1 **a)** 1:3 **b)** 1:5 **c)** 1:4 **d)** 1:4
e) 1:3.5 **f)** 1:6.5 **g)** 1:3.25 **h)** 1:0.5
i) 1:0.3 **j)** 1:3.5 **k)** 1:0.625 **l)** 1:1.8
2 **a)** 1:5 **b)** 1:50 **c)** 1:4 **d)** 1:40
e) 1:80 **f)** 1:40 **g)** 1:12.5 **h)** 1:0.2
3 1:8 **4** 1:3 **5** 1:20 **6** 1:40 000
7 1.25 parts **8** £1:8.5 krone **9** 1:2

6.2 Using Ratios
Page 66 Exercise 1
1 12 **2** 2 **3** 18 **4** 9
5 189 **6** 750 **7** 50 g **8** 35 cm
9 £56 **10** 1.98 m **11** 1500 ml
12 9 slices of courgette, 12 slices of goat's cheese
13 Lizzy is 165 cm, Dave is 185 cm
14 Max – 30 minutes, Maisie – 20 minutes
15 7 **16** 12 **17** 4 **18** 9 minutes

Page 67 Exercise 2
1 $\frac{1}{4}$ **2** $\frac{3}{5}$ **3** $\frac{4}{7}$ **4** $\frac{1}{3}$
5 $\frac{4}{13}$ **6** $\frac{7}{20}$ **7** $\frac{7}{14}=\frac{1}{2}$
8 **a)** true **b)** false **c)** false **d)** true **e)** true
9 $\frac{1}{10}$ **10** $\frac{5}{35}=\frac{1}{7}$
11 **a)** $\frac{5}{10}=\frac{1}{2}$ **b)** $\frac{3}{10}$
12 **a)** $\frac{11}{22}=\frac{1}{2}$ **b)** $\frac{3}{22}$ **c)** $\frac{14}{22}=\frac{7}{11}$

Page 68 Exercise 3
1 1:2 **2** 1:7 **3** 3:7 **4** 7:5
5 16:3 **6** 1:5:2 **7** 3:1 **8** 1:5
9 **a)** 1:4 **b)** 3:2
10 3:1 **11** 3:4:1

Page 69 Exercise 4
1 **a)** $\frac{3}{8}$ **b)** $\frac{5}{8}$ **c)** 5:8 **d)** 3:5
2 **a)** $\frac{3}{7}$ **b)** 3:7 **c)** 4:3
3 15:17 **4** 46:99
5 **a)** $\frac{9}{17}$ **b)** 3:17 **c)** 5:9:17
6 4:5

6.3 Dividing in a Given Ratio
Page 70 Exercise 1
1 **a)** £32 and £16 **b)** £12 and £36
c) £40 and £8 **d)** £28 and £20
2 **a)** 72 kg and 18 kg **b)** 70 kg and 20 kg
c) 48 kg and 42 kg **d)** 36 kg and 54 kg
3 **a)** 7 m and 49 m **b)** 28 m and 28 m
c) 40 m and 16 m **d)** 44 m and 12 m
4 **a)** 100 ml and 900 ml **b)** 500 ml and 500 ml
c) 150 ml and 850 ml **d)** 570 ml and 430 ml
5 **a)** 24 cm, 36 cm and 12 cm
b) 16 cm, 16 cm and 40 cm
c) 30 cm, 18 cm and 24 cm
d) 28 cm, 24 cm and 20 cm
6 **a)** £15, £60 and £75 **b)** £45, £15 and £90
c) £60, £70 and £20 **d)** £65, £55 and £30
7 **a)** £10 **b)** 198 g **c)** 10 kg **d)** 500 ml
8 **a)** £22.50 **b)** 21.6 g **c)** 75 kg **d)** 15 000 ml

Page 71 Exercise 2
1 Kat – 18, Lindsay – 12
2 12 sandwiches and 20 sandwiches
3 72 men and 40 women
4 Lauren – £640, Cara – £560
5 Yellow – 24 litres, red – 18 litres
6 20 **7** 525 **8** £3420

Page 71 Exercise 3
1 Nicky – 8, Jacinta – 16, Charlie – 12
2 £1500, £2500 and £2000
3 Gemma – 155 cm, Alisha – 160 cm, Omar – 175 cm
4 Raspberries – 150 g, strawberries – 225 g, redcurrants – 75 g
5 £25 **6** 40 **7** 14
8 72°, 144°, 36° and 108°
9 Length = 30 cm, width = 6 cm

6.4 Ratio Problems
Page 72 Exercise 1
1 **a)** 2:5 **b)** 1:2.5 **c)** 0.4:1
2 **a)** 2:5 **b)** $\frac{18}{63}=\frac{2}{7}$
3 **a)** $\frac{8}{9}$ **b)** 56
4 36 purple cards
5 **a)** 6:1 **b)** 36
6 **a)** $\frac{3}{5}$ **b)** 120
7 £90
8 **a)** 20 cm **b)** 50 cm

9 30 cm
10 15 books
11 Caroline's is stronger
12 a) 18   **b)** 1 : 2
13 9

Section 7 — Percentages

7.1 Percentages

Page 73   Exercise 1

1 a) 40%   **b)** 47%   **c)** 61%   **d)** 89%
2 a) 13%   **b)** 27%   **c)** 76%   **d)** 243%
3 13%   **4 a)** $\frac{46}{100}$ **b)** 46%
5 a) $\frac{12}{25}$ **b)** $\frac{48}{100}$ **c)** 48%
6 a) $\frac{45}{300}$ **b)** $\frac{15}{100}$ **c)** 15%
7 a) 44%   **b)** 66%   **c)** 15%   **d)** 210%
   e) 6%   **f)** 33%   **g)** 150%   **h)** 89%
8 a) 25%   **b)** 60%   **c)** 60%   **d)** 20%
   e) 160%   **f)** 70%   **g)** 84%   **h)** 75%
   i) 40%   **j)** 20%   **k)** 120%   **l)** 30%
9 a) 75%   **b)** 25%
10 40%   **11** 40%

Page 75   Exercise 2

1 a) 62.5%   **b)** 85%   **c)** 12.2%   **d)** 112%
   e) 28%   **f)** 40.4%   **g)** 38%   **h)** 403.2%
2 60%   **3** 45%   **4** 95%
5 a) 55%   **b)** 32.5%   **c)** 137.5%   **d)** 8%
   e) 37.5%   **f)** 82.5%   **g)** 32.4%   **h)** 353.5%
6 a) 98%   **b)** 15%   **7** 18.5%   **8** 30%

Page 76   Exercise 3

1 a) 12   **b)** 41   **c)** 7.5   **d)** 9
   e) 20   **f)** 30   **g)** 9   **h)** 27
2 a) 12   **b)** 36
3 a) 12
   b) (i) 6   **(ii)** 24   **(iii)** 30   **(iv)** 48
4 a) 9   **b)** 25   **c)** 7   **d)** 13
   e) 27   **f)** 60   **g)** 77   **h)** 77
   i) 33   **j)** 119   **k)** 225   **l)** 78
5 £59.50   **6** 4.95 m   **7** £1330

Page 76   Exercise 4

1 a) 34   **b)** 0.99   **c)** 6.3   **d)** 73.8
   e) 217.6   **f)** 77.7   **g)** 971.7   **h)** 584.73
   i) 420.67   **j)** 2320.86   **k)** 699.79   **l)** 874.56
2 8.16 kg   **3** 119.35 km   **4** 15   **5** £28.56
6 46% of £28 is larger by 34p
7 1584 ml (or 1.584 litres)

7.2 Percentages, Fractions and Decimals

Page 77   Exercise 1

1 a) (i) 50%   **(ii)** 0.5   **(iii)** $\frac{1}{2}$
   b) (i) 25%   **(ii)** 0.25   **(iii)** $\frac{1}{4}$
   c) (i) 10%   **(ii)** 0.1   **(iii)** $\frac{1}{10}$
   d) (i) 20%   **(ii)** 0.2   **(iii)** $\frac{1}{5}$
2 a) $\frac{15}{100}$ **b) (i)** 15%   **(ii)** 0.15
3 a) $0.4\dot{5}$ **b)** $45.\dot{4}\dot{5}\%$
4 a) (i) 0.75   **(ii)** $\frac{3}{4}$ **b) (i)** 0.3   **(ii)** $\frac{3}{10}$
   c) (i) 0.4   **(ii)** $\frac{2}{5}$ **d) (i)** 0.65   **(ii)** $\frac{13}{20}$
   e) (i) 1.25   **(ii)** $\frac{5}{4}$ **f) (i)** 0.95   **(ii)** $\frac{19}{20}$
   g) (i) 0.24   **(ii)** $\frac{6}{25}$ **h) (i)** 0.32   **(ii)** $\frac{8}{25}$
   i) (i) 0.48   **(ii)** $\frac{12}{25}$ **j) (i)** 0.12   **(ii)** $\frac{3}{25}$
   k) (i) 0.02   **(ii)** $\frac{1}{50}$ **l) (i)** 0.06   **(ii)** $\frac{3}{50}$
   m) (i) 0.05   **(ii)** $\frac{1}{20}$ **n) (i)** 0.13   **(ii)** $\frac{13}{100}$
   o) (i) 0.96   **(ii)** $\frac{24}{25}$ **p) (i)** 0.74   **(ii)** $\frac{37}{50}$
5 a) (i) 0.79   **(ii)** 79%   **b) (i)** 0.43   **(ii)** 43%
   c) (i) 0.3   **(ii)** 30%   **d) (i)** 0.7   **(ii)** 70%
   e) (i) 1.5   **(ii)** 150%   **f) (i)** 0.2   **(ii)** 20%
   g) (i) 0.4   **(ii)** 40%   **h) (i)** 1.4   **(ii)** 140%
   i) (i) 0.75   **(ii)** 75%   **j) (i)** 0.875   **(ii)** 87.5%
   k) (i) $0.\dot{3}$ **(ii)** $33.\dot{3}\%$ **l) (i)** $0.\dot{1}$ **(ii)** $11.\dot{1}\%$
   m) (i) $0.1\dot{3}$ **(ii)** $13.\dot{3}\%$ **n) (i)** $0.\dot{6}\dot{3}$ **(ii)** $63.\dot{6}\dot{3}\%$
   o) (i) $0.1\dot{6}$ **(ii)** $16.\dot{6}\%$ **p) (i)** 0.16   **(ii)** 16%
6 a) (i) 35%   **(ii)** $\frac{7}{20}$ **b) (i)** 86%   **(ii)** $\frac{43}{50}$
   c) (i) 70%   **(ii)** $\frac{7}{10}$ **d) (i)** 52%   **(ii)** $\frac{13}{25}$
   e) (i) 60%   **(ii)** $\frac{3}{5}$ **f) (i)** 48%   **(ii)** $\frac{12}{25}$
   g) (i) 5%   **(ii)** $\frac{1}{20}$ **h) (i)** 72%   **(ii)** $\frac{18}{25}$
   i) (i) 36%   **(ii)** $\frac{9}{25}$ **j) (i)** 40%   **(ii)** $\frac{2}{5}$
   k) (i) 1%   **(ii)** $\frac{1}{100}$ **l) (i)** 68%   **(ii)** $\frac{17}{25}$
   m) (i) 14%   **(ii)** $\frac{7}{50}$ **n) (i)** 120%   **(ii)** $\frac{6}{5}$
   o) (i) 12.5%   **(ii)** $\frac{1}{8}$ **p) (i)** 32.5%   **(ii)** $\frac{13}{40}$
7 0.86   **8** 0.08   **9** 60%
10 $\frac{9}{25}$ **11** 68%

Page 79   Exercise 2

1 a) 0.24   **b)** 0.2   **c)** $\frac{1}{5}$, 24%, 0.25
2 a) 0.35   **b)** 68%   **c)** 0.4   **d)** 90%

e) $\frac{21}{100}$ **f)** $\frac{7}{10}$ **g)** $\frac{3}{4}$ **h)** $\frac{3}{5}$

3 a) 40% **b)** 20% **c)** 1.25% **d)** $\frac{4}{9}$
  e) 8% **f)** 0.615 **g)** $\frac{22}{50}$ **h)** $\frac{7}{4}$

4 a) 25%, $\frac{2}{5}$, 0.42 **b)** 45%, $\frac{1}{2}$, 0.505
  c) 0.2%, 0.15, $\frac{1}{5}$ **d)** 0.37, $\frac{3}{8}$, 38%
  e) 0.2, 22%, $\frac{2}{9}$ **f)** 0.7%, 0.07, $\frac{7}{10}$
  g) 11%, 0.111, $\frac{1}{9}$ **h)** 12.5%, 0.13, $\frac{3}{20}$
  i) $\frac{9}{40}$, 23%, 0.25 **j)** 0.5%, 0.02, $\frac{1}{20}$
  k) 0.06%, 0.006, $\frac{3}{50}$ **l)** $\frac{6}{5}$, 1.23, 127%

5 Shop B. **6** No. **7** Oliver. **8** Team X.

Page 80 Exercise 3
1 a) 20% **b)** 30%
2 a) 40% **b)** 12% **c)** 33%
3 51% **4** 21% **5** 20%
6 20% **7** 40% **8** 25%
9 60%

7.3 Percentage Increase and Decrease
Page 81 Exercise 1
1 a) 180 **b)** 540
2 a) 36 **b)** 156
3 a) 16 **b)** 144
4 a) 16.8 **b)** 67.2
5 a) 99 **b)** 45 **c)** 75 **d)** 140
  e) 324 **f)** 176 **g)** 210 **h)** 32.5
  i) 19.8 **j)** 552 **k)** 203 **l)** 185
6 a) 30 **b)** 49.5 **c)** 18 **d)** 12
  e) 17.5 **f)** 60 **g)** 48 **h)** 75
  i) 3.3 **j)** 67.5 **k)** 91 **l)** 442

Page 81 Exercise 2
1 a) 543.9 **b)** 117.16 **c)** 75.35 **d)** 143.29
  e) 177.92 **f)** 570.84 **g)** 1614.06 **h)** 1346.97
  i) 4213.41 **j)** 1274.28 **k)** 48 180 **l)** 868 500
2 a) 70.84 **b)** 28.44 **c)** 71.34 **d)** 57.57
  e) 117.18 **f)** 118.94 **g)** 199.95 **h)** 75.87
  i) 4164.31 **j)** 5253.32 **k)** 72 240 **l)** 95 120

Page 82 Exercise 3
1 £241.50 **2** £28 175 **3** 247 acres
4 £10.50 **5** £582 **6** 2040
7 £921.85 **8** £339.45 **9** £713.73
10 £71.19 **11** 60 inches
12 a) £867.75 **b)** £798.33 **13** £31 291.40

Page 83 Exercise 4
1 a) £380 **b)** £385 **c)** Mary, by £5.
2 a) £9900 **b)** £10 540 **c)** The van, by £640
3 Jason, by 1.2 gallons. **4** Raj, by £250.
5 House A, by £4650. **6** Electricity, by £97.92.
7 Meristock, by 24 264 people (accept 24 265).

Page 84 Exercise 5
1 a) 20% **b)** 10% **c)** 15%
2 a) 20% **b)** 12% **c)** 8%
3 a) 27 **b)** $\frac{27}{45}$ **c)** 60%
4 a) 12 kg **b)** 15%
5 8% **6** 25% **7** 40% **8** 14%
9 35% **10** 60% **11** 2%
12 a) 32% **b)** 50% **c)** 66%

Page 85 Exercise 6
1 £400 **2** £20 **3** £650
4 £200 000 **5** 480 frogs, 540 newts

7.4 Compound Growth and Decay
Page 86 Exercise 1
1 a) £7.50 **b)** £4.17 **c)** £91.35
2 a) £3822.09 **b)** £3994.08
3 a) £231.20 **b)** £196.52
4 £6062.77 **5** 3 days **6** 5 hours

Page 87 Exercise 2
1 a) £1368.57 **b)** £855.58
2 £575 800 (to the nearest £100)
3 334 ants **4** 93.6 kg (to 1 d.p.)

7.5 Percentages Problems
Page 87 Exercise 1
1 10% **2 a)** £56 **b)** £104
3 a) (i) $\frac{1}{5}$ **(ii)** 20% **(iii)** 0.2
  b) (i) $\frac{4}{5}$ **(ii)** 80% **(iii)** 0.8
  c) (i) $\frac{12}{25}$ **(ii)** 48% **(iii)** 0.48
  d) (i) $\frac{8}{25}$ **(ii)** 32% **(iii)** 0.32
4 607.5 g **5** 3.36 kg **6** £0
7 6%, $\frac{2}{33}$, 0.061 **8** Kelly.
9 Shop B, by £16.10
10 a) 76.5% **b)** 294 525
11 £259.88 **12** £3526.25
13 £9.50
14 a) 18 366 **b)** 21 422
15 45.7% (to 1 d.p.) **16** £26 726.72 **17** 12%

Section 8 — Algebraic Expressions

8.1 Collecting Like Terms

Page 89   Exercise 1

1. a) $4b$ b) $3a$ c) $6x$
   d) $14p$ e) $14s$ f) $20n$

2. a) $6y$ b) $12z$ c) $4p$
   d) $5m$ e) $4y$ f) 0
   g) $-4q$ h) $5m$ i) $-y$

3. a) $3c + 2d$ b) $a + 2b$ c) $3x + y$
   d) $4m + 2n$ e) $8x + 2y$ f) $11a + 7b$
   g) $7p + 4q$ h) $3a + 7b$ i) $3b + 3c$

4. a) $3c + 11$ b) $-3x + 2$ c) $-4y + 5$
   d) $-9m + 21$ e) $3x + 10$ f) $21a + 10$

5. a) $5x + y + 12$ b) $-4a + 3b - 8$ c) $7x + 6y - 3$
   d) $5m + 2n + 4$ e) $8x - 3$ f) $21a + 7b + 7$

6. a) $14p + 7q - 4$ b) $7a - 2b + 9$
   c) $8b + 3c + 7$ d) $-13x + 13y + 2z - 5$
   e) $-11m - 5n - 1$ f) $4p + 4q - 20r - 9$

7. a) $x^2 + 5x + 5$ b) $x^2 + 7x - 2$
   c) $2x^2 + 6x + 4$ d) $3x^2 + x$
   e) $3p^2 - 2p$ f) $7p^2 + 2q$
   g) $7p^2 + pq + 3$ h) $p^2 + 4p - 2q - pq$
   i) $2b^2 + 12b + 7$

8. a) $2x^2 + 4ab - cd + 2xy$ b) $p^2 + 2pq + q^2$
   c) $b^2 + 4ab + 3b$
   d) $b^2 + 6abc + 2ab - 3bc + 5b$

9. a) $13 + \sqrt{3}$ b) $-9 - 10\sqrt{7}$ c) $-15\sqrt{5}$
   d) $-4 - 11\sqrt{10}$ e) $-1 - 7\sqrt{2}$ f) $5 - 8\sqrt{6}$

8.2 Expanding Brackets

Page 91   Exercise 1

1. a) $2a + 10$ b) $4b + 12$ c) $5d + 35$
   d) $3p + 12$ e) $4x + 32$ f) $30 - 6r$
   g) $14 + 2y$ h) $8h - 16$ i) $9q - 27$
   j) $2t + 12$ k) $4b - 16$ l) $3k + 18$
   m) $15 + 3p$ n) $42 + 7g$ o) $15 - 5y$
   p) $8a - 8b$

2. a) $xy + 5x$ b) $pq + 2p$ c) $ab + 4a$
   d) $mp + 8m$ e) $pq - 4q$ f) $5s - st$
   g) $5y + xy$ h) $n^2 - 7n$ i) $x^2 - 2x$
   j) $8p - pq$ k) $8x - x^2$ l) $ab - 12a$

Page 92   Exercise 2

1. a) a^3 b) $6a^2$ c) $16pq$ d) $21a^2$
   e) $15xy$ f) m^4 g) $48ab$ h) $48p^2$

2. a) a^2b b) $20a^3$ c) $14pq^2$ d) $8a^2b^2$

Page 92   Exercise 3

1. a) $6p + 12$ b) $20t - 40$ c) $21h + 63$
   d) $10d + 8$ e) $56k - 40$ f) $28 + 16p$
   g) $20 + 28b$ h) $12 - 6z$ i) $16 - 12m$
   j) $18 + 72v$ k) $6n - 36m$ l) $9u + 72v$

2. a) $6n - 18m$ b) $20u + 40v$ c) $35n - 42m$
   d) $3u + 24v$ e) $16x - 28y$ f) $6p - 33q$
   g) $16s - 96t$ h) $24x + 30y$

3. a) $-q - 2$ b) $-x - 7$ c) $-h - 3$
   d) $-g - 3$ e) $-4n - 8$ f) $-14 - 2r$
   g) $-24 - 40a$ h) $-20 - 5z$ i) $-6a - 24$
   j) $-7b - 14$ k) $-22 - 2c$ l) $-60 - 5d$

4. a) $-p + 3$ (or $3 - p$)   b) $-q + 5$ (or $5 - q$)
   c) $-r + 6$ (or $6 - r$)   d) $-s + 2$ (or $2 - s$)
   e) $-4u + 28$ (or $28 - 4u$)   f) $-24 + 2v$ (or $2v - 24$)
   g) $-56 + 8w$ (or $8w - 56$)   h) $-25 + 5x$ (or $5x - 25$)

5. a) $-m - 3$ b) $-n + 11$ c) $-p - 4$
   d) $-q + 7$ e) $-4r + 36$ f) $-26 - 2s$
   g) $-16 + 8t$ h) $-30 - 5u$ i) $-v^2 - 4v$
   j) $-v^2 + 5v$ k) $-12x + x^2$ l) $-4y - y^2$

6. a) $-30g + 18$ b) $-28v - 56$ c) $-10 - 8m$
   d) $-50 + 40v$ e) $-10 - 15n$ f) $-32z + 8z^2$
   g) $-12b + 6$ h) $-8y^2 - 24y$

Page 93   Exercise 4

1. a) $6z + 14$ b) $8c + 38$ c) $12u + 64$
   d) $5c + 19$ e) $9v + 57$ f) $8w + 22$
   g) $12b - 2$ h) $9t + 3$ i) $17m + 29$

2. a) $4p - 21$ b) $c - 17$ c) $4q - 16$
   d) $j - 7$ e) $4y - 18$ f) $14c - 27$

3. a) $8q + 29$ b) $-2c - 48$ c) $18q - 8$
   d) $-a - 14$ e) $17z$ f) $2q + 2$

4. a) $5z + 22$ b) $7c + 30$
   c) $7u + 31$ d) $12p^2 + 17p - 3$
   e) $14m^2 + 45m + 30$ f) $-7k^2 + 3k + 4$
   g) $42b^2 + 69b$ h) $-56t^2 + 81t + 4$
   i) $-19h^2 + 24h$

Page 94   Exercise 5

1. a) $ab + 3a + 2b + 6$ b) $jk - 5j + 4k - 20$
   c) $xy - x - 4y + 4$ d) $xy + 2x + 6y + 12$
   e) $16 + 2y + 8x + xy$ f) $9b - 27 - ab + 3a$
   g) $st + 3t - 5s - 15$ h) $yz - 3y + 12z - 36$

2. a) $2ap + 12a + 2p + 12$
   b) $5xy - 35x + 15y - 105$
   c) $3jk + 12j - 6k - 24$
   d) $8gh + 72g + 40h + 360$
   e) $2wz - 16w - 12z + 96$
   f) $6xy - 12x - 30y + 60$
   g) $27x - 9xy + 108 - 36y$
   h) $7ab - 56a - 49b + 392$

3. a) $x^2 + 11x + 24$ b) $b^2 - 2b - 8$
   c) $a^2 + a - 2$ d) $d^2 + 13d + 42$
   e) $-c^2 - 2c + 15$ f) $-y^2 + 14y - 48$
   g) $z^2 - 3z - 108$ h) $2x^2 + 6x + 4$

4. a) $x^2 + 2x + 1$ b) $x^2 + 8x + 16$
   c) $x^2 + 10x + 25$ d) $x^2 - 4x + 4$
   e) $x^2 - 6x + 9$ f) $x^2 - 14x + 49$
   g) $4x^2 + 24x + 36$ h) $2x^2 - 24x + 72$

Page 94 Exercise 6

1. a) No b) No c) Yes
   d) No e) Yes f) No
2. a) $(x+4)^2 - 4 = (x^2 + 8x + 16) - 4 = x^2 + 8x + 12$
      $(x+6)(x+2) = x^2 + 8x + 12$
      So $(x+4)^2 - 4 \equiv (x+6)(x+2)$
   b) $5(x+2) + (x^2 - 4) = 5x + 10 + x^2 - 4 = x^2 + 5x + 6$
      $(x+4)(x+1) + 2 = (x^2 + 5x + 4) + 2 = x^2 + 5x + 6$
      So $5(x+2) + (x^2 - 4) \equiv (x+4)(x+1) + 2$

8.3 Factorising

Page 95 Exercise 1

1. a) $2(a+5)$ b) $3(b+4)$ c) $5(c+3)$
   d) $4(1+3x)$ e) $3(5+y)$ f) $7(4+v)$
   g) $5(2d+7)$ h) $4(2x+3)$
2. a) $5(a+3b)$ b) $3(3c+4d)$ c) $3(x+4y)$
   d) $7(3u+v)$ e) $4(2c+3f)$ f) $5(5d+7e)$
   g) $4(3x+4y)$ h) $3(x+3y)$
3. a) $4(a^2+3b)$ b) $3(c+5d^2)$
   c) $5(c^2+5f)$ d) $6(x+2y^2)$
4. a) x b) $2y$ c) $8p$ d) $5n$
   e) $5d$ f) $8m$ g) $6a$ h) $2b$
5. a) $a(3a+7)$ b) $b(4b+19)$ c) $x(2x+9)$
   d) $y(7+15y)$ e) $d(10d+27)$ f) $y(4y+13)$
   g) $y(11+3y)$ h) $w(22+5w)$ i) $x(4x-9)$
   j) $q(21q-16)$ k) $y(15-7y)$ l) $z(27z+11)$

Page 96 Exercise 2

1. a) $5a(a+2)$ b) $4b(1+2b)$ c) $3c(c-3)$
   d) $9d(1-2d)$ e) $2f(3f+1)$ f) $7p(p+3)$
   g) $2y(1+9y)$ h) $3h(1-5h)$
2. a) $5c(2c-d)$ b) $10x(2x-y)$ c) $3x(3x+2y)$
   d) $4x(3x+2y)$ e) $2b(a-3b)$ f) $3a(2a+1)$
   g) $4x(y-2x)$ h) $2b(a+6b)$
3. a) $5p(2p+3q)$ b) $4y(3x+2y)$ c) $5a(3b-4a)$
   d) $6q(2q-3p)$ e) $3a(2a+3b)$ f) $4p(3q-2p)$
   g) $2a(4a+3b^2)$ h) $8x(3xy-2)$

Page 96 Exercise 3

1. a) $(x+3)(x+2)$ b) $(x+3)(x+4)$
   c) $(x+7)(x+1)$ d) $(x+6)(x+2)$
   e) $(x+4)(x+1)$ f) $(x+3)^2$
   g) $(x+2)(x+4)$ h) $(y+3)(y+5)$
   i) $(z+2)(z+7)$ j) $(p+1)(p+5)$
   k) $(s+4)(s+6)$ l) $(v+3)(v+8)$
2. a) $(x-1)(x+3)$ b) $(x-4)(x-2)$
   c) $(x-5)(x-2)$ d) $(x-4)(x-1)$
   e) $(x+5)(x-2)$ f) $(x+4)(x-2)$
   g) $(k-2)(k+3)$ h) $(m-4)(m+2)$
   i) $(n-3)(n+7)$ j) $(q-5)(q-3)$
   k) $(r-3)(r+9)$ l) $(u-6)(u-9)$
3. a) $3(x+2)(x+3)$ b) $2(x+3)(x+6)$
   c) $5(x-2)(x-4)$ d) $2(x+5)(x+7)$
   e) $6(x-1)(x-3)$ f) $3(x-4)(x-5)$
   g) $5(x-3)(x+5)$ h) $4(x-3)(x+2)$

Page 97 Exercise 4

1. a) $(x+5)(x-5)$ b) $(x+3)(x-3)$
   c) $(x+6)(x-6)$ d) $(x+9)(x-9)$
2. a) $4x$ b) $(4x)^2 - 3^2$ c) $(4x+3)(4x-3)$
3. a) $(2x+7)(2x-7)$ b) $(x+8)(x-8)$
   c) $(6x+2)(6x-2)$ d) $(3x+10)(3x-10)$
   e) $(b+11)(b-11)$ f) $(4z+1)(4z-1)$
   g) $(5x+4)(5x-4)$ h) $(t+12)(t-12)$
4. a) $(x+\sqrt{7})(x-\sqrt{7})$ b) $(x+\sqrt{3})(x-\sqrt{3})$
   c) $(x+\sqrt{11})(x-\sqrt{11})$ d) $5(x+\sqrt{2})(x-\sqrt{2})$

Page 97 Exercise 5 — Mixed Exercise

1. a) $2(x+2y)$ b) $x(2+x)$ c) $2x(1+2x)$
   d) $8(x+3)$ e) $m^2(7n+4p)$ f) $2y(2-3y)$
   g) $4y(5+3x)$ h) $3p(3r+2q)$
2. a) $7(4a-5b)$ b) $5a(3b-2a)$ c) $12(5x+12y)$
   d) $4rs(7t+10r)$ e) $2abc(2c-3a)$ f) $5q(p+2r)$
   g) $4m(5mn-6)$ h) $23p(q-4)$ i) $5pq(2q-3p)$
   j) $2cd(4d-3c)$ k) $7mn(2m-5n)$ l) $2pq(8q-3p)$
3. a) $(x+1)(x-5)$ b) $(t-4)^2$
   c) $(x+7)(x-7)$ d) $(y-5)(y+4)$
   e) $(x-4)(x+3)$ f) $(y+7)(y+3)$
   g) $(x+6)(x-1)$ h) $(x-9)(x+5)$
   i) $(4a+5)(4a-5)$ j) $(10x+8)(10x-8)$
   k) $(z+1)(z-1)$ l) $(6x+13)(6x-13)$

Section 9 — Equations and Inequalities

9.1 Solving Equations

Page 98 Exercise 1

1. a) $x=3$ b) $x=11$ c) $x=16$ d) $x=26$
   e) $x=15$ f) $x=6$ g) $x=2$ h) $x=11$
   i) $x=-4$ j) $x=26$ k) $x=-9$ l) $x=52$
   m) $x=35$ n) $x=49$ o) $x=49$ p) $x=-1$
2. a) $x=3$ b) $x=2$ c) $x=1$ d) $x=-5$
   e) $x=-5$ f) $x=-8$ g) $x=-6$ h) $x=-2$
3. a) $x=5$ b) $x=18$ c) $x=-16$ d) $x=-8$
   e) $x=6$ f) $x=9$ g) $x=21$ h) $x=-11$
   i) $x=21$ j) $x=22$ k) $x=-4$ l) $x=15$
4. a) $x=-0.5$ b) $x=8.9$ c) $x=-3.5$ d) $x=-2.4$
   e) $x=-0.7$ f) $x=-3.6$ g) $x=-3.71$ h) $x=5.45$

Page 99 Exercise 2

1. a) $x=5$ b) $x=3$ c) $x=6$ d) $x=11$
   e) $x=13$ f) $x=1.5$ g) $x=3.5$ h) $x=6.5$
   i) $x=1.5$ j) $x=0.2$ k) $x=0.75$ l) $x=4.5$
2. a) $x=14$ b) $x=18$ c) $x=10$ d) $x=12$
   e) $x=20$ f) $x=8$ g) $x=16$ h) $x=18$
3. a) $x=-3$ b) $x=-4$ c) $x=-2$ d) $x=-10$
   e) $x=-10$ f) $x=-1.2$ g) $x=-2$ h) $x=-0.2$
4. a) $x=-10$ b) $x=-3$ c) $x=-9$ d) $x=-5$
   e) $x=4$ f) $x=8$ g) $x=-12$ h) $x=-15$

Answers 375

5 a) $x = 4$ b) $x = -0.8$ c) $x = 0.6$
d) $x = -0.068$ e) $x = -0.6$ f) $x = 0.075$
g) $x = -0.6$ h) $x = 0.7$

Page 100 Exercise 3
1 a) $x = 6$ b) $x = 40$ c) $x = 44$ d) $x = -18$
e) $x = 7.5$ f) $x = 1.2$ g) $x = -5.5$ h) $x = -6.4$
2 a) $x = -12$ b) $x = -30$ c) $x = -11$
d) $x = -1.5$ e) $x = -5.25$ f) $x = -4.62$
g) $x = -0.64$ h) $x = -15.75$
3 a) $x = 9$ b) $x = 15$ c) $x = 14$
d) $x = 3.6$ e) $x = 1$ f) $x = -0.15$
g) $x = -0.02$ h) $x = 1.26$

Page 101 Exercise 4
1 a) $x = 7$ b) $x = 10$ c) $x = 8$ d) $x = 4$
e) $x = -4$ f) $x = -5$ g) $x = -3$ h) $x = -2$
2 a) $x = 1$ b) $x = 2$ c) $x = 3$ d) $x = 2$
e) $x = -14$ f) $x = -30$ g) $x = -20$ h) $x = -10$
3 a) $x = 10$ b) $x = 7$ c) $x = 8$ d) $x = 3$
e) $x = -3$ f) $x = -6$ g) $x = -5$ h) $x = -5.5$
4 $x = 8$
5 a) $x = 12$ b) $x = 12$ c) $x = 72$ d) $x = 20$
e) $x = -16$ f) $x = 9$ g) $x = -40$ h) $x = -21$
6 a) $20 = 5x + 10$ b) $x = 2$
7 a) $x = 1$ b) $x = 4$ c) $x = -2$ d) $x = -9$

Page 102 Exercise 5
1 a) $x = 5$ b) $x = 7$ c) $x = 9$ d) $x = 2$
e) $x = -2$ f) $x = -3$ g) $x = -5$ h) $x = -7$
i) $x = 8$ j) $x = 6$ k) $x = 12$ l) $x = 13$
m) $x = 12$ n) $x = 20$ o) $x = 10$ p) $x = 18$
q) $x = -12$ r) $x = -7$ s) $x = -9$ t) $x = -30$

9.2 Solving Harder Equations

Page 102 Exercise 1
1 a) $x = 5$ b) $x = 1$ c) $x = 3$
d) $x = 2$ e) $x = 6$ f) $x = 3$
g) $x = 8$ h) $x = 5$ i) $x = 1$
2 a) $x = 5$ b) $x = 2$ c) $x = 3$
d) $x = 2$ e) $x = 7$ f) $x = 10$
g) $x = 36$ h) $x = 6$ i) $x = 9$
3 a) $x = 0.5$ b) $x = 4.7$ c) $x = -0.6$
d) $x = -2$ e) $x = 0.7$ f) $x = -2.4$
g) $x = 8$ h) $x = 6.3$ i) $x = -9$

Page 103 Exercise 2
1 a) $x = 4$ b) $x = 3$ c) $x = 12$
d) $x = 14$ e) $x = 10$ f) $x = 14$
g) $x = 10$ h) $x = 14$ i) $x = 3$
2 a) $x = -1$ b) $x = -2$ c) $x = 10$
d) $x = 0.5$ e) $x = 3.5$ f) $x = 1.3$
g) $x = -1.6$ h) $x = 2.2$ i) $x = 5.1$
3 a) $x = 5$ b) $x = -5$ c) $x = \frac{2}{3}$

d) $x = -2$ e) $x = 0.6$ f) $x = \frac{2}{7}$
g) $x = \frac{13}{18}$ h) $x = -\frac{2}{9}$

Page 103 Exercise 3
1 a) $x = \frac{4}{5}$ b) $x = 6$ c) $x = 5$
d) $x = \frac{10}{3}$ e) $x = \frac{6}{13}$ f) $x = -6$
g) $x = 8$ h) $x = -5$ i) $x = -10$
2 a) $x = 6$ b) $x = 8$ c) $x = -10$
d) $x = -\frac{20}{3}$ e) $x = -16$ f) $x = 60$

Page 104 Exercise 4
1 a) $x = 8$ b) $x = -1$ c) $x = 5$
d) $x = 11$ e) $x = 8$ f) $x = 21$
2 a) $x = 13$ b) $x = 6$ c) $x = 4$
d) $x = 5$ e) $x = 4$ f) $x = 4$

Page 104 Exercise 5 — Mixed Exercise
1 a) $x = -\frac{3}{4}$ b) $x = -\frac{1}{4}$ c) $x = -\frac{4}{5}$
d) $x = -1$ e) $x = -6$ f) $x = -4$
g) $x = -13$ h) $x = -7$ i) $x = \frac{64}{55}$
2 a) $x = 16$ b) $x = 9$ c) $x = 12$
d) $x = 2$ e) $x = -\frac{5}{4}$ f) $x = \frac{9}{4}$
3 a) $x = 10$ b) $x = 54$ c) $x = 44.4$
d) $x = 12.6$
4 a) $x = -7$ b) $x = \frac{12}{17}$ c) $x = 4$
d) $x = 3$
5 a) $x = -17$ b) $x = -1$ c) $x = 1$

9.3 Writing Your Own Equations

Page 105 Exercise 1
1 a) 7 b) 15 c) 19 d) 29
e) 11 f) 9 g) 36 h) 112
2 a) 8 b) 12 c) 10 d) 13.5

Page 106 Exercise 2
1 a) (i) $8x + 20° = 180°$ (ii) $x = 20°$
b) (i) $7x + 110° = 180°$ (ii) $x = 10°$
c) (i) $60x = 180°$ (ii) $x = 3°$
d) (i) $10x + 40° = 180°$ (ii) $x = 14°$
e) (i) $19x - 10° = 180°$ (ii) $x = 10°$
f) (i) $13x - 15° = 180°$ (ii) $x = 15°$
2 a) (i) $10x + 16 = 146$ (ii) $x = 13$
b) (i) $4x + 26 = 196$ (ii) $x = 42.5$
3 a) $6(x + 4) = 180$ or $6x + 24 = 180$ b) $x = 26$
4 $x = 18$ **5** 34 **6** 16
7 a) $30x + 1 - y$ b) 50p (£0.50)

9.4 Solving Inequalities

Page 107 Exercise 1

1 a) $6 > 1$ b) $2 < 8$ c) $-1 > -3$ d) $-7 < 1$

2 a) x is greater than or equal to 1.
b) x is less than 7.
c) x is greater than -4.
d) x is less than or equal to 9.
e) x is less than 8.
f) x is less than or equal to -5.
g) x is greater than or equal to 3.
h) x is greater than -4.

3 a) $x > 4$ b) $x \leq 12$ c) $x \geq 8$ d) $x < 3$

4 a) 8 9 10 11 **12** 13 14 15 16
b) 18 19 20 21 **22** 23 24 25 26
c) -10 -9 -8 -7 **-6** -5 -4 -3 -2
d) -7 -6 -5 -4 **-3** -2 -1 0 1
e) 14 15 16 17 **18** 19 20 21 22
f) -29 -28 -27 -26 **-25** -24 -23 -22 -21
g) 30 31 32 33 **34** 35 36 37 38
h) 41 42 43 44 **45** 46 47 48 49
i) 53 54 55 56 **57** 58 59 60 61
j) 61 62 63 64 **65** 66 67 68 69
k) -11 -10 -9 -8 **-7** -6 -5 -4 -3
l) -8 -7 -6 -5 **-4** -3 -2 -1 0

Page 108 Exercise 2

1 a) $x > 5$
1 2 3 4 **5** 6 7 8 9
b) $x \leq 9$
5 6 7 8 **9** 10 11 12 13
c) $x \geq 16$
12 13 14 15 **16** 17 18 19 20
d) $x < 26$
22 23 24 25 **26** 27 28 29 30
e) $x \geq 30$
26 27 28 29 **30** 31 32 33 34
f) $x > -3$
-7 -6 -5 -4 **-3** -2 -1 0 1
g) $x < 2$
-2 -1 0 1 **2** 3 4 5 6
h) $x \leq -2$
-6 -5 -4 -3 **-2** -1 0 1 2

2 a) $x > 17$ b) $x < 10$ c) $x \geq 1$ d) $x \leq 13$
e) $x \geq 4$ f) $x > 13$ g) $x < -30$ h) $x \leq 5$

3 a) 6 is greater than x.   b) $x < 6$
c) 2 3 4 5 **6** 7 8 9 10

4 a) $x \leq 12$ b) $x > 4$ c) $x \geq 15$ d) $x < 14$

5 a) $x > 16$
12 13 14 15 **16** 17 18 19 20
b) $x \geq 16$
12 13 14 15 **16** 17 18 19 20
c) $x < 18$
14 15 16 17 **18** 19 20 21 22
d) $x \leq 1$
-3 -2 -1 0 **1** 2 3 4 5

6 a) $x \geq 3$ b) $x < 5$ c) $x > 4$ d) $x \leq 3$
e) $x < -4$ f) $x > -8$ g) $x \leq 3$ h) $x < 22.5$
i) $x \geq 9.5$ j) $x < 7.5$ k) $x \geq -8$ l) $x \leq -0.75$

7 a) $x \geq 6$ b) $x < 10$ c) $x < 24$ d) $x \leq 35$
e) $x < -8$ f) $x \leq 3$ g) $x \geq 11$ h) $x < -0.64$
i) $x < 6.6$ j) $x \geq -1.2$ k) $x \leq 0.18$ l) $x < -0.69$

8 a) $x < 3$ b) $x \leq 8$ c) $x \geq 2$ d) $x > 11$
e) $x \geq -12$ f) $x > 1$ g) $x < 2.1$ h) $x \leq 6.5$

9 a) $x < 1$ b) $x \geq 6$ c) $x > 22$ d) $x \leq 10$

10 a) $x \geq 14$ b) $x > 3$ c) $x < 16.8$ d) $x \leq 11.84$

Page 110 Exercise 3

1 a) 0 1 2 3 4 5 **6** 7 8
b) 11 **12** 13 14 **15** 16 17 18 19
c) **-1** 0 1 2 3 4 5 6 7 8
d) 24 **25** 26 27 28 29 **30** 31 32
e) 3 **4** 5 6 7 8 **9** 10 11

Answers 377

f) 34 35 36 37 38 39 40 41 42

g) −1 0 1 2 3 4 5 6 7

h) 35 36 37 38 39 40 41 42 43

i) −2.4 −2 −1 0 1 1.6

2 a) $4 < x \le 12$

   4 5 6 7 8 9 10 11 12

b) $6 \le x \le 16$

   6 7 8 9 10 11 12 13 14 15 16

c) $-6 \le x \le -1$

   −7 −6 −5 −4 −3 −2 −1 0 1

d) $37 \le x \le 60$

   30 35 40 45 50 55 60 65 70

e) $2.6 \le x < 7.2$

   2.5 3 3.5 4 4.5 5 5.5 6 6.5 7 7.5

f) $1.2 < x < 19.7$

   0 2 4 6 8 10 12 14 16 18 20

3 a) $4 < x < 7$ **b)** $16 < x \le 21$ **c)** $-3 < x \le 5$
   d) $6 < x \le 16$ **e)** $-3 \le x < 4$ **f)** $5.6 < x \le 8.4$

4 a) $2 < x < 4$ **b)** $4 < x \le 10$
   c) $-7 < x \le 12$ **d)** $4 < x \le 4.6$
   e) $-3.3 \le x < -2.1$ **f)** $\frac{17}{3} < x \le 9$

Page 111   Exercise 4 — Mixed Exercise

1 a) $x > 15$ **b)** $x \le 20$ **c)** $x \ge 6$
   d) $x < 28$ **e)** $x \le 9$ **f)** $x \ge 15.98$
   g) $x < 26.24$ **h)** $x > 10.74$

2 a) $x \ge 21$ **b)** $x < 9.5$ **c)** $x \ge -\frac{56}{9}$
   d) $x \le -0.9$ **e)** $x \le 12$ **f)** $x > 75$
   g) $x \ge -20$ **h)** $x < -64$

3 a) $x < 5$ **b)** $x \le -2$ **c)** $x \ge 1$
   d) $x > \frac{7}{4}$ **e)** $x < 0$ **f)** $x \le -\frac{5}{12}$
   g) $x \ge -1$ **h)** $x > \frac{79}{46}$

4 a) $x < 20$ **b)** $x \ge 23.6$ **c)** $x \le 30.6$
   d) $x > 18.8$

5 a) $-\frac{5}{2} < x < 1$ **b)** $-6 < x \le 7$ **c)** $0 < x \le 2$
   d) $-3 < x \le 11$

9.5 Simultaneous Equations

Page 111   Exercise 1

1 a) $x = 4, y = 2$ **b)** $x = 7, y = 1$
   c) $x = 7, y = 2$ **d)** $x = 5, y = 3$
   e) $x = -2, y = 4$ **f)** $x = 6, y = 1$
   g) $x = 3, y = -5$ **h)** $x = 8, y = 0$

2 a) $x = 2, y = 5$ **b)** $x = 1, y = 4$
   c) $x = 6, y = 2$ **d)** $x = 3, y = 1$
   e) $x = 5, y = 0$ **f)** $x = 3, y = 2$
   g) $x = 1, y = 6$ **h)** $x = 2, y = -2$
   i) $y = 1, d = 5$ **j)** $e = 3, r = 1$
   k) $p = 3, m = -2$ **l)** $c = 11, v = 2$

3 a) $c = 3, d = 1$ **b)** $x = 1, y = 2$
   c) $x = 4, y = 2$ **d)** $p = 5, q = -1$
   e) $u = 2, v = 1$ **f)** $k = -1, l = 3$
   g) $e = 3, f = 2$ **h)** $m = 2, n = -1$

4 $x = 40, y = 18$

5 Sherbet dip = 20p, Supa-Choc bar = 50p

9.6 Solving Quadratic Equations

Page 113   Exercise 1

1 a) $x = -2, x = 2$ **b)** $x = -1, x = 1$
   c) $x = -5, x = 5$ **d)** $x = -8, x = 8$
   e) $x = -11, x = 11$ **f)** $x = -10, x = 10$
   g) $x = -\sqrt{2}, x = \sqrt{2}$ **h)** $x = -\sqrt{7}, x = \sqrt{7}$

Page 113   Exercise 2

1 a) $x = 0, x = -8$ **b)** $x = 0, x = 5$
   c) $x = 0, x = -6$ **d)** $x = 0, x = 3$

2 a) $x = 0, x = -6$ **b)** $x = 0, x = -1$ **c)** $x = 0, x = 6$
   d) $x = 0, x = 24$ **e)** $x = 0, x = 3$ **f)** $x = 0, x = -5$
   g) $x = 0, x = 1$ **h)** $x = 0, x = 12$

Page 114   Exercise 3

1 a) $x = 5, x = 1$ **b)** $x = -2, x = -6$
   c) $x = 9, x = -7$

2 a) (i) $(x+5)(x+2)$ **(ii)** $(x+5)(x+4)$
   (iii) $(x+4)(x+9)$ **(iv)** $(x+6)(x-4)$
   b) (i) $x = -5, x = -2$ **(ii)** $x = -5, x = -4$
   (iii) $x = -4, x = -9$ **(iv)** $x = -6, x = 4$

3 a) $x = -1$ **b)** $x = -2, x = -1$
   c) $x = 3, x = 4$ **d)** $x = -2$
   e) $x = 2$ **f)** $x = -5, x = 3$
   g) $x = 6, x = 4$ **h)** $x = 3, x = 2$
   i) $x = 7, x = -3$

9.7 Equations and Inequalities Problems

Page 114   Exercise 1

1 a) $x = 4$ **b)** $x = 35$ **c)** $x = 23.5$ **d)** $x = 15$
   e) $x = 9$ **f)** $x = -12$ **g)** $x = -3$ **h)** $x = -6$
   i) $x = -63$ **j)** $x = -32$ **k)** $x = 5$ **l)** $x = -11$

2 a) $x = 4$ b) $x = \frac{3}{4}$ c) $x = 0$
   d) $x = 9$ e) $x = -16$ f) $x = -31$
   g) $x = \frac{63}{13}$ h) $x = 15$ i) $x = 1$

3 a) $x = \frac{51}{8}$ b) $x = \frac{46}{11}$ c) $x = \frac{81}{19}$
   d) $x = \frac{35}{11}$ e) $x = -\frac{128}{21}$ f) $x = \frac{15}{2}$

4 £33.75   **5** 35 pence

6 a) $5x + 30° = 180°$ b) (triangle with angles 100°, 40°, 40°)

7 (triangle with angles 68°, 47°, 65°)

8 $x = 30$ **9** $x = 31$

Page 115 Exercise 2

1 a) $x > 25$
   b) $x \leq 8$
   c) $x \geq -18$
   d) $x > -10$
   e) $x \geq 3.5$
   f) $x < -10$
   g) $x \leq 87.8$
   h) $x < -4.23$
   i) $x \geq 28$
   j) $x < 12$
   k) $x < 63$
   l) $x \leq 7$
   m) $x \geq 7$
   n) $x < 800$
   o) $x > 8$
   p) $x \leq 15$

2 a) $x \leq 11$ b) $x \geq 5$ c) $x < 13$ d) $x > 6$
   e) $x > 25$ f) $x \leq 26$ g) $x < -2$ h) $x \geq -\frac{55}{6}$

3 a) $5 < x \leq 7$
   b) $3 < x < 5$
   c) $-1 \leq x < 3$
   d) $-7 \leq x \leq -2$
   e) $1 < x < 2$
   f) $-4 < x \leq 7$

4 a) $x = -2, y = 3$ b) $p = 7, q = 1$
   c) $r = 6, s = 3$ d) $m = -2, n = -4$

5 a) $x = -6, x = 6$ b) $x = -9, x = 9$
   c) $x = -\sqrt{3}, x = \sqrt{3}$ d) $x = -\sqrt{5}, x = \sqrt{5}$
   e) $x = -3, x = 3$ f) $x = -4, x = 4$

6 a) $x = -1, x = 5$ b) $x = 2, x = 12$
   c) $x = 1, x = 6$ d) $x = 3, x = 7$
   e) $x = -3, x = -6$ f) $x = 2, x = -11$

7 $x = 2$

8 $x = 7$

9 a) $(x + 5)(x + 5)$, so $a = 5$
   b) $x = 4$

Section 10 — Formulas and Functions

10.1 Writing Formulas

Page 116 Exercise 1

1 a) $c + 6$ b) $s - 3$ c) $p - 8$ d) $r + 20$

2 a) $d - 8$ b) $6 - s$ c) $2m$ d) $\frac{1}{3}c$

3 a) $2f$ b) $3f$ c) $3f - 6$

4 $3b + 5$ **5** $8h + 18$

6 a) $0.25n$ b) $0.25n + 7$

Page 117 Exercise 2
1. $C = 3h$ 2. $T = 2k$ 3. $P = 8w$ 4. $n = a + 2$
5. $d = r - 5$ 6. $C = F + 5.5n$ 7. $C = pt + 25$
8. $C = 0.22m + 10$
9. $C = (0.8 \times 60h) + 125$ or $C = 48h + 125$

10.2 Substituting into a Formula

Page 118 Exercise 1
1. a) 11 b) 4 c) 5 d) 42
2. a) –11 b) –1 c) –7 d) –4
3. a) 6 b) 2 c) 7 d) –1
   e) 8 f) 9 g) 7 h) 21
4. a) 42 cm² b) 48 cm²
   c) 84 cm² d) 138 cm²
   e) 222 cm² f) 246 cm²
5. a) 59 °F b) 42.8 °F
   c) 75.2 °F d) 212 °F
6. a) 7.27 m/s b) 28.6 m/s c) 16.7 m/s
   d) 178 m/s e) 8000 m/s
7. a) 12 b) 16 c) –5 d) 4
   e) 4 f) 12 g) 0.75 h) 36
8. a) 55 b) 5050 c) 500 500 d) 12 502 500
9. a) –8 b) –7 c) –12 d) –14
   e) –27 f) –1 g) –29 h) 90
10. a) 1.9 b) 8 c) –12.8 d) 31.68
    e) –32.768 f) –0.4 g) 25.6 h) 137.472
11. a) 3 b) $\frac{2}{3}$ c) $-\frac{4}{9}$ d) $-\frac{1}{4}$
    e) $\frac{5}{12}$ f) $1\frac{1}{12}$ g) $2\frac{2}{3}$ h) $\frac{1}{2}$
12. a) 100 °C b) 18 °C c) –40 °C d) 37 °C
13. a) 78.5 cm² (to 1 d.p.) b) 38.5 cm² (to 1 d.p.)
    c) 387.1 cm² (to 1 d.p.) d) 128.7 cm² (to 1 d.p.)
14. a) 2.0 s (to 1 d.p.) b) 1.4 s (to 1 d.p.)
    c) 1.0 s (to 1 d.p.) d) 7.9 s (to 1 d.p.)
15. a) 12 m² b) 3 m² c) 12 m² d) 0.36 m²
16. a) 226 cm³ b) 1900 cm³
17. a) 25.1 cm³ b) 303 cm³
18. a) 38 b) 267 c) 16.24
    d) 48.3159 e) –53 f) –120.6525
19. a) 44 b) 1241.5 c) 585.466
    d) 5866.476 e) –864.2602 f) 780.3752

10.3 Rearranging Formulas

Page 121 Exercise 1
1. a) $x = y - 2$ b) $x = b + 5$ c) $x = z - 7$
   d) $x = m - 2.3$ e) $x = p + 8.4$ f) $x = z - 12$
2. a) $x = z - r$ b) $x = 3y - 4r$ c) $x = 16r - 23t$
3. a) $x = \frac{z}{4}$ b) $x = \frac{p}{17}$ c) $x = \frac{r}{4.2}$
   d) $x = \frac{s}{3.7}$ e) $x = \frac{s}{6}$ f) $x = \frac{s}{3.5}$

4. a) $x = 8y$ b) $x = 17z$ c) $x = 8.6t$
   d) $x = 4m$ e) $x = 6.1n$ f) $x = 17.4p$
5. a) $x = \frac{abc}{2}$ b) $x = \frac{t}{y}$ c) $x = \frac{uv + y}{4.2}$
   d) $x = \frac{v}{7.3w}$ e) $x = \frac{vwy}{6}$ f) $x = \frac{2z + 4}{2.2y}$
6. a) $x = -\frac{p}{3}$ b) $x = -5q$ c) $x = -\frac{n}{6}$
   d) $x = -9m$ e) $x = -\frac{r}{2.1}$ f) $x = -2.5s$
7. a) $y = \frac{5}{4}a$ b) $y = \frac{4}{3}b$ c) $y = \frac{3}{2}c$
   d) $y = \frac{11}{7}d$ e) $y = \frac{3}{10}e$ f) $y = \frac{7}{20}f$
8. a) $s = y + 4$ b) $s = 11t$ c) $s = \frac{4}{3}d$
   d) $s = \frac{5}{4}m$ e) $s = -\frac{r}{16}$ f) $s = -\frac{p}{14.2}$
   g) $s = \frac{4}{5}a$ h) $s = -\frac{7}{6}b$ i) $s = -\frac{c}{11.6}$
9. a) $h = \frac{V}{\pi r^2}$ b) (i) 2 cm (ii) 2.4 cm

Page 123 Exercise 2
1. a) $x = \frac{y - 3}{5}$ b) $x = \frac{z + 2}{8}$ c) $x = \frac{p - 18}{15}$
   d) $x = \frac{m - 3}{6}$ e) $x = \frac{n - 4}{5}$ f) $x = \frac{r + 8}{2}$
2. a) $y = 3z - 4$ b) $y = 4x - 7$ c) $y = 9s + 2$
   d) $y = 9.7t + 5.3$ e) $y = -3v - 11$ f) $y = 5w + 65$
3. a) $x = \frac{u}{4} + 2$ b) $x = \frac{v}{8} - 4$ c) $x = \frac{w}{3} + 4$
   d) $x = 8 - \frac{p}{6}$ e) $x = -\frac{q}{5} - 1$ f) $x = -5r - 5$
4. a) $y = \frac{p + 5}{4}$ b) $y = \frac{q - 4}{9}$ c) $y = \frac{r + 4}{21}$
   d) $y = \frac{s - 15}{8}$ e) $y = \frac{t + 8}{3}$ f) $y = \frac{u + 3}{13}$
5. a) $a = \frac{v - u}{t}$
   b) 7 c) 4.1 d) 9.81 (to 2 d.p.)
6. a) $c = \frac{5}{9}(f - 32)$
   b) (i) 10 (ii) $26\frac{2}{3}$ or 26.7 (1 d.p.)
   (iii) $-34\frac{4}{9}$ or –34.4 (1 d.p.) (iv) 0
7. a) $d = \sqrt{\frac{A}{21.5}}$ b) (i) 4 cm (ii) 2.5 cm
8. a) $x = \frac{P}{4} - \frac{y}{2}$ b) (i) 2 (ii) 6
9. a) $x = \frac{y}{5}$ b) $x = y - 3$ c) $x = \frac{y}{y + 1}$

10.4 Functions

Page 125 Exercise 1
1. a) $y = 11$ b) $y = 14$ c) $y = 16$ d) $y = 5$
2. a) $y = 48$ b) $x = 15$
3. a) $y = -9$ b) $x = 3$

4 a) $x \longrightarrow \boxed{\times 4} \longrightarrow \boxed{+1} \longrightarrow y$ b) $x = 4$
5 a) $y = 6x - 3$ b) $y = \dfrac{x + 2}{4}$
   c) $y = 2(x + 5)$ d) $y = \dfrac{x}{7} + 3$

10.5 Formulas and Functions Problems

Page 126   Exercise 1

1 a) $c = w - 45$ b) 80
2 a) $h = \dfrac{m - 1}{5}$ b) 7
3 a) £24   b) $n = \dfrac{C - 7.5}{0.06}$ c) 550 units
4 a) $C = 1.25n + 30$ b) £70
   c) $n = \dfrac{C - 30}{1.25}$ d) 40
5 a) $T = 35w + 25$ b) 207 minutes
   c) $w = \dfrac{T - 25}{35}$ d) 5.8 kg
6 a) $b \longrightarrow \boxed{\times 3} \longrightarrow \boxed{+ 50} \longrightarrow w$ b) 650
   c) $b \longrightarrow \boxed{\times 4} \longrightarrow \boxed{+ 50} \longrightarrow t$ d) 120

Section 11 — Sequences

11.1 Sequences — Term-to-Term Rules

Page 127   Exercise 1

1 5, 9, 13, 17, 21
2 2, 4, 8, 16, 32
3 a) 100, 94, 88, 82, 76   b) 40, 20, 10, 5, 2.5
   c) 11, –22, 44, –88, 176
4 a) 3   b) 15, 18, 21
5 a) 2   b) 48, 96, 192
6 a) (i) Add 2 to the previous term.
      (ii) 11, 13, 15
   b) (i) Multiply the previous term by 2.
      (ii) 16, 32, 64
   c) (i) Multiply the previous term by 3.
      (ii) 324, 972, 2916
   d) (i) Add 3 to the previous term.
      (ii) 16, 19, 22
   e) (i) Subtract 2 from the previous term.
      (ii) –3, –5, –7
   f) (i) Add 0.5 to the previous term.
      (ii) 3, 3.5, 4
   g) (i) Multiply the previous term by 10.
      (ii) 100, 1000, 10 000
   h) (i) Divide the previous term by 2.
      (ii) 12, 6, 3
7 a) (i) Subtract 4 from the previous term.
      (ii) –16, –20, –24
   b) (i) Multiply the previous term by 3.
      (ii) –81, –243, –729
   c) (i) Divide the previous term by 2.
      (ii) 1, 0.5, 0.25
   d) (i) Multiply the previous term by –2.
      (ii) 16, –32, 64
8 a) Add 6 to the previous term.
   b) (i) 28   (ii) 34   (iii) 46
9 a) Multiply the previous term by 3.
   b) (i) 81   (ii) 729   (iii) 6561
10 a) 7, 13, 19, 25, 31, 37
   b) 9, 5, 1, –3, –7, –11
   c) –1, –3, –9, –27, –81, –243
   d) –72, –36, –18, –9, –4.5, –2.25
   e) 0.2, 0.8, 3.2, 12.8, 51.2, 204.8
   f) –63, –55, –47, –39, –31, –23

Page 128   Exercise 2

1 a) 1, 2, 3, 4   b) 22, 28, 35
2 a) (i) 1, 2, 3, 4   (ii) 19, 25, 32
   b) (i) 2, 4, 6, 8   (ii) 35, 47, 61
   c) (i) –2, –3, –4, –5   (ii) 0, –7, –15
3 a) 1, –2, 3, –4   b) 4, –2, 5
4 8, 13, 21
5 a) 1, 2, 3, 4   b) 120, 720

Page 129   Exercise 3

1 a) (i) Add an extra triangle to the previous pattern.
      (ii) [diagram]
      (iii) 13
   b) (i) Add two extra squares, one on the right and one at the bottom of the shape.
      (ii) [diagram]
      (iii) 34
   c) (i) Add an extra square to the left of the previous pattern.
      (ii) [diagram]
      (iii) 18

Answers 381

2 a)

10   15

21

b) The difference between terms increases by 1 each time, with the first difference being 2.
c) 28

3 a) (i)

   (ii) Add two to the number of circles in the previous pattern.
   (iii) 13   **(iv)** 19

b) (i)

   (ii) Add two to the number of circles in the previous pattern.
   (iii) 14   **(iv)** 20

c) (i)

   (ii) The number of circles added increases by 2 each time. OR For each square the number of circles is its position in the sequence squared.
   (iii) 49   **(iv)** 100

11.2 Sequences — Position-to-Term Rules

Page 130   Exercise 1

1 a) 5   **b)** 7   **c)** 9   **d)** 11
2 a) 18   **b)** 16   **c)** 14   **d)** 12
3 −4, 3, 10, 17
4 a) 6, 7, 8, 9   **b)** 5, 8, 11, 14
    c) 2, 6, 10, 14   **d)** 4, 9, 14, 19
    e) 9, 8, 7, 6   **f)** −1, −5, −9, −13
    g) 2, 12, 22, 32   **h)** −10, −13, −16, −19
5 a) 2, 5, 10, 17   **b)** 3, 9, 19, 33
    c) 2, 11, 26, 47   **d)** 0, 2, 6, 12
6 a) 30   **b)** 40   **c)** 60   **d)** 220
7 a) 91   **b)** 70   **c)** 10   **d)** −20
8 a) (i) 16   **(ii)** 21   **(iii)** 111
    b) (i) 13   **(ii)** 23   **(iii)** 203
    c) (i) 29   **(ii)** 59   **(iii)** 599
    d) (i) 32   **(ii)** 52   **(iii)** 412
    e) (i) 95   **(ii)** 90   **(iii)** 0
    f) (i) 15   **(ii)** 0   **(iii)** −270
    g) (i) 492   **(ii)** 992   **(iii)** 9992
    h) (i) −10   **(ii)** 0   **(iii)** 180
9 a) (i) 8   **(ii)** 50   **(iii)** 800
    b) (i) 11   **(ii)** 53   **(iii)** 803
    c) (i) 11   **(ii)** 95   **(iii)** 1595
    d) (i) 6   **(ii)** 30   **(iii)** 420

Page 131   Exercise 2

1 a) 7   **b)** 7th
2 a) 3   **b)** 3rd
3 a) 7th   **b)** 9th   **c)** 6th   **d)** 8th
4 a) 7th   **b)** 4th
5 a) 8th   **b)** 7th   **c)** 6th   **d)** 4th
6 a) 3rd   **b)** 10th
7 a) 2nd   **b)** 5th   **c)** 7th   **d)** 9th
8 a) (i) 13   **(ii)** 201
    b) (i) 23   **(ii)** 399
9 a) 21   **b)** 55

11.3 Finding a Position-to-Term Rule

Page 132   Exercise 1

1 a) 4   **b)** $4n + a$ **c)** $a = 5$
    d) $4n + 5$
2 a) $6n + 1$ **b)** $7n − 4$ **c)** $4n$
    d) $10n − 4$ **e)** $5n$ **f)** $20n − 13$
    g) $40n + 1$ **h)** $8n − 5$
3 a) $2n − 3$ **b)** $3n − 5$ **c)** $4n − 13$
    d) $19n − 64$
4 a) $12 − 2n$ **b)** $6 − n$ **c)** $20 − 5n$
    d) $43 − 3n$ **e)** $80 − 10n$ **f)** $87 − 9n$
    g) $65 − 5n$ **h)** $108 − 8n$

382   Answers

5 a) $9 - 5n$ b) $9 - 3n$ c) $5 - 15n$
   d) $-12n - 27$
6 a) $6n - 2$ b) $5n + 2$
7 a) $3n + 1$ b) $3n + 2$
   c) (i) Each term in sequence B is 1 greater.
      (ii) The formula for sequence B is the formula for sequence A plus 1, i.e. $3n + 2 = (3n + 1) + 1$.
8 a) $5n + 1$ b) $5n + 2$
9 a) $17 - 4n$ b) $15 - 4n$

Page 133   Exercise 2

1 $2n + 1 = 54$
   $2n = 53$
   $n = 26.5$
   Since 26.5 is not a whole number, 54 is not a term in the sequence.
2 $3n - 1 = 80$
   $3n = 81$
   $n = 27$
   Since 27 is a whole number, 80 is the 27th term in the sequence.
3 $n = 11$
4 a) $5n - 1$ b) Yes, $n = 7$.
5 a) $6n + 6$ b) No.
6 a) No.   b) Yes (27th).   c) No.
   d) Yes (77th).   e) No.
7 a) Yes, $n = 13$.   b) Yes, $n = 20$.   c) No.
   d) No.   e) Yes, $n = 222$.

Section 12 — Graphs and Equations

12.1 Coordinates

Page 134   Exercise 1

1 a) (i) (0, 0)   (ii) (2, 2)   (iii) (1, 3)
      (iv) (0, 4)   (v) (4, 4)
   b) X-COORDINATE COMES FIRST
2 a) [graph with square ABCD]
   b) [graph with triangle EFG]
   c) [graph with rhombus HIJK]
   d) [graph with trapezium LMNO]

3 a) (i) SQUARE   (ii) CIRCLE   (iii) CUBOID
   b) (i)   (2, 1) (−4, 1) (4, −4) (−5, 3)
      (ii) (2, −4) (5, −2) (5, 3) (−5, 3) (−2, −4) (−5, 3)
      (iii) (4, −4) (−2, −4) (−4, 1) (−4, 5) (−3, −2) (3, 3)
            (4, 1) (−5, 3)
4 [star graph with points A, B, C, D, E, F, G, H, I, J]

Page 136   Exercise 2

1 a) X: (−5, 1), Y: (3, 5)   b) M: (−1, 3)
   c) Use a ruler to check your diagram.
2 a) (2, 2.5)   b) [graph with P, M(2, 2.5), Q]
3 a) (2, 3)   b) (3, 2)   c) (2, 2)   d) (4, 7)
4 a) (0, 2)   b) (−3, 4)   c) (2, 1)
   d) (1, 1)   e) (−2, −6.5)   f) (−2.5, −1.5)
   g) (−2.5, −1.5)   h) (−0.5, −4)
5 a) (0, 5)   b) (−3.5, 4)   c) (3.5, 3)
   d) (−0.5, −2.5)   e) (0.5, 1)   f) (0.5, 0.5)

12.2 Horizontal and Vertical Graphs

Page 137   Exercise 1

1 A: $x = -5$ B: $x = -2$ C: $y = 3$
   D: $x = 5$ E: $y = -2$
2 [graph showing lines: a) $y = 3$, b) $y = -6$, c) $y = -1$, d) $x = 2$, e) $x = 4$, f) $x = -4$]

3 a) 0   b) $y = 0$
4 $x = 0$

5 a) [graph showing horizontal line y = −2]   **b)** $y = -2$

6 a) [graph showing vertical line x = 1]   **b)** $x = 1$

7 $y = 8$ **8** $x = -2$
9 $x = 1$ **10** $y = 6$

11 a) [graph with points Q and P]   **b)** $y = -1$

12 $x = 2$

13 a) [graph showing lines x = −2 and y = 4]   **b)** $(-2, 4)$

14 a) $(2, 4)$ **b)** $(-3, 7)$ **c)** $(8, -11)$ **d)** $(-5, -13)$

12.3 Other Straight-Line Graphs

Page 138 Exercise 1

1 a)

x	0	1	2	3	4	5
y	2	3	4	5	6	7
Coords	(0, 2)	(1, 3)	(2, 4)	(3, 5)	(4, 6)	(5, 7)

b), c) [graph of line through plotted points]

2 a)

x	0	1	2	3	4	5
y	−4	−3	−2	−1	0	1
	(0, −4)	(1, −3)	(2, −2)	(3, −1)	(4, 0)	(5, 1)

b), c) [graph of line through plotted points]

3 a)

x	0	1	2	3	4
y	8	7	6	5	4
Coords	(0, 8)	(1, 7)	(2, 6)	(3, 5)	(4, 4)

b), c) [graph of descending line through plotted points]

4 a) (i)

x	−1	0	1	2
y	2	3	4	5
	(−1, 2)	(0, 3)	(1, 4)	(2, 5)

(ii) [graph of $y = x + 3$]

b) (i)

x	−1	0	1	2
y	4	5	6	7
	(−1, 4)	(0, 5)	(1, 6)	(2, 7)

(ii) [graph of $y = x + 5$]

c) (i)

x	−1	0	1	2
y	−2	−1	0	1
	(−1, −2)	(0, −1)	(1, 0)	(2, 1)

384 *Answers*

(ii) graph of $y = x - 1$

d) (i)

x	−1	0	1	2
y	−4	−3	−2	−1
	(−1, −4)	(0, −3)	(1, −2)	(2, −1)

(ii) graph of $y = x - 3$

e) (i)

x	−1	0	1	2
y	−3	0	3	6
	(−1, −3)	(0, 0)	(1, 3)	(2, 6)

(ii) graph of $y = 3x$

f) (i)

x	−1	0	1	2
y	−4	0	4	8
	(−1, −4)	(0, 0)	(1, 4)	(2, 8)

(ii) graph of $y = 4x$

g) (i)

x	−1	0	1	2
y	−0.5	0	0.5	1
	(−1, −0.5)	(0, 0)	(1, 0.5)	(2, 1)

(ii) graph of $y = \frac{x}{2}$

h) (i)

x	−1	0	1	2
y	−4	−1	2	5
	(−1, −4)	(0, −1)	(1, 2)	(2, 5)

(ii) graph of $y = 3x - 1$

i) (i)

x	−1	0	1	2
y	3	5	7	9
	(−1, 3)	(0, 5)	(1, 7)	(2, 9)

(ii) graph of $y = 2x + 5$

j) (i)

x	−1	0	1	2
y	−7	−3	1	5
	(−1, −7)	(0, −3)	(1, 1)	(2, 5)

(ii) [graph of $y = 4x - 3$]

k) (i)

x	−1	0	1	2
y	4	3	2	1
	(−1, 4)	(0, 3)	(1, 2)	(2, 1)

(ii) [graph of $y = 3 - x$]

l) (i)

x	−1	0	1	2
y	5	4	3	2
	(−1, 5)	(0, 4)	(1, 3)	(2, 2)

(ii) [graph of $y = 4 - x$]

m) (i)

x	−1	0	1	2
y	8	6	4	2
	(−1, 8)	(0, 6)	(1, 4)	(2, 2)

(ii) [graph of $y = 6 - 2x$]

n) (i)

x	−1	0	1	2
y	11	8	5	2
	(−1, 11)	(0, 8)	(1, 5)	(2, 2)

(ii) [graph of $y = 8 - 3x$]

o) (i)

x	−1	0	1	2
y	3	1	−1	−3
	(−1, 3)	(0, 1)	(1, −1)	(2, −3)

(ii) [graph of $y = 1 - 2x$]

p) (i)

x	−1	0	1	2
y	5.5	5	4.5	4
	(−1, 5.5)	(0, 5)	(1, 4.5)	(2, 4)

(ii) [graph of $y = 5 - \frac{x}{2}$]

5 a) [graph] b) [graph]

c) [graph] d) [graph]

386 *Answers*

e) [graph]

f) [graph]

Page 140   Exercise 2

1 $x = 2$ and $y = 5$

2   **a), b)** [graph showing $y = 5 - x$ and $y = x - 3$]

     c) $x = 4$ and $y = 1$

3   **a)** [graph showing $y = 7 - x$ and $y = x - 3$] $x = 5$ and $y = 2$

     b) [graph showing $y = 8 - x$ and $y = x$] $x = 4$ and $y = 4$

     c) [graph showing $y = 9 - x$ and $y = 2x$] $x = 3$ and $y = 6$

     d) [graph showing $y = 3x$ and $y = 2x + 2$] $x = 2$ and $y = 6$

     e) [graph showing $y = x + 5$ and $y = 2 - 2x$] $x = -1$ and $y = 4$

     f) [graph showing $y = x + 1$ and $y = 2x - 1$] $x = 2$ and $y = 3$

     g) [graph showing $y = 2x - 3$ and $y = 6 - x$] $x = 3$ and $y = 3$

     h) [graph showing $y = -7 - 2x$ and $y = x + 2$] $x = -3$ and $y = -1$

     i) [graph showing $y = 2x + 3$ and $y = 4x + 2$] $x = \frac{1}{2}$ and $y = 4$

4   **a)** [graph showing $y = x + 3$ and $y = x - 2$]

     b) The lines are parallel and so do not intersect. This means there are no points where both the x and the y values are the same for both lines, and so there are no solutions.

Answers   **387**

12.4 Gradients

Page 141 Exercise 1

1. a) 4 b) 3 c) Positive. d) $\frac{4}{3}$
2. a) 1 b) 4 c) –1 d) $-\frac{5}{3}$
   e) $-\frac{3}{4}$ f) $-\frac{1}{3}$ g) $\frac{3}{2}$ h) 0
3. a) (i) 1 : 2 (ii) 50% (iii) 1 in 2
   b) (i) 3 : 4 (ii) 75% (iii) 3 in 4
   c) (i) 3 : 5 (ii) 60% (iii) 3 in 5
   d) (i) 2 : 1 (ii) 200% (iii) 2 in 1
   e) (i) 5 : 4 (ii) 125% (iii) 5 in 4
4. a) Negative. b) 4 c) –5 d) $-\frac{4}{5}$
5. a) $-\frac{2}{5}$ b) $-\frac{1}{2}$ c) $\frac{2}{3}$
6. a) (i) G: (2, –5), H: (6, 6) (ii) $\frac{11}{4}$
   b) (i) I: (–10, 5), J: (30, –25) (ii) $-\frac{3}{4}$
   c) (i) Line 1: K: (–8, –25) L: (8, 35)
      Line 2: M: (–4, 30) N: (6, –15)
      (ii) Line 1: $\frac{15}{4}$ Line 2: $-\frac{9}{2}$
7. a) [graph with points U and V] b) 1
8. $\frac{1}{2}$
9. a) 3 b) 2 c) $\frac{2}{3}$
   d) $-\frac{3}{4}$ e) $-\frac{1}{2}$ f) $\frac{3}{4}$
10. a) (i) 1 : 5 (ii) 20%
    b) (i) 1 : 1 (ii) 100%
    c) (i) 2 : 1 (ii) 200%
    d) (i) 3 : 5 (ii) 60%
    e) (i) 3 : 2 (ii) 150%
    f) (i) 4 : 5 (ii) 80%
11. a) $a = 9$ b) $b = 3$ c) $c = 4$

12.5 Equations of Straight-Line Graphs

Page 143 Exercise 1

1. a) (i) 3 (ii) (0, 2) b) (i) 2 (ii) (0, –4)
   c) (i) 5 (ii) (0, –11) d) (i) –3 (ii) (0, 7)
   e) (i) 4 (ii) (0, 0) f) (i) $\frac{1}{2}$ (ii) (0, –1)
2. a) (i) –1 (ii) $(0, -\frac{1}{2})$ b) (i) –1 (ii) (0, 3)
   c) (i) 0 (ii) (0, 3)

3. $A: y = -\frac{1}{3}x + 4$ $B: y = 3x$
   $C: y = \frac{1}{3}x + 2$ $D: y = \frac{7}{3}x - 1$
   $E: y = x + 2$ $F: y = -x + 6$

4. a) [graph: (–2, 0), (0, 6), $y = 3x + 6$]
   b) [graph: (0, –2), (2, 0), $y = x – 2$]
   c) [graph: (0, –4), (2, 0), $y = 2x – 4$]
   d) [graph: (0, 5), (5, 0), $y = -x + 5$]
   e) [graph: (0, 9), (3, 0), $y = -3x + 9$]
   f) [graph: (0, 6), (3, 0), $y = -2x + 6$]

Page 144 Exercise 2

1. A and E, B and D, C and F
2. a) E.g. $y = 5x + 1$, $y = 5x + 2$, $y = 5x + 3$
   b) E.g. $x + y = 6$, $x + y = 5$, $x + y = 4$
3. (i) a), c) and g) (ii) e), h) and i)
4. b), e) and f)
5. a) $y = 3x + 5$ b) $y = 5x – 9$
   c) $y = 2x + 4$ d) $y = 5x + 3$
   e) $y = 2x + 7$ f) $y = \frac{1}{2}x - 10$
   g) $y = 4x – 15$ h) $y = 8x + 19$
   i) $y = x – 12$ j) $y = 3x + 13$
   k) $y = -9x – 2$ l) $y = -x + 16$

Page 145 Exercise 3

1. a) $y = 8x + 2$ b) $y = -x + 7$
   c) $y = 11x – 5$ d) $y = -6x – 1$
   e) $y = 3x – 2$ f) $y = 6x + 8$
2. a) $y = 2x + 1$ b) $y = 5x – 1$
   c) $y = 2x – 4$ d) $y = 3x – 8$
   e) $y = 2x – 9$ f) $y = x – 3$
   g) $y = 2x + 5$ h) $y = 3x + 2$

12.6 Quadratic Graphs

Page 146 Exercise 1

1. a)

x	–3	–2	–1	0	1	2	3
x^2	9	4	1	0	1	4	9
$x^2 + 2$	11	6	3	2	3	6	11

388 Answers

b), c)

2 a)

x	−3	−2	−1	0	1	2	3
x^2	9	4	1	0	1	4	9
$x^2 - 1$	8	3	0	−1	0	3	8

b)

3 a) (i)

x	−3	−2	−1	0	1	2	3
x^2	9	4	1	0	1	4	9
x^2	9	4	1	0	1	4	9

(ii)

b) (i)

x	−3	−2	−1	0	1	2	3
x^2	9	4	1	0	1	4	9
$x^2 + 3$	12	7	4	3	4	7	12

(ii)

c) (i)

x	−3	−2	−1	0	1	2	3
x^2	9	4	1	0	1	4	9
$x^2 - 2$	7	2	−1	−2	−1	2	7

(ii)

d) (i)

x	−3	−2	−1	0	1	2	3
x^2	9	4	1	0	1	4	9
$x^2 + 4$	13	8	5	4	5	8	13

(ii)

e) (i)

x	−3	−2	−1	0	1	2	3
x^2	9	4	1	0	1	4	9
$5 - x^2$	−4	1	4	5	4	1	−4

(ii)

f) (i)

x	−3	−2	−1	0	1	2	3
x^2	9	4	1	0	1	4	9
$10 - x^2$	1	6	9	10	9	6	1

(ii)

Answers 389

Page 147   Exercise 2

1 a)

x	−3	−2	−1	0	1	2	3
x^2	9	4	1	0	1	4	9
x	−3	−2	−1	0	1	2	3
$x^2 + x$	6	2	0	0	2	6	12

b), c) graph of $y = x^2 + x$

2 a)

x	−3	−2	−1	0	1	2	3
x^2	9	4	1	0	1	4	9
$-2x$	6	4	2	0	−2	−4	−6
$x^2 - 2x$	15	8	3	0	−1	0	3

b) graph of $y = x^2 - 2x$

3 a) (i)

x	−3	−2	−1	0	1	2	3
x^2	9	4	1	0	1	4	9
$3x$	−9	−6	−3	0	3	6	9
$x^2 + 3x$	0	−2	−2	0	4	10	18

(ii) graph of $y = x^2 + 3x$

b) (i)

x	−3	−2	−1	0	1	2	3
x^2	9	4	1	0	1	4	9
$2x$	−6	−4	−2	0	2	4	6
$x^2 + 2x$	3	0	−1	0	3	8	15

(ii) graph of $y = x^2 + 2x$

c) (i)

x	−3	−2	−1	0	1	2	3
x^2	9	4	1	0	1	4	9
$-4x$	12	8	4	0	−4	−8	−12
$x^2 - 4x$	21	12	5	0	−3	−4	−3

(ii) graph of $y = x^2 - 4x$

d) (i)

x	−3	−2	−1	0	1	2	3
x^2	9	4	1	0	1	4	9
$5x$	−15	−10	−5	0	5	10	15
$x^2 + 5x$	−6	−6	−4	0	6	14	24

(ii) graph of $y = x^2 + 5x$

e) (i)

x	−3	−2	−1	0	1	2	3
x^2	9	4	1	0	1	4	9
$-3x$	9	6	3	0	−3	−6	−9
$x^2 - 3x$	18	10	4	0	−2	−2	0

390   *Answers*

(ii) [graph of $y = x^2 - 3x$]

f) (i)

x	−3	−2	−1	0	1	2	3
x^2	9	4	1	0	1	4	9
$4x$	−12	−8	−4	0	4	8	12
$x^2 + 4x$	−3	−4	−3	0	5	12	21

(ii) [graph of $y = x^2 + 4x$]

4 a) (i)

x	−3	−2	−1	0	1	2	3
x^2	9	4	1	0	1	4	9
$2x$	−6	−4	−2	0	2	4	6
5	5	5	5	5	5	5	5
$x^2 + 2x + 5$	8	5	4	5	8	13	20

(ii) [graph of $y = x^2 + 2x + 5$]

b) (i)

x	−3	−2	−1	0	1	2	3
x^2	9	4	1	0	1	4	9
x	−3	−2	−1	0	1	2	3
−3	−3	−3	−3	−3	−3	−3	−3
$x^2 + x − 3$	3	−1	−3	−3	−1	3	9

(ii) [graph of $y = x^2 + x − 3$]

c) (i)

x	−3	−2	−1	0	1	2	3
x^2	9	4	1	0	1	4	9
$−3x$	9	6	3	0	−3	−6	−9
−2	−2	−2	−2	−2	−2	−2	−2
$x^2 − 3x − 2$	16	8	2	−2	−4	−4	−2

(ii) [graph of $y = x^2 − 3x − 2$]

d) (i)

x	−3	−2	−1	0	1	2	3
x^2	9	4	1	0	1	4	9
$−2x$	6	4	2	0	−2	−4	−6
−3	−3	−3	−3	−3	−3	−3	−3
$x^2 − 2x − 3$	12	5	0	−3	−4	−3	0

(ii) [graph of $y = x^2 − 2x − 3$]

e) (i)

x	−3	−2	−1	0	1	2	3
x^2	9	4	1	0	1	4	9
$−3x$	9	6	3	0	−3	−6	−9
−1	−1	−1	−1	−1	−1	−1	−1
$x^2 − 3x − 1$	17	9	3	−1	−3	−3	−1

Answers

(ii)

f) (i)

x	-3	-2	-1	0	1	2	3
$-x^2$	-9	-4	-1	0	-1	-4	-9
$-x$	3	2	1	0	-1	-2	-3
-1	-1	-1	-1	-1	-1	-1	-1
$-x^2-x-1$	-7	-3	-1	-1	-3	-7	-13

(ii)

Page 148 Exercise 3

1 a) $x = -4$ and $x = 0$ b) $x = -1$ and $x = 3$
  c) $x = -2$ and $x = 2$
2 a)

  b) $x = 0.7$ and $x = 4.3$ (accept 0.6 to 0.8 and 4.2 to 4.4)

For questions 3 and 4 — accept answers 0.1 more or less than those given.

3 a) $x = -4.2$ and $x = 1.2$ b) $x = -1.3$ and $x = 2.3$
  c) $x = 0.6$ and $x = 3.4$ d) $x = 1.7$ and $x = 5.3$
4 a) $x = -1$ and $x = 1$ b) $x = -1.4$ and $x = 1.4$
  c) $x = -1.7$ and $x = 1.7$ d) $x = -2$ and $x = 2$
  e) $x = -2.2$ and $x = 2.2$

Page 149 Exercise 4

1 a) maximum b) minimum c) maximum
  d) minimum e) minimum f) maximum
  g) maximum h) minimum i) maximum

2 a) $(-2.5, -2.25)$ b) $(-1.5, 6.25)$ c) $(2.5, -4.25)$
3 a) $(1, -9)$ b) $(1, 2)$ c) $(4, 16)$
  d) $(-2, 2)$ e) $(-1, 9)$ f) $(1, -13)$
4 a) $(1, -1)$ b) $(-1.5, 8.75)$ c) $(-2.5, -15.25)$
  d) $(-0.5, 11.25)$ e) $(-2, -11)$ f) $(-2, -20)$
  g) $(-0.5, 9.5)$ h) $(-1.5, -14)$ i) $(1.5, 10.5)$

12.7 Harder Graphs

Page 151 Exercise 1

1 a)

x	-3	-2	-1	0	1	2	3
x^3	-27	-8	-1	0	1	8	27

b)

x	-3	-2	-1	0	1	2	3
x^3	-27	-8	-1	0	1	8	27
x^3+5	-22	-3	4	5	6	13	32

c)

x	-3	-2	-1	0	1	2	3
$-x^3$	27	8	1	0	-1	-8	-27

392 Answers

d)

x	–3	–2	–1	0	1	2	3
5	5	5	5	5	5	5	5
$-x^3$	27	8	1	0	–1	–8	–27
$5-x^3$	32	13	6	5	4	–3	–22

e)

x	–3	–2	–1	0	1	2	3
–4	–4	–4	–4	–4	–4	–4	–4
$-x^3$	27	8	1	0	–1	–8	–27
$-4-x^3$	23	4	–3	–4	–5	–12	–31

2 $y = x^3 + 3$

3 $y = x^3 - 3x + 7$

Page 152 Exercise 2

1 B, C, E and G

2 a)

x	–5	–4	–2	–1	–0.5	–0.1
$\frac{2}{x}$	–0.4	–0.5	–1	–2	–4	–20

x	0.1	0.5	1	2	4	5
$\frac{2}{x}$	20	4	2	1	0.5	0.4

b)

x	–5	–4	–2	–1	–0.5	–0.1
$-\frac{1}{x}$	0.2	0.25	0.5	1	2	10

x	0.1	0.5	1	2	4	5
$-\frac{1}{x}$	–10	–2	–1	–0.5	–0.25	–0.2

12.8 Graphs and Equations Problems

Page 153 Exercise 1

1 a), b) — this is a kite.

2 (–1, 3)

3 a) (i) 2 **(ii)** (0, 3)
 b) (i) 3 **(ii)** (0, 8)
 c) (i) 4 **(ii)** (0, –5)
 d) (i) –1 **(ii)** (0, 3)
 e) (i) 3 **(ii)** $(0, \frac{1}{2})$
 f) (i) $-\frac{2}{3}$ **(ii)** (0, –1)

4 $x = 11$ **5** $y = 7$

Answers 393

6 AB: –1 CD: –2 EF: $\frac{2}{7}$

7 A: $x = -5$ B: $y = x^2$ C: $y = x$ D: $y = -4$

8 a) 5   **b)** 3   **c)** –1   **d)** –4

9 a) A: (1, 5) B: (4, 5) C: (6, 3)
  D: (4, 1) E: (1, 1)
  b) (2.5, 5)   **c)** (5, 4)   **d)** $x = 1$ **e)** –1

10 a), **b)**, **c)**, **d)**

11 a)

x	–3	–2	–1	0	1	2	3
y	11	10	9	8	7	6	5
	(–3, 11)	(–2, 10)	(–1, 9)	(0, 8)	(1, 7)	(2, 6)	(3, 5)

b)

12 a)

x	–3	–2	–1	0	1	2	3
y	–4	–2	0	2	4	6	8
	(–3, –4)	(–2, –2)	(–1, 0)	(0, 2)	(1, 4)	(2, 6)	(3, 8)

b)   **c)** $x = 1.5$

13 a)   **b)** $y = 2 - 3x$

14 a) $\frac{1}{10}$ **b)** $y = 3$

15 $y = 2x + 8$

16 a) E.g.   **b)** E.g.

c)

17 $x = -2.3$, $x = 1.3$

18 a)

x	–4	–3	–2	–1	0	1	2
x^2	16	9	4	1	0	1	4
$5x$	–20	–15	–10	–5	0	5	10
$x^2 + 5x$	–4	–6	–6	–4	0	6	14

b)   **c)** (–2.5, –6.25)

394 *Answers*

19 a) [Graph of $y = x^3 - 6x^2 + 12x - 5$]

b) The graph crosses the x-axis at $x = 0.6$ (to 1 d.p.)
(Accept x-values from 0.5 to 0.7)

Section 13 — Real-Life Graphs

13.1 Interpreting Real-Life Graphs

Page 155   Exercise 1

For Questions 1-4, accept answers that are within £5 or €5 of the given answer.

1 a) €60   b) €290   c) €130   d) €340
2 a) £40   b) £170   c) £310   d) £370
3 £110
4 a) €490   b) £400   c) France

For Questions 5-8, accept answers that are within £1 or $1 of the given answer.

5 a) $16   b) $48   c) $70   d) $98
6 a) £6   b) £46   c) £34   d) £25
7 a) £36   b) £72
8 a) $64   b) $128

For Questions 9 and 11, accept answers that are within 10p of the given answer. For Questions 10 and 12, accept answers that are within 10 g of the given answer.

9 a) £1.80   b) £6.80   c) £1.10   d) £7.30
10 a) 280 g   b) 500 g   c) 120 g   d) 210 g
11 a) £7.20   b) £14.40
12 1.12 kg (or 1120 g)
13 a) 24 mph *(accept answers between 23.5-24.5 mph)*
   b) 43 km/h *(accept answers between 42-44 km/h)*
14 2.5 mph *(accept answers between 2-3 mph)*
15 Spain, by 5 mph (or 8 km/h) *(accept 4-6 mph or 6-10 km/h).*

Page 157   Exercise 2

1 a) D   b) A   c) C   d) B
2 a) Oven 1   b) Oven 2
   c) Between 60 and 80 seconds
   d) Between 144 and 156 seconds
   e) (i) 84 seconds *(accept answers between 82-86 seconds)*
      (ii) 150 °C

f) E.g. The gradients show the change in the temperature of each oven per unit of time — this is the rate at which the temperature of each oven changes.

3 a) The water got steadily deeper for about an hour, then steadily shallower for about 6 hours. Finally it got steadily deeper for about 5 hours.
   b) 09.20   c) 1.2 m
   d) 13.00 and 17.45   e) 2 hours 15 minutes

4 a) (i) 5 cm   (ii) 5 cm   (iii) 5 cm
   b) (i) 10 cm   (ii) 4.5 cm (iii) 2.5 cm
   c) The depth of water in vase P increases steadily while the depth of water in vase Q increases quickly at first then more slowly as the vase fills up. This means that when the vases are nearly empty the depth of water in vase Q increases quicker than the depth of water in vase P, but as the vases fill up the depth of water in vase Q increases at a slower rate than the depth of water in vase P.

13.2 Drawing Real-Life Graphs

Page 159   Exercise 1

Your answers to this exercise may differ slightly depending on the accuracy of your graphs.

1 a)
No. Days	1	2	3	4	5
Cost (£)	60	100	140	180	220

b) [Graph: cost (£) vs days, linear]

c) (i) £300   (ii) 6 days

2 a)
Weight (kg)	1	2	3	4	5
Time (minutes)	60	95	130	165	200

b)

c) 2.4 kg

3 a)

b) £390   c) 5 nights

4 a)

b) £15.50   c) 7 parcels

5 a)

b) 25.6 mpg

6 a)

b) 0.9 kg

Section 14 — Proportion

14.1 Direct Proportion

Page 161   Exercise 1

1 a) £70   b) £175   c) £700
2 a) €11.40   b) €22.80   c) €114   d) €969
3 £54   4 3 kg
5 a) £13.50   b) £63   c) £270
6 a) 3 books   b) 8 books
7 4 DVDs   8 13 builders   9 5 kilograms
10 £13.86

Page 162   Exercise 2

1 a) 52 minutes   b) 20 km
2 a) 357 km   b) 56 litres
3 a) 73.50 Swiss francs   b) £20
4 a) 14 eggs   b) 12 servings   c) 16.5 g

396   *Answers*

Page 162 Exercise 3
1. The bag of 10 apples
2. The small (240 ml) cup
3. The pack of 10 sausages

Page 163 Exercise 4
1. Graph C — it is a straight line through the origin.
2. a) [graph with points (0, 0) and (20, 8) on x-y axes]
   b) [graph with points (0, 0) and (80, 15) on t-s axes]

Page 164 Exercise 5
1. a) (i)

x	8	12
y	2	3

   (ii) [graph]

   b) (i)

x	4	8
y	3	6

   (ii) [graph]

   c) (i)

x	2	7	10	12
y	6	21	30	36

   (ii) [graph]

   d) (i)

x	−2	0	3	6
y	−10	0	15	30

   (ii) [graph]

Page 164 Exercise 6
1. a) $s = 20t$ b) $s = 260$
   c) [graph with points (0, 0), (4, 80), (13, 260) on t-s axes]

2. a) $j = 3h$ b) $j = 120$
   c) [graph with points (0, 0), (5, 15), (40, 120) on h-j axes]

3. a) $r = 1.5t$
   b) [graph]

4. a) [graph] b) $p = 28$

5. a) [graph with points (0, 0) and (27, 2.7) on g-f axes] b) $f = 2.1$

14.2 Inverse Proportion

Page 165 Exercise 1
1. 1 hour
2. 2 hours
3. 16 minutes
4. 1 hour 20 minutes
5. a) 155 days b) 8 builders

Page 165 Exercise 2
1. 4 hours
2. 9 days
3. 72 minutes
4. 75 minutes
5. 2 hours 24 minutes
6. a) 6 weeks b) 23 workers

Page 166 Exercise 3
1. Graph A — as x increases, y decreases so they're inversely proportional.
2. $y = \frac{4}{x}$ and $yx = 9$
3. a)
x	12	6
y	15	30

b)
x	11	22
y	4	2

c)
x	2	4	8	10
y	80	40	20	16

d)
x	2.5	7
y	25.2	9

e)
x	0.5	3	6	30
y	180	30	15	3

f)
x	0.25	4	20	100
y	320	20	4	0.8

4. a)
q	0.2	0.4	0.5	1	2	4	5	10
p	10	5	4	2	1	0.5	0.4	0.2

b) [graph]

14.3 Proportion Problems

Page 167 Exercise 1
1. £96
2. a) R 8750 b) £150.89 (to the nearest penny)
3. 7.2 minutes (or 7 minutes 12 seconds)
4. a) 10 days b) 36 chickens
5. a)
a	2	4	10	80
b	20	40	100	800

b)
a	2	4	10	80
b	20	10	4	0.5

6. a) [graph] b) [graph]

7. a) True b) False c) True
8. a) $y = 15$ b) $x = 240$ c) $y = \frac{120}{x}$

Section 15 — Angles and 2D Shapes

15.1 Basic Angle Properties

Page 168 Exercise 1
1. $a = 90°$ $b = 65°$ $c = 120°$ $d = 60°$
   $e = 327°$ $f = 70°$ $g = 270°$ $h = 123°$
2. $a = 18°$ $b = 56°$ $c = 140°$ $d = 40°$
3. $a = 127°$ $b = 28°$ $c = 113°$ $d = 62°$ $e = 107°$

Page 169 Exercise 2
1. $a = 35°$ $b = 60°$ $c = 33°$ $d = 45°$ $e = 60°$
   $f = 72°$ $g = 53°$ $h = 30°$
2. a) TRUE. Angle $EOB = 43° + 72° + 65° = 180°$
   b) TRUE. EOB is a straight line, and angle $AOB = 90°$, so angle $AOE = 90°$ too.
   c) TRUE. Angle $FOC = 25° + 90° + 65° = 180°$
   d) FALSE. Since FC is a straight line, $p = 180° - 72° = 108°$
3. $a = 50°$ $b = 90°$ $c = 55°$ $d = 100°$
4. Angle $AOB = 59° + 65° + 58° = 182°$ so AB cannot be straight
5. a) 70°, 40°, 30° b) $m = 220°$

15.2 Triangles

Page 170 Exercise 1

1. **a)** Scalene; right-angled
   b) Equilateral; acute-angled
   c) Isosceles; acute-angled
   d) Isosceles; right-angled
2. $a = 53°$ $b = 22°$ $c = 15°$ $d = 16°$
3. $e = 73°$ $f = 41°$ $g = 52°$ $h = 49°$ $i = 131°$
4. $a = 20°$ $b = 10°$ $c = 60°$ $d = 60°$
5. $a = 30°$ $b = 120°$ $c = 70°$ $d = 45°$ $e = 36°$
   $f = 66°$ $g = 114°$
6. **a)** $x = 60°$ **b)** $y = 120°$
7. **a)** $p = 125°$ **b)** $q = 110°$

15.3 Parallel and Intersecting Lines

Page 172 Exercise 1

1. $a = 40°$ $b = 160°$ $c = 75°$ $d = 105°$ $e = 90°$
   $f = 90°$ $g = 90°$
2. **a)** $v = 44°$
   b) $w = 44°$ — it is an opposite angle (formed by two straight lines crossing) to the 44° angle v.
3. $a = 81°$ $b = 49°$ $c = 60°$ $d = 63°$ $e = 47°$
   $f = 70°$ $g = 54°$ $h = 48°$ $i = 78°$
4. $w = 64°$ $x = 64°$ $y = 52°$ $z = 76°$

Page 173 Exercise 2

1. $a = 120°$ $b = 72°$ $c = 35°$ $d = 98°$ $e = 82°$
   $f = 98°$ $g = 45°$ $h = 45°$ $i = 48°$ $j = 132°$
2. **a)** $x = 42°$
   b) x is alternate to an angle of 42° as the floors are parallel and the stairs are a straight line crossing them.
3. $a = 73°$ $b = 46°$ $c = 61°$ $d = 65°$ $e = 65°$
   $f = 50°$ $g = 116°$ $h = 64°$ $i = 52°$

Page 174 Exercise 3

1. $a = 135°$ $b = 72°$ $c = 111°$ $d = 100°$ $e = 128°$
   $f = 128°$ $g = 128°$ $h = 52°$ $i = 108°$ $j = 72°$
   $k = 132°$ $l = 48°$
2. $h = 141°$ $i = 39°$ $j = 39°$ $k = 105°$ $l = 75°$
   $m = 75°$ $n = 75°$ $o = 75°$ $p = 105°$ $q = 105°$
   $r = 78°$ $s = 102°$ $t = 102°$ $u = 78°$ $v = 102°$
   $w = 78°$ $x = 102°$
3. $y = 81°$
4. $a = 65°$ $b = 115°$ $c = 65°$ $d = 115°$ $e = 69°$
   $f = 69°$ $g = 111°$ $h = 111°$ $i = 69°$ $j = 114°$
   $k = 66°$ $l = 24°$

Page 175 Exercise 4 — Mixed Exercise

1. $a = 130°$, opposite an angle of 130°
   $b = 130°$, corresponding to a
   $c = 37°$, corresponding to an angle of 37°
   $d = 143°$, $d = 180° - 37°$
   $e = 143°$, corresponding to d
   $f = 143°$, opposite d
   $g = 143°$, corresponding to f
   $h = 37°$, opposite an angle of 37°
   $i = 37°$, corresponding to h
   $j = 60°$, opposite an angle of 60°
   $k = 60°$, alternate to j
   $l = 120°$, $l = 180° - k$
   $m = 55°$, corresponding to an angle of 55°
   $n = 125°$, $n = 180° - m$
   $o = 65°$, corresponding to an angle of 65°
   $p = 40°$, alternate to an angle of 40°
   $q = 75°$, $q = 180° - 65° - 40°$
   $r = 115°$, corresponding to an angle of 115°
   $s = 115°$, corresponding to an angle of 115°
   $t = 58°$, allied with an angle of 122°
   $u = 40°$, $u = 180° - 30° - 110°$
   $v = 52°$, $2v = 180° - 76° = 104°$ so $v = 52°$
   $w = 52°$, alternate to v
2. $w = 48°$, opposite an angle of 48°
   $x = 48°$, corresponding to w
   $y = 84°$, $y = 180° - 48° - 48°$
   $z = 84°$, opposite y

15.4 Quadrilaterals

Page 176 Exercise 1

1. $a = 112°$ $b = 92°$ $c = 90°$ $d = 70°$ $e = 109°$

Page 176 Exercise 2

1. [grid diagram]
2. E.g. [grid diagram]
3. **a)** They are the same length.
   b) 90°
   c) (iii)

Page 177 Exercise 3

1. **a)** [grid diagram] **b)** E.g. [grid diagram]
2. $a = 122°$ $b = 72°$ $c = 108°$ $d = 118°$ $e = 62°$
   $f = 51°$ $g = 129°$ $h = 70°$

Page 178 Exercise 4

1. **a)** d **b)** Q **c)** S
2. $a = 113°$ $b = 111°$ $c = 90°$ $d = 70°$ $e = 99°$

Answers **399**

Page 179 Exercise 5

1. **a)** parallel **b)** two pairs **c)** one pair **d)** one pair **e)** 360°
2. $a = 120°$ $b = 120°$ $c = 60°$ $d = 74°$ $e = 116°$ $f = 56°$

Page 179 Exercise 6 — Mixed Exercise

1. **a)** parallelogram **b)** rectangle **c)** kite **d)** trapezium **e)** square
2. **a)** square, rhombus
   b) square, rectangle
   c) square, rhombus, rectangle, parallelogram, kite
   d) square, rectangle, parallelogram, rhombus
   e) square, rectangle, parallelogram, trapezium, rhombus
   f) trapezium
3. $a = 128°$ $b = 116°$ $c = 82°$ $d = 60°$ $e = 120°$ $f = 114°$ $g = 230°$ $h = 130°$ $i = 62°$ $j = 118°$ $k = 62°$ $l = 54°$ $m = 54°$ $n = 36°$ $o = 77°$ $p = 103°$ $q = 77°$
4. 138°
5. both 80°
6. both 127°
7. both 110°

15.5 Interior and Exterior Angles

Page 181 Exercise 1

1. **a)** 360° **b)** 900° **c)** 1080° **d)** 1260°
2. **a)** 720° **b)** 1440° **c)** 1800° **d)** 3240°
3. **a)** One triangle is partly outside the original shape.
   b) [diagram]
   c) 720° **d)** 265°
4. $a = 118°$ $b = 247°$ $c = 210°$
5. **a)** 900° **b)** 128.57°
6. **a)** 135° **b)** 140° **c)** 144°
7. **a)** 100°
   b) No — not all the interior angles are equal.

Page 182 Exercise 2

1. **a)** $a = 72°$ **b)** $b = 108°$
2. **a) (i)** 51.43° **(ii)** 45° **(iii)** 40°
   b) (i) 128.57° **(ii)** 135° **(iii)** 140°
3. $a = 54°$ $b = 56°$ $c = 74°$ $d = 135°$
4. **a)** 53° **b)** 40° **c)** 35° **d)** 40°
5. **a)** 8 sides, Octagon
   b) [octagon diagram]
   c) 135° **d)** 1080°

6. **a) (i)** 6 sides **(ii)** 120° **(iii)** 720°
   b) (i) 4 sides **(ii)** 90° **(iii)** 360°
   c) (i) 9 sides **(ii)** 140° **(iii)** 1260°
   d) (i) 3 sides **(ii)** 60° **(iii)** 180°
   e) (i) 36 sides **(ii)** 170° **(iii)** 6120°
   f) (i) 40 sides **(ii)** 171° **(iii)** 6840°
   g) (i) 60 sides **(ii)** 174° **(iii)** 10 440°
   h) (i) 72 sides **(ii)** 175° **(iii)** 12 600°
   i) (i) 90 sides **(ii)** 176° **(iii)** 15 840°
   j) (i) 120 sides **(ii)** 177° **(iii)** 21 240°
7. $x = 10°$ $y = 100°$ $z = 20°$

15.6 Symmetry

Page 184 Exercise 1

1. **a)** 1 line of symmetry
   b) 1 line of symmetry
   c) no lines of symmetry
   d) no lines of symmetry
   e) 2 lines of symmetry
   f) 1 line of symmetry
   g) 5 lines of symmetry
   h) 4 lines of symmetry
2. **a)** 2 lines of symmetry
   b) 2 lines of symmetry
   c) no lines of symmetry
   d) 1 line of symmetry

e) 5 lines of symmetry

f) 6 lines of symmetry

g) 7 lines of symmetry

h) 8 lines of symmetry

Page 185   Exercise 2

1 a) 2   b) 6   c) 1   d) 2
   e) 1   f) 1   g) 2   h) 2
   i) 3   j) 7

2 a) rotational symmetry order 4
   b) rotational symmetry order 1
   c) rotational symmetry order 1
   d) rotational symmetry order 1
   e) rotational symmetry order 5
   f) rotational symmetry order 6
   g) rotational symmetry order 8
   h) rotational symmetry order 10

Page 186   Exercise 3 — Mixed Exercise

1 a) (i) 3 lines of symmetry
      (ii) rotational symmetry order 3
   b) (i) no lines of symmetry
      (ii) rotational symmetry order 1
   c) (i) 4 lines of symmetry
      (ii) rotational symmetry order 4
   d) (i) 1 line of symmetry
      (ii) rotational symmetry order 1

2 a) B   b) A   c) D   d) C

3

4

5

6

15.7 Angles and 2D Shapes Problems

Page 187   Exercise 1

1 $a = 18°$ $b = 62°$ $c = 53°$ $d = 127°$ $e = 127°$
   $f = 45°$ $g = 186°$ $h = 94°$ $i = 72°$ $j = 59°$
   $k = 75°$ $l = 58°$ $m = 47°$ $n = 47°$

2 $r = 82°$ $s = 103°$ $t = 59°$ $u = 62°$ $v = 28°$
   $w = 71°$ $x = 95°$ $y = 92°$

3 $o = 28°$ $p = 56°$ $q = 118°$ $r = 103°$

4 a) A, B, C, D, F, G
   b) F   c) B   d) A, G

5 $a = 58°$ $b = 70°$ $c = 66°$ $d = 294°$ $e = 66°$
   $f = 66°$ $g = 114°$ $h = 114°$

6 $a = 61°$ $b = 119°$ $c = 43°$ $d = 43°$ $e = 98°$
   $f = 98°$ $g = 91°$ $h = 91°$ $i = 89°$ $j = 78°$
   $k = 78°$ $l = 102°$ $m = 58°$ $n = 125°$ $o = 55°$
   $p = 35°$ $q = 33°$ $r = 327°$

7 No. Angle BAC + Angle $ACD = 178°$ not $180°$

8 a) $720°$ b) $x = 70°$

9 a) $540°$ b) $y = 110°$

10 $w = 270°$ $z = 117°$

11 $p = 34°$

12 a) $a = 105°$ b) $b = 165°$ $c = 146°$

13 a) $x = 60°$ b) $y = 120°$

14 $x = 45°$ $y = 90°$

Answers   401

Section 16 — Units, Measuring and Estimating

16.1 Reading Scales

Page 189   Exercise 1

1. **a)** A 3 cm   B 7 cm   C 9.5 cm
   b) A 10 cm   B 45 cm   C 75 cm
   c) A 28 cm   B 46 cm   C 52 cm
2. **a)** 7 mm   **b)** 4 mm   **c)** 8 mm
3. **a)** 9 g   **b)** 5.3 kg
   c) 20 tonnes **d)** 4.35 kg
4. 160 g   5 65 ml
6. **a)** 400 ml   **b)** 0.25 cm^3
   c) 3.75 l   **d)** 0.75 cm^3

Page 191   Exercise 2

1. **a)** lower bound = 9.5 cm, upper bound = 10.5 cm
   b) lower bound = 14.5 g, upper bound = 15.5 g
   c) lower bound = 22.5 km, upper bound = 23.5 km
   d) lower bound = 17.5 l, upper bound = 18.5 l
   e) lower bound = 56.5 mm, upper bound = 57.5 mm
   f) lower bound = 132.5 ml, upper bound = 133.5 ml
2. **a)** lower bound = 172.5 cm, upper bound = 177.5 cm
   b) lower bound = 885 km, upper bound = 895 km
   c) lower bound = 227.5 g, upper bound = 232.5 g
   d) lower bound = 62.5 l, upper bound = 67.5 l
   e) lower bound = 2050 l, upper bound = 2150 l
   f) lower bound = 19 m, upper bound = 21 m
3. 5.75 cm^3 4 10.5 m, 10.7 m
5. **a)** 24 °C
   b) No, the minimum possible temperature is 22 °C
6. Yes, the maximum width of the table is 96 cm
7. 95 g, 105 g   8 10 cm (175 cm – 165 cm)

16.2 Converting Metric Units — Length, Mass and Volume

Page 192   Exercise 1

1. **a)** 20 mm   **b)** 3000 ml   **c)** 4100 mg
   d) 15 cm^3 **e)** 126.7 ml   **f)** 2000 m
   g) 250 cl   **h)** 2300 kg
2. **a)** 4 m   **b)** 3.4 km   **c)** 0.5 m
   d) 3 kg   **e)** 2 l   **f)** 0.5 l
   g) 0.246 tonnes **h)** 5 l
3. **a)** 0.2 cm   **b)** 3000 g   **c)** 12 700 ml
   d) 37.9 cm   **e)** 3 tonnes   **f)** 0.4 g
   g) 0.123 l   **h)** 0.05116 kg   **i)** 1.2 l
   j) 2.7165 m   **k)** 0.0223 g   **l)** 1.05 m
4. **a)** 1200 g   **b)** 40 servings
5. 6 bottles
6. **a)** 500 cm   **b)** 5000 mm
7. **a)** 20 000 cm   **b)** 600 000 g   **c)** 400 000 cm
   d) 231 000 mg **e)** 62 000 mm   **f)** 3400 mm

8. **a)** 0.001 m   **b)** 0.003 kg
   c) 0.15 l   **d)** 0.001532 tonnes
   e) 0.01005 km **f)** 0.003023 kg
9. 6
10. **a)** 500 laps   **b)** 200 km

Page 193   Exercise 2

1. **a)** 78.5 l   **b)** 7.54 tonnes
   c) 5801 cm   **d)** 23 240 m
   e) 3.575 kg   **f)** 1395 cm
   g) 1250 ml   **h)** 723.5 cm
   i) 1204 kg   **j)** 13 111.1 m
2. 3800 g   3 1600 m
4. 0.05 kg   5 741.4 kg
6. Yes. Their total weight with equipment is 0.2262 tonnes.

Page 193   Exercise 3

1. 8 days
2. 14.8 km
3. 7 packs to make sure there is enough
4. **a)** 750 l   **b)** 267 days
5. **a)** 1.6025 kg   **b)** 8 people

16.3 Converting Units — Area and Volume

Page 195   Exercise 1

1. **a)** 2000 m × 3000 m = 6 000 000 m^2
   b) 2 km × 3 km = 6 km^2 × 1 000 000 = 6 000 000 m^2
2. **a)** 20 mm × 40 mm = 800 mm^2
   b) 800 ÷ 100 = 8 cm^2
3. **a)** 2600 mm^2 **b)** 36 000 m^2
   c) 170 mm^2 **d)** 10 500 cm^2
   e) 70 000 m^2 **f)** 12 000 cm^2
4. **a)** 0.84 cm^2 **b)** 0.175 m^2 **c)** 290 cm^2
   d) 3.15 km^2 **e)** 85 cm^2 **f)** 0.17 m^2
5. 3 bottles
6. 33.24 m^2
7. **a)** 85 000 cm^2 **b)** 8.5 m^2
8. **a)** 6.5 cm^2 **b)** 650 mm^2
9. **a)** 1 200 000 mm^2 **b)** 10 000 000 cm^2
   c) 0.0605 m^2 **d)** 0.0673 km^2
   e) 50 m^2 **f)** 5 000 000 mm^2

Page 196   Exercise 2

1. **a)** 1.5 m × 3 m × 2 m = 9 m^3
   b) 150 cm × 300 cm × 200 cm = 9 000 000 cm^3
   9 000 000 ÷ 1 000 000 = 9 m^3
2. **a)** 1 000 000 m^3 **b)** 15 000 mm^3
   c) 200 000 cm^3 **d)** 55 mm^3
   e) 1 200 000 000 m^3 **f)** 17 600 000 cm^3
   g) 435 000 000 m^3 **h)** 6 700 000 000 cm^3
   i) 0.045 mm^3

3 **a)** 0.134 m³ **b)** 16 cm³
  c) 0.003 m³ **d)** 453.6 cm³
  e) 0.00000015 km³ **f)** 0.091475 cm³
  g) 0.0000359 m³ **h)** 131.4 cm³
  i) 0.0000179 km³

4 0.002 m³

5 **a)** 595 cm³ **b)** 140 cm³ **c)** 455 000 mm³

6 35 771 complete bricks

7 482485.5 mm³

8 **a)** 40 glasses **b)** 525 000 mm³

9 **a)** 1125 m³ **b)** 1 125 000 000 cm³
  c) 1 125 000 litres

10 **a)** 560 000 cm³ **b)** 560 000 000 mm³

16.4 Metric and Imperial Units

In this topic there are sometimes alternative answers, depending on which conversion factor is used to convert between the metric and imperial systems.

Page 197 Exercise 1

1 **a)** 24 inches **b)** 12 feet **c)** 4 pints
  d) 56 pounds **e)** 72 pints **f)** 10 800 feet

2 **a)** 2 pounds **b)** 4 stone **c)** 5 yards
  d) 5 feet **e)** 4 gallons **f)** 3 stone

3 **a)** 10 cm
  b) 84 g (or 85 g / 86 g)
  c) 9 litres
  d) 64 000 g (or 62 720 g / 63 000 g / 63 636 g)
  e) 450 cm **f)** 40 km **g)** 6.75 cm
  h) 2.57 litres (or 2.53 litres) **i)** 207 cm

4 **a)** 5 miles **b)** 100 pints (or 101 pints)
  c) 2 stone **d)** 2 feet **e)** 10 inches
  f) 10 miles **g)** 2 ounces
  h) 16.5 pounds (or 16.4 pounds / 16.7 pounds)
  i) 30 miles

5 4 laps

6 **a)** 5 jugs **b)** 0.15 litres (or 0.19 litres)

7 56.25 mph **8** 562.5 miles

9 **a)** 1620 cm **b)** 16.2 m

10 **a)** 2.25 kg (or 2.24 kg / 2.27 kg / 2.29 kg)
  b) 3.3 m **c)** 6.4 kg (or 6.3 kg)
  d) 13 500 ml (or 13 680 ml)
  e) 18 m **f)** 8.25 m
  g) 9120 ml (or 9000 ml)
  h) 160 kg (or 157 kg / 158 kg / 159 kg)

11 **a)** 1.4 pints
  b) 0.5 stone
  c) 0.1875 miles
  d) 1 stone
  e) 48 ounces (or 47 ounces)
  f) 4.9 pints (or 5 pints)
  g) 352 ounces
    (or 350 ounces / 356 ounces / 357 ounces)
  h) 3 feet

Page 198 Exercise 2

1 **a) (i)** 68 ounces **(ii)** 4 pounds 4 ounces
  b) (i) 30 ounces **(ii)** 1 pound 14 ounces
  c) (i) 96 ounces **(ii)** 6 pounds (and 0 ounces)
  d) (i) 175 ounces **(ii)** 10 pounds 15 ounces
  e) (i) 35 ounces **(ii)** 2 pounds 3 ounces

2 **a)** 6 feet 8 inches **b)** 1 foot 9 inches
  c) 5000 feet **d)** 2 feet 6 inches
  e) 2 inches

3 No, Maddie is too short at 132.5 cm.
  (Or convert 140 cm to 4 feet 8 inches.)

4 No, they need 784 g / 787.5 g.
  (Or convert 750 g to 1 pound 11 ounces.)

Page 199 Exercise 3 — Mixed Exercise

1 **a)** 3.5 m **b)** 7 kg **c)** 10 miles
  d) 9 litres **e)** 1.5 kg **f)** 5 stone
  g) 160 stone **h)** 10 litres

2 £35.91 (or £36.39) **3** 2 litres

4 550 miles (or 543 miles)

5 **a)** 1540 ml (or 1525 ml)
  b) 20 kg (or 19.7 kg / 19.8 kg / 19.9 kg)
  c) 17.97 m **d)** 50.89 km
  e) 10.9 kg (or 10.8 kg) **f)** 730 cm
  g) 5815 ml (or 5781 ml) **h)** 723.5 cm

6 No, their total combined weight is less than 740 kg.

16.5 Estimating in Real Life

Page 200 Exercise 1

1 **a)** centimetres (or millimetres)
  b) grams **c)** metres
  d) millimetres (or centimetres)
  e) tonnes **f)** kilograms (or grams)
  g) kilometres

2 **a)** probably between 2 m and 3 m
  b) between 4 m and 5 m
  c) around 2.5 m
  d) between 1.5 m and 2 m
  e) between 20 cm and 25 cm
  f) between 200 litres and 300 litres

3 around 7 m **4** between 2 m and 2.5 m

5 length ≈ 11 m, height ≈ 3.6 m

6 The dinosaur is about 3 times as tall as the chicken and 7 times as long. So if you reckon the height and length of an average chicken are around 30 cm, the dinosaur will be around 0.9 m tall and 2.1 m long.

7 The rhino is about 6 times as tall as the cat. So if you reckon the height of an average cat is around 25 cm, the rhino will be around 1.5 m tall.

Section 17 — Speed, Density, Pressure

17.1 Speed, Distance, Time Calculations

Page 201 Exercise 1

1. **a)** 15 km/h **b)** 20 km/h **c)** 30 mph
   d) 4 m/s **e)** 6000 km/h **f)** 35 mph
2. **a)** 40 km/h **b)** 16 km/h **c)** 25 m/s
   d) 0.1 cm/s **e)** 600 mph **f)** 7800 m/s
   g) 1.5 m/s **h)** 1.25 m/s
3. **a)** 20 km/h **b)** 6 km/h **c)** 12 km/h
   d) 3 km/h **e)** 2.5 km/h **f)** 14 km/h

Page 202 Exercise 2

1. **a)** 40 km **b)** 50 miles **c)** 500 m
   d) 72 km **e)** 135 m **f)** 175 miles
2. **a)** 2 h **b)** 5 s **c)** 3 s **d)** 2.5 h
   e) 0.5 s **f)** 0.25 h (or 15 minutes)
3. 120 miles **4** 980 miles **5** 0.16 s
6. 5 hours **7** 6 minutes **8** 1.875 miles
9. **a)** 180 km/h **b)** 20 m/s **c)** 11.5 m/s
   d) 95.4 km/h **e)** 15.66 km/h **f)** 12.6 m/s
10. 5 m/s **11** 28 800 km/h **12** 0.3 m/min

Page 203 Exercise 3 — Mixed Exercise

1. 4 m/s **2** 25 m **3** 2.5 h **4** 28 m/s
5. 405 cm **6** 0.75 s **7** 4.05 km
8. **a)** 54 km/h **b)** 15 m/s
9. **a)** 0.008 m/s **b)** 0.0288 km/h
10. 22.5 seconds

17.2 Density, Mass, Volume Calculations

Page 203 Exercise 1

1. **a)** 4 kg/m³ **b)** 60 kg/m³
   c) 9 kg/m³ **d)** 250 kg/m³
   e) 50 kg/m³ **f)** 90 kg/m³
2. **a)** Volume = $\frac{\text{Mass}}{\text{Density}}$
   b) (i) 5 m³ **(ii)** 50 m³
   (iii) 20 m³ **(iv)** 4 m³
3. **a)** Mass = Volume × Density **b)** 1044 kg
4. 0.092 kg **5** 2700 kg/m³

17.3 Pressure, Force, Area Calculations

Page 204 Exercise 1

1. **a)** 9 N/cm² **b)** 25 N/m²
   c) 1200 N/m² **d)** 8 N/cm²
2. **a)** 6 cm² **b)** 7 m²
   c) 4 cm² **d)** 3 m²
3. **a)** 1500 N **b)** 1080 N
4. 2 N
5. **a)** 5 N/cm² **b)** 50 000 N/m²

17.4 Distance-Time Graphs

Page 205 Exercise 1

1. **a)** *[graph]* **b)** *[graph]*
   c) (i) 70 km **(ii)** *[graph]*
2. **a)** *[graph]* **b)** *[graph]*
   c) *[graph]*
3. *[graph]* **4** *[graph]*
5. *[graph]*
6. *[graph]*
7. **a) (i)** 1 hour **(ii)** 50 miles
   b) 1 hour
   c) (i) 11:00 am **(ii)** 2 hours

404 *Answers*

8 a) The person travels 5 km in 2 hours. They rest for 1 hour. They then continue their journey for another 1 hour, during which time they travel a further 3 km. They then stop for 30 minutes. Finally, they travel back to their starting point in 1.5 hours.

b) The person travels 1 km in 1 hour. They rest for 30 minutes. They then continue their journey for another 30 minutes, during which time they travel a further 0.5 km. They then stop for 15 minutes. They then continue their journey for 30 minutes, and cover a further 2 km, before stopping for 15 minutes.

c) The person travels 35 miles in 45 minutes. They rest for 45 minutes. They then travel 15 miles in 30 minutes back towards their starting point before stopping for a further 30 minutes. They then continue their journey away from the starting point for another 20 miles, which takes 30 minutes.

Page 207   Exercise 2

1 a) The second stage, since the graph for that part of the journey is steeper.
   b) (i) 2 km   (ii) 4 km/h
   c) 12 km/h

2 a) Between 13:30 and 14:30, since the graph between those times is steepest.
   b) (i) 1 hour   (ii) 3 km   (iii) 3 km/h
   c) 2 km/h   d) 4.5 km/h

3 a) (i) 40 km/h   (ii) 33.3 km/h (to 1 d.p.)
   b) and d)

   c) 1.5 hours

4 a)

b)

Section 18 — Scale Drawings and Bearings

18.1 Scale Drawings

Page 209   Exercise 1

1 a) (i) 2 km   (ii) 3 km   (iii) 11 km
      (iv) 1.5 km   (v) 0.25 km   (vi) 0.125 km
   b) (i) 10 cm   (ii) 16 cm   (iii) 28 cm
      (iv) 7 cm   (v) 1 cm   (vi) 1.4 cm

2 a) 700 km   b) 150 km   c) 80 km
   d) 622 km   e) 301 km   f) 430 km

3 a) 3 cm   b) 12 cm   c) 20 cm
   d) 0.5 cm   e) 0.2 cm   f) 0.3 cm

4 a) 5.4 m by 3 m   b) 6.4 m by 4.4 m
   c) 3.7 m by 2.8 m d) 1.8 m by 2.7 m

5 1 cm : 40 km   6 a) 1 cm : 3 km b) 21 km

7 a) 8 cm   b) 36 cm
   c) 42 cm   d) 23.6 cm

8 1.6 cm

9 a) Width = 57 cm, Depth = 30 cm
   b) Width = 66 cm, Depth = 45 cm

10 a) 1 cm : 50 m   b) (i) 75 m   (ii) 125 m

Page 210   Exercise 2

1 a) (i) 7 m   (ii) 24.5 m   (iii) 77 m
      (iv) 34.65 m   (v) 50.75 m   (vi) 89.95 m
   b) (i) 2 cm   (ii) 2.5 cm   (iii) 0.5 cm
      (iv) 0.6 cm   (v) 2.7 cm   (vi) 0.42 cm

2 a) 3 m   b) 8.25 m   c) 4.125 m
   d) 5.925 m   e) 18.075 m   f) 12.9 m

3 a) 0.3 m or 30 cm   b) 1.4 m or 140 cm
   c) 0.84 m or 84 cm   d) 0.12 m or 12 cm
   e) 1 m or 100 cm   f) 0.43 m or 43 cm

4 a) 2 m   b) 1.4 m   c) 1.28 m   d) 0.96 m

5 2.68 cm

6 a) 4 cm   b) 6 cm   c) 20 cm   d) 1.2 cm

7 a) 7.5 cm   b) 11.25 cm   c) 4.5 cm

8 a) 1 cm : 1.5 km   b) 1 : 150 000

9 a) 1 cm : 15 m   b) 4 cm

10 a) 1 : 600   b) 7.2 m   c) 0.75 cm

11 a) 1.2 km   b) 3 km   c) 2.64 km

Answers   405

Page 212 Exercise 3

Your answers to this exercise should be accurate scale drawings with the measurements shown.

1 [Scale drawing: outer rectangle 19 cm × 13 cm, with 8 cm × 3 cm and 5 cm × 3 cm cutouts]

2 [Scale drawing with measurements: 15 cm, 3 cm, 3.75 cm, 5 cm, 4.5 cm, 3 cm, 5 cm, 3 cm]

3 a) [Scale drawing with measurements: 1 cm, 1 cm, 6 cm, 5 cm, 6 cm, 2 cm, 3 cm, 9 cm, 3 cm, 10 cm, 3 cm, 19 cm]

b) Width = 1.5 m, height = 2.25 m.

4 a) [Scale drawing: 11 cm top, 8 cm left, 14 cm bottom, 2.5 cm right]

b) 14 m - 15 m

18.2 Bearings

Page 213 Exercise 1

1 a) 090° **b)** 045° **c)** 180° **d)** 270°
  e) 225° **f)** 315°

2 a) 062° **b)** 130° **c)** 227° **d)** 301°
  e) 071° **f)** 113° **g)** 187° **h)** 288°

3 065°

4 a) 21° **b)** 23° **c)** 75°
  d) 63° **e)** 45° **f)** 48°

5 [Diagram showing compass directions with points a, b, c, d, e, f from O, with North reference]

Page 214 Exercise 2

1 038°   **2** 305°   **3** 130°
4 203°   **5** 281°
6 a) 020° **b)** 130° **c)** 260°
  d) 297° **e)** 195° **f)** 279°
7 a) 32° **b)** 032°
8 a) 270° **b)** 090°
9 a) 135° **b)** 315°
10 a) 112° **b)** 292°
11 a) 055° **b)** 143° **c)** 244° **d)** 326°
   e) 235° **f)** 323° **g)** 064° **h)** 146°

Page 215 Exercise 3

1 a) (i) 250 km, 050°   **(ii)** 190 km, 125°
  b) 340-350 km

2 [Diagram: Tirana to Skopje, bearing 048°, distance 5 cm]

3 [Diagram: Bonn to Salzburg, bearing 125°, distance 6 cm]

4 [Diagram: Budapest to Madrid, bearing 242°, distance 2 cm]

5

[Diagram: Bern — Budapest, 263°, 4 cm, N arrow]

6 a) (i) 300 km (ii) 450 km (iii) 580 km
   b) (i) 060°   (ii) 140°   (iii) 290°

18.3 Scale Drawings and Bearings Problems

Page 216 Exercise 1
1 a) 180°   b) 270°   c) 225°
2 a) 1 cm : 1 km   b) 14.9 km   c) 310°
3 a) [Diagram: N, 110°, 3.9 cm, 020°, 2.3 cm]
   b) 90°
4 a) [Diagram: N, 100°, 3 cm, 055°, 4 cm]
   b) 3200-3250 m (shown by 6.4-6.5 cm on diagram)
   c) 255°
5 a) [Diagram: Start and End path]   b) 22-23 m
6 a) [Diagram: Doncaster, Leicester, King's Lynn]
   b) 090°
   c) (i) 180°   (ii) 135°
   d) (i) 270°   (ii) 315°

Section 19 — Pythagoras and Trigonometry

19.1 Pythagoras' Theorem

Page 217 Exercise 1
1 a) 5 cm   b) 13 mm   c) 30 cm
   d) 34 m   e) 6.71 cm   f) 73.54 m
   g) 2.5 m   h) 7.75 cm   i) 6.36 km
   j) 13.57 mm   k) 1.39 m   l) 3.30 m
2 10.63 cm
3 a) 8.60 cm   b) 11.70 cm   c) 6.58 mm
4 6.65 cm   5 216.33 m   6 25 m
7 1110 m   8 5.98 cm
9 a) 8.38 cm   b) 4.19 cm
10 6.40 units 11 30.46 cm

Page 219 Exercise 2
1 a) 5 cm   b) 5.66 cm   c) 8.49 mm
   d) 24 cm   e) 40 cm   f) 25.61 mm
   g) 4.53 m   h) 14.77 km   i) 3.89 cm
   j) 174.28 mm   k) 9.00 m   l) 247.18 cm
2 a) 7.94 cm   b) 11.53 m
   c) 10.53 mm   d) 14.53 cm
3 15.99 cm   4 0.79 m   5 3.20 m   6 8.66 cm
7 18.73 cm   8 12.36 m 9 1.88 m   10 747 km
11 111 km   12 0.57 m

Page 220 Exercise 3 — Mixed Exercise
1 4.37 m   2 94.58 km   3 10.89 m
4 Yes   5 2.12 m   6 100 m
7 Yes   8 1.96 m   9 8.66 cm
10 a) 8.06 units b) 4.47 units   c) 6.71 units
11 a) 9 m   b) 22.5 m   c) 13.5 m
12 931   13 18.97 units   14 Marrow, by 0.12 km
15 24.97 m   16 10.52 cm   17 10.42 cm

19.2 Trigonometry — Sin, Cos and Tan

Page 222 Exercise 1
1 a) $a = 4.39$ cm   b) $b = 9.33$ cm
   c) $c = 1.06$ cm   d) $d = 8.02$ cm
   e) $p = 7.96$ cm   f) $q = 35.8$ cm
   g) $r = 6.30$ cm   h) $s = 4.58$ cm
2 $m = 11.9$ cm   3 $n = 18.7$ cm
4 a) $a = 68.0°$ b) $b = 45.6°$ c) $c = 47.5°$
5 a) $d = 80.4°$ b) $e = 33.7°$ c) $f = 60.1°$

Page 223 Exercise 2
1 a) 60°   b) 45°   c) 60°   d) 30°
2 a) $\sqrt{3}$ m   b) 1 cm   c) 8 mm   d) 1 m

Answers 407

3 $\tan 45° + \sin 60° = 1 + \frac{\sqrt{3}}{2} = \frac{2}{2} + \frac{\sqrt{3}}{2}$
$= \frac{2 + \sqrt{3}}{2}$

4 $\sqrt{3}$ mm **5** 7 cm

19.3 Pythagoras and Trigonometry Problems

Page 224   Exercise 1
1 309 km
2 a) $a = 5.83$ cm   b) $b = 17.5$ cm
   c) $c = 15.0$ cm   d) $d = 2.40$ m
3 $m = 19.5°$ 4 19.8 m   5 7.8 units
6 a) $a = 3 + 3\sqrt{3}$ cm   b) 12 cm
7 $x = 60°$ 8 45.0°   9 120.8°

Section 20 — Vectors

20.1 Column Vectors

Page 225   Exercise 1
1

2 $\mathbf{a} = \begin{pmatrix}4\\0\end{pmatrix}$ $\mathbf{b} = \begin{pmatrix}-1\\-1\end{pmatrix}$ $\mathbf{c} = \begin{pmatrix}2\\6\end{pmatrix}$ $\mathbf{d} = \begin{pmatrix}-3\\0\end{pmatrix}$

   $\mathbf{e} = \begin{pmatrix}-4\\-1\end{pmatrix}$ $\mathbf{f} = \begin{pmatrix}2\\3.5\end{pmatrix}$ $\mathbf{g} = \begin{pmatrix}-4\\-3\end{pmatrix}$ $\mathbf{h} = \begin{pmatrix}-2\\2\end{pmatrix}$

   $\mathbf{p} = \begin{pmatrix}9\\1\end{pmatrix}$ $\mathbf{q} = \begin{pmatrix}2\\-6\end{pmatrix}$ $\mathbf{r} = \begin{pmatrix}5\\-3.5\end{pmatrix}$ $\mathbf{s} = \begin{pmatrix}-2\\-3\end{pmatrix}$

3 a) $\begin{pmatrix}-3\\9\end{pmatrix}$ b) $\begin{pmatrix}-5\\15\end{pmatrix}$ c) $\begin{pmatrix}-1.5\\4.5\end{pmatrix}$ d) $\begin{pmatrix}2\\-6\end{pmatrix}$

4 a) d   b) g   c) b   d) e

Page 227   Exercise 2
1 a) $\begin{pmatrix}8\\6\end{pmatrix}$ b) $\begin{pmatrix}5\\5\end{pmatrix}$

   c) $\begin{pmatrix}-3\\9\end{pmatrix}$ d) $\begin{pmatrix}-5\\7\end{pmatrix}$

   e) $\begin{pmatrix}4\\2\end{pmatrix}$ f) $\begin{pmatrix}4\\-4\end{pmatrix}$

   g) $\begin{pmatrix}4\\-3\end{pmatrix}$ h) $\begin{pmatrix}-9\\-2\end{pmatrix}$

2 a) $\begin{pmatrix}-1\\2\end{pmatrix}$ b) $\begin{pmatrix}-3\\1\end{pmatrix}$ c) $\begin{pmatrix}0\\11\end{pmatrix}$ d) $\begin{pmatrix}6\\7\end{pmatrix}$

   e) $\begin{pmatrix}4\\-5\end{pmatrix}$ f) $\begin{pmatrix}3\\-3\end{pmatrix}$ g) $\begin{pmatrix}-4\\6\end{pmatrix}$ h) $\begin{pmatrix}5\\26\end{pmatrix}$

3 a) $\begin{pmatrix}7\\7\end{pmatrix}$ b) $\begin{pmatrix}8\\1\end{pmatrix}$ c) $\begin{pmatrix}-7\\4\end{pmatrix}$ d) $\begin{pmatrix}14\\30\end{pmatrix}$

   e) $\begin{pmatrix}19\\14\end{pmatrix}$ f) $\begin{pmatrix}10\\8\end{pmatrix}$ g) $\begin{pmatrix}21\\45\end{pmatrix}$ h) $\begin{pmatrix}21\\10\end{pmatrix}$

4 a) $\begin{pmatrix}2\\4\end{pmatrix}$ b)

   c) The vectors are parallel because $\mathbf{u} + 2\mathbf{v} = 2\mathbf{w}$

Page 228   Exercise 3
1 a) 3a   b) 3b
   c) –3b   d) a + 2b
   e) –a – 2b   f) 2a – 5b
   g) 5a – 8b   h) a – 4b

20.2 Vectors Problems

Page 228 Exercise 1

1. a) $a = \begin{pmatrix} 3 \\ 4 \end{pmatrix}$ $b = \begin{pmatrix} 4 \\ -2 \end{pmatrix}$ $c = \begin{pmatrix} -2 \\ -4 \end{pmatrix}$ $d = \begin{pmatrix} -4 \\ -1 \end{pmatrix}$

   $e = \begin{pmatrix} 4 \\ -1 \end{pmatrix}$ $f = \begin{pmatrix} 1 \\ 4 \end{pmatrix}$ $g = \begin{pmatrix} 0 \\ -5 \end{pmatrix}$ $h = \begin{pmatrix} 1 \\ -4 \end{pmatrix}$

   b) b   c) g   d) d, e, f and h

2. a) $\begin{pmatrix} 12 \\ -9 \end{pmatrix}$ b) $\begin{pmatrix} -1 \\ 9 \end{pmatrix}$ c) $\begin{pmatrix} -9 \\ 11 \end{pmatrix}$ d) $\begin{pmatrix} -1 \\ 16 \end{pmatrix}$

3. a) $a + b = \begin{pmatrix} 4 \\ -1 \end{pmatrix}$

   b) $e - d = \begin{pmatrix} -1 \\ 8 \end{pmatrix}$

   c) a and f   d) b and e   e) e   f) f

Page 229 Exercise 2

1. a) −4p   b) −p   c) q + p
   d) −p − q   e) 3p − q   f) −4p + q

2. a) (i) −a − b   (ii) −a + b   b) parallelogram

3. a) 4a   b) 3c   c) 3a
   d) 2c   e) −3c + 4a   f) −4a + 3c

4. E.g.
   a) p and −r + q   b) q and p + r
   c) r and q − p   d) −q and −r − p
   e) −p and r − q   f) −r and p − q

Section 21 — Constructions

21.1 Circles

Page 230 Exercise 1

1. a) 6 cm   b) 4 cm   c) 70 mm   d) 56 mm
2. a) 4 cm   b) 5 mm   c) 9.5 mm   d) 2.4 cm
3. a) 8 cm   b) 12 cm   c) 60 mm   d) 50 m
   e) 5.6 m   f) 9.2 mm   g) 7.4 m   h) 98 mm
   i) 110 m   j) 8.4 mm
4. a) 1 cm   b) 6 cm   c) 7 m   d) 14 mm
   e) 0.7 m   f) 1.4 cm   g) 28.5 mm   h) 2.15 cm
   i) 0.4 m   j) 0.01 cm

5. Measure your diagrams — they should be as follows:
   a) 4 cm, 8 cm   b) 5 cm, 10 cm
   c) 40 mm, 80 mm   d) 3 cm, 6 cm
   e) 3.5 cm, 7 cm   f) 11.5 mm, 23 mm

Page 231 Exercise 2

1. a) chord   b) diameter   c) tangent
   d) radius   e) sector   f) circumference
   g) arc   h) segment

2. A: radius   B: diameter   C: circumference
   D: tangent   E: sector   F: segment

3. Your diagram should look something like this:
   a) chord   b) arc   c) tangent   d) diameter

21.2 Lines, Angles and Triangles

Page 232 Exercise 1

1. $a = 40°$ $b = 3.9$ cm - 4 cm $c = 4.9$ cm - 5 cm
   $d = 65°$ $e = 4.4$ cm - 4.5 cm $f = 2.9$ cm - 3 cm
   $g = 120°$ $h = 4.8$ cm $i = 1.8$ cm

2. a) and b) 30°, 70°, 6 cm

3. a) and b) 130°, 170°, 8.5 cm

4 a) [triangle with angles 102°, 52°, 26°]
b) [triangle with angles 45°, 45°, 90°]

Page 233   Exercise 2

1 If you've drawn the triangles accurately, your answers should be as follows:
a) $l = 5.0$ cm - 5.1 cm   b) $l = 6.1$ cm - 6.2 cm
c) $l = 8.8$ cm - 8.9 cm   d) $l = 5.6$ cm - 5.7 cm

2 a) (i) [triangle A, B, C with angle A = 55°, angle C = 35°, AB = 4 cm]
(ii) [triangle with angle A = 22°, angle B = 107°, AB = 8 cm]
(iii) [triangle with angle A = 65°, angle B = 30°, AB = 6.5 cm]
(iv) [triangle with angle A = 120°, angle B = 28°, AB = 7.2 cm]

b) (i)   3.2 cm - 3.3 cm   (ii) 3.8 cm - 3.9 cm
   (iii) 5.9 cm - 6.0 cm   (iv) 11.7 cm - 11.8 cm

3 [equilateral triangle, all sides 4 cm, all angles 60°]

4 3.5 km - 3.6 km

Page 234   Exercise 3

1 If you've drawn the triangles accurately, your answers should be as follows:
a) $l = 13$ cm   b) $l = 5.5$ cm - 5.6 cm
c) $l = 4.8$ cm - 4.9 cm d) $l = 110$ mm

2 a) (i) [triangle with angle B = 40°, AB = 6 cm, BC = 7 cm]
(ii) [triangle with angle B = 110°, AB = 4 cm, BC = 3 cm]
(iii) [triangle with angle B = 20°, AB = 65 mm, BC = 53 mm]
(iv) [triangle with angle B = 45°, AB = 45 mm, BC = 45 mm]

b) (i)   4.5 cm - 4.6 cm   (ii) 5.7 cm - 5.8 cm
   (iii) 23 mm - 24 mm   (iv) 34 mm - 35 mm

3 [isosceles triangle, two sides 5 cm with 50° between them]

4 a) and b) [angle PSR = 60°, SP = 5 cm, SR = 5 cm]
c) 120°
d) [parallelogram PQRS with angles 120°, 60°, 60°, 120°, sides 5 cm]

5 a) [parallelogram with sides 6 cm, angles 40° and 140°]
b) [parallelogram with sides 4.5 cm, angles 70° and 110°]

Page 235   Exercise 4

1 Measure all 3 sides of your triangles and check the lengths are correct.

2 Measure all 3 sides of your triangles and check the lengths are correct.

410   *Answers*

3 Measure all 3 sides of your triangle and check the lengths are correct.

4

Exeter — 4.7 cm — Yeovil — 2.7 cm — Weymouth — 5.4 cm — Exeter

21.3 Constructions
Page 236 Exercise 1

1 P ←5 cm→ Q

2 X — 9 cm — Y

3 A ←7 cm→ B

4 a) A ←6 cm→ B

b) Use part **a)** to get: rhombus ACBD with AB = 6 cm, diagonal 8 cm.

5 a), b), c) circle constructions with points A, B, C, D

d) They meet at the circle's centre.

Page 237 Exercise 2

1 a) 50°/50° **b)** 70°/70° **c)** 48°/48° **d)** 22°/22° **e)** 25°/25° **f)** 35°/35° **g)** 10°/10° **h)** 32.5°/32.5°

2 a) triangle **b)** triangle with angle bisectors — They intersect at a single point.

3 a) Triangle with A, B, C; 55°/55°, BC = 5 cm, AB = 5 cm.

b) ABCD is a kite. (AB = 5 cm, BC = 5 cm, CD = 8 cm, 55°/55°)

Page 238 Exercise 3

1 Triangle XYZ with perpendicular construction.

2 P, Q, R construction — **or** — alternative P, Q, R construction

3 a), b) and c) Graph with points A, B, C plotted on grid from 0 to 10.

4 a) [triangle diagram]
   b) [triangle with construction arcs diagram]
   They intersect at a single point.

5 a) [triangle DEF with DF = 6 cm, DE = 5 cm, angle D = 55°]
   b) [triangle DEF with point G, angle D = 55°]
   c) FG = 4.9 cm, area = 12.3 cm²

Page 239   Exercise 4

1 Measure the length of AB and the size of the angle in your diagram to check they are correct.
2 Measure the 3 sides and angles in your triangle to check they are correct.
   [equilateral triangle with sides 6 cm and angles 60°]

Page 239   Exercise 5

1 Measure the length of AB and the size of the angle in your diagram to check they are correct.
2 Measure the length of AB and the sizes of the 3 angles in your triangle to check they are correct.
   [right triangle ABC with angle A = 60°, angle B = 30°, AB = 7 cm]
3 Measure the sides and angles in your triangle to check they are correct.
   [triangle PQR with angle R = 120°, angles P and Q = 30°, PQ = 8 cm]

Page 240   Exercise 6

1 Measure your angle to check that it is a right angle.
2 Measure the sides of your rectangle and check the lengths are correct. Measure each angle to check they are right angles.

Page 240   Exercise 7

1 Measure your angle to check that it is 45°.
2 [triangle ABC with angles A and B = 45°, AB = 8 cm]

   Measure AB to check the length is correct. Measure angles CAB and CBA to check they are 45°.

Page 241   Exercise 8

1 [perpendicular bisector construction of AB through P]

2 [parallel lines construction and parallelogram]

3 a) [equilateral triangle construction with 60° angles, base 10 cm]
   b) [triangle with 60° angles, base 10 cm, side 3 cm to C]
   c) [trapezium/triangle construction with D and C]

Page 241   Exercise 9 — Mixed Exercise

1 a) [angle of 60° at A, AB = 8 cm]
   b) [parallelogram ABCD with sides 8 cm and angles 60°]

2 a) [equilateral triangle with sides 5.8 cm, angle 60°]
   b) [isosceles triangle with perpendicular bisector construction]

412   Answers

3 a)

b) 75°

4

Construct an angle of 60°. Then bisect that angle once to get an angle of 30°. Then bisect this angle of 30° to construct an angle of 15°.

21.4 Loci
Page 242   Exercise 1

1

2 a)   **b)**

3   **4**

5

6 a) P •←— 5 cm —→• Q

b)

c)

d) The points marked with dots are both 3 cm from P and 4 cm from Q.

7 a)

b)

8 a)   **b)**

9 a)   **b)** Locus of points shown by black line.

Page 243   Exercise 2

1 a) P •←— 3 cm —→• L

b)

Answers **413**

2 Location of treasure marked by the dot.

3 Location of bonfire marked by the dot.

4 a) $A \bullet \!\!\leftarrow\!\! 5\text{ cm}\!\!\rightarrow\!\!\bullet B$
   b) Shaded area shows where they could meet.

5 Shaded regions show where the dog can move.
   a)   b)

Section 22 — Area and Perimeter

22.1 Rectangles and Triangles

Page 244   Exercise 1

1 a) 12 cm   b) 28 m   c) 20 cm
   d) 20 cm   e) 43 m   f) 90 mm
   g) 16.8 cm   h) 31.8 mm   i) 25.9 m

Page 245   Exercise 2

1 a) 50 cm^2 b) 18 m^2 c) 16 mm^2
   d) 33 m^2 e) 121 cm^2 f) 10 mm^2
   g) 6 cm^2 h) 176 cm^2 i) 25 cm^2

Page 246   Exercise 3 — Mixed Exercise

1 a) (i) 9 cm   (ii) 4.34 cm^2
   b) (i) 8.4 mm   (ii) 3.41 mm^2
   c) (i) 7.2 cm   (ii) 3.24 cm^2
2 a) (i) 16 cm   (ii) 16 cm^2
   b) (i) 28 m   (ii) 48 m^2
   c) (i) 76 mm   (ii) 345 mm^2
   d) (i) 68 m   (ii) 289 m^2
   e) (i) 53 m   (ii) 95.46 m^2
   f) (i) 22.8 mm   (ii) 21.6 mm^2

3 a) (i) 24 cm   (ii) 26.8 cm^2
   b) (i) 26 m   (ii) 26.95 m^2
   c) (i) 42.8 mm   (ii) 65.8 mm^2
   d) (i) 30 mm   (ii) 25.6 mm^2
   e) (i) 31.5 m   (ii) 50 m^2
   f) (i) 36 m   (ii) 40.15 m^2
4 a) 407 m^2 b) 81.6 m
5 a) 5.88 m^2 b) 9.8 m
6 27
7 a) 67.5 m^2 b) 0.25 m^2 c) 270
8 a) 100 cm   b) 1416 cm^2

Page 247   Exercise 4

1 a) 68 m^2 b) 108 m^2 c) 148 mm^2
2 a) (i) 50 cm   (ii) 136 cm^2
   b) (i) 30 cm   (ii) 47 cm^2
   c) (i) 92 mm   (ii) 334 mm^2
3 a) 56 m^2 b) 75 cm^2

22.2 Other Quadrilaterals

Page 248   Exercise 1

1 a) 28 cm^2 b) 8 m^2 c) 48 mm^2
   d) 54 mm^2 e) 630 m^2 f) 47.56 mm^2
2 50.84 cm^2
3 The square has the larger area. The vertical height of the rhombus (a special type of parallelogram) is less than 6 cm, so its area will be less than the area of the square.

Page 249   Exercise 2

1 a) 28 m^2 b) 90 mm^2 c) 40 mm^2
   d) 19.475 cm^2 e) 313.95 mm^2 f) 0.1375 cm^2
2 90 m^2
3 They have the same area, since they have the same vertical height, and ½(9 + 3) = 6.

Page 250   Exercise 3 — Mixed Exercise

1 a) 22 cm^2 b) 210 m^2 c) 937.5 mm^2
   d) 288 mm^2 e) 50.6 cm^2 f) 5.25 m^2
2 116.16 cm^2
3 a) 1800 cm^2 b) 1200 cm^2

Page 251   Exercise 4

1 a) 82.5 cm^2 b) 139 mm^2
2 a) (i) 96 mm^2 (ii) 46 mm
   b) (i) 89.25 m^2 (ii) 34 m
   c) (i) 336 m^2 (ii) 88 m
   d) (i) 810 m^2 (ii) 150 m

22.3 Circumference of a Circle

The answers in this topic have been calculated using the π button on a calculator.

Page 252 Exercise 1

1. a) 25.1 cm b) 37.7 cm c) 6.3 cm
   d) 31.4 cm e) 94.2 mm f) 15.7 mm
   g) 22.0 m h) 28.3 cm

2. a) $d = 4$ cm, so $C = 12.6$ cm
   b) $d = 3$ mm, so $C = 9.4$ mm
   c) $d = 5$ cm, so $C = 15.7$ cm
   d) $d = 1$ m, so $C = 3.1$ m
   e) $d = 3.4$ cm, so $C = 10.7$ cm
   f) $d = 2.6$ mm, so $C = 8.2$ mm
   g) $d = 5.2$ m, so $C = 16.3$ m
   h) $d = 22.2$ mm, so $C = 69.7$ mm

3. a) 12.6 cm b) 25.1 mm c) 28.3 m
   d) 18.8 cm e) 69.1 m f) 138.2 cm
   g) 88.0 km h) 219.9 mm i) 7.9 m
   j) 11.9 cm k) 0.6 km l) 19.8 mm

Page 253 Exercise 2

1. a) 10.3 cm b) 66.8 mm
   c) 10.3 m d) 36.0 cm

2. a) 16.3 cm b) 61.1 mm c) 15.9 cm
   d) 32.1 mm e) 50.1 mm f) 13.4 cm

Page 254 Exercise 3

1. 9.4 m 2. 62.8 cm 3. 78.5 cm 4. 144.5 m
5. 264 cm 6. 110 mm (or 11 cm) 7. 35.8 km
8. a) 345.6 cm b) 172.8 cm
9. 2857 m (to nearest m) 10. 703 m (to nearest m)
11. 50.3 m 12. 8.1 m 13. 25.1 cm

22.4 Area of a Circle

The answers in this topic have been calculated using the π button on a calculator.

Page 255 Exercise 1

1. a) 12.6 cm² b) 314.2 mm²
   c) 28.3 m² d) 2827.4 mm²

2. a) $r = 4$ cm, so $A = 50.3$ cm²
   b) $r = 25$ mm, so $A = 1963.5$ mm²
   c) $r = 3.5$ m, so $A = 38.5$ m²
   d) $r = 6$ mm, so $A = 113.1$ mm²

3. a) 113.1 mm² b) 78.5 cm² c) 50.3 m²
   d) 132.7 cm² e) 56.7 mm² f) 9.6 m²
   g) 113.1 km² h) 380.1 cm² i) 5.3 m²
   j) 1520.5 mm² k) 1.1 mm² l) 3.5 m²

4. 38.5 m² 5. 50.3 cm² 6. 132.7 cm²
7. 40.7 m² 8. 2.0 km² 9. 21.2 cm²
10. a) 5.3 cm²
    b) A 2p coin has the greater area (of 5.3 cm², the combined area of two 5p coins is 5.1 cm²).

11. The circle, with an area of 452.4 mm². (The rectangle has an area of 440 mm².)
12. 39.3 cm² 13. 3.1 cm²

Page 257 Exercise 2

1. a) 77.0 cm² b) 139.3 mm² c) 59.3 cm²
   d) 22.3 cm² e) 116.5 cm² f) 146.3 mm²
   g) 158.5 cm² h) 178.5 mm² i) 10.3 cm²

2. 9.8 m² 3. 2.4 m² 4. 28.3 cm²
5. 1714.2 m² 6. 1.9 cm² 7. 15.7 m²
8. a) 353.4 cm²
   b) 3646.6 cm²

22.5 Arcs and Sectors of Circles

The answers in this topic have been calculated using the π button on a calculator.

Page 258 Exercise 1

1. a) arc length $\frac{\pi}{4}$ cm, sector area $\frac{3\pi}{8}$ cm²
   b) arc length $\frac{20\pi}{9}$ cm, sector area $\frac{40\pi}{9}$ cm²
   c) arc length $\frac{5\pi}{2}$ cm, sector area $\frac{25\pi}{2}$ cm²
   d) arc length $\frac{10\pi}{3}$ cm, sector area $\frac{25\pi}{3}$ cm²

2. a) sector area 82.10 cm², arc length 29.85 cm
   b) sector area 198.20 in², arc length 37.75 in
   c) sector area 403.38 in², arc length 67.23 in
   d) sector area 69.32 m², arc length 21.33 m

22.6 Area and Perimeter Problems

The answers in this topic have been calculated using the π button on a calculator.

Page 258 Exercise 1

1. a) 11.3 m² b) 2128.3 mm² c) 216 mm²
2. a) $P = 12.6$ cm; $A = 10.3$ cm²
   b) $P = 754.0$ m; $A = 27\,879.6$ m²
   c) $P = 15.1$ cm; $A = 6.6$ cm²
3. a) 36.2 cm² b) 34.8 cm²
4. 1608.5 m² 5. 120 cm²
6. arc length 1.88 cm, sector area 8.48 cm²
7. 18.4 cm
8. arc length $\frac{10\pi}{9}$ m, sector area $\frac{25\pi}{9}$ m²
9. They both have the same area ($= a^2$).

Page 260 Exercise 2

1. 40.7 m 2. 14.3 cm 3. 3.0 cm 4. 9.2 feet
5. 5.1 km 6. 25.5 m

Page 260 Exercise 3

1. 4.9 cm 2. 3.0 m 3. 6.3 m 4. 17.5 m

Section 23 — 3D Shapes

23.1 Nets

Page 261   Exercise 1

1. **a)** 6 faces, 8 vertices, 12 edges
   b) 5 faces, 6 vertices, 9 edges
   c) 4 faces, 4 vertices, 6 edges
   d) 5 faces, 5 vertices, 8 edges

2. **a)** Cube   **b)** Triangular Prism
   c) Tetrahedron   **d)** Square-based Pyramid
   e) Cylinder

3. A, B and C

Page 262   Exercise 2

1. **a)** (i) 0   (ii) 4   **b)** (i) 6   (ii) 0
   c) (i) 1   (ii) 4

2. 8

3. No, a cuboid has 6 faces but this net is made up of only 5 rectangles.

4. No, a cube has 6 faces but this net is made up of 7 squares.

5. **a)** Square-based Pyramid
   b) Cuboid
   c) Triangular Prism

6. **a)** 2   **b)** 2   **c)** 2   **d)** 0
7. **a)** 1   **b)** 1   **c)** 1   **d)** 0
8. C

Page 263   Exercise 3

1. **a)** E.g.   **b)** E.g.
2. **a)** E.g.   **b)** E.g.
   c) E.g.   **d)** E.g.
   e) E.g.   **f)** E.g.
   g) E.g.   **h)** E.g.

3. **a)** E.g.   **b)** E.g.
   c) E.g.   **d)** E.g.
   e) E.g.   **f)** E.g.

23.2 Plans and Elevations

Page 265   Exercise 1

1. **a)**   **b)**
2. **a)**   **b)**
3. **a)** Plan View

   Front Elevation   Side Elevation

416   *Answers*

b) [Plan View, Front Elevation, Side Elevation]

c) [Plan View, Front Elevation, Side Elevation]

d) [Plan View, Front Elevation, Side Elevation]

4 B   **5** P

6 a) [Plan View, Front Elevation, Side Elevation]

b) [Plan View, Front Elevation, Side Elevation]

c) [Plan View, Front Elevation, Side Elevation]

d) [Plan View, Front Elevation, Side Elevation]

e) [Plan View, Front Elevation, Side Elevation]

f) [Plan View, Front Elevation, Side Elevation]

g) [Plan View, Front Elevation, Side Elevation]

h) [Plan View, Front Elevation, Side Elevation]

Page 266   Exercise 2

1 a) [Plan View 1 cm × 1 cm, Front Elevation 1 cm × 1 cm, Side Elevation 1 cm × 1 cm]

Answers 417

b)

Plan View: rectangle 3 cm × 1 cm
Front Elevation: rectangle 3 cm × 1 cm
Side Elevation: square 1 cm × 1 cm

c)

Plan View: square 2 cm × 2 cm
Front Elevation: rectangle 2 cm × 5 cm
Side Elevation: rectangle 2 cm × 5 cm

d)

Plan View: rectangle 2 cm × 6 cm
Front Elevation: right triangle, base 2 cm, height 5 cm
Side Elevation: rectangle 6 cm × 5 cm

e)

Plan View: rectangle 1 cm × 4 cm (with vertical line)
Front Elevation: triangle, base 1 cm, height 3 cm
Side Elevation: rectangle 4 cm × 3 cm

f)

Plan View: square 2 cm × 2 cm with X inside
Front Elevation: triangle, base 2 cm, height 3 cm
Side Elevation: triangle, base 2 cm, height 3 cm

2 a)

Plan View: circle, radius 2 cm
Front Elevation: square 4 cm × 5 cm
Side Elevation: square 4 cm × 5 cm

b)

Plan View: rectangle 2 cm × 6 cm
Front Elevation: circle, diameter 2 cm
Side Elevation: rectangle 6 cm × 2 cm

c)

Plan View: circle, radius 3 cm
Front Elevation: triangle, base 6 cm, height 6 cm
Side Elevation: triangle, base 6 cm, height 6 cm

3 a)

Plan View: square 2 cm × 2 cm
Front Elevation: square 2 cm × 2 cm
Side Elevation: square 2 cm × 2 cm

b) E.g.

Plan View: rectangle 2 cm × 5 cm
Front Elevation: rectangle 2 cm × 1 cm
Side Elevation: rectangle 5 cm × 1 cm

c) E.g.

Plan View: circle, radius 3 cm
Front Elevation: rectangle 6 cm × 4 cm
Side Elevation: rectangle 6 cm × 4 cm

d) E.g.

Plan View: circle, radius 1 cm
Front Elevation: triangle, base 2 cm, height 4 cm
Side Elevation: triangle, base 2 cm, height 4 cm

e) E.g.

Plan View: rectangle 3 cm × 4 cm (with vertical line)
Front Elevation: triangle, base 3 cm, height 5 cm
Side Elevation: rectangle 4 cm × 5 cm

418   *Answers*

f) E.g.

3 cm × 3 cm Plan View

Front Elevation 5 cm × 3 cm

Side Elevation 5 cm × 3 cm

23.3 Isometric Drawings

Page 267 Exercise 1

1 a) b) c) d)

2 a) b) c) d)

3 a) b)
c) E.g. d) E.g.
e) E.g. f) E.g.

4 a) b) c) d) e) f)

Page 269 Exercise 2

1 a) b) c) d) e)

2 a) b) c) d) e)

3 a) b) c)

Answers **419**

23.4 Volume

Page 270   Exercise 1

1. **a)** 5 cm³   **b)** 4 cm³   **c)** 8 cm³   **d)** 7 cm³
2. **a)** 30 cm³   **b)** 10 m³   **c)** 28 cm³
   d) 84 mm³   **e)** 27 cm³   **f)** 64 m³
3. **a)** 6 cm³   **b)** 24 cm³   **c)** 70 m³
   d) 1600 cm³   **e)** 31.5 cm³   **f)** 756 m³
   g) 130 mm³   **h)** 35.136 mm³   **i)** 200.564 cm³
4. 32.768 mm³   5. By 0.06 m³ (box A is bigger).
6. No.   7. 3312 cm³
8. **a)** 20 cm³   **b)** 6 cm³
9. 1.2 cm
10. **a)** 0.45 m³   **b)** 0.225 m³   **c)** 0.4 m

Page 271   Exercise 2

1. **a)** 6 cm³   **b)** 54 cm³   **c)** 9 m³
   d) 12.25 cm³   **e)** 16.1875 mm³   **f)** 105.56 mm³
2. **a)** 28 cm³   **b)** 30 cm³
   c) 22.5 cm³   **d)** 15.71 cm³ (to 2 d.p.)
3. **a)** 60 cm³   **b)** 66 cm³
   c) 33.93 cm³ (to 2 d.p.)   **d)** 101.2 cm³
4. **a)** 624 cm³   **b)** 8.463 m³
   c) 904.78 m³ (to 2 d.p.)   **d)** 282.74 mm³ (to 2 d.p.)
   e) 18.9 m³
5. **a)** 14.4 m³   **b)** 80 cm³   **c)** 33 mm³   **d)** 9 m³
6. **a)** 30 cm³   **b)** 60 cm³   **c)** 80 cm³   **d)** 51 cm³

Page 273   Exercise 3

1. **a)** 36π cm³   **b)** 972π cm³   **c)** 4500π m³
   d) $12\,348\pi$ mm³   **e)** 4.5π m³
2. **a)** 33.51 cm³   **b)** 2144.66 m³
   c) 3705.97 mm³   **d)** 16 210.17 m³
   e) 1057.40 cm³
3. 18.0 cm

Page 273   Exercise 4

1. **a)** 100π m³   **b)** 392π cm³
   c) 600π m³   **d)** 1650π mm³
2. **a)** 768π cm³   **b)** 12π cm³   **c)** 756π cm³
3. 2199.11 cm³

Page 274   Exercise 5

1. **a)** 60 cm³   **b)** 8 m³
2. 120 cm³   3. 90 cm³
4. 108 m³   5. 8 cm

Page 274   Exercise 6

1. **a)** 40 cm³ per second   **b)** 180 litres per minute
   c) 77 m³ per minute   **d)** 18.75 litres per hour
2. 30 minutes   3. 106 minutes

23.5 Surface Area

Page 275   Exercise 1

1. 12 cm²   2. **a)** 1 cm²   **b)** 6 cm²
3. **a)** 4 m²   **b)** 24 m²
4. **a)** 8 m²   **b)** 12 m²   **c)** 6 m²   **d)** 52 m²
5. **a)** 54 cm²   **b)** 38 cm²   **c)** 23 m²   **d)** 57.5 m²
6. **a)** 390 mm²   **b)** 31.6 m²
   c) 72 cm²   **d)** 174 cm²
7. **a)** 150 m²   **b)** 216 mm²   **c)** 48 m²
   d) 135.5 m²   **e)** 64 cm²
8. **a)** 11.69 m²   **b)** 3 tins

Page 277   Exercise 2

1. **a)** [diagram: rectangle 6 cm by 2π cm with circles of radius 1 cm]
   b) Circular faces have area 3.14 cm²
   Rectangular surface has area 37.70 cm²
   c) 44.0 cm²
2. **a)** [diagram: rectangle 4π cm by 2 cm with circles of radius 2 cm]
   b) Circular faces have area 12.57 cm²
   Rectangular surface has area 25.13 cm²
   c) 50.3 cm²
3. **a)** 31.42 cm²   **b)** 226.19 m²   **c)** 276.46 mm²
   d) 131.95 m²   **e)** 12.82 m²   **f)** 51.90 mm²
   g) 8.17 m²   **h)** 207.35 m²
4. **a)** 113.1 m²   **b)** 471.2 mm²   **c)** 1694.1 cm²
   d) 1537.9 m²   **e)** 2.5 m²
5. **a)** 19.10 m²   **b)** 2 tins
6. **a)** 98.14 m²   **b)** 883.3 m²
7. 3.27 m²

Page 278   Exercise 3

1. **a)** 16π cm²   **b)** 100π cm²   **c)** 196π m²
   d) 324π mm²   **e)** 441π m²
2. **a)** 78.54 cm²   **b)** 633.47 m²
   c) 1576.33 mm²   **d)** 4680.85 m²
   e) 299.26 cm²
3. **a)** 90π m²   **b)** 224π cm²   **c)** 480π m²
4. **a)** 804.25 m²   **b)** 204.20 cm²
   c) 15.21 m²   **d)** 95.19 cm²
5. 4.6 cm

Page 279 Exercise 4 — Mixed Exercise

1. **a)** E.g. **b)** 72 cm²

2. **a)** 113.10 cm² **b)** 226.19 cm²
3. **a)** 54 cm² **b)** 40 cm² **c)** 72 cm² **d)** 78 cm²
4. **a)** 1000 m² **b)** £450
5. **a)** 12 m **b)** E.g.

   c) 510 m²
6. **a)** 65 cm **b)** 6776π cm²
7. 4 : 1
8. **a)** Your drawing should look like this:
   Measure the lengths on your drawing to check it is correct.
   b) 3.4 m **c)** 46 m²
   d) £28 **e)** £51

23.6 3D Shapes Problems

Page 280 Exercise 1

1. **a)** E.g. P, Q

   b) P Plan View, Front Elevation, Side Elevation

   Q Plan View, Front Elevation, Side Elevation

   c) P, Q

   d) P 36 cm³ Q 24 cm³
   e) P 72 cm² Q 60 cm²

2. **a)** E.g. **b)** 42.41 cm²
3. **a)** 512 cm³ **b)** 12 288 cm³
4. **a)** E.g. **b)** E.g.
5. **a)** E.g. **b)** 4 cm

   c) Plan View, Front Elevation, Side Elevation

Answers **421**

d)

6 a) 22 619 cm^3 b) 283 cm^3 c) 80 jars
7 a) 9 cm^2 b) 3 cm c) 27 cm^3
   d) 10.8 seconds e)

8 a) 473.09 cm^3 b) 29.6 cm × 22.2 cm × 11 cm
   c) 7228.32 cm^3 d) 1551.2 cm^3
9 a) 1 : 4 b) 9 : 22
10 294 cm^3
11 a) 2 : 3 b) 4 : 9 c) 8 : 27
12 a) 1244.07 cm^3 b) 215.98 cm^3
    c) 1028.1 cm^3 d) 4.29 cm^3 e) 240 sheets
13 a) 16.00 mm b) 2238 mm^2
    c) 10 000 mm^3 d) 2146 mm^3
14 a) 324π m^3 b) (i) 15 m (ii) 216π m^2
    c) 228π m^3

Section 24 — Transformations

24.1 Reflection

Page 283   Exercise 1
1 a)–h)

Page 284   Exercise 2
1 a), b)

   A$_1$(−4, 6)   A(4, 6)
   B$_1$(−6, 4)   E(2, 4)   B(6, 4)
   E$_1$(−2, 4)
   C$_1$(−6, 1) D$_1$(−2, 1)   D(2, 1)   C(6, 1)

   c) The x-coordinates become negative in the reflected shape, and the y-coordinates stay the same.

2 a)
   b)
3 a) (i)
      (ii)

b) The sign of the *y*-coordinate is reversed (so a positive *y*-coordinate becomes negative, and a negative *y*-coordinate becomes positive), while the *x*-coordinate stays the same.

4 a) (1, −2) **b)** (3, 0) **c)** (−2, −4)
d) (−1, 3) **e)** (−2, 2)

5 a) (−4, 5) **b)** (−7, 2) **c)** (1, 3)
d) (3, −1) **e)** (4, −8)

6 a), b), c)

d) The *y*-axis.

Page 285 Exercise 3

1 a), b), c)

d) $y = 7$

2 a), b), c), d)

e) $x = 1$

Page 286 Exercise 4

1 a), b)

c) The *x*-coordinate becomes the *y*-coordinate, and the *y*-coordinate becomes the *x*-coordinate.

2 a)

b)

3 a) (2, 1) **b)** (0, 3) **c)** (4, −2)
d) (−3, −1) **e)** (−2, −2)

24.2 Rotation

Page 287 Exercise 1

1 a) **b)**

2 a) **b)**

3 a) **b)**

c) **d)**

Answers 423

4 a), b) [diagrams]

5 a), b), c) [diagrams]

6 a), b) [diagrams]

7 a), b) [diagram with triangles A and B on coordinate grid]

8 a), b), c), d) [diagram with shapes A, B, C, D on coordinate grid]

9 a), b), c), d) [diagram with shapes A, B, C, D on coordinate grid]

10 a), b), c) [diagram showing X(4, 2) and Y(−4, −2)]

11 a), b), c) [diagram showing A(−2, 1), B(−2, 6), C(4, 1), C₁(8, 3), B₁(3, −3), A₁(8, −3)]

12 $D_1(6, 2)$, $E_1(6, -5)$, $F_1(1, -5)$

Page 290   Exercise 2

1 a) Rotation of 90° clockwise (or 270° anticlockwise) about the origin.
b) Rotation of 90° anticlockwise (or 270° clockwise) about the origin.

2 a) Rotation of 180° about the origin.
b) Rotation of 180° about (0, 2).

3 a) Rotation of 180° about (0, 3).
b) Rotation of 90° anticlockwise (or 270° clockwise) about (0, 2).

4 a) Rotation of 90° anticlockwise (or 270° clockwise) about (−1, 7).
b) Rotation of 90° clockwise (or 270° anticlockwise) about (1, −2).

5 a) Rotation of 180° about (0, 6).
b) Rotation of 90° anticlockwise (or 270° clockwise) about (−2, 7).
c) Rotation of 90° clockwise (or 270° anticlockwise) about (1, 8).

6 a) [diagram showing triangles X, Y, Z, V, W, U]
b) Rotation of 90° anticlockwise (or 270° clockwise) about (−2, 1).

24.3 Translations

Page 291   Exercise 1

1 a) 1 to the right, 1 up   b) 2 to the right
   c) 3 to the right, 1 down   d) 2 to the left, 6 up
   e) 3 to the left, 2 down   f) 5 to the left

2 a) [diagram with shapes A, B, C, D, E]   b) [diagram with shapes P, Q, R, S, T]

3 a), b)

c) The x-coordinates of the image points are always 10 less than those of the original points.
The y-coordinates of the image points are always 1 less than the originals.

4 a) $(3, -3)$ b) $(6, -4)$ c) $(7, -6)$
    d) $(2, -9)$ e) $(0, 1)$ f) $(5, -6)$

5 a) $(-2, 4)$ b) $(-1, 9)$ c) $(-6, 5)$
    d) $(3, 2)$ e) $(-5, -3)$ f) $(-7, 8)$

6 $D_1(-1, 3), E_1(1, 0), F_1(2, 2)$

7 $P_1(-3, -4), Q_1(1, -3), R_1(-1, -1), S_1(-4, -2)$

Page 292   Exercise 2

1 a) $\begin{pmatrix} 1 \\ 2 \end{pmatrix}$ b) $\begin{pmatrix} 1 \\ -2 \end{pmatrix}$ c) $\begin{pmatrix} -2 \\ 0 \end{pmatrix}$ d) $\begin{pmatrix} 0 \\ -3 \end{pmatrix}$

   e) $\begin{pmatrix} -4 \\ -3 \end{pmatrix}$ f) $\begin{pmatrix} 6 \\ 7 \end{pmatrix}$ g) $\begin{pmatrix} -5 \\ 2 \end{pmatrix}$ h) $\begin{pmatrix} 0 \\ 6 \end{pmatrix}$

2 a) 2 units to the right, 3 units down
   b) $\begin{pmatrix} 2 \\ -3 \end{pmatrix}$ c) $\begin{pmatrix} 2 \\ -4 \end{pmatrix}$

3 a) $\begin{pmatrix} 4 \\ -3 \end{pmatrix}$ b) $\begin{pmatrix} 9 \\ 0 \end{pmatrix}$ c) $\begin{pmatrix} -5 \\ -3 \end{pmatrix}$
   d) $\begin{pmatrix} 4 \\ -5 \end{pmatrix}$ e) $\begin{pmatrix} -13 \\ 5 \end{pmatrix}$ f) $\begin{pmatrix} -9 \\ 2 \end{pmatrix}$

4 a) $\begin{pmatrix} 0 \\ -5 \end{pmatrix}$ b) $\begin{pmatrix} 8 \\ 0 \end{pmatrix}$ c) $\begin{pmatrix} 13 \\ 1 \end{pmatrix}$
   d) $\begin{pmatrix} -8 \\ 0 \end{pmatrix}$ e) $\begin{pmatrix} -13 \\ -6 \end{pmatrix}$ f) $\begin{pmatrix} -8 \\ 5 \end{pmatrix}$

5 a)   b) $\begin{pmatrix} 3 \\ 4 \end{pmatrix}$

6 a) $\begin{pmatrix} -1 \\ 2 \end{pmatrix}$ b) $\begin{pmatrix} 1 \\ -2 \end{pmatrix}$

Page 294   Exercise 3

1 a) $\begin{pmatrix} 3 \\ -5 \end{pmatrix}$ b) $\begin{pmatrix} -3 \\ 5 \end{pmatrix}$

   c) The x and y coordinates have changed signs.

2 $\begin{pmatrix} -1 \\ 4 \end{pmatrix}$

3 a), b), c), d)

4 $D(0, -4), E(-3, 0), F(4, -2)$

24.4 Enlargements

Page 295   Exercise 1

1 a)   b)   c)   d)

2 a)   b)   c)

3 a) 5 cm square (5 cm × 5 cm)
   b) 10 cm × 5 cm rectangle
   c) right triangle, 10 cm × 7.5 cm
   d) L-shape, 5 cm, 10 cm, 5 cm, 10 cm

Page 295   Exercise 2

1 a)   b)   c)

2 a)   b)   c)

3 4 cm   **4** 3 cm × 7 cm

Page 296   Exercise 3

1 a)   b)

c) [graph]   d) [graph]

2 a), b), c), d) [graph showing shapes A, B, C, D]

3 a), b) [graph showing triangle with points P, Q, R]

4 a) (i) 4 units (ii) 4 units (iii) 4 units (iv) 4 units
   b) (i) 8 units (ii) 8 units (iii) 8 units (iv) 8 units
   c) [graph showing squares ABCD and A₁B₁C₁D₁]

5 [graph showing four shapes]

6 a), b) [graph showing trapezium with XYZW inside]

7 a) (i) 3 units (ii) 3 units (iii) 0 units
   b) (i) 6 units (ii) 6 units (iii) 0 units
   c) [graph showing triangles PQR and P₁Q₁R₁]

8 [graph showing four shapes]

9 a), b) [graph with KLMN and L₁M₁N₁]   c) [graph with K₂L₂M₂N₂]

Page 298 Exercise 4

1 a), b), c), d) [graph showing shapes A, B, C, D]

2 a), b), c), d) [graph showing shapes A, B, C, D]

Page 299 Exercise 5

1 a) Scale factor 2, centre (2, 10)
   b) Scale factor 2, centre (6, 10)
   c) Scale factor 3, centre (11, 9)

2 a) Scale factor $\frac{1}{2}$, centre (1, 1)
   b) Scale factor $\frac{1}{2}$, centre (6, 5)
   c) Scale factor $\frac{1}{3}$, centre (5, 4)

Page 299 Exercise 6

1 a) [graph with WXYZ]   perimeter of $WXYZ$ is 8 units
   b) [graph with $W_1X_1Y_1Z_1$]
   c) perimeter of $W_1X_1Y_1Z_1$ is 15 units

2 a) 36 cm **b)** 100 m **c)** 180 m

3 a) area of $ABCD$ is 9 square units

b)

c) area of $A_1B_1C_1D_1$ is 36 square units

4 a) 16 cm² **b)** 36 cm² **c)** 135 m² **d)** 40 m²

5 a) 12 cm³
b) 2 cm, 8 cm, 6 cm   **c)** 96 cm³

6 a) 40 cm³ **b)** 64 cm³ **c)** 27 cm³
d) 216 m³ **e)** 500 m³

24.5 Combinations of Transformations

Page 301 Exercise 1

1 a)

b)

2

3

4 a), b) (i) **(ii)**

c) (i) **(ii)**

5 a)

b) (i) **(ii)**

c) (i) **(ii)**

Page 303 Exercise 2

1 a)

Answers 427

b)

c)

d)

e) P_2 and P_3 are identical, and Q_2 and Q_3 are identical.

2

d) Rotation of 180° about (0, 0)

3

c) Rotation of 90° clockwise about (0, 0)

4

Rotation of 180° about (3, 1)

24.6 Congruence and Similarity

Page 304 Exercise 1

1 A is congruent to G, B is congruent to J, C is congruent to F, D is congruent to H, E is congruent to I.

2 a) D **b)** H **c)** I **d)** N **e)** Q **f)** V

Page 305 Exercise 2

1 a) Yes. Two sides and the angle between on one triangle are the same as two sides and the angle between on the other triangle.
b) No. The two angles shown are the same, but the corresponding sides are not equal.
c) Yes, all the sides are the same in both triangles.
d) No. Their hypotenuses are different, so they cannot be congruent.

2 a) E.g. Missing angle in first triangle: $180° - 75° - 50° = 55°$ so two angles and one corresponding side are the same in both triangles.
b) Using Pythagoras' theorem the hypotenuse of the triangle on the right is 5 cm. Both triangles have a right angle, the same hypotenuse and another side the same, so they are congruent.

Page 306 Exercise 3

1 A, C and F are similar
B, E and K are similar
D, G and I are similar
H, J and L are similar

2 a) A and B **b)** D and F **c)** H and I
d) J and L **e)** M and N **f)** Q and R

Page 307 Exercise 4

1 a) All the angles in one triangle are the same as the angles in the other triangle.
b) All the sides in one triangle are in the same ratio as the corresponding sides in the other triangle.
c) All the angles in one triangle are the same as the angles in the other triangle.
d) Two sides in one triangle are in the same ratio as the corresponding sides in the other triangle and the angle between them is the same in both triangles.

2 a) Similar — the angles are the same in both triangles.
b) Similar — corresponding sides are in the same ratio.
c) Similar — 2 corresponding sides are in the same ratio and the angle between them is the same.
d) Not similar.
e) Similar — 2 corresponding sides are in the same ratio and the angle between them is the same.
f) Not similar.

Page 309 Exercise 5

1. **a)** (i) 100° (ii) 55° **b)** 110°
2. **a)** (i) angle *ABC* (ii) angle *ACB* (iii) angle *BAC*
   b) 1 : 3
   c) (i) 7.5 m (ii) 4 m
3. **a)** 6 cm **b)** 10 cm **c)** 5 cm
4. **a)** 1.5 m **b)** 5.4 m **c)** 3.6 m
5. **a)** 34°
   It forms a pair of opposite angles with angle *ZXY*.
   b) angle *XRQ*
   c) 1 : 2
   d) (i) 8 m (ii) 7 m
6. $a = 110°$, $b = 45°$, $c = 25°$, $d = 25°$, $e = 5.385$ cm, $f = 8$ cm

Section 25 — Collecting Data

25.1 Using Different Types of Data

Page 310 Exercise 1

1. **a)** Primary data **b)** Secondary data
2. Primary data
3. Secondary data
4. Primary data
5. **a)** Data needed — girls' answers to some questions about school dinners.
   Method of collecting — e.g. Nikita could ask all the girls in her class to fill in a questionnaire.
   b) Primary data
6. **a)** Data needed — colours of cars passing Dan's house in the 30-minute interval.
   Method of collecting — e.g. Dan could observe cars passing his house and note the colour of each car in a tally chart.
   b) Primary data
7. **a)** Data needed — daily rainfall figures for London and Manchester last August.
   Method of collecting — e.g. Anne could look for rainfall figures on the internet.
   b) Secondary data
8. **a)** Data needed — the distance an identical ball can be thrown by the boys and girls in his class.
   Method of collecting — e.g. Rohan could ask everyone in the class to throw the same ball as far as they can. He could measure the distances and record them in a table, along with whether each thrower was male or female.
   b) Primary data
9. **a)** Data needed — one set of data consists of the temperature readings in Jim's garden taken at 10 am each day. The other set consists of the Met Office's temperatures recorded for Jim's area at the same time.
   Method of collecting — e.g. Jim could collect the data from his garden by taking readings from a thermometer. He can get the Met Office temperatures from their website. He should record both temperatures for each day in a table.
   b) Data collected in Jim's garden is primary data. The Met Office data is secondary data.

Page 311 Exercise 2

1. Discrete
2. Qualitative
3. Discrete
4. Discrete
5. Continuous
6. Continuous
7. Qualitative
8. Continuous
9. Continuous
10. Qualitative
11. **a)** One set of data consists of the average number of chocolate bars eaten each week by each pupil. The other set consists of the times it takes these pupils to run 100 metres.
    b) Gemma could ask each pupil how many chocolate bars they eat on average each week.
    She could time how long it takes each pupil to run 100 m and record the data in a table, along with the chocolate bar data.
    c) The chocolate data is discrete data, and the running times data is continuous data.
    d) Both sets of data are primary data.

25.2 Data-Collection Sheets and Questionnaires

Page 312 Exercise 1

1. There is no tally column.
   The rows do not cover all the possible answers.
2. **a)**

Visits	Tally	Frequency
0		
1		
2		
3		
More than 3		

b)

Destination	Tally	Frequency
UK		
Europe		
USA		
Asia		
Other		

3. **a)** E.g.

Transport	Tally	Frequency
Walking		
Car		
Train		
Bus		
Bicycle		
Other		

b)

Days	Tally	Frequency
28		
29		
30		
31		

Answers

Page 313 Exercise 2

1 a) There is no row for someone who went to the cinema 0 times — the lowest possible answer is 1. The classes are overlapping.

No. of trips	Tally	Frequency
0-10		
11-20		
21-30		
31-40		
41 or more		

b) There are gaps between data classes. The classes do not cover all possible results.

No. of people	Tally	Frequency
0 - 5000		
5001 - 10 000		
10 001 - 15 000		
15 001 - 20 000		
20 001 - 25000		

c) The classes are overlapping. There are not enough classes.

Time (t mins)	Tally	Frequency
$t \leq 1$		
$1 < t \leq 2$		
$2 < t \leq 3$		
$3 < t \leq 4$		
$t > 4$		

d) There are gaps between classes. The classes do not cover all possible results.

Weight (w kg)	Tally	Frequency
$w \leq 3$		
$3 < w \leq 3.5$		
$3.5 < w \leq 4$		
$w > 4$		

2 a) E.g. $5 \leq h \leq 10$ $10 < h \leq 15$ $15 < h \leq 20$, $20 < h \leq 25$ $h > 25$
b) E.g. 0-4   5-8   9-12   13-16   17-20
c) E.g. $w \leq 180$ $180 < w \leq 190$ $190 < w \leq 200$, $200 < w \leq 210$ $w > 210$
d) E.g. $v \leq 260$ $260 < v \leq 270$ $270 < v \leq 280$ $280 < v \leq 290$ $290 < v \leq 300$

3 a) E.g.

Time (t hrs)	Tally	Frequency
$t \leq 5$		
$5 < t \leq 10$		
$10 < t \leq 20$		
$20 < t \leq 40$		
$t > 40$		

b) E.g.

No. of pairs	Tally	Frequency
0 - 4		
5 - 8		
9 - 12		
13 - 16		
17 or more		

c) E.g.

Length (s cm)	Tally	Frequency
$s \leq 15$		
$15 < s \leq 20$		
$20 < s \leq 25$		
$25 < s \leq 30$		
$s > 30$		

d) E.g.

Distance (d km)	Tally	Frequency
$d \leq 5$		
$5 < d \leq 10$		
$10 < d \leq 20$		
$20 < d \leq 40$		
$d > 40$		

Page 314 Exercise 3

1 a) There are not enough hair colour data classes. The age classes overlap. The data is for adults and does not need a data class for 0-15 years.

b) E.g.

Hair Colour	Age in whole years					
	18 - 30	31 - 45	46 - 60	61 - 75	76 or more
Blonde					
Light brown					
Dark brown					
Ginger					
Grey					
Other					

2 a)

Season	Gender	
	Male	Female
Spring		
Summer		
Autumn		
Winter		

b)

Music	Age Group	
	Adult	Child
Pop		
Classical		
Rock		

c) E.g.

Time spent (t hours)	School Year				
	7	8	9	10	11
$t \leq 1$					
$1 < t \leq 2$					
$2 < t \leq 3$					
$3 < t \leq 4$					

3 a) E.g.

TV time (t hours)	Age Group	
	Adult	Child
$t \leq 1$		
$1 < t \leq 2$		
$2 < t \leq 3$		
$3 < t \leq 4$		
$t > 4$		

Answers

b) E.g.

Transport	School Year				
	7	8	9	10	11
Walking					
Bus					
Car					
Bicycle					
Train					
Other					

c) E.g.

Height (h cm)	No. of fruit portions eaten				
	0 - 2	3 - 4	5 - 6	7 - 10	11 or more
$h \leq 120$					
$120 < h \leq 140$					
$140 < h \leq 160$					
$160 < h \leq 180$					
$h > 180$					

Page 314 Exercise 4

1 E.g.

No. of people	Tally	Frequency
1		
2		
3		
4		
5 or more		

2

Hair rating	Age Group	
	Adult	Child
1		
2		
3		
4		
5		

3 E.g.

Pocket Money	Tally	Frequency
0 - £2.00		
£2.01 - £4.00		
£4.01 - £6.00		
£6.01 - £8.00		
£8.01 or more		

4 E.g.

TV time per week (t hours)	Sport time per week (s hours)			
	$s \leq 5$	$5 < s \leq 10$	$10 < s \leq 20$	$s > 20$
$t \leq 5$				
$5 < t \leq 10$				
$10 < t \leq 20$				
$t > 20$				

Page 316 Exercise 5

1 E.g. one from: it's too vague / it's hard to answer because there are no options or time span given / it could be difficult to analyse the data because the answers could all be different.

2 It's a leading question, so the results could be biased.

3 E.g. this might be a sensitive issue for people, so there should be options where people can tick a range of weights rather than stating their exact weight.

4 There is no tick box for 'no pets'.

5 The tick boxes overlap.

Page 316 Exercise 6

1 The tick boxes should be changed so they don't overlap. E.g. *How much time do you spend reading each week on average?*

1 hour or less ☐
More than 1 hour, but no more than 2 hours ☐
More than 2 hours, but no more than 3 hours ☐
More than 3 hours, but no more than 4 hours ☐
More than 4 hours ☐

2 There should be a tick box added for "other", and possibly more options e.g. "Documentary" or "News". E.g. *What's your favourite type of TV programme? Tick one box.*

Comedy ☐ *Soap* ☐ *Reality* ☐ *Sport* ☐
Documentary ☐ *News* ☐ *Other* ☐

3 Reword the question so it is not a leading question. E.g. *Do you think the gym should open a squash court or a tennis court?*

Page 316 Exercise 7

1 Include a time span and tick boxes which cover all possible answers and do not overlap.
E.g. "*How many times, on average, do you use the gym each week?*"
You could include boxes such as "I don't use the gym", "Less than once a week", "1-2 times", "More than 2 times".

2 Include a tick box for each day of the week, and make it clear that more than one can be selected.
E.g. "*On which day(s) of the week do you usually shop at the supermarket? You may tick more than one box.*"

3 Include tick boxes to cover all possible opinions.
E.g. "*What do you think about the length of the dance class?*" You could include boxes such as "Much too short", "A bit too short", "About right", "A bit too long", "Much too long".

25.3 Sampling and Bias

Page 317 Exercise 1

1 The population is all the students of that university, and the sample is the students who complete the questionnaire.

2 E.g. It would take far too long to time all 216 pupils, and a smaller sample would create less disruption in the school routine.

3 E.g. It would be highly impractical and time-consuming to interview everyone in the town.

4 E.g. It would take a long time to test all the matches, and Jim wouldn't have any matches left to use at the end of it.

5 E.g. Kelly's sample is far too small and her results could easily be very unrepresentative of the whole audience.

6   E.g. There is a random element to the results of tossing a coin, so different samples will usually give different results.

7   Alfie's sample was bigger and would be expected to be more accurate — therefore, "chocolate" is more likely to be the most popular flavour.

8   E.g. Nikhil's idea is best, as only tasting one cake would not be accurate, and tasting 50 out of the 200 would take too long and use up a quarter of their cakes.

Page 318   Exercise 2

1   Barry's friends could easily have similar opinions about the film.

2   Animal rights activists are more likely to want vegetarian food, so the sample will be biased in favour of vegetarian food.

3   People using the library on a Monday are unlikely to want it to close on a Monday, so the sample will be biased away from a Monday closure.

4   People at work probably won't be able to answer the phone in the afternoon, so the only replies they will get will be from people who don't work, home workers, and people with the day off.

Page 318   Exercise 3

1   E.g. The dentist could assign each of the adult patients on his database a number, generate 20 random numbers with a computer or calculator, and match the numbers to the patients to create the sample.

2   E.g. The teacher could put all the names of Year 7 pupils into a hat, then mix them up and pick 50 at random.

3   E.g. The manager could assign each of the female members on her database a number, generate 40 random numbers with a computer or calculator, and match the numbers to the members to create the sample.

Page 318   Exercise 4

1   George's sample will be a much higher percentage of the total number of pupils, and Stuart's sample is not random. For example, it could be a group of friends who may all support the same football team.

2   E.g. Seema's sample, being taken on a Sunday morning, may include a lower than usual percentage of churchgoers (if they are at church at the time) or a higher than usual percentage (if they are going to/from church). It would be better to conduct the survey on a weekday evening when far fewer people will be at work or at (or going to/from) a place of worship. Also, people chosen at random in the street may not even live in that street. So instead, Seema could pick 20 house numbers from her street at random and knock on the doors, asking one person from each house.

3   E.g. The management could select 20 employees from each branch by assigning each employee at the branch a number, generating 20 random numbers using a computer or calculator, and matching those numbers to the numbered employees.

4   E.g. If the factory runs for 24 hours a day, test one freshly made component roughly every 30 minutes (or at 50 random times throughout the day).

Section 26 — Analysing Data

26.1 Using Lists and Tables

Page 319   Exercise 1

1   a)

Type of Music	Tally	Frequency
Classical	|	1
Indie	|||	3
Pop	|||| ||||	9
Rock	|||	3
Other	||||	4

   b) (i) 1   (ii) Pop   (iii) 20

2   a)

Weight (g)	Tally	Frequency
117	|||	3
118	||	2
119	||	2
120	||||	4
121	||||	4
122	|	1

   b) 120 g and 121 g

3   a)

Age (years)	Tally	Frequency
0-9	|||| ||	7
10-19	||||	4
20-29	|||| |	6
30-39	|||| |||	8
40-49	|||| |||	8
50-59	|||| ||||	9
60-69	|||	3
70-79	||||	4
80-89	|	1

   b) The 50-59 age group is the most common.

4   a)

Mark	Tally	Frequency
20-29	||||	4
30-39	|||| ||||	9
40-49	||||	5
50-59	|||	3
60-69	|||| ||||	10
70-79	|||	3
80-89	|||| ||	7
90-100	|||| ||||	9

432   *Answers*

b) 29
c) No, because the grouping used means the table doesn't show how many students in the 50-59 group scored less than 55 (and so failed), and how many scored 55 or over (and so passed).

26.2 Averages and Range

Page 320 Exercise 1
1. a) 8   b) 6   c) 8
2. 58   3. 78 seconds   4. red

Page 321 Exercise 2
1. a) 5   b) 6   c) 13
2. a) 3.8   b) 16.5   c) 3
3. 58   4. 81 seconds   5. 7
6. 16.9

Page 322 Exercise 3
1. a) 5.6   b) 6.33 (to 2 d.p.)   c) 13.125
2. a) 3.68   b) 18.075   c) 3.125
3. 60.2 marks (to 1 d.p.)
4. 83 seconds
5. a) mean = 3.25, median = 2.5, mode = 2
   b) mean = 3, median = 3, mode = 3
6. 10   7. 15.3

Page 322 Exercise 4
1. a) 5   b) 7   c) 9
2. a) 4.1   b) 6.19   c) 1
3. 52   4. 17 seconds   5. 2 or 11

Page 323 Exercise 5
1. a) 1   b) 2
   c) (i) 5   (ii) 8   (iii) 7   (iv) 5   (v) 2
   d) 45   e) 27   f) 1.67 (to 2 d.p.)
2. a) 4   b) 3   c) 3.07 (to 2 d.p.)
   d) 4
3. a) 18.5 °C   b) 18.5 °C
   c) E.g. The student's garden has experienced some fairly typical June temperatures for the UK.

Page 325 Exercise 6
1. a) 16-20   b) 11-15   c) 12.2   d) 19
2. a) 58 g   b) 80 g
   c) E.g. You don't know where the data values lie within the groups. The one tangerine in the $0 \leq w < 20$ g group could weigh 19 g, in which case the actual range would be no greater than 61 g.
3. a) 11-15 hours   b) 11-15 hours   c) 11.0 hours

Page 325 Exercise 7 — Mixed Exercise
1. a) (i) 138 cm   (ii) 137 cm   (iii) 142 cm
   b) 33 cm

2. a) (i) £5.04   (ii) £5.00   (iii) £5.00
   b) £1.58
3. a) (i) 6.49 cm   (ii) 6.35 cm   (iii) 4.3 cm
   b) 4.7 cm
4. a) 0   b) 20   c) 1
   d) (i) 20   (ii) 1   e) 3
5. a) 3   b) 2.7   c) 3
   d) More goals were scored on average than in the previous year.
6. a) $1.6 < h \leq 1.7$ b) $1.6 < h \leq 1.7$
   c) 1.695 m   d) 0.4 m
7. 72 g and 75 g
8. a) 14 days
   b) E.g. Most of the data is much closer together than the range suggests, so the range is not a good measure of spread. The range is affected by the data value 17, which is an outlier.
   c) E.g. There are two modes for this data, 3 and 6, so the mode does not give a good indication of the average value of the data.
9. a) Test 1: 14.25   Test 2: 10.5
   b) Test 1: 14   Test 2: 9
   c) E.g. The mean score was higher in Test 1, so the score achieved was generally higher in that test. The range of scores was lower in Test 2, so there was less variation in the scores in Test 2.
10. a) 2   b) 2   c) 2.375   d) 5

26.3 Two-Way Tables

Page 327 Exercise 1
1. a)

	Walk	Car	Total
Boys	12	6	18
Girls	16	3	19
Total	28	9	37

b)

	Walk	Car	Total
Boys	16	9	25
Girls	18	4	22
Total	34	13	47

c)

	Walk	Bus	Car	Total
Boys	9	5	3	17
Girls	5	8	6	19
Total	14	13	9	36

d)

	Walk	Bus	Car	Total
Boys	10	12	8	30
Girls	11	15	4	30
Total	21	27	12	60

2. a)

	Germany	France	Spain	Total
Male	16	7	12	35
Female	18	4	16	38
Total	34	11	28	73

b) 4   c) 16   d) 28
e) 38   f) 73

Answers

3 a)

	Chocolate	Crisps	Jellies	Total
Male	3	5	10	18
Female	3	7	2	12
Total	6	12	12	30

b) 12   **c)** 2   **d)** 16.7% (to 1 d.p.)

4 a)

	Red	Black	Blue	White	Total
Cars	8	7	4	3	22
Vans	2	2	1	10	15
Motorbikes	2	1	1	2	6
Total	12	10	6	15	43

b) 1   **c)** 15
d) (i) 51.2% (to 1 d.p.)   **(ii)** 34.9% (to 1 d.p.)
(iii) 27.9% (to 1 d.p.)

26.4 Bar Charts and Pictograms

Page 328   Exercise 1

1 Bar chart: Frequency vs Meal (Pie & Chips 11, Pasta 3, Baked potato 7, Baguette 10, Salad 4)

2 Bar chart: Frequency vs Bus (Number 7: 6, Number 23: 5, Coastlander 2, X94: 3, 12a: 2)

3 Bar chart: Frequency vs Drink (Espresso 23, Latte 19, Cappuccino 12, Mocha 15, Tea 22, Other 9)

4 a) Bar chart: Cups of tea vs Name, Morning and Afternoon (Nigel 3/2, Ali 2/1, Raul 1/4, Kate 3/3, Ailsa 0/0, Jan 0/2)

b) $\frac{2}{5}$

5 a) Bar chart: Rainy days vs Season, Plymouth and Aberdeen (Spring ~38/45, Summer 40/47, Autumn 48/53, Winter 52/53)

b) E.g. Aberdeen has more rainy days than Plymouth each season. The difference between the two cities is smallest in the winter.

Page 330   Exercise 2

1

Theme Park	👤👤👤👤👤👤👤
Bowling	👤👤👤👤👤
Cinema	👤👤👤 (half)
Boat Trip	👤👤 (half)

Key: 👤 represents 2 members

2 a) (i) 40   **(ii)** 30 (or "approximately 30")

b)

Monday	🍬🍬🍬
Tuesday	🍬🍬
Wednesday	🍬🍬 (half)
Thursday	🍬
Friday	🍬🍬🍬
Saturday	🍬🍬🍬🍬 (bit)
Sunday	

Key: 🍬 represents 20 packets of sweets

3 a) 10   **b)** Number 1   **c)** 39

26.5 Stem and Leaf Diagrams

Page 331   Exercise 1

1 a)
```
4 | 1 8
5 | 1 4 9
6 | 5 5 9
7 | 4
8 | 0 6 9
```
Key: 4 | 1 means 41

b)
```
1 | 2 5 5 7
2 | 4 6 7
3 | 1 6 9
4 | 1 1
```
Key: 1 | 2 means 12

c)
```
4 | 2 6
5 | 4 9
6 | 3 6 7
7 | 1 4
8 | 3 7
9 | 4
```
Key: 4 | 1 means 41

2 a)

3	1	4				Key: 3 | 1 means 3.1
4	0	4	9	4		
5	3	7	9	4	1	7
6	0	1				
7	7	1				

b)

20	3	5			Key: 20 | 1 means 201
30	1	4			
40	2	9	9	4	3	2
50	0	1	3		
60	6	8	1		

3

0	0	0	0	1	3	6
1	1	3	6		Key: 0 | 1 means 0.1 cm
2	0	5	7		
3	1	6	8		
4	1				

Page 331   Exercise 2

1 a) 32   **b)** 20   **c)** 27
2 a) 61   **b)** 7   **c)** 6
3 a)

10	2	6				Key: 10 | 1 means 10.1 seconds
11	4	7				
12	4	8	9			
13	1	3	6	9	9	9
14	2					
15	4					
16						
17	3					

b) 13.9 seconds   **c)** 7.1 seconds   **d)** 7

4 a) (i) 72 bpm   **(ii)** 77 bpm
b) These people's average heart rate was greater after exercise.

26.6 Pie Charts

Page 333   Exercise 1

1 a) 60   **b)** 6°
c) Black 150°, Silver 102°, Red 48°, Other 60°
d)

2 a) 36
b) Carlisle 130°, Kendal 90°, Millom 80°, Bristol 60°
c)

3

4

5

6 a) 48
b) Plain 135°, Salt and Vinegar 97.5°, Cheese and Onion 75°, Other 52.5°
c)

7

8

9

Page 335   Exercise 2

1   Set 1 : Q Set 2 : P Set 3 : S Set 4 : R
2 a) Pepperoni   **b)** $\frac{1}{4}$ **c)** 60   **d)** 6
3 a) Yes   **b)** Yes   **c)** No
d) No. The pie charts do not represent times, just the proportion of homework tasks set for each subject.

4 a) The area of the circle used to represent Pixie is much bigger than it should be. Only a fifth of the people surveyed said they use Pixie, but the diagram suggests that over half of them use it.

b)

(Pie chart: Use Pixie 72°, Use another brand)

5 a) 50+   **b)** $\frac{1}{10}$ **c)** 120
 d) (i) 24   **(ii)** 12   **e)** 40   **f)** 15

26.7 Time Series

Page 337   Exercise 1

1 a) (Time series graph of Gas used (m³) across Spring/Summer/Autumn/Winter for 2012, 2013, 2014)

b) E.g. The amount of gas they use rises through autumn and winter. It then decreases in spring and drops further in summer, before rising again in autumn.

c) E.g. Overall there is a slight downward trend in the amount of gas they use.

2 (Graph of Max. temperature (°C) by month for Sydney and London, a) and b) labelled)

c) E.g. The London graph peaks in July, when the Sydney graph is at its lowest. The Sydney graph peaks in February, when the London graph is very low. Warmer temperatures in one city correspond to lower temperatures in the other city.

3 a) E.g. The number of sunglasses sold increases from spring to summer, then falls in autumn and again in winter, before rising again the next spring.

b) E.g. There is an overall upward trend in the number of sunglasses sold.

c) E.g. The scale on the vertical axis is inconsistent. At the lower end of the axis, the numbers on the scale increase in increments of 20 and each grid square represents 10 pairs of sunglasses. But after 100 it increases in increments of 40 and each square represents 20 pairs of sunglasses. This makes it hard to interpret the graph.

26.8 Scatter Graphs

Page 338   Exercise 1

1 a) 5   **b)** Day 8   **c)** 2

2 (Scatter graph: Ice creams sold vs Temperature (°C))

3 (Scatter graph: No. of baby teeth vs Age (Years))

Page 339   Exercise 2

1 a) Weak negative correlation.
  b) No correlation.
  c) Strong positive correlation.

2 a) Positive correlation — as it gets warmer, people will probably be more likely to buy ice cream.
  b) Negative correlation — as it gets colder, people will probably be more likely to buy hot chocolate.
  c) No correlation — there probably isn't any connection between how hot it is and how much bread people buy.
  d) Positive correlation — as a child grows, he or she gets taller.
  e) Positive correlation — most people will probably drive more slowly in an area with a low speed limit.

Page 340   Exercise 3

1 a) Yes, the points will lie close to a straight line.
  b) No, the points are randomly scattered.
  c) Yes, most of the points will lie close to a straight line. There are 3 outliers which don't match the general pattern and so can be ignored.

2 a) Strong negative correlation OR the more time spent watching TV, the less time was spent on homework.
  b) 1 hour   **c)** 1.5 hours
3 a) Strong positive correlation OR the higher the tree, the wider the trunk.
  b) Width = 40 cm, height = 23 m
  c) 65 cm   **d)** 20 m
4 a), b)

(Scatter graph: Cost of car (×£1000) vs Mileage of car (×1000), with line of best fit showing negative correlation.)

  c) About £2300.   **d)** About 21 000 miles
5 a), b)

(Two scatter graphs: Drinks sold Machine 1 vs Temperature (°C), and Drinks sold Machine 2 vs Temperature (°C), both with lines of best fit showing positive correlation.)

  c) Machine 1: 20 drinks. Machine 2: 22 drinks.
  d) E.g. 3 °C is well below the temperature range for this data, so the relationship shown by this data may not apply at such a low temperature.
  e) E.g. No — just because the two things are correlated does not mean that one thing causes the other. They both could be influenced by a third variable.

Section 27 — Probability

27.1 Probability — The Basics

Page 342   Exercise 1

1 a) Evens   **b)** Impossible   **c)** Impossible   **d)** Evens
  e) Certain   **f)** Unlikely   **g)** Evens   **h)** Likely

2   f)   d)   b)   c) e)   a)
  Impossible Unlikely Evens Likely Certain

3 a) A   **b)** L
  c) P: 1   A: 2   R: 1   L: 3   E: 1

Page 343   Exercise 2

1 a) D   **b)** C   **c)** A   **d)** B   **e)** E
2 a) C   **b)** A   **c)** D   **d)** B
3   c) (i)   c) (ii)   b)   a)
  0    $\frac{1}{4}$ $\frac{1}{2}$ $\frac{3}{4}$ 1

27.2 Calculating Probabilities

Page 345   Exercise 1

1 a) 2   **b)** 52   **c)** 10   **d)** 8
  e) 7   **f)** 365 (or 366 for a leap year)
2 a) 6   **b)** $\frac{1}{6}$ **c)** $\frac{1}{3}$
3 a) $\frac{1}{6}$ **b)** $\frac{1}{6}$ **c)** 0   **d)** $\frac{1}{3}$
  e) $\frac{1}{3}$ **f)** $\frac{2}{3}$
4 a) $\frac{1}{9}$ **b)** $\frac{2}{9}$ **c)** $\frac{4}{9}$ **d)** $\frac{5}{9}$
5 a) $\frac{1}{4}$ **b)** $\frac{1}{3}$ **c)** $\frac{2}{3}$ **d)** $\frac{3}{4}$
6 a) $\frac{1}{8}$ **b)** $\frac{3}{16}$ **c)** $\frac{1}{16}$ **d)** $\frac{1}{8}$
  e) $\frac{3}{8}$ **f)** $\frac{3}{8}$ **g)** $\frac{15}{16}$ **h)** 0
7 a) $\frac{1}{4}$ **b)** $\frac{1}{13}$ **c)** $\frac{1}{2}$ **d)** $\frac{1}{52}$
  e) $\frac{3}{4}$ **f)** $\frac{2}{13}$
8 a) (spinner with 2, 2, 2 marked)   **b)** (spinner with 3, 3, 3, 3 marked)   **c)** (spinner with 5, 5, 6, 6 marked)

The unmarked sections can be any number different from the ones already shown on the spinner.

Page 345   Exercise 2

1 a) $\frac{1}{12}$ **b)** $\frac{1}{366}$
2 $\frac{1}{39}$
3 a) $\frac{1}{9}$ **b) (i)** 7   **(ii)** $\frac{7}{18}$

4 a) $\frac{1}{100}$ **b)** $\frac{1}{100}$

5 It takes no account of how good the team is or how good their opponents are. The three outcomes are not equally likely.

Page 346 Exercise 3

1 a) Yes **b)** No **c)** No
2 a) Yes **b)** No **c)** No
   d) No **e)** No
3 0.8 **4** $\frac{3}{8}$ **5** 75%
6 0.55 **7** 0.26
8 a) 0.55 **b)** 0.8

Page 347 Exercise 4

1 0.3
2 a) 0.3 **b)** 0.9
3 0.45 **4** $\frac{3}{8}$ **5** 40

Page 348 Exercise 5 — Mixed Exercise

1 a) (i) $\frac{2}{5}$ **(ii)** $\frac{1}{3}$ **(iii)** $\frac{2}{3}$
  b) (i) $\frac{5}{18}$ **(ii)** $\frac{13}{18}$ **(iii)** $\frac{2}{3}$
2 a) $\frac{3}{8}$ **b)** $\frac{7}{8}$
3 a) $\frac{1}{2}$ **b)** $\frac{1}{3}$
  c) These are not mutually exclusive outcomes that cover all the possibilities. (The two events aren't mutually exclusive, because if 6 is rolled, then both events have happened. And the outcomes 1 and 5 are not included in either event.)

27.3 Listing Outcomes

Page 349 Exercise 1

1 a)

1st coin	2nd coin
Heads	Heads
Heads	Tails
Tails	Heads
Tails	Tails

b)

Dice	Coin
1	Heads
1	Tails
2	Heads
2	Tails
3	Heads
3	Tails
4	Heads
4	Tails
5	Heads
5	Tails
6	Heads
6	Tails

2

1st ball	2nd ball
Green	Green
Green	Blue
Blue	Green
Blue	Blue

3

1st spin	2nd spin
Blue	Blue
Blue	Purple
Blue	Orange
Purple	Blue
Purple	Purple
Purple	Orange
Orange	Blue
Orange	Purple
Orange	Orange

4 a)

Burger	Drink
Hamburger	Cola
Hamburger	Lemonade
Hamburger	Coffee
Cheeseburger	Cola
Cheeseburger	Lemonade
Cheeseburger	Coffee
Veggie burger	Cola
Veggie burger	Lemonade
Veggie burger	Coffee

  b) $\frac{1}{9}$ **c)** $\frac{1}{3}$

5 a)

1st spin	2nd spin
1	1
1	2
1	3
2	1
2	2
2	3
3	1
3	2
3	3

  b) $\frac{1}{9}$ **c)** $\frac{1}{3}$

6 a)

1st toss	2nd toss	3rd toss
Heads	Heads	Heads
Heads	Heads	Tails
Heads	Tails	Heads
Heads	Tails	Tails
Tails	Heads	Heads
Tails	Heads	Tails
Tails	Tails	Heads
Tails	Tails	Tails

  b) (i) $\frac{1}{8}$ **(ii)** $\frac{3}{8}$

Page 350 Exercise 2

1 a)

	1	2	3	4	5	6
H	H1	H2	H3	H4	H5	H6
T	T1	T2	T3	T4	T5	T6

b)

	Red	White	Blue
Red	RR	RW	RB
White	WR	WW	WB
Blue	BR	BW	BB

2 a)

	1	2	3	4	5	6
1	2	3	4	5	6	7
2	3	4	5	6	7	8
3	4	5	6	7	8	9
4	5	6	7	8	9	10
5	6	7	8	9	10	11
6	7	8	9	10	11	12

b) 36

c) (i) $\frac{5}{36}$ **(ii)** $\frac{1}{36}$ **(iii)** 0   **(iv)** $\frac{7}{12}$
   (v) $\frac{5}{18}$ **(vi)** $\frac{1}{2}$

3 a)

	B	G	G	Y
B	BB	BG	BG	BY
G	GB	GG	GG	GY
Y	YB	YG	YG	YY

b) (i) $\frac{1}{12}$ **(ii)** $\frac{1}{6}$ **(iii)** $\frac{1}{3}$ **(iv)** $\frac{1}{2}$

Page 350 Exercise 3

1 a)

	1	2	3	4	5	6
A	A1	A2	A3	A4	A5	A6
B	B1	B2	B3	B4	B5	B6
C	C1	C2	C3	C4	C5	C6
D	D1	D2	D3	D4	D5	D6

b) (i) $\frac{1}{24}$ **(ii)** $\frac{1}{24}$ **(iii)** $\frac{1}{12}$ **(iv)** $\frac{1}{8}$
   (v) $\frac{1}{8}$ **(vi)** $\frac{1}{6}$

2 a)

	\multicolumn{5}{c}{Asha's score (2nd number)}
Hayley's score (1st number)	1	2	3	4	5
1	1,1	1,2	1,3	1,4	1,5
2	2,1	2,2	2,3	2,4	2,5
3	3,1	3,2	3,3	3,4	3,5
4	4,1	4,2	4,3	4,4	4,5
5	5,1	5,2	5,3	5,4	5,5

b) $\frac{2}{5}$ **c)** $\frac{4}{25}$

27.4 Probability from Experiments

Page 351 Exercise 1

1 a) $\frac{17}{50}$ **b)** $\frac{33}{50}$

2 a) Red $\frac{49}{100}$, green $\frac{17}{50}$, yellow $\frac{2}{25}$, blue $\frac{9}{100}$
   b) Perform the experiment more times.

3 a) $\frac{13}{50}$ **b)** $\frac{9}{50}$
   c) Jason's should be more accurate as he has performed the experiment more times.

4 a) (i) 0.452   **(ii)** 0.237   **b)** 0.089

5 $\frac{5}{6}$

6 a) $\frac{8}{15}$ **b)** $\frac{7}{15}$

7 $\frac{2}{5}$

8 Lilia could examine the recent records of her team's previous matches against a similar level of opposition, count the number of wins and divide it by the total number of matches in those records.

Page 352 Exercise 2

1 a) 15   **b)** 45   **c)** 75   **d)** 750
2 a) 20   **b)** 20   **c)** 60   **d)** 100
3 a) 20   **b)** 100   **c)** 160
4 12

Page 353 Exercise 3

1 a)

Gender — Over 6 foot tall?
100 → Male 60 → Yes 22, No 38
100 → Female 40 → Yes 6, No 34

b)

Travel to work by train? — Late for work?
500 → Yes 380 → Yes 240, No 140
500 → No 120 → Yes 22, No 98

2 a) E.g.

Said their vision was fine? — Passed test?
720 → Yes 640 → Yes 460, No 180
720 → No 80 → Yes 30, No 50

b) $\frac{5}{8}$

c) $\frac{23}{36}$

Page 354 Exercise 4 — Mixed Exercise

1. **a)** Blue 0.22, Green 0.21, White 0.18, Pink 0.39
   b) Blue 0.25, Green 0.25, White 0.25, Pink 0.25
   c) The spinner seems biased as the relative frequencies for white and pink are a long way away from the theoretical probability.

2. **a)** 20 times.
   b) The dice may be biased as the number 4 comes up much more than expected.
   c) Perform the experiment more times.

3. **a)**

	Amy	Steve	Hal
No. of tosses	20	60	100
No. of heads	12	33	49
Relative frequency	0.6	0.55	0.49

   b) Hal's should be the most accurate, as he has performed the experiment the most times.
   c) The coin seems fair, as the expected frequency of heads is 0.5 and Hal's results are very near that.

4. **a)** E.g.

   [Tree diagram: 800 → Yes 555 → Brown eyes? Yes 220, No 335; No 245 → Yes 105, No 140]

   b) $\frac{11}{40} = 0.275$ **c)** 550

27.5 The AND / OR Rules

Page 355 Exercise 1

1. **a)** $\frac{1}{12}$ **b)** $\frac{1}{4}$ **c)** $\frac{1}{6}$
   d) $\frac{1}{4}$ **e)** $\frac{1}{6}$ **f)** $\frac{1}{6}$

2. **a)** 90% or 0.9   **b)** 85% or 0.85
   c) 1.5% or 0.015   **d)** 76.5% or 0.765

3. **a)** $\frac{1}{4} = 0.25$ **b)** $\frac{9}{100} = 0.09$ **c)** $\frac{49}{100} = 0.49$

Page 356 Exercise 2

1. **a)** 0.6   **b)** 0.9   **c)** 0.5
2. **a)** 0.54   **b)** 0.4   **c)** 0.6   **d)** 0.66
3. **a)** $\frac{1}{3}$ **b)** $\frac{2}{3}$ **c)** $\frac{2}{3}$
4. **a)** $\frac{13}{20}$ **b)** $\frac{9}{20}$
5. **a)** $\frac{28}{52} = \frac{7}{13}$ **b)** $\frac{22}{52} = \frac{11}{26}$
6. No, having glasses and having blonde hair are not mutually exclusive (some people could have both) so you can't just add the probabilities unless you know that none of the pupils both wear glasses and have blonde hair.

27.6 Tree Diagrams

Page 357 Exercise 1

1. **a)** [Tree diagram: 1st: 0.6 R, 0.4 B; 2nd from R: 0.6 R, 0.4 B; 2nd from B: 0.6 R, 0.4 B]

   b) [Tree diagram: 1st: 0.5 R, 0.3 B, 0.2 G; 2nd from R: 0.5 R, 0.3 B, 0.2 G; 2nd from B: 0.5 R, 0.3 B, 0.2 G; 2nd from G: 0.5 R, 0.3 B, 0.2 G]

2. **a)** [Tree diagram: 1st: 0.65 H, 0.35 T; 2nd from H: 0.65 H, 0.35 T; 2nd from T: 0.65 H, 0.35 T]

   b) [Tree diagram: 1st: 0.3 P, 0.7 B; 2nd from P: 0.3 P, 0.7 B; 2nd from B: 0.3 P, 0.7 B]

   c) [Tree diagram: 1st: 0.7 W, 0.1 D, 0.2 L; 2nd from each: 0.7 W, 0.1 D, 0.2 L]

440 *Answers*

3 a)

	1st	2nd
	0.8 — F	0.8 — F
		0.2 — J
	0.2 — J	0.8 — F
		0.2 — J

b) 0.64

4 a)

Sally / Jesse tree:
- $\frac{1}{3}$ Comedy → $\frac{2}{5}$ Comedy, $\frac{3}{5}$ Not a comedy
- $\frac{2}{3}$ Not a comedy → $\frac{2}{5}$ Comedy, $\frac{3}{5}$ Not a comedy

b) $\frac{2}{5} = 0.4$ **c)** $\frac{3}{5} = 0.6$

5 a)

Saturday / Sunday tree:
- 0.7 Goes to cinema → 0.2 Goes to cinema, 0.8 Doesn't go to cinema
- 0.3 Doesn't go to cinema → 0.6 Goes to cinema, 0.4 Doesn't go to cinema

b) 0.14   **c)** 0.74

6 a)

1st name / 2nd name tree:
- $\frac{16}{30}$ Boy → $\frac{15}{29}$ Boy, $\frac{14}{29}$ Girl
- $\frac{14}{30}$ Girl → $\frac{16}{29}$ Boy, $\frac{13}{29}$ Girl

b) $\frac{8}{29}$ **c)** $\frac{224}{435}$

27.7 Sets and Venn Diagrams

Page 358   Exercise 1

1 a) (i) {12, 14, 16, 18, 20, 22, 24}
  (ii) {2, 3, 5, 7, 11, 13, 17, 19, 23, 29}
  (iii) {1, 4, 9, 16, 25, 36, 49, 64, 81, 100, 121, 144, 169, 196}
  (iv) {1, 2, 3, 5, 6, 10, 15, 30}
b) (i) 7   **(ii)** 10   **(iii)** 14   **(iv)** 8

2 a) {1, 2, 4, 5, 6, 7, 8}   **b)** {2, 4, 8}

3 a) 4   **b)** 6
  c) {2, 4, 5, 6, 8}   **d)** {1, 2, 3, 5, 6, 7, 8, 9}
  e) {1, 4, 7}   **f)** {3, 9}
  g) 8   **h)** {2, 3, 4, 5, 6, 8, 9}
  i) {1, 7}   **j)** {1, 2, 4, 5, 6, 7, 8}

Page 359   Exercise 2

1 a) Venn diagram: A = {5}, A∩B = {1, 3}, B = {7}; outside: 2, 4, 6, 8, 9, 10

b) Venn diagram: A = {2, 4}, A∩B = {3, 5}, B = {1, 7, 9}; outside: 6, 8, 10

c) Venn diagram: A = {2, 10}, A∩B = {6}, B = {1, 3, 9}; outside: 4, 5, 7, 8

d) Venn diagram: A = {2, 4, 5, 6}, A∩B = {3}, B = {1, 7}; outside: 8, 9, 10

2 a) $\frac{19}{50} = 0.38$ **b)** $\frac{87}{200} = 0.435$ **c)** $\frac{1}{20} = 0.05$
   d) $\frac{103}{200} = 0.515$ **e)** $\frac{57}{100} = 0.57$ **f)** $\frac{27}{200} = 0.135$

3 a) $\frac{75}{137}$ **b)** $\frac{60}{137}$ **c)** $\frac{16}{137}$

4 a) Venn diagram: A = {1, 9}, A∩B = {3, 5, 7}, B = {2}; outside: 4, 6, 8, 10

b) (i) $\frac{2}{5} = 0.4$ **(ii)** $\frac{3}{10} = 0.3$ **(iii)** $\frac{1}{5} = 0.2$

5 a) Venn diagram: M = {8}, M∩E = {15}, E = {3}; outside: 4

b) (i) $\frac{1}{2}$ **(ii)** $\frac{4}{15}$ **(iii)** $\frac{1}{10}$ **(iv)** $\frac{2}{15}$

Index

3D shapes 261-282
   isometric drawings 267-269
   nets 262-264
   projections 264-267
   surface area 275-280
   volume 270-274

A

acute-angled triangles 170
addition
   decimals 9-11
   fractions 48-51
   negative numbers 1-2
   whole numbers 3-4
algebraic expressions 89-97, 116-117
allied angles 174-175
alternate angles 173
AND rule 355
angle bisectors 237
angles 168-183
   allied 174-175
   alternate 173
   around a point 168-169
   constructing 239-240
   corresponding 174-175
   exterior 182-183
   in quadrilaterals 176-180
   interior 180-182
   in triangles 170-171
   measuring 232
   on a straight line 168-169
   opposite 172
   right 168-169
approximations 18-25
arcs 231, 258
area
   and enlargements 299-300
   circles 255-257
   composite shapes 247, 249-251, 256-257
   converting units 194-195
   parallelograms 248
   rectangles 245-246
   squares 245-246
   trapeziums 249
   triangles 245-246
averages 320-326

B

bar charts 328-329
bearings 213-216
bias 317-318, 353-354
BODMAS 15-16

C

cancelling fractions 43-45
centre of
   enlargement 296-299
   rotation 287

chords 231
circles 230-231
   area 255-257
   of a sector 258
circumference 231, 252-253
collecting data 310-318
   questionnaires 315-317
   sampling 317-318
   tally charts 312-313
   two-way tables 314-315
collecting like terms 89-90
column vectors 225-228
common
   denominators 46-48
   factors 35-36, 40-41
   multiples 34, 38-40
complement of a set 358
composite shapes 247, 250-251, 253-257
compound growth and decay 86-87
compound inequalities 25, 109-110
cones 273, 278
congruence 304-305
constructions 233-241
   angle bisectors 237
   angles 239-240
   parallel lines 241
   perpendicular bisectors 236
   perpendicular from point to line 238
continuous data 311
converting units 192-199
   areas 194-195
   density 203-204
   imperial units 197-199
   metric units 192-194
   pressure 204
   speed 202-203
   volumes 195-196
coordinates 134-136
correlation 339-341
corresponding angles 174-175
cos 221-223
cube numbers 26
cube roots 27-28
cubic graphs 150-151
cuboids
   surface area 275-276
   volume 270-271
cylinders 261, 263
   surface area 276-277
   volume 271-272

D

data
   collection 310-318
   continuous 311
   discrete 311
   primary 310-311
   qualitative 311
   quantitative 311

   secondary 310-311
decimals 7-15, 56-60
   arithmetic 9-15
   converting
      to fractions 59-60, 77-80
      to percentages 77-80
   ordering 8-9
   recurring 56-57, 60
   rounding 19-20
   terminating 56-59
denominators 42
density 203-204
diameter 230, 252-253
difference of two squares 97
direct proportion 161-164, 167
discrete data 311
distance-time graphs 205-208
division
   decimals 11-12, 14-15
   fractions 54-56
   negative numbers 2-3
   whole numbers 6-7

E

edges 261
elements of a set 358-359
elevations 264-269
enlargements 294-300
   area 299-300
   perimeter 299
   scale factors 294-296
   volume 299-300
equations
   of straight lines 136-137, 143-145
   quadratic 113-115
   simultaneous 111-113
   solving 98-104
   writing 105-107
equilateral triangles 170
equivalent fractions 42-44
error intervals 25
estimating 23-24
   measurements 199-200
expanding brackets 91-94
expected frequency 352
expressions 116-117
   collecting like terms 89-90
   expanding brackets 91-93
   factorising 95-97
   quadratic 96-97
   simplifying 89-95
exterior angles 182-183

F

faces 261
factorising 95-97
   quadratics 96-97, 113-114

442   *Index*

factors 35-36
  common 35-36
  highest common 40-41
  prime 37-38
  trees 37-38
fair 317-318, 353-354
formulas 116-126
  rearranging 121-124
  substituting into 118-121
  writing 116-117
fractions 42-62
  addition 48-51
  converting
    to decimals 56-60, 77-80
    to percentages 77-80
  division 54-56
  equivalent 42-44
  improper 44-45
  mixed numbers 44-45
  multiplication 51-54
  ordering 46-47
  reciprocals 54-56
  simplifying 43-44
  subtraction 48-51
frequency tables 319-320
  averages and range 323-326
  grouped 319-320
frequency trees 353
front elevation 264-267
frustums 273
functions 124-125

G

gradient 140-142, 157-158
  distance-time graphs 207
graphs 134-154
  cubic 150-151
  distance-time 205-208
  interpreting 155-158
  quadratic 146-150
  real-life 155-160
  reciprocal 152
  straight-line 136-145
  y-intercept 143-145
grouped frequency tables 319-320
  averages and range 324-326

H

HCF (highest common factor) 40-41
horizontal lines 136-137
hypotenuse 217, 221

I

identities 94
imperial units 197-199
improper fractions 44-45
index notation 28-29
indices 28-32
  laws of 30-32
inequalities
  compound 25, 109-110
  solving 107-110

interior angles 180-182
intersecting lines 172-175
intersection of sets 358
inverse proportion 165-167
isometric drawings 267-269
isosceles triangles 170

K

kites 178

L

laws of indices 30-32
LCM (least common multiple) 38-40
like terms 89
line graphs 336-337
lines
  intersecting 172-175
  of best fit 339-341
  parallel 173-175
  perpendicular 168-169
line symmetry 184
loci 242-243

M

map scales 209-212
mean 320, 322
  from a frequency table 323-326
measurements 189-191
  estimating 199-200
measuring angles 232
median 320-321
  from a frequency table 323-326
  from a stem and leaf diagram 331-332
metric units 192-194
  converting to imperial units 197-199
midpoint of a line segment 135-136
mixed numbers 44-45, 50-51
mode 320-321
  from a frequency table 323-326
  from a stem and leaf diagram 331-332
multiples 34
  common 34
  least common 38-41
multiplication
  decimals 11-13
  fractions 51-54
  negative numbers 2-3
  whole numbers 4-5
mutually exclusive events 346-347

N

negative correlation 339
negative numbers 1-3
nets 262-264
nth term 130-133
numerators 42

O

obtuse-angled triangles 170
opposite angles 172

ordering
  decimals 8-9
  fractions 46-47
order of operations 15-16
OR rule 355-356
outcomes 344-350
  listing 348-350

P

parallel lines 144-145, 173-175
  constructing 241
parallelograms 177, 248
percentages 73-85
  converting
    to decimals 77-80
    to fractions 77-84
  decrease 80-85
  increase 80-85
  with a calculator 76-77, 81
  without a calculator 75-76, 80-84
perimeter 244
  and enlargements 299
  composite shapes 247, 250-251, 253-255
perpendicular
  bisector 236
  from point to line 238
  lines 168-169
pictograms 329-330
pie charts 332-336
place value 7-9
plan view 264-269
polygons 180-184
  exterior angles 182-183
  interior angles 180-182
  regular 180
population 316-318
position-to-term rules 130-133
positive correlation 339
powers 26, 28-32
  laws of indices 30-32
pressure 204
primary data 310-311
prime factors 37-38
prime numbers 36-38
prisms 261
  surface area 275-276
  volume 271-272
probability 342-359
  AND rule 355
  calculating 344-348
  experimental 351-352
  frequency trees 353
  listing outcomes 348-350
  OR rule 355-356
  scale 342-344
  tree diagrams 356-357
proportion 161-167
  direct 161-164
  inverse 165-167
protractors 232-234
pyramids 274, 276
Pythagoras' theorem 217-221

Index 443

Q

quadratic equations 113-115
quadratic expressions 96-97
quadratic graphs 146-150
   drawing 146-148
   to solve quadratic equations 148-149
   turning points 149-150
quadrilaterals 176-180
qualitative data 311
quantitative data 311
questionnaires 315-316

R

radius 230, 252-253
range 322
   from a frequency table 323-326
   from a stem and leaf diagram 331-332
rates of change 157-158
rates of flow 274
ratios 63-72
   dividing in a given 70-71
   part : whole 69
   simplifying 63-65
real-life graphs 155-160
rearranging formulas 121-124
reciprocal graphs 152
reciprocals 54-56
rectangles 176-177
   area 245-246
   perimeter 244
recurring decimals 56-57, 60
reflections 283-286
regular polygons 180
relative frequency 351-352
rhombuses 177
right-angled triangles 170
   Pythagoras' theorem 217-221
   Trigonometry 221-224
right angles 168-170
   constructing 240
roots 27-28
rotation 287-290
rotational symmetry 185
rounding
   decimal places 19-20
   errors 25
   significant figures 21-22
   whole numbers 18-19

S

sampling 316-318
scalars 226
scale
   drawings 209-212
   factors 294-296
   readings 189-191
scalene triangles 170
scatter graphs 338-341
   correlation 339-341
   lines of best fit 339-341
secondary data 310-311
sectors 231, 258
segments 231
sequences 127-133
   nth term 130-133
   position-to-term rules 130-133
   term-to-term rules 127-129
sets 358-359
side elevation 264-267
significant figures 21-22
similarity 306-309
simplifying
   expressions 89-95
   fractions 43-44
   ratios 63-65
simultaneous equations 111-113
sin 221-223
solving
   equations 98-104, 111-115
   inequalities 107-111
speed 201-203, 207-208
spheres 272-273, 278
square numbers 26
square roots 27-28
squares 176-177
   area 245-246
   perimeter 244
standard form 32-33
stem and leaf diagrams 330-332
straight-line graphs 136-145
   drawing 138-139
   equations 136-137, 143-145
   gradients 140-142
subject of a formula 121
substituting into formulas 118-121
subtraction
   decimals 9-11
   fractions 48-51
   negative numbers 1-2
   whole numbers 3-4
surface area 275-280
   cones 278
   cuboids 275-276
   cylinders 276-277
   prisms 275-276
   pyramids 276
   spheres 278
symmetry 184-186
   line 184
   rotational 185

T

tables
   frequency 319-320, 323-326
   two-way 327-328, 349-350
tally charts 312-314, 319-320
tan 221-223
tangents 231
terminating decimals 56-59
term-to-term rules 127-129
time series 336-337
transformations 283-303
   enlargements 294-300
   reflections 283-286
   rotations 287-290
trapeziums 178-179, 249
translations 291-294
tree diagrams 356-357
trends 336-337
triangles 170-171, 180
   acute-angled 170
   angles in 170-171
   area 245-246
   congruent 305-306
   drawing 233-235
   equilateral 170
   isosceles 170
   obtuse-angled 170
   perimeter 244
   Pythagoras' theorem 217-221
   right-angled 170
   scalene 170
   similar 307-309
trigonometry 221-224
   common values 223
   formulas 221
truncating numbers 25
turning points 149-150
two-way tables 314, 327-328, 349-350

U

union of sets 358
unit conversions 192-199
universal set 358

V

vectors 225-229, 291
   addition 226-227
   subtraction 226-227
   vector geometry 229
Venn diagrams 358-359
vertex 261
vertical lines 136-137
volume 270-274
   and enlargements 299-300
   cones 273
   converting units 195-196
   cuboids 270-271
   cylinders 271-272
   frustums 273
   prisms 271-272
   pyramids 274
   spheres 272-273

W

whole numbers
   arithmetic 3-7
   rounding 18-19

X

x-coordinates 134

Y

y-coordinates 134
y-intercepts 143-144